Kernelization

Preprocessing, or data reduction, is a standard technique for simplifying and speeding up computation. Written by a team of experts in the field, this book introduces a rapidly developing area of preprocessing analysis known as kernelization.

The authors provide an overview of basic methods and important results, with accessible explanations of the most recent advances in the area, such as meta-kernelization, representative sets, polynomial lower bounds and lossy kernelization. The text is divided into four parts, which cover the different theoretical aspects of the area: upper bounds, meta-theorems, lower bounds and beyond kernelization. The methods are demonstrated through extensive examples.

Written to be self-contained, the book only requires a basic background in algorithmics and will be of use to professionals, researchers and graduate students in theoretical computer science, optimization, combinatorics and related fields.

FEDOR V. FOMIN is Professor of Computer Science at the University of Bergen. He is known for his work in algorithms and graph theory. He has coauthored two books, *Exact Exponential Algorithms* and *Parameterized Algorithms*, and received the EATCS Nerode prizes in 2015 and 2017 for his work on bidimensionality and Measure and Conquer, respectively.

DANIEL LOKSHTANOV is Professor of Informatics at the University of Bergen and Associate Professor at UC Santa Barbara. His main research interests are in graph algorithms, parameterized algorithms, and complexity. He is a coauthor of *Parameterized Algorithms* and a recipient of the Meltzer prize, the Bergen Research Foundation young researcher grant and an ERC starting grant on parameterized algorithms.

SAKET SAURABH is Professor of Theoretical Computer Science at the Institute of Mathematical Sciences, Chennai, and Professor of Computer Science at the University of Bergen. He has made important contributions to every aspect of parametrized complexity and kernelization, especially to general purpose results in kernelization and applications of extremal combinatorics in designing parameterized algorithms. He is a coauthor of *Parameterized Algorithms*.

MEIRAV ZEHAVI is Assistant Professor of Computer Science at Ben-Gurion University. Her research interests lie primarily in the field of parameterized complexity. In her PhD studies, she received three best student paper awards.

Kernelization
Theory of Parameterized Preprocessing

FEDOR V. FOMIN
University of Bergen

DANIEL LOKSHTANOV
University of Bergen and University California Santa Barbara

SAKET SAURABH
Institute of Mathematical Sciences and University of Bergen

MEIRAV ZEHAVI
Ben-Gurion University

CAMBRIDGE
UNIVERSITY PRESS

University Printing House, Cambridge CB2 8BS, United Kingdom

One Liberty Plaza, 20th Floor, New York, NY 10006, USA

477 Williamstown Road, Port Melbourne, VIC 3207, Australia

314–321, 3rd Floor, Plot 3, Splendor Forum, Jasola District Centre,
New Delhi – 110025, India

79 Anson Road, #06–04/06, Singapore 079906

Cambridge University Press is part of the University of Cambridge.

It furthers the University's mission by disseminating knowledge in the pursuit of
education, learning, and research at the highest international levels of excellence.

www.cambridge.org
Information on this title: www.cambridge.org/9781107057760
DOI: 10.1017/9781107415157

© Fedor V. Fomin, Daniel Lokshtanov, Saket Saurabh, and Meirav Zehavi 2019

This publication is in copyright. Subject to statutory exception
and to the provisions of relevant collective licensing agreements,
no reproduction of any part may take place without the written
permission of Cambridge University Press.

First published 2019

A catalogue record for this publication is available from the British Library.

Library of Congress Cataloging-in-Publication Data
Names: Fomin, Fedor V., author. | Lokshtanov, Daniel, 1984– author. |
Saurabh, Saket, author. | Zehavi, Meirav, author.
Title: Kernelization : theory of parameterized preprocessing / Fedor V. Fomin, University of
Bergen, Norway, Daniel Lokshtanov, University of Bergen, Norway, Saket Saurabh,
University of Bergen, Norway, Meirav Zehavi, University of Bergen, Norway.
Description: First edition. | Cambridge : Cambridge University Press, 2019. |
Includes bibliographical references and index.
Identifiers: LCCN 2018030108 | ISBN 9781107057760 (hardback)
Subjects: LCSH: Electronic data processing–Data preparation. |
Data reduction. | Kernel functions. | Parameter estimation.
Classification: LCC QA76.9.D345 F66 2019 | DDC 005.7/2–dc23
LC record available at https://lccn.loc.gov/2018030108

ISBN 978-1-107-05776-0 Hardback

Cambridge University Press has no responsibility for the persistence or accuracy
of URLs for external or third-party internet websites referred to in this publication
and does not guarantee that any content on such websites is, or will remain,
accurate or appropriate.

Contents

	Preface	*page* xi
	Acknowledgments	xiv
1	**What Is a Kernel?**	1
1.1	Introduction	1
1.2	Kernelization: Formal Definition	6
	PART I UPPER BOUNDS	13
2	**Warm Up**	15
2.1	Trivial Kernelization	16
2.2	VERTEX COVER	18
2.3	FEEDBACK ARC SET IN TOURNAMENTS	21
2.4	DOMINATING SET in Graphs of Girth at Least 5	22
2.5	Alternative Parameterization for VERTEX COVER	25
2.6	EDGE CLIQUE COVER	28
3	**Inductive Priorities**	32
3.1	Priorities for MAX LEAF SUBTREE	33
3.2	Priorities for FEEDBACK VERTEX SET	40
4	**Crown Decomposition**	50
4.1	Crown Decomposition	51
4.2	VERTEX COVER and DUAL COLORING	52
4.3	MAXIMUM SATISFIABILITY	55
4.4	LONGEST CYCLE Parameterized by Vertex Cover	57

5	**Expansion Lemma**	61
5.1	Expansion Lemma	61
5.2	CLUSTER VERTEX DELETION: Bounding the Number of Cliques	65
5.3	Weighted Expansion Lemma	66
5.4	Component Order Connectivity	70
5.5	FEEDBACK VERTEX SET	73
6	**Linear Programming**	84
6.1	The Theorem of Nemhauser and Trotter	84
6.2	2-SAT of Minimum Weight	89
6.3	Reduction of MIN-WEIGHT-2-IP to MIN-ONES-2-SAT	92
6.4	COMPONENT ORDER CONNECTIVITY	96
7	**Hypertrees**	105
7.1	Hypertrees and Partition-Connectedness	105
7.2	SET SPLITTING	108
7.3	MAX-INTERNAL SPANNING TREE	114
8	**Sunflower Lemma**	121
8.1	Sunflower Lemma	121
8.2	d-HITTING SET	122
8.3	d-SET PACKING	123
8.4	Domination in Degenerate Graphs	124
8.5	Domination in $K_{i,j}$-Free Graphs	128
9	**Modules**	133
9.1	Modular Partition	133
9.2	CLUSTER EDITING	139
9.3	COGRAPH COMPLETION	147
9.4	FAST Revisited	158
10	**Matroids**	164
10.1	Matroid Basics	164
10.2	Cut-Flow Data Structure	169
10.3	Kernel for ODD CYCLE TRANSVERSAL	173
11	**Representative Families**	183
11.1	Introduction to Representative Sets	183
11.2	Computing Representative Families	185
11.3	Kernel for VERTEX COVER	191
11.4	DIGRAPH PAIR CUT	192

11.5	An Abstraction	199
11.6	Combinatorial Approach	202
12	**Greedy Packing**	**217**
12.1	SET COVER	218
12.2	MAX-LIN-2 above Average	222
12.3	MAX-Er-SAT	231
13	**Euler's Formula**	**237**
13.1	Preliminaries on Planar Graphs	237
13.2	Simple Planar Kernels	238
13.3	Planar FEEDBACK VERTEX SET	243
	PART II META THEOREMS	255
14	**Introduction to Treewidth**	**257**
14.1	Properties of Tree Decompositions	259
14.2	Computing Treewidth	262
14.3	Nice Tree Decompositions	265
14.4	Dynamic Programming	268
14.5	Treewidth and **MSO$_2$**	279
14.6	Obstructions to Bounded Treewidth	286
15	**Bidimensionality and Protrusions**	**297**
15.1	Bidimensional Problems	298
15.2	Separability and Treewidth Modulators	301
15.3	Protrusion Decompositions	306
15.4	Kernel for DOMINATING SET on Planar Graphs	309
16	**Surgery on Graphs**	**316**
16.1	Boundaried Graphs and Finite Integer Index	319
16.2	Which Problems Have Finite Integer Index?	323
16.3	A General Reduction Rule	327
16.4	Kernelization in Quadratic Running Time	333
16.5	Linear Time Algorithm	340
	PART III LOWER BOUNDS	357
17	**Framework**	**359**
17.1	OR-Distillation	360
17.2	Cross-Composition	366
17.3	Examples of Compositions	369

18	**Instance Selectors**	377
18.1	DISJOINT FACTORS	379
18.2	SAT Parameterized by the Number of Variables	381
18.3	Colored Red-Blue Dominating Set	383
19	**Polynomial Parameter Transformation**	389
19.1	Packing Paths and Cycles	390
19.2	RED-BLUE DOMINATING SET	392
20	**Polynomial Lower Bounds**	398
20.1	Weak Cross-Composition	398
20.2	Lower Bound for VERTEX COVER	401
20.3	Lower Bound for d-HITTING SET	404
20.4	RAMSEY	408
21	**Extending Distillation**	412
21.1	Oracle Communication Protocol	412
21.2	Hardness of Communication	414
21.3	Lower Bounds for POINT LINE COVER	418
21.4	Lower Bounds Using Co-Nondeterminism	424
21.5	AND-Distillations and AND-Compositions	425
	PART IV BEYOND KERNELIZATION	427
22	**Turing Kernelization**	429
22.1	MAX LEAF SUBTREE	431
22.2	PLANAR LONGEST CYCLE	431
23	**Lossy Kernelization**	440
23.1	Framework	441
23.2	Cycle Packing	455
23.3	Partial Vertex Cover	457
23.4	Connected Vertex Cover	458
23.5	Steiner Tree	461
Appendix A	**Open Problems**	467
A.1	Polynomial Kernels	467
A.2	Structural Kernelization Bounds	469
A.3	Deterministic Kernels	471
A.4	Turing Kernels	472

Appendix B	**Graphs and SAT Notation**	474
Appendix C	**Problem Definitions**	477
References		483
Author Index		505
Index		510

Preface

Preprocessing, also known as *data reduction*, is one of the basic and most natural types of heuristic algorithms. The idea of preprocessing information to speed up computations can be traced much before the invention of the first computers. The book *Mirifici Logarithmorum Canonis Descriptio* (A Description of the Admirable Table of Logarithm) authored by Napier (1550–1617), who is credited with the invention of logarithms, was published in 1614. A quote (Eves 1969) attributed to Laplace states that this table, "by shortening the labours, doubled the life of the astronomer."

As a strategy of coping with hard problems, preprocessing is universally employed in almost every implementation, ranging from lossless data compression and navigation systems to microarray data analysis for the classification of cancer types. The "gold standard" successes in software development for hard problems, such as CPLEX for integer linear programming, depend heavily on sophisticated preprocessing routines. However, even very simple preprocessing can be surprisingly effective.

Developing rigorous mathematical theories that explain the behavior of practical algorithms and heuristics has become an increasingly important challenge in the theory of computing for the twenty-first century. Addressing issues central to the theory of computing, the report of Condon et al. (1999) states:

> "While theoretical work on models of computation and methods for analyzing algorithms has had enormous payoff, we are not done. In many situations, simple algorithms do well. We don't understand why! It is apparent that worst-case analysis does not provide useful insights on the performance of algorithms and heuristics and our models of computation need to be further developed and refined."

A natural question in this regard is how to measure the quality of preprocessing rules proposed for a specific problem, yet for a long time the mathematical analysis of polynomial time preprocessing algorithms was neglected. One central reason for this anomaly stems from the following observation: Showing that in polynomial time an instance I of an NP-hard problem can be replaced by an equivalent instance whose size is smaller than the size of I implies that P = NP with classical computation. The situation has changed drastically with the advent of mulivariate complexity theory, known as *parameterized complexity*. By combining tools from parameterized complexity and classical complexity it has become possible to derive upper and lower bounds on sizes of reduced instances, or so-called *kernels*. According to Fellows (2006),

> "It has become clear, however, that far from being trivial and uninteresting, pre-processing has unexpected practical power for real world input distributions, and is mathematically a much deeper subject than has generally been understood."

The foundations of kernelization are rooted in parameterized complexity: the classical book by Downey and Fellows (1999) mentions the method of reduction to a problem kernel as one of the basic tools to tackle problems in parameterized complexity. Indeed, for a parameterized problem, admitting an exponential kernel is roughly equivalent to being fixed-parameter tractable. However, some problems admit polynomial or even linear kernels! It is thus natural to ask whether for a parameterized problem admitting a *polynomial* kernel is also roughly equivalent to being fixed-parameter tractable. On the one hand, there is a growing number of examples of polynomial kernelization, scattered with the development of various algorithmic tools. On the other hand, some fixed-parameter tractable problems are only known to admit exponential kernels despite many attempts to prove that they do have polynomial kernels. The breakthrough work of Bodlaender et al. (2009b) showed that under reasonable complexity-theoretic assumptions, there exist fixed-parameter tractable problems that simply cannot have a kernel of polynomial size! This result led to a flurry of research activity in the field of kernelization, propagating kernelization algorithms for concrete parameterized problems and kernel lower-bound techniques.

Kernelization is an emerging subarea of algorithms and complexity. Despite its dynamic state, we believe the time is ripe for surveying major results and summarizing the current status of the field. The objective of this book is to provide a valuable overview of basic methods, important results and current issues. We have tried to make the presentation accessible not only to the specialists working in this field but also to a more general audience of students and researchers in computer science, operations research, optimization, combinatorics and other areas related to the study of algorithmic solutions of hard optimization problems. Parts of this book were used to teach courses on kernelization for graduate students in Bergen and Chennai.

The content of the book is divided into four parts. The first part, "Upper Bounds," provides a thorough overview of main algorithmic techniques employed to obtain polynomial kernels. After discussing the design of simple reduction rules, it shows how classical tools from combinatorial optimization, especially min-max theorems, are used in kernelization. Among other methods, this part presents combinatorial matroid-based methods as well as probabilistic techniques. The second part, "Meta Theorems," explores relations between logic and combinatorial structures. By gaining deep understanding of these relations, we can devise general rather than problem-specific kernelization techniques. The third part, "Lower Bounds," is devoted to aspects of complexity theory. This part explains cases in which we do not expect that there exist efficient data reductions, and provides insights into the reasons that underlie our pessimism. The book also contains a fourth part, "Beyond Kernalization," which discusses topics that do not fit into the previous parts, such as the notion of Turing and lossy kernels.

Using the Book for Teaching

The book is self-contained, and it can be used as the main textbook for a course on kernelization. Prior knowledge assumed includes only basic knowledge of algorithmics. For an introductory course on kernelization, we suggest to teach material covered in Parts I and III. In particular, we suggest to teach Chapters 2–4, Chapter 5 (without Sections 5.3 and 5.4), Chapter 6 (without Section 6.4), Chapter 8 and Chapters 17–19. Missing sections in Chapters 5 and 6, and the whole of Chapters 7, 12 and 13 can be used for a more extensive course. The book can also serve as a companion book to *Parameterized Algorithms* by Cygan et al. (2015) for teaching a course on parameterized algorithms.

At the end of each chapter we provide sections with exercises, hints to exercises, and bibliographical notes. Many of the exercises complement the main narrative and cover important results that have to be omitted due to space constraints. We use (✐) and (☠) to identify easy and challenging exercises. Following the common practice for textbooks, we try to minimize the occurrence of bibliographical and historical references in the main text by moving them to bibliographic notes. These notes can also guide the reader on to further reading.

Acknowledgments

Many of our colleagues helped with valuable advices, comments, corrections and suggestions. We are grateful for feedback from Faisal Abu-Khzam, Marek Cygan, Pål Drange, Markus Sortland Dregi, Bart M. Jansen, Mike Fellows, Petr Golovach, Gregory Gutin, Stefan Kratsch, Neeldhara Misra, Rolf Möhring, Christophe Paul, Marcin and Michał Pilipczuks, Venkatesh Raman, Ignasi Sau, Sigve Sæther, Dimitrios M. Thilikos, Magnus Wahlström and Mingyu Xiao.

Our work has received funding from the European Research Council under the European Union's Seventh Framework Programme (FP/2007-2013)/ERC Grant Agreements No. 267959 (Rigorous Theory of Preprocessing), 306992 (Parameterized Approximation), and 715744 (Pareto-Optimal Parameterized Algorithms), from the Bergen Research Foundation and the University of Bergen through project "BeHard," and the Norwegian Research Council through project "MULTIVAL."

1
What Is a Kernel?

Every block of stone has a statue inside it and it is the task of the sculptor to discover it.

(—Michelangelo Buonarroti (1475–1564))

1.1 Introduction

Preprocessing (*data reduction* or *kernelization*) is a computation that transforms input data into "something simpler" by partially solving the problem associated with it. Preprocessing is an integral part of almost any application: Both systematic and intuitive approaches to tackle difficult problems often involve it. Even in our everyday lives, we often rely on preprocessing, sometimes without noticing it. Before we delve into the formal details, let us start our acquaintance with preprocessing by considering several examples.

Let us first look at the simple chess puzzle depicted in Fig. 1.1. In the given board position, we ask if White can checkmate the Black king in two moves. A naive approach for solving this puzzle would be to try all possible moves of White, all possible moves of Black, and then all possible moves of White. This gives us a huge number of possible moves—the time required to solve this puzzle with this approach would be much longer than a human life. However, a reader with some experience of playing chess will find the solution easily: First we move the white knight to f7, checking the black king. Next, the black king has to move to either h8 or to h7, and in both cases it is checkmated once the white rook is moved to h5. So how we are able to solve such problems? The answer is that while at first look the position on the board looks complicated, most of the pieces on the board, like white pieces on the first three rows or black pieces on the first three columns, are irrelevant to the solution. See the right-hand board in Fig. 1.1. An experienced player could see the important patterns

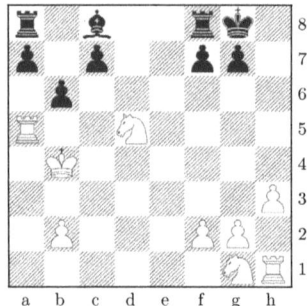 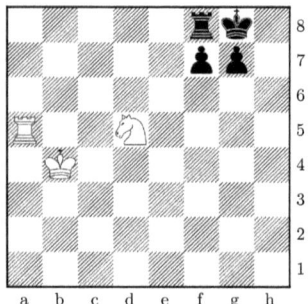

Figure 1.1 Can White checkmate in two moves? The initial puzzle and an "equivalent" reduced puzzle.

immediately, which allows the player to ignore the irrelevant information and concentrate only on the essential part of the puzzle. In this case, the player reduces the given problem to a seemingly simpler problem, and only then tries to solve it.

In this example, we were able to successfully simplify a problem by relying on intuition and acquired experience. However, we did not truly give a *sound* rule, having provable correctness, to reduce the complexity of the problem—this will be our goal in later examples. Moreover, in this context we also ask ourselves whether we can turn our intuitive arguments into generic rules that can be applied to all chess compositions. While there exist many rules for good openings, middle games and endings in chess, turning intuition into generic rules is not an easy task, and this is why the game is so interesting!

Let consider more generic rules in the context of another popular game, Sudoku (see Fig. 1.2). Sudoku is a number-placement puzzle, which is played over a 9×9 grid that is divided into 3×3 subgrids called "boxes." Some of the cells of the grid are already filled with some numbers. The objective is to fill each of the empty cells with a number between 1 and 9 such that each number appears exactly once in each row, column and box. While an unexperienced Sudoku-solver will try to use a brute force to guess the missing numbers this approach would work only for very simple examples. The experienced puzzle-solver has a number of preprocessing rules under her belt that allow her to reduce the puzzle to a state in which a brute-force approach can solve the problem within reasonable time.

Several known such preprocessing techniques solve most easy puzzles. For more difficult puzzles preprocessing is used to decrease the number of cases one should analyze to find a solution, whereas the solution is obtained by

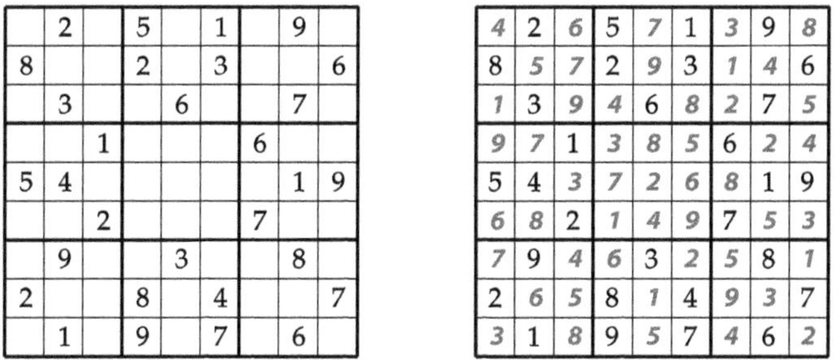

1.1 Introduction

	2		5	1		9		
8			2		3			6
	3			6			7	
		1				6		
5	4						1	9
		2			7			
	9		3			8		
2			8	4				7
	1		9	7		6		

4	2	6	5	7	1	3	9	8
8	5	7	2	9	3	1	4	6
1	3	9	4	6	8	2	7	5
9	7	1	3	8	5	6	2	4
5	4	3	7	2	6	8	1	9
6	8	2	1	4	9	7	5	3
7	9	4	6	3	2	5	8	1
2	6	5	8	1	4	9	3	7
3	1	8	9	5	7	4	6	2

Figure 1.2 A solution to a Sudoku puzzle.

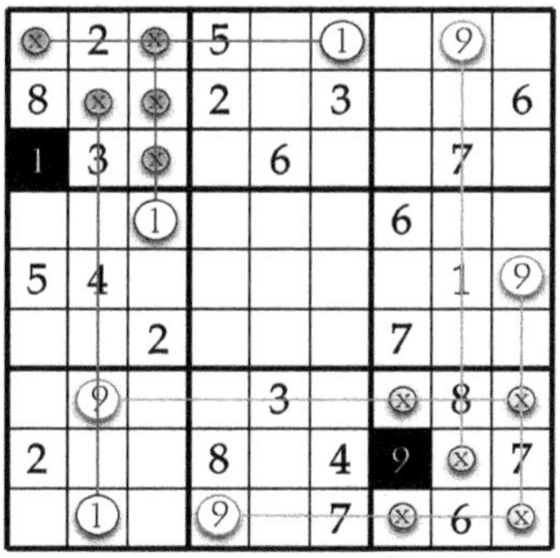

Figure 1.3 Applying the cross-hatching rule to the top-left and bottom-right boxes.

combining preprocessing with other approaches. For example, one such well-known preprocessing technique is *cross-hatching*. The cross-hatching rule is applied to 3×3 boxes. Let us look at the top-left box of the sample puzzle in Fig. 1.2. Because all numbers between 1 and 9 must appear in this box, the six empty cells should be filled with the numbers $1, 4, 5, 6, 7$ and 9. Let us attempt to find an empty cell that can be filled in with the missing number 1. To identify such a cell, we use the fact that any number can appear only once per row and once per column. As illustrated in Fig. 1.3, we thus discover a unique cell that can accommodate the number 1. In the bottom-right box, cross-hatching identifies a unique cell that can accommodate the number 9.

Although many rules were devised for solving Sudoku puzzles, none provides a generic solution to every puzzle. Thus while, for Sudoku, one can formalize what a reduction is, we are not able to predict whether reductions will solve the puzzle or even if they simplify the instance.

In both examples, to solve the problem at hand, we first simplify, and only then go about solving it. While in the chess puzzle we based our reduction solely on our intuition and experience, in the Sudoku puzzle we attempted to formalize the preprocessing rules. But is it possible not only to formalize what a preprocessing rule is but also to analyze the impact of preprocessing rigorously?

In all examples discussed so far, we did not try to analyze the potential impact of implemented reduction rules. We know that in some cases reduction rules will simplify instances significantly, but we have no idea if they will be useful for all instances or only for some of them. We would like to examine this issue in the context of NP-complete problems, which constitute a very large class of interesting combinatorial problems. It is widely believed that no NP-complete problem can be solved efficiently, that is, by a polynomial time algorithm. Is it possible to design reduction rules that can reduce a hard problem, say, by 5 percent while not solving it? At first glance, this idea can never work unless P is equal to NP. Indeed, consider for example the following NP-complete problem VERTEX COVER. Here we are given an n-vertex graph G and integer k. The task is to decide whether G contains a vertex cover S of size at most k, that is a set such that every edge of G has at least one endpoint in S. VERTEX COVER is known to be NP-complete. Suppose that we have a polynomial time algorithm that is able to reduce the problem to an equivalent instance of smaller size. Say, this algorithm outputs a new graph G' on $n-1$ vertices and integer k' such that G has a vertex cover of size at most k if and only if G' has a vertex cover of size at most k'. In this situation, we could have applied the algorithm repeatedly at most n times, eventually solving the problem optimally in polynomial time. This would imply that P is equal to NP and thus the existence of such a preprocessing algorithm is highly unlikely. Similar arguments are valid for any NP-hard problem. However, before hastily determining that we have reached a dead end, let us look at another example.

In our last example, we have a set of pebbles lying on a table, and we ask if we can cover all pebbles with k sticks. In other words, we are given a finite set of points in the plane, and we need to decide if all these points can be covered by at most k lines (see Fig. 1.4). This problem is known under the name POINT LINE COVER. We say that the integer k is the *parameter* associated with our problem instance. If there are n points, we can trivially solve the problem by trying all possible ways to draw k lines. Every line is characterized by two points, so this procedure will require roughly $n^{\mathcal{O}(k)}$ steps.

But before trying all combinations, let us perform some much less time-consuming operations. Toward this end, let us consider the following simple yet powerful observation: If there is a line L covering at least $k+1$

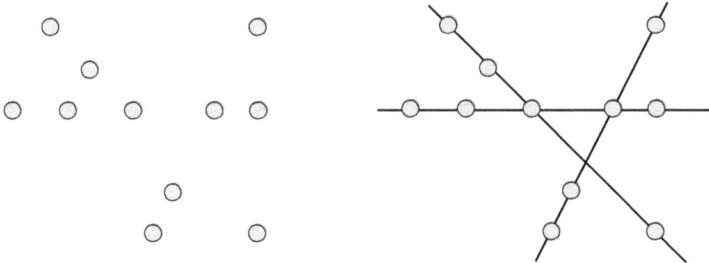

Figure 1.4 Covering all points with three lines.

points, then this line should belong to every solution (that is, at most k lines that cover all points). Indeed, if we do not use this line L, then all the points it covers have to be covered by other lines, which will require at least $k+1$ lines. Specifically, this means that if our instance has a solution, then it necessarily contains L, and therefore the instance obtained by deleting all points covered by L and decrementing the budget k by 1 also has a solution. In the other direction, it is clear that if our new instance has a solution, then the original one also has a solution. We thus conclude that solving the original problem instance is equivalent to solving the instance obtained by deleting all points covered by L and decrementing the budget k by 1. In other words, we can apply the following *reduction rule*.

> **Reduction Rule** Reduction Rule If there is a line L covering more than k points, remove all points covered by L and decrement the parameter k by one.

This reduction rule is *sound*: The reduced problem instance has a solution if and only if the original problem instance has a solution. The naive implementation of the reduction rule takes time $\mathcal{O}(n^3)$: For each pair of points, we check if the line through it covers at least $k+1$ points. After each application of the reduction rule, we obtain an instance with a smaller number of points. Thus, after exhaustive repeated application of this rule, we arrive at one of the following situations.

- We end up having an instance in which no points are left, in which case the problem has been solved.
- The parameter k is zero but some points are left. In this case, the problem does not have solution.

- Neither of the two previous conditions is true, yet the reduction rule cannot be applied.

What would be the number of points in an irreducible instance corresponding to the last case? Because no line can cover more than k points, we deduce that if we are left with more than k^2 points, the problem does not have solution. We have thus managed, without solving the problem, to reduce the size of the problem from n to k^2! Moreover, we were able to estimate the size of the reduced problem as a function of the parameter k. This leads us to the striking realization that polynomial-time algorithms hold provable power over exact solutions to hard problems; rather than being able to find those solutions, they are able to provably reduce input sizes without changing the answer.

It is easy to show that the decision version of our puzzle problem—determining whether a given set of points can be covered by at most k lines—is NP-complete. While we cannot claim that our reduction rule always reduces the number of points by 5 percent, we are still able to prove that the size of the reduced problem does not exceed some function of the parameter k. Such a reduced instance is called a *kernel* of the problem, and the theory of efficient parameterized reductions, also known as *kernelization*, is the subject of this book.

1.2 Kernelization: Formal Definition

To define kernelization formally, we need to define what a parameterized problem is. The algorithmic and complexity theory studying parameterized problems is called *parameterized complexity*.

Definition 1.1 A *parameterized problem* is a language $L \subseteq \Sigma^* \times \mathbb{N}$, where Σ is a fixed, finite alphabet. For an instance $(x, k) \in \Sigma^* \times \mathbb{N}$, k is called the *parameter*.

For example, an instance of POINT LINE COVER parameterized by the solution size is a pair (S, k), where we expect S to be a set of points on a plane encoded as a string over Σ, and k is a positive integer. Specifically, a pair (S, k) is a yes-instance, which belongs to the POINT LINE COVER parameterized language, if and only if the string S correctly encodes a set of points, which we will also denote by S, and moreover this set of points can be covered by k lines. Similarly, an instance of the CNF-SAT problem (satisfiability of propositional formulas in conjunctive normal form), parameterized by the number of variables, is a pair (φ, n), where we expect φ to be the input formula

1.2 Kernelization: Formal Definition

encoded as a string over Σ and n to be the number of variables of φ. That is, a pair (φ, n) belongs to the CNF-SAT parameterized language if and only if the string φ correctly encodes a CNF formula with n variables, and the formula is satisfiable.

We define the size of an instance (x, k) of a parameterized problem as $|x|+k$. One interpretation of this convention is that, when given to the algorithm on the input, the parameter k is encoded in unary.

The notion of kernelization is tightly linked to the notion of *fixed-parameter tractability* (FPT) of parameterized problems. Before we formally define what a kernel is, let us first briefly discuss this basic notion, which serves as background to our story. Fixed-parameter algorithms are the class of exact algorithms where the exponential blowup in the running time is restricted to a small parameter associated with the input instance. That is, the running time of such an algorithm on an input of size n is of the form $\mathcal{O}(f(k) n^c)$, where k is a parameter that is typically small compared to n, $f(k)$ is a (typically super-polynomial) function of k that does not involve n, and c is a constant. Formally,

Definition 1.2 A parameterized problem $L \subseteq \Sigma^* \times \mathbb{N}$ is called *fixed-parameter tractable* if there exists an algorithm $\mathcal{A}$ (called a *fixed-parameter algorithm*), a computable function $f: \mathbb{N} \to \mathbb{N}$, and a constant c with the following property. Given any $(x, k) \in \Sigma^* \times \mathbb{N}$, the algorithm $\mathcal{A}$ correctly decides whether $(x, k) \in L$ in time bounded by $f(k) \cdot |x|^c$. The complexity class containing all fixed-parameter tractable problems is called FPT.

The assumption that f is a computable function is aligned with the book by Cygan et al. (2015). This assumption helps to avoid running into trouble when developing complexity theory for fixed-parameter tractability.

We briefly remark that there is a hierarchy of intractable parameterized problem classes above FPT. The main ones are the following.

$$\text{FPT} \subseteq \text{M}[1] \subseteq \text{W}[1] \subseteq \text{M}[2] \subseteq \text{W}[1] \subseteq \cdots \subseteq \text{W}[P] \subseteq \text{XP}$$

The principal analog of the classical intractability class NP is W[1]. In particular, a fundamental problem complete for W[1] is the k-STEP HALTING PROBLEM FOR NONDETERMINISTIC TURING MACHINES (with unlimited nondeterminism and alphabet size). This completeness result provides an analog of Cook's theorem in classical complexity. A convenient source of W[1]-hardness reductions is provided by the result that CLIQUE is complete for

W[1]. Other highlights of this theory are that DOMINATING SET is complete for W[2], and that FPT=M[1] if and only if the *exponential time hypothesis* fails. The classical reference on parameterized complexity is the book by Downey and Fellows (1999). A rich collection of books for further reading about parameterized complexity is provided in the "Bibliographic Notes" to this chapter.

Let us now turn our attention back to the notion of *kernelization*, which is formally defined as follows.

Definition 1.3 Let L be a parameterized problem over a finite alphabet Σ. A *kernelization algorithm*, or in short, a *kernelization*, for L is an algorithm with the following property. For any given $(x, k) \in \Sigma^* \times \mathbb{N}$, it outputs in time polynomial in $|(x, k)|$ a string $x' \in \Sigma^*$ and an integer $k' \in \mathbb{N}$ such that

$$((x, k) \in L \iff (x', k') \in L) \text{ and } |x'|, k' \leq h(k),$$

where h is an arbitrary computable function. If K is a kernelization for L, then for every instance (x, k) of L, the result of running K on the input (x, k) is called the kernel of (x, k) (under K). The function h is referred to as the *size* of the kernel. If h is a polynomial function, then we say that the kernel is polynomial.

We remark that in the preceding definition, the function h is not unique. However, in the context of a specific function h known to serve as an upper bound on the size of our kernel, it is conventional to refer to this function h as the size of the kernel.

We often say that a problem L admits a kernel of size h, meaning that every instance of L has a kernel of size h. We also often say that L admits a kernel with property Π, meaning that every instance of L has a kernel with property Π. For example, saying that VERTEX COVER admits a kernel with $\mathcal{O}(k)$ vertices and $\mathcal{O}(k^2)$ edges is a short way of saying that there is a kernelization algorithm K such that for every instance (G, k) of the problem, K outputs a kernel with $\mathcal{O}(k)$ vertices and $\mathcal{O}(k^2)$ edges.

While the running times of kernelization algorithms are of clear importance, the optimization of this aspect is not the topic of this book. However, we remark that, lately, there is some growing interest in optimizing this aspect of kernelization as well, in particular in the design of linear-time kernelization algorithms. Here, linear time means that the running time of the algorithm is linear in $|x|$, but it can be nonlinear in k.

1.2 Kernelization: Formal Definition

It is easy to see that if a decidable (parameterized) problem admits a kernelization for some function f, then the problem is FPT: For every instance of the problem, we call a polynomial time kernelization algorithm, and then we use a decision algorithm to identify if the resulting instance is valid. Because the size of the kernel is bounded by some function of the parameter, the running time of the decision algorithm depends only on the parameter. Interestingly, the converse also holds, that is, if a problem is FPT then it admits a kernelization. The proof of this fact is quite simple, and we present it here.

Theorem 1.4 *If a parameterized problem L is* FPT *then it admits a kernelization.*

Proof: Suppose that there is an algorithm deciding if $(x, k) \in L$ in time $f(k)|x|^c$ for some computable function f and constant c. On the one hand, if $|x| \geq f(k)$, then we run the decision algorithm on the instance in time $f(k)|x|^c \leq |x|^{c+1}$. If the decision algorithm outputs yes, the kernelization algorithm outputs a constant size yes-instance, and if the decision algorithm outputs no, the kernelization algorithm outputs a constant size no-instance. On the other hand, if $|x| < f(k)$, then the kernelization algorithm outputs x. This yields a kernel of size $f(k)$ for the problem. □

Theorem 1.4 shows that kernelization can be seen as an alternative definition of FPT problems. So to decide if a parameterized problem has a kernel, we can employ many known tools already given by parameterized complexity. But what if we are interested in kernels that are as small as possible? The size of a kernel obtained using Theorem 1.4 equals the dependence on k in the running time of the best known fixed-parameter algorithm for the problem, which is usually exponential. Can we find better kernels? The answer is yes, we can, but not always. For many problems we can obtain polynomial kernels, but under reasonable complexity-theoretic assumptions, there exist FPT problems that do not admit kernels of polynomial size.

Finally, if the input and output instances are associated with *different* problems, then the weaker notion of *compression* replaces the one of kernelization. In several parts of this book polynomial compression will be used to obtain polynomial kernels. Also the notion of compression will be very useful in the theory of lower bounds for polynomial kernels. Formally, we have the following weaker form of Definition 1.3.

Definition 1.5 A *polynomial compression* of a parameterized language $Q \subseteq \Sigma^* \times \mathbb{N}$ into a language $R \subseteq \Sigma^*$ is an algorithm that takes as input an instance $(x, k) \in \Sigma^* \times \mathbb{N}$, works in time polynomial in $|x| + k$, and returns a string y such that:

(i) $|y| \leq p(k)$ for some polynomial $p(\cdot)$, and
(ii) $y \in R$ if and only if $(x, k) \in Q$.

If $|\Sigma| = 2$, the polynomial $p(\cdot)$ will be called the *bitsize* of the compression.

In some cases, we will write of a polynomial compression without specifying the target language R. This means that there exists a polynomial compression into some language R.

Of course, a polynomial kernel is also a polynomial compression. We just treat the output kernel as an instance of the unparameterized version of Q. Here, by an *unparameterized version* of a parameterized language Q we mean a classic language $\tilde{Q} \subseteq \Sigma^*$ where the parameter is appended in unary after the instance (with some separator symbol to distinguish the start of the parameter from the end of the input). The main difference between polynomial compression and kernelization is that the polynomial compression is allowed to output an instance of *any* language R, even an undecidable one.

When R is reducible in polynomial time back to Q, then the combination of compression and the reduction yields a polynomial kernel for Q. In particular, every problem in NP can be reduced in polynomial time by a deterministic Turing machine to any NP-hard problem. The following theorem about polynomial compression and kernelization will be used in several places in this book.

Theorem 1.6 *Let $Q \subseteq \Sigma^* \times \mathbb{N}$ be a parameterized language and $R \subseteq \Sigma^*$ be a language such that the unparameterized version of $Q \subseteq \Sigma^* \times \mathbb{N}$ is NP-hard and $R \subseteq \Sigma^*$ is in NP. If there is a polynomial compression of Q into R, then Q admits a polynomial kernel.*

Proof: Let (x, k) be an instance of Q. Then the application of a polynomial compression to (x, k) results in a string y such that $|y| = k^{\mathcal{O}(1)}$ and $y \in R$ if and only if $(x, k) \in Q$. Because $\tilde{Q}$ is NP-hard and R is in NP, there is a polynomial time many-to-one reduction f from R to $\tilde{Q}$. Let $z = f(y)$. Because the time of the reduction is polynomial in the size of y, we have that it runs in time $k^{\mathcal{O}(1)}$ and hence $|z| = k^{\mathcal{O}(1)}$. Also we have that $z \in \tilde{Q}$ if and only if $y \in R$. Let us remind that z is an instance of the unparameterized version of Q, and thus we can rewrite z as an equivalent instance $(x', k') \in Q$. This two-step polynomial-time algorithm is the desired kernelization algorithm for Q. □

Two things are worth a remark. Theorem 1.6 does not imply a polynomial kernel when we have a polynomial compression in a language that is not in NP. There are examples of natural problems for which we are able to obtain a polynomial compression but to a language R of much higher complexity than Q, and we do not know if polynomial kernels exist for such problems.

While Theorem 1.6 states the existence of a polynomial kernel, its proof does not explain how to construct such a kernel. The proof of Cook-Levin theorem constructs a reduction from any problem in NP to CNF-SAT. This reduction, combined with an NP-hardness proof for Q, provides a constructive kernel for Q.

Bibliographic Notes

The classical reference on parameterized complexity is the book by Downey and Fellows (1999). In this book, Downey and Fellows also introduced the concept of reduction to a problem kernel. For more updated material we refer to the books by Flum and Grohe (2006); Niedermeier (2006); Downey and Fellows (2013); and Cygan et al. (2015). Each of these books contains a part devoted to kernelization. Theorem 1.4 on the equivalence of kernelization and FPT is due to Cai et al. (1997). For surveys on kernelization we refer to Bodlaender (2009); Fomin and Saurabh (2014); Guo and Niedermeier (2007a); Hüffner et al. (2008); and Misra et al. (2011). Approaches to solving Sudoku puzzles, including formulations of integer programs, are given by Kaibel and Koch (2006) and Bartlett et al. (2008).

We remark that Theorem 1.6 was first observed by Bodlaender et al. (2011). An example of a compression for which a kernelization is not known is given in Wahlström (2013) for a problem in which one is interested in finding a cycle through specific vertices given as input. As noted in this chapter, in this book we do not optimize running times of kernelization algorithms, except one chapter on meta-kernelization. However, this is also an aspect of interest in the design of kernels. For a recent example of a linear-time kernelization algorithm for the FEEDBACK VERTEX SET problem, we refer to Iwata (2017).

PART I
Upper Bounds

2
Warm Up

In this warm-up chapter we provide simple examples of kernelization algorithms and reduction rules. Our examples include kernels for MAX-3-SAT, PLANAR INDEPENDENT SET, VERTEX COVER, FEEDBACK ARC SET IN TOURNAMENTS, DOMINATING SET in graphs of girth 5, VERTEX COVER parameterized by degree-1 modulator and EDGE CLIQUE COVER.

Sometimes even very simple arguments can result in a kernel. Such arguments are often formulated as reduction rules. In fact, the design of sets of reduction rules is the most common approach to obtain kernelization algorithms. Reduction rules transform a problem instance to an equivalent instance having beneficial properties, whose size is usually smaller than the size of the original problem instance. Standard arguments that analyze such rules are often formulated as follows. Suppose that we applied our set of reduction rules exhaustively. In other words, the current problem instance is *irreducible* subject to our rules. Then, the size of the current problem instance is bounded appropriately, which results in a bound on the size of the kernel.

Formally, a *data reduction rule*, or simply, a reduction rule, for a parameterized problem Q is a function $\varphi \colon \Sigma^* \times \mathbb{N} \to \Sigma^* \times \mathbb{N}$ that maps an instance (I, k) of Q to an equivalent instance (I', k') of Q. Here, we assume that φ is computable in time polynomial in $|I|$ and k, and we say that two instances of Q are *equivalent* if $(I, k) \in Q$ if and only if $(I', k') \in Q$. Usually, but not always, $|I'| < |I|$ or $k' < k$. In other words, it is often the case that φ reduces the size of the instance or the parameter. The guarantee that a reduction rule φ translates a problem instance to an equivalent instance is referred to as the *safeness* or *soundness* of φ. In this book, we use the phrases *a rule is safe* and *the safeness of a reduction rule*.

Some reduction rules can be complicated both to design and to analyze. However, simple rules whose analysis is straightforward occasionally already result in polynomial kernels—this chapter presents such examples. The simplest reduction rule is the one that does nothing, and for some problems such a strategy is just fine. For example, suppose that our task is to decide if a cubic graph G (i.e., graph with all vertex degrees at most 3) contains an independent set of size at least k. By the classical result from Graph Theory called Brook's theorem, every graph with maximum degree Δ can be properly colored in at most $\Delta + 1$ colors. Moreover, such a coloring can be obtained in polynomial time. Because each color class in proper coloring is an independent set, G should contain an independent set of size at least $|V(G)|/4$. Thus, if $|V(G)| \geq 4k$, it contains an independent set of size k and, moreover, such a set can be found in polynomial time. Otherwise, G has at most $4k$ vertices, and thus the problem admits a kernel with at most $4k$ vertices.

Next, we give examples of other such "trivial" kernels for MAX-3-SAT and PLANAR INDEPENDENT SET. Then we proceed with examples of basic reduction rules, when trivial operations like deleting a vertex or an edge, or reversing directions of arcs, result in kernels. Here, we consider the problems VERTEX COVER, FEEDBACK ARC SET IN TOURNAMENTS, VERTEX COVER, FEEDBACK ARC SET IN TOURNAMENTS (FAST), DOMINATING SET in graphs of girth 5, VERTEX COVER parameterized by the number of vertices whose removal leaves only isolated edges and vertices and EDGE CLIQUE COVER.

2.1 Trivial Kernelization

In some situations, one can directly conclude that a given problem instance is already a kernel. We start by giving two examples of such "trivial" kernels.

MAX-3-SAT. In the CNF-SAT problem (satisfiability of propositional formulas in conjunctive normal form), we are given a Boolean formula that is a conjunction of clauses, where every clause is a disjunction of literals. The question is whether there exists a truth assignment to variables that satisfies all clauses. In the optimization version of this problem, namely MAXIMUM SATISFIABILITY, the task is to find a truth assignment satisfying the maximum number of clauses. We consider a special case of MAXIMUM SATISFIABILITY, called MAX-3-SAT, where every clause is of size at most 3. That is, in MAX-3-SAT we are given a 3-CNF formula φ and a nonnegative integer k, and the task is to decide whether there exists a truth assignment satisfying at least k clauses of φ.

2.1 Trivial Kernelization

Lemma 2.1 MAX-3-SAT *admits a kernel with at most $2k$ clauses and $6k$ variables.*

Proof: Let (φ, k) be an instance of MAX-3-SAT, and let m and n denote its number of clauses and its number of variables, respectively. Let ψ be a truth assignment to the variables of φ. We define $\neg\psi$ to be the assignment obtained by complementing the assignment of ψ. Thus ψ assigns $\delta \in \{\top, \bot\}$ to some variable x then $\neg\psi$ assigns $\neg\delta$ to x. In other words, $\neg\psi$ is the bitwise complement of ψ. So if the parameter k is smaller than $m/2$, there exists an assignment that satisfies at least k clauses and, therefore (φ, k) is a yes-instance. Otherwise, $m \leq 2k$ and so $n \leq 6k$, which implies that the input is a kernel of the desired size. □

PLANAR INDEPENDENT SET. Our second example of a "trivial" kernel concerns the special case of INDEPENDENT SET on planar graphs. Let us recall that a set of pairwise nonadjacent vertices is called an *independent set*, and that a graph is planar if it can be drawn on the plane in such a way that its edges intersect only at vertices. In PLANAR INDEPENDENT SET, we are given a planar graph G and a nonnegative integer k. The task is to decide whether G has an independent set of size k.

Lemma 2.2 PLANAR INDEPENDENT SET *admits a kernel with at most $4(k-1)$ vertices.*

Proof: By one of the most fundamental theorems in Graph Theory, the Four Color Theorem, there is a coloring of the vertices of every planar graph that uses only four colors and such that vertices of the same color form an independent set. This theorem implies that if a planar graph has at least $4k - 3$ vertices, it has an independent set of size k, and thus we have a yes-instance at hand. Otherwise the number of vertices in the graph is at most $4k - 4$, and therefore (G, k) is a kernel with the desired property. □

Let us note that it is important that we restricted the problem to planar graphs. On general graphs, INDEPENDENT SET is W[1]-hard, which means that the existence of a (not even polynomial) kernel for this problem is highly unlikely.

The arguments used in the proof Lemma 2.2 are trivially extendable to the case when input graph is colorable in a constant number of colors. However, it is not known whether PLANAR INDEPENDENT SET admits a kernel with $4k - 5$ vertices. In fact, to the best of our knowledge, it is open whether an independent set of size at least $n/4 + 1$ in an n-vertex planar graph can be found in polynomial time.

2.2 VERTEX COVER

In this section we discuss a kernelization algorithm for VERTEX COVER that is based on simple, intuitive rules. Let us remind that a vertex set S is a *vertex cover* of a graph G if $G - S$ does not contain edges. In the VERTEX COVER problem, we are given a graph G and integer k, the task is to decide whether G has a vertex cover of size at most k.

The first reduction rule is based on the following trivial observation: If the graph G has an isolated vertex, the removal of this vertex does not change the solution, and this operation can be implemented in polynomial time. Thus, the following rule is safe.

> **Reduction VC.1** If G contains an isolated vertex v, remove v from G. The resulting instance is $(G - v, k)$.

The second rule is also based on a simple observation: If G contains a vertex of degree larger than k, then this vertex should belong to every vertex cover of size at most k. Indeed, the correctness of this claim follows from the argument that if v does not belong to some vertex cover, then this vertex cover must contain at least $k + 1$ other vertices to cover the edges incident to v. Thus, the following reduction is also safe.

> **Reduction VC.2** If G contains a vertex v of degree at least $k + 1$, remove v (along with edges incident to v) from G and decrement the parameter k by 1. The resulting instance is $(G - v, k - 1)$.

Reduction Rules VC.1 and VC.2 are already sufficient to deduce that VERTEX COVER admits a polynomial kernel:

Lemma 2.3 VERTEX COVER *admits a kernel with at most* $k(k+1)$ *vertices and* k^2 *edges.*

Proof: Let (G', k') be an instance of VERTEX COVER obtained from (G, k) by exhaustively applying Rules VC.1 and VC.2. Note that $k' \leq k$, and that G has a vertex cover of size at most k if and only if G' has a vertex cover of size at most k'. Because we can no longer apply Rule VC.1, G' has no isolated vertices. Thus for any vertex cover C of G', every vertex of $G' - C$ should be adjacent to some vertex from C. Because we cannot apply Rule VC.2, every vertex of G' is of degree at most k'. Therefore, if G' has more than $k'(k'+1) \leq k(k+1)$ vertices, (G', k') is a no-instance. Moreover, every edge of G' must be covered by a vertex, and every vertex can cover at most k' edges. Hence, if G' has more than $(k')^2 \le k^2$ edges, we again deduce that (G', k') is a no-instance. To conclude, we have shown that if we can apply neither Rule VC.1 nor Rule VC.2, the irreducible graph has at most $k(k+1)$ vertices and k^2 edges.

Finally, all rules can be easily performed in polynomial time. □

Because the design of this kernelization was rather simple, let us try to add more rules and see if we can obtain a better kernel. The next rule is also very intuitive. If a graph has a vertex v of degree 1, there is always an optimal solution containing the neighbor of v rather than v. We add a rule capturing this observation:

> **Reduction VC.3** If G contains a vertex v of degree 1, remove v and its neighbor from G, and decrement the parameter k by 1. The resulting instance is $(G - N[v], k - 1)$.

Once Rule VC.3 cannot be applied, the graph G' has no vertices of degree 1. Hence, $|V(G')| \le |E(G')|$. We have already proved that in the case of a yes-instance, we have $|E(G')| \le k^2$. Thus by adding the new rule, we have established that VERTEX COVER admits a kernel with at most k^2 vertices.

If all vertices of a graph G are of degree at least 3, then $|V(G)| \le 2|E(G)|/3$. Thus, if we found a reduction rule that gets rid of vertices of degree 2, we would have obtained a kernel with at most $2k^2/3$ vertices. Such a rule exists, but it is slightly more complicated than the previous ones. We have to distinguish between two different cases depending on whether the neighbors of the degree-2 vertex are adjacent. If the neighbors u and w of a degree-2 vertex v are adjacent, then every vertex cover should contain at least two vertices of the triangle formed by v, u and w. Hence to construct an optimal solution, among v, u and w, we can choose only u and w. This shows that the following rule is safe.

> **Reduction VC.4** If G contains a degree-2 vertex v whose neighbors u and w are adjacent, remove v, u and w from G, and decrement the parameter k by 2. The resulting instance is $(G - N[v], k - 2)$.

In case a vertex of degree 2 is adjacent to two nonadjacent vertices, we apply the following rule.

> **Reduction VC.5** If G contains a degree-2 vertex v whose neighbors u and w are nonadjacent, construct a new graph G' from G by identifying u and w and removing v (see Fig. 2.1), and decrement the parameter k by 1. The resulting instance is $(G', k - 1)$.

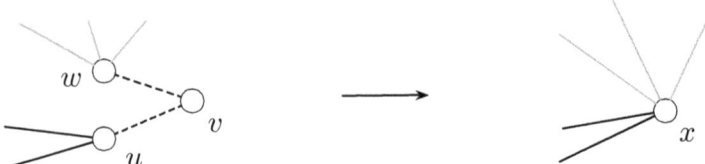

Figure 2.1 Rule VC.5.

Let us argue that Rule VC.5 is safe. For this purpose, let X be a vertex cover of G' of size $k-1$, and let x be the vertex of G' obtained by identifying u and w. On the one hand, if $x \in X$, then $(X \setminus \{x\}) \cup \{u, w\}$ is a vertex cover of G of size k. On the other hand, if $x \notin X$, then $X \cup \{v\}$ is a vertex cover of G of size k. Thus if G' has a vertex cover of size $k-1$, then G has a vertex cover of size at most k.

In the opposite direction, let Y be a vertex cover of G of size k. If both u and w belong to Y, then $(Y \setminus \{u, w, v\}) \cup \{x\}$ is a vertex cover in G' of size at most $k-1$. If exactly one of u, w belongs to Y, then v should belong to Y, in which case $(Y \setminus \{u, w, v\}) \cup \{x\}$ is vertex cover of G' of size $k-1$. Finally, if $u, w \notin Y$, then $v \in Y$, and therefore $Y \setminus \{v\}$ is a vertex cover of G' of size $k-1$.

We have proved that both Rules VC.4 and VC.5 are safe. After we apply all rules exhaustively, the resulting graph will have at most $2k^2/3$ vertices and k^2 edges. Clearly, each of the rules can be implemented in polynomial time. Thus we arrive at the following lemma.

Lemma 2.4 VERTEX COVER *admits a kernel with at most* $2k^2/3$ *vertices and* k^2 *edges.*

A natural idea to improve the kernel would be to design reduction rules that can handle vertices of degree 3. However, coming up with such rules is much more challenging. One of the reasons to that is that VERTEX COVER is NP-complete already on graphs with vertices of degree at most 3. However this does not exclude a possibility of obtaining a better kernel for VERTEX COVER, we just have to adapt another approaches. In Chapters 4 and 6, we use different ideas to construct kernels for VERTEX COVER with at most $2k$ vertices. We complement these results in Chapter 20 by arguing that it is highly unlikely that VERTEX COVER admits a kernel of size $k^{2-\varepsilon}$ for any $\varepsilon > 0$. Thus the bound on the number of edges in the kernels presented in this section is asymptotically tight.

2.3 Feedback Arc Set in Tournaments

In this section we discuss a kernel for FEEDBACK ARC SET IN TOURNAMENTS (FAST). A *tournament* is a directed graph T such that for every pair of vertices $u, v \in V(T)$, there is exactly one arc in T: either uv or vu. A set of arcs A of T is called a *feedback arc set* if every cycle of T contains an arc from A. In other words, the removal of A from T turns it into an acyclic graph. We remark that acyclic tournaments are often said to be *transitive*. In FAST, we are given a tournament T and a nonnegative integer k. The task is to decide whether T has a feedback arc set of size at most k.

Deletions of arcs of tournaments can result in graphs that are not tournaments anymore. Due to this fact, reversing (redirecting) arcs is much more convenient than deleting arcs. We leave the proof of the following lemma as an exercise (Problem 2.5).

Lemma 2.5 *A graph is acyclic if and only if it is possible to order its vertices in a way such that for every arc uv, it holds that $u < v$. Moreover, such an ordering can be found in polynomial time.*

An ordering of an acyclic graph in Lemma 2.5 is called *transitive*.

Lemma 2.6 FAST *admits a kernel with at most $k^2 + 2k$ vertices.*

Proof: By Lemma 2.5, a tournament T has a feedback arc set of size at most k if and only if it can be turned into an acyclic tournament by reversing at most k arcs (see also Problem 2.6). In what follows, we reverse arcs and use the term *triangle* to refer to a directed triangle. We present two simple reduction rules that can be easily implemented to run in polynomial time.

> **Reduction FAST.1** If there exists an arc uv that belongs to more than k distinct triangles, construct a new tournament T' from T by reversing uv. The new instance is $(T', k-1)$.

> **Reduction FAST.2** If there exists a vertex v that is not contained in any triangle, delete v from T. The new instance is $(T - v, k)$.

To see that the first rule is safe, note that if we do not reverse uv, we have to reverse at least one arc from each of $k+1$ distinct triangles containing uv. Thus, uv belongs to every feedback arc set of size at most k.

Let us now argue that Rule FAST.2 is safe. Let X be the set of heads of the arcs whose tail is v, and let Y be the set of tails of the arcs whose head is v.

Because T is a tournament, (X, Y) is a partition of $V(T) \setminus \{v\}$. Because v is not contained in any triangle in T, we have that there is no arc from X to Y. Moreover, for any pair of feedback arc sets A_1 and A_2 of the tournaments $T[X]$ and $T[Y]$, respectively, the set $A_1 \cup A_2$ is a feedback arc set of T. Thus, (T, k) is a yes-instance if and only if $(T - v, k)$ is a yes-instance.

Finally, we show that in any reduced yes-instance, T has at most $k(k + 2)$ vertices. Let A be a feedback arc set of T of size at most k. For every arc $e \in A$, aside from the two endpoints of e, there are at most k vertices that are contained in a triangle containing e because otherwise the first rule would have applied. Because every triangle in T contains an arc of A and every vertex of T is in a triangle, we have that T has at most $k(k + 2)$ vertices. □

2.4 DOMINATING SET in Graphs of Girth at Least 5

Let us remind that a vertex set S is a *dominating set* of a graph G if every vertex of G either belongs to S or has a neighbor in S. In the DOMINATING SET problem, we are given a graph G and integer k, and the task is to decide whether G has a dominating set of size at most k. The DOMINATING SET problem it is known to be W[2]-complete, and thus it is highly unlikely that it admits a kernel (not even an exponential kernel). The problem remains W[2]-complete on bipartite graphs and hence on graphs without cycles of length 3. In this section, we show that if a graph G has no cycles of lengths 3 and 4, that is, G is a graph of girth at least 5, then kernelization is possible by means of simple reduction rules. Moreover, the kernel will be polynomial.

In our kernelization algorithm, it is convenient to work with the colored version of domination called *red-white-black domination*. Here, we are given a graph F whose vertices are colored in three colors: *red*, *white* and *black*. The meaning of the colors is the following:

Red: The vertex has already been included in the dominating set D' that we are trying to construct.
White: The vertex has not been included in the set D', but it is dominated by some vertex in D'.
Black: The vertex is not dominated by any vertex of D'.

A set $D \subseteq V(F)$ is an *rwb-dominating set* if every black vertex $v \notin D$ is adjacent to some vertex of D, that is, D dominates black vertices.

Let R, W and B be the sets of vertices of the graph F colored red, white and black, respectively. We say that F is an *rwb-graph* if

2.4 DOMINATING SET in Graphs of Girth at Least 5

- Every white vertex is a neighbor of a red vertex.
- Black vertices have no red neighbors.

In what follows, we apply reduction rules on **rwb**-graphs. Initially, we are given an input graph G, and we color all its vertices black. After every application of a reduction rule, we obtain an **rwb**-graph F with $V(F) = R \cup W \cup B$, $|R| \leq k$, and such that F has an **rwb**-dominating set of size $k - |R|$ if and only if (G, k) is a yes-instance. Obviously, the first **rwb**-graph F, obtained from G by coloring all vertices black, satisfies this condition.

The following lemma essentially shows that if an **rwb**-graph of girth at least 5 has a black or white vertex dominating more than k black vertices, then such a vertex must belong to every solution of size at most $k - |R|$.

Lemma 2.7 *Let F be an **rwb**-graph of girth at least 5 with $|R| \leq k$, and let $V(F) = R \cup W \cup B$. Let v be a black or white vertex with more than $k - |R|$ black neighbors. Then, v belongs to every **rwb**-dominating set of size at most $k - |R|$.*

Proof: Let D be an **rwb**-dominating set of size $k - |R|$, that is, D dominates all black vertices in F. Targeting a contradiction, let us assume that $v \notin D$. Let X be the set of black neighbors of v that are not in D, and let Y be the set of black neighbors of v in D. It holds that $|X| + |Y| > k - |R|$. Observe that for every vertex $u \in X$, there is a neighbor $u_d \in D$ that is not in Y because otherwise v, u and u_d form a cycle of length 3. Similarly, for every pair of vertices $u, w \in X$, $u \neq w$ implies that $u_d \neq w_d$ because otherwise v, u, u_d, w and v form a cycle of length 4. This means that $|D| \geq |X| + |Y| > k - |R|$, which is a contradiction. □

Given an **rwb**-graph F, Lemma 2.7 suggests the following simple reduction rule.

Reduction DS.1 If there is a white or a black vertex v having more than $k - |R|$ black neighbors, then color v red and color its black neighbors white.

It should be clear that the following reduction rule is safe and does not decrease the girth of a graph.

Reduction DS.2 If a white vertex v is not adjacent to a black vertex, delete v.

For each **rwb**-graph F with $V(F) = R \cup W \cup B$ obtained after applying any of the preceding rules, we have that F has an **rwb**-dominating set of size $k - |R|$

if and only if G has a dominating set of size k. Thus, if at some moment we arrive at a graph with $|R| > k$, this implies that (G, k) is a no-instance.

Now, we estimate the size of an irreducible colored graph.

Lemma 2.8 *Let F be an rwb-graph with $V(F) = R \cup W \cup B$ and of girth at least 5, such that Rules DS.1 and DS.2 cannot be applied to F. Then, if F has an rwb-dominating set of size $k - |R|$, it has at most $k^3 + k^2 + k$ vertices.*

Proof: Suppose that F has an rwb-dominating set of size $k - |R|$. We argue then that each of $|R|$, $|B|$ and $|W|$ is bounded by a function of k.

First of all, $|R| \le k$ because otherwise F is a no-instance. By Rule DS.1, every vertex colored white or black has at most $k - |R|$ black neighbors. We also know that no red vertex has a black neighbor. Moreover, at most $k - |R|$ black or white vertices should dominate all black vertices. Thus, because each black or white can dominate at most k black vertices, we deduce that $|B| \le k^2$.

It remains to argue that $|W| \le k^3$. Toward this end, we show that every black vertex has at most k white neighbors. Because $|B| \le k^2$ and every white vertex is adjacent to some black vertex (due to Rule DS.2), the conclusion will follow. We start by noting that every white vertex has a red neighbor. Moreover, the white neighbors of any black vertex have distinct red neighbors, that is, if w_1 and w_2 are white neighbors of a black vertex b, then the sets of red neighbors of w_1 and of w_2 do not overlap. Indeed, if w_1 and w_2 had a common red neighbor r, then b, w_1, r and w_2 would have formed a cycle of length 4. Because $|R| \le k$, we have that a black vertex can have at most k white neighbors. □

We conclude with the following theorem.

Theorem 2.9 DOMINATING SET *on graphs of girth at least 5 has a kernel with at most $k^3 + k^2 + 2k$ vertices.*

Proof: For an instance (G, k) of DOMINATING SET, we construct a colored graph by coloring all vertices of G black. Afterward we apply Rules DS.1 and DS.2 exhaustively. Each of the rules runs in polynomial time. Let $F = (R \cup W \cup B, E)$ be the resulting rwb-graph. Note that F has an rwb-dominating set of size $k - |R|$ if and only if G has a dominating set of size k. Because none of the rules decreases girth, the girth of F is also at least five. Hence if F has more than $k^3 + k^2 + k$ vertices, by Lemma 2.8 we have that G is a no-instance.

We construct a noncolored graph G' from F by attaching a pendant vertex to every red vertex of F and uncoloring all vertices. The new graph G' has at most $k^3 + k^2 + k + |R| \le k^3 + k^2 + 2k$ vertices, its girth is at most the girth of G, and it is easy to check that G' has a dominating set of size k if and only if

F has an rwb-dominating set of size $k - |R|$. Thus, (G', k) is a yes-instance if and only if (G, k) is a yes-instance. □

2.5 Alternative Parameterization for VERTEX COVER

So far we have studied parameterized problems with respect to "natural" parameterizations, which are usually the sizes of their solutions. However, in many cases it is very interesting to see how other parameterizations influence the complexity of the problem. In this book, we consider several examples of such problems. We start with an alternative parameterization for VERTEX COVER.

Toward presenting the alternative parameterization, consider some vertex cover S of a graph G. The graph $G - S$ has no edges, and thus every vertex of $G - S$ is of degree 0. For an integer d, we say that a vertex set S of a graph G is a *degree-d modulator* if all vertices of $G - S$ are of degree at most d. For example, every vertex cover is a degree-0 modulator, and, of course, every degree-d modulator is also a degree-$(d + 1)$ modulator. Because the size of a degree-1 modulator can be smaller than the size of a vertex cover, that is, a degree-0 modulator, it is reasonable to consider kernelization for a "stronger" parameterization.

We define the VERTEX COVER (DEGREE-1-MODULATOR) problem (vertex cover parameterized by degree-1 modulator) as follows. Given a graph G, a degree-1 modulator S of size k and an integer ℓ, the task is to decide whether G contain a vertex cover of size at most ℓ. In the rest of this section, we prove the following theorem.

Theorem 2.10 VERTEX COVER (DEGREE-1-MODULATOR) *admits a kernel with* $\mathcal{O}(k^3)$ *vertices.*

Let us note that the kernel obtained in Theorem 2.10 is incomparable to a kernel for VERTEX COVER from Theorem 2.4. While one kernel is for a stronger parameterization, the size of another kernel has a better dependence on the parameter.

Let (G, S, ℓ), $|S| = k$ be an instance of VERTEX COVER (DEGREE-1-MODULATOR). Thus, every vertex of $F = G - S$ is of degree at most 1 in F. We assume that G has no isolated vertices, otherwise we delete these vertices. According to the degrees of the vertices in F, we partition F into two sets, one of 0-F-degree vertices and the other of 1-F-degree vertices.

The first reduction rule is similar to the degree reduction rule designed for VERTEX COVER.

> **Reduction VC/1D.1** If there is a vertex $s \in S$ adjacent to more than $|S|$ 0-F-degree vertices of F, then delete s and decrease ℓ by 1. The new instance is $(G - s, S \setminus \{s\}, \ell - 1)$.

Reduction Rule VC/1D.1 is safe for the following reason: There is always a minimum vertex cover of G containing s. Indeed, if a vertex cover C of G does not contain s, then all the neighbors of s from F should be in C. However, the set obtained from C by deleting the 0-F-degree neighbors of s and adding all the missing vertices from S to C is also a vertex cover of size at most $|C|$. By using similar arguments, we also have that the following rule is safe.

> **Reduction VC/1D.2** If there is a vertex $s \in S$ such that the neighborhood $N_G(s)$ of s contains more than $|S|$ pairs of adjacent 1-F-degree vertices of F, then delete s and decrease ℓ by 1. The new instance is $(G - s, S \setminus \{s\}, \ell - 1)$.

If there is a vertex v in F that has no neighbors in S, then because G has no isolated vertices, v should be adjacent to some vertex u of F. In this situation, the vertex v is not only a degree-1 vertex in F, but it is also a degree-1 vertex in G. Hence there is always a minimum vertex cover containing u and excluding v. This brings us to the following reduction rule.

> **Reduction VC/1D.3** If there is a vertex $v \in V(F)$ that is not adjacent to any vertex of S, delete v and its neighbor u from $V(F)$, and decrease ℓ by 1. The new instance is $(G - \{u, v\}, S, \ell - 1)$.

Our next reduction rule is the following.

> **Reduction VC/1D.4** If there is a pair of nonadjacent vertices $s, t \in S$ such that the neighborhood $N_G(s) \cup N_G(t)$ contains more than $|S|$ pairs of adjacent 1-F-degree vertices of F, then add the edge st to G. Let G' be resulting graph. Then, the new instance is (G', S, ℓ).

Reduction Rule VC/1D.4 is safe because there is always a minimum vertex cover of G containing at least one vertex among s and t. Indeed, every vertex cover C not containing s and t should contain all vertices in $N_G(s) \cup N_G(t)$. By adding to C all vertices of S and removing at least $|S| + 1$ vertices (one from

2.5 Alternative Parameterization for VERTEX COVER

each of the pairs of adjacent vertices in $N_G(s) \cup N_G(t)$), we obtain a smaller vertex cover.

Our last reduction rule is the following.

> **Reduction VC/1D.5** Let $u, v \in V(F)$ be a pair of adjacent vertices such that $N_G(u) \cap N_G(v) = \emptyset$, and for every pair of vertices $s \in S \cap N_G(u)$ and $t \in S \cap N_G(v)$, s is adjacent to t. Then, delete u and v and decrease ℓ by 1. The new instance is $(G - \{u, v\}, S, \ell - 1)$.

Lemma 2.11 *Reduction Rule VC/1D.5 is safe.*

Proof: The safeness of Reduction Rule VC/1D.5 is based on the observation that if its conditions hold, there is always a minimum vertex cover C containing the open neighborhood (in G) of exactly one of the vertices u and v. First, note that as the vertices u and v are adjacent, at least one of them should belong to every vertex cover of G. Thus, if G has a vertex cover C of size at most ℓ, then $G \setminus \{u, v\}$ has a vertex cover of size $\ell - 1$.

Let us now show that if $G \setminus \{u, v\}$ has a vertex cover C' of size at most $\ell - 1$, then G has a vertex cover of size at most ℓ. Because the graph induced by the open neighborhoods of u and v in S contains a complete bipartite graph with bipartition $(N_G(u) \cap S, N_G(v) \cap S)$ as a subgraph, either all the vertices of $N_G(u) \cap S$ or all the vertices of $N_G(v) \cap S$ should belong to C. Let us assume w.l.o.g that $N_G(u) \cap S \subseteq C'$. Then, $C' \cup \{v\}$ is a vertex cover of G, which concludes proof that the reduction rule is safe. □

Each of the reduction rules can be easily implemented to run in polynomial time. Thus, it remains to argue that every irreducible instance is of size $\mathcal{O}(|S|^3)$. Due to Rule VC/1D.1, the number of 0-F-degree vertices of G is at most $|S|^2$. Moreover, due to Rule VC/1D.2, the number of pairs of adjacent 1-F-degree vertices having a common neighbor in S is at most $|S|^2$. But how many other pairs of adjacent 1-F-degree vertices can belong to G?

By Rule VC/1D.3, every 1-F-degree vertex should have a neighbor in S. Then, by Rule VC/1D.5, for every pair of adjacent vertices $u, v \in V(F)$ that do not have a common neighbor, there is a neighbor $s \in S$ of u and a neighbor $t \in S$ of v that are distinct and non adjacent. However, by Rule VC/1D.4, the union of the neighborhoods of two nonadjacent vertices in S contains at most $|S|$ pairs of adjacent vertices from F. Thus, the number of pairs of adjacent 1-F-degree vertices is at most $|S|^2 + \binom{|S|}{2} \cdot |S|$, and hence the total number of vertices of G is $\mathcal{O}(|S|^3)$. This concludes the proof of Theorem 2.10.

2.6 EDGE CLIQUE COVER

Unfortunately, some problems are only known to have kernels of exponential sizes. As we will see later, there are convincing arguments that, for some problems, this is the best we can hope for. One such example is EDGE CLIQUE COVER, for which we present a data reduction that results in a kernel of exponential size. In EDGE CLIQUE COVER, we are given a graph G and a non negative integer k. The task is to decide whether the edges of G can be covered by at most k cliques. In what follows, recall that we use $N[v]$ to denote the *closed* neighborhood of a vertex v in G.

Reduction ECC.1 Remove isolated vertices.

Reduction ECC.2 If there is an edge uv whose endpoints have exactly the same closed neighborhood, that is, $N[u] = N[v]$, then contract uv. In case uv was an isolated edge, also decrease k by 1.

Theorem 2.12 EDGE CLIQUE COVER *admits a kernel with at most 2^k vertices.*

Proof: Because the removal of isolated vertices does not change the solution, Rule ECC.1 is safe. Let us now argue that Rule ECC.2 is also safe. Because the removal of any isolated edge decreases the minimum size of a clique cover by exactly 1, we next assume that uv is not an isolated edge. Let G' denote the graph obtained from G by contracting uv. Because the contraction of an edge cannot increase the minimum size of a clique cover, it holds that if G has a clique cover of size at most k, so does G'. To prove the other direction, let $C_1, \ldots, C_k$ be a clique cover of G', and let w be the vertex of G' that is the result of the contraction of uv. Because uv was not an isolated edge in G, w is not an isolated vertex in G', and therefore it is contained in at least one of the cliques. Thus, because $N[u] = N[v]$, by replacing w by u and v in each of the cliques C_i, $1 \leq i \leq k$, which contains w, we obtain a clique cover for G.

Next, let G be a graph to which both rules do not apply and that has a clique cover $C_1, \ldots, C_k$. We claim that G has at most 2^k vertices. Targeting a contradiction, let us assume that G has more than 2^k vertices. We assign a binary vector b_v of length k to each vertex $v \in V$, where bit i, $1 \leq i \leq k$, is set to 1 if and only if v is contained in the clique C_i. Because there are only 2^k possible vectors, there must be distinct vertices $u, v \in V(G)$ such that $b_u = b_v$. If $b_u = b_v$ is the zero vector, the first rule is applicable. Thus, $b_u = b_v$ is not the zero vector, which implies that u and v have the same *closed* neighborhood, and, in particular, u and v are adjacent. In this case, the second reduction rule is applicable, and thus we necessarily reach a contradiction. $\square$

Exercises

Problem 2.1 ($\mathscr{D}$)   Prove that the size of a graph that is irreducible subject to Reduction Rules VC.1, VC.3 and VC.4 cannot be bounded by a function of k only. Here, we do not apply Reduction Rule VC.2.

Problem 2.2   In the ODD SUBGRAPH problem, we are given a graph G and an integer k. The task is to decide whether G has a subgraph on k edges where all vertices are of odd degrees. Prove that the problem admits a kernel with $O(k^2)$ vertices.

Problem 2.3   In the CLUSTER EDITING problem, we are given a graph G and integer k. The task is to decide whether G can be transformed into a disjoint union of cliques by adding or deleting at most k edges in total, that is, by at most k editing operations. Prove that the problem admits a kernel with $\mathcal{O}(k^2)$ vertices.

Problem 2.4   In Section 1.1, we gave a kernel with k^2 points for the POINT LINE COVER problem. Prove that POINT LINE COVER admits a kernel with k^2-c points for some $c \geq 1$.

Problem 2.5   Prove Lemma 2.5.

Problem 2.6   Let D be a directed graph and F be a minimal feedback arc set of D. Let D' be the graph obtained from D by reversing the arcs of F in D. Show that D' is acyclic, and that the requirement of minimality from F is necessary, that is, without it the statement is not correct.

Problem 2.7   Give a kernel of size $k^{\mathcal{O}(1)}$ for the LONGEST CYCLE (VC) problem. Given a graph G, a vertex cover S of G of size k and an integer ℓ, the objective of this problem is to decide whether G contains a cycle on at least ℓ vertices.

Problem 2.8   The input of the TEST COVER problem consists of a set V of n vertices, and a collection $\mathcal{E} = \{E_1, \ldots, E_m\}$ of distinct subsets of V, called tests. A test E_q separates a pair v_i, v_j of vertices if $|\{v_i, v_j\} \cap E_q| = 1$. A subcollection $\mathcal{T} \subseteq \mathcal{E}$ is a test cover if each pair v_i, v_j of distinct vertices is separated by a test in $\mathcal{T}$. The task is to decide whether an instance $(V, \mathcal{E})$ of TEST COVER has a test cover of size at most k. Let r be a positive integer.

The TEST r-COVER problem is the TEST COVER problem in which $n \geq r$ and $|E_j| \leq r$ for each $j \in \{1, \ldots, m\}$. Prove that TEST r-COVER has a kernel with $\mathcal{O}(k)$ vertices and $\mathcal{O}(k^r)$ tests.

Problem 2.9 (☠) Let G be a graph with n vertices. A bijection $\sigma : V(G) \to \{1, \ldots, n\}$ is a linear ordering of G. For a linear ordering σ of G, the cost of an edge $xy \in E(G)$ is $c(xy) = |\sigma(x) - \sigma(y)|$ and the net cost of σ is $\sum_{e \in E}(c(e) - 1)$. In the NET LINEAR ARRANGEMENT problem, given a graph G and a parameter k, decide whether there is a linear ordering of G of net cost at most k. Prove that NET LINEAR ARRANGEMENT admits a kernel with $\mathcal{O}(k)$ vertices and edges.

Problem 2.10 In the $(k, n-k)$-MAXCUT problem, we are given a graph G, and integers k and p. The task is to decide whether there is a partition $A \uplus B$ of $V(G)$ such that $|A| = k$ and G has at least p edges with one endpoint in A and the other endpoint in B. Give a kernel of size $p^{\mathcal{O}(1)}$ for this problem.

Problem 2.11 (☠) VERTEX COVER (FVS) is the problem of computing a vertex cover of size at most ℓ parameterized by the size k of a minimum feedback vertex set. Show that this problem admits a polynomial kernel.

Problem 2.12 (☠) VERTEX COVER (DEGREE-2-MODULATOR) is the problem of computing a vertex cover of size at most ℓ parameterized by the size k of a minimum degree-2 modulator. Show that this problem admits a polynomial kernel.

Bibliographic Notes

The classical reference on parameterized complexity is the book of Downey and Fellows (1999). For more updated material we refer to the books of Flum and Grohe (2006), Niedermeier (2006), Downey and Fellows (2013) and Cygan et al. (2015).

Because INDEPENDENT SET admits "trivial" kernelization on graphs of bounded vertex degree when parameterized by the size of the solution, it is more natural to study this problem with different "above guarantee" parameterizations. Dvořák and Lidický (2017) have shown that the problem of deciding whether an n-vertex graph G with maximum vertex degree Δ contains an independent set of size at least $n/\Delta + k$, admits a kernel with $\mathcal{O}(k)$ vertices. See also Dvorak and Mnich (2014).

The design of reduction rules for VERTEX COVER of the type discussed in this chapter is often called Buss kernelization, attributed to Sam Buss in (Buss and Goldsmith, 1993). A more refined set of reduction rules for VERTEX COVER was introduced by Balasubramanian et al. (1998). The kernelization algorithm for FAST follows the lines provided by Dom et al. (2010). An improved kernel with $(2+\varepsilon)k$ vertices, where $\varepsilon > 0$, was obtained by Bessy et al. (2011) (see also Chapter 9). The kernel for DOMINATING SET on graphs of large girth is due to Raman and Saurabh (2008). As a complete bipartite graph $K_{2,2}$ is a cycle on four vertices, the following result of Philip et al. (2012) is a generalization of Theorem 2.9: For every fixed i,j, DOMINATING SET has a kernel of size $\mathcal{O}(k^h)$ in graphs containing no $K_{i,j}$ as a subgraph, where $h = 2(\min\{i,j\})^2$ depends only on i and j. Kernelization for DOMINATING SET on other classes of sparse graphs is discussed in chapters of this book on meta-theorems. A polynomial kernel for $(k, n-k)$-MAXCUT, given as Problem 2.10, was obtained in (Saurabh and Zehavi, 2016). Problems 2.8 and 2.9 are taken from Gutin et al. (2013b) and Gutin et al. (2013a), respectively. We remark that NET LINEAR ARRANGEMENT is an above guarantee version of a problem called OPTIMAL LINEAR ARRANGEMENT. An exponential kernel for EDGE CLIQUE COVER was given by Gramm et al. (2008) (see also Gyárfás, 1990). Cygan et al. (2011) showed that EDGE CLIQUE COVER does not admit a kernel of polynomial size unless the polynomial time hierarchy collapses to the third level.

The paper of Niedermeier (2010) discusses different aspects of parameterization by different parameters, and the thesis of Jansen (2013), as well as Fomin et al. (2014) discusses kernelization algorithms for different problems parameterized by vertex cover. A result generalizing the polynomial kernel for VERTEX COVER (DEGREE-1-MODULATOR), given as Problem 2.11, provides a kernel with $\mathcal{O}(k^3)$ vertices for VERTEX COVER (FVS) and was obtained by Jansen and Bodlaender (2013). Later, an improved kernel for VERTEX COVER (DEGREE-1-MODULATOR), a kernel for VERTEX COVER (DEGREE-2-MODULATOR) and related results were given by Majumdar et al. (2015). Recently, Fomin and Strømme (2016) gave a polynomial kernel for VERTEX COVER parameterized by the size of a vertex set whose removal results in a graph where each connected component has at most one cycle, called pseudoforest modulator. They also show that VERTEX COVER parameterized by the size of a vertex set whose removal results in a graph where no two cycles share a vertex, called a mock forest modulator, is unlikely to admit a polynomial kernel.

3
Inductive Priorities

In this chapter we introduce the method of inductive priorities. This method can be seen as a systematic way of obtaining reduction rules. We exemplify this method by providing kernels for MAX LEAF SUBTREE and FEEDBACK VERTEX SET.

We have seen already several examples of kernelization algorithms based on reduction rules. So far we were only explaining why and how reduction rules work. But how to come up with such rules? We do not know a universal recipe for making reductions—normally this is a creative process requiring deep insight into the structural properties of the problem. However, in some situations the following "direct" attack can be successful.

Suppose that we have some initial solution at hand, which can be of low quality. The manner in which the initial solution is obtained depends on the problem in question, and it can involve the use of greedy arguments or approximation algorithms. We implement simple rules that aim to improve the quality of the initial solution. Once we reach a boundary situation, where no further improvement is possible, we seek reasons underlying this stalemate. Such a strategy brings us either to additional reduction rules or to a reasonable upper bound on the size of the current instance. As a result, we may either solve the problem or obtain a kernel.

This approach is known as the *method of inductive priorities*; it can be viewed as a systematic way to design reduction rules. We exemplify this method by providing kernels for MAX LEAF SUBTREE and FEEDBACK VERTEX SET. While the kernels given in this chapter are not the best possible, the approach used to obtain them sheds some light on the manner in which one can systematically design kernelization algorithms.

3.1 Priorities for MAX LEAF SUBTREE

In this section, we demonstrate how to use the method of inductive priorities in the context of the NONBLOCKER problem. In this problem, we are given a graph G and a nonnegative integer k. The task is to decide whether G has a subtree with at least k leaves. We refer the reader to the "Bibliographic Notes" for the relation between this problem and the more well-known MAX LEAF SPANNING TREE problem. In what follows, we always assume that the input graph G is connected. This assumption is crucial: Without the connectivity requirement, MAX LEAF SUBTREE does not admit a polynomial kernel under a reasonable complexity-theoretic assumption (see "Bibliographic Notes" for further references). Notice that because G is connected, if there exists a solution, then there also exists a solution that is a spanning tree. Indeed, extending a subtree cannot decrease the number of leaves it contains.

> On a high level, we employ the following strategy. First of all, given the (connected) input graph G, we obtain some spanning tree, say a tree constructed by using depth-first search. If this tree contains at least k leaves, we have already solved the problem. Otherwise, we try to improve it. If we succeed to obtain a tree with a larger number of leaves, we restart the procedure using the new tree. The most interesting case occurs at the moment we cannot improve our spanning tree. In this case we start to analyze the structure of the graph and the tree, and this will bring us either to a new reduction idea or to a bound on the size of the graph.

To articulate the structure that a bound on the *max leaf number* imposes, we seek to prove (for the best possible constant c) the following generic lemma regarding the kernelization for the problem:

Boundary Lemma. *Let G be a connected graph, and suppose that (G, k) is a "reduced" yes-instance of* MAX LEAF SUBTREE *such that $(G, k+1)$ is a no-instance. Then, $|V(G)| \leq ck$. (Here c is a small constant that we will clarify in the following text.)*

The lemma says that if G is reduced (where the meaning of *reduced* is still to be determined), contains a tree with k leaves and does not contain a tree with

$k+1$ leaves, then the number of vertices in G is at most ck. Hence, once we have proved this lemma, we know that if G is reduced but has more than ck vertices, then either (G,k) is a no-instance or $(G, k+1)$ is a yes-instance. Then, if G is reduced but has more than ck vertices, one way to proceed is to find some operation that modifies the graph G so that the resulting graph G' is smaller, while satisfying two conditions: if (G,k) is a no-instance, then so is (G',k), and if $(G, k+1)$ is a yes-instance, then so is (G',k). In the context of MAX LEAF SUBTREE, a possible operation is simply the one that contracts any edge so that the resulting graph remains a connected graph. Afterward, we restart the application of the reduction rules. Thus, to obtain a kernel, it is sufficient to prove such a Boundary Lemma. Later, we present another argument why it is sufficient to prove the Boundary Lemma to obtain our kernel, which does not require the use of the preceding operation.

Obtaining a Boundary Lemma involves two crucial strategic choices:

(1) A choice of a *witness structure* for the hypothesis that (G,k) is a yes-instance. In the context of MAX LEAF SUBTREE, a possible witness structure is simply a tree with k leaves.
(2) A choice of inductive priorities. To illustrate the methodology for MAX LEAF SUBTREE, we give two examples where one is an extension of the other.

The structure of the proof is "by minimum counterexample," where we assume that (G,k) is a yes-instance while $(G, k+1)$ is a no-instance. Here, the arguments are guided by the inductive priorities established by (2), which involve reference to (1). Generally, given the inductive priorities, the proof consists of a series of structural claims that eventually lead to a detailed structural picture at the "boundary," and thereby to a bound on the size of G that is the conclusion.

We will describe three natural reduction rules. After the application of these rules, we will be able to derive some properties that the structure of the input should satisfy. Let us begin by explaining the intuition that leads to the design of these reduction rules, and then state the rules. To this end, we consider a combinatorial result due to Linial and Sturtevant (1987) and Kleitman and West (1991), which we do not prove here. This combinatorial result (stated in the following text) implies that if G is a connected graph with minimum vertex degree at least 3, then we already have a kernel. While we are not able to apply this result (because we are not able to reduce the graph appropriately), it shades light on which vertices are to be handled if one is interested in a kernel. Indeed, inspired by this result, we will try to eliminate certain degree-1 and degree-2 vertices in G, though we will not be able to eliminate all of them. Formally, this result is stated as follows.

Theorem 3.1 (Linial and Sturtevant [1987]; Kleitman and West [1991])
Every connected graph G with minimum vertex degree at least 3 has a spanning tree with at least $|V(G)|/4 + 2$ leaves. Moreover, such a spanning tree can be found in polynomial time.

By Theorem 3.1, if we were to succeed in safely eliminating all vertices of degrees 1 and 2, then either the reduced graph G would have had more than $4k$ vertices, in which case (G, k) is automatically a yes-instance, or the reduced graph G would have had at most $4k$ vertices, in which case we are also done. While vertices of degree 1 can be "shaved off" (though this task is not as easy as in the case of VERTEX COVER), with degree-2 vertices the situation is much more delicate. We will not get rid of all vertices of degrees 1 and 2, but nevertheless, we will target these vertices and be able to obtain a kernel by doing so.

The first rule is the following.

Reduction ML.1 Let u be a vertex of degree 1 in (the connected graph) G adjacent to a vertex v of degree 2 in G. Delete u from G. The new instance is $(G - u, k)$.

To see that this rule is safe, note that if G contains a tree with k leaves, then it also has a spanning tree T with at least k leaves such that u is a leaf of T. The vertex v is of degree 2 in T, and therefore the deletion of u does not decrease the number of leaves in T—once the vertex u is deleted, the vertex v becomes a new leaf.

Let us remind that an edge uv is a *bridge* in a graph G if its deletion increases the number of connected components in G. Because a bridge should be contained in every spanning tree of G, we deduce that the following reduction rule is safe.

Reduction ML.2 If an edge uv is a bridge in G and neither u nor v is of degree 1, then contract uv. The new instance of the problem is $(G/uv, k)$.

Our final rule is the following.

Reduction ML.3 If u and v are two adjacent vertices of degree 2 (where uv is not a bridge), then delete the edge uv from G. The new instance of the problem is $(G - uv, k)$.

This rule is safe for the following reason. Let T be a spanning tree of G with k leaves. If uv is not an edge of T, then the deletion of uv does not change T.

If uv belongs to T, then because uv is not a bridge, there is another edge xy in G such that T', obtained from $T - uv$ by adding xy, is a tree. By adding xy, we eliminate at most two leaves from T while after deleting uv, the vertices u and v become leaves. Thus T' also has at least k leaves and therefore the rule is safe.

We say that the graph G is *reduced* if none of the preceding reduction rules can be applied to it.

We first show how to obtain the following Boundary Lemma.

Lemma 3.2 (Max-Leaf Boundary Lemma I) *Let G be a reduced connected graph. Suppose that (G, k) is a yes-instance of* MAX LEAF SUBTREE, *and that $(G, k + 1)$ is a no-instance of this problem. Then, $|V(G)| \leq 7k$.*

Proof: Targeting a contradiction, let us assume that the lemma does not hold. For a given integer k, we assume that there is a counterexample, which is a connected graph G such that:

(i) (G, k) is a reduced instance of MAX LEAF SUBTREE,
(ii) (G, k) is a yes-instance of MAX LEAF SUBTREE,
(iii) $(G, k + 1)$ is a no-instance of MAX LEAF SUBTREE, and
(iv) $|V(G)| > 7k$.

Because (G, k) is a yes-instance, it contains a witness structure, which is a tree subgraph T of G with k leaves. Among all such counterexamples, consider one where the witness subgraph tree T has the maximum number of vertices. In the case of MAX LEAF SUBTREE, this choice simply means that T is a spanning tree.

Due to our choice of inductive priorities, we immediately conclude that the set of "outsiders" $O = V(G) \setminus V(T)$ is simply empty. Let L denote the set of leaves of T, I the set of internal (nonleaf) vertices of T, $B \subseteq I$ the set *branch vertices* of T (the nonleaf, internal vertices of T that have degree at least 3 with respect to T) and J the set *subdivider vertices* of T (the nonbranch, internal vertices of T that have degree 2 with respect to T). An illustrative example is given in Fig. 3.1. Recall that we already know that $O = \emptyset$, which clearly simplifies our picture.

Because we need to discuss the structure of the tree T in more detail, we introduce the following terminology. A path $bj_1 \cdots j_r b'$ in T, where $b, b' \in B \cup L$ are branch or leaf vertices of T and the vertices j_i for $i \in \{1, \ldots, r\}$ are subdivider vertices of T, is termed a *subdivided edge* of T. To be able to refer to the length of the path $bj_1 \cdots j_r b'$, we say that b and b' are joined by an *r-subdivided edge* in T. Note that a 0-subdivided edge is just an ordinary edge of T.

3.1 Priorities for MAX LEAF SUBTREE

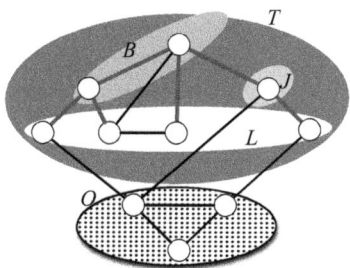

Figure 3.1 A witness tree T, and the vertex sets B, L, J and O.

Figure 3.2 An illustration for Claim 3.4.

We also need the following lemma, whose proof is left as an exercise.

Lemma 3.3 *Let T be a tree. Then,*

- $|B| \leq |L| - 2$ *and*
- *The number of subdivided edges is at most $|L|$.*

Next, we must bound the size of T. By Lemma 3.3,

$$|B| \leq k - 2. \tag{3.1}$$

We proceed by proving several claims that reveal some properties of the structure of T.

Claim 3.4 The subgraph of G induced by the vertices of a subdivided edge of T is a path.

The claim is trivially true for an r-subdivided edge where $r = 0$, so suppose that $r \geq 1$. In this case, as shown in Fig. 3.2, we can reengineer T to have $k+1$ leaves, which results in a contradiction to the assumption that $(G, k+1)$ is a no-instance.

Claim 3.5 There are no r-subdivided edges in T for $r \geq 6$.

Proof: Suppose, by way of contradiction, that we have a subdivided edge $bj_1 \cdots j_r b'$ in T where $b, b' \in B \cup L$ and $r \geq 6$. Because G is a reduced graph,

Figure 3.3 An illustration for Claim 3.5.

at least one vertex among j_3 and j_4 is of degree more than 2 in G. Without loss of generality, suppose that j_3 is adjacent in G to a vertex outside the subdivided edge. Then, we can reengineer T to have $k+1$ leaves as shown in Fig. 3.3, which results in a contradiction. ⌋

We are ready to conclude the proof of the Boundary Lemma. We know that

$$|V(G)| = |L| + |B| + |J| + |O|.$$

We have that $|L| = k$. By Lemma 3.3, $|B| \leq k - 2$. By Lemma 3.3 and Claim 3.5, $|J| \leq 5k$. Finally, recall that $O = \emptyset$, and thus $|V(G)| \leq 7k$. □

We now show that it is possible to further improve the bound by introducing another Boundary Lemma.

Lemma 3.6 (Max-Leaf Boundary Lemma II) *Let G be a reduced connected graph. Suppose (G, k) is a yes-instance of* MAX LEAF SUBTREE, *and that $(G, k+1)$ is a no-instance of this problem. Then, $|V(G)| \leq 5k$.*

Proof: The proof is again by minimum counterexample. Witnessing that (G, k) is a yes-instance, we have a spanning tree T with k leaves, as in the proof of Boundary Lemma I. Here we need to further analyze the structure of T, and therefore we rely on another inductive priority. We choose some arbitrary vertex s in G, and view this vertex as the root of T. The possible counterexample that we entertain in our argument is one where

(1) T is a spanning tree, and among all counterexamples satisfying this requirement, one where
(2) The sum over all leaves $l \in L$ of the distance in T from s to l is minimized.

All the structural claims derived in the proof of Boundary Lemma I hold here as well because all we have done is to introduce one additional inductive priority. This additional priority allows us to establish a stronger version of Claim 3.5.

Claim 3.7 There are no r-subdivided edges in T for $r \geq 4$ that do not contain s.

Proof: Suppose, by way of contradiction, that we have an r-subdivided edge $bj_1 \cdots j_r b'$ in T, where $b, b' \in B \cup L$ and $r \geq 4$. The deletion of the vertices $j_1, \ldots, j_r$ splits T into two subtrees. Let T_b be the subtree containing b, and let $T_{b'}$ the subtree containing b'. Without loss of generality, let us assume that the root of T, s, lies in the subtree $T_{b'}$. The vertices j_1 and j_2 cannot be adjacent to vertices in $T_{b'}$, else we can reengineer T to have $k+1$ leaves, as in the proof of Claim 3.5. By Claim 3.4 and because G is irreducible (in particular, j_1 and j_2 do not both have degree 2 in G), at least one among j_1 or j_2 is adjacent by an edge e to a vertex x of T_b. Let us add the edge e to T and remove the edge xu that is the first edge on the path in T from x to b. In this manner, we obtain a tree T' with the same number of leaves as T as every vertex that is a leaf in T, including possibly x, is also a leaf in T'. However, we have thus improved priority (2), reaching a contradiction. Indeed, the distance between s and every leaf outside the subtree of x has not changed, while the distance between s and every leaf in this subtree has decreased by at least 1. This concludes the proof of the claim, from which we derive the correctness of the Boundary Lemma. ⌐

□

The proofs of the Boundary Lemmata almost directly yield a kernelization algorithm for MAX LEAF SUBTREE.

Theorem 3.8 *The* MAX LEAF SUBTREE *problem on connected graphs admits a kernel with at most $5k$ vertices.*

Proof: While in the statement of the Boundary Lemma we require that $(G, k+1)$ is a no-instance, the only property of a no-instance that we need is that none of the negations of the conditions of Claims 3.4–3.7 holds. In the kernelization algorithm, we first apply our reduction rules to handle some degree-1 vertices and two adjacent degree-2 vertices (Rules ML.1, ML.2 and ML.3), obtaining a reduced graph. Each of these rules can be clearly implemented in polynomial time. Then, in this graph we build (in polynomial time) a spanning tree T with ℓ leaves. If $\ell \geq k$, we have thus solved the problem. Otherwise, we try to modify T by making use of the analysis of any of Claims 3.4–3.7 whose negation is satisfied. Here, if no negation is satisfied, we correctly conclude that (G, k) is a no-instance. Again, each of the checks for the satisfaction of the appropriate condition and the modification described in the proof is easily implementable in polynomial time. If we succeed in constructing a tree T' with more than ℓ leaves, then we restart the process with $T := T'$. Thus, if we do not already find a solution or conclude that a solution does not exist, we end up in the situation in which the conditions of Claims 3.4–3.7 hold. However, in this case (if (G, k) is a yes-instance), the number of vertices in the graph is at most $5k$. □

3.2 Priorities for FEEDBACK VERTEX SET

Our second example of the method of inductive priorities concerns the FEEDBACK VERTEX SET problem. Let us remind that a set $S \subseteq V(G)$ is a *feedback vertex set* of G if S contains at least one vertex from each cycle in G. That is, $G - S$ is a forest. In the FEEDBACK VERTEX SET problem, we are given a graph G and a nonnegative integer k, and the task is to decide whether G has a feedback vertex set of size at most k.

With more deep arguments, it is possible to show that FEEDBACK VERTEX SET admits a kernel with $\mathcal{O}(k^2)$ vertices (see Section 5.5). In this section, we show how inductive priorities lead us to the design of reduction rules reducing the problem to a kernel with $\mathcal{O}(k^3)$ vertices. Here, we assume that graphs can have multiple edges and loops, and that there exist at most two parallel edges between each pair of vertices. If two vertices are connected by two parallel edges, we say that they are connected by a *double edge*.

We begin by computing some feedback vertex set F, say one that is obtained by a constant factor approximation algorithm. The strategy we present now differs from the one employed to handle MAX LEAF SUBTREE in the following sense. While in the previous section we tried to modify the current witness to obtain one that contains more leaves, here we do not try to modify F to obtain a smaller feedback vertex set. Instead, we will try to create double edges. Let us briefly explain the intuition indicating why the addition of double edges simplifies the instance at hand. Every double edge "contributes" to any feedback vertex set by ensuring that at least one of its points should be selected. Thus, every new double edge provides additional information on the structure of any feedback vertex set of the graph. The interesting case occurs at the moment we cannot add new double edges. In this case, we analyze the structure of the graph G and the forest $G - F$, and this results in new ideas for reduction rules.

Let us first give two simple reduction rules. The first rule is based on the observation that no vertex of degree at most 1 can be a part of any cycle. Thus, the following rule is safe.

3.2 Priorities for FEEDBACK VERTEX SET

Reduction FVS.1 (Degree-1 Rule) If G has a vertex v of degree at most 1, remove it from the graph. The new instance is $(G - v, k)$.

The second rule is based on the observation that if a vertex of degree 2 belongs to a minimum feedback vertex set, then another minimum feedback vertex set can be obtained by swapping this vertex with one of its neighbors.

Reduction FVS.2 (Degree-2 Rule) If G has a vertex x of degree 2 adjacent to vertices y and z, such that $y, z \neq x$, then construct a graph G' from G as follows. Remove x, and if y and z are not connected by a double edge, then add a new edge yz (even if y and z were adjacent earlier). The new instance is (G', k).

If both the preceding reduction rules are not applicable to the graph G, we still cannot bound the size of G as we desire. To see this, take a complete bipartite graph H with bipartition (A, B), where A is of size k and B is arbitrarily large. Such a graph has feedback vertex set of size k and all its vertices are of degree more than 2. Thus, Rules FVS.1 and FVS.2 are not applicable to such graphs; in particular, we cannot bound the sizes of such graphs by a function of k.

In the following Boundary Lemma we purposely use the term *reduced* vaguely, that is, without yet defining what it means. A formally correct way of stating this lemma would be to provide all reduction rules first, and then to define a reduced instance as one to which these rules do not apply. However, we find the current order much more instructive when explaining how new reduction rules are designed.

Lemma 3.9 (FVS Boundary Lemma) *If (G, k) is a reduced yes-instance of* FEEDBACK VERTEX SET, *then* $|V(G)| \leq 10k^3 + 9k^2 - 3k$.

Proof: Suppose we are given a feedback vertex set F whose size is "close" to k, say at most $2k$. For our purposes, any size that is a constant times k would be fine. Because later we would like to turn our combinatorial arguments into a kernelization algorithm, we select $2k$ to be able to employ a known 2-approximation polynomial-time algorithm for FEEDBACK VERTEX SET. The graph $T = G - F$, obtained from G by removing F, is a forest. We partition the vertex set of T according to the degrees of the vertices in T:

- T_1 is the set of leaves in T, that is, the vertices of degree at most 1,
- T_2 is the set of vertices of degree 2 in T, and
- T_3 is the set of vertices of degree at least 3 in T.

We start by estimating the number of vertices in T_1. So far, there is no reason why the size of T_1 should be bounded: In the complete bipartite graph H with bipartition (A, B) such that $|A| = k$ and $|B| = n$, a feedback vertex set $F = A$ leaves us with $T_1 = B$, whose size cannot be bounded by any function of k. However, if T_1 is large enough, then due to Rule FVS.1, some pairs of vertices in F have many common neighbors in T_1. Moreover, due to Rule FVS.2, if a pair $f, g \in F$ has many common neighbors in T_1, then there are a great deal of cycles containing both f and g. Thus, every optimal feedback vertex set should contain at least one of these vertices. Let us formalize this intuition.

> **Reduction FVS.3** If there are two vertices $f, g \in F$ that are not connected by a double edge and that have at least $k + 2$ common neighbors in T_1, that is, $|T_1 \cap N(f) \cap N(g)| \geq k + 2$, then construct a new graph G' from G by connecting f and g by a double edge. The new instance is (G', k).

Claim 3.10 Reduction Rule FVS.3 is safe.

Proof: Every feedback vertex set in G' is also a feedback vertex set in G. Now, let us show that every feedback vertex set in G is also a feedback vertex set in G'. To this end, let S be a feedback vertex set of size k in G. At least one of f and g should belong to every feedback vertex set of size at most k because otherwise we need at least $k + 1$ vertices to hit all the cycles passing through f and g. Thus, at least one of f and g belongs to S, and therefore S is a feedback vertex set in G' as well. ⌐

The reduction rule adding a double edge exposes the structure of a feedback vertex set: The presence of a double edge indicates that at least one of its endpoints should be in every solution. However, this rule does not decrease the number of vertices in the graph. Coming back to our running example of the complete bipartite graph H, after applying Reduction Rule FVS.3 we can end up in the situation in which every pair of vertices in A is connected by a double edge. Accordingly, we define the notion of a *double clique*: We say that a set of vertices $C \subset F$ is a double clique if every pair of vertices in C is connected by a double edge. Let us note that a single vertex is also a double clique. In this context, we observe that if the neighborhood of a vertex $v \in T_1$ is a double clique C, then either all or all but one of the vertices of C should belong to every feedback vertex set. Can we use this observation to get rid of vertices from T_1 whose neighborhood is a double clique?

We next employ different reductions depending on whether a vertex v from T_1 is isolated in T. If the vertex v is isolated in T and has a double clique

3.2 Priorities for FEEDBACK VERTEX SET

as its neighborhood, we would like to delete it. However, we should be a bit careful here because if v is connected to some vertices in C by double edges, its deletion can change the size of the solution. We fix this case by adding loops to vertices adjacent to v.

> **Reduction FVS.4** Let $v \in T_1$ be an isolated vertex in T. If the set $C = N(v) \cap F$ is a double clique, then construct the following graph G' from G: Add a loop to every vertex $x \in C$ connected to v by a double edge and delete it v. The new instance is (G', k).

Claim 3.11 Reduction Rule FVS.4 is safe.

Proof: Let S be a feedback vertex set in G of size k. Because C is a double clique, at most one vertex of C does not belong to S. Hence we can assume that $v \notin S$, otherwise the set $(S - v) \cup C$ is also a feedback vertex set of size k in G and we could have taken it in the first place. Then, if the graph $G' - S$ contain a cycle, this cycle is a loop at some vertex $x \in C \setminus S$. This loop does not exist in the graph $G - S$ as it is acyclic, hence it appears in G' because of the double edge vx in G. However, because S does not contain v and x, the double edge is a cycle in $G - S$, which is a contradiction.

For the opposite direction, let S be a feedback vertex set in G'. If $G - S$ contains a cycle, then this cycle is a double edge vx for some $x \in C$. However, then $G' - S$ contains a loop at x, and thus it is not acyclic, which is a contradiction. ⌐

For the second case, where v is not isolated, we apply a slightly different reduction.

> **Reduction FVS.5** Let $v \in T_1$ be a none-isolated vertex of T. Let u be (the unique) neighbor of v in T. If the set $C = N(v) \cap F$ is a double clique, then contract the edge uv. We denote the new vertex resulting from this edge-contraction by v (see Fig. 3.4). The new instance is $(G/uv, k)$.

Claim 3.12 Reduction Rule FVS.5 is safe.

Proof: Denote $G' = G/uv$. Note that every feedback vertex set of G is also a feedback vertex set of G', and hence one direction of the proof of trivial.

For the opposite direction, we claim that every feedback vertex set S of G' is also a feedback vertex set of G. Suppose, by way of contradiction, that this is not the case, and therefore $G - S$ contains a cycle Q. This cycle should pass

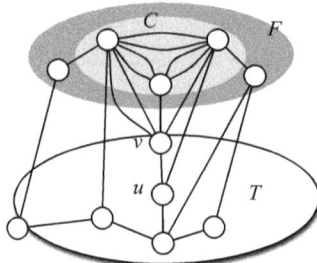 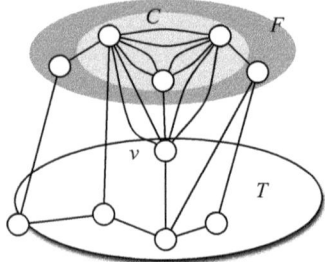

Figure 3.4 When the neighborhood of a leaf v in T is a double clique C, we can contract the edge uv.

through v and at least one vertex $x \in C$. Because C is a double clique and $G' - S$ acyclic, x is the only vertex of C contained in Q. Because $x \notin S$, we have that xv is not a double edge in G, and thus Q contains at least three vertices. Hence, Q should contain edge uv, but then the cycle obtained from Q by contracting uv is a cycle in $G' - S$, contradicting the choice of S as a feedback vertex set of G'. ⌐

At this point, we are already able to bound $|T_1|$. Because Reduction Rule FVS.2 cannot be applied to G, we have that every $v \in T_1$ has at least two neighbors in F. Then, due to Reduction Rules FVS.4 and FVS.5, for every $v \in T_1$, the neighborhood $N(v)$ in F contains a pair of vertices $f, g \in F$ that are not connected by a double edge. By Reduction Rule FVS.3, the common neighborhood in T_1 of each such pair $f, g \in F$ is of size at most $k + 1$, and the total number of pairs does not exceed $\binom{|F|}{2}$. We arrive at the following bound

$$|T_1| \leq \binom{|F|}{2}(k+1) \leq \binom{2k}{2}(k+1) = k(k+1)(2k-1). \quad (3.2)$$

By Lemma 3.3, we have that

$$|T_3| \leq |T_1|. \quad (3.3)$$

To bound the size of T_2, we proceed as follows. Let $\mathcal{E}$ be the set of *subdivided edges*, that is, the set of paths in T with endpoints in T_1 and T_3 and all inner edges from T_2. By Lemma 3.3, the number of subdivided edges from $\mathcal{E}$ is at most $|T_1|$. However, we are not yet done as an irreducible graph can still have long subdivided edges. How can we deal with such paths? Well, just as in the case of T_1, long paths create pairs of vertices in F having many short paths between them. In this situation, the promising strategy is to add double edges as in the case of T_1, and then use a reduction similar to Reduction Rule FVS.5.

However, this will not be sufficient. The difference between the current case and the case of T_1 is that in the latter one, due to degree-1 and degree-2 reduction rules, every vertex from T_1 should have at least two neighbors in F. This is not the true for T_2, so we should handle separately the "flower" case, that is, the case in which a vertex from F is adjacent to many vertices from T_2. In this context, we notice that if a vertex v from F is adjacent to many vertices in T_2, there should be a great deal of cycles intersecting only at v, and therefore v should be in every solution of size k. Thus, our strategy will be the following: We first fix the "flower" case, and then proceed in a way similar to the one taken to bound the size of T_1.

To follows our strategy, we first compute a matching M in T that maximizes the number of matched vertices from T_2. We say that two vertices $u, v \in V(T_2)$ are *matched* if $uv \in M$. It is easy to check that for every subdivided edge path E, there are at most two nonmatched vertices of degree 2. Hence, the number of vertices in $V(E) \setminus V(M)$, and thus the total number of nonmatched vertices from T_2, is at most $2|T_1|$.

Now, notice that a vertex in T_2 is either a matched vertex or a nonmatched vertex. To bound the number of matched vertices, we separately consider pairs of matched vertices with a common neighbor in F, and pairs with disjoint neighborhoods in F. The following reduction rule handles the pairs of vertices of the first type.

Reduction FVS.6 If there is a vertex $f \in F$ adjacent to more than k pairs of vertices matched by M, then delete v and reduce the parameter k by 1. The new instance is $(G - v, k - 1)$.

Claim 3.13 Reduction Rule FVS.6 is safe.

Proof: If f is adjacent to $k+1$ pairs of matched vertices, then G contains $k+1$ triangles intersecting only at f. Thus, every feedback vertex set of size k should contain f. ⌐

Let $f, g \in F$. We say that the pair $\{f, g\}$ is *adjacent* to a matched pair $\{u, v\}$ if either $u \in N(f) \cap N(g)$ or both $u \in N(f)$ and $v \in N(g)$. To reduce the number of pairs of matched vertices with disjoint neighborhoods, we use two new reductions. The first one among them can be seen as an extension of Reduction Rule FVS.3 for pairs of matched vertices.

Reduction FVS.7 If vertices $f, g \in F$ are adjacent to more than $k + 2$ pairs of matched vertices, then construct a new graph G' by connecting f and g by a double edge. The new instance is (G', k).

Claim 3.14 Reduction Rule FVS.7 is safe.

Proof: After observing that at least one of the vertices f and g should be in every feedback vertex set with at most k vertices, the proof of this claim is similar to the proof of Claim 3.10. ⌋

The following reduction is an adaptation of Reduction Rule FVS.3 to pairs of matched vertices.

> **Reduction FVS.8** Let u, v be matched vertices such that $N(u) \cap F$ and $N(v) \cap F$ are disjoint. If $(N(u) \cup N(v)) \cap F$ is a double clique, then contract edge uv. The new instance is $(G/uv, k)$.

Claim 3.15 Reduction Rule FVS.8 is safe.

Proof: The proof of this claim is almost identical to the proof of Claim 3.15, and we leave it as an exercise. ⌋

We are now ready to upper bound the size of T_2. As we have already mentioned, the number of nonmatched vertices is at most $2|T_1|$. Thanks to Reduction Rule FVS.6, we have that the number of matched pairs whose endpoints have a common neighbor in F is at most $k|F| \leq 2k^2$, and thus the number of vertices in these pairs is at most $4k^2$. Due to Reduction Rules FVS.7 and FVS.8, we can bound the number of pairs which endpoints have disjoint neighborhoods in F as follows. For every pair $uv \in M$ of matched vertices such that $N(u) \cap F$ and $N(v) \cap F$ are disjoint, we have that $(N(u) \cup N(v)) \cap F$ contains a pair of vertices not connected by a double edge. Hence, the number of such matched pairs is at most $\binom{|F|}{2}(k+1) \leq k(k+1)(2k-1)$.

Thus,

$$|T_2| \leq 2|T_1| + 4k^2 + k(k+1)(2k-1).$$

The total number of vertices in T is

$$|T_1| + |T_2| + |T_3|.$$

By (3.2) and (3.3), we have that

$$|V(T)| \leq 4|T_1| + 4k^2 + k(k+1)(2k-1) \leq 4k^2 + 5k(k+1)(2k-1).$$

We conclude that the total number of vertices in G is at most

$$|V(T)| + |F| \leq 2k + 4k^2 + 5k(k+1)(2k-1) = 10k^3 + 9k^2 - 3k.$$

□

As in the case of MAX LEAF SUBTREE, the proof of the Boundary Lemma can be easily transformed into a kernelization algorithm, providing a kernel with $\mathcal{O}(k^3)$ vertices for FEEDBACK VERTEX SET.

For our kernelization algorithm we need a constant factor approximation algorithm for FEEDBACK VERTEX SET. The proof of the following theorem can be found in Bafna et al. (1999).

Theorem 3.16 *There is a polynomial time algorithm that for a given graph G outputs a feedback vertex set whose size is at most twice the minimum size of a feedback vertex set in G.*

Now everything is settled to prove the main result of this section.

Theorem 3.17 FEEDBACK VERTEX SET *admits a kernel with $\mathcal{O}(k^3)$ vertices.*

Proof: We start with an approximation algorithm described in Theorem 3.16. For a given instance (G,k), this algorithm returns a feedback vertex set whose size is at most twice the size of an optimal one. Thus, if the output is a set of size more than $2k$, we conclude that (G,k) is a no-instance. Otherwise, we have a feedback vertex set F of size at most k.

Now, we exhaustively apply Reduction Rules FVS.1–FVS.8. Each of these reduction rules is clearly implementable in polynomial time. If we obtain a reduced instance with at most $10k^3 + 9k^2 - 3k$ vertices, we are done. Otherwise, by Lemma 3.9, we conclude that (G,k) is a no-instance. □

Exercises

Problem 3.1 (✎) Prove Lemma 3.3.

Problem 3.2 (♟) Prove the following claim. For every $r \geq 1$, there is a constant c such that every connected graph G with ck vertices and no r-subdivided edges has a spanning tree with at least k leaves.

Problem 3.3 (♟) In a graph G, a set of vertices X is called a *nonblocker set* if every vertex in X has a neighbor outside X. In other words, the complement $V(G) \setminus X$ of a nonblocker X is a dominating set in G. In the NON-BLOCKER problem, we are given a graph G and an integer k, and the task is to decide whether G contains a nonblocker set of size at least k. By McCuaig and Shepherd (1989), every graph G with at least eight vertices and without vertices of degree 1 has a dominating set of size at most $\frac{2}{5}|V(G)|$. Use this to construct a Boundary Lemma and a polynomial kernel for NONBLOCKER.

Problem 3.4 (☠) In a digraph G, a set of vertices X is called a *directed nonblocker set* if every vertex in X has an outgoing neighbor outside X. In the directed version of the NONBLOCKER problem, we are given a digraph G and an integer k, and the task is to decide whether G contains a directed nonblocker set of size at least k. Prove that this version has a kernel with $k^2 + k - 1$ vertices.

Problem 3.5 In $K_{1,d}$-PACKING, we are given a graph G and an integer k, and the task is to decide whether G contains at least k vertex-disjoint copies of the star $K_{1,d}$ with d leaves. Use the method of inductive priorities to obtain a kernel with $\mathcal{O}(kd^3 + k^2d^2)$ vertices for $K_{1,d}$-PACKING.

Problem 3.6 (✎) Prove Claim 3.15.

Bibliographic Notes

The MAX LEAF SUBTREE was generally studied as a mean to analyze MAX LEAF SPANNING TREE, where given a graph G and an integer k, we ask whether G contains a spanning tree with at least k leaves. It is easy to see that (G, k) is a yes-instance of MAX LEAF SUBTREE if and only if it is a yes-instance of MAX LEAF SPANNING TREE. The MAX LEAF SPANNING TREE problem has gained more interest because it is the parameteric dual of the CONNECTED DOMINATING SET problem: Given a spanning tree T of G with at least k leaves, the set of internal vertices of T is a connected dominating set of size at most $n - k$ in G, and given a connected dominating set D of size at most $n - k$ in G, by taking a spanning tree of $G[D]$ and attaching to it the vertices in $G - D$ as leaves, we obtain a spanning tree of G with at least k leaves. We chose to focus on MAX LEAF SUBTREE rather than MAX LEAF SPANNING TREE to exemplify the use of inductive properties; in particular, in MAX LEAF SUBTREE it is very natural to choose a counterexample of maximum size as the first priority, and hence it serves as a good intuitive example.

The first kernelization algorithm for MAX LEAF SUBTREE appeared in Bonsma et al. (2003). Our presentation of a kernel for MAX LEAF SUBTREE follows the work of Fellows and Rosamond (2007) and Fellows et al. (2009) on inductive priorities. Currently, the smallest known kernel for MAX LEAF SUBTREE on connected graphs with at most $3.75k$ vertices is claimed in Estivill-Castro et al. (2005). In the general case, where the input graph is not required to be connected, MAX LEAF SUBTREE does not admit a polynomial kernel. However, it admits a polynomial Turing kernelization, see Chapter 22. Jansen (2012) extends the kernelization algorithm to weighted graphs. The kernelization issues of the directed version of the problem, namely DIRECTED MAX LEAF, are discussed in Binkele-Raible et al. (2012); Daligault and Thomassé (2009), and Daligault et al. (2010).

We note that Exercise 3.2 is taken from Appendix A in Jansen (2012). The thesis of Prieto (2005) is devoted to the systematic study of the method of inductive priorities. In particular, Exercise 3.5 is taken from Prieto and Sloper (2006) (see also Xiao 2017b). Exercises 3.3 and 3.4 are taken from Dehne et al. (2006) and Gutin et al. (2011a), respectively.

Constant-factor approximation algorithms for feedback vertex set are due to Bafna et al. (1999) and Bar-Yehuda et al. (1998). Kernelization algorithm for FEEDBACK VERTEX SET by making use of inductive priorities resulting in kernel of size $\mathcal{O}(k^{11})$ was given by Burrage et al. (2006). It was improved to $\mathcal{O}(k^3)$ by Bodlaender and van Dijk (2010). The quadratic kernel of Thomassé (2010) uses more powerful combinatorial techniques and is discussed in detail in Section 5.5. Our presentation here is an adaptation of the kernel from Fomin et al. (2012b) for a more general $\mathcal{F}$-DELETION problem.

4
Crown Decomposition

In this chapter we study a graph structure that resembles a crown. We show how to design reduction rules that are based on the existence (or absence) of such a structure. In this context, we examine the VERTEX COVER, DUAL COLORING, MAXIMUM SATISFIABILITY and LONGEST CYCLE problems.

A general technique to obtain kernels is based on the analysis of a graph structure that resembles a crown, known as a Crown decomposition. The foundations of this technique are the classical theorems of Kőnig and Hall. The first theorem, known as Kőnig's Minimax Theorem, is the following statement about bipartite graphs.

Theorem 4.1 (Kőnig's theorem, Kőnig [1916]) *Let G be a bipartite graph. Then, the minimum size of a vertex cover in G is equal to the maximum size of a matching in G.*

To state the second theorem, known as Hall's Theorem, let us first remind that for a vertex set $X \subseteq V(G)$, we let $N(X)$ denote the set of vertices in $V(G) \setminus X$ adjacent to vertices from X. When G is a bipartite graph with bipartition (A, B) and M is a matching in G, we say that M is a *matching of A into B* if all the vertices of A are covered (saturated, matched) by M. In other words, for every vertex in A, there exists at least one edge in M that contains that vertex as an endpoint.

Theorem 4.2 (Hall's theorem, Hall [1935]) *Let G be a bipartite graph with bipartition (A, B). Then, G has a matching of A into B if and only if $|N(X)| \geq |X|$ for all $X \subseteq A$.*

4.1 Crown Decomposition

We will also be using an algorithmic version of Kőnig's Theorem, which is due to Hopcroft and Karp (1973). For the proof of the (nonstandard) second claim of the theorem, see Cygan et al. (2015, Exercise 2.21).

Theorem 4.3 (Hopcroft-Karp algorithm, Hopcroft and Karp [1973]) *Let G be an undirected bipartite graph with bipartition A and B, on n vertices and m edges. Then we can find a maximum matching as well as a minimum vertex cover of G in time $\mathcal{O}(m\sqrt{n})$. Furthermore, in time $\mathcal{O}(m\sqrt{n})$ either we can find a matching saturating A or an inclusion-wise minimal set $X \subseteq A$ such that $|N(X)| < |X|$.*

4.1 Crown Decomposition

Definition 4.4 A crown decomposition of a graph G is a partition of $V(G)$ into three sets, C, H and R, where C and H are nonempty and the following properties are satisfied.

(i) The set C, $C \neq \emptyset$, is an independent set.
(ii) There does not exist an edge with one endpoint in C and the other endpoint in R, that is, H separates C and R.
(iii) There is a matching of H into C. In other words, let E' be the set of edges with one endpoint in C and the other endpoint in H. Then, E' contains a matching of size $|H|$.

A crown decomposition can be seen as a Crown (C) put on a Head (H) of a Royal body (R). Fig. 4.1 illustrates an example of a crown decomposition.

The following lemma lies at the heart of kernelization algorithms that make use of crown decompositions.

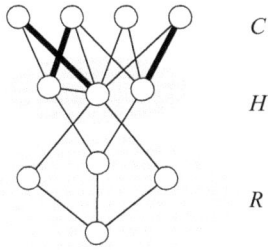

Figure 4.1 A crown decomposition: The set C is an independent set, H separates C and R, and there exists a matching of H into C.

Lemma 4.5 (Crown Lemma) *Let G be a graph without isolated vertices and with at least $3k + 1$ vertices. Then, there is a polynomial time algorithm that either*

- *Finds a matching of size $k + 1$ in G, or*
- *Finds a crown decomposition of G.*

Proof: We first find a maximal matching M in G. This can be done by a greedy insertion of edges. If the size of M is $k + 1$, we are done. Hence, let us next assume that $|M| \leq k$, and let V_M be the set of the endpoints of the edges in M. Note that $|V_M| \leq 2k$. Because M is a maximal matching, the set of the remaining vertices, $I = V(G) \setminus V_M$, is an independent set.

Let us examine the bipartite graph G_{I,V_M} formed by the edges of G with one endpoint in V_M and the other endpoint in I. If the size of the maximum matching in G_{I,V_M} is at least $k + 1$, then we are done. Thus, we next assume that G_{I,V_M} has no matching of size $k + 1$. By Kőnig's Theorem, the minimum size of a vertex cover in the bipartite graph G_{I,V_M} is equal to the maximum size of matching. Moreover, by Theorem 4.3, we can compute a minimum-sized vertex cover, X, of G_{I,V_M} in polynomial time.

If no vertex of X belongs to V_M, then every vertex of I should belong to X (because G has no isolated vertices). But then $|I| \leq k$, implying that G has at most

$$|I| + |V_M| \leq k + 2k = 3k$$

vertices, which is a contradiction.

Hence, $X \cap V_M \neq \emptyset$. We obtain a crown decomposition (C, H, R) as follows. We define the head as $H = X \cap V_M$ and the crown as $C = I \setminus X$. Obviously, C is an independent set. Moreover, because X is a vertex cover in G_{I,V_M}, every vertex of C can be adjacent only to vertices of H. By Kőnig's Theorem, G_{I,V_M} contains a matching of size $|X|$. Every edge of this matching has exactly one endpoint in X, and thus the edges of this matching with endpoints in H form a matching of H into C. □

4.2 VERTEX COVER and DUAL COLORING

In this section we show how the Crown Lemma can be used to obtain kernels for the VERTEX COVER and DUAL COLORING problems. Let us start with VERTEX COVER. We remark that later, in Chapter 6, we also show how to construct a kernel for VERTEX COVER by making use of linear programming. Here, we focus only on crown decompositions. Given a crown decomposition

4.2 VERTEX COVER and DUAL COLORING

(C, H, R) of G, we first observe that one can reduce the instance (G, k) of VERTEX COVER by applying the following reduction rule.

> **Reduction VC.6** (Crown Reduction for Vertex Cover)   Let (C, H, R) be a crown decomposition of G. Construct a new instance of the problem, (G', k'), by removing $H \cup C$ from G and reducing k by $|H|$. In other words, $G' = G[R]$ and $k' = k - |H|$.

We first prove that the Crown Reduction Rule is safe.

Lemma 4.6 *Let (G', k') be the result of an application of the Crown Reduction Rule. Then, (G, k) is a yes-instance of* VERTEX COVER *if and only if (G', k') is a yes-instance of* VERTEX COVER.

Proof: We need to show that G has a vertex cover of size k if and only if $G' = G[R]$ has a vertex cover of size $k' = k - |H|$. For the first direction, let S be a vertex cover of G of size k. By the properties of a crown decomposition, there is a matching M of H into C. This matching is of size $|H|$ and it saturates every vertex of H. Thus, as each vertex cover must pick at least one vertex from each of the edges in M, we have that $|S \cap (H \cup C)| \geq |H|$. Hence, the number of vertices in S covering the edges not incident with any vertex in $H \cup C$ is at most $k - |H|$.

For the other direction, we simply observe that if S' is a vertex cover of size $k - |H|$ for G', then $S' \cup H$ is a vertex cover of size k for G.   □

Next, we show how the Crown Reduction Rule can be used to obtain a kernel with $3k$ vertices.

Theorem 4.7 VERTEX COVER *admits a kernel with at most $3k$ vertices.*

Proof: Given an instance (G, k) of VERTEX COVER, we perform the following operations. First, apply Reduction Rule VC.1: Delete all isolated vertices of G.

If G contains at most $3k$ vertices, then (G, k) is the desired kernel. Otherwise, we use the Crown Reduction Lemma (Lemma 4.5). If G has a matching of size $k+1$, then to cover these edges we need at least $k+1$ vertices, and therefore we answer no. Otherwise, we construct in polynomial time a crown decomposition (C, H, R). Then, we apply the Crown Reduction Rule. The application of this rule results in an equivalent instance (G', k'), where $G' = G[R]$ and $k' = k - |H|$. We repeat the preceding procedure with each reduced instance until we either obtain a no answer or reach a kernel with $3k$ vertices.   □

In our next example, we would like to properly color the vertex set of a graph. Specifically, a *k-coloring* of an undirected graph G is a function $c : V(G) \rightarrow \{1, 2, \ldots, k\}$ that assigns a color to each vertex of the graph such that adjacent vertices have different colors. The smallest k for which G has a k-coloring is called the *chromatic number* of G, and it is denoted by $\chi(G)$. It is well known that deciding if $\chi(G)$ is at most 3 is an NP-complete problem. Thus, to analyze the chromatic number from the perspective of Parameterized Complexity, we consider the parameterization called DUAL COLORING. Formally, given an n-vertex graph G and a nonnegative integer k, the DUAL COLORING problem asks whether G has a $(n - k)$-coloring.

We would like to analyze a crown decomposition of the complement of the input graph. In this context, recall that the *complement* of an undirected graph G, denoted by $\overline{G}$, is the graph on the vertex set $V(G)$ and whose edge set is $E(\overline{G}) = \{\{u, v\} \mid \{u, v\} \notin E(G), u \neq v\}$. In what follows, we would rely on the observation that coloring an n-vertex graph with $(n - k)$ colors is equivalent to covering the complement of the graph by $(n - k)$ cliques.

Given a crown decomposition (C, H, R) of $\overline{G}$, we apply a reduction rule that is exactly the Crown Rule presented for VERTEX COVER, where the only difference is that this time we use a crown decomposition of $\overline{G}$ rather than G. Formally, the rule is stated as follows.

> **Reduction DC.1** (Crown Reduction for Dual Coloring) Let (C, H, R) be a crown decomposition of $\overline{G}$. Construct a new instance of the problem, (G', k'), by deleting $H \cup C$ from G and reducing k by $|H|$. In other words, $G' = G[R]$ and $k' = k - |H|$.

The following lemma shows that Rule DC.1 is safe.

Lemma 4.8 *Let (G', k') be the result of an application of the Crown Reduction Rule. Then, (G, k) is a yes-instance of* DUAL COLORING *if and only if (G', k') is a yes-instance of* DUAL COLORING.

Proof: We need to show that G is $(|V(G)| - k)$-colorable if and only if $G' = G[R]$ is $(|V(G')| - k')$-colorable, where $k' = k - |H|$.

For the first direction, let c be a $(|V(G)| - k)$-coloring of G. Because C is a clique, all the vertices in C are assigned different colors by c. None of these colors can be reused to color any of the vertices of R because every vertex in R is adjacent to all the vertices in C. Thus, the number of color using which c colors $G' = G[R]$ is at most

$$(|V(G)| - k) - |C| = |V(G)| - (|C| + |H|) - (k - |H|) = |V(G')| - k'.$$

For the second direction, let c' be a $(|V(G')| - k')$-coloring of G'. We introduce $|C|$ new colors to color the vertices in C. Because there is a matching M of H into C in $\overline{G}$, we can use the $|C|$ colors from the coloring of C to color H as well: For every vertex $u \in H$, we select the color of the vertex from C matched by M to u. Thus, the number of colors that we used to color G is at most

$$(|V(G')| - k') + |C| = |V(G)| - (|C| + |H|) - (k - |H|) + |C| = |V(G)| - k.$$

□

Theorem 4.9 DUAL COLORING *admits a kernel with at most* $3k - 3$ *vertices.*

Proof: Let (G, k) denote an instance of DUAL COLORING, where G is a graph on n vertices. First, suppose that the complement $\overline{G}$ of G contains an isolated vertex v. Then, in G this vertex v is adjacent to all other vertices, and thus (G, k) is a yes-instance if and only if $(G - v, k - 1)$ is a yes-instance. Hence, in this case, we can reduce the instance.

Let us now assume that $\overline{G}$ does not have isolated vertices. In this case, we apply the Crown Lemma on $\overline{G}$. If $\overline{G}$ has a matching M of size k, then G is $(n-k)$-colorable. Indeed, the endpoints of every edge of M can be colored with the same color. If $\overline{G}$ has no matching M of size k, then either $n \leq 3(k-1)$, or G can be reduced by making use of the Crown Reduction Rule for DUAL COLORING. □

4.3 MAXIMUM SATISFIABILITY

Our next example concerns MAXIMUM SATISFIABILITY. Here, for a given CNF formula φ with n variables and m clauses, and a nonnegative integer k, the objective is to decide whether φ has a truth assignment satisfying at least k clauses.

By the following lemma, we can always assume that the instance of MAXIMUM SATISFIABILITY contains at most $2k$ clauses.

Lemma 4.10 *If* $m \geq 2k$, *then* (φ, k) *is a yes-instance of* MAXIMUM SATISFIABILITY.

Proof: We already used this argument in the proof of Lemma 2.1: Let ψ be a truth assignment to the variables of φ and $\neg \psi$ be the assignment obtained by complementing the assignment of ψ. Then at least one of ψ and $\neg \psi$ satisfies at least $m/2$ clauses of φ. Hence if $m \geq 2k$, then (φ, k) is a yes-instance. □

In what follows we give a kernel with at most k variables.

In the design of the kernel, we use the notion of the *variable-clause incidence graph* of φ, which is a bipartite graph with bipartition (X, Y), defined as follows. The sets X and Y correspond to the set of variables of φ and the set of clauses of φ, respectively. For a vertex $x \in X$, we refer to x as both the vertex in G_φ and the corresponding variable in φ. Similarly, for a vertex $c \in Y$, we refer to c as both the vertex in G_φ and the corresponding clause in φ. The graph G_φ has an edge between a variable $x \in X$ and a clause $c \in Y$ if and only if c contains either x or the negation of x.

We proceed with the construction of the kernel.

Theorem 4.11 MAXIMUM SATISFIABILITY *admits a kernel with at most k variables and $2k$ clauses.*

Proof: Let φ be a CNF formula with n variables and m clauses. By Lemma 4.10, we may assume that $m \leq 2k$. If $n \leq k$, then there is nothing to prove.

Suppose that φ has at least k variables. Let G_φ be the variable-clause incidence graph of φ with bipartition (X, Y). If there is a matching of X into Y in G_φ, then there is a truth assignment satisfying at least $|X| \geq k$ clauses. Indeed, in this case we set each variable in X in such a way that the clause matched to it becomes satisfied. We now show that if G_φ does not have a matching of X into Y, then in polynomial time we can either reduce (F, k) to an equivalent smaller instance or find an assignment to the variables satisfying at least k clauses.

By making use of Theorem 4.3, in polynomial time we can find

- Either a matching of X into Y, or
- A nonempty inclusion-wise minimal set $C \subseteq X$ such that $|N(C)| < |C|$.

If we found a matching then we are done, as we have already argued that in such a case we can satisfy at least $|X| \geq k$ clauses. Thus, suppose that we found a nonempty inclusion-wise minimal set $C \subseteq X$ such that $|N(C)| < |C|$. Denote $H = N(C)$ and $R = V(G_\varphi) \setminus (C \cup H)$. Clearly, $G[C]$ is an independent set. Also because $H = N(C)$, H separates C and R. Furthermore, due to the minimality of C, for every vertex $x \in C$, we have $|N(C')| \geq |C'|$ for all $C' \subseteq C \setminus \{x\}$. Therefore, by Hall's Theorem, there exists a matching of $C \setminus \{x\}$ into H. Because $|C| > |H|$, we have that a matching of $C \setminus \{x\}$ into H is in fact the matching of H into C. Hence, (C, H, R) is a crown decomposition of G_φ.

We claim that all clauses in H are satisfied in every truth assignment to the variables satisfying the maximum number of clauses. Indeed, consider any truth assignment ψ that does not satisfy all clauses in H. For every variable y in $C \setminus \{x\}$, change the value of y such that the clause in H matched to y

is satisfied. Let ψ' be the new assignment obtained from ψ in this manner. Because $N(C) \subseteq H$ and ψ' satisfies all clauses in H, more clauses are satisfied by ψ' than by ψ. Hence, ψ could not have been an assignment satisfying the maximum number of clauses.

The preceding argument shows that (φ, k) is a yes-instance of MAXIMUM SATISFIABILITY if and only if $(\varphi \setminus H, k - |H|)$ is a yes-instance of this problem. This claim gives rise to the following reduction rule.

Reduction MSat.1 (Crown Reduction for Max Sat)   Let (φ, k) and H be as in the preceding text. Then remove H from φ and decrease k by $|H|$. That is, $(\varphi \setminus H, k - |H|)$ is the new instance.

By repeating the preceding arguments and applying Reduction Rule MSat.1, we obtain the desired kernel. □

4.4 LONGEST CYCLE Parameterized by Vertex Cover

In this section we employ crown decompositions to obtain the kernel for the LONGEST CYCLE problem parameterized by vertex cover. Here, we are given a graph G, integers k and ℓ and a vertex cover S of G such that $|S| = k$. The parameter is k, and the task is to decide whether G contains a cycle on ℓ vertices.

We proceed directly to show how crown decompositions can be used to obtain a kernel for LONGEST CYCLE (VC) with $\mathcal{O}(k^2)$ vertices.

Theorem 4.12 LONGEST CYCLE (VC) *admits a kernel with* $\mathcal{O}(k^2)$ *vertices.*

Proof: Let (G, k, ℓ, S) be an instance of LONGEST CYCLE (VC). Because S is a vertex cover, we have that $I = V(G) \setminus S$ is an independent set. We construct an auxiliary bipartite graph G_S, where each of the vertices in one set of the bipartition represents an unordered pair of elements from S, and the other set of the bipartition is simply I. Thus, G_S has $\binom{k}{2} + |I|$ vertices. The graph G_S contains an edge between a pair $\{u, v\} \in \binom{S}{2}$ and $x \in I$ if $x \in N_G(u) \cap N_G(v)$.

By Theorem 4.3, in polynomial time we can find in G_S either a matching saturating I or an inclusion-wise minimal set $C \subseteq I$ such that $|N(C)| < |C|$. If we found a matching, then we are done—in this case $|I| \leq \binom{k}{2}$ and G has $|S| + |I| = \mathcal{O}(k^2)$ vertices.

Thus, suppose that we found a nonempty inclusion-wise minimal set $C \subseteq I$ such that $|N_{G_S}(C)| < |C|$. We put $H = N_{G_S}(C)$ and $R = V(G_S) \setminus (C \cup H)$.

We claim that (C, H, R) is the crown decomposition of G_S. Indeed, $G[C]$ is an independent set and H separates C and R. Furthermore, due to the choice of C, for every vertex $x \in C$, we have that $|N(C')| \geq |C'|$ for all $C' \subseteq C \setminus \{x\}$. Therefore there is a matching of $C \setminus x$ into H. Because $|C| > |H|$, we have that every matching of $C \setminus \{x\}$ into H is in fact a matching of H into C. Hence, (C, H, R) is a crown decomposition of G_S.

We define the following reduction rule.

> **Reduction LC.1** Find a matching M saturating H in G_S. Let x be (the unique) vertex of C that is not saturated by M. Delete x from G. That is, $(G - x, S, k, \ell)$ is the new instance.

To prove that Reduction Rule LC.1 is safe, let us consider the new instance $(G - x, S, k, \ell)$ of LONGEST CYCLE (VC). We claim that (G, S, k, ℓ) is a yes-instance if and only if $(G - x, S, k, \ell)$ is a yes-instance. The reverse direction is trivial because $G - x$ is a subgraph of G and thus every cycle in $G - x$ is also a cycle in G. For the forward direction, let L be a cycle of length ℓ in G and let $\{a_1, \ldots, a_q\}$ be the set of vertices of L that belong to C. Let x_i and y_i be the neighbors of a_i in L. Clearly, $\{x_i, y_i\} \in H$. Let $b_i \in C$ be the vertex matched to $\{x_i, y_i\}$ by M, and note that $b_i \neq x$. Now, we obtain a new cycle L' from L by replacing the vertex a_i by b_i for every $i \in \{1, \ldots, q\}$. In particular, if $x = a_i$ for some $i \in \{1, \ldots, q\}$, then it is replaced by $b_i \neq x$. Therefore, the construction of G_S ensures that L' is a cycle of length ℓ avoiding x. Thus, we have shown that if G has a cycle of length ℓ, then so does $G - x$.

We have shown that either the graph already contains at most $\mathcal{O}(k^2)$ vertices or we can obtain an equivalent instance by deleting a vertex from the graph. Moreover, the desired vertex can be found in polynomial time. By applying the arguments and the reduction rule, we obtain the desired kernel. This completes the proof. □

In Chapter 5, with the help of a tool called the Expansion Lemma, we show how to extend ideas relevant to crown decompositions to additional problems.

Exercises

Problem 4.1 In the MAX-INTERNAL SPANNING TREE problem, we are given graph G and an integer k. The task is to decide whether G has a spanning tree of G with at least k internal vertices. Prove that MAX-INTERNAL SPANNING TREE/VC admits a kernel with $\mathcal{O}(\ell^2)$ vertices, where ℓ is the vertex cover number of G.

Problem 4.2 Prove that MAX-INTERNAL SPANNING TREE admits a kernel with $\mathcal{O}(k^2)$ vertices.

Problem 4.3 In the d-SET PACKING problem, we are given a universe U, a family $\mathcal{A}$ of sets over U, where each set in $\mathcal{A}$ is of size at most d, and an integer k. The task is to decide whether there exists a family $\mathcal{A}' \subseteq \mathcal{A}$ of k pairwise-disjoint sets. Prove that this problem admits a kernel with $\mathcal{O}(k^d)$ elements, where d is a fixed constant.

Problem 4.4 (☠) Prove that the d-SET PACKING problem admits a kernel with $\mathcal{O}(k^{d-1})$ elements, where d is a fixed constant.

Problem 4.5 (☠) In the d-HITTING SET problem, we are given a universe U, a family $\mathcal{A}$ of sets over U, where each set in $\mathcal{A}$ is of size at most d, and an integer k. The task is to decide whether there exists a set $X \subseteq U$ of size at most k that has a nonempty intersection with every set of $\mathcal{A}$. Prove that this problem admits a kernel with $\mathcal{O}(k^{d-1})$ elements, where d is a fixed constant.

Bibliographic Notes

Hall's Theorem (Theorem 4.2) is due to Hall (1935), see also the book of Lovász and Plummer (2009). Kőnig's Minimax Theorem (Theorem 4.1) is attributed to Kőnig (1916). The first chapter of the book (Lovász and Plummer, 2009) contains a nice historical overview on the development of the matching problem. The algorithm finding a minimum-size vertex cover and maximum-size matching in bipartite graphs in time $\mathcal{O}(\sqrt{n}m)$ is due to Hopcroft and Karp (1973) and Karzanov (1974). We refer to Chapter 16 of Schrijver's book (2003) for an overview of maximum-size matching algorithms on bipartite graphs.

The bound obtained on the kernel for VERTEX COVER in Theorem 4.7 can be further improved to $2k$ with much more sophisticated use of crown decomposition (folklore). The Crown Rule was introduced by Chor et al. (2004), see also Fellows (2003). Implementation issues of kernelization algorithms for vertex cover that are relevant to the Crown Rule are discussed in Abu-Khzam et al. (2004). Theorem 4.11 is due to Lokshtanov (2009), and Theorem 4.12 is due to Bodlaender et al. (2013).

Exercises 4.1 and 4.2 are based on the paper of Prieto and Sloper (2005), which used the technique of crown decomposition to obtain a quadratic kernel for MAX-INTERNAL SPANNING TREE. Exercises 4.4 and 4.5 are due to Abu-Khzam, who used this technique to obtain a kernel for d-SET PACKING with at most $\mathcal{O}(k^{d-1})$ elements (see Abu-Khzam, 2010a), and a kernel for d-HITTING SET with at most $(2d-1)k^{d-1}+k$ elements (Abu-Khzam, 2010b). For other examples of problems where crown decompositions and related variations of these structures were employed to obtain kernels, we refer to the papers Wang et al., 2010; Prieto and Sloper, 2005, 2006; Fellows et al., 2004; Moser, 2009; and Chlebík and Chlebíková, 2008.

5
Expansion Lemma

In this chapter we generalize the notion of a crown decomposition. We thus derive a powerful method that is employed to design polynomial kernels for COMPONENT ORDER CONNECTIVITY and FEEDBACK VERTEX SET.

In the previous chapter, we showed how crown decompositions can be used to obtain polynomial kernels for a variety of problems. The foundation of the method was Hall's Theorem, and the construction of crown decompositions further relied on König's Theorem. We proceed by introducing a powerful variation of Hall's Theorem, which is called the Expansion Lemma. Here, König's Theorem again comes into play in the proof of the lemma. In fact, the Expansion Lemma can be viewed as König's Theorem in an auxiliary graph. This lemma essentially says that if one side of a bipartition of a bipartite graph is much larger than the other side, then we can find more than one matching, where the distinct matchings are, of course, pairwise edge-disjoint, and exploit these matchings to obtain a polynomial kernel, even when the problem in question exhibits a nonlocal behavior. In this context, our example would consider FEEDBACK VERTEX SET. We also give a weighted version of the Expansion Lemma, whose formulation is very close to the one of the SANTA CLAUS problem studied in combinatorial optimization. We employ this version to design a polynomial kernel for a generalization of VERTEX COVER, called COMPONENT ORDER CONNECTIVITY.

5.1 Expansion Lemma

Toward the presentation of the Expansion Lemma, we first note that a *q-star*, $q \geq 1$, is a graph with $q + 1$ vertices such that one vertex is of degree q and all

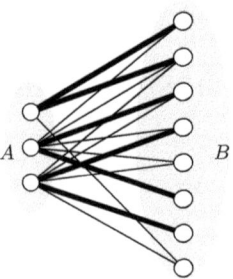

Figure 5.1 The set A has a 2-expansion into B.

other vertices are of degree 1. Let G be a bipartite graph with vertex bipartition (A, B). A set of edges $M \subseteq E(G)$ is called a *q-expansion*, $q \geq 1$, of A into B if

- Every vertex of A is incident with exactly q edges of M, and
- M saturates exactly $q|A|$ vertices in B.

Let us note that the expansion saturates all the vertices of A (see Fig. 5.1). Moreover, for every $u, v \in A$, $u \neq v$, the set of vertices adjacent to u using edges of M does not intersect the set of vertices adjacent to v using edges of M. Thus, every vertex v of A could be thought of as the center of a star with its q leaves in B, overall resulting in $|A|$ stars that are vertex-disjoint. Furthermore, the collection of these stars also forms a family of q edge-disjoint matchings, with each matching saturating A.

Let us remind that by Hall's Theorem (Theorem 4.2), a bipartite graph with bipartition (A, B) has a matching of A into B if and only if $|N(X)| \geq |X|$ for all $X \subseteq A$. The following lemma is an extension of this result.

Lemma 5.1 *Let G be a bipartite graph with bipartition (A, B). Then, there is a q-expansion of A into B if and only if $|N(X)| \geq q|X|$ for all $X \subseteq A$.*

Proof: In one direction, note that if A has a q-expansion into B, then trivially $|N(X)| \geq q|X|$ for all $X \subseteq A$.

To prove the opposite direction, we construct a new bipartite graph G' with bipartition (A', B) from G as follows. For every vertex $v \in A$, we add $(q - 1)$ copies of v, where the neighborhood of each of these copies in B is the same neighborhood of v in B. We would like to prove that there is a matching M of A' into B in G'. If we prove this claim, then by identifying the endpoints of M corresponding to copies of the same vertex from A, we obtain a q-expansion in G. It suffices to check that the assumptions of Hall's Theorem are satisfied by G'. Suppose, by way of contradiction, that there is a set $X \subseteq A'$ such that $|N_{G'}(X)| < |X|$. Without loss of generality, we can assume that if X contains

5.1 Expansion Lemma   63

some copy of some vertex v, then it contains all the copies of v, as inserting all the remaining copies increases $|X|$ but does not change $|N_{G'}(X)|$. Hence, the set X in A' naturally corresponds to a set X_A of size $|X|/q$ in A, namely, the set of vertices whose copies are in X. However, we then have that $|N_G(X_A)| = |N_{G'}(X)| < |X| = q|X_A|$, which is a contradiction. Thus, A' has a matching into B, which implies that A has a q-expansion into B. □

Lemma 5.2 (Expansion Lemma) *Let q be a positive integer, and G be a bipartite graph with vertex bipartition (A, B) such that*

(i) $|B| \geq q|A|$, and
(ii) There are no isolated vertices in B.

Then, there exist nonempty vertex sets $X \subseteq A$ and $Y \subseteq B$ such that

- *X has a q-expansion into Y and*
- *No vertex in Y has a neighbor outside X, that is, $N(Y) \subseteq X$.*

Furthermore, the sets X and Y can be found in time $\mathcal{O}(mn^{1.5})$.

Let us remark that the sets X, Y and $V(G) \setminus (X \cup Y)$ form a crown decomposition of G with a property stronger than one of an arbitrary crown decomposition—not only can every vertex of X be matched to a distinct vertex in Y, but there is a q-expansion of X into Y.

We proceed with the proof of the Expansion Lemma.

Proof: The proof is based on induction on $|A|$. In the basis, where $|A| = 1$, the lemma holds trivially. Next, suppose that that $|A| \geq 2$.

We apply Lemma 5.1 to G. If A has a q-expansion into B, we are done. Otherwise, there is a (nonempty) set $Z \subseteq A$ such that $|N(Z)| < q|Z|$. We construct the graph G' by removing Z and $N(Z)$ from G. We claim that G' satisfies the assumptions of the lemma. Indeed, because the number of vertices we removed from B is smaller than q times the number of vertices we removed from A, we have that G' satisfies (i). Moreover, no vertex from $B \setminus N(Z)$ has a neighbor in Z, and therefore G' also satisfies (ii). Note that $Z \neq A$, because otherwise $N(A) = B$ (as there are no isolated vertices in B) and then $|B| \geq |A|$. By the inductive hypothesis for G', there are nonempty sets $X \subseteq A \setminus Z$ and $Y \subseteq B \setminus N(Z)$ such that both X has a q-expansion into Y and $N_{G'}(Y) \subseteq X$. Because $Y \subseteq B \setminus N(Z)$, we have that no vertex in Y has a neighbor in Z. Hence, $N_{G'}(Y) = N_G(Y) \subseteq X$ and the pair (X, Y) satisfies all the required properties.

Finally, let us analyze the running time of the algorithm that is the naive algorithmic interpretation of the inductive proof of the lemma. We claim that the running time of this algorithm can be bounded by $\mathcal{O}(mn^{1.5})$. Note that when $|A| \geq 2$, we have that one vertex is removed from the side A of the bipartition, and therefore the number of iterations of the algorithm is bounded by $|A| = \mathcal{O}(n/q)$. In each iteration, the algorithm invokes the procedure given by Theorem 4.3 on a graph with at most $q|A| + |B| \leq 2|B| = \mathcal{O}(n)$ vertices and qm edges. Thus, the running time of one iteration is bounded by $\mathcal{O}(qm\sqrt{n})$. Overall, we have that the total running time is bounded by $\mathcal{O}(mn^{1.5})$. □

Sometimes the following slightly stronger version of the Expansion Lemma is handy.

Lemma 5.3 *Let q be a positive integer, and G be a bipartite graph with vertex bipartition (A, B) such that*

- $|B| > \ell q$, *where ℓ is the size of the maximum matching in G, and*
- *There are no isolated vertices in B.*

Then, there exist nonempty vertex sets $X \subseteq A$ and $Y \subseteq B$ such that

- *X has a q-expansion in Y, and*
- *No vertex in Y has a neighbor outside X, that is, $N(Y) \subseteq X$.*

Furthermore, the sets X and Y can be found in time $\mathcal{O}(mn^{1.5})$.

Proof: Let C be a minimum vertex cover of G and M be a maximum matching of G. By Kőnig's Minimax Theorem (Theorem 4.1), we have that $|C| = |M|$ and that C contains exactly one vertex of every edge of M. Let $A' = A \cap C$ capture the vertices in A that belong to the vertex cover C, and let $B' = N(A') \setminus C$ capture the neighbors in B of these vertices that lie outside the vertex cover C. We claim that the set A' is not empty. Suppose, by way of contradiction, that this claim is false. Then, we have that $C \subseteq B$. However, $|C| = |M| \leq |B|/q < |B|$, which means that $B \setminus C$ is not empty. Because B does not contain isolated vertices, we have that $B \setminus C$ contains vertices incident to edges that are not covered by C. We have thus reached a contradiction, and therefore $A' \neq \emptyset$.

Let $G' = G[A' \cup B']$. We now verify that G' satisfies conditions of Lemma 5.2. For (i), by definition B' does not contain isolated vertices in G'. For (ii), observe that $B \setminus B' \subseteq C$. Indeed, vertices of $B \setminus B'$ that are not in C cannot be incident to vertices in $N(A')$ (by the definition of B'), which means that they are incident to edges not covered by C as they are not isolated, and hence such vertices cannot exist. Therefore, $C = A' \cup (B \setminus B')$, which implies the following.

$$|B'| = |B| - |B \setminus B'| \geq q|C| - |B \setminus B'|$$
$$= q|A' \cup (B \setminus B')| - |B \setminus B'|$$
$$\geq (q-1)|A' \cup (B \setminus B')| + |A'| + |B \setminus B'| - |B \setminus B'| \geq q|A'|.$$

By Lemma 5.2, we can find nonempty sets $X \subseteq A'$ and $Y \subseteq B'$, such that there is a q-expansion of X into Y and $N_{G'}(Y) \subseteq X$. However, note that in G, the vertices of the set $Y \subseteq B'$ cannot have neighbors outside A' because edges connecting them to these neighbors would not be covered by C. Hence, pair (X, Y) is feasible also for G.

Finally, let us analyze the running time of the algorithm directly suggested by the preceding arguments. By Theorem 4.3, a minimum vertex cover and maximum matching in a bipartite graph can be found in time $\mathcal{O}(m\sqrt{n})$. Because application of Lemma 5.2 can be performed in time $\mathcal{O}(mn^{1.5})$, we have that the total running time is bounded by $\mathcal{O}(mn^{1.5})$. □

5.2 CLUSTER VERTEX DELETION: Bounding the Number of Cliques

In the CLUSTER VERTEX DELETION problem, we are given an undirected graph G and an integer k, and the task is to decide if there exists a set X of at most k vertices of G such that $G - X$ is a cluster graph. Here, a cluster graph is a graph where every connected component is a clique. Observe that a graph is a cluster graph if and only if it does not have an induced P_3, that is, and induced path on three vertices. In this section, we suppose that we have an approximate solution S, that is, $G - S$ is a cluster graph. It is easy to obtain such a set S of size at most $3k$ or conclude that we have a no-instance as follows. Initially, $S = \emptyset$, and as long as $G - S$ has a induced P_3, we insert all of its vertices into S. At the end, if $|S| > 3k$, we have a no-instance. We will show how a simple application of the Expansion Lemma bounds the number of cliques in $G - S$. This is the first step of the currently best kernel for this problem (see the "Bibliographic Notes" in this chapter). Let us denote the set of cliques in $G - S$ by $\mathcal{C}$.

First, we have the following simple rule, whose safeness is obvious.

Reduction CVD.1 If there exists $C \in \mathcal{C}$ such that no vertex in C has a neighbor in S, then remove C from G. The new instance is $(G \setminus C, k)$.

Now, we define the bipartite graph B by setting one side of the bipartition to be S and the other side to be $\mathcal{C}$, such that there exists an edge between $s \in S$ and $C \in \mathcal{C}$ if and only if s is adjacent to at least one vertex in C. Here, we slightly abuse notation. Specifically, we mean that each clique in $\mathcal{C}$ is represented by a unique vertex in $V(B)$, and we refer to both the clique and the corresponding vertex identically. Note that by Reduction Rule CVD.1, no clique in $\mathcal{C}$ is an isolated vertex in B. We can thus apply the following rule, where we rely on the Expansion Lemma. It should be clear that the conditions required to apply the algorithm provided by this lemma are satisfied.

> **Reduction CVD.2** If $|\mathcal{C}| \geq 2|S|$, then call the algorithm provided by the Expansion Lemma (Lemma 5.3) to compute sets $X \subseteq S$ and $\mathcal{Y} \subseteq \mathcal{C}$ such that X has a 2-expansion into $\mathcal{Y}$ in B and $N_B(\mathcal{Y}) \subseteq X$. The new instance is $(G \setminus X, k - |X|)$.

We now argue that this rule is safe.

Lemma 5.4 *Reduction Rule CVD.2 is safe.*

Proof: In one direction, it is clear that if $S^\star$ is a solution to $(G \setminus X, k - |X|)$, then $S^\star \cup X$ is a solution to (G, k). For the other direction, let $S^\star$ be a solution to (G, k). We denote $S' = (S^\star \setminus V(\mathcal{Y})) \cup X$. Notice that for all $s \in X$, there exists an induced P_3 in G of the form $u - s - v$ where u is any vertex in one clique associated to s by the 2-expansion that is adjacent to s and v is any vertex in the other clique associated to s by the 2-expansion that is adjacent to s. The existence of such u and v is implied by the definition of the edges of B. Thus, as $S^\star$ is a solution to (G, k), we have that $|X \setminus S^\star| \leq |S^\star \cap V(\mathcal{Y})|$, and hence $|S'| \leq |S^\star| \leq k$. Note that $G \setminus S'$ consists of *(i)* the collection of cliques $\mathcal{Y}$ that are isolated in $G \setminus S'$, and *(i)* a subgraph of $G \setminus S^\star$. Thus, as $G \setminus S^\star$ does not contain any induced P_3, we derive that $G \setminus S'$ also does not contain any induced P_3. We conclude that S' is a solution to (G, k), and as $X \subseteq S'$, we have that $S' \setminus X$ is a solution to $(G \setminus X, k - |X|)$. Thus, $(G \setminus X, k - |X|)$ is a yes-instance. □

Due to Reduction Rule CVD.2, we have that $|\mathcal{C}| \leq 6k$.

5.3 Weighted Expansion Lemma

In this section we prove a weighted version of the Expansion Lemma. For a weighted graph G and its weight function $w : V(G) \to \{1, \ldots, W\}$, given a subset $X \subseteq V(G)$, we let $w(X)$ denote the sum of the weights of the vertices in X, that is, $\sum_{x \in X} w(x)$. Because we will be working with weights, it will be more convenient to think of expansions as function. In particular, a function $f : B \to A$ is called a *weighted q-expansion*, $q \geq 1$, of A into B if

5.3 Weighted Expansion Lemma

- For every $b \in B, f(b) \in N(b)$, and
- For every $a \in A, w(f^{-1}(a)) \geq q - W + 1$.

Toward the proof of the Weighted Expansion Lemma, we first prove the following lemma.

Lemma 5.5 *Let q be a positive integer, G be a bipartite graph with vertex bipartition (A, B), and $w : B \to \{1, \ldots, W\}$ such that*

(i) *There are no isolated vertices in B, and*
(ii) *For every $A' \subseteq A$, $w(N(A')) \geq q|A'|$.*

Then, there is a weighted q-expansion $f : B \to A$ of A into B. Moreover, such a function f can be found in time $\mathcal{O}(qm\sqrt{n}W^{1.5} + mn)$.

Proof: We start by constructing a new (unweighted) bipartite graph G' with bipartition (A, B') from G. For every vertex $v \in B$, we add $w(v)$ copies of v to B', where all of the copies of v have the same neighborhood in A as v. Clearly, for every $A' \subseteq A$, $|N_{G'}(A')| \geq q|A'|$. Thus, by Lemma 5.1, there is a q-expansion of A into B', and such an expansion can found in time $\mathcal{O}(qm\sqrt{n}W^{1.5})$ because $|V(G')| \leq W \cdot |V(G)|$ and $|E(G')| \leq W \cdot |E(G)|$. Hence, for every vertex $u \in A$, there exists a q-star $\mathcal{S}_u$ where u is the center of star and for every $u_1, u_2 \in A, u_1 \neq u_2$, we have that $\mathcal{S}_{u_1}$ and $\mathcal{S}_{u_2}$ are pairwise vertex-disjoint. In what follows, we construct a function f with the desired properties using the q-expansion in G'.

For every vertex $u \in A$, let $H(u) \subseteq B'$ denote the set of vertices in B' that belong to $\mathcal{S}_u$. Furthermore, let $H^*(u)$ be the subset of vertices w in B such that at least one copy of w belongs to $H^*(u)$. For $w \in H^*(u)$, let $d^u(w)$ denote the number of copies of w in $H(u)$. Now, we construct an auxiliary bipartite graph G^* with vertex sets A and B. We add an edge between $u \in A$ and $v \in B$ if and only if $v \in H^*(u)$. We also define a weight function $w^* : E(G^*) \to \{1, \ldots, W\}$ as follows: for $uv \in E(G^*)$ with $u \in A$ and $v \in B$, $w^*(uv) = d^u(v)$. It is convenient to view $w^*(uv)$ as the weight $w(v)$ of v being "fractionally assigned to u." Under this interpretation, our objective using f is to assign the weights of the vertices of B to the vertices in A integrally, albeit at some loss. Observe that for every $u \in A$, the sum of the weights of the edges incident to u in G^* is at least q. That is, for every $u \in A$,

$$\sum_{v \in N_{G^*}(u)} w^*(uv) \geq q.$$

We now modify the graph G^* and the weight function w^* so that G^* would become acyclic, while maintaining that for every $u \in A$, the sum of the weights

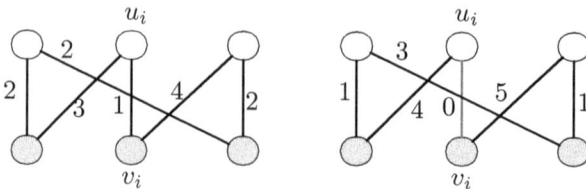

Figure 5.2 The left side of the figure shows the cycle C, and the right side shows the result of alternately decreasing or increasing weights of edges by 1, starting with the edge $u_i v_i$.

of the edges incident to u in G^* is at least q. To this end, suppose that G^* is not yet acyclic. Then, there exists a cycle, say $C = u_1 v_1 \cdots u_\ell v_\ell$, where $u_i \in A$ and $v_i \in B$ for all $i \in \{1, \ldots, \ell\}$. By construction, the weight of every edge is a positive integer and thus the minimum weight among the edges in the cycle C, denoted by x, is at least 1. Pick an edge that has weight x in C, which w.l.o.g. we denote by $u_i v_i$ (it could also be that the edge is of the form $v_i u_j$ where $j = (i+1) \mod (\ell + 1)$). We now traverse the cycle C in clockwise direction, starting with the edge $u_i v_i$, and alternately either decreasing the weight of the currently visited edge by x or increasing the weight of this edge by x. We start by decreasing the weight of $u_i v_i$ by x (see Fig. 5.2 for an illustrative example). In particular, in the new assignment $w^*(u_i v_i) = 0$. We remark that if the edge would have been $v_i u_j$, then again we would have performed the same procedure though we would have then started with the reduction of the weight of $v_i u_j$ by x. Observe that the weight function w^* only changes for the edges in the cycle C. Furthermore, because G^* is bipartite and thus $|C|$ is even, we have that for every $u \in A$, the sum of the weights of the edges incident to u in G^* with respect to the new assignment is also at least q. Now, we remove all the edges e in G^* for which $w^*(e) = 0$. We repeat the preceding procedure with the new graph and weight function until G^* becomes a forest. Observe that this procedure is applied less than $|E(G^*)| \leq m$ times (where here we refer to the original graph G^*), and that each application can be executed in time $\mathcal{O}(|V(G^*)|) = \mathcal{O}(n)$. Thus, this process can be performed in time $\mathcal{O}(mn)$.

Let T be a tree in G^*. We root T at some vertex in A, say $u \in A$. Now, we are ready to define the mapping f from B to A. We first define this mapping for vertices of $B \cap V(T)$. For every vertex $v \in B$, we map v to its parent. To obtain the entire map f, we perform this action separately for every tree in G^*. By construction, we have that for every $b \in B$, $f(b) \in N_G(b)$. Moreover, note that because G^* is a forest, every neighbor of a vertex $a \in A$ is its child except possibly one (the parent in case a is not the root). Let child(a) denote the children of a in T. Thus,

$$w(f^{-1}(a)) = \sum_{b \in \text{child}(a)} w(b) \geq \sum_{b \in \text{child}(a)} w^*(ab). \tag{5.1}$$

Because $\sum_{b \in N_{G^*}(a)} w^*(ab) \geq q$, this yields that if a is the root, then $w(f^{-1}(a)) \geq q$.

Now, suppose that a is not the root, and let p denote the parent of a in T. Then,

$$\sum_{b \in \text{child}(a)} w^*(ab) \geq q - w^*(pa).$$

However, because T is rooted at some vertex from A, the vertex p has at least two neighbors in T: a and the parent of p. Because every edge in G^* has weight at least 1 and every vertex of B in G has weight at most W, this implies that $w^*(ap) \leq W - 1$. Therefore,

$$w(f^{-1}(a)) \geq q - (W - 1).$$

This completes the proof that f satisfies the two properties that define a weighted q-expansion, and it can be found in time $\mathcal{O}(qm\sqrt{n}W^{1.5} + mn)$. □

Using Lemma 5.5, we prove the Weighted Expansion Lemma.

Lemma 5.6 (Weighted Expansion Lemma) *Let q be a positive integer, G be a bipartite graph with vertex bipartition (A, B), and $w : B \to \{1, \ldots, W\}$ such that*

(i) $w(B) \geq q|A|$, and
(ii) There are no isolated vertices in B.

Then, there exist nonempty vertex sets $X \subseteq A$ and $Y \subseteq B$ and a function $f : Y \to X$ such that

- *f is a weighted q-expansion of X into Y, and*
- *No vertex in Y has a neighbor outside X, that is, $N(Y) \subseteq X$.*

Furthermore, the sets X and Y and the function f can be found in time $\mathcal{O}(mn^{1.5}W^{2.5})$.

Proof: We start by constructing a new bipartite graph G' with vertex bipartition (A, B') from G. For every vertex $v \in B$, we add $w(v) - 1$ copies of v to B' (in addition to v), and let all the copies of the vertex v have the same neighborhood in A as v. Clearly, $|B'| \geq q|A|$. By Lemma 5.2, there exist nonempty vertex sets $X \subseteq A$ and $Y' \subseteq B'$ such that

- X has a q-expansion into Y', and
- No vertex in Y' has a neighbor outside X, that is, $N(Y') \subseteq X$.

Clearly, the sets X and Y' can be found in time $\mathcal{O}(mn^{1.5}W^{2.5})$ because $|V(G')| = |A| + \sum_{b \in B} w(b) \leq (W+1) \cdot |V(G)|$ and $|E(G')| \leq W \cdot |E(G)|$. By the q-expansion property, for every vertex $u \in X$, we have a q-star $\mathcal{S}_u$ where u is the center of the star and for all $u_1, u_2 \in X$, $u_1 \neq u_2$, we have that $\mathcal{S}_{u_1}$ and $\mathcal{S}_{u_2}$ are pairwise vertex-disjoint. Let $Y \subseteq B$ denote the set of vertices that have at least one copy in Y'. Because $N_G(Y) = N_{G'}(Y')$ and $N(Y') \subseteq X$, we have that that $N(Y) \subseteq N(X)$.

Next, we would like to use Lemma 5.5 with respect to $G[X \cup Y]$, and thus we need to show that for every $X' \subseteq X$, $w(N(X')) \geq q|X'|$. Note that by construction, Y does not contain isolated vertices. For every vertex $u \in X$, let $H(u) \subseteq Y'$ denote the set of vertices in Y' that belong to $\mathcal{S}_u$, and let $H^*(u)$ denote the subset of vertices in Y that have at least one copy in $H(u)$. For $z \in H^*(u)$, let $d^u(z)$ denote the number of copies of z in $H(u)$. Clearly, $\sum_{u \in X} d^u(z) \leq w(z)$. Moreover, because X has a q-expansion into Y, for all $u \in X$, $\sum_{z \in H^*(u)} d^u(z) = q$. We thus have that for all $X' \subseteq X$,

$$w(N(X')) = \sum_{z \in N(X')} w(z) \geq \sum_{z \in N(X')} \sum_{u \in X'} d^u(z)$$
$$= \sum_{u \in X'} \sum_{z \in H^*(u)} d^u(z) = \sum_{u \in X'} q$$
$$= q|X'|$$

This implies that X and Y satisfy the premises given in Lemma 5.5, and thus there exists a function $f : Y \to X$ such that for every $y \in Y$, $f(y) \in N(y)$, for all $x \in X$, $w(f^{-1}(x)) \geq q - (W-1)$. Moreover, by Lemma 5.5, such a function f can be found in time $\mathcal{O}(qm\sqrt{n}W^{1.5} + mn)$, which is upper bounded by $\mathcal{O}(mn^{1.5}W^{2.5})$. This completes the proof. □

5.4 Component Order Connectivity

In the COMPONENT ORDER CONNECTIVITY problem, we are given an undirected graph G, and positive integers k and ℓ. The objective is to determine whether there exists a vertex set $X \subseteq V(G)$ of size at most k such that every connected component of $G - X$ has at most ℓ vertices. Observe that for $\ell = 1$, this corresponds to the classical VERTEX COVER problem. We remark that it is possible to design a kernel with $\mathcal{O}(\ell^3 k)$ vertices using the unweighted version

5.4 Component Order Connectivity

of the Expansion Lemma; in fact, one can obtain a kernel with $\mathcal{O}(k\ell^2 \log \ell)$ vertices using this approach (see Problem 5.2). Here, we design a kernel with $\mathcal{O}(\ell^2 k)$ vertices for COMPONENT ORDER CONNECTIVITY using the Weighted Expansion Lemma. In the next chapter, we also see how method based on linear programming can further reduce the size of the kernel to have only $\mathcal{O}(\ell k)$ vertices.

Theorem 5.7 COMPONENT ORDER CONNECTIVITY *admits a kernel with* $\mathcal{O}(\ell^2 k)$ *vertices.*

Proof: Our kernelization algorithm starts by greedily computing an approximate solution A to COMPONENT ORDER CONNECTIVITY, as is shown in Fig. 5.3.

Algorithm ApproximatingCOC.
Input: A graph G and an integer ℓ.
Output: A set $A \subseteq V(G)$ such that every connected component of $G - A$ has at most ℓ vertices.

$A := \emptyset$
while *there exists a connected set Z of size $\ell + 1$ in G* **do**
  set $G := G - Z$
  $A := A \cup Z$

Figure 5.3 Algorithm ApproximatingCOC.

In ApproximatingCOC, to find a connected set Z of size $\ell + 1$ (if one exists), we first check whether there is a connected component C in G of size at least $\ell + 1$. If the answer is positive, then we compute a breadth-first search tree (BFS) from some vertex of that component, terminating the computation when the size becomes exactly equal to $\ell + 1$. Because at least one vertex of every connected set of size $\ell + 1$ should be in every solution for COMPONENT ORDER CONNECTIVITY, and the connected sets considered by ApproximatingCOC are pairwise disjoint, we have that ApproximatingCOC is an $(\ell+1)$-approximation algorithm for COMPONENT ORDER CONNECTIVITY.

We compute an approximate solution A as described in the preceding text. If $|A| > (\ell + 1)k$, then we return that (G, k, ℓ) is a no-instance. Thus, from now onward, we assume that we have an approximate solution A to COMPONENT ORDER CONNECTIVITY of size at most $(\ell + 1)k$. Let $Q = G - A$. Then, every connected component of Q is of size at most ℓ. We proceed by applying the following simple reduction rule, whose correctness is evident.

Reduction COC.1 If there exists a connected component C of G such that $|C| \leq \ell$, then delete C. The new instance is $(G - C, k, \ell)$.

We apply Reduction Rule COC.1 exhaustively. Now, we construct a bipartite graph G' with bipartition (A, B), where A is the approximate solution, that is defined as follows. First, for every connected component C of Q, we have a vertex v_c in B. Second, there is an edge between a vertex $u \in A$ and $v_c \in B$ if and only if u has a neighbor in the connected component C. This completes the description of the bipartite graph G'. We also define a weight function $w : B \to \{1, \ldots \ell\}$ as follows: for every vertex $v_c \in B$, the weight of v_c is $|V(C)| \leq \ell$, that is, the size of the connected component it represents. This brings to the following reduction rule.

Reduction COC.2 If $|B| \geq (2\ell - 1)|A|$, then apply the Weighted Expansion Lemma (Lemma 5.6) to obtain sets $X \subseteq A$ and $Y \subseteq B$ with the properties described in its statement. Delete X and the connected components corresponding to the vertices in Y. The new instance is $(G - X - (\bigcup_{v_c \in Y} C), k - |X|, \ell)$.

Claim 5.8 Reduction Rule COC.2 is safe.

Proof Let $T = \bigcup_{v_c \in Y} V(C)$. We want to show that G admits a solution of size at most k if and only if $G' = G - X - T$ admits a solution of size at most $k' = k - |X|$. In one direction, let S be a solution with respect to G of size at most k. By the properties of the Weighted Expansion Lemma (Lemma 5.6), there is a function $f : Y \to X$ such that

- For all $b \in Y, f(b) \in N(b)$,
- For all $a \in X$, $w(f^{-1}(a)) \geq \ell$, and
- No vertex in Y has a neighbor outside X, that is, $N(Y) \subseteq X$.

Thus, we have that $N(T) \subseteq X$. Furthermore, because $w(f^{-1}(a)) \geq \ell$, we have that

$$\sum_{v_c \in f^{-1}(a)} |V(C)| \geq \ell.$$

For every $a \in X$, let

$$C_a = \{a\} \cup \bigcup_{v_c \in f^{-1}(a)} V(C).$$

Clearly, for two distinct vertices a_1 and a_2 in X, the sets $\mathcal{C}_{a_1}$ and $\mathcal{C}_{a_2}$ are pairwise disjoint. Furthermore, because S is a solution, it must contain at least one vertex from each set $\mathcal{C}_a$, $a \in X$ because $G[\mathcal{C}_a]$ is connected and has size at least $\ell + 1$. Let $H = S \cap (T \cup X)$. Then, $|H| \geq |X|$. Let $S^* = (S \setminus H) \cup X$. Because $|H| \geq |X|$, we have that $|S^*| \leq k$. Every connected component of $G[T]$ has size at most ℓ, and after deleting S^*, each such connected component also becomes the connected component of $G - S^*$. Furthermore, for every two connected components C and C' of $G - S$ that have no vertex from T, there does not exist a connected component of $G - S^*$ that contains both a vertex of C and a vertex of C'. Thus, we have that $G - S^*$ does not have any connected component of size at least ℓ.

Hence, we have that $S^* \setminus X$ is a solution with respect to G'. Indeed, this follows from the fact that G' is an induced subgraph of G and $S^* \cap V(G') = S^* \setminus X$. This completes the proof of the forward direction.

Let us now consider the reverse direction. To this end, let S' be a solution of of size at most $k - |X|$ with respect to G'. Then, we simply note that $S' \cup X$ is a solution of size at most k for G. This concludes the proof.

After an exhaustive application of Reduction Rules COC.1 and COC.2, either we already have concluded that the given instance is a no-instance or we have that $|A| \leq (\ell + 1)k$ and $|V(Q)| \leq (2\ell - 1)|A|$. Thus, the total number of vertices in the graph is upper bounded by

$$|V(G)| = |A| + |V(Q)| \leq 2\ell|A| \leq 2\ell(\ell + 1)k.$$

This concludes the proof. □

5.5 FEEDBACK VERTEX SET

In Section 3.2, we gave a kernel with $\mathcal{O}(k^3)$ vertices for FEEDBACK VERTEX SET. In this section, we show how to obtain a better kernel.

We start with simple preprocessing rules (the Degree-1 and Degree-2 Rules already used in Section 3.2), which remove nonessential vertices from the input graph without affecting the size of a minimum feedback vertex set. Graphs resulting from applications of these rules may have loops and parallel edges, and this is why in this section we work with multigraphs. Then, we show that after the application of these rules, a clever application of the Expansion Lemma brings us to a quadratic kernel for FEEDBACK VERTEX SET. More precisely, to obtain a quadratic kernel, we implement the following plan.

- With simple reduction rules we eliminate vertices of degree at most 2. Afterward, we rely on the fact that the number of edges and vertices in a graph with minimum vertex degree 3, maximum vertex degree Δ and a feedback vertex set of size k, is upper bounded by $\mathcal{O}(k\Delta)$. Thus, if the maximum vertex degree Δ of the reduced graph is bounded by $\mathcal{O}(k)$, then we already have a quadratic kernel at hand.
- We next modify the instance so that every vertex would be of degree $\mathcal{O}(k)$. This is the most difficult part of the proof. The reduction is based on two ideas, described in the following text.
- First, we show that for every vertex v, it is possible in polynomial time to either identify that v belongs to $k+1$ cycles pairwise intersecting only in v (in which case v should belong to every feedback vertex set of size at most k), or to construct a set H_v of size at most $3k$ that does not contain v but hits all cycles passing through v.
- Second, we use the Expansion Lemma to design another reduction rule, which for a given vertex v and a set H_v hitting all cycles containing v, deletes and adds some edges incident to v. The exhaustive application of this rule results in an equivalent instance, where every vertex is of degree at most $\mathcal{O}(k)$. At this point, we derive a quadratic kernel.

Let G be an undirected multigraph. We start by applying Degree-1 and Degree-2 Rules (Reduction Rules FVS.1 and FVS.2). Next, note that any feedback vertex set has to destroy all existing loops. However, the only way to destroy a loop is to delete its only vertex. Thus, we have the following rule.

> **Reduction FVS.9** Let (G, k), $k \geq 1$, be an instance of FEEDBACK VERTEX SET. If G has a vertex x with a self-loop, then remove x and decrease the parameter k by 1. The resulting instance is $(G - x, k - 1)$.

We apply Reduction Rules FVS.1, FVS.2 and FVS.9 to G as long as possible. Let (G', k') be the resulting instance of FEEDBACK VERTEX SET. Then, (G, k) is a yes-instance if and only if (G', k') is. If $k' = 0$ and G' is not a forest, then we conclude that G does not have a feedback vertex set of size at most k. Otherwise, the degree of every vertex of G' is at least 3. The graph G' can be constructed in time $\mathcal{O}(mk)$, where m is the number of edges of G. Indeed, each application of Rule FVS.9 decreases k by 1, and each exhaustive application of Rules FVS.1 and FVS.2 can be performed in time $\mathcal{O}(m)$. Thus, we have the following lemma.

Lemma 5.9 *Given an undirected multigraph G with m edges and a positive integer k, in time $O(mk)$ we can*

- *Either conclude that G has no feedback vertex set of size k, or*
- *Produce a multigraph G' with minimum degree 3 and a positive integer k' such that G has a feedback vertex set of size k if and only if G' has a feedback vertex set of size k'.*

We first obtain a kernel for FEEDBACK VERTEX SET on graphs whose maximum degree is bounded by Δ. Here, we rely on the observation that for this class of graphs, the size of any feedback vertex is linear in n.

Lemma 5.10 *Let G be a graph on n vertices with minimum degree $\delta \geq 3$ and maximum degree Δ. Then, the size of a minimum feedback vertex set of G is larger than $n(\delta - 2)/(2(\Delta - 1))$.*

Proof: Let F be a minimum feedback vertex set of G, and let E_F be the set of edges with at least one endpoint in F. Because $G - F$ is a forest, it contains at most $n - |F| - 1$ edges, and therefore $|E_F| \geq |E(G)| - (n - |F| - 1)$. Thus,

$$\Delta|F| \geq |E_F| \geq |E(G)| - n + |F| + 1 > n\delta/2 - n + |F|,$$

which implies

$$(\Delta - 1)|F| > n(\delta - 2)/2.$$

We thus have that $|F| > n(\delta - 2)/(2(\Delta - 1))$. $\square$

Lemma 5.10 implies the following lemma.

Lemma 5.11 *Let $\mathcal{G}$ be the class of graphs of maximum vertex degree at most Δ. Then, FEEDBACK VERTEX SET on $\mathcal{G}$ admits a kernel of size $\mathcal{O}(k\Delta)$.*

Proof: Given a graph $G \in \mathcal{G}$, we first apply Lemma 5.9 to obtain an equivalent instance (G', k'), where the graph G' has minimum vertex degree at least 3. Let n be the number of vertices in G'. By Lemma 5.10, every minimum feedback vertex set of G' must have size at least $n(\delta - 2)/(2(\Delta - 1)) \geq n/(2(\Delta - 1))$. Hence, if $k' < n/(2(\Delta - 1))$, then we return that G does not have a feedback vertex set of size at most k. Thus $k' \geq n/2(\Delta - 1)$, and hence $n \leq 2k'(\Delta - 1)$. Furthermore, every graph with a feedback vertex set of size at most k' and maximum degree Δ has at most $k'\Delta + (n - 1)$ edges: There are at most $k'\Delta$ edges incident to the vertices of the feedback vertex set, and at most $(n - 1)$

edges in the forest. Hence if (G', k') is a yes-instance, the number of edges in G' is at most

$$k'\Delta + (n-1) < k'\Delta + 2k'(\Delta - 1) = 3k'\Delta - 2k'.$$

Therefore, if G' has at least $3k'\Delta - 2k'$ edges, we return that G does not have a feedback vertex set of size at most k. Otherwise, $|V(G')| = \mathcal{O}(k\Delta)$ and $|E(G')| = \mathcal{O}(k\Delta)$, and thus the lemma follows. □

Next, we describe additional reduction rules that allowsus to bound the maximum degree of a yes-instance of FEEDBACK VERTEX SET by a linear function of k. This together with Lemma 5.11 would imply a quadratic kernel for FEEDBACK VERTEX SET.

Our next rule is analogous to the one in Section 2.2 handling vertices of high degree in the context of VERTEX COVER. Toward the formulation of this rule, we introduce a notion of x-flower of G for a vertex $x \in V(G)$. Given a vertex x of G, an *x-flower of order k* is a set of k cycles pairwise intersecting exactly at x.

If G has a x-flower of order $k + 1$, then the vertex x should belong to every feedback vertex set of size at most k, as otherwise we would have needed at least $k + 1$ vertices to hit all cycles passing through x. Thus, the following rule is safe.

Reduction FVS.10 Let (G, k) be an instance of FEEDBACK VERTEX SET. If G has an x-flower of order at least $k + 1$, then remove x and decrease the parameter k by 1. The resulting instance is $(G - x, k - 1)$.

The correctness of Reduction rule FVS.10 is clear. Next, we describe how we can potentially find a vertex x, if there exists one, which has an x-flower of order at least $k + 1$. More precisely, we prove the following lemma.

Lemma 5.12 *Let G be a multigraph and x be a vertex of G without a self-loop. Then, in polynomial time we can correctly satisfy one of the following requirements.*

- *Decide that (G, k) is a no-instance of* FEEDBACK VERTEX SET;
- *Determine whether there is an x-flower of order $k + 1$; and*
- *Find a set of vertices $Z \subseteq V(G) \setminus \{x\}$ of size at most $3k$ intersecting every cycle containing x.*

Proof: As we have already discussed in Section 3.2, FEEDBACK VERTEX SET admits a factor 2 approximation algorithm. That is, there is a polynomial time algorithm that returns a feedback vertex set S of size at most 2OPT, where

5.5 FEEDBACK VERTEX SET

OPT is the size of the smallest feedback vertex set of G. We first call this algorithm to obtain a feedback vertex set S of size at most 2OPT. If $|S| > 2k$, we immediately return that (G, k) is a no-instance of FEEDBACK VERTEX SET. Thus, from now onward, we assume that $|S| \leq 2k$.

If $x \notin S$ then we return S as Z. Indeed, S intersects every cycle in G, and in particular, every cycle passing through x. So from now on, we assume that both $|S| \leq 2k$ and $x \in S$.

The set S is a feedback vertex set, and thus $F = G - S$ is a forest. Let N_x denote the set of neighbors of x in F. That is, $N_x = N(x) \cap V(F)$. Our objective is to find either a set $\mathcal{P}$ of $k + 1$ vertex disjoint paths in F whose endpoints belong to N_x or a set X of size at most k such that every connected component of $F - X$ contains at most one vertex from N_x. In other words, in the latter case the graph $F - X$ has no path between any pair of vertices in N_x. Notice that in the former case, we can use the paths in $\mathcal{P}$ to construct a x-flower of order $k + 1$, and in the latter case, $Z := (S \cup X) \setminus \{x\}$ is a set of size at most $3k$ that intersects every cycle containing x.

Let $T_1, \ldots, T_\ell$ denote the trees in $G - S$. We root each of the trees at some arbitrarily chosen vertex r_i. Now, for each tree T_i, we proceed as follows. Let N_x^i denote the set of neighbors of x in T_i, that is, $N_x^i = N(x) \cap V(T_i)$. Moreover, let H denote the set of pairs formed by vertices in N_x^i, that is, $H = \{\{u, v\} \mid u, v \in N_x^i\}$. For every pair of vertices $\{u, v\} \in H$, let a_{uv} denote the least common ancestor of u and v in T_i. Observe that a_{uv} could, of course, be equal to u or v (when the path from the root r_i to u is a subpath of the path from the root to v or the other way round). Now, we sort these ancestors in a list L, possibly with multiple occurrences of one ancestor, by decreasing order of their depth. (The depth of a vertex in a rooted tree is the length of the path from the root to that vertex.) Finally, as long as the list L is nonempty, we perform the following operations.

(i) Let $\{u, v\}$ denote a pair for which a_{uv} is the first vertex in the list L. Observe that because we sorted the list, the unique path P_{uv} between u and v in the tree T_i does not contain any other vertex of N_x^i besides u and v.
(ii) Add a_{uv} to X.
(iii) Add P_{uv} to $\mathcal{P}$.
(iv) Delete all pairs from H containing at least one vertex among u and v, and delete all vertices $a_{u'v'}$ from L such that there is no path between u' and v' in $T_i - X$.
(v) Observe that in the current H there is no pair of vertices $\{u', v'\}$ such that at least one of the vertices u' and v' belongs to the the subtree rooted at a_{uv} in T_i. Thus, we delete the subtree rooted at a_{uv} from T_i.

We repeat this process for each tree T_i. Clearly, the preceding process can be implemented in polynomial time. Observe that the last item ensures that any two distinct paths $P_i, P_j \in \mathcal{P}$ are pairwise vertex-disjoint and their endpoints belong to N_x. By construction, the set X has the property that in the graph $F - X$ there is no path between any pair of vertices in N_x. In addition, we have that $|X| = |\mathcal{P}|$.

Finally, we show the desired assertion. If $|X| > k$, then we return that there is an x-flower of order $k + 1$, guaranteed by the paths in $\mathcal{P}$. Else, we return $Z := S \cup X \subseteq V(G) \setminus \{x\}$ of size at most $3k$ intersecting every cycle containing x. This concludes the proof. □

We apply Reduction Rules FVS.1, FVS.2, FVS.9 and FVS.10 on the input instance as long as possible. Let (G, k) be the resulting instance of FEEDBACK VERTEX SET. Observe that now G does not contain any vertex with a self-loop, there is no x-flower of order at least $k + 1$ and the minimum degree of G is at least 3. Next, we show how to bound the maximum degree of the the graph by applying the Expansion Lemma.

q-Expansion Rule with $q = 2$. Given an instance (G, k), we show that if there is a vertex v of degree larger than $11k$, then we can reduce its degree by repeatedly applying the Expansion Lemma with $q = 2$. To this end, let v be a vertex of degree larger than $11k$. Due to our application of Reduction Rule FVS.10, we have that there is no v-flower of order $k+1$. By Lemma 5.12, there exists a set H_v of size at most $3k$ that intersects every cycle passing through v and such that $v \notin H_v$.

Consider the graph $G - (H_v \cup \{v\})$. Let the components of this graph that contain a neighbor of v be $C_1, C_2, \ldots, C_t$. Note that v cannot have more than one neighbor in any component C_i, else $C_i \cup \{v\}$ would contain a cycle, which would contradict the fact that H_v intersects all cycles passing through v. Also note that we can next assume that at most k of the components C_i can contain a cycle—indeed, otherwise we immediately conclude that G does not have a feedback vertex set of size at most k. We rename the components C_i that are trees by $D_1, D_2, \ldots, D_s$. An illustrative example is given by Fig. 5.4. From now onward, we only work with components $D_1, D_2, \ldots, D_s$.

We say that a component D_i, $1 \leq i \leq s$ is *adjacent* to H_v if there exist vertices $u \in D_i$ and $w \in H_v$ such that $uw \in E(G)$. We argue that every component D_i is adjacent to H_v. Indeed, observe that D_i is a tree and hence it has a vertex x of degree 1 in D_i. However, every vertex of G is of degree at least 3, thus x should be adjacent to at least two vertices outside D_i, and hence it is adjacent to at least one vertex of H_v.

5.5 Feedback Vertex Set

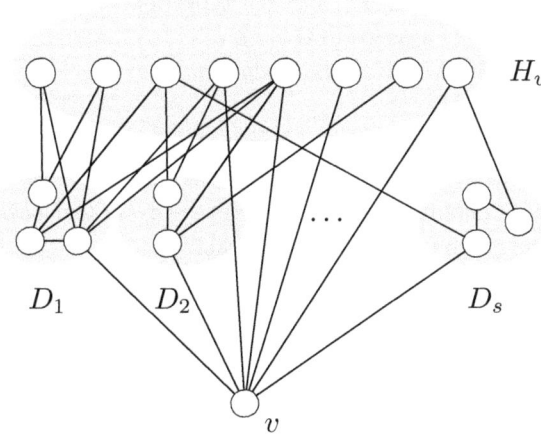

Figure 5.4 The vertex v, vertex set H_v hitting all cycles containing v and acyclic connected components D_i of $G \setminus (H_v \cup v)$.

Let us proceed by first stating the following simple reduction rule. This rule is based on the observation that if a pair of vertices uw is joined by more that two multiple edges, one of these edges can be safely removed.

Reduction FVS.11 Let (G, k) be an instance of FEEDBACK VERTEX SET. If G has a pair of vertices u and w joined by at least three multiple edges, then delete one of these edges. Let G' denote the resulting graph. Then, the new instance is (G', k).

After an exhaustive application of Reduction Rule FVS.11, every pair of vertices have at most two edges connecting them. In particular, for every vertex $u \in H_v$, there are at most two edges between u and v. Let p be the number of vertices in H_v connected to v by two edges. Notice that because there are no v-flowers of order at least $k + 1$, $p \leq k$. Because $|H_v| \leq 3k$, there are at most

$$2p + (|H_v| - p) = p + |H_v| \leq 4k$$

edges from v to vertices in H_v. Because v sends at most one edge to each component C_i and all but at most k components C_i are trees, it follows that if $d(v) > 11k$, then the number s of components D_i is larger than $6k$.

We consider a bipartite graph $\mathcal{B}$ with vertex bipartition (H_v, D), where in the set $D = \{d_1, \ldots, d_s\}$, each vertex d_i corresponds to a component D_i. For $u \in H_v$, we add the edge ud_i if there is a vertex $w \in D_i$ such that $uw \in E(G)$.

Observe that $|D| > 6k \geq 2|H_v|$, and that no vertex in D is isolated (because the minimum degree of a vertex in G is 3).

Now we are ready to state our last reduction rule.

> **Reduction FVS.12** Let (G, k) be an instance of FEEDBACK VERTEX SET, v be a vertex of degree larger than $11k$ and H_v be a set of size at most $3k$ that does not contain v and intersects every cycle that passes through v. Construct the graph G_R from G as follows.
>
> - Let $T \subseteq D$ and $S \subseteq H_v$ be the sets obtained by applying the Expansion Lemma with $q = 2$, $A = H_v$ and $B = D$. The set S has $|S|$ 2-stars with both leaves in T, and $N(T) = S$ in the graph $\mathcal{B}$;
> - Delete from G all the edges of the form vu for all $u \in D_i$ such that $d_i \in T$; and
> - Add edges between v and vertices in S such that for every $w \in S$, there would be two parallel edges between v and w.
>
> The new instance is (G_R, k).

By Lemma 5.12, every step of Reduction Rule FVS.12 can be performed in polynomial time. Let us also remark that the rule cannot be applied more than $|E(G)|$ times. To see this, let $\mu(u)$ be the number of neighbors of a vertex u that are each connected to u by a single edge. Any application of the reduction rule does not increase value of the function μ for any vertex of G, and it decreases this value for the vertex v. Thus, every application of the reduction rule strictly decreases the following measure of the graph G:

$$\sum_{u \in V(G)} \mu(u).$$

Let G_R be the graph obtained after applying Reduction Rule FVS.12. We next prove the correctness of the rule.

Lemma 5.13 *Reduction Rule FVS.12 is safe.*

Proof: We first show that if G_R has a feedback vertex set W of size at most k, then the same feedback vertex set W also hits all the cycles in G. Observe that either $v \in W$ or $S \subseteq W$. First, suppose that $v \in W$. Then, the graphs $G_R - v$ and $G - v$ are identical. Therefore, the set $W \setminus \{v\}$, which is a feedback vertex set of $G_R - v$, is also a feedback vertex set of $G - v$. This shows that W is a feedback vertex set of size at most k of G. The case in which $S \subseteq W$ is similar. In this case, the only differences between G_R and G are the lack of edges from v to D_i for all $d_i \in T$, and the presence of extra edges between v and S. However, by the definition of a 2-expansion, every cycle in G passing through D_i, for any $d_i \in T$, should also pass through a vertex of S. Thus, the set W indeed hits all the cycles in G.

Next, we prove that if (G, k) is a yes-instance, then (G_R, k) is a yes-instance. Let W be a feedback vertex set of size k in G. If $v \in W$ or $S \subseteq W$, then arguing as in the preceding text, it is easy to show that W is also a feedback vertex set in G_R. In what follows, we prove that whenever there is a feedback vertex set of size at most k in G, there also exists a feedback vertex set of size at most k that contains either v or all the vertices of S. This will complete the proof of the lemma.

Consider a feedback vertex set W that does not contain v as well as at least one vertex from S. Note that the $|S|$ 2-stars in $\mathcal{B}[S \cup T]$, along with v, correspond to cycles centered at v in G that pairwise intersect only at v. Thus, such a feedback vertex set the set W must pick at least one vertex from each component D_i such that $d_i \in T$. Let $\mathcal{D}$ be the collection of components D_i such that $d_i \in T$. Moreover, let X denote the set of all vertices of W that appear in sets $D_i \in \mathcal{D}$. Consider the feedback vertex set W' obtained from W by removing X and adding S, that is, $W' := (W \setminus X) \cup S$.

We now argue that W' is also a feedback vertex set of size at most k. Indeed, let S' be the set of vertices in S that do not already belong to W. Then, for *every* vertex in S', there exists a distinct vertex in $\mathcal{D}$ that the set W had to pick in hit the cycle formed by the corresponding 2-star. Formally, there exists $X' \subseteq X$ such that there is a bijection between S' and X', implying that $|W'| \le |W| \le k$.

Finally, observe that W' must also hit all the cycles in G. If not, there exists a cycle M that contains some vertex $u \in X$. Hence, $u \in D_i$ for some i. The vertices of D_i induce a tree, so M should contain other vertices of G. Because M contains no vertex of S, there should be at least two edges of M between from v and D_i. However, by the definition of H_v, there is exactly one edge from v to D_i, hence W' is a feedback vertex set. This concludes the proof of the lemma. $\square$

Theorem 5.14 FEEDBACK VERTEX SET *admits a kernel with $\mathcal{O}(k^2)$ vertices and edges.*

Proof: Let (G, k) be an instance of FEEDBACK VERTEX SET, and let (G', k'), $k' \le k$, be an instance of the problem obtained after an exhaustive application of Reduction Rules FVS.1, FVS.2, FVS.9, FVS.10, FVS.11 and FVS.12. All these rules can be performed in polynomial time, and we have shown that each of them is safe. Thus, (G', k') is a yes-instance of FEEDBACK VERTEX SET if and only if (G, k) is a yes-instance. Every vertex of G' is of degree at least 3 and at most $11k$. Thus, by Lemma 5.11, the graph G' has at most $\mathcal{O}(k' \cdot 11k') = \mathcal{O}(k^2)$ vertices and edges. □

Exercises

Problem 5.1 Obtain a kernel with $\mathcal{O}(k^3)$ vertices and $\mathcal{O}(k^3)$ edges for WEIGHTED FEEDBACK VERTEX SET.

Problem 5.2 This problem concerns polynomial kernels for COMPONENT ORDER CONNECTIVITY that do not build upon the Weighted Expansion Lemma.

(i) Obtain a kernel with $\mathcal{O}(\ell^3 k)$ vertices for COMPONENT ORDER CONNECTIVITY using the unweighted version of the Expansion Lemma.
(ii) Obtain a kernel with $\mathcal{O}(k\ell^2 \log \ell)$ vertices for COMPONENT ORDER CONNECTIVITY using the unweighted version of the Expansion Lemma.

Problem 5.3 Obtain a polynomial kernel for INDEPENDENT FEEDBACK VERTEX SET, where given a graph G and a parameter k, we seek a set $S \subseteq V(G)$ of size at most k that is both a feedback vertex set and an independent set.

Problem 5.4 Obtain a polynomial kernel for EVEN CYCLE TRANSVERSAL, where given a graph G and a parameter k, we seek a set $S \subseteq V(G)$ of size at most k that intersects all even cycles of G.

Problem 5.5 Obtain a polynomial kernel for BLOCK DELETION SET, where given a graph G and a parameter k, we seek a set $S \subseteq V(G)$ of size at most k such that $G - S$ is a *block graph*, that is, every biconnected component (block) of $G - S$ should be a clique.

Problem 5.6 Obtain a polynomial kernel for SIMULTANEOUS FEEDBACK VERTEX SET, which is defined as follows. The input consists of an edge-colored graph G and a parameter k, and the task is to remove at most k vertices from G so that the resulting graph does not have any monochromatic cycle. Here, the parameter is $k + \alpha$, where α is the number of distinct colors of the edges of G.

Problem 5.7 Obtain a polynomial kernel for ALMOST INDUCED MATCHING. In this problem, given a graph G and a parameter k, the goal is to decide whether we can delete at most k vertices from G so that the resulting graph will be an induced matching.

Problem 5.8 Obtain a polynomial kernel for VERTEX COVER (DEGREE-2-MODULATOR). Recall (from Chapter 2) that this problem is the one of computing a vertex cover of size at most ℓ parameterized by the size k of a minimum degree-2 modulator.

Bibliographic Notes

The Expansion Lemma, in a form slightly different than the one presented here, appeared in the PhD thesis of Prieto (2005), see also Thomassé (2010, Theorem 2.3). Here, we follow the variant of this lemma as considered by Fomin et al. (2011c). A kernel with $\mathcal{O}(k^{\frac{5}{3}})$ vertices for CLUSTER VERTEX DELETION was given by Le et al. (2018). The kernel for FEEDBACK VERTEX SET given in this chapter is due to Thomassé (2010). This result improves on the previous works of Bodlaender and van Dijk (2010) and Burrage et al. (2006). We remark that the proof of Thomassé (2010) relies on a classical theorem of Gallai (1961). The use of a weighted variant of the Expansion Lemma to obtain a kernel for COMPONENT ORDER CONNECTIVITY is due to Kumar and Lokshtanov (2016), which improved upon a kernel given by Drange et al. (2016b). Simultaneously, the use of a similar weighted variant to obtain a kernel for this problem (with a larger number of vertices) was given by Xiao (2017a).

Kernelization algorithms for problems involving the removal of k vertices so that the resulting graph would not contain a fixed graph H as a minor are discussed in Fomin et al. (2011c). Note that FEEDBACK VERTEX SET is a special case of this problem for $H = K_3$. In the context of the exercises given in this chapter, we remark that a kernel for INDEPENDENT FEEDBACK VERTEX SET, which relies on the Expansion Lemma, was given by Misra et al. (2012a). Moreover, a polynomial kernel for EVEN CYCLE TRANSVERSAL was given by Misra et al. (2012b), polynomial kernels for BLOCK DELETION SET were given by Kim and Kwon (2017) and Agrawal et al. (2016a), a polynomial kernel for SIMULTANEOUS FEEDBACK VERTEX SET was give by Agrawal et al. (2016b) and a polynomial kernel for ALMOST INDUCED MATCHING was given by Xiao and Kou (2016). Finally, we remind that results related to VERTEX COVER (DEGREE-2-MODULATOR) were discussed in Chapter 2.

6
Linear Programming

In this chapter we give a kernel for VERTEX COVER based on Linear Programming. We then show how this approach can be extended to more general problems, namely, MIN-ONES-2-SAT and MIN-WEIGHT-2-IP. Afterward, we further consider the COMPONENT ORDER CONNECTIVITY problem, and present a kernel of size $\mathcal{O}(\ell k)$, improving upon the one given in Chapter 5, Section 4.

6.1 The Theorem of Nemhauser and Trotter

One of the classical results in algorithms is a polynomial-time algorithm to solve LINEAR PROGRAMMING (LP). Making use of LP has been proved to be extremely useful in the design of approximation algorithms. In particular, a common approach in approximation algorithms for problems in NP is to formulate a problem as an *Integer Linear Programming* (IP) problem, an LP with the additional restriction that the variables must take integer values. Because IP is NP-complete, we do not hope to solve it in polynomial time. Instead we settle for an approximate solution by solving the corresponding *linear programming relaxation* of the IP, which is just the IP without the integrality constraint on the variables. A (not necessarily optimal) solution to the IP is obtained by rounding the variables in an optimal solution to the LP relaxation in an appropriate way. In this chapter, we show that LP can also be utilized to obtain kernels.

We begin by showing how to obtain a kernel with at most $2k$ vertices for VERTEX COVER by applying LP. Given a graph G and integer k, we construct an IP with n variables, one variable x_v for each vertex $v \in V(G)$. Setting the variable x_v to 1 means that v goes into the vertex cover, while setting x_v to 0 means that v does not go into the vertex cover. This yields the following IP

6.1 The Theorem of Nemhauser and Trotter

formulation

$$
\begin{array}{ll}
\text{Min} & \sum_{v \in V(G)} x_v \\
\text{subject to} & x_u + x_v \geq 1 \quad \text{for every } uv \in E(G) \\
& x_v \in \{0, 1\} \quad \text{for every } v \in V(G)
\end{array}
\quad \text{(VC)}
$$

Clearly, the optimal value of (VC) is at most k if and only if G has a vertex cover of size at most k. We relax the IP by replacing the constraint $x_v \in \{0, 1\}$ for every $v \in V(G)$ with the constraint $0 \leq x_v \leq 1$ for every $v \in V(G)$. In other words, we obtain the following linear program $L(G)$.

$$
\begin{array}{ll}
\text{Min} & \sum_{v \in V(G)} x_v \\
\text{subject to} & x_u + x_v \geq 1 \quad \text{for every } uv \in E(G) \\
& 0 \leq x_v \leq 1 \quad \text{for every } v \in V(G)
\end{array}
\quad \text{(VC-LP)}
$$

Let us remark that the constraints $x_v \leq 1$ can be omitted because every optimal solution of $L(G)$ satisfies these constraints.

Let us fix some optimal solution of $L(G)$. In this solution the vertices of G obtain some fractional values from $[0, 1]$. We partition $V(G)$ according to these fractional values into three sets as follows.

- V_0 is the set of vertices whose fractional values are smaller than $\frac{1}{2}$;
- V_1 is the set of vertices whose fractional values are larger than $\frac{1}{2}$; and
- $V_{\frac{1}{2}}$ is the set of vertices whose fractional values are $\frac{1}{2}$.

Theorem 6.1 (Nemhauser-Trotter's Theorem) *There is a minimum vertex cover OPT of G such that*

$$V_1 \subseteq OPT \subseteq V_1 \cup V_{\frac{1}{2}}.$$

Proof: Let *OPT* be a minimum vertex cover such that $V_0 \cap OPT \neq \emptyset$. Every vertex of V_0 can have a neighbor only in V_1 and thus the set

$$OPT' = (OPT \setminus V_0) \cup V_1$$

is also a vertex cover in G.

If

$$|V_0 \cap OPT| \geq |V_1 \setminus OPT|,$$

then the set OPT' is a vertex cover satisfying the conditions of the theorem. We argue that

$$|V_0 \cap OPT| < |V_1 \setminus OPT|$$

cannot occur. Targeting a contradiction, assume the converse. We define

$$\varepsilon = \min\left\{\left|x_v - \frac{1}{2}\right| \mid v \in V_0 \cup V_1\right\}.$$

Now, decrease the fractional values of vertices from $V_1 \setminus OPT$ by ε and increase the values of vertices from $V_0 \cap OPT$ by ε. In other words, we define $(y_v)_{v \in V(G)}$ as

$$y_v = \begin{cases} x_v - \varepsilon & \text{if } v \in V_1 \setminus OPT, \\ x_v + \varepsilon & \text{if } v \in V_0 \cap OPT, \\ x_v & \text{otherwise.} \end{cases}$$

Then,

$$\sum_{v \in V(G)} y_v < \sum_{v \in V(G)} x_v.$$

To see that $(y_v)_{v \in V(G)}$ satisfies the constraints of $L(G)$, we have to check that for every edge $uv \in E(G)$, $y_u + y_v \geq 1$. Because only the values of variables corresponding to vertices from $V_1 \setminus OPT$ decreased, the only interesting case to consider is when at least one endpoint of edge uv, say u, is in $V_1 \setminus OPT$. Because OPT is a vertex cover, we have that $v \in OPT$. If $v \in V_0 \cap OPT$, then

$$y_u + y_v = x_u - \varepsilon + x_v + \varepsilon \geq 1.$$

If $v \in V_{\frac{1}{2}}$, then

$$y_u + y_v = x_u - \varepsilon + x_v \geq \frac{1}{2} + \frac{1}{2} = 1.$$

Finally, if $v \in V_1$, then

$$y_u + y_v \geq \frac{1}{2} + \frac{1}{2} = 1.$$

Thus $(y_v)_{v \in V(G)}$ is a lower weight fractional solution of $L(G)$, contradicting the assumption that we started from an optimal LP solution. □

Another property of $L(G)$, which is not used in our kernelization, is that it always has an optimal solution with fractional values in range $\{0, \frac{1}{2}, 1\}$, that is, a *half-integral solution*.

Theorem 6.2 VERTEX COVER *admits a kernel with at most 2k vertices.*

Proof: Let (G, k) be an instance of VERTEX COVER. Let $L(G)$ be the corresponding linear program. By solving $L(G)$ in polynomial time, we partition vertex set $V(G)$ into sets V_0, $V_{\frac{1}{2}}$, and V_1. Let us define $G' = G[V_{\frac{1}{2}}]$ and $k' = k - |V_1|$.

6.1 The Theorem of Nemhauser and Trotter

We claim that (G, k) is a yes-instance of VERTEX COVER if and only if (G', k') is. Let S be a vertex cover in G of size k. Then, $S' = S \cap V_{\frac{1}{2}}$ is a vertex cover in G'. By Lemma 6.1, we can assume that $V_1 \subseteq S \subseteq V_1 \cup V_{\frac{1}{2}}$. Thus, the size of S' is $k - |V_1| = k'$.

For the opposite direction, let S' be a vertex cover in G'. For every solution of $L(G)$, every edge with an endpoint from V_0 should have an endpoint in V_1. Hence, $S = S' \cup V_1$ is a vertex cover in G and the size of this vertex cover is $k' + |V_1| = k$.

Finally, if (G, k) is a yes-instance, the weight of every fractional solution of $L(G)$ is at most k. Because for every vertex $v \in V_{\frac{1}{2}}$ the value x_v is $\frac{1}{2}$, we have that $|V_{\frac{1}{2}}| \leq 2k$. Hence, G' corresponds to a kernel with at most $2k$ vertices. □

The preceding proof can also be viewed as an exhibition of a crown decomposition. More precisely, if G has more than $2k$ vertices, then $V_0 \neq \emptyset$, and $(V_0, V_1, V_{\frac{1}{2}})$ is a crown decomposition. Indeed, V_0 is an independent set, and there is no edge with an endpoint in V_0 and an endpoint in $V_{\frac{1}{2}}$. In addition, if there does not exist a matching of V_1 into V_0, then there is $U \subseteq V_1$ such that $|N(U) \cap V_0| < |U|$. In this case, raising the values corresponding to the vertices in $N(U) \cap V_0$ while lowering those corresponding to the vertices in U results in a contradiction to the optimality of our solution of $L(G)$.

Moreover, Nemhauser-Trotter's Theorem (Theorem 6.1) also yields a 2-approximation algorithm for the vertex cover problem. Indeed, let k be the size of a minimum vertex cover in G. On the one hand, the set of vertices $V_{\frac{1}{2}} \cup V_1$ forms a vertex cover. On the other hand, the value of any optimal solution of the linear program $L(G)$ is always at most k. Thus,

$$\frac{1}{2}(|V_{\frac{1}{2}}| + |V_1|) \leq k.$$

Hence,

$$\frac{|V_{\frac{1}{2}}| + |V_1|}{k} \leq 2.$$

However, in general, kernelization reductions do not necessarily preserve approximation ratio.

While it is possible to solve linear programs in polynomial time, usually such solutions are less efficient than combinatorial algorithms. The specific structure of the LP-relaxation of the VERTEX COVER problem (VC-LP) gives rise to a combinatorial algorithm based on a reduction to the problem of finding a maximum matching in a bipartite graph. In the following lemma, we use

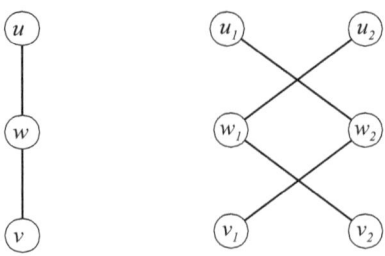

Figure 6.1 Constructing the graph H from a graph G.

the fact that a maximum-size matching and minimum-size vertex cover in a bipartite graph with n vertices and m edges can be found in time $\mathcal{O}(m\sqrt{n})$.

We also need the classical result about matchings in bipartite graphs discussed in Chapter 4, namely, Theorem 4.1.

Now we are ready to give a faster kernelization for vertex cover.

Lemma 6.3 *For a graph G with n vertices and m edges, the kernel of Theorem 6.2 can be computed in time $\mathcal{O}(m\sqrt{n})$.*

Proof: We reduce the problem of solving LP (VC-LP) to a problem of finding a minimum-size vertex cover in the following bipartite graph H. Its vertex set consists of two copies V_1 and V_2 of the vertex set of G. Thus every vertex $v \in V(G)$ has two copies, $v_1 \in V_1$ and $v_2 \in V_2$, in H. For every edge $uv \in E(G)$, we have edges u_1v_2 and v_1u_2 in H. See Fig. 6.1 for an example of the construction of H.

Let S be a minimum vertex cover in H. We can find the set S in time $\mathcal{O}(m\sqrt{n})$. We define a vector $(x_v)_{v \in V(G)}$ as follows: if both vertices v_1 and v_2 are in S, then $x_v = 1$; if exactly one of the vertices v_1 and v_2 is in S, then $x_v = 1/2$ and if none of the vertices v_1 and v_2 is in S, then $x_v = 0$. Thus,

$$\sum_{v \in V(G)} x_v = \frac{|S|}{2}.$$

Because S is a vertex cover in H, we have that for every edge $uv \in E(G)$ at least two vertices from u_1, u_2, v_1, and v_2 should be in S. Thus, $x_u + x_v \geq 1$ and the vector $(x_v)_{v \in V(G)}$ satisfies the constraints of $L(G)$.

To show that $(x_v)_{v \in V(G)}$ is an optimal solution of $L(G)$, we argue as follows. Let $(y_v)_{v \in V(G)}$ be an optimal solution of $L(G)$. For every vertex v_i, $i = 1, 2$, of H, we assign the weight $w(v_i) = y_v$. This weight assignment is a fractional vertex cover of H, that is, for every edge $v_1u_2 \in E(H)$, $w(v_1) + w(u_2) \geq 1$. On the one hand, we have that

$$\sum_{v \in V(G)} y_v = \frac{1}{2} \sum_{v \in V(G)} (w(v_1) + w(v_2)).$$

On the other hand, the value of any fractional solution is at least the size of a maximum matching. By Kőnig's Theorem (Theorem 4.1), the size of maximum matching is at least $|S|$. Hence,

$$\sum_{v \in V(G)} y_v = \frac{1}{2} \sum_{v \in V(G)} (w(v_1) + w(v_2)) \geq \frac{|S|}{2} = \sum_{v \in V(G)} x_v.$$

This means that $(x_v)_{v \in V(G)}$ is an optimal solution of $L(G)$. □

Let us note that the solution of LP produced in Lemma 6.3 is half-integral, that is, all its values are within $\{0, 1/2, 1\}$.

6.2 2-SAT of Minimum Weight

Let us recall some fundamental notions. Let $X = \{x_1, x_2, \ldots, x_n\}$ be a set of *Boolean variables*. A variable or a negated variable is called a *literal*. Let $L = L(X) = \{x_1, \overline{x_1}, x_2, \overline{x_2}, \ldots, x_n, \overline{x_n}\}$ be the set of literals over X. A disjunction $c = (\ell_1 \vee \ell_2 \vee \cdots \vee \ell_t)$ of literals $\ell_i \in L(X)$, $i \in \{1, 2, \ldots, t\}$, is called a *clause* over X. As usual, we demand that a literal appears at most once in a clause, and that a clause does not contain both a variable x_i and its negation $\overline{x_i}$. We represent a clause c by the set $\{\ell_1, \ell_2, \ldots, \ell_t\}$ of its literals. A conjunction $F = (c_1 \wedge c_2 \wedge \cdots \wedge c_r)$ of clauses is called a Boolean formula in *conjunctive normal form* (CNF). We represent F by the set $\{c_1, c_2, \ldots, c_m\}$ of its clauses and call it a *CNF formula*. If each clause of a CNF formula consists of at most k literals then it is called a *k-CNF formula*. By $\emptyset$ we denote the empty formula, which is a tautology, and thus satisfiable by definition.

A *truth assignment* t from X to $\{0, 1\}$ assigns Boolean values (0 = false, 1 = true) to the variables of X, and thus also to the literals of $L(X)$. A clause c is *satisfied* by an assignment t if it contains at least one true literal within this assignment. A CNF formula F is *satisfiable* if there is a truth assignment t such that the formula F evaluates to true, that is, every clause is satisfied. The *weight* of a satisfying assignment t is the number of 1s assigned to variables.

For example, consider the following 3-CNF formula:

$$(x_1 \vee x_2 \vee \overline{x_3}) \wedge (\overline{x_1} \vee \overline{x_2}) \wedge (\overline{x_1} \vee \overline{x_3}).$$

It is satisfied by the truth assignment x_1 = true, x_2 = false and x_3 = false. The weight of this assignment is one.

6 Linear Programming

It is well known that deciding if a given 2-CNF formula has a satisfying assignment can be done in polynomial time. However, the version of the problem where we seek for a satisfying assignment of minimum weight is NP-complete. In this section, we consider the parameterized version of the problem, defined as follows. Given a 2-CNF formula F and a nonnegative integer k, the MIN-ONES-2-SAT problem asks to determine whether F has a satisfying assignment of weight at most k.

Let us remark that MIN-ONES-2-SAT is a generalization of VERTEX COVER. This is because VERTEX COVER can be encoded as an instance of MIN-ONES-2-SAT, with edges corresponding to clauses and vertices corresponding to variables. Moreover, in this formula all literals occur only positively.

It is easy to show that if for a 2-CNF formula F, every literal occurs only positively, then F has a satisfying assignment of weight k if and only if the graph G_F, whose vertex set is the set of variables of F and two vertices are adjacent in G_F if and only if they are in the same clause in F, has a vertex cover of size k. What we show in this section, is that MIN-ONES-2-SAT in general form is also equivalent to VERTEX COVER.

Let (F, k) be an instance of MIN-ONES-2-SAT, and let $C(F)$ be the set of clauses in F with literals corresponding to variables among $x_1, x_2, \ldots, x_n$. We define the *implication digraph* D_F of F as follows. The vertices of (the directed graph) D_F correspond to the literals $\ell_1, \ell_2, \ldots, \ell_{2n}$ of F, that is, $V(D_F) = \{x_1, x_2, \ldots, x_n, \bar{x}_1, \bar{x}_2, \ldots, \bar{x}_n\}$. For every clause $(\ell_i \vee \ell_j)$, there are two arcs in D, $(\bar{\ell}_i, \ell_j)$ and $(\bar{\ell}_j, \ell_i)$. In this context, recall that $\bar{\bar{x}} = x$. See Fig. 6.2 with an example of an implication digraph.

We need the following property of implication digraphs.

Lemma 6.4 *If D_F contains a path from ℓ_1 to ℓ_2, then for every satisfying truth assignment t, $t(\ell_1) = 1$ implies that $t(\ell_2) = 1$.*

Proof: Observe that F contains a clause of the form $\bar{x} \vee y$ when D_F contains the arc (x, y). Further, every clause takes the value 1 under every satisfying truth assignment. Thus, by the fact that t is a satisfying truth assignment and by the definition of D_F, we have that for every arc (x, y) of D_F, $t(x) = 1$ implies

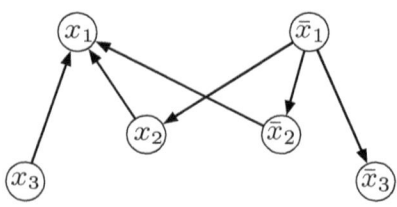

Figure 6.2 The implication digraph of $(x_1 \vee \bar{x}_2) \wedge (x_1 \vee \bar{x}_3) \wedge (x_1 \vee x_2)$.

$t(y) = 1$. Now the claim follows easily by induction on the length of a shortest (ℓ_1, ℓ_2)-path in D_F. □

The *closure* F^* of a formula F is the smallest formula that contains all the clauses of F as well as all the clauses $(\ell_1 \vee \ell_2)$ such that ℓ_1 and ℓ_2 are literals for which there is a directed path from $\bar{\ell}_1$ to ℓ_2 in D_F. The closure of F is computable in polynomial time by computing the transitive closure of the implication digraph D_F.

Theorem 6.5 *Given a 2-CNF formula F, let F^* be the* closure *of F, and F_+^* be the set of all clauses of F^* where both literals occur positively. Let G be the graph that has one vertex for every variable in F_+^*, and $uv \in E(G)$ if and only if $(u \vee v) \in C(F_+^*)$. Then, F has a satisfying assignment of weight at most k if and only if G has a vertex cover of size at most k.*

Proof: Suppose that F has a satisfying assignment of weight at most k. Then, the same satisfying assignment is a satisfying assignment of F^* as well. Indeed, if $c = (\ell_1 \vee \ell_2)$ is in $C(F^*) \setminus C(F)$, then there is a directed path from $\bar{\ell}_1$ to ℓ_2, by construction. Hence, if the satisfying assignment of F sets ℓ_1 to false, then $\bar{\ell}_1$ is set to true, and therefore by Lemma 6.4, ℓ_2 is set to true, thus satisfying c. This implies that F_+^*, a subformula of F^*, has a satisfying assignment of weight at most k. But because every literal in F_+^* occurs only positively, for any satisfying assignment of F_+^*, the variables assigned 1 correspond to a minimum vertex cover of G. Thus, G has a vertex cover of size at most k.

Conversely, let S be a *minimal* vertex cover of size k. Let t be the truth assignment corresponding to a minimum-sized vertex cover, say S, of size at most k in G. More precisely, for every variable x, define $t(x) = 1$ if $x \in S$, and $t(x) = 0$ otherwise. Then, t is a satisfying assignment of F_+^* of weight at most k. We now show that t is in fact a satisfying assignment of F^*. Targeting toward a contradiction, we assume that there is a clause c in F^* that is not satisfied by t. Because c is not a clause of F_+^*, we have only two possible cases: either $c = (x \vee \bar{y})$ or $c = (\bar{x} \vee \bar{y})$, for some variables x and y.

Case 1. If $c = (x \vee \bar{y})$ is not satisfied by t, then we have that $t(x) = 0$, or equivalently $t(\bar{x}) = 1$, and $t(y) = 1$. This means that $x \notin S$ and $y \in S$. The vertex cover S is minimal, and therefore there exists a vertex $z \notin S$ that is adjacent to y. Because of the manner in which the assignment t is obtained from S, we have that the clause $(y \vee z)$ belongs to F_+^* and that $t(z) = 0$. Notice that the implication graph D_{F^*} of F^* has arcs from $\bar{x}$ to $\bar{y}$ and from $\bar{y}$ to z, and therefore it has a path from $\bar{x}$ to z. This means that the clause $(x \vee z)$ belongs to F^*, and in particular it belongs to F_+^*. Thus, xz is an edge in G. However, because $x, z \notin S$ and S is a vertex cover, this is a contradiction.

Case 2. If $c = (\bar{x} \vee \bar{y})$ is not satisfied by t, then $t(x) = t(y) = 1$. This means that $x, y \in S$. The vertex cover S is minimal, and therefore there exist vertices $z_1, z_2 \notin S$ such that z_1 is adjacent to x and z_2 is adjacent to y. Because of the manner in which the assignment t is obtained from S, we have that the clauses $(x \vee z_1)$ and $(y \vee z_2)$ belong to F_+^*, and that $t(z_1) = t(z_2) = 0$. Now, notice that the implication graph D_{F^*} of F^* has an arc from $\bar{z}_1$ to x, an arc from x to $\bar{y}$ and an arc from $\bar{y}$ to z_2, and therefore it has a path from $\bar{z}_1$ to z_2. This means that the clause $(z_1 \vee z_2)$ belongs to F^*, and in particular it belongs to F_+^*. Thus, $z_1 z_2$ is an edge in G. However, because $z_1, z_2 \notin S$ and S is a vertex cover, this is a contradiction.

In both cases, the assumption that t is not a satisfying assignment of F^* brings us to a contradiction. Thus, F^* has a satisfying assignment of weight at most k. □

By Theorem 6.5, we have the following corollary.

Corollary 6.6 MIN-ONES-2-SAT *has a kernel with at most 2k literals.*

Proof: Let (F, k) be an instance of MIN-ONES-2-SAT. We use Theorem 6.5 to reduce the problem to an instance (G, k) of VERTEX COVER. Then, we use Theorem 6.2 to obtain a kernel with $2k$ vertices for the instance of VERTEX COVER. Let (G', k'), where $|V(G')| \le 2k$ and $k' \le k$, be the result of this transformation. Finally, we translate (G', k') into a 2-SAT CNF formula F' with every literal appearing positively. The formula F' has at most $2k$ literals, and it has a satisfying assignment of weight at most k' if and only if G' has a vertex cover of size at most k'. Thus, F' has a satisfying assignment of weight at most k' if and only if G has a vertex cover of size at most k, which in turn occurs if and only if F has a satisfying assignment of weight at most k'. This completes the proof. □

6.3 Reduction of MIN-WEIGHT-2-IP to MIN-ONES-2-SAT

Integer programming with two variables per inequality is defined as follows.

$$\begin{array}{ll} \text{Min} & \sum_{i=1}^{n} x_i \\ \text{subject to} & a_{\ell i} x_i + a_{\ell j} x_j \ge b_\ell \\ & 0 \le x_i \le u_i \\ & x_i \text{ is an integer} \quad 1 \le i \le n,\ 1 \le \ell \le m \end{array} \quad \text{(IP2)}$$

6.3 Reduction of MIN-WEIGHT-2-IP to MIN-ONES-2-SAT

Here, we assume without loss of generality that u_i, $1 \leq i \leq n$, is an integer. Program (IP2) with $a_{ij} = b_i = u_i = 1$, $i \in \{1, \ldots, n\}$ is precisely (VC), the program corresponding to VERTEX COVER. With values $a_{ij}, b_i \in \{-1, 0, 1\}$ and $u_i = 1$, (IP2) captures the MIN-ONES-2-SAT problem. Indeed, every instance of the problem associated with

$$\begin{array}{ll} \text{Min} & \sum_{i=1}^{n} x_i \\ \text{subject to} & a_{\ell i} x_i + a_{\ell j} x_j \geq b_\ell \\ & a_{\ell i}, b_\ell \in \{-1, 0, 1\} \\ & x_i \in \{0, 1\}, \qquad 1 \leq i \leq n,\ 1 \leq \ell \leq m \end{array} \qquad \text{(2SAT)}$$

can be transformed into an instance of 2-SAT as follows. First, note that we can assume that none of the inequalities $x_i + x_j \geq 0$, $x_i + x_j \geq -1$, and $x_i - x_j \geq -1$ occurs in (2SAT) just because these inequalities hold for all values of $x_i, x_j \in \{0, 1\}$ and thus are superfluous. Moreover, $-x_i - x_j \geq 1$ can never occur. Each inequality from (2SAT) is transformed into one or two clauses according to the following table.

Inequality	Clause
$x_i + x_j \geq 1$	$(i \vee j)$
$x_i - x_j \geq 1$	$(i) \wedge (\bar{j})$
$x_i - x_j \geq 0$	$(i \vee \bar{j})$
$-x_i - x_j \geq 0$	$(\bar{i}) \wedge (\bar{j})$
$-x_i - x_j \geq -1$	$(\bar{i} \vee \bar{j})$

The resulting 2-CNF formula has n variables, and it has weight at most k if and only if the optimum value of the objective function in (2SAT) is at most k. Similarly, every 2-CNF formula can be encoded in the form (2SAT).

The following theorem shows the equivalence of (IP2) and (2SAT).

Theorem 6.7 *Let P be an instance of (IP2) with n variables. Then, there is an instance Q of (2SAT) with at most $n \cdot \max_{1 \leq i \leq n} u_i$ variables such that P has a feasible solution of value at most k if and only if Q has a satisfying assignment of weight at most k.*

Proof: The proof is constructive, resulting in an algorithmic transformation of P into Q. In Q, we represent every variable x_i of P, $0 \leq x_i \leq u_i < \infty$, $1 \leq i \leq n$, by u_i binary variables $x_{i,\ell} \in \{0, 1\}$, $1 \leq \ell \leq u_i$. The objective function to minimize in Q is

$$\sum_{i=1}^{n} \sum_{\ell=1}^{u_i} x_{i,\ell}.$$

We enforce the following constraints on variables in Q:

$$x_{i,\ell} \geq x_{i,\ell+1} \text{ for } 1 \leq \ell \leq u_i. \tag{6.1}$$

In what follows, we describe additional constraints such that the vector $(x_i)_{1 \leq i \leq n}$ is a feasible solution of P if and only if the vector $(x_{i,\ell})_{1 \leq i \leq n, 1 \leq \ell \leq u_i}$ defined by

$$x_{i,\ell} = 1 \text{ if and only if } x_i \geq \ell \tag{6.2}$$

is a feasible solution of Q. If we succeed in constructing such a system of constraints, we also succeed in the proof of the theorem. Indeed, by (6.1) and (6.2), there is a one-to-one correspondence between x_i and the u_i-tuple $(x_{i,1}, x_{i,2}, \ldots, x_{i,u_i})$ characterized by $x_{i,\ell} = 1$ if and only if $x_i \geq \ell$. Thus,

$$x_i = \sum_{\ell=1}^{u_i} x_{i,\ell},$$

and system P has a feasible solution of value k if and only if Q does.

To obtain the system of constraints forcing (6.2), we perform the following transformation for every $t \in \{1, \ldots, m\}$. Take one of the equations in P:

$$a_{ti}x_i + a_{tj}x_j \geq b_t.$$

Depending on the values of the coefficients a_{ti}, a_{tj}, several cases are to be distinguished. We consider only the case with both a_{ti}, a_{tj} being positive, as the other cases can be handled in a similar way. In this case we can assume that $b_t > 0$ because with $b_t \leq 0$ this constraint is superfluous. If $a_{ti}u_i + a_{tj}u_j = b_t$, then in every feasible solution of P, we should have $x_i = u_i$ and $x_j = u_j$, and thus the instance can be simplified by deleting these variables. Thus without loss of generality, we can assume that

$$0 < b_t < a_{ti}u_i + a_{tj}u_j. \tag{6.3}$$

For $\ell \in \{0, 1, \ldots, u_i\}$, we put

$$\alpha_{t\ell} = \left\lceil \frac{b_t - \ell a_{ti}}{a_{tj}} \right\rceil - 1.$$

Let us observe that for each $\ell \geq 0$, we cannot have both $x_i \leq \ell$ and $x_j \leq \alpha_{t\ell}$. Indeed, if it were the case, then

$$a_{ti}x_i + a_{tj}x_j \leq a_{ti}\ell + a_{tj}\alpha_{t\ell} < b_t,$$

contradicting the inequality $a_{ti}x_i + a_{tj}x_j \geq b_t$. Hence, for every ℓ, we have that

$$x_i \geq \ell + 1, \text{ or } x_j \geq \alpha_{t\ell} + 1. \tag{6.4}$$

6.3 Reduction of MIN-WEIGHT-2-IP to MIN-ONES-2-SAT

Moreover, if (6.4) holds for every ℓ, then $a_{ti}x_i + a_{tj}x_j \geq b_t$.

To express (6.4) in terms of constraints for the variables $x_{i\ell}$, for every ℓ, we proceed as follows (exhaustiveness follows from (6.3)).

- If $0 \leq \ell \leq u_i - 1$ and $0 \leq \alpha_{t\ell} \leq u_j - 1$, then (6.4) holds if and only if $x_{i,\ell+1} = 1$ or $x_{j,\alpha_{t\ell}+1} = 1$. Equivalently, (6.4) holds if and only if

$$x_{i,\ell+1} + x_{j,\alpha_{t\ell}+1} \geq 1.$$

- If $0 \leq \ell \leq u_i - 1$ and $\alpha_{t\ell} = u_j$, then by (6.4), we have that $x_i \geq \ell + 1$. Therefore,

$$x_{i,\ell+1} = 1.$$

- If $\ell = u_i$, then by (6.4), $x_j \geq \alpha_{t\ell} + 1$, in which case $\alpha_{t\ell} \leq u_j - 1$. Hence, the new constraint is

$$x_{j,\alpha_{t\ell}+1} = 1.$$

The description of the system of constraints for Q is complete. To conclude, let vector $(x_i)_{1 \leq i \leq n}$ be a feasible solution of P. Then (6.4) holds. Hence the vector $(x_{i,\ell})_{1 \leq i \leq n, 1 \leq \ell \leq u_i}$ defined by (6.2) is a feasible solution of Q. In the opposite direction, if $(x_{i,\ell})_{1 \leq i \leq n, 1 \leq \ell \leq u_i}$ is a feasible solution for Q, then $(x_i)_{1 \leq i \leq n}$ defined by (6.2) satisfies (6.4), and thus is a feasible solution for P. □

In Section 6.2, we have shown the equivalence of MIN-ONES-2-SAT and VERTEX COVER. Now we can use Theorem 6.7 to reduce the parameterized version of (IP2) to MIN-ONES-2-SAT. The parameterized version of (IP2), MIN-WEIGHT-2-IP, is defined as follows: Given an instance I of (IP2) and a nonnegative integer k, the task is to decide whether I has a feasible solution of weight at most k.

Corollary 6.8 MIN-WEIGHT-2-IP *with constraint values bounded by a polynomial of the input length admits a kernel with at most 2k variables.*

Proof: Let (I, k) be an instance of MIN-WEIGHT-2-IP. By making use of Theorem 6.7, we construct an instance (I', k) of MIN-ONES-2-SAT. This construction is done in time polynomial in $|I|$ and the maximum value of the constraint bounds u_i in (I, k), which is polynomial. By Corollary 6.6, (I', k) has a kernel with at most $2k$ variables. As we discussed in the beginning of this section, every instance of 2-SAT can be encoded as an integer program of the form (2SAT), which is the special case of (IP2). As this program has at most $2k$ variables, the proof is complete. □

6.4 Component Order Connectivity

In the strategy we employed to solve Component Order Connectivity in Section 5.4, we constructed a bipartite graph where one side of the bipartition was an approximate solution A. As the size of A could already be $(\ell + 1)k$, and in addition we required the other side B to be of size at least $(2\ell - 1)|A|$ to be able to derive the desired expansion, we obtained a kernel with $\mathcal{O}(\ell^2 k)$ vertices. If we were to replace A by a solution of size k, we could have obtained a kernel with only $\mathcal{O}(\ell k)$ vertices. However, if we had a solution of size k at hand, then we would have no problem to solve in the first place. Then, how can we devise a reduction rule that is similar to Rule COC.2, but that concerns a solution of size k rather than the approximate solution A? Here, the use of LP comes into play.

For this purpose, we seek a pair (X, Y) of subsets of vertices where we know it is safe to delete X using the arguments we considered in the proof of the safeness of Rule COC.2. However, now we do not have disjoint sets, A and B, so that $X \subseteq A$ and $Y \subseteq B$. Formally, we seek a pair defined as follows.

Definition 6.9 For a graph G, a pair (X, Y) of vertex-disjoint subsets of $V(G)$ is *reducible* if the following conditions are satisfied.

- $N(Y) \subseteq X$.
- Let $\mathcal{C}$ be the set of connected components of $G[Y]$. Then, the size of every component in $\mathcal{C}$ is at most ℓ.
- There exists a function $f \colon \mathcal{C} \to X$, such that
  - for all $C \in \mathcal{C}, f(C) \in N(V(C))$, and
  - for all $x \in X$, $\sum_{C \in f^{-1}(x)} |V(C)| \geq \ell$.

In addition, if there exists $x \in X$ such that $\sum_{C \in f^{-1}(x)} |V(C)| \geq 2\ell$, then (X, Y) is *strictly reducible*.

The usefulness of the definition of strictness will become clear when we discuss how to compute a reducible pair. Before we proceed to present this computation, let us first see that if we had such a pair at hand, that would indeed be useful.

Lemma 6.10 *Let (X, Y) be a reducible pair. Then, if (G, k, ℓ) is a yes-instance of* Component Order Connectivity, *then there exists a solution S such that $X \subseteq S$ and $S \cap Y = \emptyset$.*

Proof: Let f be a function that witnesses that (X, Y) is a reducible pair. Observe that for all $C \in \mathcal{C}, f(C) \in N(V(C))$, and for all $x \in X$, $\sum_{C \in f^{-1}(x)} |V(C)| \geq \ell$.

Thus, for every solution S and for every $x \in X$, we have that $S \cap (\{x\} \cup V(f^{-1}(x))) \neq \emptyset$. (By $V(f^{-1}(x))$ we refer to the union of the vertex sets of the connected components in $f^{-1}(x)$.) Furthermore, because $N(Y) \subseteq X$, we derive that for any solution S, we have that $(S \setminus Y) \cup X$ is a solution as well. This concludes the proof. □

In what follows, we first argue that if $n \geq 2\ell k + 1$ and we have a yes-instance at hand, then there exists a strictly reducible pair. Afterward, we use LP to find such a pair.

6.4.1 Existence of a Reducible Pair

We would not always work directly with a reducible pair, but with a slightly different notion that is defined as follows.

Definition 6.11 For a graph G, a pair (X, Y) of vertex-disjoint subsets of $V(G)$ is *fractionally reducible*, or *f-reducible* for short, if the following conditions are satisfied.

- $N(Y) \subseteq X$.
- Let $\mathcal{C}$ be the set of connected components of $G[Y]$. Then, the size of every component in $\mathcal{C}$ is at most ℓ.
- There exists a function $g \colon \mathcal{C} \times X \to \mathbb{N} \cup \{0\}$, such that
    - for all $C \in \mathcal{C}$ and $x \in X$ such that $g(C, x) \neq 0$, $x \in N(V(C))$,
    - for all $x \in X$, $\sum_{C \in \mathcal{C}} g(C, x) \geq 2\ell - 1$ and
    - for all $C \in \mathcal{C}$, $\sum_{x \in X} g(C, x) = |V(C)|$.

In addition, if there exists $x \in X$ such that $\sum_{C \in \mathcal{C}} g(C, x) \geq 2\ell$, then (X, Y) is *strictly f-reducible*.

We say that a (resp. strictly) f-reducible pair (X, Y) is *minimal* if there does not exist a (resp. strictly) reducible pair (X', Y') such that $X' \subsetneq X$ and $Y' \subseteq Y$. Let us first claim that if we had a partition (A, B) of $V(G)$ and we only looked for an f-reducible pair (X, Y) such that $X \subseteq A$ and $Y \subseteq B$, then this task is in fact easy. Later, we see how to deduce a partition (A, B) of $V(G)$ that will capture an f-reducible pair (if one exists) in time $n^{\mathcal{O}(\ell)}$ rather than 2^n (the number of all partitions).

Lemma 6.12 *Given a pair (A, B) of vertex-disjoint subsets of $V(G)$, there is a polynomial-time algorithm to compute an f-reducible pair (X, Y) such that $X \subseteq A$ and $Y \subseteq B$ or decide that such a pair does not exist.*

The proof of Lemma 6.12, based on the methods discussed in Chapter 5, is given as Exercise 6.1. The main tool in the proof of the existence of a reducible pair is based on the Weighted Expansion Lemma (Lemma 5.6). Let us now highlight an appropriate stronger version of it that is of independent interest. The statement of this variant is as follows.

Lemma 6.13 *Let q be a positive integer, G be a bipartite graph with vertex bipartition (A, B), and $w : B \to \{1, \ldots, W\}$ such that*

(i) $w(B) \geq q|A|$ (resp. $w(B) \geq q|A| + 1$), and
(ii) there are no isolated vertices in B.

Then, there exist nonempty vertex sets $X \subseteq A$ and $Y \subseteq B$ and a function $f : Y \to X$ such that

- *For all $b \in Y, f(b) \in N(b)$,*
- *For all $a \in X, w(f^{-1}(a)) \geq q - (W - 1)$,*
- *There exists $a \in X$ such that $w(f^{-1}(a)) \geq q$ (resp. $w(f^{-1}(a)) \geq q + 1$) and*
- *No vertex in Y has a neighbor outside X, that is, $N(Y) \subseteq X$.*

Furthermore, the sets X and Y and the function f can be found in time $\mathcal{O}(mn^{1.5}W^{2.5})$.

The proof of this lemma follows the lines of the proof of Lemma 5.6, and it is given as Exercises 6.2 and 6.3. Having Lemma 6.13 at hand, we argue about the existence of f-reducible pairs and (standard) reducible pairs. The proof of the first lemma is given as Exercise 6.4.

Lemma 6.14 *Suppose that $n \geq 2\ell k$ (resp. $n \geq 2\ell k + 1$) and (G, k, ℓ) is a yes-instance of* COMPONENT ORDER CONNECTIVITY *to which Rule COC.1 is not applicable. Let S be a solution for (G, k, ℓ). Then, there exists a (resp. strictly) f-reducible pair (X, Y) such that $X \subseteq S$.*

Let us now consider the existence and computation of standard reducible pairs given f-reducible pairs.

Lemma 6.15 *Let (A, B) be a (resp. strictly) f-reducible pair. Then, there exists a (resp. strictly) reducible pair (X, Y) such that $X \subseteq A$ and $Y \subseteq B$, and such a pair can be found in polynomial time.*

Proof: We construct a bipartite graph as in Section 5.4. More precisely, we have a bipartite graph G' with bipartition $(A, \widetilde{B})$, which is defined as follows. First, for every connected component C of $G[B]$, we have a vertex v_c in $\widetilde{B}$. Second, there is an edge between a vertex $u \in A$ and $v_c \in \widetilde{B}$ if and only if u

has a neighbor in the connected component C. Moreover, we define $w : \widetilde{B} \to \{1,\ldots,\ell\}$ as follows: for every vertex $v_c \in \widetilde{B}$, the weight of v_c is $|V(C)| \leq \ell$. Because (A, B) is a (resp. strictly) f-reducible pair, we have that $w(\widetilde{B}) \geq (2\ell - 1)|A|$ (resp. $w(\widetilde{B}) \geq (2\ell - 1)|A| + 1$), and that there are no isolated vertices in $\widetilde{B}$. Thus, by Lemma 6.13, there exist nonempty vertex sets $X \subseteq A$ and $\widetilde{Y} \subseteq \widetilde{B}$, and a function $f : \widetilde{Y} \to X$ such that

- For all $b \in \widetilde{Y}, f(b) \in N(b)$,
- For all $a \in X, w(f^{-1}(a)) \geq (2\ell - 1) - (\ell - 1) = \ell$,
- There exists $a \in X$ such that $w(f^{-1}(a)) \geq 2\ell - 1$ (resp. $w(f^{-1}(a)) \geq (2\ell - 1) + 1 = 2\ell$) and
- No vertex in $\widetilde{Y}$ has a neighbor outside X, that is, $N(\widetilde{Y}) \subseteq X$.

Denote $Y = \bigcup_{v_c \in \widetilde{Y}} V(C)$. Then, because $N(B) \subseteq A$, the preceding properties immediately imply that (X, Y) is a (resp. strictly) reducible pair. □

6.4.2 Computation of a Reducible Pair

In light of Lemmata 6.10, 6.14 and 6.15, it remains to show how to compute a reducible pair efficiently. Here, we shall obtain a running time $n^{\mathcal{O}(\ell)}$, which means that we would have a kernel for any fixed ℓ. We remark that the running time can be "sped up" to $2^{\mathcal{O}(\ell)} n^{\mathcal{O}(1)}$ by using a method, called *color coding*, to design parameterized algorithms. By the arguments we have so far, we deduce that to conclude our task, it would be sufficient to find a pair (A, B) of vertex-disjoint subsets of $V(G)$ that capture an f-reducible pair (X, Y), that is, $X \subseteq A$ and $Y \subseteq B$.

Toward the computation of a reducible pair, we encode our instance (G, k, ℓ) of COMPONENT ORDER CONNECTIVITY as an IP problem. We introduce $n = |V(G)|$ variables, one variable x_v for each vertex $v \in V(G)$. Setting the variable x_v to 1 means that v is in S (the solution we seek), while setting $x_v = 0$ means that v is not in S. To ensure that S contains a vertex from every connected set of size $\ell+1$, we can introduce constraints $\sum_{v \in C} x_v \geq 1$ where C is a connected set of size $\ell + 1$. The size of S is given by $\sum_{v \in V(G)} x_v$. This gives us the following IP formulation:

Min $\quad \sum_{v \in V(G)} x_v$
subject to $\quad \sum_{v \in C} x_v \geq 1 \quad$ for every connected set C of size $\ell + 1$
$\qquad\qquad x_v \in \{0, 1\} \quad$ for every $v \in V(G)$

(COC-IP)

Note that there are $n^{\mathcal{O}(\ell)}$ connected sets of size at most ℓ in a graph on n vertices. Hence, providing an explicit IP requires $n^{\mathcal{O}(\ell)}$ time, which forms the bottleneck for the running time of the kernelization algorithm that follows. We denote by (COC-LP) the LP relaxation of (COC-IP) obtained by replacing the constraint $x_v \in \{0, 1\}$ with the constraint $0 \leq x_v \leq 1$. By an optimal LP solution S_L with weight L, we refer to the set of values assigned to each variable whose total cost (given by $\sum_{v \in V(G)} x_v$) is L. For a set of vertices $X \subseteq V(G)$, $X = 1$ ($X = 0$) denotes that every variable corresponding to vertices in X is set to 1 (0). In what follows, we show that for a strictly reducible pair (X, Y), at least one vertex in X would correspond to a variable set to 1, and that, in turn, would imply that all vertices in X would correspond to variables set to 1 while all vertices in Y would correspond to variables set to 0. Having these arguments at hand, we can then turn to compute a reducible pair. To this end, we first need the following lemma.

Lemma 6.16 *Let S_L be an optimal LP solution for (COC-LP) such that $x_v = 1$ for some $v \in V(G)$. Then, S_L restricted to $\{x_u \mid u \in V(G) \setminus \{v\}\}$ is an optimal LP solution for $G - v$ of value $L - 1$.*

Proof: First, note that S_L restricted to $\{x_u \mid u \in V(G) \setminus \{v\}\}$ is a feasible solution for $G - v$ of value $L - 1$. Suppose, by way of contradiction, that $G - v$ has a solution $S_{L'}$ such that $L' < L - 1$. Then, by extending $S_{L'}$ to assign 1 to x_v, we obtain a solution for G of value smaller than L. This contradicts the optimality of S_L, and thus we conclude the proof. □

As a corollary of this lemma, we have the following result.

Corollary 6.17 *Let S_L be an optimal LP solution for (COC-LP) such that $X = 1$ for some $X \subseteq V(G)$. Then, S_L restricted to $\{x_u \mid u \in V(G) \setminus X\}$ is an optimal LP solution for $G - X$ of value $L - |X|$.*

We now proceed to prove the two lemmata that would imply the existence of an f-reducible pair (X, Y) where X is set to 1 and Y is set to 0.

Lemma 6.18 *Let (X, Y) be a strictly reducible pair. Then, every optimal LP solution for (COC-LP) sets at least one variable corresponding to a vertex in X to 1.*

Proof: Let f be a function that witnesses that (X, Y) is a strictly reducible pair, and let S_L be an optimal solution for (COC-LP). Then, there exists $v \in X$ such that $\sum_{C \in f^{-1}(v)} |V(C)| \geq 2\ell$. We claim that $x_v = 1$, which would conclude the proof. Suppose, by way of contradiction, that $x_v \neq 1$, which implies that $x_v < 1$ (because S_L is optimal).

Because (X, Y) is a reducible pair, we have that every connected component of $G[Y]$ has size at most ℓ. Because $N(Y) \subseteq X$, from any LP solution S_L, a feasible LP solution can be obtained by setting $X = 1$ and $Y = 0$. Because S_L is optimal, we deduce that $\sum_{w \in X \cup Y} x_w \leq |X|$ is satisfied by S_L. Now, note that for all $u \in X$, we have that $G[\{u\} \cup V(f^{-1}(u))]$ is a connected graph on at least $\ell + 1$ vertices, which means that $\sum_{w \in \{u\} \cup V(f^{-1}(w))} x_w \geq 1$ is satisfied by S_L. From this, we get that for all $u \in X$, $\sum_{w \in \{u\} \cup V(f^{-1}(u))} x_w = 1$ is satisfied by S_L. In particular, $\sum_{w \in \{v\} \cup V(f^{-1}(v))} x_w = 1$ is satisfied by S_L. Because $x_v < 1$, there exists $C' \in f^{-1}(v)$ such that $\sum_{w \in V(C')} x_w > 0$ is satisfied by S_L. This means that $\sum_{w \in \{v\} \cup V(f^{-1}(v)) \setminus V(C')} x_w < 1$ is satisfied by S_L. However, every connected component in $G[Y]$ has at most ℓ vertices, and hence because $\sum_{C \in f^{-1}(v)} |V(C)| \geq 2\ell$, we have that $\{v\} \cup V(f^{-1}(v)) \setminus V(C')$ is a connected set on at least $\ell + 1$ vertices. This contradicts the feasibility of S_L. □

By Lemma 6.15, we have the following corollary of Lemma 6.18.

Corollary 6.19 *Let (X, Y) be a strictly f-reducible pair. Then, every optimal LP solution for (COC-LP) sets at least one variable corresponding to a vertex in X to 1.*

Lemma 6.20 *Suppose that (G, k, ℓ) is an instance of* COMPONENT ORDER CONNECTIVITY *to which Rule COC.1 is not applicable. Let (X, Y) be a minimal strictly f-reducible pair, and let S_L be an optimal LP solution. If there exists a vertex $v \in X$ such that S_L sets $x_v = 1$, then S_L also sets $X = 1$ and $Y = 0$.*

Proof: Let v be a vertex in X such that S_L sets x_v to 1. Let $X' \subseteq X$ be the set of all vertices in X whose variables are set to 1 by S_L. We claim that $X' = X$, which would conclude the proof. Suppose, by way of contradiction, that this claim is false. Let $\mathcal{C}$ denote the set of connected components of $G[Y]$, and let $\mathcal{C}'$ denote the set of connected components $C \in \mathcal{C}$ such that $N(V(C)) \subseteq X'$. Moreover, denote $Y' = \bigcup_{C \in \mathcal{C}'} V(C)$. Because (X, Y) is minimal and $X' \subsetneq X$, we have that $(\widehat{X}, \widehat{Y})$ is not a strictly f-reducible pair for any $\widehat{X} \subseteq X'$ and $\widehat{Y} \subseteq Y$. Note that X' is a solution to the instance $(G[X' \cup Y'], |X'|, \ell)$ of COMPONENT ORDER CONNECTIVITY, and hence $G[Y']$ has no connected component on at most ℓ vertices. By Lemma 6.14, if $|Y'| \geq (2\ell - 1)|X'| + 1$, then $(G[X' \cup Y'], |X'|, \ell)$ has a strictly f-reducible pair (X'', Y'') such that $X'' \subseteq X'$. Because $N(Y'') \subseteq N(X')$, this means that (X'', Y'') is a strictly f-reducible pair also with respect to G, which is a contradiction. This implies that $|Y'| \leq (2\ell - 1)|X'|$. Because (X, Y) is a strictly f-reducible pair, we have that $|Y| \geq (2\ell - 1)|X| + 1$. Therefore, $|Y \setminus Y'| \geq (2\ell - 1)|X| + 1 - (2\ell - 1)|X'| = (2\ell - 1)|X \setminus X'| + 1$.

In addition, let $S_{L'}$ be defined as S_L when restricted to the graph $G - X'$. By Corollary 6.17, we have that $S_{L'}$ is an optimal LP solution for $G - X'$. By Corollary 6.19, because $S_{L'}$ does not set any variable in $X \setminus X'$ to 1, we have that $(\widehat{X}, \widehat{Y})$ is not a strictly f-reducible pair with respect to $G - X'$ for any

$\widehat{X} \subseteq X \setminus X'$ and $\widehat{Y} \subseteq V(G - X') \setminus \widehat{X}$. Now, note that $X \setminus X'$ is a solution for $G[(X \setminus X') \cup (Y \setminus Y')]$. Moreover, as (X, Y) is an f-reducible pair and every component in $G[Y \setminus Y']$ has a vertex that is a neighbor of a vertex in $X \setminus X'$, we have that $G[(X \setminus X') \cup (Y \setminus Y')]$ has no connected component on at most ℓ vertices. However, because $|Y \setminus Y'| \geq (2\ell - 1)|X \setminus X'| + 1$, this means that Lemma 6.15 implies that $G[(X \setminus X') \cup (Y \setminus Y')]$ has a strictly f-reducible pair (X'', Y'') such that $X'' \subseteq X \setminus X'$. Because $N(Y'') \subseteq X$, this in turn means that (X'', Y'') is a strictly f-reducible pair also with respect to $G - X'$. Thus, we have reached a contradiction. From this we conclude that $X = 1$ is satisfied by S_L. In turn, because S_L is optimal, we have that $Y = 0$ is also satisfied by S_L. Indeed, otherwise by modifying S_L to set $Y = 0$, we obtain a feasible solution that contradicts the optimality of S_L. This concludes the proof. □

We are now ready to show how to compute a reducible pair.

Lemma 6.21 *There exists an $n^{\mathcal{O}(\ell)}$-time algorithm that, given an instance (G, k, ℓ) of* COMPONENT ORDER CONNECTIVITY *on at least $2\ell k + 1$ vertices to which Rule COC.1 is not applicable, either finds a reducible pair (X, Y) or concludes that (G, k, ℓ) is a no-instance.*

Proof: Our algorithm consists of three steps, defined as follows:

- **Step 1.** Solve (COC-LP) in time polynomial in the size of the program, that is, $n^{\mathcal{O}(\ell)}$. Let A and B be the sets of vertices that the LP solution has set to 1 and 0, respectively.
- **Step 2.** Call the polynomial-time algorithm given by Lemma 6.12 to compute an f-reducible pair (X, Y) such that $X \subseteq A$ and $Y \subseteq B$ or decide that such a pair does not exist. In the former case, proceed to the third step, and in the latter case, conclude that (G, k, ℓ) is a no-instance.
- **Step 3.** Call the polynomial-time algorithm given by Lemma 6.15 to compute a reducible pair (X', Y') such that $X' \subseteq X$ and $Y' \subseteq Y$.

Clearly, the algorithm runs in polynomial time. Due to Lemma 6.15, to conclude the correctness of the algorithm, it remains to show that if the algorithm concludes in Step 2 that (G, k, ℓ) is a no-instance, then this conclusion is correct. By Lemma 6.14, if (G, k, ℓ) is a yes-instance, then there exists a strictly f-reducible pair, and in particular this means that there exists a minimal strictly f-reducible pair (P, Q). By Corollary 6.19 and Lemma 6.20, this means that if (G, k, ℓ) is a yes-instance, then in Step 1 we obtain a partition (A, B) such that $P \subseteq A$ and $Q \subseteq B$. However, this means that if (G, k, ℓ) is a yes-instance, then the algorithm will not wrongly conclude in Step 2 that it is a no-instance. □

6.4.3 Putting It All Together

The kernelization algorithm consists of the exhaustive application of Rule COC.1 and the following rule.

Reduction COC.3 If $n \geq 2\ell k + 1$, then call the algorithm in Lemma 6.21 to compute an f-reducible pair (X, Y). Delete X and Y from G and decrease k by $|X|$. The new instance is $(G - (X \cup Y), k - |X|, \ell)$.

The safeness of this rule follows from Lemma 6.10. After exhaustively applying this rule, we end up with a graph on at most $2k\ell$ vertices. Thus, we have proved the following theorem.

Theorem 6.22 *For any fixed ℓ,* COMPONENT ORDER CONNECTIVITY *admits a kernel with $2\ell k$ vertices.*

Exercises

Problem 6.1 Prove Lemma 6.12.

Problem 6.2 Toward the proof of Lemma 6.13, prove the following results.

- Observe that the proof of Lemma 5.5 also shows that the following more general statement holds:

    Lemma 6.23 *Let q be a positive integer, G be a bipartite graph with vertex bipartition (A, B), and $w : B \to \{1, \ldots, W\}$ such that*

    (i) There are no isolated vertices in B and
    (ii) For every $A' \subseteq A$, $w(N(A')) \geq q|A'|$.

    Then, there exists a function $f : B \to A$ such that

    - *For every $b \in B$, $f(b) \in N(b)$,*
    - *For every $a \in A$, $w(f^{-1}(a)) \geq q - W + 1$ and*
    - *There exists $a \in A$ such that $w(f^{-1}(a)) \geq q$.*

    Furthermore, such a function f can be found in time $\mathcal{O}(qm\sqrt{n}W^{1.5} + mn)$.

- Prove the following variant of Lemma 5.5.

    Lemma 6.24 *Let q be a positive integer, G be a bipartite graph with vertex bipartition (A, B), and $w : B \to \{1, \ldots, W\}$ such that*

(i) There are no isolated vertices in B,
(ii) For every $A' \subseteq A$, $w(N(A')) \geq q|A'|$ and
(iii) $w(B) \geq q|A| + 1$.

Then, there exists a function $f : B \to A$ such that

- For every $b \in B$, $f(b) \in N(b)$,
- For every $a \in A$, $w(f^{-1}(a)) \geq q - W + 1$ and
- There exists $a \in A$ such that $w(f^{-1}(a)) \geq q + 1$.

Furthermore, such a function f can be found in time $\mathcal{O}(qm\sqrt{n}W^{1.5} + mn)$.

Problem 6.3   Prove Lemma 6.13.

Problem 6.4   Prove Lemma 6.14.

Bibliographic Notes

Nemhauser-Trotter's Theorem (Theorem 6.1) is a classical result from Combinatorial Optimization by Nemhauser and Trotter (1974). Our proof of this theorem mimics the proof from Khuller (2002). The application of Nemhauser-Trotter's Theorem to design a kernel for VERTEX COVER (Theorem 6.2) was observed by Chen et al. (2001). The relation between this result and a crown decomposition was addressed in Abu-Khzam et al. (2007) and Chlebík and Chlebíková (2008). It is an open question if there is a kernel for VERTEX COVER with $(2-\varepsilon)k$ vertices for some $\varepsilon > 0$. Based on the work of Soleimanfallah and Yeo (2011), Lampis (2011) obtained a kernel with $2k - c\log k$ vertices, where c is some constant. The kernelization based on Nemhauser-Trotter's Theorem can also be used to obtain a kernel for the weighted version of the vertex cover problem. If we parameterize the problem by the weight W of the solution, then Nemhauser-Trotter's Theorem provides us a kernel with $2W$ vertices. A generalization of Nemhauser-Trotter's Theorem to obtain polynomial kernels for vertex removal problems to graphs of constant degree d is due to Fellows et al. (2011). This generalization was extended in Xiao (2017b) to obtain linear kernels for any constant d.

Relations between (VC), (IP2) and (2SAT) are well known in combinatorial optimization, see for example, chapter 3 of Hochbaum (1997). The parameterized reduction of Theorem 6.5 is from Misra et al. (2010). Theorem 6.7 is attributed to Feder in Hochbaum (1997). The proof of this theorem follows the proof from chapter 3 of Hochbaum (1997). The kernelization algorithm for COMPONENT ORDER CONNECTIVITY is due to Kumar and Lokshtanov (2016).

7
Hypertrees

In this chapter we give two examples of kernelization algorithms based on a deep min-max theorem about partition-connectedness of hypertrees. The examples we consider concern the SET SPLITTING and MAX-INTERNAL SPANNING TREE problems.

7.1 Hypertrees and Partition-Connectedness

Let H be a hypergraph with vertex set $V(H)$ and hyperedge set $E(H)$, where a hyperedge $e \in E(H)$ is a subset of $V(H)$. With every hypergraph H we associate a graph as follows: The *primal graph* (also called the *Gaifmann graph*) of H, denoted by $P(H)$, has the same vertices as H, and two vertices $u, v \in V(H)$ are adjacent in $P(H)$ if there is a hyperedge $e \in E(H)$ such that $u, v \in e$. We say that H is *connected* or has r components if the corresponding primal graph $P(H)$ is connected or has r components, respectively. Now, we define notions related to forests in hypergraphs.

Definition 7.1 Let H be a hypergraph. A subset $F \subseteq E(H)$ of hyperedges is a *hyperforest* if every hyperedge $e \in F$ can be shrunk into an edge e' (i.e., $e' \subseteq e$ contains exactly two vertices from e) in such a way that the graph T with vertex set $V(T) = V(H)$ and edge set $E(T) = F' = \{e' \mid e \in F\}$ forms a forest (in the usual sense). A hyperforest with $|V(H)| - 1$ hyperedges is called a *hypertree*.

Observe that if F is a hypertree, then its set of shrunk edges F' forms a spanning tree on $V(T)$. In terms of graphs, the definition of a hyperforest can be interpreted in the following way. With every hypergraph H, we associate an *incidence* graph, which is a bipartite graph $G_H = (U, V, E)$ with $U = E(H)$ and $V = V(H)$. Vertices $e \in U$ and $v \in V$ are adjacent in G_H if and only if

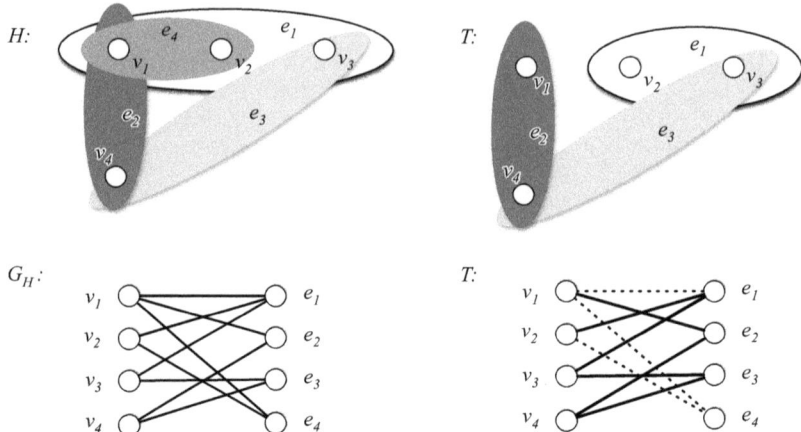

Figure 7.1 A hypergraph H with hyperedges $e_1 = \{v_1, v_2, v_3\}$, $e_2 = \{v_1, v_4\}$, $e_3 = \{v_3, v_4\}$ and $e_4 = \{v_1, v_2\}$. The subset of hyperedges $F = \{e_1, e_2, e_3\}$ is a hypertree.

$v \in e$ in H. Then, a subset of hyperedges F is a hyperforest if and only if G_H contains a forest T such that the degree of every vertex $e \in F$ in T is 2. See Fig. 7.1.

A natural question that arises at this point asks how can we test whether a hypergraph H contains a hypertree? Furthermore, if there exists one, then how do we find it? In the context of these questions, we need the following classical result of Lovász.

Theorem 7.2 *Let F be a subset of hyperedges of a hypergraph H. The following are equivalent*

(i) *F is a hyperforest;*
(ii) *For every subset X of F, $|\cup X| \geq |X| + 1$, where $\cup X$ denotes the set of all vertices belonging to at least one hyperedges in X.*

Condition (*ii*) of Theorem 7.2 is strongly related to the condition of Hall's Theorem (Theorem 4.2). For the induced subgraph $A = (U, V, E)$ of the incidence graph G_H with $U = F$ and $V = \cup F$, condition (*ii*) says that $|N(X)| \geq |X| + 1$ for all $X \subseteq U$. This is why this condition is also called the *strong Hall's condition*, where strong stands for the extra plus one added to the usual Hall's condition.

Another notion of connectivity that is associated with hypergraphs is called *partition-connectedness*. To define this notion, let H be a hypergraph. The

7.1 Hypertrees and Partition-Connectedness

border of a partition $\mathcal{P} = \{V_1, \ldots, V_p\}$ of $V(H)$ is the set $\delta(\mathcal{P})$ of hyperedges of H such that each of the hyperedges from $\delta(\mathcal{P})$ intersects at least two parts of $\mathcal{P}$.

Definition 7.3 A hypergraph H is called *partition-connected* if $|\delta(\mathcal{P})| \geq |\mathcal{P}| - 1$ for every partition $\mathcal{P}$ of $V(H)$.

For example, it is easy to show by induction on the number of partitions, that a graph is connected if and only if it is partition-connected. Because a graph is connected if and only if it contains a spanning tree, we have that every graph is partition-connected if and only if it contains a spanning tree.

The following theorem is due to Frank, Király, and Kriesell, and it generalizes our observation from graphs to hypergraphs.

Theorem 7.4 *A hypergraph H contains a hypertree if and only if H is partition-connected.*

Next, we present an algorithm based on Theorem 7.4.

Theorem 7.5 *Let H be a hypergraph. In polynomial time, one can find either a hypertree T in H or a partition $\mathcal{P} = \{V_1, \ldots, V_p\}$ of $V(H)$ such that $|\delta(\mathcal{P})| \leq |\mathcal{P}| - 2$.*

Proof: The proof sketch relies on the notion of a matroid—readers unfamiliar with this notion are referred to Chapter 10. Lorea proved that $\mathcal{M}_H = (E, \mathcal{F})$, where $\mathcal{F}$ is the set of hyperforests of H, is a matroid (see Frank et al. [2003] or Loréa [1975]), called the *hypergraphic matroid*. Observe that when this definition is restricted to graphs, it simply corresponds to a graphic matroid.

We first a polyomial-time algorithm that constructs a hypertree, if one exists, greedily. We start with an empty hyperforest, and iteratively try to grow our current hyperforest by adding new hyperedges. When inspecting a new hyperedge, we either reject or accept its addition to our current hyperforest, depending on whether by adding it we still have a hyperforest. When we can no longer add hyperedges, we check whether our current hyperforest is a hypertree; if it is not, then we turn to seek the desired partition as described in the following text. Observe that if H has a hypertree, then due to axiom (I3) (in Definition 10.1) satisfied by the matroid $\mathcal{M}_H = (E, \mathcal{F})$, it is guaranteed that our greedy process will indeed find a hypertree (Exercise 7.1). The only question that remains to be answered in this context asks us how to test efficiently if a given set of hyperedges forms a hyperforest. In other words, by Theorem 7.2, we have to determine if the strong Hall's condition holds. However, this can be easily done in polynomial time as follows. For every subhypergraph $H \setminus v$ of H, where $v \in V(H)$ and $H \setminus v$ is the hypergraph consisting of all the hyperedges $e \setminus v$ for $e \in E(H)$, we test whether the standard Hall's condition is satisfied (Theorem 4.2).

Given a hypertree, we can also find a way to shrunk its hyperedges to obtain a spanning tree in polynomial time. For this, consider any hyperedge e of the hypertree with more than two vertices (if none exists, we already have our tree). Observe that one of the vertices $v \in e$ can be deleted from e in such a way that we still have a hypertree (Exercise 7.2). We find such a vertex by checking the strong Hall's condition for every choice of $e \setminus v$ where $v \in e$. This implies that we need to apply the algorithm to test the strong Hall condition at most $|V|$ times to obtain the desired spanning tree. Consequently, there exists a polynomial time algorithm that can find a contracted spanning tree out of a partition-connected hypergraph.

We now turn to the co-NP certificate, that is, we want to exhibit a partition $\mathcal{P}$ of $V(H)$ such that $|\delta(\mathcal{P})| < |\mathcal{P}| - 1$ when H is not partition-connected. The algorithm simply tries to contract every pair of vertices in $H = (V, E)$ and checks if the resulting hypergraph is partition-connected. When it is not, we contract the two vertices and recurse. We stop when the resulting hypergraph H' is not partition-connected, and every contraction results in a partition-connected hypergraph. Observe then that if a partition $\mathcal{P}$ of H' is such that $|\delta(\mathcal{P})| < |\mathcal{P}| - 1$ and $\mathcal{P}$ has a part that is not a singleton, then contracting two vertices of this part results in a non partition-connected hypergraph. Hence, when we stop, we have a singleton partition at hand. This singleton partition corresponds to the partition of H that gives our co-NP certificate. □

7.2 SET SPLITTING

Let f be a function from the vertex set of a hypergraph H to $\{0, 1\}$. We say that f *splits* a hyperedge e if there exist two vertices $u, v \in e$ such that $f(u) = 0$ and $f(v) = 1$. If the function f splits all of the hyperedges of H, then it is often referred to as a *2-coloring* of H. Let us remind that a (proper) coloring of a graph is an assignment of colors to its vertices so that no edge is monochromatic. Similarly, note that a 2-coloring of a hypergraph is also an assignment of colors to its vertices so that no hyperedge is monochromatic.

The problem of coloring a hypergraph in two colors is mostly known as the SET SPLITTING problem. Formally, the input for this problem consists of a hypergraph H and a positive integer k. The objective is to decide where there exists a function $f : V(H) \to \{0, 1\}$ that splits at least k hyperedges in H.

7.2 SET SPLITTING

A special case of SET SPLITTING, where the input hypergraph H is a graph, is a parameterized version of the well-known MAXCUT problem.

We will obtain a kernel for SET SPLITTING with at most k vertices and $2k$ hyperedges using the hypergraph machinery developed in the previous section. To obtain our kernel, we implement the following plan.

- With simple reduction rules, we eliminate all hyperedges of size one, bound the number of hyperedges by $2k$ and show that the primal graph is connected.
- Using the hypergraph machinery we show that the reduced hypergraph has at most $k + 1$ vertices. This is the most difficult part of the proof, and it is based on the following idea.
- If a hypergraph contains no hypertree, then in polynomial time we can identify a non empty subset of hyperedges that can always be split. This allows us to reduce the instance.
- Otherwise, the hypergraph contains a hypertree. In this case, we show that a hypergraph with more than k vertices is always a yes-instance.

We start with the following simple reduction rule.

Reduction SS.1 Let (H, k) be an instance of SET SPLITTING with an edge $e \in E(H)$ such that $|V(e)| = 1$. Then, output the new instance $(H \setminus \{e\}, k)$.

Next, we present a lemma that allows us to bound the number of hyperedges in any no-instance.

Lemma 7.6 *Let H be a hypergraph with vertex set $V(H)$ and edge set $E(H) = \{e_1, \ldots, e_m\}$, such that for all $i \in \{1, \ldots, m\}$, $r_i = |V(e_i)| \geq 2$. Then, there exists $f : V(H) \to \{0, 1\}$ splitting at least $\frac{m}{2}$ hyperedges.*

Proof: Let $f : V(H) \to \{0, 1\}$ be a function assigning each vertex in $V(H)$ either 0 or 1, each with probability $\frac{1}{2}$. Then, a hyperedge e_i is not split only if all the elements in the set $V(e_i)$ are mapped to the same value, which happens with probability $\frac{2}{2^{r_i}} = \frac{1}{2^{r_i-1}}$. Let X_i be a $\{0, 1\}$ random variable that takes the value 1 if e_i gets split, and 0 otherwise. Let $X = \sum_{i=1}^{m} X_i$. By the linearity of expectation, the expected value of the random variable X is given by

$$E[X] = \sum_{i=1}^{m} E[X_i] = \sum_{i=1}^{m} \left(\frac{2^{r_i} - 2}{2^{r_i}} \right) = \sum_{i=1}^{m} \left(1 - \frac{1}{2^{r_i-1}} \right).$$

Because $r_i \geq 2$, we have that $E[X] \geq \frac{m}{2}$. Hence, there is a function f splitting at least $m/2$ hyperedges. This concludes the proof of lemma. □

We apply Rule SS.1 to (H, k) as long as it is possible. Let (H', k) be the resulting instance of SET SPLITTING. Then, (H, k) is a yes-instance if and only if (H', k) is. Without loss of generality we will denote the resulting instance also by (H, k). By Lemma 7.6, we have that if an instance (H, k) of SET SPLITTING without hyperedges of size 1 has more than $2k$ hyperegdes, then (H, k) is a yes-instance. Thus in this case, we can replace (H, k) by a trivial yes-instance, say by the instance $(C_4, 4)$, that is, a graph consisting of a cycle of length 4 and $k = 4$.

We formalize these arguments with the following reduction rule.

Reduction SS.2 Let (H, k) be an instance of SET SPLITTING without hyperedges of size 1. If $|E(H)| \geq 2k$, then replace (H, k) by a trivial yes-instance.

At this point we have already obtained a kernel with at most $2k$ hyperedges. By adding the following reduction rule, it is possible to bound the number of vertices in the kernel by $\mathcal{O}(k^2)$. We leave the proof of this claim as an exercise (Exercise 7.3).

Reduction SS.3 Let (H, k) be an instance of SET SPLITTING. If H contain a hyperedge e with at least k vertices, then output the new instance $(H \setminus \{e\}, k - 1)$.

Next, we present a reduction rule that applies when the hypergraph H is disconnected, that is, when its primal graph $P(H)$ is disconnected.

Reduction SS.4 Let (H, k) be an instance of SET SPLITTING such that $P(H)$ has connected components $C_1, \ldots, C_t$. Let $v_1, \ldots, v_t$ be vertices such that $v_i \in C_i$. Construct a hypergraph H' from H by unifying the vertices $v_1, \ldots, v_t$. Thus, $V(H') = V(H) \setminus \{v_2, \ldots, v_t\}$, and for every hyperedge $e \in E(H)$, we have an hyperedge edge $e' \in E(H')$ such that $e' = e$ if $v_i \notin e$ for every i, and $e' = e \setminus \{v_2, \ldots, v_t\} \cup \{v_1\}$ otherwise. The new instance is (H', k).

We leave the proof of the correctness of this rule as an exercise (Exercise 7.4).

Lemma 7.7 *Let (H, k) be an instance of* SET SPLITTING. *If H is connected and does not contain a hypertree, then there is a polynomial time algorithm finding a non empty subset of hyperedges X such that (H, k) is a yes-instance if and only if $(H \setminus X, k - |X|)$ is a yes-instance. Here, $H \setminus X$ is obtained from H by deleting the hyperedges in X.*

Proof: If H has no hypertree, then by Theorem 7.4, it is not partition-connected. This means that there is a partition $\mathcal{P} = \{V_1, \ldots, V_p\}$ of $V(H)$ such that $|\delta(\mathcal{P})| \leq p - 2$. Moreover, such a partition can be found in polynomial time.

We proceed by induction on $|\delta(\mathcal{P})|$ to prove the following claim.

Claim 7.8 *There is a non empty subset $X \subseteq E(H)$ such that for every function $f : V(H) \to \{0, 1\}$, there is a function $g : V(H) \to \{0, 1\}$ such that*

- *Every hyperedge split by f is also split by g and*
- *All hyperedges from X are split by g.*

If we also show how to find such a set X in polynomial time, then the proof of the lemma will follow from the claim. Indeed, (H, k) is a yes-instance if and only if $(H \setminus X, k - |X|)$ is a yes-instance.

When $|\delta(\mathcal{P})| = 1$, because H is connected, we have that there is a unique hyperedge e such that $e \cap V_i \neq \emptyset$ for all $i \in \{1, \ldots, p\}$. Let $f : V(H) \to \{0, 1\}$ be a 2-coloring of H. We claim that it is possible to select $\{e\}$ as the desired set X. If f splits e, then there is nothing to show. Thus, we next assume that this is not the case. Then, from every set V_i, the hyperedge e contains vertices colored with the same color. Thus, by flipping colors in V_1, that is, by taking function

$$g(v) = \begin{cases} f(v), & \text{if } v \notin V_1, \\ 1 - f(v), & \text{if } v \in V_1, \end{cases}$$

we split e. Because no hyperedge except e belongs to $\delta(\mathcal{P})$, $g(v)$ splits every edge that was split by f. This proves the base of induction.

To prove the inductive step, let $\mathcal{P} = \{V_1, \ldots, V_p\}$ be a partition of $V(H)$ with $\delta(\mathcal{P}) = \{e_1, e_2, \ldots, e_t\}$, $t \leq p - 2$.

We construct an auxiliary bipartite graph $G_\mathcal{P} = (V_\mathcal{P}, V_E, E_G)$. One set of the bipartition is $V_\mathcal{P} = \{V_1, V_2, \ldots, V_p\}$ and the other side is $V_E = \{e_1, e_2, \ldots, e_t\}$. There is an edge between $e_i \in V_E$ and $V_j \in V_\mathcal{P}$ in $G_\mathcal{P}$ if and only if $e_i \cap V_j \neq \emptyset$ in H.

We have to consider two cases:

(a) There is no matching in $G_\mathcal{P}$ that saturates V_E and
(b) There is a matching in $G_\mathcal{P}$ that saturates V_E.

In the first case, by Hall's Theorem, there is a nonempty subset $A \subset V_E$ such that $|N_G(A)| < |A|$. Moreover, such a set A can be found in polynomial time. We take $Y = \delta(\mathcal{P}) \setminus \{e \mid e \in A\}$. Clearly, $1 \leq |Y| < t$. Without loss of generality, we can assume that the sets of H corresponding to $N_G(A)$ have indices from $\ell + 1$ to p for some $\ell < p$. Consider the following partition of H, $\mathcal{P}' = \{V_1, \ldots, V_\ell, V'\}$, where $V' = \bigcup_{\ell+1 \leq i \leq p} V_i$. Then, $Y = \delta(\mathcal{P}')$. Because

$$|Y| = |V_E| - |A| \leq (p-2) - |A| < (p-2) - |N_G(A)| = \ell - 2 \leq |\mathcal{P}'| - 1,$$

we have that $|\delta(\mathcal{P}')| \leq |\mathcal{P}'| - 2$, which means that we can resolve this case by using the inductive assumption.

For the second case, suppose there is a matching $M = \{m_1, \ldots, m_t\}$ in $G_\mathcal{P}$ that saturates V_E. Without loss of generality, let us assume that every edge m_i of M is of the form $e_i V_i$, $1 \leq i \leq t$. Let $V_{t+1}, \ldots, V_p$ be the sets corresponding to the vertices of $V_\mathcal{P}$ unsaturated by M. We want to order the pairs $e_i V_i$ in such a way that for every $i \in \{1, \ldots, t\}$, vertex e_i is adjacent to V_j for some $j > i$. An example of such an ordering is illustrated in the left half of Fig. 7.2.

We construct this ordering in a greedy way, starting from the last pair $e_t V_t$. For $i = t, \ldots, 1$, we seek a vertex e_ℓ, $1 \leq \ell \leq t$, such that e_ℓ is adjacent to V_j for some $j > i$, and if it is found, we swap the positions of e_ℓ and e_i in the ordering. When $i = t$, we necessarily succeed in making a swap because H is connected, and hence there exists a vertex e_ℓ adjacent to V_j for some $j > t$.

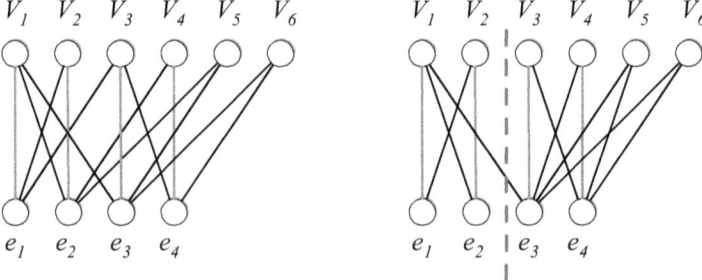

Figure 7.2 In the left graph, for every $i \in \{1, 2, 3, 4\}$, e_i has at least one neighbor among $V_{i+1}, \ldots, V_6$. In the right graph, there is no edge connecting vertices e_1 and e_2 with $V_3, \ldots, V_6$. In this case we apply the inductive assumption for $Y = \{e_3, e_4\}$.

7.2 SET SPLITTING

If we got stuck while constructing such an ordering, this means that for some $\ell < t$, we found a subset of hyperedges $A = \{e_1, \ldots, e_\ell\}$ such that none of these hyperedges contains vertices from any of the sets $V_{\ell+1}, V_{\ell+2}, \ldots, V_p$ (see, e.g., Fig. 7.2). In this situation, we take the partition $\mathcal{P}' = (V_{\ell+1}, V_{\ell+2}, \ldots, V_p, V')$, where $V' = V_1 \cup V_2 \cup \cdots \cup V_\ell$. Then, the set $Y = \delta(\mathcal{P}) \setminus A = \delta(\mathcal{P}')$ is a set of size at most $p - 2 - |A| = p - 2 - \ell = |\mathcal{P}'| - 3$. Because $\ell < t$, we have that $|Y| < |\delta(\mathcal{P})|$, and we can apply the inductive assumption. Thus, in what follows, we assume that we succeed to construct the desired ordering.

Let f be a 2-coloring of H. As in the base case, we observe that flipping colors in the sets V_i, $1 \leq i \leq p$, does not change which hyperedges outside $\delta(\mathcal{P})$ are split. We now describe a t-step procedure of flopping colors of sets V_i. At the i-th step, the procedure tries to flip colors (if necessary) of the set V_{t+1-i} such that after flipping, the following condition holds:

Hyperedges $e_{t+1-i}, \ldots, e_t$ are not monochromatic. Moreover, for every $j \geq t + 1 - i$, there are two differently colored vertices in $e_j \cap (V_j \cup V_{j+1} \cup \cdots \cup V_p)$.

Let us remark that at the t-th step of the procedure, all hyperedges of $\delta(\mathcal{P})$ will be split.

The procedure starts with the set V_t and then proceeds to flip the colorings of the sets V_i in decreasing order. By our choice of the ordering, the hyperedge e_t has a vertex from a set V_i, $i > t$. In addition, it also has a vertex from the set V_t. If all the vertices from $V_t, V_{t+1}, \ldots, V_p$ that are in e_t are monochromatic according to the coloring f, we flip the colors of V_t. The new coloring splits e_t. Moreover, we did not change which hyperedges outside $\delta(\mathcal{P})$ are split. At the i-th step, if the desired condition does not hold, we flip the coloring of V_{t+1-i}, thus splitting e_{t+1-i}. This flipping does not change which hyperedges $e_j \in \delta(\mathcal{P})$ such that $j > t + 1 - i$ are split, as well as which hyperedges outside $\delta(\mathcal{P})$ are split.

We set $X = \delta(\mathcal{P})$, and this completes the inductive proof of the claim.

It remains to observe that by Theorem 7.5, in polynomial time it can either be deduced that H is a hypertree or a partition $\mathcal{P} = \{V_1, \ldots, V_p\}$ of $V(H)$ such that $|\delta(\mathcal{P})| \leq p - 2$ can be found. Because in both cases the set X is constructed in polynomial time from $\mathcal{P}$, this concludes the proof of the lemma. □

Lemma 7.7 naturally gives rise to a reduction rule for the SET SPLITTING problem.

Reduction SS.5 Let (H, k) be an instance of SET SPLITTING such that H is connected and contains no hypertree. Use Lemma 7.7 to identify a set $X \subseteq E(H)$ and output the new instance $(H \setminus X, k - |X|)$.

We are now ready to prove the main result of this section.

Theorem 7.9 SET SPLITTING *admits a kernel with $2k$ sets and k elements.*

Proof: Given an instance (H, k) of SET SPLITTING, we first obtain an equivalent instance with at most $2k$ hyperedges and at most $2k^2$ vertices, see Exercise 7.3. We then apply Reduction Rules SS.1, SS.4 and SS.5 exhaustively. Let (H', k') be the reduced instance. Because all our rules can only reduce k, we have that $k' \leq k$. Let H' have n vertices and $m \leq 2k$ hyperedges. We show that if $n > k'$ then (H', k') is a yes-instance. In particular, Because Reduction Rule SS.5 cannot be applied, H' contains a hypertree.

By Theorem 7.5, we can find in polynomial time a hypertree with a set of hyperedges F of H'. Let us remark that $|F| = n - 1$. The incidence graph of the hypertree is a tree with all vertices corresponding to F of degree 2 (see Fig. 7.1). If we contract these vertices of degree 2, the result is a tree on n vertices. A tree is also a bipartite graph and, therefore a tree admits a (proper) graph coloring in two colors. Exactly the same coloring of the vertices of H splits all hyperedges of F, whose number is $n - 1$. Thus if $n > k'$, then (H', k') is a yes-instance. This concludes the proof. □

7.3 MAX-INTERNAL SPANNING TREE

A vertex of a tree is an *internal* vertex if its degree is at least 2. In other words, every non leaf vertex of a tree is internal. Here, we study the MAX-INTERNAL SPANNING TREE (IST) problem, where given an undirected graph G and a non negative integer k, the objective is to decide whether there exists a spanning tree T of G having at least k internal vertices. This problem is a natural generalization of the HAMILTONIAN PATH problem—every n-vertex graph has a Hamiltonian path if and only if it has a spanning tree with $n - 2$ internal vertices.

In this section we give a linear-vertex kernel for IST. This result is also interesting because, as we shall see later in Part 3, the parameterized version of the HAMILTONIAN PATH—find a path of length at least k—is unlikely to have a polynomial kernel.

Let (G, k) be an instance of IST. We assume that G is connected because otherwise (G, k) is trivially a no-instance. We show that IST has a $3k$-vertex kernel.

7.3 MAX-INTERNAL SPANNING TREE

The algorithm is based on the following combinatorial lemma, which is interesting on its own. The proof of this lemma is based on Theorem 7.4, and it can be found in Section 7.3.1. For two disjoint sets $X, Y \subseteq V(G)$, we denote by $B(X, Y)$ the bipartite graph obtained from $G[X \cup Y]$ by removing all edges with both endpoints in X or in Y.

Lemma 7.10 *If $n \geq 3$, and I is an independent set of G of cardinality at least $2n/3$, then there are nonempty subsets $S \subseteq V(G) \setminus I$ and $L \subseteq I$ such that*

(i) $N(L) = S$, and
(ii) $B(S, L)$ has a spanning tree such that all vertices of S and $|S| - 1$ vertices of L are internal.

Moreover, given such a set I, such subsets S and L can be found in time polynomial in the size of G.

Now, we give the description of the kernelization algorithm and use Lemma 7.10 to prove its correctness. The algorithm consists of the following reduction rules.

Reduction IST.1 If $n \leq 3k$, then output (G, k) as the kernel. In this case, (G, k) is a $3k$-vertex kernel. Otherwise, proceed to Rule IST.3.

Reduction IST.2 Choose an arbitrary vertex $v \in V$ and run DFS (depth first search) from v. If the DFS tree T has at least k internal vertices, then the algorithm has found a solution. Otherwise, as $n > 3k$, T has at least $2n/3 + 2$ leaves, and because all leaves but the root of the DFS tree are pairwise nonadjacent, the algorithm found an independent set of G of cardinality at least $2n/3$; then, proceed to Rule IST.3.

Reduction IST.3 Find nonempty subsets of vertices $S, L \subseteq V$ as in Lemma 7.10. If $|S| = 1$, then go to Rule IST.1 with $(G \setminus L, k-1)$. Otherwise, add a new vertex v_S and make it adjacent to every vertex in $N(S) \setminus L$, add a new vertex v_L and make it adjacent to v_S, remove all vertices of $S \cup L$ and denote the new graph by G_R. Now, consider the following cases.

(i) If $S \cup L = V(G)$, then go to Rule IST.1 with
   $(G_R, \max\{k - 2|S| + 1, 0\})$.
(ii) Otherwise, go to Rule IST.1 with $(G_R, \max\{k - 2|S| + 2, 0\})$.

To prove the safeness of Rule IST.3, we need the following lemma. Here, S and L are as in Lemma 7.10. If T is a tree and X a vertex set, we denote by $i_T(X)$ the number of vertices of X that are internal in T.

Lemma 7.11 *If G has a spanning tree with at least k internal vertices, then G has a spanning tree with at least k internal vertices where all the vertices of S and exactly $|S| - 1$ vertices of L are internal.*

Proof: Let T be a spanning tree of G with k internal vertices. Denote by F the forest obtained from T by removing all edges incident to L. Then, as long as there exist two vertices of S that are in the same connected component of F, remove an edge from F incident to one of these two vertices. Now, obtain the spanning tree T' by adding the edges of a spanning tree of $B(S, L)$ to F in which all vertices of S and $|S| - 1$ vertices of L are internal (see Lemma 7.10). Clearly, all vertices of S and $|S| - 1$ vertices of L are internal in T'. It remains to show that T' has at least as many internal vertices as T.

Let $U := V(G) \setminus (S \cup L)$. Then, we have that $i_T(L) \leq \sum_{u \in L} d_T(u) - |L|$ as every vertex in a tree has degree at least 1 and internal vertices have degree at least 2. We also have $i_{T'}(U) \geq i_T(U) - (|L| + |S| - 1 - \sum_{u \in L} d_T(u))$ as at most $|S| - 1 - (\sum_{u \in L} d_T(u) - |L|)$ edges incident to S are removed from F to separate $F \setminus L$ into $|S|$ connected components, one for each vertex of S. Thus,

$$\begin{aligned}
i_{T'}(V) &= i_{T'}(U) + i_{T'}(S \cup L) \\
&\geq i_T(U) - \left(|L| + |S| - 1 - \sum_{u \in L} d_T(u)\right) + i_{T'}(S \cup L) \\
&= i_T(U) + \left(\sum_{u \in L} d_T(u) - |L|\right) - |S| + 1 + i_{T'}(S \cup L) \\
&\geq i_T(U) + i_T(L) - |S| + 1 + i_{T'}(S \cup L) \\
&= i_T(U) + i_T(L) - (|S| - 1) + (|S| + |S| - 1) \\
&= i_T(U) + i_T(L) + |S| \\
&\geq i_T(U) + i_T(L) + i_T(S) \\
&= i_T(V).
\end{aligned}$$

This finishes the proof of the lemma. □

Lemma 7.12 *Rule IST.3 is safe, $|V_R| < |V|$, and $k' \leq k$.*

Proof: We only consider the more difficult case in which $|S| > 1$ and $V(G) \neq S \cup L$, and leave the other two cases as an exercise (Exercise 7.6). We claim first that the resulting graph $G_R = (V_R, E_R)$ has a spanning tree with at least

$k' = k - 2|S| + 2$ internal vertices if and only if the original graph G has a spanning tree with at least k internal vertices. Indeed, assume G has a spanning tree with $\ell \geq k$ internal vertices. Then, let $B(S, L)$ be as in Lemma 7.10 and T be a spanning tree of G with ℓ internal vertices such that all vertices of S and $|S| - 1$ vertices of L are internal (which exists by Lemma 7.11). Because $T[S \cup L]$ is connected, every two distinct vertices $u, v \in N_T(S) \setminus L$ are in different connected components of $T \setminus (L \cup S)$. But this means that the graph T' obtained from $T \setminus (L \cup S)$ by connecting v_S to all neighbors of S in $T \setminus (S \cup L)$ is also a tree in which the degree of every vertex in $N_G(S) \setminus L$ is unchanged. The graph T'' obtained from T' by adding v_L and connecting v_L to v_S is also a tree. Then T'' has exactly $\ell - 2|S| + 2$ internal vertices.

In the opposite direction, if G_R has a tree T'' with $\ell - 2|S| + 2$ internal vertices, then all neighbors of v_S in T'' are in different components of $T'' \setminus \{v_S\}$. By Lemma 7.10 we know that $B(S, L)$ has a spanning tree T_{SL} such that all the vertices of S and $|S| - 1$ vertices of L are internal. We obtain a spanning tree T of G by considering the forest $T^* = (T'' \setminus \{v_S, v_L\}) \cup T_{SL}$, and adding edges between different components to make it connected as follows. For each vertex $u \in N_{T''}(v_S) \setminus \{v_L\}$, add an edge uv to T^* for some $uv \in E(G)$ such that $v \in S$. By construction we know that such an edge always exists. Moreover, the degrees of the vertices in $N_G(S) \setminus L$ are the same in T as in T''. Thus T is a spanning tree with ℓ internal vertices.

Finally, as $|S| \geq 2$ L is not empty, $|L \cup S| \geq 3$ and therefore $|V_R| < |V|$ and $k' \leq k$. □

As Rule IST.3 compresses the graph, we conclude with the following theorem.

Theorem 7.13 *IST admits a 3k-vertex kernel.*

7.3.1 Proof of Lemma 7.10

In this section we provide the proof of Lemma 7.10. Let G be a connected graph on n vertices, I be an independent set of G of cardinality at least $2n/3$ and $C := V(G) \setminus I$. We can assume that in the bipartite graph $B(I, C)$, no vertex of C is isolated because otherwise we would have been able to add this vertex to I.

The proof of the following lemma is based on Theorem 7.4.

Lemma 7.14 *There exist nonempty sets $S \subseteq C$ and $L \subseteq I$ such that*

- *$B(S, L)$ has a spanning tree in which all the vertices of L have degree at most 2,*

- S has 2-expansion in L and
- $N(L) = S$.

Moreover, such sets S and L can be found in time polynomial in the size of G.

Proof: As $|I| \geq 2n/3$, by Expansion Lemma (Lemma 5.2), we can find in polynomial time nonempty sets $S' \subseteq C$ and $L' \subseteq I$ such that $N(L') = S'$ and S' has a 2-expansion into L'. We prove that there exist nonempty sets $S \subseteq S'$ and $L \subseteq L'$ satisfying the conditions of the lemma.

The proof is by induction on $|S'|$. If $|S'| = 1$, the lemma holds with $S := S'$ and $L := L'$.

Now, we prove the inductive step. Let $H = (S', E')$ be the hypergraph with edge set $E' = \{N(v) \mid v \in L'\}$. First, consider the case in which H contains a hypertree. Then, it has $|S'| - 1$ hyperedges, and we obtain a tree $T_{S'}$ on S' by shrinking these edges (as in Theorem 7.5). We use $T_{S'}$ to find a subtree T' of $B(S', L')$ spanning S' as follows: For every edge $e = uv$ of $T_{S'}$, there exists a hyperedge corresponding to it and hence a unique vertex, say w, in L'; we delete the edge $e = uv$ from $T_{S'}$ and add the edges wu and wv to $T_{S'}$. Observe that the resulting subtree T' of $B(S', L')$ has the property that every vertex of L' that belongs to T' has degree 2 in T'. Finally, we extend T' to a spanning tree of $B(S', L')$ by adding the remaining vertices of L' as pendant vertices. All these steps can be clearly performed in time polynomial in the size of G. Thus, S' and L' are the sets of vertices we are looking for.

Second, consider the case in which H does not contain a hypertree. Then, H is not partition-connected by Theorem 7.4. Then, we use Theorem 7.5 to find in polynomial time a partition $\mathcal{P} = \{P_1, P_2, \ldots, P_\ell\}$ of S' such that its border $\delta(\mathcal{P})$ contains at most $\ell - 2$ hyperedges of H. Let b_i be the number of hyperedges completely contained in P_i, where $1 \leq i \leq \ell$. Then there is j, $1 \leq j \leq \ell$, such that $b_j \geq 2|P_j|$. Indeed, otherwise $|L'| \leq (\ell-2)+\sum_{i=1}^{\ell}(2|P_i|-1) < 2|S'|$, which contradicts the choice of L' and S' as S' has an 2-expansion in L'. Let $X := P_j$ and $Y := \{w \in L' \mid N(w) \subseteq P_j\}$. We know that $|Y| \geq 2|X|$ and hence by Expansion Lemma there exist $S^* \subseteq X$ and $L^* \subseteq Y$ such that S^* has a 2-expansion into L^* and $N(L^*) = S^*$. Thus, by the inductive assumption, there exist $S \subseteq S^*$ and $L \subseteq L^*$ with the desired properties. □

Let S and L be as in Lemma 7.14. In what follows, we will prove that there exists a spanning tree of $B(S, L)$ such that all the vertices of S and exactly $|S| - 1$ vertices of L are internal. Note that there cannot be more than $2|S| - 1$ internal vertices in a spanning tree of $B(S, L)$, as then cycles are created. By Lemma 7.14, we know that there exists a spanning tree of $B(S, L)$ in which $|S| - 1$ vertices of L have degree exactly 2. Moreover, because S

has a 2-expansion into L in $B(S,L)$, there exist two edge-disjoint matchings M_1 and M_2 in $B(S,L)$ such that both matchings saturate S. We refer to the edges in $M_1 \cup M_2$ as *favorite edges*.

Lemma 7.15 *$B(S,L)$ has a spanning tree T such that all the vertices of S and $|S|-1$ vertices of L are internal in T.*

Proof: Let T be a spanning tree of $B(S,L)$ in which all vertices of L have degree at most 2, obtained using Lemma 7.14. As T is a tree, exactly $|S|-1$ vertices of L have degree 2 in T. As long as a vertex $v \in S$ is not internal in T, add a favorite edge uv to T, which is not yet in T ($u \in L$), and remove an appropriate edge from the tree that is incident to u so that T remains a spanning tree. The vertex v thus becomes internal, and the degree of u in T remains unchanged. As u is only incident to one favorite edge, this rule increases the number of favorite edges in T even though it is possible that some other vertex in S has become a leaf. We apply this rule until it is no longer possible, and note that this rule can only be applied at most $|S|$ times. In the end, all the vertices of S are internal and $|S|-1$ vertices among L are internal as their degrees remained the same. □

To conclude the proof of Lemma 7.10, we observe that $S \subseteq C$, $L \subseteq I$ and $N(L) = S$ (by the construction of S and L). Moreover, by Lemma 7.15, $B(S,L)$ has a spanning tree in which all the vertices of S and $|S|-1$ vertices of L are internal.

Exercises

Problem 7.1 (✐) Prove that the greedy procedure of 7.5 is guaranteed to find a hypertree if one exists.

Problem 7.2 (✐) Prove that, given a hypertree T of a hypergraph H along with a hyperedge of more than two vertices, one of the vertices of e can be deleted from e so that the T remains a hypertree.

Problem 7.3 (✐) Show that Reduction Rule SS.3 is safe, and obtain a kernel with $\mathcal{O}(k^2)$ vertices and $2k$ hyperedges for SET SPLITTING.

Problem 7.4 Prove that Reduction Rule SS.4 is safe.

Problem 7.5 Prove that by using a 2-expansion (see Chapter 5), it can be shown that SET SPLITTING admits a kernel with $2k$ vertices and $4k$ hyperedges.

Problem 7.6 Prove Lemma 7.12 for the cases in which $|S|=1$ or $V(G) = S \cup L$.

Bibliographic Notes

Theorem 7.2 (in a more general form) was proved by Lovász (1970) and Theorem 7.4 is due to Frank et al. (2003).

Our presentation of a kernelization algorithm for SET SPLITTING follows Lokshtanov and Saurabh (2009). Several previous results were given in Chen and Lu (2009), Dehne et al. (2003, 2004), and Lokshtanov and Sloper (2005). For MAX-INTERNAL SPANNING TREE, Prieto and Sloper (2003) provided an $O(k^3)$-vertex kernel and then improved it to $O(k^2)$ in Prieto and Sloper (2005). Our presentation is based on Fomin et al. (2013). A kernel with $2k$ vertices was announced by Li et al. (2017).

8
Sunflower Lemma

In this chapter we show how a fundamental tool from extremal combinatorics can be used to design kernelization algorithm. Extremal combinatorics is a an area of combinatorial mathematics dealing with problems of the following nature—for a specific property of finite objects (graphs, sets, vectors, etc.), how many objects with this property can there be? We will focus on a tool called Sunflower lemma, which is a classical result of Erdős and Rado from 1960.

8.1 Sunflower Lemma

In this section we introduce a classical result of Erdős and Rado and present some of its applications to kernelization. In the literature, this result is known as the Sunflower lemma or as the Erdős-Rado lemma. We first define the terminology used in the statement of the lemma. A *sunflower* with k *petals* and a *core* Y is a collection of sets $S_1, \ldots, S_k$ such that $S_i \cap S_j = Y$ for all $i \neq j$; the sets $S_i \setminus Y$ are called petals and we require *none of them to be empty*. Note that a family of pairwise disjoint sets is a sunflower (with an empty core).

Lemma 8.1 *Let $\mathcal{F}$ be a family of sets (without duplicates) over a universe U, such that each set in $\mathcal{F}$ has cardinality d. If $|\mathcal{F}| > d!\,(k-1)^d$, then $\mathcal{F}$ contains a sunflower with k petals and such a sunflower can be computed in time polynomial in $|\mathcal{F}|$, $|U|$ and k.*

Proof: We prove the lemma by induction on d. For $d = 1$, that is, for a family of singletons, the statement trivially holds. Next, suppose that $d \geq 2$.

Let $\mathcal{G} = \{S_1, \ldots, S_\ell\} \subseteq \mathcal{F}$ be an inclusion-wise maximal family of pairwise disjoint sets in $\mathcal{F}$. If $\ell \geq k$, then $\mathcal{G}$ is a sunflower with at least k petals. Thus we assume that $\ell < k$. Let $S = \bigcup_{i=1}^{\ell} S_i$. Then, $|S| \leq d(k-1)$. Because $\mathcal{G}$ is maximal, every set $A \in \mathcal{F}$ intersects at least one set from $\mathcal{G}$, that is, $A \cap S \neq \emptyset$. Therefore, there is an element $u \in \mathcal{U}$ contained in at least

$$\frac{|\mathcal{F}|}{|S|} > \frac{d!\,(k-1)^d}{d(k-1)} = (d-1)!\,(k-1)^{d-1}$$

sets from $\mathcal{F}$. We take all sets of $\mathcal{F}$ containing this element u, and construct a family $\mathcal{F}'$ of sets of cardinality $d-1$ by removing from each set the element u. Because $|\mathcal{F}'| > (d-1)!\,(k-1)^{d-1}$, by the induction hypothesis, $\mathcal{F}'$ contains a sunflower $\{S_1', \ldots, S_k'\}$ with k petals. Then, $\{S_1' \cup \{u\}, \ldots, S_k' \cup \{u\}\}$ is a sunflower in $\mathcal{F}$ with k petals.

The proof can be easily transformed into a polynomial-time algorithm, as follows. Greedily select a maximal set of pairwise disjoint sets. If the size of this set is at least k, then return this set. Otherwise, find an element u contained in the maximum number of sets in $\mathcal{F}$, and call the algorithm recursively on sets of cardinality $d-1$, obtained from deleting u from the sets containing it. □

Theorem 8.2 (Sunflower Lemma) *Let $\mathcal{F}$ be a family of sets (without duplicates) over a universe U, such that each set in $\mathcal{F}$ has cardinality at most d. If $|\mathcal{F}| > d \cdot d!\,(k-1)^d$, then $\mathcal{F}$ contains a sunflower with k petals and such a sunflower can be computed in time polynomial in $|\mathcal{F}|$, $|U|$ and k.*

Proof: We prove the theorem by applying Lemma 8.1. Let $\mathcal{F}_\ell$, $\ell \leq d$, be the subfamily of $\mathcal{F}$ such that each set in F_ℓ has size exactly ℓ. Because $|\mathcal{F}| > d \cdot d!\,(k-1)^d$, there exists an integer $\ell \leq d$ such that $|\mathcal{F}_\ell| > d!\,(k-1)^d$. By applying Lemma 8.1 to F_ℓ, we get the desired result. □

8.2 d-Hitting Set

As a first application of the sunflower lemma, we give a kernel for d-Hitting Set. In this problem, we are given a family $\mathcal{A}$ of sets over a universe U, where each set in $\mathcal{A}$ has cardinality at most d, and a nonnegative integer k. The objective is to decide whether there is a subset $H \subseteq U$ of size at most k such that H contains at least one element from each set in $\mathcal{A}$.

Theorem 8.3 *d-Hitting Set admits a kernel with at most $d \cdot d!\,k^d$ sets and at most $d^2 \cdot d!\,k^d$ elements.*

Proof: The heart of the proof is the observation that if $\mathcal{A}$ contains a sunflower

$$\mathcal{S} = \{S_1, \ldots, S_{k+1}\}$$

of cardinality $k + 1$, then every hitting set H of $\mathcal{A}$ of cardinality at most k intersects the core Y of the sunflower $\mathcal{S}$. Indeed, if H does not intersect Y, it should intersect each of the $k + 1$ disjoint petals $S_i \setminus Y$. This leads to the following reduction rule.

> **Reduction HS.1** Let $(U, \mathcal{A}, k)$ be an instance of d-HITTING SET such that $\mathcal{A}$ contains a sunflower $\mathcal{S} = \{S_1, \ldots, S_{k+1}\}$ of cardinality $k + 1$ with core Y. Then, return $(U', \mathcal{A}', k)$, where $\mathcal{A}' = (\mathcal{A} \setminus \mathcal{S}) \cup \{Y\}$ and $U' = \bigcup_{X \in \mathcal{A}'} X$.

Note that when we delete sets, we do not delete the elements contained in these sets but only those that do not belong to any of the remaining sets. Then, the instances $(U, \mathcal{A}, k)$ and $(U', \mathcal{A}', k)$ are equivalent, that is, $(U, \mathcal{A})$ contains a hitting set of size k if and only if $(U, \mathcal{A}')$ does.

The kernelization algorithm is as follows. If the number of sets in $\mathcal{A}$ is larger than $d \cdot d! \, k^d$, then the kernelization algorithm applies the Sunflower lemma (Theorem 8.2) to find a sunflower of size $k + 1$, and applies Reduction HS.1 to this sunflower.

It applies this procedure exhaustively and obtains a new family of sets $\mathcal{A}'$ of size at most $d \cdot d! \, k^d$. If $\emptyset \in \mathcal{A}'$ (i.e., at some point a sunflower with an empty core has been discovered), then the algorithm concludes that there is no hitting set of size at most k and returns that the given instance is a no-instance. Otherwise, every set contains at most d elements, and thus the number of elements in the kernel is at most $d! \, k^d \cdot d^2$. □

8.3 d-SET PACKING

In the last section, as an application of the Sunflower lemma, we gave a kernel for d-HITTING SET. In this section, we demonstrate the versatility of the Sunflower lemma by applying it to design polynomial kernel for a packing problem, namely, d-SET PACKING. In this problem we are given a family $\mathcal{A}$ of sets over a universe U, where each set in $\mathcal{A}$ has cardinality at most d, and a nonnegative integer k. The objective is to decide whether there is a subfamily $\mathcal{P} \subseteq \mathcal{A}$ of size at least k such that the sets in $\mathcal{P}$ are pairwise disjoint.

Theorem 8.4 d-SET PACKING *admits a kernel with at most* $d \cdot d! \, ((k-1)d+1)^d$ *sets and at most* $d^2 \cdot d! \cdot ((k-1)d+1)^d$ *elements.*

Proof: Set $\ell = (k-1)d$. Here, the crucial observation is that if $\mathcal{A}$ contains a sunflower

$$\mathcal{S} = \{S_1, \ldots, S_{\ell+2}\}$$

of cardinality $\ell + 2$, then we can arbitrarily delete any of the petals from the sunflower and obtain an equivalent instance. In particular, we have the following reduction rule.

> **Reduction SP.1** Let $(U, \mathcal{A}, k)$ be an instance of d-SET PACKING and assume that $\mathcal{A}$ contains a sunflower $\mathcal{S} = \{S_1, \ldots, S_{\ell+2}\}$ of cardinality $\ell + 2$ with core Y. Then return $(U', \mathcal{A}', k)$, where $\mathcal{A}' = \mathcal{A} \setminus \{S_1\}$ and $U' = \bigcup_{X \in \mathcal{A}'} X$.

We next show that Reduction SP.1 is safe. First observe that if $(U', \mathcal{A}', k)$ has a subfamily $\mathcal{P} \subseteq \mathcal{A}'$ of size at least k such that sets in $\mathcal{P}$ are pairwise disjoint, then so does $(U, \mathcal{A}, k)$. Now we show the forward direction of the proof. Let $\mathcal{P} \subseteq \mathcal{A}$ be a subfamily of size *exactly* k such that sets in $\mathcal{P}$ are pairwise disjoint. For the proof we will modify $\mathcal{P}$ and obtain a subfamily $\mathcal{P}' \subseteq \mathcal{A}'$ of size k such that sets in $\mathcal{P}'$ are pairwise disjoint. If $S_1 \notin \mathcal{P}$ then $\mathcal{P}$ is also a solution for $(U', \mathcal{A}', k)$, and thus in this case we take $\mathcal{P}$ as $\mathcal{P}'$. Thus, from now onward we assume that $S_1 \in \mathcal{P}$. Let $W = \bigcup_{X \in \mathcal{P} \setminus \{S_1\}} X$. Observe that $|W| \leq (k-1)d$. This together with the fact that the sets in $\mathcal{P}$ are pairwise disjoint implies that the number of sets in $\mathcal{S} \setminus \{S_1\}$ that contain elements from W is upper bounded by $(k-1)d$. Thus, as $|\mathcal{S} \setminus \{S_1\}| \geq \ell + 1$, there is a set $X \in \mathcal{S} \setminus \{S_1\}$ that does not contain any element from W. This in turn implies that $\mathcal{P}' = (\mathcal{P} \setminus \{S_1\}) \cup X$ is a subfamily of $\mathcal{A}'$ of size k such that sets in $\mathcal{P}'$ are pairwise disjoint.

The kernelization algorithm is as follows. If the number of sets in $\mathcal{A}$ is larger than $d \cdot d! \cdot (\ell+1)^d$, then the kernelization algorithm uses the Sunflower lemma (Theorem 8.2) to find a sunflower of size $\ell+2$, and applies Reduction Rule 8.4 to this sunflower. It applies this procedure exhaustively, and thus eventually obtains a new family of sets $\mathcal{A}'$ of size at most $d \cdot d! \cdot (\ell+1)^d$. Because every set contains at most d elements, the number of elements in the kernel is at most $d^2 \cdot d! \cdot ((k-1)d+1)^d$. This concludes the proof. □

8.4 Domination in Degenerate Graphs

In Section 2.4 we discussed a kernelization for DOMINATING SET on graphs with girth of at least 5. In this section we give a kernel for DOMINATING SET on another class of graphs, namely, *d-degenerate* graphs.

Let $d \geq 1$ be an integer. A graph G is *d-degenerate* if every subgraph of G has a vertex of degree at most d. For example, every forest is 1-degenerate

8.4 Domination in Degenerate Graphs

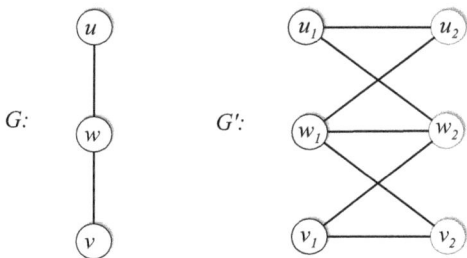

Figure 8.1 Constructing a red-blue graph G' from a graph G.

because every subgraph of a forest, which is also a forest, contains a vertex of degree at most 1. More generally, graphs of treewidth at most d are d-degenerate. Moreover, every d-regular graph is trivially d-degenerate, and every planar graph has a vertex of degree at most 5, and thus any planar graph is 5-degenerate.

Graphs of bounded degeneracy are sparse—the number of edges in a d-degenerate n-vertex graph is at most dn. We show that for every d, DOMINATING SET on d-degenerate graphs admits a compression to DOMINATING SET on $(d+1)$-degenerate graphs with $k^{\mathcal{O}(d^2)}$ vertices. Toward this we define an auxiliary problem called RED-BLUE DOMINATING SET. In the RED-BLUE DOMINATING SET problem, we are given a bipartite graph G with $V(G)$ being bipartitioned into (B,R) and a nonnegative integer k. The goal is to decide whether there exists a subset $D \subseteq R$ such that $N(D) = B$. We refer to vertices from B as *blue*, vertices of R as *red*, and to the graph as a *red-blue graph*. A subset $D \subseteq R$ is a *red-blue dominating set* if $N(D) = B$. In other words, every blue vertex is adjacent to at least one vertex in D.

It is easy to establish an equivalence of the two dominating problems. For a d-degenerate graph G, we construct a $(d+1)$-degenerate bipartite red-blue graph G' by taking two disjoint copies of $V(G)$, one for B and one for R, and making every blue vertex $v \in B$ adjacent to all the copies of the vertices of $N_G[v]$ in R. See Fig. 8.1. We leave it as an exercise to show that G has a dominating set of size k if and only if G' has a red-blue dominating set of size k (Exercise 8.1).

For a given bipartite d-degenerate red-blue graph G, we construct a $(d+1)$-degenerate graph G' by adding two new vertices u and w. We make u adjacent to all red vertices and w adjacent only to u. See Fig. 8.2. Again, we leave it to the reader as an exercise to show that G' is $(d+1)$-degenerate and that G has a red-blue dominating set of size k if and only if G' has a dominating set of size $k+1$ (Exercise 8.2).

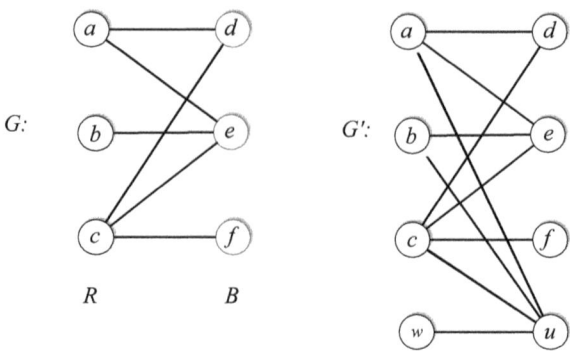

Figure 8.2 Constructing a graph G' from a red-blue graph G.

We are now ready to prove the following theorem.

Theorem 8.5 *For every $d \geq 0$,* DOMINATING SET *on d-degenerate graphs admits a compression to* DOMINATING SET *on $(d+2)$-degenerate graphs with $k^{\mathcal{O}(d^2)}$ vertices.*

Proof: We prove that RED-BLUE DOMINATING SET admits a kernel with $k^{\mathcal{O}(d^2)}$ vertices on d-degenerate graphs. By the discussion preceding the theorem statement, this will proof the theorem.

Let G be a d-degenerate red-blue graph whose vertex set is partitioned into R (red vertices) and B (blue vertices). Let R_s be the set of vertices of R of degree at most $2d$ and let $R_\ell = R \setminus R_s$. Thus, every vertex of R_s is of "small" degree (at most $2d$) and every vertex of R_ℓ is of "large" degree (larger than $2d$). Let $H = G[R_\ell \cup B]$. We claim that the average degree of the vertices from B in H is at most $2d$. Specifically,

$$\sum_{v \in B} d_H(v) \leq 2d \cdot |B|. \tag{8.1}$$

Indeed, because degeneracy is a hereditary property, we have that the graph H is d-degenerate. Thus,

$$|E(H)| \leq d \cdot |V(H)| = d(|R_\ell| + |B|).$$

We observe that $|B| \geq |R_\ell|$, or else,

$$|E(H)| = \sum_{v \in R_\ell} d_H(v) \geq 2d \cdot |R_\ell| > d(|R_\ell| + |B|), \tag{8.2}$$

8.4 Domination in Degenerate Graphs

which is a contradiction. Hence, $|R_\ell| + |B| \leq 2|B|$, and

$$\sum_{v \in B} d_H(v) = |E(H)| \leq d(|R_\ell| + |B|) \leq 2d \cdot |B|.$$

This concludes the proof of (8.1).

Now we claim that at least $|B|/2$ vertices of B have degree at most $4d$ in H. Indeed, if it was not the case, then

$$\sum_{v \in B} d_H(v) > 4d \cdot |B|/2 = 2d \cdot |B|,$$

contradicting (8.1).

To use the Sunflower lemma (Theorem 8.2), we construct a family of sets $\mathcal{F}$ over a universe U: The vertices of R_ℓ form the universe U (i.e., $R_\ell = U$), and for every vertex $b \in B$, there is a corresponding set $F_b \in \mathcal{F}$ that consists of the neighbors of b in H (i.e., $F_b = N_H(b)$).

As we have already shown, at least half of the vertices of B are of degree at most $4d$ in H. Thus if $|B| > 2 \cdot 4d \cdot (4d)! \, (2dk + k)^{4d}$, then there are more than $4d \cdot (4d)! \, (2dk+k)^{4d}$ sets of size at most $4d$ in $\mathcal{F}$. In this case, by the Sunflower lemma, $\mathcal{F}$ contains a sunflower with $(2dk + k + 1)$ petals. Moreover, each of the sets of this sunflower is of size at most $4d$. Let $Y \subseteq R_\ell$, $|Y| \leq 4d$, be the core of the sunflower.

We observe that every red-blue dominating set D in G of size at most k contains a vertex from Y. Indeed, every vertex of R_s can dominate at most $2d$ vertices of B, and thus at least $k + 1$ petals of the sunflower (and thus the corresponding vertices of B) are not hit by $D \cap R_s$. Thus if D does not intersect Y, it should intersect at least $k + 1$ disjoint petals, which is a contradiction. Hence $D \cap Y \neq \emptyset$. This leads to the following reduction rule.

> **Reduction DS.3** If $\mathcal{F}$ contains a sunflower with $(2dk + k + 1)$ petals, we construct a new graph G' by deleting all the vertices of B corresponding to these petals, and adding to B a new blue vertex y and making it adjacent to all the vertices of Y.

To prove that Reduction Rule DS.3 is safe, we show that G has a red-blue dominating set of size k if and only if G' does. Let D be a dominating set in G of size k. Because $D \cap Y \neq \emptyset$, we have that D also dominates y in G', and thus D is a dominating set in G'. In the opposite direction, if D is a dominating set in G', then it should contain a vertex from Y to dominate y. However, then D dominates all vertices of B as well.

We will view G' as a subgraph of G. Toward this observe that we could obtain G' from G as follows: Delete all but one of the vertices of B corresponding to petals, and for the remaining vertex, delete all the edges incident to it but not incident to any vertex in Y. Because G' is a subgraph of G, it is also d-degenerate, and thus we can apply Reduction Rule DS.3 to the new graph until we obtain a graph with blue set of size at most $8d \cdot (4d)! \, (2dk+k)^{4d}$. By Equation 8.2, we also know that the number of vertices of large degree, R_ℓ, is at most $|B|$. To bound the number of small degree vertices in R, we need another reduction rule.

> **Reduction DS.4** If there are $u, v \in R_s$, $u \neq v$, such that $N_G(u) \subseteq N_G(v)$, then delete u.

Rule DS.4 is trivially safe and can be implemented in polynomial time. Because the vertices in R_s are of degree at most $2d$, there are at most

$$\sum_{i=0}^{2d} \binom{|B|}{i}$$

vertices remaining in R_s after the exhaustive application of Rule DS.4. Thus, the number of vertices in an irreducible red-blue graph for which none of the Rules DS.3 and DS.4 can be applied, is at most

$$\begin{aligned}
|B| + |R_\ell| + |R_s| &\leq 2|B| + \sum_{i=0}^{2d} \binom{|B|}{i} \\
&\leq |B|^{\mathcal{O}(d)} \\
&\leq (8d \cdot (4d)! \, (2dk+k)^{4d})^{\mathcal{O}(d)} \\
&\leq = k^{\mathcal{O}(d^2)}.
\end{aligned}$$

This completes the proof. $\square$

8.5 Domination in $K_{i,j}$-Free Graphs

In this section we give a polynomial compression for RED-BLUE DOMINATING SET when the input graph excludes $K_{i,j}$ as a subgraph. Here, $K_{i,j}$ is the complete bipartite graph with one side of the bipartition of size i and and the other of size j. Let us note that because every $K_{d,d}$-free graph is also d-degenerate, Theorem 8.7 addresses a class of graphs that is more general than the one considered by Theorem 8.5. The general strategy of both theorems is

8.5 Domination in $K_{i,j}$-Free Graphs

similar—we want to identify the set of vertices in R intersecting every red-blue dominating set of size at most k, and then use this set to apply a reduction rule.

We start with an auxiliary counting lemma that will be a critical component of the kernelization algorithm for RED-BLUE DOMINATING SET, and that will also be useful in the context of other kernelization algorithms. Here, a bipartite graph G with $V(G)$ being partitioned into R and B is said to be *B-twinless* if there do not exist distinct vertices $u, v \in B$ such that $N(u) = N(v)$.

Lemma 8.6 *Let G be a bipartite graph with $V(G)$ being partitioned into R and B. If G is B-twinless and excludes $K_{i,j}$ as a subgraph, then*

$$|B| \leq \sum_{q<i} \binom{|R|}{q} + (j-1)\binom{|R|}{i}.$$

Proof: For every $X \in \binom{R}{i}$, let $F(X)$ denote the set of vertices $w \in B$ such that $X \subseteq N(w)$. And for every $q < i$ and $Y \in \binom{R}{q}$ let $F(Y)$ denote the set of vertices $w \in B$ such that $Y = N(w)$. Let $\mathcal{P}$ denote $\bigcup_{q<i} \binom{R}{q}$. Between G is a B-twinless bipartite graph, we have that for every $Y \in \mathcal{P}$, $|F(Y)| \leq 1$. Furthermore, G excludes $K_{i,j}$ as a subgraph and thus for every $X \in \binom{R}{i}$, $|F(X)| \leq j$. Note that every vertex in B either belongs to $F(Y)$ for some $Y \in \mathcal{P}$, or to $F(X)$ for some $X \in \binom{R}{i}$. This implies that

$$|B| \leq \sum_{Y \in \mathcal{P}} |F(Y)| + \sum_{X \in \binom{R}{i}} |F(X)| \leq \sum_{q<i} \binom{|R|}{q} + (j-1)\binom{|R|}{i}.$$

This concludes the proof of the lemma. □

Compression Algorithm. As in the previous section, the main component of our compression algorithm is a kernel for RED-BLUE DOMINATING SET. In the design of this kernelization algorithm, the goal is to devise reduction rules so that one can bound the size of R. This together with Lemma 8.6 will imply the desired kernel.

Theorem 8.7 *For every $1 \leq i \leq j$, DOMINATING SET on graphs excluding $K_{i,j}$ as a subgraph admits a compression to DOMINATING SET on graphs excluding $K_{i+1,i+j+1}$ as a subgraph with $k^{\mathcal{O}(ij)}$ vertices and edges.*

Proof: As in the proof of Theorem 8.5 from the previous section, to prove the theorem it is sufficient to give a kernel for RED-BLUE DOMINATING SET (see also Exercises 8.1 and 8.2).

Let $G = (B, R, E)$ be a bipartite graph with $|B| = m$ and $|R| = n$. Our main reduction rule is based on the following claim.

Claim 8.8 If there exists a vertex $u \in R$ such that $|N(u)| \geq ik^{j-1}$, then in polynomial time we can find a set $S \subseteq R$ of size at most $j - 1$ that intersects every red-blue dominating set of size at most k of G.

Proof: Suppose that there exists $u \in R$ such that $|N(u)| \geq ik^{j-1}$. Let $S = \{u_1, u_2, \ldots, u_p\} \subseteq R$ be a maximal set such that for all $\ell \leq p$ we have that

$$\bigcap_{x=1}^{\ell} N(u_x) \geq ik^{j-\ell}.$$

Such a set S can be found in polynomial time by greedily selecting vertices. Observe that $p \leq j - 1$, else it would imply an existence of $K_{i,j}$ in G.

We claim that every red-blue dominating set D of size at most k of G intersects S. Let $I = \bigcap_{x=1}^{p} N(u_x)$, and note that $|I| \geq ik^{j-p}$. Moreover, for every vertex $w \in R \setminus S$, we have that $|N(w) \cap I| < ik^{i-p-1}$. Thus if $D \cap S = \emptyset$, then k vertices cannot dominate the vertices in I. This implies that $D \cap S \neq \emptyset$. □

> **Reduction DS.5** Let $S = \{u_1, \ldots, u_p\}$ be the output of the algorithm of Claim 8.8, and denote $I = N(S)$.
>
> (i) If $|S| = 1$, then return $(G', k - 1)$, where G' is the subgraph of G induced by $(B \setminus N(u_1), R \setminus u_1)$.
> (ii) If $|S| > 1$, then pick a vertex $w \in I$ and construct the graph G' from G as follows. Remove all the vertices of I from B with the exception of w, and remove all edges incident to w apart from the incident to both w and a vertex in S. Return (G', k).

Claim 8.9 Reduction Rule DS.5 is safe.

Proof: We first give a proof for the case in which $|S| = 1$. By Claim 8.8 we know that u_1 is part of every red-blue dominating set of size at most k. Thus, one the one hand, if W is a red-blue dominating set of size at most k of G, then clearly $W \setminus \{u_1\}$ is a red-blue dominating set of size at most $k - 1$ of G'. On the other hand, given any red-blue dominating set of size at most $k - 1$ of G', we can obtain a red-blue dominating set of size at most k of G by adding u_1 to it.

Next we prove the case in which $|S| \geq 2$. Let $B' = (B \setminus I) \cup \{w\}$ and W be a red-blue dominating set of size at most k of G. We will show that W is also a red-blue dominating set of size at most k for G'. By Claim 8.8 we know that $W \cap S \neq \emptyset$. This implies that w is dominated by a vertex in $W \cap S$. The adjacencies of vertices in B' (other than w) in G' are the same as in G and thus they are also dominated by W in G'. For the reverse direction observe that $N_{G'}(w) = S$ and thus any red-blue dominating set of size at most k of G' must contain a vertex of S. Together with the fact that $I = \bigcap_{x \in S} N(u_x)$, we have that every red-blue dominating set W of size at most k of G' is also a red-blue dominating set of G. This completes the proof of safeness. □

We apply Reduction Rule DS.4 to the vertices of R and Reduction Rule DS.5 to G exhaustively. Clearly, this can be done in polynomial time. Let (G, k) be an irreducible instance, that is, none of the two reduction rules can be applied to (G, k). The irreducible instance has the following properties.

(a) G is an R-twinless bipartite graph. That is, there are no vertices $u, v \in R$ such that $N(u) = N(v)$.
(b) Every vertex in R has degree at most ik^{j-1}.

If $k = 0$ and $B \neq \emptyset$, then return that (G, k) is a no-instance, and else if $k = 0$, then return that (G, k) is a yes-instance. Next assume that $k \geq 1$. Because every vertex in R has degree at most ik^{j-1}, every k vertices of R can dominate at most ik^j vertices. Thus, if $|B| > ik^j$ we can return that (G, k) is a no-instance. Else, we have that $|B| \leq ik^j$ and thus by Theorem 8.6 (with the roles of R and B swapped), we have that

$$|R| \leq 2(j-1) \cdot \left(\frac{|B|e}{i}\right)^{2i} \leq 2(j-1)e^{2i}k^{2ij}.$$

This implies that $|V(G)| = |R| + |B| \leq 2(j-1)e^{2i}k^{2ij} + ik^j$ and $|E(G)| \leq ik^{j-1}|R| \leq ik^{j-1}2(j-1)e^{2i}k^{2ij} \leq 2ije^{2i}k^{2ij+j-1}$. Hence after an exhaustive application of the reduction rules, the obtained graph is of size $k^{\mathcal{O}(ij)}$. This concludes the proof of the theorem. □

Exercises

Problem 8.1 (✎) Given a graph G, construct a bipartite red-blue graph G' by taking two disjoint copies of $V(G)$, one for B and one for R, and making every blue vertex $v \in B$ adjacent to all the copies of the vertices of $N_G[v]$ in R. Show that G has a dominating set of size k if and only if G' has a red-blue dominating set of size k.

Furthermore, prove that if G is d-degenerate, then G' is $(d+1)$-degenerate, and if G excludes $K_{i,j}$ as a subgraph, then G' excludes $K_{i,i+j}$ as a subgraph.

Problem 8.2 (✎) Given a bipartite d-degenerate red-blue graph G, construct a $(d+1)$-degenerate graph G' by adding two new vertices u and w. Make u

adjacent to all red vertices and w adjacent only to u. Show that G' is $(d+1)$-degenerate and that G has a red-blue dominating set of size k if and only if G' has a dominating set of size $k+1$.

Furthermore, prove that if G is d-degenerate, then G' is $(d+1)$-degenerate, and if G excludes $K_{i,j}$ as a subgraph, then G' excludes $K_{i+1,j+1}$ as a subgraph.

Problem 8.3 Consider the following counting version of d-HITTING SET. The input consists of a family $\mathcal{A}$ of sets over a universe U, where each set in $\mathcal{A}$ has cardinality at most d, and nonnegative integers k and t. The objective is to decide whether $\mathcal{A}$ has at least t minimal hitting set of size at most k. Can the kernelization algorithm for d-HITTING SET, given in Section 8.2, be adapted to solve this counting version of HITTING SET?

Problem 8.4 Consider the question addressed by Exercise 8.3 also in the context of d-SET PACKING and DOMINATING SET.

Bibliographic Notes

For a nice introduction to extremal combinatorics, we refer to the book of Jukna (2011). Sunflower lemma is due to Erdős and Rado (1960). The proof of Theorem 8.2 and the kernelization for d-HITTING SET follow the lines of Flum and Grohe (2006). Abu-Khzam (2010b) showed that a better kernel for d-HITTING SET with at most $(2d-1)k^{d-1} + k$ elements can be obtained by making use of crown decompositions. Our presentation of the kernelization algorithm for d-degenerate graphs follows the work of Cygan et al. (2017) who also have shown that the problem has no kernel of size $k^{(d-1)(d-3)-\varepsilon}$ for any $\varepsilon > 0$ unless coNP⊆NP/poly. See also Philip et al. (2012) and Telle and Villanger (2012) for kernels for DOMINATING SET on $K_{i,j}$-free graphs.

9
Modules

In this chapter we discuss the notion of modules, which forms the basis of techniques to design polynomial time algorithms for various problems on several graph classes. Here, we show its utility in the context of kernelization algorithms. Specifically, we use modular partitions to obtain kernels for CLUSTER EDITING, COGRAPH COMPLETION and FAST.

We begin with a brief introduction to modules and modular partitions. Afterward, we show how these notions can be exploited to design kernelization algorithms for CLUSTER EDITING, COGRAPH COMPLETION and FAST.

9.1 Modular Partition

Modular partition is a partition of a (directed or undirected) graph into subsets of vertices called modules. Let us start by giving the definition of a module in the context of undirected graphs. We will extend this notion to directed graphs later.

Definition 9.1 Given an undirected graph G, a subset $M \subseteq V(G)$ is called a *module* if for every $u, v \in M$, we have $N(u) \setminus M = N(v) \setminus M$. In other words, for every $x \in V(G) \setminus M$ x is adjacent to either all the vertices of M or none of the vertices of M.

Thus, all vertices of a module have exactly the same neighbors outside the module. A simple example of a module is a connected component of a graph: Every vertex of the same connected component has the same (empty) set of neighbors outside the component. A few other simple examples of modules M of a graph G are $M = V(G)$, $M = \emptyset$ and $M = \{v\}$ for any $v \in V(G)$. If M is a module of any of these three types (empty, all vertices or single vertex), then it is called *trivial*. Moreover, graph G is *prime* if all its modules are trivial.

Before we turn to discuss several interesting properties of module, we need to introduce a few more definitions.

Definition 9.2 Given a graph G, a module M of G is a *strong module* if it does not overlap with any other module of G. In other words, for every module M' of G, one of the following holds: $M' \cap M = \emptyset$; $M' \subseteq M$; $M \subseteq M'$.

While connected components of graphs are modules, it is not true that a module is necessarily a connected component or a set of connected components. In particular, a module can be a proper subset of a connected component. Note that the set of modules of a graph G and the set of modules of the complement $\overline{G}$ of G are identical—if M is a module in G, then it remains a module in $\overline{G}$.

Let us remind that we use $A \subset B$ to state that A is a *proper* subset of B. A module M is *maximal* with respect to a set $S \subseteq V(G)$ of vertices if $M \subset S$ and there is no module M' such that $M \subset M' \subset S$. If the set S is not specified, it is assumed that $S = V(G)$. Let us note that by definition, a maximal module is always a proper subset of the vertex set of G. Moreover, observe that every two distinct maximal strong modules are disjoint, see Exercise 9.4.

Definition 9.3 Let $\mathcal{P} = \{M_1, \ldots, M_k\}$ be a partition of the vertex set of a graph G. If for every i, $1 \leq i \leq k$, M_i is a module of G, then $\mathcal{P}$ is a *modular partition* (or *congruence partition*) of G.

The partitions $\mathcal{P} = \{V(G)\}$ and $\mathcal{P} = \{\{x\} \mid x \in V(G)\}$ are said to be the trivial modular partitions of G. Any other modular partition is called a *nontrivial modular partition*. A modular partition $\mathcal{P}$ containing only maximal modules is a *maximal modular partition*. For a graph G, we denote by $\mathcal{M}(G)$ the set of all maximal modules of G. Recall that by definition, every maximal module is a proper subset of $V(G)$. The following result shows that when both G and $\overline{G}$ are connected, then $\mathcal{M}(G)$ partitions $V(G)$.

Lemma 9.4 *If both the graphs G and $\overline{G}$ are connected, then $\mathcal{M}(G)$ partitions $V(G)$. In fact, $\mathcal{M}(G)$ is the unique maximal modular partition of G.*

Proof: Let $M_1, M_2 \in \mathcal{M}(G)$. Suppose, by way of contradiction, that $I = M_1 \cap M_2 \neq \emptyset$. First, suppose that $M_1 \cup M_2 \subset V(G)$. However, as M_1 and M_2 are modules, the neighborhood of every vertex in $M_1 \cup M_2$ outside $M_1 \cup M_2$ is the same as the neighborhood of any vertex in I. Thus, $M_1 \cup M_2$ is a nontrivial module properly containing M_1 and M_2, contradicting the maximality of both M_1 and M_2.

9.1 Modular Partition

Second, suppose that $M_1 \cup M_2 = V(G)$. Because G is connected, there is an edge uv with $u \in M_1 \setminus I$ and $v \in M_2$. Thus, because M_2 is a module, we have that u is adjacent to all the vertices of M_2, including those in I. However, as M_1 is also a module, every vertex in M_1 is adjacent to every vertex in $M_2 \setminus I$. This means that in $\overline{G}$, M_1 and $M_2 \setminus I$ do not belong to a single connected component, and therefore $\overline{G}$ is not connected. As we have reached a contradiction, this completes the proof. □

The unique partition defined in Lemma 9.4 depends on the fact that both G and $\overline{G}$ are connected. However, this may not be the case in general. For the general case, given a graph G, we define the following specific modular partition of G.

$$\mathcal{SP}(G) = \begin{cases} \bigcup_{C_i} \mathcal{SP}(C_i) & \text{if } G \text{ is disconnected,} \\ \bigcup_{\overline{C_i}} \mathcal{SP}(\overline{C_i}) & \text{if } \overline{G} \text{ is disconnected,} \\ \mathcal{M}(G) & \text{if } G \text{ and } \overline{G} \text{ are connected.} \end{cases}$$

Here, the C_is and $\overline{C_i}$s are connected components of G and $\overline{G}$, respectively.

Lemma 9.5 *Let G be a graph, then $\mathcal{SP}(G)$ can be computed in polynomial time.*

Proof: If G or $\overline{G}$ are disconnected, we proceed by recursively handling the connected components of G or $\overline{G}$, respectively. Else, when both G and $\overline{G}$ are connected, then by Lemma 9.4, $\mathcal{M}(G)$ is the unique maximal modular partition of G. We next show how to compute in polynomial time all maximal modules of G, which will imply the correctness of the lemma.

Let u and v be a pair of vertices of G. The crucial observation is that if u and v belong to the same nontrivial module M, then all vertices from the symmetric difference $N(u) \triangle N(v) = (N(u) \setminus N(v)) \cup (N(v) \setminus N(u))$ should also belong to M. For a vertex set $X \subset V(G)$, we define a procedure called modular-closure(X), which outputs a module containing X. The procedure performs the following operation until it constructs a module: If X contains a pair of vertices u and v such that $N(u) \setminus X \neq N(v) \setminus X$, then $X := X \cup (N(u) \triangle N(v))$. Let us note that for every $X \subset V(G)$,

- If modular-closure(X) = $V(G)$, then there is no maximal module containing X and
- If modular-closure(X) $\subset V(G)$, then modular-closure(X) is a nontrivial module.

Algorithm `ComputeMaximalModule`(G, v).
Input: A graph G such that G and $\overline{G}$ are connected and vertex $v \in V(G)$.
Output: The maximal module M containing v.

$M \leftarrow \{v\}$;
forall the $u \notin M$ **do**
  Compute $M_u = $ modular-closure$(M \cup \{u\})$;
  if $M_u \subset V(G)$ **then**
    $M \leftarrow M_u$;

Figure 9.1 Algorithm `ComputeMaximalModule`.

For every vertex v, there is a unique maximal module M containing v. Algorithm `ComputeMaximalModule`, presented in Fig. 9.1, computes this module.

The correctness of the algorithm is due to the following observation. Let M^* be the maximal module containing v, and let M' be a module such that $M' \subset M^*$. For any vertex $u \in M^* \setminus M'$, because M^* is the unique maximal module containing $M' \cup \{u\}$, we have that modular-closure$(M' \cup \{u\}) \subseteq M^*$. However, if $u \notin M^*$, then again as M^* is unique, modular-closure$(M' \cup \{u\}) = V(G)$. Thus, if when the algorithm examines a vertex u, modular-closure$(M' \cup \{u\})$ returns $V(G)$, then $u \notin M^*$. Otherwise, if modular-closure$(M' \cup \{u\})$ returns a nontrivial module, then modular-closure$(M' \cup \{u\}) \subseteq M^*$. Because with each correct guess of $u \in M^*$ we increase the size of the set M, the algorithm terminates in at most n steps, outputting the unique maximal module containing v.

Now, we proceed to analyze the running time. As usual, let n be the number of vertices in G and m be the number of edges in G. Here, we do not attempt to optimize the running time, but only seek to prove that it is polynomial. To compute modular-closure(X), we examine all pairs of vertices from X, whose number is $\mathcal{O}(n^2)$. For each such pair u, v, we need to find a vertex from $N(u) \triangle N(v) \setminus X$ or to conclude that $N(u) \triangle N(v) \setminus X = \emptyset$. Both can be easily performed in time $\mathcal{O}(n+m)$. At every step, we either finish the computation of modular-closure(X) or increase the size of the set X by at least one. Thus, the total number of steps to compute modular-closure(X) is $\mathcal{O}(n^4 m)$. Algorithm `ComputeMaximalModule` calls the procedure modular-closure at most n times, and thus runs in time $\mathcal{O}(n^5 m)$. By running the algorithm for each vertex v, we compute the set of all maximal modules in time $\mathcal{O}(n^6 m)$. □

Let us remark that while the construction of $\mathcal{SP}(G)$ in the proof Lemma 9.5 is performed in time $\mathcal{O}(n^6 m)$, there are several involved algorithms computing

9.1 Modular Partition 137

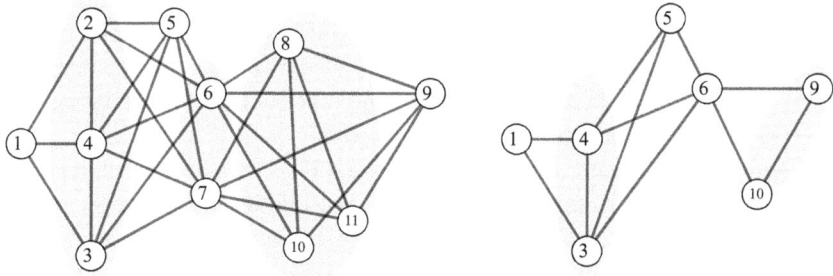

Figure 9.2 A modular partition and the corresponding quotient graph.

modular partitions in *linear* time $\mathcal{O}(n + m)$. See the "Bibliographic notes" section for the references.

If M_1 and M_2 are disjoint modules, then either every vertex of M_1 is a neighbor of every vertex of M_2, or no vertex of M_1 is adjacent to any vertex of M_2; see Exercise 9.3. Thus, the relationship between two disjoint modules is either "adjacent" or "nonadjacent." By making use of this observation, we can define a *quotient graph*. The vertices of the quotient graph are the parts (or modules) belonging to the modular partition $\mathcal{P}$.

Definition 9.6 With a modular partition $\mathcal{P} = \{M_1, \ldots, M_k\}$ of graph G, we associate a k-vertex *quotient graph* $G_{/\mathcal{P}}$, whose vertices are in one-to-one correspondence with the parts of $\mathcal{P}$. Two vertices v_i and v_j of $G_{/\mathcal{P}}$ are adjacent if and only if the corresponding modules M_i and M_j are adjacent in G.

In the left part of Fig. 9.2 we have a graph G, where the grey sets specify the nontrivial modules of G. The partition

$$\mathcal{Q} = \{\{1\}, \{2, 3\}, \{4\}, \{5\}, \{6, 7\}, \{9\}, \{8, 10, 11\}\}$$

is a modular partition of G. The quotient graph $G_{/\mathcal{Q}}$, depicted on the right with a representative vertex for each module of $\mathcal{Q}$, has two nontrivial modules (the sets $\{3, 4\}$ and $\{9, 10\}$). The maximal modular partition of G is $\mathcal{P} = \{\{1\}, \{2, 3, 4\}, \{5\}, \{6, 7\}, \{8, 9, 10, 11\}\}$.

In the case in which $\mathcal{P} = \{V(G)\}$, the quotient graph $G_{/\mathcal{P}}$ is just the one-vertex graph, while when $\mathcal{P} = \{\{x\} | x \in V(G)\}$, we have that $G_{/\mathcal{P}} = G$.

Let M be a nontrivial module. Then, M and the one-element subsets of $V(G) \setminus M$ form a nontrivial modular partition of $V(G)$. Thus the existence of a nontrivial module implies the existence of a nontrivial modular partition. In general, many (or all) members of $\mathcal{P}$ can be nontrivial modules. If $\mathcal{P}$ is a nontrivial modular partition, then $G_{/\mathcal{P}}$ is a compact representation of all the edges that have endpoints in different partition classes of $\mathcal{P}$. For each module $M \in \mathcal{P}$, the subgraph $G[M]$ induced by M is called a *factor*, and it displays all edges with both endpoints in M. Therefore, the edges of G can be reconstructed given only the quotient graph $G_{/\mathcal{P}}$ and its factors.

When $G[M]$ is a factor of a modular quotient $G_{/\mathcal{P}}$, it is possible that $G[M]$ can be recursively decomposed into factors and quotients. Each level of the recursion gives rise to a quotient. As a base case, the graph has only one vertex. The graph G can be reconstructed inductively by reconstructing the factors in a bottom-up fashion, inverting the steps of the decomposition by combining the current factors and quotient at each level.

For the purpose of this chapter, we only need the notions of the specific partition $\mathcal{SP}(G)$ defined previously and its quotient graph. However, we remark that there are several kernelization algorithms in the literature that are based on the more general notion of modular decomposition.

Modules having desirable properties. In the following sections we will be interested in modules with some specific structure. For example, we could demand that a module M is a clique, a cograph or an acyclic digraph (when we discuss to directed graphs). More generally, let $\mathcal{G}$ be a hereditary graph class. Then, we define the notions of $\mathcal{G}$-module, $\mathcal{G}$-modular partition and $\mathcal{G}$-modular decomposition as follows.

Definition 9.7 A module M is a $\mathcal{G}$-*module* if the induced subgraph $G[M]$ belongs to $\mathcal{G}$. A modular partition $\mathcal{P} = \{M_1, \ldots, M_\ell\}$ is a $\mathcal{G}$-*modular partition* if each M_i is a $\mathcal{G}$-module. For a graph G, by $\mathcal{G}\text{-}\mathcal{M}(G)$ we denote the set of all maximal $\mathcal{G}$-modules of G.

We extend the notion of a special partition of a graph to a special partition of a graph with respect to $\mathcal{G}$-modules as follows.

$$\mathcal{G}\text{-}\mathcal{SP}(G) = \begin{cases} \bigcup_{C_i} \mathcal{G}\text{-}\mathcal{SP}(C_i) & \text{if } G \text{ is disconnected,} \\ \bigcup_{C_i} \mathcal{G}\text{-}\mathcal{SP}(\overline{C_i}) & \text{if } \overline{G} \text{ is disconnected,} \\ \mathcal{G}\text{-}\mathcal{M}(G) & \text{if } G \text{ and } \overline{G} \text{ are connected.} \end{cases}$$

Here, the C_is and $\overline{C_i}$s are the connected components of G and $\overline{G}$, respectively.

The proof of the following lemma is almost identical to the proof of Lemma 9.5; we leave it as Exercise 9.6.

Lemma 9.8 *Let $\mathcal{G}$ be either the set of all cliques or the set of all independent sets, and G be an undirected graph. Then, $\mathcal{G}\text{-}\mathcal{SP}(G)$ can be computed in polynomial time.*

Let us note that by making using of Lemma 9.8, we are able to find in polynomial time a maximal clique-module in $\mathcal{G}\text{-}\mathcal{M}(G)$, as well as to construct the quotient graph corresponding to $\mathcal{G}\text{-}\mathcal{SP}(G)$.

9.2 CLUSTER EDITING

Our first example of kernelization algorithms based on the structure of modules is for CLUSTER EDITING. A graph is a *cluster graph* if each of its connected components is a complete graph (clique). Thus, a cluster graph is a disjoint union of complete graphs. We will be refer to the connected components of a cluster graph as clusters. We study the following problem: For a given graph G, can we transform G into a cluster graph by "editing" at most k adjacencies, that is, by adding or deleting at most k edges?

More formally, let G be a graph. Then, $F \subseteq V(G) \times V(G)$ is called a *cluster editing set* for G if the graph $G \triangle F$, which is the graph with vertex set $V(G)$ and edge set $E(G) \triangle F$, is a cluster graph. Here, $E(G) \triangle F$ is the symmetric difference between $E(G)$ and F. In CLUSTER EDITING, we are given a graph G and an integer k, and the task is to decide whether there is a cluster editing set for G of size at most k. CLUSTER EDITING is known to be NP-complete. We will show how to obtain a kernel for this problem when the parameter is the size of the editing set k.

Let $\mathcal{C}$ be the class of graphs consisting of all complete graphs. This is a hereditary graph class, and every maximal $\mathcal{C}$-module of a graph G is a maximal clique-module.

Definition 9.9 *A critical clique of a graph G is a maximal $\mathcal{C}$-module.*

In other words, a critical clique of G is a clique C such that all the vertices of C have the same set of neighbors in $V(G) \setminus C$, and C is inclusion maximal under this property. Let us highlight the most crucial properties of critical cliques first, and show how these properties almost immediately bring us a $\mathcal{O}(k^2)$-vertex kernel for CLUSTER EDITING.

- Out first observation is that if we have a connected component C in G which is a clique, then we can safely remove C from G as this does not change the answer.

- Suppose that G can be transformed into a cluster graph by modifying at most k adjacencies. This means that at most $2k$ vertices of G are affected by the modification, that is, incident to edges that are removed from G or added to G. Because we deleted isolated cliques, this also means that in the resulting cluster graph each cluster contains at least one affected vertex.
- How do unaffected vertices look like? First, it does not make any sense to "split" critical cliques. In other words, it is possible to prove that there is an optimal solution, such that in the resulting cluster graph, every critical clique K of G is contained in some cluster of the resulting graph. Thus, every maximal $\mathcal{C}$-module of G is also a $\mathcal{C}$-module in this solution. Another observation is that one cluster cannot contain more than one unaffected clique. Thus, every cluster consists of at most one unaffected clique and some affected vertices. To bound the maximum number of vertices contained in an unaffected critical clique, we need another reduction rule.
- The reduction rule is based on the observation that if at least one vertex of a critical clique K is unaffected, then all vertices of K should be unaffected. Therefore, if we have a critical clique K with at least $2k+1$ vertices, this clique should be unaffected. Thus, if K has strictly more than $2k+1$ vertices, we can safely remove a vertex from it. Hence, after this reduction rule, we can assume that each critical clique has at most $2k+1$ vertices.
- To conclude, every cluster graph G' obtained from the reduced graph G has the following structure. Each of its clusters contains at least one affected and at most $2k+1$ unaffected vertices. Because the total number of affected vertices is at most $2k$, we have that the number of vertices in G', and hence in G, is $\mathcal{O}(k^2)$.

In what follows, we prove the claimed properties of critical cliques and also show how a more careful estimation of the number of unaffected vertices results in vertex-linear kernel for the problem.

We denote the set of all critical cliques by $\mathcal{C}\text{-}\mathcal{M}(G)$. The proof of the following lemma is very similar to the proof of Lemma 9.4.

Lemma 9.10 *If G is not a complete graph, then $\mathcal{C}\text{-}\mathcal{M}(G)$ partitions $V(G)$. Moreover, $\mathcal{C}\text{-}\mathcal{M}(G)$ is the unique maximal $\mathcal{C}$-modular partition of G.*

Proof: Let $M_1, M_2 \in \mathcal{C}\text{-}\mathcal{M}(G)$ be distinct critical cliques. To prove the lemma, we need to show that M_1 and M_2 are disjoint. Suppose, by way of contradiction, that $I = M_1 \cap M_2 \neq \emptyset$. Then, $M_1 \cup M_2$ is a module (see Exercise 9.2). Because M_2 is a clique, each vertex of I is adjacent to all vertices of $M_2 \setminus I$. Then, because M_1 is a module, each vertex of M_1 is adjacent to all vertices of $M_2 \setminus I$. Because M_1 is a clique, we overall derive that $M_1 \cup M_2$ is a clique, and hence it is a clique-module. Because M_1 and M_2 are maximal clique-modules, $M_1 \cup M_2$ cannot be a nontrivial module, and thus $M_1 \cup M_2 = V(G)$. However, this means that G is a complete graph, which is a contradiction. $\square$

A cluster editing set $F \subseteq V \times V$ of minimum size is referred to as a *minimum cluster editing set*, or just as a *minimum editing set*. The following lemma explains the relations between critical cliques and minimum editing sets.

Lemma 9.11 *Let F be a minimum editing set of a graph G. For every critical clique K of G, there is a clique in the cluster graph $G \triangle F$ containing K.*

Proof: Targeting toward a contradiction, let us assume that for some critical clique K there are two distinct maximal cliques C_1 and C_2 in $G \triangle F$ such that both $K_1 = K \cap C_1$ and $K_2 = K \cap C_2$ are nonempty. Furthermore, we define C_1^1 as the set of vertices of $C_1 \setminus K_1$ having neighbors (in G) in K, and we define $C_1^2 = C_1 \setminus (K_1 \cup C_1^1)$. Similarly, the set C_2^1 is the set of vertices of $C_2 \setminus K_2$ with neighbors in K and $C_2^2 = C_2 \setminus (K_2 \cup C_2^1)$. See Fig. 9.3. Let us note that because K is a module, every vertex of C_1^1 and of C_2^1 is adjacent to all vertices of K.

On the one hand, note that all the edges of G between K_1 and K_2 should be deleted by F. Moreover, all edges between K_1 and C_2^1 as well as between K_2 and C_1^1 have to be deleted. On the other hand, all edges between K_1 and C_1^2 and between K_2 and C_2^2 should be added.

Let us assume first that $|C_1^1| + |C_2^2| \leq |C_1^2| + |C_2^1|$. Then, we construct another cluster graph from $G \triangle F$ by moving K_1 from C_1 to C_2. By doing this,

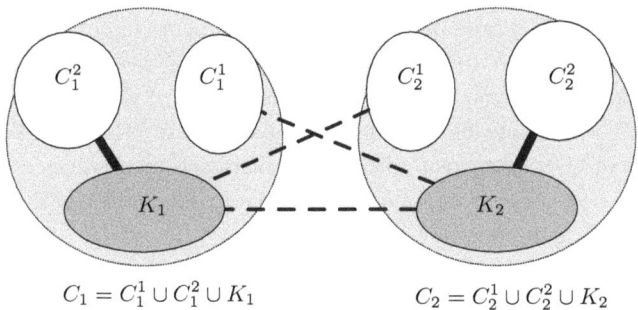

Figure 9.3 The dashed lines indicate edge deletions and the thick lines indicate edge additions, both incident to K_1 and K_2.

we no longer need to delete edges between K_1 and K_2 and between K_1 and C_2^1. We also do not need to add edges between K_1 and C_1^2. Thus, by moving K_1 to C_2 we "gain"

$$|K_1| \cdot |K_2| + |K_1| \cdot (|C_1^2| + |C_2^1|)$$

edits. On the other hand, now we have to delete edges between K_1 and C_1^1 and add edges between K_1 and C_2^2. Hence, we "lose"

$$|K_1| \cdot (|C_1^1| + |C_2^2|)$$

edits. However,

$$|K_1| \cdot (|C_1^1| + |C_2^2|) \leq |K_1| \cdot (|C_1^2| + |C_2^1|) < |K_1| \cdot |K_2| + |K_1| \cdot (|C_1^2| + |C_2^1|).$$

This means that F is a not a minimum editing set, which is a contradiction. Thus, $|C_1^1| + |C_2^2| \leq |C_1^2| + |C_2^1|$ cannot occur, and hence $|C_1^1| + |C_2^2| > |C_1^2| + |C_2^1|$.

Now, having $|C_1^1| + |C_2^2| > |C_1^2| + |C_2^1|$, we construct another cluster graph from $G \triangle F$ by moving K_2 from C_2 to C_1. However, in this case we "gain"

$$|K_1| \cdot |K_2| + |K_2| \cdot (|C_1^1| + |C_2^2|)$$

edits, while we "lose" only

$$|K_2| \cdot (|C_1^2| + |C_2^1|)$$

edits. This again contradicts the minimum choice of F, excluding the option $|C_1^1| + |C_2^2| > |C_1^2| + |C_2^1|$ as well. As at least one of the cases should have held, our assumption that K is contained in two different clusters is wrong. This completes the proof. □

Let $\mathcal{P} = \mathcal{C}\text{-}\mathcal{M}(G)$ be a partition of G into critical cliques. Let us remind that by Observation 9.3, for every distinct $M_1, M_2 \in \mathcal{P}$, either every vertex of M_1 is a neighbor of every vertex of M_2, or no vertex of M_1 is adjacent to any vertex of M_2. We denote the corresponding quotient graph by $G_{/\mathcal{P}}$. We refer to the vertices of $G_{/\mathcal{P}}$ as nodes to distinguish them and the vertices of G. Thus, the nodes of $G_{/\mathcal{P}}$ are critical cliques, and two nodes are adjacent if and only if the corresponding modules are.

Let K be a critical clique of G and N_K be the set of critical cliques corresponding to the nodes of quotient graph $G_{/\mathcal{P}}$ that are adjacent to K. By Lemma 9.11, we know that for every minimum editing set F of G, K should be contained in some clique C of $G \triangle F$. The next lemma provides more information on the structure of C.

Lemma 9.12 *Let K be a critical clique of G such that*

$$|K| \geq |\bigcup_{K' \in N_K} K'|.$$

Then, there exists a minimum editing set F of G such that the maximal clique C of $G \triangle F$ containing K is a subset of

$$\bigcup_{K' \in N_K} K' \cup K.$$

Proof: Let F be a minimum editing set of G. By Lemma 9.11, we have that $K \subseteq C$ for some maximal clique C of $G \triangle F$. We set $X = \bigcup_{K' \in N_K} K' \cup K$ and define $D = C \setminus X$. Suppose that $D \neq \emptyset$, else the proof is complete. Then, we transform $G \triangle F$ into cluster graph $G \triangle F'$ by deleting D from C and making a new cluster D. Because no vertex from D is adjacent to a vertex from K in G, we have that F should contain $|D| \cdot |K|$ edges between D and K. However, in F', one has to delete the edges of G between $C \cap X$, which by the condition of the lemma, is at most $|\bigcup_{K' \in N_K} K'| \cdot |D| \leq |K| \cdot |D|$. Thus, $|F'| \leq |F|$, and the clique of $G \triangle F'$ containing K is a subset of X. □

The next lemma refines Lemma 9.12. It provides conditions under which it is possible to characterize the maximal clique C of a cluster graph containing a critical clique K of G. For a critical clique K, we denote by N_K^2 the set of critical cliques corresponding to the nodes of the quotient graph $G_{/\mathcal{P}}$ at distance exactly two in $G_{/\mathcal{P}}$ from the node K.

Lemma 9.13 *Let K be a critical clique of G such that*

$$|K| \geq |\bigcup_{K' \in N_K} K'| + |\bigcup_{K' \in N_K^2} K'|.$$

Then, there exists a minimum editing set F of G such that the maximal clique C of $G \triangle F$ containing K is

$$C = \bigcup_{K' \in N_K} K' \cup K.$$

Proof: Let $X = \bigcup_{K' \in N_K} K' \cup K$ and $Y = \bigcup_{K' \in N_K^2} K'$. By Lemmata 9.11 and 9.12, there is a minimum editing set F of G and a maximal clique C of $G \triangle F$ such that $K \subseteq C \subseteq X$. Let us assume that $X' = X \setminus C \neq \emptyset$, else we are done. Then by Lemma 9.11, there is a critical clique $K' \in N_K$ such that $K' \subseteq X'$. Also by the same lemma, there is a maximal clique C' of $G \triangle F$ containing K'.

We construct a new cluster graph $G \triangle F'$ from $G \triangle F$ by moving K' from C' to C. The critical cliques of G corresponding to the neighbors of the node K' in the quotient graph form a subset of $N_K^2 \cup \{K\}$. Then by Lemma 9.12, we have that $C' \subseteq Y$ and by moving K' to C we "lose" at most $|K'| \cdot |Y|$ deleted edges and at most $|K'| \cdot |X|$ added edges. However, we "gain" $|K'| \cdot |K|$ edges that have to be deleted from G in F. Because $|K| \geq |X| + |Y|$, we obtain that the size of the editing set F' is at most $|F|$. As we can repeat this procedure until $X' = \emptyset$, this completes the proof. □

We are now ready to state two reduction rules. The first reduction rule is very natural—if there is an isolated clique in G, it is already a cluster, so there is no need to edit it.

Reduction CE.1 Compute a partition $\mathcal{P} = \mathcal{C}\text{-}\mathcal{M}(G)$ of G into critical cliques. If the quotient graph $G_{/\mathcal{P}}$ contains an isolated node, remove the corresponding critical clique K from G. The new instance is $(G - K, k)$.

Lemma 9.14 *Reduction Rule CE.1 is safe and can be implemented in polynomial time.*

Proof: The rule is safe because isolated critical cliques are connected components of G and require no modifications. By Lemma 9.8, the rule can be implemented in polynomial time. □

The second reduction rule is based on Lemma 9.13.

Reduction CE.2 If there is critical clique K such that

$$|K| \geq |\bigcup_{K' \in N_K} K'| + |\bigcup_{K' \in N_K^2} K'|,$$

then delete from G the set of vertices

$$C = \bigcup_{K' \in N_K} K' \cup K.$$

Let p be the number of edges in G between $G - C$ and C, and let q be the number of nonedges (i.e., the number of edges in the complement) in $G[C]$. The new instance is $(G - C, k - p - q)$.

Let us remark that if our reduction rule outputs an instance with a negative parameter, we conclude that we have a no-instance.

Lemma 9.15 *Reduction Rule CE.2 is safe and can be implemented in polynomial time.*

Proof: The rule is safe by Lemma 9.13. It can be implemented in polynomial time by Lemma 9.8. □

We are ready to proof the main result of this section.

Theorem 9.16 CLUSTER EDITING *admits a 6k-vertex kernel.*

Proof: We apply Reduction Rules CE.1 and CE.2 exhaustively. By Lemmata 9.14 and 9.15, these rules are safe and can be implemented in polynomial time.

Let G be a graph irreducible subject to Reduction Rules CE.1 and CE.2. If (G, k) is a yes-instance, then there is an editing set F of size at most k such that $G \triangle F$ is a cluster graph. If a vertex of G is an endpoint of some edge or nonedge from F, we call such a vertex *affected*. All other vertices of G are called *unaffected*. The number of affected vertices is at most $2k$. We want to bound the number of unaffected vertices of G.

Let us note that due to Reduction Rule CE.1, every maximal clique C of $G \triangle F$ contains affected vertices. Let $U(C)$ be the set of unaffected vertices of C and let $v \in U(C)$. By Lemma 9.11, C should contain a critical clique K containing v. Because K is a module in G and $v \in K$ is unaffected, all vertices of K are unaffected and thus $K \subseteq U(C)$. Moreover, $K = U(C)$. Indeed, if there was another unaffected critical clique $K' \subseteq U(C)$, then $K' \cup K$ also forms a clique-module in G contradicting the maximality of the critical clique K. Thus if C contains unaffected vertices, all these vertices belong to one critical clique K. Then all vertices of the critical cliques from N_K are affected and belong to C. Also because vertices of K are unaffected, all vertices of cliques from N_K^2 cannot be in C and hence are affected. Thus each critical clique consists entirely of either affected or unaffected vertices. We denote the family of critical cliques containing unaffected vertices by $\mathcal{U}$. To bound the number of vertices contained in unaffected critical cliques, we observe that by Reduction Rule CE.2, for every $K \in \mathcal{U}$,

$$|K| < |\bigcup_{K' \in N_K} K'| + |\bigcup_{K' \in N_K^2} K'|.$$

Thus the total number of unaffected vertices is

$$\sum_{K \in \mathcal{U}} |K| < \sum_{K \in \mathcal{U}} \left(|\bigcup_{K' \in N_K} K'| + |\bigcup_{K' \in N_K^2} K'| \right).$$

For every unaffected critical clique K all its neighbors are in the same cluster, and because K is the only unaffected critical clique in this cluster, we have that

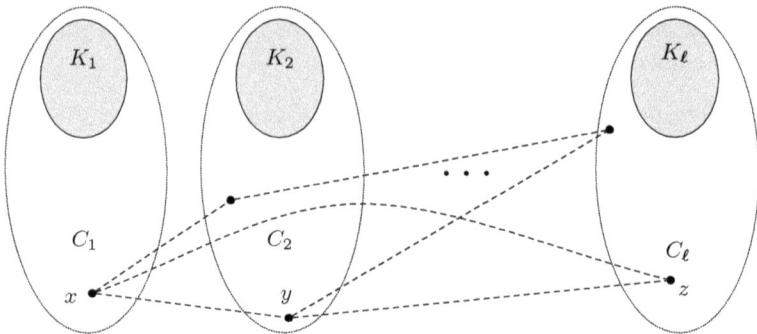

Figure 9.4 Clusters $C_1, \ldots, C_\ell$. Each of the clusters C_i contains a unique unaffected critical clique K_i. The dashed lines indicate edges of G between clusters that have to be deleted.

every affected vertex is counted at most once in the summand $\bigcup_{K' \in N_K} |K'|$. Thus

$$\sum_{K \in \mathcal{U}} |\bigcup_{K' \in N_K} K'| \leq 2k.$$

The vertices of cliques from N_K^2 cannot be in the same cluster as K, and therefore they are affected. It can occur that an affected vertex x is counted in $|\bigcup_{K' \in N_K^2} K'|$ several times. Let $C_1, \ldots, C_\ell$ be the clusters of the resulting cluster graph and K_i be the corresponding unaffected critical cliques contained in these clusters; see Fig. 9.4. If an affected vertex from some cluster is adjacent to affected vertices from other clusters, then this vertex can occur in N_K^2 for several unaffected critical cliques K. For example, in Fig. 9.4, affected vertex y from cluster C_2 is adjacent in G to affected vertices $x \in C_1$ and $z \in C_\ell$ and is counted in $|\bigcup_{K' \in N_K^2} K'|$ at least twice (for $K = K_1$ and $K = K_\ell$). However, the number of times an affected vertex v is counted in $\bigcup_{K' \in N_K^2} |K'|$ does not exceed the number of edges in G going from v to other clusters, and thus does not exceed the number of editing edges of F incident to v. Hence

$$\sum_{K \in \mathcal{U}} |\bigcup_{K' \in N_K^2} K'| \leq 2|F| \leq 2k.$$

We have that the number of unaffected vertices does not exceed $4k$. Because the number of affected vertices is at most $2k$, we have that the total number of vertices in a reduced graph G is at most $6k$. □

9.3 COGRAPH COMPLETION

Let us finally remark that the kernelization algorithm of Theorem 9.16 can be implemented in time $\mathcal{O}(n^3)$, see Exercise 9.7.

9.3 COGRAPH COMPLETION

Cluster graphs, studied in the previous section, can be characterized as graphs having no induced path on three vertices, or P_3-free graphs. Let P_4 be a path on four vertices. A graph G is called a *cograph* if it does not contain P_4 as an induced subgraph. In other words, no four vertices of G induce a P_4. In this section, we would like to analyze such graphs. Let us note that the complement of P_4 is again P_4, and thus the complement $\overline{G}$ of a cograph G is also a cograph.

Let G be a graph. A set $F \subseteq V(G) \times V(G)$ is called a *cograph completion set* for G if the graph $G+F$ with vertex set $V(G)$ and edge set $E(G) \cup F$ is a cograph. In other words, F is a set of nonedges of G such that adding F to G turns it into a cograph. Because a complete graph is a cograph, a cograph completion set always exists. However, identifying the minimum size cograph completion set is a NP-hard optimization problem. We define COGRAPH COMPLETION as follows. For a graph G and a nonnegative integer k, the task is to decide whether there is a cograph completion set for G of cardinality at most k.

A useful property of cographs is that they can be decomposed by making use of two operations, namely disjoint union $\dot{\cup}$ and join $\otimes$. We begin by defining these operations.

Let G and H be disjoint graphs, that is, $V(G) \cap V(H) = \emptyset$. The *disjoint union (parallel composition)* of G and H is the graph $G \dot{\cup} H$ with the vertex set $V(G) \cup V(H)$ and the edge set $E(G) \cup E(H)$. We use $G \otimes H$ to denote the *join (serial composition)* of disjoint graphs G and H: $G \otimes H$ is the graph with the vertex set $V(G) \cup V(G)$ and the edge set $E(G) \cup E(H) \cup \{uv \colon u \in V(G), \in V(H)\})$.

If we have two cographs G_1 and G_2, then clearly their disjoint union $G_1 \dot{\cup} G_2$ is also a cograph. Moreover, if a graph G is a join $G_1 \otimes G_2$, then every P_4 in G entirely belongs to either G_1 or G_2. Therefore, if G_1 and G_2 are cographs, then so is $G_1 \otimes G_2$. It is interesting that the opposite is also true, as formally stated as follows.

Definition 9.17 We say that a graph G is $\{\dot{\cup}, \otimes\}$-decomposable if one of the following conditions is fulfilled:

- $|V(G)| = 1$;
- There are $\{\dot{\cup}, \otimes\}$-decomposable graphs $G_1, \ldots, G_k$ such that $G = G_1 \dot{\cup} G_2 \dot{\cup} \cdots \dot{\cup} G_k$ or

- There are $\{\dot{\cup}, \otimes\}$-decomposable graphs $G_1, \ldots, G_k$ such that $G = G_1 \otimes G_2 \otimes \cdots \otimes G_k$.

We leave the proof of the following lemma as an exercise (Exercise 9.8)

Lemma 9.18 *A graph G is a cograph if and only if it is $\{\dot{\cup}, \otimes\}$-decomposable.*

By Lemma 9.18, with each cograph G one can associate a labeled tree called the *cotree* T_G. Cotree T_G has the following properties:

(i) Each internal vertex v of T_G has label$(v) \in \{\dot{\cup}, \otimes\}$.
(ii) There is a bijection τ between the set of leaves of T_G and $V(G)$.
(iii) To each vertex $v \in (T_G)$ we assign the subgraph G_v of G as follows:

   (a) If v is a leaf then $G_v = (\{\tau(v)\}, \emptyset)$.
   (b) If v is an internal vertex and label$(v) = \dot{\cup}$ then $G_v = G_u \dot{\cup} G_w$, where u, w are the children of v.
   (c) If v is an internal vertex and label$(v) = \otimes$ then $G_v = G_u \times G_w$, where u, w are the children of v.

Notice that if r is the root of T_G then $G_r = G$. It is always possible to construct T_G such that no pair of adjacent nodes of T_G have the same label. In other words, for every node labeled by $\dot{\cup}$, all its children are either leaves or labeled by $\otimes$ and for every node labeled by $\otimes$, all its children are either leaves or labeled by $\dot{\cup}$. We will always assume that we have a cotree with this property. Moreover, it is possible to show that such a tree can be constructed in time $\mathcal{O}(n + m)$. (Such a construction will not be given here.) See Fig. 9.5 with an example of a cograph and its cotree.

9.3.1 Minimum Completions and Properties of Modules

A cograph completion set $F \subseteq V(G) \times V(G)$ of minimum size is referred to as a *minimum cograph completion set*, or just as a *minimum completion set*. Let $\mathcal{C}$ be the class of cographs. Our reduction rules are based on properties of $\mathcal{C}$-modules and minimum completion sets.

If an input graph G has a connected component G_1 that is a cograph, then a cograph H with minimum number of edges containing G can be obtained from a disjoint union of a minimum cograph supergraph containing $G - V(G_1)$ and G_1. Similarly, if G has a *universal* cograph G_1, that is, every vertex of G_1 is adjacent to all vertices of $V(G) \setminus V(G_1)$, then a cograph H with minimum number of edges containing G can be obtained from a join of a

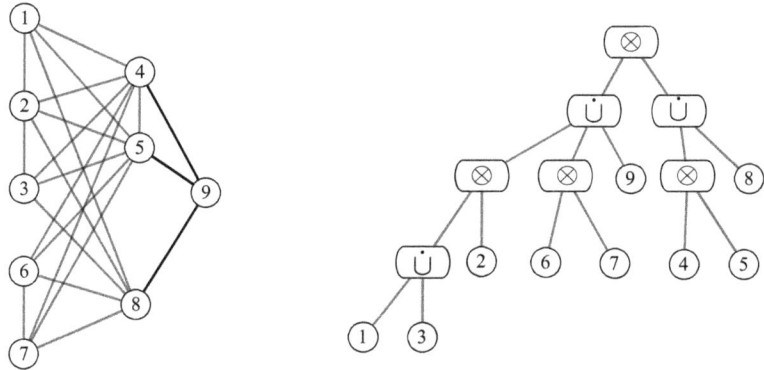

Figure 9.5 An example of a cograph and its cotree.

minimum cograph supergraph containing $G - V(G_1)$ and G_1. We summarize these observations in the following lemma.

Lemma 9.19 *Let G be graph and G_1 be a cograph such that either $G = G_1 \dot{\cup} G_2$ or $G = G_1 \otimes G_2$. Then F is a minimum completion set of G if and only if F is a minimum completion set of $G - V(G_1)$.*

Our next goal is to show that for each module there is a minimum completion set "preserving" this module. To this end, we need the following lemma.

Lemma 9.20 *If M is a module of G, then for every set of vertices X inducing a P_4 in G, either $X \subseteq M$, or $|X \cap M| \leq 1$.*

Proof: We want to prove that if a P_4, say P, intersects a module M, then the intersection consists of exactly four vertices or exactly one vertex. If P intersects M and is not contained in M, then there is an edge xy of P such that $x \notin M$ and $y \in M$. If P contains three vertices from M, then all these vertices (M is a module) are also adjacent to x, which cannot occur in a P_4. Thus, next suppose by way of contradiction that P contains exactly two vertices $y, z \in M$ and exactly two vertices outside $w, x \notin M$, else the proof is complete. Because M is module, y and z are both adjacent to x. Then the only way to construct P from these vertices is to make w adjacent to z but not to y, or to y but not to z. However, in both cases we obtain a contradiction to the assumption that M is a module. □

We now turn to consider the preservation of modules.

Lemma 9.21 *Let G be a graph and M be a module of G. There is a minimum completion set F of G such that M is a module in the graph $G + F$.*

Proof: Let F be a minimum completion set of G and let M be a module in G. Suppose that M is not a module in $G + F$. Then, in the graph $G + F$ we select a vertex v of M with the minimum number of neighbors in $V(G) \setminus M$. Let N_v be the set of neighbors of v outside M, that is,

$$N_v = \{u \mid u \in V(G) \setminus M \text{ and } uv \in E(G) \cup F\}.$$

We construct a new set F' from F. The only difference between F and F' lies in edges between M and $V(G) \setminus M$. For every vertex $u \in M$, we delete all edges of F incident to u and a vertex of $V(G) \setminus M$, and make u adjacent to N_v. Then, $|F'| \leq |F|$ (due to our specific choice of v), and in the graph $G + F'$, the set M is a module—the neighborhood of every vertex of M outside M is exactly N_v.

It remains to show is that F' is a completion set. Assume that it is not. Then there is an induced P_4 in $G + F'$. Let V_P be the vertex set of this P_4. Because all edges of $F \triangle F'$ are between M and $V(G) \setminus M$, the set V_P can be entirely contained neither in M nor in $V(G) \setminus M$. Moreover, by Lemma 9.20 and because M is a module in $G + F'$, we have that V_P cannot contain two or three vertices of M. The only possibility left then is that V_P contains exactly one vertex $w \in M$. Because M is a module in $G + F'$, we have that set $V_P \setminus \{w\} \cup \{v\}$ also induces a P_4 in $G + F'$, and hence in $G + F$. However, this is a contradiction. Therefore, F' is a completion set, and because $|F'| \leq |F|$, F' is a minimum completion set. □

The following lemma exhibits a useful behavior of modules under minimum completions. If M is a module of a graph G, then computing a minimum completion set of G can be separated into two independent tasks: finding a minimum completion set of $G[M]$ and finding a minimum completion set of the remaining part of the graph. In particular, for the reduction rules discussed later, this argument will allow us to transform M into a simple clique-module and then to deal with a new graph and $G[M]$ separately. Specifically, we need the following lemma.

Lemma 9.22 *Let G be graph and M be a module of G. Let G_1 be the graph obtained from G by turning M into a clique and G_2 be a graph isomorphic to G[M]. Then (G, k) is a yes-instance of* COGRAPH COMPLETION *if and only if $(G' := G_1 \dot\cup G_2, k)$ is.*

Proof: Let F be a minimum completion set of graph G such that M is a module in $G + F$ (the existence of such F is guaranteed by Lemma 9.21). Now, let F_M

be the set of edges of F with both endpoints in M. In the graph $G + F$, module M induces a cograph, and thus G_2 can be completed into a cograph by adding at most $|F_M|$ edges. We claim that $G_1 + (F \setminus F_M)$ is a cograph. Indeed, if this is not the case, this graph should contain a set of vertices X inducing a P_4. Let us note that M should contain more than one vertex from X because otherwise X induces P_4 in $G + F$ as well. Because M is a module in $G + F$, and hence in $G_1 + (F \setminus F_M)$, by Lemma 9.20, M should contain X. However, in G_1 the vertices of M form a clique, and thus X cannot induce P_4 in $G_1 + (F \setminus F_M)$. However, this is a contradiction to our choice of X. Therefore, there is a completion of G' into a cograph with at most $|F|$ edges.

The proof of the opposite direction, which states that there is a minimum completion of G' that can be transformed into a minimum completion of G, is similar. This proof is given as Exercise 9.9. □

The next lemma will be used to reduce the sizes of clique-modules.

Lemma 9.23 *Let G be a graph and M be a clique-module of G such that $|M| > k + 1$. Let G' be the graph obtained from G by removing all but $k + 1$ vertices from M. Then, (G, k) is a yes-instance of* COGRAPH COMPLETION *if and only if (G', k) is.*

Proof: If (G, k) is a yes-instance, then by Lemma 9.21, there is a minimum completion F, $|F| \leq k$, of G such that M is a module in $G + F$. Thus either no edge or at least $|M|$ edges of F cross from M to $V(G) \setminus M$. This yields that if the size of M is more than k, no edge of F is incident to M. In this situation, G' has a cograph completion set of size k if and only if G does. □

9.3.2 Reduction Rules

Having established several properties of modules, we are ready to state our reduction rules. The safeness of the first two reduction rules follows from Lemma 9.19. Both rules are clearly implementable in polynomial time.

> **Reduction CC.1** If G contains a connected component C that is a cograph, then delete C from G. The new instance is $(G - C, k)$.

> **Reduction CC.2** If G contains a vertex subset $V_1 \subseteq V(G)$ inducing a universal cograph, that is, such that $G_1 = G[V_1]$ is a cograph and $G = G_1 \otimes (G - V_1)$, then delete V_1 from G. The new instance is $(G - V_1, k)$.

The safeness of the following reduction rule follows from Lemma 9.22. Recall that by Lemma 9.5, we can compute the graph $\mathcal{SP}(G)$, which provides complete information about maximal modules, in polynomial time. This allows us to implement the rule in polynomial time.

Reduction CC.3 If G contains a module M that is not a clique-module and such that $G[M]$ is not a connected component of G, then construct the following graphs. Let G_1 be the graph obtained from G by turning M into a clique, G_2 be a graph isomorphic to $G[M]$ and $G' := G_1 \dot\cup G_2$. The new instance is (G', k).

The next rule is safe by Lemma 9.23. It also can be implemented in polynomial time because a maximal clique-module can be found in polynomial time by Lemma 9.13.

Reduction CC.4 If G contains a clique-module M such that $|M| > k+1$, then construct G' from G by removing all but $k+1$ vertices from M. The new instance is (G', k).

We will need one more reduction rule, which will be used to handle a scenario, occurring in the proof of Theorem 9.29, where a cotree of the resulting cograph can contain a long path with unaffected vertices.

Reduction CC.5 Let x and y be nonadjacent vertices of G, such that there is a set $\mathcal{P}$ of $k+1$ induced P_4s of the form form $v - y - u - x$, such that every pair of distinct P_4s from $\mathcal{P}$ has exactly x and y in common. Then, construct G' from G by adding the edge xy. The new instance is $(G', k-1)$. See Fig. 9.6.

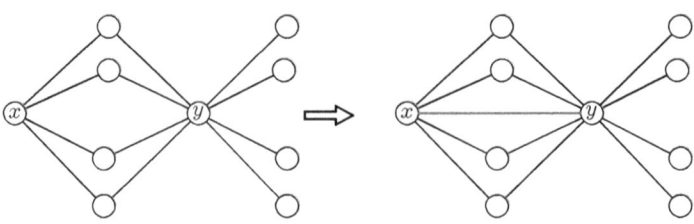

Figure 9.6 An example of an application of Reduction Rule CC.5 for $k = 3$.

Lemma 9.24 *Reduction Rule CC.5 is safe and can be implemented in polynomial time.*

Proof: The edge xy has to be added because otherwise we need at least $k+1$ edges to eliminate all P_4s from $\mathcal{P}$.

To decide in polynomial time if a pair of nonadjacent vertices x and y satisfies conditions of the rule, we do the following. For every pair of nonadjacent vertices x, y, define $X = N_G(x) \cap N_G(y)$ and $Y = N_G(y) \setminus N_G(x)$, and construct a bipartite graph G_{xy} with bipartition (X, Y) such that $u \in X$ is adjacent to $v \in Y$ if and only if uv is not an edge of G. It is easy to check that a vertex set $\{x, y, u, v\}$ induces a P_4 in G of the form form $v - y - u - x$ if and only of u is not adjacent to v in G_{xy}. Thus, checking the conditions of the reduction rule is reduced to checking if the constructed bipartite graph G_{xy} has a matching of size $k+1$, which can be done in polynomial time. □

9.3.3 Least Common Ancestor Closure

Before completing the polynomial kernel for COGRAPH COMPLETION, we take a short detour and discuss an operation on vertex sets in rooted trees. This operation turns out to be useful in many different settings.

Let T be a rooted tree and u and v be vertices in $V(T)$. We allow u and v to be the same vertex. We define the *least common ancestor* $\text{LCA}(u, v)$ of u and v to be the lowermost node x, which is an ancestor both of u and of v. We are now ready to define the least common ancestor closure of a vertex set.

Definition 9.25 Let T be a rooted tree and S be a set of vertices in T. We define the *least common ancestor closure* of S to be the set

$$\text{LCA-Closure}(S) = \{LCA(u, v) \colon u, v \in S\}.$$

Here u and v are not necessarily distinct.

Next we show that for any set S, the set LCA-Closure(S) is actually closed under the least common ancestor operation. Thus, LCA-Closure(S) is the smallest superset of S that is closed under taking least common ancestors, explaining the name "least common ancestor closure."

Lemma 9.26 *Let T be a rooted tree, $S \subset V(T)$ and $M = \text{LCA-Closure}(S)$. Then,* $\text{LCA-Closure}(M) = M$.

Proof: First observe that $M \subseteq \text{LCA-Closure}(M)$ because every vertex v satisfies $v = \text{LCA}(v, v)$. We now show that $\text{LCA-Closure}(M) \subseteq M$. Toward a contradiction, suppose this claim is false, and let $x \in \text{LCA-Closure}(M) \setminus M$.

Then, $x = \text{LCA}(u,v)$ where u and v are both in M. Because x is not in M, it follows that u and v belong to different subtrees below x. Because u belongs to LCA-Closure(S), it follows that $u \in S$ or u has a descendant $u' \in S$. If $u \in S$, then we set $u' = u$. Similarly, either $v \in S$, in which case we set $v' = v$, or v has a descendant $v' \in S$. Thus, u' and v' are both in S, and x is the least common ancestor of u' and v', contradicting that $x \notin M$. □

The properties of $M = \text{LCA-Closure}(S)$ that make this operation useful are that each connected component of $T - M$ has at most two neighbors, and that the size of M is bounded linearly in the size of S. We now prove these two properties.

Lemma 9.27 *Let T be a rooted tree, $S \subseteq V(T)$ and $M = \text{LCA-Closure}(S)$. Then, each connected component C of $T - M$ satisfies $|N(C)| \leq 2$.*

Proof: Let C be some connected component of $T - M$. Let r be the unique vertex in C that is closest to the root of T. Note that each vertex in C is a descendant of r. Thus, all neighbors of C, except for the parent of r, are descendants of r. It follows that if $|N(C)| \geq 3$ then there are two distinct vertices $u, v \in N(C)$ that both are descendants of r. Because C is a component of $T - M$, it follows that u and v are both in M. Let $x = \text{LCA}(u,v)$. By Lemma 9.26, we have that $x \in M$. However, both u and v are descendants of r, and therefore x must be a descendant of r as well. But then $x \in C$, contradicting that $C \cap M = \emptyset$. □

Lemma 9.28 *Let T be a rooted tree, $S \subseteq V(T)$ and $M = \text{LCA-Closure}(S)$. Then, $|M| \leq 2|S| - 1$.*

Proof: It suffices to show that $|M \setminus S| \leq |S| - 1$. Consider a vertex u in $M \setminus S$. We have that u is the least common ancestor of two different nodes of S. Thus, there are at least two different subtrees of T rooted at u containing vertices from S. Let now T' be the tree obtained from T by repeatedly contracting edges that do not have both endpoints in M. Because there are at least two different subtrees of T rooted at u containing vertices from S, u must have at least two children in T'. Thus the degree of u in T' is at least 3, unless u is the root of T', in which case u has degree at least 2. It follows that the sum of the degrees of all the vertices in T' is at least $|S| + 3|M \setminus S| - 1$. Because T' has $|M|$ vertices and $|M| - 1 = |S| + |M \setminus S| - 1$ edges, it follows that

$$2|S| + 2|M \setminus S| - 2 \geq |S| + 3|M \setminus S| - 1.$$

Rearranging the terms of this inequality completes the proof the lemma. □

9.3.4 Putting Things Together: Kernel for COGRAPH COMPLETION

We are ready to proceed to the main theorem of this section. However, before we present the proof, let us outline the main ideas.

- For a reduced connected graph G, we consider its minimum completion set F of size at most k. Thus, $G+F$ is a cograph. In the cotree T of $G+F$ the leaves of T correspond to vertices of G, and other nodes of T (we call them nodes to distinguish them from vertices of G) correspond to join and union operations. There are at most $2k$ vertices of G adjacent to edges of F. We say that the nodes in the LCA-Closure of these vertices in T are *affected nodes*. Thus, there are at most $4k$ affected nodes. To bound the size of G, we want to bound the number of nodes of T.
- The crucial observation is that if we take an unaffected node a such that the subtree T_a rooted at a has no affected nodes as well, then the set of leaves of T_a is a module in G. But then by Reduction Rule CC.3, the leaves of T_a form a clique in G, while by Reduction Rule CC.4, the size of this clique is at most $k+1$.
- Thus to bound the number of vertices in T it is sufficient to bound the maximum number of unaffected nodes that can occur on a path between two affected nodes. Here it is possible to show that the length of such a path cannot be larger than $3k+5$ because otherwise it is possible to show that G contains $k+1$ disjoint P_4s on the same endpoints, and thus Reduction Rule CC.5 should have come into play.
- Finally, if G is not connected, then by Reduction Rule CC.1, every connected component of G is not a cograph. Thus G cannot have more than k connected components, and we can apply kernelization for each connected component individually.

Theorem 9.29 COGRAPH COMPLETION *admits a kernel with $\mathcal{O}(k^3)$ vertices.*

Proof: Let G be a graph such that none of the preceding reduction rules can be applied to it. Let us assume first that G is connected and consider the case in which G is non-connected later. Let F be a minimum completion set of size at most k. Thus $G + F$ is a cograph. Let T be a cotree of $G + F$. We bound the number of vertices in G by bounding the number of nodes in T.

The leaves of T correspond to the vertices of $G + F$, and slightly abusing the notation, we will not distinguish between leaves of T and vertices of G. We call a node of tree T *affected* if it is either a leaf incident to an edge of F, or is a least common ancestor of two affected nodes. In other words, the set of affected nodes of T is the least ancestor closure of leaves incident to edges of F. Because there are at most $2|F|$ vertices incident to edges of F, by Lemma 9.28, the total number of affected nodes is at most $4|F|$.

Let a be a node of T. The subtree T_a of T rooted at a has the following property, crucial for our analysis:

Claim 9.30 If there is no edge of F with one endpoint being a leaf of T_a and the other endpoint outside T_a, then the leaves of T_a form a module in G. In this case, by Reduction Rules CC.3 and CC.4, the leaves of T_a form (in G) a clique of size at most $k + 1$.

Let us note that the root r of T is affected and labeled by $\otimes$. Indeed, if r was labeled by $\dot{\cup}$, then $G + F$, and hence G, is not connected. Thus, r is labeled by $\otimes$. If r was unaffected, then it should have contained a child a such that the subtree T_a rooted at a has no affected nodes. But then the leaves of T_a induce a cograph that is universal in G. By Reduction Rule CC.2, such vertices have to be removed from G.

We claim now that

Claim 9.31 No path in T from the root to a leaf can contain more that $3k + 5$ consecutive unaffected nodes.

Proof of the claim: Suppose that there is a path P in T from the root r to a leaf containing at least $3k + 5$ consecutive unaffected nodes. We select a subpath of P of unaffected nodes of the form $x_1 x_2 \cdots x_{3k+5}$ with x_1 being the closest node to r. We claim that there is an affected leaf x such that

- x is a descendant of node x_{2k+3} and
- There is a leaf y that is not in the subtree rooted at x_1 and $xy \in F$. See Fig. 9.7.

Indeed, by Claim 9.30, if there is no edge of F from $T_{x_{2k+3}}$ to some node y outside $T_{x_{2k+3}}$, then the leaves of $T_{x_{2k+3}}$ form a module M in G. In this case, by Reduction Rules CC.4 and CC.3, the size of M is at most $k+1$. However, $T_{x_{2k+3}}$ contains at least $k+2$ leaves, which is a contradiction. Because all nodes x_i are unaffected, we conclude that the node y should be outside not only $T_{x_{2k+3}}$, but T_{x_1} as well.

By the preceding arguments, we can select a subpath

$$P' = u_1 s_1 u_2 s_2 \cdots u_{k+1} s_{k+1}$$

of P rooted at u_1 with the following properties. In path P' all vertices are unaffected, s_i is the child of u_i and u_1 is the end of P' closest to r. Every node u_i is labeled by the union label $\dot{\cup}$, and every node s_i is labeled by the serial

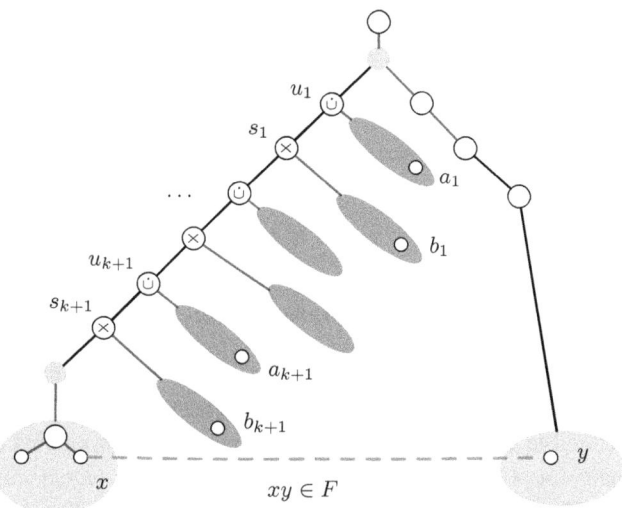

Figure 9.7 Path P' in T.

composition label $\otimes$. Moreover, there is an affected leaf x that is a descendant of node s_{k+1} and this leaf is adjacent in F to a leaf y that is not in the subtree rooted at u_1. See Fig. 9.7.

Because $xy \in F$, we know that x and y are nonadjacent in G. For every node u_i and s_i, all branches rooted at these nodes, except the one containing leaf x, consist only of unaffected nodes. Thus for every $i \in \{1, \ldots, k+1\}$, we can select nonaffected leaf-descendants a_i of u_i and b_i of s_i. Because a_i is unaffected and u_i is a union node, we have that $a_i x \notin E(G)$. Similarly, we have that $b_i x \in E(G)$. Because $xy \in F$ and vertices a_i and b_i are unaffected for $i \in \{1, \ldots, k+1\}$, we conclude that y is adjacent to all vertices a_i and b_i. Thus each quadruple $\{x, y, a_i, b_i\}$ induces a P_4 in G of the form $a_i - y - b_i - x$; see Fig. 9.8. Then, by Reduction Rule CC.5, x and y should be adjacent in G. This is a contradiction, and the claim follows. □

We continue with the proof of the theorem.

Let T' be a minimal subtree of T spanning all affected nodes. Because the number of affected nodes is at most $4|F|$, by Claim 9.31, the number of nodes in T' is at most $4|F| \cdot (3k+5)$. By Claim 9.30, the union of unaffected branches of T rooted at one vertex of T' is a module, and thus of size at most $k+1$. Hence the total number of nodes in T, and thus also the vertices in G, is in $\mathcal{O}(|F| \cdot k^2)$. Thus if G is a reduced connected graph, then it has $\mathcal{O}(|F| \cdot k^2)$ vertices.

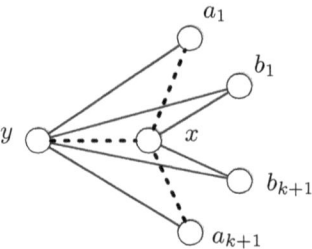

Figure 9.8 Constructing $k+1$ P_4s in G.

If G is not connected, it has at most k connected components. Indeed, by Reduction Rule CC.1, every connected component of G is not a cograph. Thus an irreducible graph with more than k connected components is trivially a no-instance. Let $G_1, G_2, \ldots, G_\ell$, $\ell \leq k$, be the connected components of G, and let F_i be a minimum completion set for G_i. Then by applying kernelization arguments for each connected component, we obtain a kernel with $\sum_{1 \leq i \leq \ell} \mathcal{O}(|F_i| \cdot k^2)$ vertices. Because $\sum_{1 \leq i \leq \ell} |F_i| \leq k$, we obtain a kernel with $\mathcal{O}(k^3)$ vertices and the theorem follows. □

9.4 FAST Revisited

In the beginning of the book (Section 2.3) we gave an example of a simple $\mathcal{O}(k^2)$-vertex kernel for the problem of reverting at most k arcs in a tournament to obtain an acyclic graph, the FAST problem. Now we use modules to present a better kernel. To this end, we first need to extend the notion of module to directed graphs.

Definition 9.32 A *module* of a digraph D is a subset $M \subseteq V(D)$, such that for every $u, v \in M$, we have $N^+(u) \setminus M = N^+(v) \setminus M$ and $N^-(u) \setminus M = N^-(v) \setminus M$, where $N^-(v), N^+(v)$ are the sets of in-neighbors and out-neighbors of v, respectively.

As in undirected graphs, we can define strong and nontrivial modules. In tournaments we will be interested in a special type of modules, namely *maximal transitive-modules*. A module M is a *maximal transitive-module* if $M \neq V(T)$, M induces an acyclic tournament and there is no nontrivial transitive module properly containing M.

In a manner similar to the case of undirected graphs, we have the following result about modules in tournaments. We leave the proof of the theorem as Exercise 9.11.

9.4 FAST Revisited

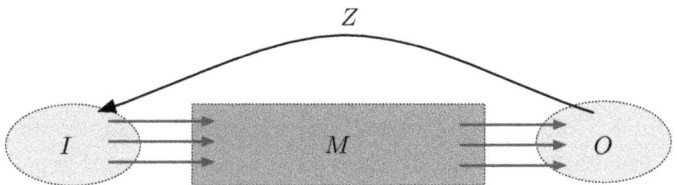

Figure 9.9 An illustration for Reduction Rule FAST.3.

Theorem 9.33 *Let T be a tournament. Then, the maximal transitive-modules of T form a partition of $V(T)$. Moreover, such a partition can be found in polynomial time.*

Before we proceed, ket us recall the following useful observation (Exercise 2.6) about FAST: instead of deleting the arcs of a feedback arc set F, one can obtain an acyclic graph also by reversing the arcs of F.

As we discussed in Section 2.3, a combination of Reduction Rules FAST.1 and FAST.2 brings us to a kernel for FAST with a quadratic number of vertices. We now add a new reduction rule. This rule allows us to obtain a kernel with a subquadratic number of vertices.

Reduction FAST.3 Let M be a maximal transitive-module and I and O be the sets of in-neighbors and out-neighbors of the vertices of M in tournament T, respectively. Let Z be the set of arcs uv such that $u \in O$ and $v \in I$. See Fig. 9.9. If $|M| \geq |Z|$, then construct the new tournament T' from T by reversing all arcs from Z. The new instance is $(T', k - |Z|)$.

Lemma 9.34 *Reduction Rule FAST.3 is safe and can be applied in polynomial time.*

Proof: Let k_I be the size of a minimum feedback arc set for $T[I]$, and k_O be the size of a minimum feedback arc set for $T[O]$. The crucial observation is that because M is a module and $|M| \geq |Z|$, we have that the union of Z and the set of arcs from I to M and from M to O contains at least $|Z|$ arc-disjoint triangles. Thus, the size of every feedback arc set of T is at least $k_I + k_O + |Z|$. However, a feedback vertex set of size $k_I + k_O + |Z|$ can be obtained by reversing k_I arcs in $T[I]$, k_O arcs in $T[O]$ and the arcs of Z. To see that the resulting tournament is transitive, one can take the following transitive ordering. First we position the vertices of I, then we take a transitive ordering of M, and then of O.

Thus, the minimum size of a feedback arc set for T is $k_I + k_O + |Z|$, and by reversing arcs of Z, we obtain a tournament with a feedback arc set of size $k_I + k_O$. This implies that the rule is safe. Because by Theorem 9.33, we can find a partition of T into maximal transitive-modules in polynomial time, it follows that the reduction rule can be also implemented in polynomial time. □

We are ready to estimate the size of the kernel obtained from Reduction Rules FAST.2, FAST.1 and FAST.3.

Theorem 9.35 FAST *admits a kernel with* $\mathcal{O}(k\sqrt{k})$ *vertices.*

Proof: Let (T,k) be a yes-instance of FAST that has been reduced according to Reduction Rules FAST.2, FAST.1 and FAST.3. We claim that T has $\mathcal{O}(k\sqrt{k})$ vertices.

Let F be a feedback arc set of T of size at most k and let T' be the tournament obtained from T by reversing all the arcs from F. By Lemma 2.5, T' admits a transitive ordering $\sigma = v_1, v_2, \ldots, v_n$. We order the vertices of T according to σ. Then each arc of F in this ordering is a *backward* arc, that is each of the arcs of F is of the form $v_j v_i$, where $i < j$. For a backward arc $e = v_j v_i$, the *span* of e is the set $S(e) = \{v_i, \ldots, v_j\}$. The number of vertices in $S(e)$ is called the *length* of e and is denoted by $\ell(e)$. Thus, for every arc $e = v_i v_j$, $\ell(e) = |i-j|+1$. For every vertex $v \in S(e)$, we say that e is *above* v.

We say that a vertex is *affected* if it is incident with some arc in F. The number of affected vertices is at most $2|F| \leq 2k$. Reduction Rule FAST.2 ensures that vertices v_1 and v_n are affected. Indeed, if v_1 is not affected then it is a source vertex in T (vertex with in-degree 0), hence it is not part of any triangle and Reduction Rule FAST.2 would have applied. We can similarly argue for the last vertex v_n.

Next, we argue that there is no backward arc e of length greater than $2k+2$. Assume to the contrary that $e = uv$ is a backward arc with $\ell(e) > 2k+2$ and let $S(e) = \{v, x_1, x_2, \ldots, x_{2k+1}, \ldots, u\}$. Consider the collection of triples $\mathcal{T} = \{vx_i u \mid 1 \leq i \leq 2k\}$ and observe that at most k of these triples can contain an arc from $F \setminus \{e\}$; hence, there exist at least $k+1$ triplets in $\mathcal{T}$ which correspond to distinct triangles all containing e. However, then e would have been reversed by an application of Reduction Rule FAST.1. Thus, there is no backward arc e of length greater than $2k+2$ in T according to the ordering σ, and therefore $\sum_{e \in F} \ell(e) \leq k(2k+2)$.

Note between two consecutive affected vertices we can have only one maximal transitive-module of T. We denote by t_i the number of vertices in these modules, where $i \in \{1, \ldots, 2k-1\}$. Thus the number of unaffected vertices does not exceed $\sum_{i=1}^{2k-1} t_i$. Thanks to Reduction Rule FAST.3, there are at least t_i backward arcs above every module with t_i vertices, each of length at least t_i. This implies that

$$\sum_{i=1}^{2k-1} t_i^2 \le \sum_{e \in F} \ell(e) \le 2k^2 + 2k.$$

By making use of the Cauchy-Schwarz inequality, we derive that

$$\sum_{i=1}^{2k-1} t_i = \sum_{i=1}^{2k-1} t_i \cdot 1 \le \sqrt{\sum_{i=1}^{2k-1} t_i^2 \cdot \sum_{i=1}^{2k-1} 1} \le \sqrt{(2k^2 + 2k) \cdot (2k - 1)}$$

$$= \sqrt{4k^3 + 2k^2 - 2k}.$$

Thus, every reduced yes-instance has at most $\sqrt{4k^3 + 2k^2 - 2k} + 2k = \mathcal{O}(k\sqrt{k})$ vertices. □

Exercises

Problem 9.1 (✐) If M is a module in G, then it is also a module in $\overline{G}$.

Problem 9.2 (✐) Let M_1 and M_2 be two modules of G whose intersection is nonempty. Show that the following vertex sets are modules:

(i) $M_1 \cup M_2$;
(ii) $M_1 \cap M_2$;
(iii) $M_1 \triangle M_2 = (M_1 \cup M_2) \setminus (M_1 \cap M_2)$; and
(iv) $M_1 \setminus M_2$.

Problem 9.3 (✐) If M_1 and M_2 are disjoint modules, then either every vertex of M_1 is a neighbor of every vertex of M_2, or no vertex of M_1 is adjacent to any vertex of M_2.

Problem 9.4 Every two distinct maximal strong modules M_1 and M_2 are disjoint.

Problem 9.5 If X is a module of G and Y is a subset of X, then Y is a module of G if and only if it is a module of $G[X]$.

Problem 9.6 Let $\mathcal{G}$ be either the set of all cliques or the set of all independent sets, and G be an undirected graph. Show that $\mathcal{G}$-$\mathcal{SP}(G)$ can be computed in polynomial time.

Problem 9.7 Show that Reduction Rules CE.1 and CE.2 can be implemented in $\mathcal{O}(n^3)$ time.

Problem 9.8 Prove Lemma 9.18: A graph G is a cograph if and only if it is $\{\dot{\cup}, \otimes\}$-decomposable.

Problem 9.9 Prove the reverse direction of Lemma 9.22.

Problem 9.10 Show the following:

- A cograph is a graph all of whose induced subgraphs have the property that every maximal clique intersects every maximal independent set in a single vertex.
- A cograph is a graph G in which every nontrivial induced subgraph F has at least two vertices with the same neighborhood in F.
- A cograph is a graph in which the complement of every connected induced subgraph is disconnected.

Problem 9.11 Prove Theorem 9.33.

Bibliographic Notes

Modular partitions is a classical subject in Graph Theory and algorithms. Modules and their decompositions were introduced by Gallai (1967) in his study of the structure of comparability graphs. We refer to the surveys Möhring and Radermacher (1984), and Habib and Paul (2010) for detailed discussions on different generalizations and applications of modules. The first linear time algorithm to compute the modular decomposition tree of a graph is due to McConnell and Spinrad (1999); see the survey Habib and Paul (2010) for additional references to different types of algorithms for modular decompositions. For a simple time $\mathcal{O}(n+m)$ algorithm finding strong modules in a tournament, see the work of McConnell and de Montgolfier (2005). Corneil et al. (1985) gave an $O(n+m)$ algorithm for determining whether a given graph G is a cograph and, if so, for constructing the corresponding cotree.

The first polynomial kernel for CLUSTER EDITING was given by Gramm et al. (2005). Our presentation of the $6k$-vertex kernel for CLUSTER EDITING follows Guo (2009), which also gave a $4k$-vertex kernel. Later, Cao and Chen (2012) and Chen and Meng (2012) gave a $2k$-vertex kernel. The CLUSTER EDITING was proven to be NP-hard independently by Shamir et al. (2004), Chen et al. (2003) and Bansal et al. (2004). Our presentation of the kernel for

COGRAPH COMPLETION follows Guillemot et al. (2013), who also gave a kernel for the editing version of the problem.

COGRAPH COMPLETION is a special case of a more general problem, $\mathcal{F}$-COMPLETION, where for a family of graphs $\mathcal{F}$, the task is to decide whether there exists a supergraph $G + FS$ of G, such that $|F| \leq k$ and $G + F$ contains no graph from $\mathcal{F}$ as an induced subgraph. COGRAPH COMPLETION is $\mathcal{F}$-COMPLETION for $\mathcal{F} = \{P_4\}$. Even for the case of finite families $\mathcal{F}$, we do not know when $\mathcal{F}$-COMPLETION admits a polynomial kernel. Guo (2007) initiated the study of kernelization algorithms for $\mathcal{F}$-COMPLETION in the case when the forbidden set $\mathcal{F}$ contains the graph C_4 and some other classes of C_4-free graphs. Kratsch and Wahlström (2009) have shown that there exists a set $\mathcal{F}$ consisting of one graph on seven vertices for which $\mathcal{F}$-COMPLETION does not admit a polynomial kernel. Guillemot et al. (2013) showed that when $\mathcal{F} = \{\overline{P}_{13}\}$, where $\overline{P}_{13}$ is the complement of a path on 13 vertices, $\mathcal{F}$-COMPLETION has no polynomial kernel. These results were significantly improved by Cai and Cai (2015): For $\mathcal{F} = \{P_\ell\}$ or $\mathcal{F} = \{C_\ell\}$, the problems $\mathcal{F}$-COMPLETION and $\mathcal{F}$-DELETION admit a polynomial kernel if and only if the forbidden graph has at most three edges. Much less is known for $\mathcal{F}$-EDITING.

The first polynomial kernel for FAST with $\mathcal{O}(k^2)$ vertices is due to Dom et al. (2010). The kernel with $\mathcal{O}(k^{1.5})$ vertices presented in this chapter is from the work of Bessy et al. (2011), who also gave a kernel with $(2 + \varepsilon)k$ vertices. For bipartite tournaments, polynomials kernels of sizes $\mathcal{O}(k^3)$ and $\mathcal{O}(k^3)$, which are based on the use of modules, were given by Misra et al. (2013) and Xiao and Guo (2015), respectively. For FEEDBACK VERTEX SET IN TOURNAMENTS, the best known kernel has $\mathcal{O}(k^{1.5})$ vertices due to Le et al. (2018).

10
Matroids

Matroids generalize several fundamental notions from Graph Theory and linear algebra, and they are employed as a powerful tool in combinatorial optimization. In this chapter, as well as the next one, we describe techniques based on matroids that are used to design kernelization algorithms. To make these chapters self-contained, we start by providing all necessary basic definitions. For a broader overview on matroids, we refer to the bibliography provided at the end of this chapter.

In this chapter, we introduce the notion of a matroid. We will see that matroids, particularly linear matroids, can represent information compactly. Here, we will see the Cut-Flow data structure as an example of such representation. In turn, we will utilize this data structure to obtain a (randomized) polynomial compression for the ODD CYCLE TRANSVERSAL problem. Apart from the possibility of representing information compactly, matroids also give rise to the application of the irrelevant vertex technique, as we will see in the next chapter.

10.1 Matroid Basics

Let us begin by defining the notion of a matroid.

Definition 10.1 A pair $M = (E, \mathcal{I})$, where E is a ground set and $\mathcal{I}$ is a family of subsets (called *independent sets*) of E, is a *matroid* if it satisfies the following conditions, called *matroid axioms*:

(I1) $\phi \in \mathcal{I}$.
(I2) If $A' \subseteq A$ and $A \in \mathcal{I}$ then $A' \in \mathcal{I}$.
(I3) If $A, B \in \mathcal{I}$ and $|A| < |B|$, then there is $e \in (B \setminus A)$ such that $A \cup \{e\} \in \mathcal{I}$.

Axiom (I2) is also called an *hereditary property*, and a pair $(E, \mathcal{I})$ satisfying only axiom (I2) is called a *hereditary family*. An inclusion-wise maximal set in $\mathcal{I}$ is a *basis* of the matroid M. Using axiom (I3) it is easy to show that all the bases of a matroid are of the same size. This size is called the *rank* of the matroid M, and it is denoted by rank(M). The *rank* of a subset $A \subseteq E$ is the maximum size of an independent set contained in A.

Let us give several examples of well-known matroids. The first example comes from linear algebra. Let us take a look at any finite subset E of a vector space. Every subset of a linearly independent subset of E is also linearly independent. By the basic theorem of linear algebra known as Steinitz exchange lemma, for every linearly independent sets A and B such that $|A| < |B|$, there is $e \in B$ such that $A \cup \{e\}$ is linearly independent. Thus, the following defines a matroid.

Linear and representable matroids. Let A be a matrix over an arbitrary field $\mathbb{F}$, and let E be the set of columns of A. We associate a matroid $M = (E, \mathcal{I})$ with A as follows. A set $X \subseteq E$ is independent (i.e., $X \in \mathcal{I}$) if the columns in X are linearly independent over $\mathbb{F}$. The matroids that can be defined by such a construction are called *linear matroids*, and if a matroid can be defined by a matrix A over a field $\mathbb{F}$, then we say that the matroid is representable over $\mathbb{F}$. That is, a matroid $M = (E, \mathcal{I})$ of rank d is representable over a field $\mathbb{F}$ if there exist vectors in $\mathbb{F}^d$ corresponding to the elements in E such that linearly independent sets of vectors correspond to independent sets of the matroid. Then, a matroid $M = (E, \mathcal{I})$ is called *representable* or *linear* if it is representable over some field $\mathbb{F}$.

We will use the following product defined on matroids. Let $M_1 = (E_1, \mathcal{I}_1)$, $M_2 = (E_2, \mathcal{I}_2), \ldots, M_t = (E_t, \mathcal{I}_t)$ be linear matroids with $E_i \cap E_j = \emptyset$ for all $1 \leq i \neq j \leq t$. The *direct sum* $M_1 \oplus \cdots \oplus M_t$ is the matroid $M = (E, \mathcal{I})$ with $E := \bigcup_{i=1}^t E_i$, where $X \subseteq E$ is independent if and only if $X \cap E_i \in \mathcal{I}_i$ for all $1 \leq i \leq t$. Let $A_1, A_2, \ldots, A_t$ be representation matrices of $M_1 = (E_1, \mathcal{I}_1)$, $M_2 = (E_2, \mathcal{I}_2), \ldots, M_t = (E_t, \mathcal{I}_t)$, respectively, such that all these representations are over the same field. Then,

$$A_M = \begin{pmatrix} A_1 & 0 & 0 & \cdots & 0 \\ 0 & A_2 & 0 & \cdots & 0 \\ \vdots & \vdots & \vdots & \ddots & \vdots \\ 0 & 0 & 0 & \cdots & A_t \end{pmatrix}$$

is a representation matrix of $M_1 \oplus \cdots \oplus M_t$ over the same field. We thus obtain the following.

Proposition 10.2 *Given representations of matroids $M_1, \ldots, M_t$ over the same field $\mathbb{F}$, a representation of their direct sum can be found in polynomial time.*

Uniform and partition matroids. A pair $M = (E, \mathcal{I})$ over an n-element ground set E is called a *uniform matroid* if the family of independent sets is given by $\mathcal{I} = \{A \subseteq E \mid |A| \leq k\}$, where k is some nonnegative integer. This matroid is also denoted by $U_{n,k}$. Every uniform matroid is linear, and it can be represented over any finite field $\mathbb{F}$ with at least n nonzero elements by a $k \times n$ matrix A_M as follows. Let $x_1, \ldots, x_n$ be n distinct nonzero elements of $\mathbb{F}$. Then, $A_M[i,j]$ is defined to be x_j^{i-1}. That is,

$$A_M = \begin{pmatrix} 1 & 1 & 1 & \cdots & 1 \\ x_1 & x_2 & x_3 & \cdots & x_n \\ x_1^2 & x_2^2 & x_3^2 & \cdots & x_n^2 \\ \vdots & \vdots & \vdots & \ddots & \vdots \\ x_1^{k-1} & x_2^{k-1} & x_3^{k-1} & \cdots & x_n^{k-1} \end{pmatrix}$$

This matrix A_M is known as the *Vandermonde matrix*. Observe that for $U_{n,k}$ to be representable by A_M over $\mathbb{F}$, we need that the determinant of each $k \times k$ submatrix of A_M must not vanish over $\mathbb{F}$. Any set of k columns, corresponding to $x_{i_1}, \ldots, x_{i_k}$, by itself forms a Vandermonde matrix, whose determinant is given by

$$\prod_{1 \leq j < l \leq k} (x_{i_j} - x_{i_l}).$$

Combining this with the fact that $x_1, \ldots, x_n$ are n distinct nonzero elements of $\mathbb{F}$, we conclude that every subset of size at most k of the ground set is independent, while clearly each larger subset is dependent. Note that this means that a representation of the uniform matroid $U_{n,k}$ can be stored using $\mathcal{O}(nk \log n)$ bits.

A *partition matroid* $M = (E, \mathcal{I})$ is defined by a ground set E being partitioned into (disjoint) sets $E_1, \ldots, E_\ell$ and by ℓ nonnegative integers $k_1, \ldots, k_\ell$. A set $X \subseteq E$ is independent if and only if $|X \cap E_i| \leq k_i$ for all $i \in \{1, \ldots, \ell\}$. Observe that a partition matroid is a direct sum of uniform matroids $U_{|E_1|, k_1}, \cdots, U_{|E_\ell|, k_\ell}$. Thus, by Proposition 10.2 and the fact that a uniform matroid $U_{n,k}$ is representable over any field $\mathbb{F}$ with at least n nonzero elements, we have the following.

Proposition 10.3 *A representation over any field of size larger than n of a partition matroid with an n-element ground set can be constructed in polynomial time.*

Graphic matroids. Given a graph G, a *graphic matroid* $M = (E, \mathcal{I})$ is defined by setting the elements in E to be the edges of G (i.e., $E = E(G)$), where $F \subseteq E(G)$ is in $\mathcal{I}$ if it forms a spanning forest in G. The graphic matroid is representable over any field of size at least 2. Indeed, consider the incidence matrix A_M of G with a row for each vertex $i \in V(G)$ and a column for each edge $e = ij \in E(G)$. In the column corresponding to $e = ij$, all entries are 0, except for the entries i and j, where one of them contains 1 and the other contains -1 (the choice of which entry contains the 1 is arbitrary). This is a representation over reals. To obtain a representation over a field $\mathbb{F}$, one simply needs to take the representation given previously (over the reals) and replace every -1 by the additive inverse of 1. Thus, we obtain the following proposition.

Proposition 10.4 *Graphic matroids are representable over any field of size at least 2.*

Dual Matroids. The dual of a matroid $M = (E, \mathcal{I})$ is the matroid $M^\star = (E, \mathcal{I}^\star)$ where a subset $A \subseteq E$ belongs to $\mathcal{I}^\star$ if and only if M has a basis disjoint from A. Equivalently, the dual of a matroid M is the matroid $M^\star$ whose basis sets are the complements of the basis sets of M. Note that duality is an involution, that is, $(M^\star)^\star = M$. For a simple example of duality, observe that the dual of the uniform matroid $U_{n,k}$ is the uniform matroid $U_{n,n-k}$. For another example of duality, let us consider a graph G. The cographic matroid corresponding to G, which is the dual of the graphic matroid corresponding to G, is defined as the matroid $M = (E, \mathcal{I})$ where $E = E(G)$ and $\mathcal{I} = \{F \subseteq E \mid G - F \text{ is connected}\}$ (see Exercises 10.1 and 10.2). Finally, we state the following proposition (see Exercise 10.3).

Proposition 10.5 *Given a representation of a matroid M, a representation of the dual of M over the same field can be found in polynomial time.*

Transversal matroids. Let G be a bipartite graph with the vertex set $V(G)$ being partitioned to A and B. The *transversal matroid* M of G has A as its ground set, and a subset $X \subseteq A$ is independent in M if and only if there is a matching that covers (saturates) X. That is, X is independent if and only if there is an injective mapping $\phi \colon X \to B$ such that $\phi(v)$ is a neighbor of v for every $v \in X$. Let us now consider the computation of a representation of a transversal matroid. For this purpose, we first state the well-known Schwartz-Zippel lemma.

Proposition 10.6 (DeMillo and Lipton [1978]; Zippel [1979]; Schwartz [1980]) *Let $p(x_1, x_2, \ldots, x_n)$ be a nonzero polynomial of n variables and degree at most d over the finite field $\mathbb{F}$. Then, for $a_1, a_2, \ldots, a_n \in \mathbb{F}$ selected independently and uniformly at random:* $\Pr(p(a_1, a_2, \ldots, a_n) \neq 0) \geq 1 - d/|\mathbb{F}|$.

In the context of the representation given in the following text, by one-sided error we mean that dependent sets in the graph would be preserved, but independent sets in the graph might not be preserved. Specifically, if the procedure returns a matrix R, then with some (low) probability, some subsets of $X \subseteq A$ may be independent in M but dependent in the matroid represented by R.

Theorem 10.7 *There exists a one-sided error randomized polynomial time algorithm that, given a bipartite graph G with vertex bipartition (A, B), outputs a representation of the transversal matroid M corresponding to G over the rationals.*

Sketch: Denote $A = \{a_1, a_2, \ldots, a_{|A|}\}$ and $B = \{b_1, b_2, \ldots, b_{|B|}\}$. Let R_M be a $|B| \times |A|$ matrix where for all $i \in \{1, 2, \ldots, |A|\}$ and $j \in \{1, 2, \ldots, |B|\}$, we define $R_M[j, i]$ as follows:

- If a_i and b_j are adjacent in G, then $R_M[j, i]$ is a randomly chosen integer between 1 and $10 \cdot |A| \cdot 2^{|A|}$.
- Otherwise, $R_M[j, i] = 0$.

By relying on Proposition 10.6, it can be shown that with high probability, R_M is a representation of M (see Exercise 10.4). □

We remark that a polynomial time deterministic computation of a representation of a transversal matroid is not known.

Gammoids. Let D be a directed graph, and let S and T be (not necessarily disjoint) subsets $V(D)$. Here, S is called the source set of the gammoid, and T is called the sink set of the gammoid. We say that a set $X \subseteq T$ is *linked* to S, if there exist $|X|$ vertex disjoint paths going from S to X. Note that here we require that the paths are entirely disjoint, not only internally disjoint. Furthermore, zero-length paths are also allowed if $X \cap S \neq \emptyset$. The *gammoid M* corresponding to D, S and T is a matroid whose ground set is T, and where a subset $X \subseteq T$ is independent in M if and only if X is linked to S. In case $T = V(D)$, the gammoid M is called a *strict gammoid*.

A transversal matroid is in particular a gammoid, and the dual of a strict gammoid is a transversal matroid. To see the former claim, given a bipartite graph G with bipartition (A, B), direct the edges of G from B to A, and define $S = B$ and $T = A$. The proof of the latter claim is given as an exercise (Exercise 10.5). Thus, by relying on Proposition 10.5 and Theorem 10.7, we can prove a weaker version of the following theorem (see Exercise 10.6). To obtain explicit bound on compressions sizes by using the following theorem, we also specify bit-length in its statement.

Theorem 10.8 (Kratsch and Wahlström [2014]) *There exists a randomized polynomial time algorithm with one-sided error bounded by ϵ that, given a directed graph D with subsets S and T of V(D), outputs a representation A_M of the gammoid M corresponding to D, S and T over the rationals. Moreover, the entries in A_M are of bit-length $\mathcal{O}(\min\{|T|, |S|\log|T|\} + \log(1/\epsilon) + \log|V(D)|)$, and its size is $|S| \times |T|$.*

10.2 Cut-Flow Data Structure

In this section we develop a data structure based on representations of matroids, which is a crucial component of forthcoming polynomial kernels for several parameterized problems. We start with some definitions and notations. Let D be a directed graph and S and T be (not necessarily disjoint) subsets of $V(D)$. We use $\text{mvdp}_D(S,T)$ to denote the maximum number of (fully) vertex disjoint paths from S to T, and by $\text{mincut}_D(S,T)$ we denote the minimum number of vertices required to disconnect T from S in D. Note that vertices used to disconnected S from T can belong to the sets S and T. By the classical Menger's theorem, it is well known that $\text{mvdp}_D(S,T) = \text{mincut}_D(S,T)$ and that $\text{mvdp}_D(S,T)$ can be computed in polynomial time.

The data structure that we want to build should serve the following purpose. Given a directed graph D and a subset $X \subseteq V(D)$, for every partition of $X = S \cup T \cup R \cup U$ we want to store the maximum number of vertex disjoints paths from S to T in $D - R$. Moreover, for every such partition X, we want to compute $\text{mvdp}_{D-R}(S,T)$ in time polynomial in $|X|$ and $\log|V(D)|$. It is trivial to construct such a structure of size $\mathcal{O}(4^{|X|} \cdot \log|V(D)|)$ by keeping the required number of paths for every partition of X into four sets. However, this structure is not sufficiently good for us—the size of the structure that we require should be bounded by a polynomial of $|X|$ and $\log|V(D)|$.

More precisely, the formulation of our current task is as follows.

Given a digraph D and a subset $X \subseteq V(D)$ of vertices (called *terminals*), the PARTITION CUT-FLOW problem asks to output a data structure of size polynomial in $|X|$ and $\log|V(D)|$ such that any query

For a given a partition of $X = S \cup T \cup R \cup U$, what is $\text{mvdp}_{D-R}(S,T)$?

can be answered in time polynomial in $|X|$ and $\log|V(D)|$.

We proceed in three steps:

a) Describing the data structure,
b) Explaining how to answer a query, and
c) Analyzing the time required to answer a query.

We implement the following approach to create the required data structure.

- For a given digraph D with terminal set X, we construct a gammoid $M = (E, \mathcal{I})$. By using Theorem 10.8, we also construct a representation matrix A_M of M.
- The gammoid M would have the following property: For every partition $P = (S, T, R, U)$ of X, it is possible in polynomial time to compute a subset of elements I_P of M such that T is linked to S in $D - R$ if and only if I_P is independent in M.
- Thus, to answer the query on the number of paths from S to T in $D - R$, we only need to compute I_P and its rank.
- Finally, to compute the rank of I_P, we refer to our representation matrix A_M of M. Specifically, the computation of the rank of I_P can be done in polynomial time using Gaussian elimination.

Description of the data structure. Let $X' = \{x' \mid x \in X\}$ be a vertex set that is a copy of X. The vertices x' and x are called *conjugates* of each other. Add X' and the arc set $\{(x', x) \mid x \in X\}$ to D, and let the resulting digraph be D'. Consider the gammoid M whose source set is X' and whose sink set is $X \cup X'$. That is, the matroid $M = (E, \mathcal{I})$ is defined by $E = X \cup X'$, where $\mathcal{I}$ contains the subsets of $X \cup X'$ that are linked to X'. Let A_M be a representation matrix of M.

The matrix A_M will be the required data structure. By Theorem 10.8, given a fixed $\epsilon > 0$, the representation A_M of M can be computed in randomized polynomial time with one-sided error bounded by ϵ, and so that A_M would be a matrix over the rationals with entries of bit-length $\mathcal{O}(|X| \log |X| + \log(1/\epsilon) + \log |V(D)|)$ and size (not the number of bits) $|X| \times 2|X|$. Thus, for a fixed $\epsilon > 0$, the number of bits of the representation is $\mathcal{O}(|X|^3 \log |X| + |X|^2 \log |V(D)|)$.

Answering a query. Now we show that for every partition of $X = S \cup T \cup R \cup U$, we can find the maximum number of vertex disjoint paths between S and T in $D - R$ by computing the rank of the appropriate set of columns in A_M. Toward

10.2 Cut-Flow Data Structure

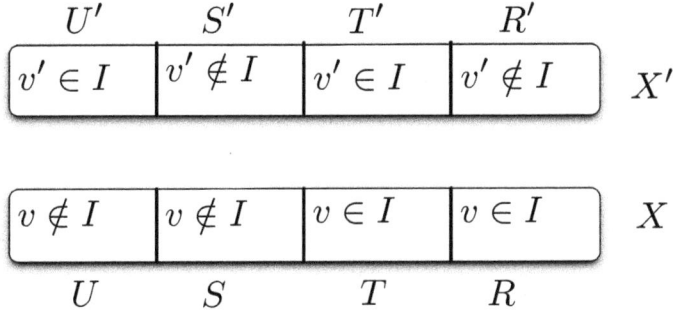

Figure 10.1 Constructing the partition $P_I = (S, T, R, U)$ from I.

this, we first establish a one-to-one correspondence between subsets of $X \cup X'$ and partitions of X. For every $I \subseteq X \cup X'$, we define a partition of X, called P_I, as follows:

- S contains all the vertices $v \in X$ with $v, v' \notin I$,
- T contains all the vertices $v \in X$ with $v, v' \in I$,
- R contains all the vertices $v \in X$ with $v \in I$ but $v' \notin I$, and
- $U = X \setminus (R \cup T \cup S)$, that is, U contains all the vertices $v \in X$ with $v \notin I$ but $v' \in I$.

See Fig 10.1 for an illustration. For a partition $P = (S, T, R, U)$ of X, the corresponding subset I_P of $X \cup X'$ (which *may not be independent*) is $T \cup R \cup T' \cup U'$. Observe that, for every subset $I \subseteq X \cup X'$,

$$I_{P_I} = I.$$

Toward our main goal, we prove the following important lemma.

Lemma 10.9 *A set $I \subseteq X \cup X'$ is independent in the gammoid M if and only if T is linked to S in $D - R$. Here, T and S are the subsets in the partition P_I corresponding to I.*

Proof: We first show the forward direction of the proof. Let $I \subseteq X \cup X'$ be an independent set in M. Thus there exists a set $\mathcal{P}$ of $|I|$ vertex disjoint paths from X' to I. For every vertex $v' \in X' \cap I = T' \cup U'$, the only path from a vertex in X' to v' is the one consisting only of v' as every vertex in X' and, in particular v', has in-degree 0. For every vertex $w \in R$, there is a path in $\mathcal{P}$ that is either of the form $w'w$ or of the form $v'v \cdots w$ with $v' \in S'$. In latter case, we can replace the path $v'v \cdots w$ by $w'w$; this replacement is possible as the only out-neighbor of w' is w, and thus w' does not appear on any other path in $\mathcal{P}$. These arguments imply that for every vertex $w \in T$, there exists a path in $\mathcal{P}$ of the form $v'v \cdots w$ where $v' \in S'$. All these paths do not contain any vertex of R, are vertex disjoint and in fact $v \cdots w$ is a path in $D - R$. This implies that T is linked to S in $D - R$.

For the opposite direction, let T be linked to S in $D - R$. Let us remind that for every subset $I \subseteq X \cup X'$, $I_{P_I} = I$. To construct vertex disjoint paths from X' to I, we proceed as follows. For the vertices $v' \in X' \cap I = T' \cup U'$, we select the paths v', and for the vertices $w \in R$, we select the paths $w'w$. Finally, for a path $v \cdots w$ from S to T in $D-R$ (corresponding to a witness of T being linked to S), where $v \in S$ and $w \in T$, we select a path from S' to T by appending v' to it, that is, we select $v'v \cdots w$. Because we have thus shown that there exist $|I|$ vertex disjoint paths from X' to I, we derive that I is independent. This completes the proof. □

Using Lemma 10.9, we prove the following lemma.

Lemma 10.10 *Let $P = (S, T, R, U)$ be a partition of X, and let $I_P \subseteq X \cup X'$ be the set corresponding to P, that is, $I_P = T \cup R \cup T' \cup U'$. Then,*

$$\mathrm{mvdp}_{D-R}(S, T) = \mathrm{rank}(I_P) - |X \setminus S|.$$

Proof: Let $\mathcal{P} = \{P_1, \ldots, P_\ell\}$ be a maximum-sized collection of vertex disjoint paths from S to T in $D-R$, and let $T^* \subseteq T$ be the set of endpoints in T of these paths. Clearly, $\mathrm{mvdp}_{D-R}(S, T) = |T^*|$. Because T^* is linked to S in $D - R$, by Lemma 10.9 we have that $U' \cup T' \cup R \cup T^* \subseteq I_P$ is an independent set of the gammoid. Moreover, if the gammoid has a larger independent set Q that is contained in I_P, then $|Q \cap T| > |T^*|$; however, by Lemma 10.9 we have that $Q \cap T$ is linked to S, which is a contradiction to our choice of T^*. Therefore, $U' \cup T' \cup R \cup T^*$ is the largest sized independent set of the gammoid among all the independent sets contained in I_P. That is, $\mathrm{rank}(I_P) = |U'|+|T'|+|R|+|T^*|$. This implies that

$$\begin{aligned}
\mathrm{mvdp}_{D-R}(S, T) &= |T^*| \\
&= \mathrm{rank}(I_P) - |U'| - |T'| - |R| \\
&= \mathrm{rank}(I_P) - |U| - |T| - |R| \\
&= \mathrm{rank}(I_P) - |X \setminus S|.
\end{aligned}$$

This completes the proof. □

So to answer the query, we perform the following computation:

> Given a partition of $P = (S, T, R, U)$ of X, return $\text{rank}(I_P) - |X \setminus S|$.

The correctness of the answer is justified by Lemma 10.10.

Query time. To answer the query, we have to compute the maximum size of a set of linearly independent columns among the columns corresponding to I_P in A_M. This can be done in time $\mathcal{O}(|X|^\omega \log |V(D)|)$. Here, $\omega < 2.3727$ is the exponent of the best matrix multiplication algorithm.

We summarize the preceding in the following theorem.

Theorem 10.11 *For every $\epsilon > 0$, there is a randomized polynomial time algorithm with one-sided error bounded by ϵ that, given a digraph D and subset of terminals X, outputs a data structure for the PARTITION CUT-FLOW problem with output size $\mathcal{O}(|X|^3 \log |X| + |X|^2 \log |V(D)|)$ and query time $\mathcal{O}(|X|^\omega \log |V(D)|)$.*

10.3 Kernel for ODD CYCLE TRANSVERSAL

Let G be an undirected graph and $O \subseteq V$ such that $G - O$ is a bipartite graph. For an undirected graph G, we say that a subset $O \subseteq V(G)$ is an *odd cycle transversal* of G if $G - O$ is a bipartite graph. In the ODD CYCLE TRANSVERSAL problem, we are given an undirected graph G and a nonnegative integer k. The task is to decide whether G has an odd cycle transversal of size at most k.

To obtain a polynomial kernel for ODD CYCLE TRANSVERSAL, we initially employ an FPT algorithm for this problem. This algorithm will not only be used in a black box manner by the kernelization algorithm, but the ideas underlying its design will be repeated in later steps of the kernelization algorithm, "encoded" succinctly using matroids. Thus, we first present the FPT algorithm in detail.

10.3.1 FPT Algorithm

Iterative compression algorithm for ODD CYCLE TRANSVERSAL. The FPT algorithm for ODD CYCLE TRANSVERSAL is based on the so-called technique of *iterative compression*. The scheme of algorithms relying on this technique is based on a *compression routine*, which is an algorithm that, given a problem instance and a corresponding solution, either calculates a smaller solution or proves that the given solution is of minimum size. The point is that if the compression routine runs in FPT time, then by applying the routine iteratively, we also obtain an FPT algorithm.

We solve ODD CYCLE TRANSVERSAL in the following three steps.

Step 1: (Auxiliary problem) Solve the following auxiliary annotated problem on bipartite graphs:

> Given a bipartite graph G, two sets $B, W \subseteq V(G)$, and an integer k, find a set S of at most k vertices such that $G - S$ has a proper 2-coloring with white and black colors where $B \setminus S$ is black and $W \setminus S$ is white.

Step 2: (Compression routine) Use Step 1 to solve the following problem on general graphs:

> Given a graph G, an integer k, and a set Q of $k + 1$ vertices such that $G - Q$ is bipartite, find a set S of k vertices such that $G - S$ is bipartite.

Step 3: Apply the idea of iterative compression.

Solving the annotated problem. Let B, W be some vertex subsets of a bipartite graph G. We can view the vertices in B and W as vertices precolored in black and white, respectively, by some coloring function f_0. We want to find a set S of size at most k such that the graph $G - S$ has a proper 2-coloring f^* called an *extension*, which extends the precoloring of $B \cup W$ (i.e., the vertices in B and W retain their predetermined colors). To find such a coloring, we proceed as follows. First, we fix an arbitrary 2-coloring f of G in black and white. Let this coloring correspond to the bipartition (B_0, W_0), where B_0 and W_0 denote the sets of vertices colored black and white, respectively. Clearly, such a coloring f exists as G is a bipartite graph. Now, observe that in terms of coloring functions, our objective is to find a set S of at most k vertices such that $G - S$ has *another* 2-coloring f^* in black and white such that $B \setminus S$ is black and $W \setminus S$ is white.

Observe that the vertices of Change$(f_0, f) = C := (B_0 \cap W) \cup (W_0 \cap B)$ should either belong to S or have different colors with respect to f and f^*. That is, for all $v \in C$, either $v \in S$ or $f(v) \neq f^*(v)$. Similarly, every vertex of Retain$(f_0, f) = R := (B_0 \cap B) \cup (W_0 \cap W)$ should either belong to S or have the same color with respect to f and f^*. That is, for all $v \in R$, either

10.3 Kernel for ODD CYCLE TRANSVERSAL

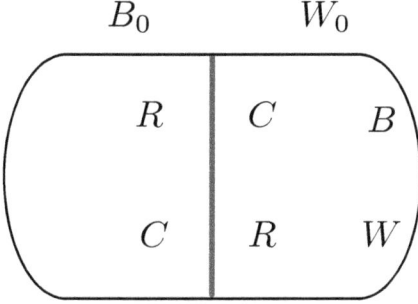

Figure 10.2 The sets C and R.

$v \in S$ or $f(v) = f^\star(v)$. The diagram in Fig. 10.2 illustrates this argument. Let us summarize this observation in the following statement.

Lemma 10.12 *Let G be a bipartite graph with bipartition corresponding to a coloring f, and let f_0 be a precoloring of some of the vertices of G. For any subset $S \subseteq V(G)$ and extension $f^\star$ of f_0 for $G - S$, it holds that* **(i)** *for all $v \in$ Change(f_0,f), either $v \in S$ or $f(v) \neq f^\star(v)$, and* **(ii)** *for all $v \in$ Retain(f_0,f), either $v \in S$ or $f(v) = f^\star(v)$.*

The following lemma will be used to solve the annotated problem.

Lemma 10.13 *Let G be a bipartite graph with bipartition corresponding to a coloring f, and let f_0 be a precoloring of some of the vertices of G. For any subset $S \subseteq V(G)$, $G - S$ has an extension $f^\star$ of f_0 if and only if S separates $C =$ Change(f_0,f) and $R =$ Retain(f_0,f), that is, no component of $G - S$ contains vertices from both $C \setminus S$ and $R \setminus S$.*

Furthermore, a set S of size at most k such that $G - S$ has an extension $f^\star$, if one exists, can be found in time $\mathcal{O}(k|E(G)|)$.

Proof: We first prove the forward direction of the statement. To this end, let $S \subseteq V(G)$ be a subset such that $G - S$ has an extension $f^\star$ of f_0. Every vertex in $G - S$ either changes its color or retains its color with respect to f and $f^\star$. Adjacent vertices do the same as f or $f^\star$ are proper colorings of G. Thus, the vertices of every connected component of $G - S$ either all flip their colors or all keep their colors. In other words, either for all the vertices v of the component we have that $f(v) \neq f^\star(v)$, or for all the vertices v of the component we have that $f(v) = f^\star(v)$. By Lemma 10.12, this implies that S separates C and R.

For the backward direction, let $S \subseteq V(G)$ be a subset that separates C and R. We construct a coloring $f^\star$ of G as follows. Flip the coloring with respect to

f of the vertices of those components of $G - S$ that contain vertices from $C \setminus S$. As S separates C and R, no vertex of R has its color flipped. Because f is a proper 2-coloring of G, so is $f^\star$. Thus, by the definition of $f^\star$, it is an extension of f_0 with respect to $G - S$ (see Fig. 10.2).

To find a separator of size at most k separating C and R, one can use classical max-flow min-cut techniques. In particular, our goal can be achieved in time $\mathcal{O}(k|E(G)|)$ using k iterations of the Ford-Fulkerson algorithm. □

Compression. In this step, we implement the compression routine. To this end, we first prove the following lemma.

Lemma 10.14 *Let G be a graph, and $Q \subseteq V(G)$ be a subset such that $G - Q$ is a bipartite graph with bipartition (B, W). Let f be the proper 2-coloring corresponding to (B, W). For any subset $S \subseteq V(G)$, $G - S$ is a bipartite graph if and only if there exists a partition (Q_B, Q_W, Q_S) of Q such that Q_B and Q_W are independent sets, $Q_S = Q \cap S$ and S separates $C = \text{Change}(f_0, f)$ and $R = \text{Retain}(f_0, f)$, where f_0 is the function that colors $N_G(Q_W) \setminus Q$ black and $N_G(Q_B) \setminus Q$ white.*

Furthermore, a set S of size at most k such that $G - S$ is a bipartite graph, if one exists, can be found in time $\mathcal{O}(3^{|Q|} \cdot k|E(G)|)$.

Proof: For the forward direction, let $S \subseteq V(G)$ be a subset such that $G - S$ is a bipartite graph, and let $f^\star$ be a proper 2-coloring corresponding to a bipartition $(B^\star, W^\star)$ of $G - S$. Every vertex $v \in Q$ belongs to either S or $G - S$, where in the latter case either $f^\star(v)$ is black or $f^\star(v)$ is white. This observation leads to the partition (Q_B, Q_W, Q_S) of Q, where $Q_S = Q \cap S$, $Q_B = Q \cap B^\star$ and $Q_W = Q \cap W^\star$. Clearly, Q_B and Q_W are independent sets. Let f_0 be the function that colors $N_G(Q_W) \setminus Q$ black and $N_G(Q_B) \setminus Q$ white. Now, observe that the neighbors of Q_B in $G - Q$ must be either colored white or deleted by S. Similarly, the neighbors of Q_W in $G - Q$, say B, must be either colored black or deleted by S. Therefore, $f^\star$ is an extension of f_0. By Lemma 10.13, this means that S separates C and R.

For the reverse direction, let $S \subseteq V(G)$ be a subset for which there exists a partition (Q_B, Q_W, Q_S) of Q such that Q_B and Q_W are independent sets, $Q_S = Q \cap S$ and S separates C and R. By Lemma 10.13, $G - S$ has an extension $f^\star$ of f_0, and let $(B^\star, W^\star)$ denote its corresponding bipartition. Now, note that $(B^\star \cup Q_B, W^\star \cup Q_W)$ is a bipartition of $G - S$. Indeed, Q_B and Q_W are independent sets, and as $f^\star$ is a proper 2-coloring of $G - S$, $B^\star$ and $W^\star$ are also independent sets. Furthermore, as $f^\star$ extends f_0, the neighbors of every vertex v in $Q_B \cup Q_W$ are not in the same side as v in $(B^\star \cup Q_B, W^\star \cup Q_W)$. Thus, $G - S$ is a bipartite graph.

Finally, to compute the desired set S, we first branch into at most $3^{|Q|}$ cases to consider every partition (Q_B, Q_W, Q_S) of Q such that Q_B and Q_W are independent sets. In every branch, we seek a subset $S' \subseteq V(G) \setminus Q_S$ of size at most $k - |Q_S|$ such that S' separates C and R. By Lemma 10.13, this step can be carried out in time $\mathcal{O}(k|E(G)|)$. Overall, we can thus find a set S of size at most k such that $G - S$ is a bipartite graph, if one exists, in time $\mathcal{O}(3^{|Q|} \cdot k|E(G)|)$. □

As a corollary to Lemma 10.14, we have the following result.

Corollary 10.15 *For a given graph G, an integer k and a set Q of $k+1$ vertices such that $G-Q$ is a bipartite graph, it can be determined in time $\mathcal{O}(3^k \cdot k|E(G)|)$ if there exists a subset $S \subseteq V(G)$ of k vertices such that $G - S$ is a bipartite graph, where if the answer is positive, such a subset S is outputted.*

Iterative compression. The final question that we need to address in the context of the FPT algorithm is how to obtain a solution of size $k + 1$. Luckily, this comes almost for free: We build such a solution iteratively. Take an arbitrary ordering $(v_1, \ldots, v_n)$ of $V(G)$ and let G_i be the graph induced by $\{v_1, \ldots, v_i\}$. For every i, we find a set S_i of size k such that $G_i - S_i$ is bipartite. For G_k, the set $S_k = \{v_1, \ldots, v_k\}$ is a trivial solution. If S_{i-1} is known, then $Q_i = S_{i-1} \cup \{v_i\}$ is a set of size $k + 1$ whose deletion makes G_i bipartite. We use Corollary 10.15 to find a suitable S_i in time $\mathcal{O}(3^k \cdot k|E(G_i)|)$. If for some $i \leq n$ we reach the conclusion that G_i does not have a solution of size k, then G also does not have a solution of size k. Else, S_n is a solution of size at most k for $G_n = G$.

The compression algorithm is called n times and thus the whole algorithm runs in time $\mathcal{O}(3^k \cdot k|V(G)| \cdot |E(G)|)$. Thus, we obtain the following theorem.

Theorem 10.16 ODD CYCLE TRANSVERSAL *is solvable in time* $\mathcal{O}(3^k \cdot k \cdot |V(G)| \cdot |E(G)|)$.

10.3.2 Compression

Reformulation of the compression step. To obtain the desired kernelization algorithm, we need to reformulate the compression step so that we can apply Theorem 10.11. Given a graph G and a set Q such that $G - Q$ is bipartite, we define another graph G' as follows. Let $(\widehat{A}, \widehat{B})$ be a fixed bipartition of $G - Q$. We take two copies of the set Q, denoted by $Q_a = \{q_a \mid q \in Q\}$ and $Q_b = \{q_b \mid q \in Q\}$. The vertex set of G' is $A \cup B \cup Q_a \cup Q_b$. The edges within

$G'[\widehat{A} \cup \widehat{B}]$ are the same as within G, while for every vertex $q \in Q$, the vertex q_a is connected to all the vertices in $N_G(q) \cap \widehat{B}$ and the vertex q_b is connected to all the vertices in $N_G(q) \cap \widehat{A}$.

Let (S', T', R') be a partition of $Q_a \cup Q_b$. We say that (S', T', R') is a *valid partition* if for every $q \in Q$,

- For every $q \in Q$, either $|\{q_a, q_b\} \cap S'| = |\{q_a, q_b\} \cap T'| = 1$ or $|\{q_a, q_b\} \cap R'| = 2$ and
- $\{q \in Q \mid q_a \in S'\}$ and $\{q \in Q \mid q_b \in S'\}$ are independent sets.

Given a graph G and vertex subsets S' and T' of $V(G)$, we say that X is a *vertex cut-set* of S' and T' if in $G - X$ there is no path between a pair of vertices s, t such that $s \in S'$ and $t \in T'$. Let us remind that by $\text{mincut}_G(S', T')$ we denote the minimum size of a vertex cut-set of S' and T' in G.

Lemma 10.17 *Let G be a graph and $Q \subseteq V(G)$ be such that $G - Q$ is bipartite with bipartition $(\widehat{A}, \widehat{B})$. Then, the size of the minimum odd cycle transversal of G is the minimum over all valid partitions (S', T', R') of $Q_a \cup Q_b$ of the following value:*

$$\frac{|R'|}{2} + \text{mincut}_{G'-R'}(S', T').$$

Proof: Let us denote $(B, W) = (\widehat{A}, \widehat{B})$, and define f as the proper 2-coloring corresponding to this bipartition of $G - Q$. For the forward direction, let S be an odd cycle transversal of G. By Lemma 10.14, there exists a partition (Q_B, Q_W, Q_S) of Q such that Q_B and Q_W are independent sets, $Q_S = Q \cap S$ and S separates $C = \text{Change}(f_0, f)$ and $R = \text{Retain}(f_0, f)$, where f_0 is the function that colors $N_G(Q_W) \setminus Q$ black and $N_G(Q_B) \setminus Q$ white. Observe that $C = (N_G(Q_B) \cap B) \cup (N_G(Q_W) \cap W)$ and $R = (N_G(Q_B) \cap W) \cup (N_G(Q_W) \cap B)$. Let us define a partition (S', T', R') of $Q_a \cup Q_b$ as follows: $S' = \{q_a \mid q \in Q_B\} \cup \{q_b \mid q \in Q_W\}$, $T' = \{q_b \mid q \in Q_B\} \cup \{q_a \mid q \in Q_W\}$, $R' = \{q_a \mid q \in Q_S\} \cup \{q_b \mid q \in Q_S\}$. Clearly, for every $q \in Q$, either $|\{q_a, q_b\} \cap S'| = |\{q_a, q_b\} \cap T'| = 1$ or $|\{q_a, q_b\} \cap R'| = 2$. Moreover, because Q_B and Q_W are independent sets, we have that $\{q \in Q \mid q_a \in S'\}$ and $\{q \in Q \mid q_b \in S'\}$ are independent sets. Thus, (S', T', R') is a valid partition. Hence, to conclude the proof of this direction, it remains to show that $\text{mincut}_{G'-R'}(S', T') \leq |S \setminus Q|$, as this would imply that $\frac{|R'|}{2} + \text{mincut}_{G'-R'}(S', T') \leq |S|$. For this purpose, it is enough to show that $S \setminus Q$ separates S' and T' in $G' - R'$. However, this follows as we argued that S separates $(N_G(Q_B) \cap B) \cup (N_G(Q_W) \cap W)$ and $(N_G(Q_B) \cap W) \cup (N_G(Q_W) \cap B)$ in G.

For the reverse direction, let (S', T', R') be a valid partition of $Q_a \cup Q_b$. Let X be a vertex cut of minimum size between S' and T' in $G - R'$. We define S

10.3 Kernel for ODD CYCLE TRANSVERSAL

as the union of $\{q \in Q \mid q_a \in R'\}$ and $(X \setminus Q) \cup \{q \in Q \mid \{q_a, q_b\} \cap X \neq \emptyset\}$. Note that $S \subseteq V(G)$ and $|S| \leq \frac{|R'|}{2} + \text{mincut}_{G'-R'}(S', T')$. Thus, it remains to prove that $G - S$ is a bipartite graph. By Lemma 10.14, to show that $G - S$ is a bipartite graph, it is sufficient to show that there exists a partition (Q_B, Q_W, Q_S) of Q such that Q_B and Q_W are independent sets, $Q_S = Q \cap S$ and S separates $C = \text{Change}(f_0, f)$ and $R = \text{Retain}(f_0, f)$, where f_0 is the function that colors $N_G(Q_W) \setminus Q$ black and $N_G(Q_B) \setminus Q$ white. To this end, we define $Q_B = \{q \in Q \setminus S \mid q_a \in S'\}$, $Q_W = \{q \in Q \setminus S \mid q_b \in S'\}$ and $Q_S = Q \cap S$. As (S', T', R') is a valid partition, we immediately have that Q_B and Q_W are independent sets. Moreover, as X separates S' and T' in $G - R'$, we have that S separates $(N_G(Q_B) \cap W) \cup (N_G(Q_W) \cap B)$ and $(N_G(Q_B) \cap B) \cup (N_G(Q_W) \cap W)$ in G. Recall that f colors B black and W white, and f_0 colors $N_G(Q_W) \setminus Q$ black and $N_G(Q_B) \setminus Q$ white. Thus, we have that $C = (N_G(Q_B) \cap B) \cup (N_G(Q_W) \cap W)$ and $R = (N_G(Q_B) \cap W) \cup (N_G(Q_W) \cap B)$, which concludes the proof. $\square$

Compression. Now, we are prepared to proceed to the compression algorithm for ODD CYCLE TRANSVERSAL. The compression algorithm is a combination of Lemma 10.17 and Theorem 10.11. Here, the target problem Compressed Odd Cycle Transversal (COMPRESSED OCT) is defined as follows. Given a set Q' with partition (Q_a, Q_b), a Cut-Flow data structure corresponding to Q', and a parameter k, the objective of COMPRESSED OCT is to determine whether there exists a valid partition (S', T', R') of Q' such that $\frac{|R'|}{2} + \text{mincut}_{D'-R'}(S', T') \leq k$. Here, only the subgraph $D'[Q']$ of the digraph D' is given explicitly.

Let G be an input graph on n vertices. Observe that to exploit Lemma 10.17, we need a set $Q \subseteq V(G)$ be such that $G - Q$ is bipartite. To obtain the desired Q we make use of a known $\alpha\sqrt{\log n}$ factor approximation algorithm for the optimization version of the ODD CYCLE TRANSVERSAL problem:

Proposition 10.18 *For some fixed α, ODD CYCLE TRANSVERSAL admits a polynomial time algorithm that, given an instance of ODD CYCLE TRANSVERSAL, outputs a set Q that is an odd cycle transversal of G of size $\alpha\sqrt{\log n} \cdot OPT$, where OPT is the minimum size of an odd cycle transversal of G.*

Next, we outline the steps involved in designing the compression algorithm for ODD CYCLE TRANSVERSAL.

(i) If $k \leq \log n$, then run the $\mathcal{O}(3^k mn)$ time algorithm of Theorem 10.16 to find a solution in polynomial time, after which return a trivial yes- or no-instance accordingly.

(ii) Apply the known $\alpha\sqrt{\log n}$ approximation algorithm for ODD CYCLE TRANSVERSAL to find an approximate solution Q. If $|Q| > k\alpha\sqrt{\log n}$, then output a trivial no-instance.

(iii) At this stage, we have $k > \log n$ and $|Q| \leq k\alpha\sqrt{\log n}$. Thus, $|Q| = \mathcal{O}(k^{1.5})$.
(iv) For the graph G and subset $Q \subseteq V(G)$, we construct the graph G' described in Section 10.3.2. To utilize Theorem 10.11, we translate G into a digraph. To this end, let D' be the digraph obtained from G' by replacing every edge by a directed cycle of length two, that is, two arcs with different directions. By adding these double arcs, the reachability relationships between vertices in G and D are the same. Let A_M be the matrix (i.e., the data structure) returned by Theorem 10.11 by taking D' as the input digraph and $Q_a \cup Q_b$ as a set of terminals.
(v) By Theorem 10.11, the size of A_M in terms of bits is at most $\mathcal{O}(k^{4.5}\log k)$.
(vi) The output instance of COMPRESSED OCT (defined before Proposition 10.18) is $(Q_a \cup Q_b, D'[Q_a \cup Q_b], A_M, k)$.

From Lemma 10.17 and Theorem 10.11, we derive the correctness of the above procedure:

Lemma 10.19 *The* ODD CYCLE TRANSVERSAL *admits a randomized compression of size* $\mathcal{O}(k^{4.5}\log k)$ *into* COMPRESSED OCT.

Before we proceed, let us clarify that by randomized compression, we mean that with high probability (say, some constant close to 1), the input and output instances are equivalent.

10.3.3 Kernel

Finally, let us show that Lemma 10.19 in fact implies that ODD CYCLE TRANSVERSAL admits a polynomial kernel. To this end, first note that ODD CYCLE TRANSVERSAL is an NP-hard problem. Furthermore, we have that COMPRESSED OCT is in NP. Indeed, given an instance $(Q_a \cup Q_b, D'[Q_a \cup Q_b], A_M, k)$ of COMPRESSED OCT, observe that a nondeterministic Turing machine can "guess" a partition (S', T', R'), verify that the partition is valid in polynomial time (using $D'[Q_a \cup Q_b]$), and then verifying that $\frac{|R'|}{2} + \text{mincut}_{D'-R'}(S', T') \leq k$ (using A_M). Thus, there exists a polynomial-time algorithm that, given an instance of COMPRESSED OCT, translates it into an equivalent instance of COMPRESSED OCT (see Theorem 1.6). Combined with Lemma 10.19, this results in the following theorem.

Theorem 10.20 ODD CYCLE TRANSVERSAL *admits a randomized polynomial kernel.*

Exercises

Problem 10.1 (✐) Based on the matroid axioms, verify that the following families indeed form matroids.

(i) Let G be a graph. Let $M = (E, \mathcal{I})$ be a matroid defined on G, where $E = E(G)$ and $\mathcal{I}$ contains all *forests* of G. (**Graphic Matroid**)
(ii) Let G be a connected graph. Let $M = (E, \mathcal{I})$ be a matroid defined on G, where $E = E(G)$ and $\mathcal{I}$ contains all $F \subseteq E(G)$ such that the graph G' obtained from G by deleting edges of F is connected. (**Co-Graphic Matroid**)

Problem 10.2 Let G be a graph. Prove that the dual of the graphic matroid corresponding to G is the cographic matroid corresponding to G.

Problem 10.3 Prove Proposition 10.5.

Problem 10.4 Complete the proof of Proposition 10.7.

Problem 10.5 Prove every strict gammoid is the dual of a transversal matroid. (Hint: Given a strict gammoid corresponding to D, S and $T = V(D)$, construct a bipartite graph G with bipartition $A = V(D)$ and $B = \{v' : v \in V(D) \setminus S\}$, such that there is an edge between $v \in A$ and $u' \in B$ if $v = u$ or there is an arc from v to u in D.)

Problem 10.6 Prove the following weaker version of Theorem 10.8: There exists a one-sided error randomized polynomial time algorithm that, given a directed graph D with subsets S and T of $V(D)$, outputs a representation of the gammoid M corresponding to D, S and T over the rationals. Here, it is not requested to bound the bit-length of the entries.

(Hint: Given a gammoid, extend its target set. First use Exercise 10.4, and then use Exercise 10.5. Afterward, remember to restrict the target set.)

Problem 10.7 Let $M_1 = (E_1, \mathcal{I}_1)$ and $M_2 = (E_2, \mathcal{I}_2)$ be two matroids such that $E_1 = E_2 = E$. Define $M_1 \cap M_2$ as $M = (E, \mathcal{I})$ such that $X \in \mathcal{I}$ if and only if $X \in \mathcal{I}_1$ and $X \in \mathcal{I}_2$. Is M always a matroid? (**Matroid Intersection**)

Problem 10.8 Express the following as intersections of (possibly more than two) matroids.

(i) Finding a maximum matching in a bipartite graph.
(ii) Testing whether a graph contains two edge disjoint spanning trees.
(iii) Finding a Hamiltonian path in a directed graph D between a pair of vertices s and t of D.

Bibliographic Notes

In this chapter, we have only touched the surface of the deep and well-studied area of Matroid Theory. We refer to the textbook of Welsh (2010) as well as the books of Oxley (2010) and Lawler (2001) for an introduction to the field. For applications of matroids to the design of parameterized algorithms, we refer the book of Cygan et al. (2015). We remark that Propositions 10.2 and 10.3 can be found as Propositions 3.4 and 3.5, respectively, in Marx (2009). Moreover, Theorem 10.8 can be found in Kratsch and Wahlström (2014). The randomized representation of transversal matroids can be found in the memorandum of Edmonds and Fulkerson (1965) (see also Marx, 2009). Recently, a deterministic quasipolynomial representation was given by Lokshtanov et al. (2018). We also refer to Perfect (1968) for the context of gammoids.

The randomized polynomial kernel for ODD CYCLE TRANSVERSAL is based on Kratsch and Wahlström (2014). We remark that a deterministic polynomial kernel for ODD CYCLE TRANSVERSAL is not known. Let us also point out another work where the approach of matrix representation (which does not have to be based on matroids) has been considered: Wahlström (2013) presented a compression for the problem of finding a cycle through specific vertices given as input. Interestingly, here the output problem is not known to be in NP, and hence we do not obtain a kernel.

In this chapter, we have also referred to Ford-Fulkerson algorithm, which can be found in Ford Jr. and Fulkerson (1956). Menger's theorem is due to Menger (1927). The most recent bound $\omega < 2.3728639$ for the matrix multiplication exponent is given in Gall (2014). The technique of iterative compression was introduced by Reed et al. (2004) to solve ODD CYCLE TRANSVERSAL, and additional applications of this technique to design parameterized algorithms are given in Cygan et al. (2015). A faster algorithm for ODD CYCLE TRANSVERSAL was given in Lokshtanov et al. (2014). The $\alpha\sqrt{\log n}$ factor approximation algorithm ODD CYCLE TRANSVERSAL is due to Agarwal et al. (2005).

11
Representative Families

In the previous chapter, we used succinct representations of matroids to derive a kernel for ODD CYCLE TRANSVERSAL of polynomial size. In this chapter, we discuss kernelization algorithms that find vertices or edges that are irrelevant and thus can be safely deleted. The tools that we use to identify irrelevant vertices or edges are based on linear algebra and matroid theory. In what follows, we first motivate these tools by giving as an example a parameterized algorithm for LONGEST PATH, and then we formalize the notion of a representative set. This is followed by an efficient algorithm to compute these combinatorial objects together with several applications of representative sets in kernelization algorithms.

11.1 Introduction to Representative Sets

Let us consider the classical dynamic programming algorithm for HAMILTONIAN PATH, where for a given n-vertex graph G, the task is to determine whether there exists a path visiting each vertex of G exactly once. Such a path is called a Hamiltonian path. A trivial algorithm would be to try all possible vertex permutations of G, and for each permutation, check whether it corresponds to a simple path. This approach will take $\mathcal{O}(n! \cdot n)$ steps. By making use of dynamic programming, it is possible to solve HAMILTONIAN PATH in time $\mathcal{O}(2^n \cdot n^2)$.

Let G be an input graph and W be a matrix. The rows of W are indexed by the vertices in $V(G) = \{v_1, \ldots, v_n\}$, and the columns of W are indexed by the integers in $\{1, \ldots, n-1\}$. The matrix entry $W[v_j, i]$ stores all sets $X \subseteq V(G)$ such that $|X| = i$ and G has at least one path of length $i - 1$ ending at v_j and using only the vertices of X. Observe that in W we are only storing sets and not permutations of vertices. That is, while it is possible that there exist many paths ending at v_j with internal vertices taken from X, rather than storing the order in which each of them visits X, we only store the set X. This implies that the size of the family stored at $W[v_j, i]$ is at most $\binom{n}{i}$. We can fill the matrix as follows. For $i = 1$, the family stored in every entry $W[v_j, i]$ consists only of $\{v_j\}$. For $w \in V(G)$, we use the notation $W[w, i-1] \bullet \{v_j\}$ to denote the family of all sets of size i that can be formed from the union of a set from $W[w, i-1]$ and $\{v_j\}$. In other words,

$$W[w, i-1] \bullet \{v_j\} = \{X \cup \{v_j\} \mid X \in W[w, i-1] \text{ and } v_j \notin X\}.$$

Then, we are able to compute the family of sets $W[v_j, i]$ by making use of the following formula:

$$W[v_j, i] = \bigcup_{w \in N(v_j)} W[w, i-1] \bullet \{v_j\}.$$

Clearly, if for some $v_j \in V(G)$ the family $W[v_j, n]$ is nonempty, then G has a Hamiltonian path ending at v_j. It is also easy to see that the running time of the algorithm is $\mathcal{O}(2^n n^2)$.

Let us now try to adapt these arguments to the following parameterized version of the HAMILTONIAN PATH problem. Recall that in the LONGEST PATH problem, we are given a graph G and a non negative integer k. The task is to decide whether G contains a path of length at least k.

Observe that we can solve the problem by restricting the columns of the matrix W to $\{1, \ldots, k+1\}$. However, the running time of this algorithm is dominated by $\mathcal{O}(\binom{n}{k+1})$, which is roughly $n^{\mathcal{O}(k)}$. A natural question that arises here is whether we can improve the running time by pruning the family stored at $W[v_j, i]$. However, what should be the property of the pruned family $\widehat{W}[v_j, i] \subseteq W[v_j, i]$? To explain this property precisely, we will use the following notations. Let A be a set of size i and B be a set of size $k - i$. We say that a path P on $k+1$ vertices is of $Av_{j+1}B$-*type* if the first i vertices of P belong to A, the $(i+1)$-th vertex is v_j, and the last $k - i$ vertices belong to B. By taking a closer look at the algorithm for HAMILTONIAN PATH, we want the families $\widehat{W}[v_j, i]$ to satisfy the following property:

> Let P be a path on $k+1$ vertices of $Av_j B$-type with $|A| = i$ and $|B| = k-i$. Then, $A \cup \{v_j\}$ clearly belongs to $W[v_j, i]$. In this case, it is not mandatory to store $A \cup \{v_j\}$, but we would like to have at least one set $\hat{A} \in \widehat{W}[v_j, i]$ such that there is a $(k+1)$-vertex path P' of $\hat{A} v_j B$-type.

Thus, for the purpose of the dynamic programming algorithm, it is sufficient to store $\widehat{W}[v_j, i]$ rather than $W[v_j, i]$. The next question is how large should the set $\widehat{W}[v_j, i]$ be and how fast can it be computed.

To address the first question, let $\widehat{W}[v_j, i]$ be a minimal subfamily of $W[v_j, i]$ that satisfies the required property. Minimality implies that for every $A \in \widehat{W}[v_j, i]$, there exists a set B of size $k - i$ such that **(i)** there is a path on $k + 1$ vertices of Av_jB-type, and **(ii)** for each $A' \in \widehat{W}[v_j, i]$ such that $A' \neq A$, there is no $(k + 1)$-vertex path of $A'v_jB$-type. An upper bound of the size of $\widehat{W}[v_j, i]$ can be obtained by considering the following classical problem in extremal combinatorics. Let U be universe and $A_i, B_i \subseteq U$, $i \in \{1, \ldots, t\}$ be sets such that each A_i is of size p and each B_i is of size q. Furthermore, $A_i \cap B_j = \emptyset$ if and only if $i = j$. The classical theorem of Bollobás implies that t is at most $\binom{p+q}{p}$. The crucial observation here is that t does not depend on the size of the universe U. This shows that the size of $\widehat{W}[v_j, i]$ is at most $\binom{k}{i}$. The family $\widehat{W}[v_j, i]$ is called a $(k - i)$-*representative family*.

To address the second question, we need efficient algorithms computing representative families. The kernelization algorithms of this chapter are based on a generalization of the result of Bollobás to a subspace variant proved by Lovász and a corresponding efficient computation. This generalization is discussed in the following section.

11.2 Computing Representative Families

In this section, we give an algorithm to find a small q-representative family for a given family. For the sake of brevity, we use the following notations: $[n] = \{1, \ldots, n\}$ and $\binom{[n]}{i} = \{X \mid X \subseteq [n], |X| = i\}$. Moreover, we use the following operations on families of sets.

Definition 11.1 Given two families of sets $\mathcal{A}$ and $\mathcal{B}$, we define

(•) $\mathcal{A} \bullet \mathcal{B} = \{X \cup Y \mid X \in \mathcal{A}, Y \in \mathcal{B}, X \cap Y = \emptyset\}$.
  Let $\mathcal{A}_1, \ldots, \mathcal{A}_r$ be r families. Then,

$$\overset{\bullet}{\prod_{i \in [r]}} \mathcal{A}_i = \mathcal{A}_1 \bullet \cdots \bullet \mathcal{A}_r.$$

(○) $\mathcal{A} \circ \mathcal{B} = \{A \cup B \colon A \in \mathcal{A}, B \in \mathcal{B}\}$.
(+) For a set X, we define $\mathcal{A} + X = \{A \cup X \colon A \in \mathcal{A}\}$.

We start with the formal definition of a q-*representative family*.

Definition 11.2 (*q*-**representative family**) Given a matroid $M = (E, \mathcal{I})$ and a family $\mathcal{S}$ of subsets of E, we say that a subfamily $\widehat{\mathcal{S}} \subseteq \mathcal{S}$ is *q-representative* for $\mathcal{S}$ if the following holds: for every set $Y \subseteq E$ of size at most q, if there is a set $X \in \mathcal{S}$ disjoint from Y with $X \cup Y \in \mathcal{I}$, then there is a set $\widehat{X} \in \widehat{\mathcal{S}}$ disjoint from Y with $\widehat{X} \cup Y \in \mathcal{I}$. If $\widehat{\mathcal{S}} \subseteq \mathcal{S}$ is *q*-representative for $\mathcal{S}$ we write $\widehat{\mathcal{S}} \subseteq^q_{rep} \mathcal{S}$.

In other words, if some independent set in $\mathcal{S}$ can be extended to a larger independent set by adding some q new elements, then there is a set in $\widehat{\mathcal{S}}$ that can be extended by adding the same q elements. A weighted variant of *q*-representative families is defined as follows. It is useful for solving problems where we are looking for objects of maximum or minimum weight.

Definition 11.3 (**min/max *q*-representative family**) Given a matroid $M = (E, \mathcal{I})$, a family $\mathcal{S}$ of subsets of E and a nonnegative weight function $w : \mathcal{S} \to \mathbb{N}$, we say that a subfamily $\widehat{\mathcal{S}} \subseteq \mathcal{S}$ is *min q-representative* (*max q-representative*) for $\mathcal{S}$ if the following holds: for every set $Y \subseteq E$ of size at most q, if there is a set $X \in \mathcal{S}$ disjoint from Y with $X \cup Y \in \mathcal{I}$, then there is a set $\widehat{X} \in \widehat{\mathcal{S}}$ disjoint from Y such that

(i) $\widehat{X} \cup Y \in \mathcal{I}$; and
(ii) $w(\widehat{X}) \leq w(X)$ ($w(\widehat{X}) \geq w(X)$).

We use $\widehat{\mathcal{S}} \subseteq^q_{minrep} \mathcal{S}$ ($\widehat{\mathcal{S}} \subseteq^q_{maxrep} \mathcal{S}$) to denote a min *q*-representative (max *q*-representative) family for $\mathcal{S}$.

We say that a family $\mathcal{S} = \{S_1, \ldots, S_t\}$ of sets is a *p-family* if each set in $\mathcal{S}$ is of size p.

We start by three lemmata providing basic results about representative sets. We prove them for unweighted representative families, but they can be easily modified to work for the weighted variant.

Lemma 11.4 *Let $M = (E, \mathcal{I})$ be a matroid and $\mathcal{S}$ be a family of subsets of E. If $\mathcal{S}' \subseteq^q_{rep} \mathcal{S}$ and $\widehat{\mathcal{S}} \subseteq^q_{rep} \mathcal{S}'$, then $\widehat{\mathcal{S}} \subseteq^q_{rep} \mathcal{S}$.*

Proof: Let $Y \subseteq E$ of size at most q such that there is a set $X \in \mathcal{S}$ disjoint from Y with $X \cup Y \in \mathcal{I}$. By the definition of a *q*-representative family, we have that there is a set $X' \in \mathcal{S}'$ disjoint from Y with $X' \cup Y \in \mathcal{I}$. Now, because $\widehat{\mathcal{S}} \subseteq^q_{rep} \mathcal{S}'$, there exists $\widehat{X} \in \widehat{\mathcal{S}}$ disjoint from Y with $\widehat{X} \cup Y \in \mathcal{I}$. $\square$

Lemma 11.5 *Let $M = (E, \mathcal{I})$ be a matroid and $\mathcal{S}$ be a family of subsets of E. If $\mathcal{S} = \mathcal{S}_1 \cup \cdots \cup \mathcal{S}_\ell$ and $\widehat{\mathcal{S}}_i \subseteq^q_{rep} \mathcal{S}_i$, then $\bigcup_{i=1}^\ell \widehat{\mathcal{S}}_i \subseteq^q_{rep} \mathcal{S}$.*

Proof: Let $Y \subseteq E$ be an independent set of size at most q such that there is a set $X \in \mathcal{S}$ disjoint from Y with $X \cup Y \in \mathcal{I}$. Because $\mathcal{S} = \mathcal{S}_1 \cup \cdots \cup \mathcal{S}_\ell$, there exists an i such that $X \in \mathcal{S}_i$. This implies that there exists $\widehat{X} \in \widehat{\mathcal{S}}_i \subseteq \cup_{i=1}^{\ell}\widehat{\mathcal{S}}_i$ disjoint from Y with $\widehat{X} \cup Y \in \mathcal{I}$. □

Lemma 11.6 *Let $M = (E, \mathcal{I})$ be a matroid of rank k, $\mathcal{S}_1$ be a p_1-family of independent sets, $\mathcal{S}_2$ be a p_2-family of independent sets, $\widehat{\mathcal{S}}_1 \subseteq_{rep}^{k-p_1} \mathcal{S}_1$, and $\widehat{\mathcal{S}}_2 \subseteq_{rep}^{k-p_2} \mathcal{S}_2$. Then, $\widehat{\mathcal{S}}_1 \bullet \widehat{\mathcal{S}}_2 \subseteq_{rep}^{k-p_1-p_2} \mathcal{S}_1 \bullet \mathcal{S}_2$.*

Proof: Let $Y \subseteq E$ of size at most $q = k - p_1 - p_2$ such that there is a set $X \in \mathcal{S}_1 \bullet \mathcal{S}_2$ disjoint from Y with $X \cup Y \in \mathcal{I}$. This implies that there exist $X_1 \in \mathcal{S}_1$ and $X_2 \in \mathcal{S}_2$ such that $X_1 \cup X_2 = X$ and $X_1 \cap X_2 = \emptyset$. Because $\widehat{\mathcal{S}}_1 \subseteq_{rep}^{k-p_1} \mathcal{S}_1$, we have that there exists $\widehat{X}_1 \in \widehat{\mathcal{S}}_1$ such that $\widehat{X}_1 \cup X_2 \cup Y \in \mathcal{I}$ and $\widehat{X}_1 \cap (X_2 \cup Y) = \emptyset$. Now because $\widehat{\mathcal{S}}_2 \subseteq_{rep}^{k-p_2} \mathcal{S}_2$, we have that there exists $\widehat{X}_2 \in \widehat{\mathcal{S}}_2$ such that $\widehat{X}_1 \cup \widehat{X}_2 \cup Y \in \mathcal{I}$ and $\widehat{X}_2 \cap (\widehat{X}_1 \cup Y) = \emptyset$. This shows that $\widehat{X}_1 \cup \widehat{X}_2 \in \widehat{\mathcal{S}}_1 \bullet \widehat{\mathcal{S}}_2$ and $\widehat{X}_1 \cup \widehat{X}_2 \cup Y \in \mathcal{I}$, and thus $\widehat{\mathcal{S}}_1 \bullet \widehat{\mathcal{S}}_2 \subseteq_{rep}^{k-p_1-p_2} \mathcal{S}_1 \bullet \mathcal{S}_2$. □

In what follows, we prove the following. Given a representable matroid $M = (E, \mathcal{I})$ of rank $k = p + q$ with its representation matrix A_M, a p-family of independent sets $\mathcal{S}$, and a nonnegative weight function $w : \mathcal{S} \to \mathbb{N}$, we can compute $\widehat{\mathcal{S}} \subseteq_{minrep}^{q} \mathcal{S}$ and $\widehat{\mathcal{S}} \subseteq_{maxrep}^{q} \mathcal{S}$ of size $\binom{p+q}{p}$ deterministically in time $\mathcal{O}\left(\binom{p+q}{p}tp^\omega + t\binom{p+q}{q}^{\omega-1}\right)$. We use ω to denote the matrix multiplication exponent. The current best-known bound on ω is $\omega < 2.373$.

For our proof we need the following well-known generalized Laplace expansion of determinants. For a matrix $A = (a_{ij})$, the row set and the column set are denoted by $\mathbf{R}(A)$ and $\mathbf{C}(A)$, respectively. For $I \subseteq \mathbf{R}(A)$ and $J \subseteq \mathbf{C}(A)$, $A[I, J] = (a_{ij} \mid i \in I, j \in J)$ refers to the submatrix (or minor) of A with the row set I and the column set J. For $I \subseteq [n]$, let $\bar{I} = [n] \setminus I$ and $\sum I = \sum_{i \in I} i$.

Proposition 11.7 (Generalized Laplace expansion) *For an $n \times n$ matrix A and $J \subseteq \mathbf{C}(A) = [n]$, it holds that*

$$\det(A) = \sum_{I \subseteq [n], |I| = |J|} (-1)^{\sum I + \sum J} \det(A[I, J]) \det(A[\bar{I}, \bar{J}])$$

The proof of Generalized Laplace expansion can be found in most of the textbooks on linear algebra, see "Bibliographic notes" section for a reference, and we omit it here.

We always assume that the number of rows in the representation matrix A_M of M over a field $\mathbb{F}$ is equal to $\text{rank}(M) = \text{rank}(A_M)$. Otherwise, using Gaussian elimination we can obtain a matrix of the desired kind in polynomial time.

Theorem 11.8 *Let $M = (E, \mathcal{I})$ be a linear matroid of rank $p + q = k$, $\mathcal{S} = \{S_1, \ldots, S_t\}$ be a p-family of independent sets and $w : \mathcal{S} \to \mathbb{N}$ be a non negative weight function. Then there exists $\widehat{\mathcal{S}} \subseteq_{minrep}^q \mathcal{S}$ ($\widehat{\mathcal{S}} \subseteq_{maxrep}^q \mathcal{S}$) of size $\binom{p+q}{p}$. Moreover, given a representation A_M of M over a field $\mathbb{F}$, we can find $\widehat{\mathcal{S}} \subseteq_{minrep}^q \mathcal{S}$ ($\widehat{\mathcal{S}} \subseteq_{maxrep}^q \mathcal{S}$) of size at most $\binom{p+q}{p}$ in $\mathcal{O}\left(\binom{p+q}{p} t p^\omega + t \binom{p+q}{q}^{\omega-1}\right)$ operations over $\mathbb{F}$.*

Proof: We only show how to find $\widehat{\mathcal{S}} \subseteq_{minrep}^q \mathcal{S}$ in the claimed running time. The proof for $\widehat{\mathcal{S}} \subseteq_{maxrep}^q \mathcal{S}$ is analogous, and for that case we only point out the places where the proof differs. If $t \leq \binom{k}{p}$, then we can take $\widehat{\mathcal{S}} = \mathcal{S}$. Clearly, in this case $\widehat{\mathcal{S}} \subseteq_{minrep}^q \mathcal{S}$. So from now onward we always assume that $t > \binom{k}{p}$. For the proof we view the representation matrix A_M as a vector space over $\mathbb{F}$ and each set $S_i \in \mathcal{S}$ as a subspace of this vector space. With every element $e \in E$, let x_e be the corresponding k-dimensional column in A_M. Observe that each $x_e \in \mathbb{F}^k$. For each subspace $S_i \in \mathcal{S}$, $i \in [t]$, we associate a vector $\vec{s}_i = \bigwedge_{j \in S_i} x_j$ in $\mathbb{F}^{\binom{k}{p}}$ as follows. In exterior algebra terminology, the vector $\vec{s}_i$ is a wedge product of the vectors corresponding to elements in S_i. For a set $S \in \mathcal{S}$ and $I \in \binom{[k]}{p}$, we define $s[I] = \det(A_M[I, S])$.

We also define

$$\vec{s}_i = (s_i[I])_{I \in \binom{[k]}{p}}.$$

Thus, the entries of the vector $\vec{s}_i$ are the values of $\det(A_M[I, S_i])$, where I runs through all the p sized subsets of rows of A_M.

Let $H_{\mathcal{S}} = (\vec{s}_1, \ldots, \vec{s}_t)$ be the $\binom{k}{p} \times t$ matrix obtained by taking $\vec{s}_i$ as columns. Now we define a weight function $w' : \mathbf{C}(H_{\mathcal{S}}) \to \mathbb{R}^+$ on the set of columns of $H_{\mathcal{S}}$. For the column $\vec{s}_i$ corresponding to $S_i \in \mathcal{S}$, we define $w'(\vec{s}_i) = w(S_i)$. Let $\mathcal{W}$ be a set of columns of $H_{\mathcal{S}}$ that are linearly independent over $\mathbb{F}$, such that the size of $\mathcal{W}$ is equal to rank$(H_{\mathcal{S}})$ and $\mathcal{W}$ is of minimum total weight with respect to the weight function w'. That is, $\mathcal{W}$ is a minimum weight column basis of $H_{\mathcal{S}}$. Because the row-rank of a matrix is equal to the column-rank, we have that $|\mathcal{W}| = $ rank$(H_{\mathcal{S}}) \leq \binom{k}{p}$. We define $\widehat{\mathcal{S}} = \{S_\alpha \mid \vec{s}_\alpha \in \mathcal{W}\}$. Let $|\widehat{\mathcal{S}}| = \ell$. Because $|\mathcal{W}| = |\widehat{\mathcal{S}}|$, we have that $\ell \leq \binom{k}{p}$. Without loss of generality, let $\widehat{\mathcal{S}} = \{S_i \mid 1 \leq i \leq \ell\}$ (else we can rename these sets) and $\mathcal{W} = \{\vec{s}_1 \ldots, \vec{s}_\ell\}$. The only thing that remains to show is that indeed $\widehat{\mathcal{S}} \subseteq_{minrep}^q \mathcal{S}$.

Let $S_\beta \in \mathcal{S}$ be such that $S_\beta \notin \widehat{\mathcal{S}}$. We show that if there is a set $Y \subseteq E$ of size at most q such that $S_\beta \cap Y = \emptyset$ and $S_\beta \cup Y \in \mathcal{I}$, then there exists a set $\widehat{S}_\beta \in \widehat{\mathcal{S}}$ disjoint from Y such that $\widehat{S}_\beta \cup Y \in \mathcal{I}$ and $w(\widehat{S}_\beta) \leq w(S_\beta)$. Let us first consider the case $|Y| = q$. Because $S_\beta \cap Y = \emptyset$, it follows that

11.2 Computing Representative Families

$|S_\beta \cup Y| = p + q = k$. Furthermore, because $S_\beta \cup Y \in \mathcal{I}$, we have that the columns corresponding to $S_\beta \cup Y$ in A_M are linearly independent over $\mathbb{F}$; that is, $\det(A_M[\mathbf{R}(A_M), S_\beta \cup Y]) \neq 0$.

Recall that $\vec{s}_\beta = \left(s_\beta[I]\right)_{I \in \binom{[k]}{p}}$, where $s_\beta[I] = \det(A_M[I, S_\beta])$. Similarly, we define $y[L] = \det(A_M[L, Y])$ and

$$\vec{y} = (y[L])_{L \in \binom{[k]}{q}}.$$

Let $J = S_\beta$. Then, $\sum J = \sum_{j \in S_\beta} j$. Define

$$\gamma(\vec{s}_\beta, \vec{y}) = \sum_{I \in \binom{[k]}{p}} (-1)^{\sum I + \sum J} s_\beta[I] \cdot y[\bar{I}].$$

Because $\binom{k}{p} = \binom{k}{k-p} = \binom{k}{q}$, the preceding formula is well defined. Observe that by Proposition 11.7, we have that $\gamma(\vec{s}_\beta, \vec{y}) = \det(A_M[\mathbf{R}(A_M), S_\beta \cup Y]) \neq 0$. We also know that $\vec{s}_\beta$ can be written as a linear combination of vectors in $\mathcal{W} = \{\vec{s}_1, \vec{s}_2, \ldots, \vec{s}_\ell\}$. That is, $\vec{s}_\beta = \sum_{i=1}^{\ell} \lambda_i \vec{s}_i$, $\lambda_i \in \mathbb{F}$, and for some i, $\lambda_i \neq 0$. Thus,

$$\gamma(\vec{s}_\beta, \vec{y}) = \sum_I (-1)^{\sum I + \sum J} s_\beta[I] \cdot y[\bar{I}]$$

$$= \sum_I (-1)^{\sum I + \sum J} \left(\sum_{i=1}^{\ell} \lambda_i s_i[I]\right) y[\bar{I}]$$

$$= \sum_{i=1}^{\ell} \lambda_i \left(\sum_I (-1)^{\sum I + \sum J} s_i[I] y[\bar{I}]\right)$$

$$= \sum_{i=1}^{\ell} \lambda_i \det(A_M[\mathbf{R}(A_M), S_i \cup Y]) \quad \text{(by Proposition 11.7)}.$$

Define

$$\mathsf{sup}(S_\beta) = \left\{ S_i \,\middle|\, S_i \in \widehat{\mathcal{S}}, \, \lambda_i \det(A_M[\mathbf{R}(A_M), S_i \cup Y]) \neq 0 \right\}.$$

Because $\gamma(\vec{s}_\beta, \vec{y}) \neq 0$, we have that

$$\sum_{i=1}^{\ell} \lambda_i \det(A_M[\mathbf{R}(A_M), S_i \cup Y]) \neq 0$$

and thus $\mathsf{sup}(S_\beta) \neq \emptyset$. Observe that for all $S \in \mathsf{sup}(S_\beta)$ we have that $\det(A_M[\mathbf{R}(A_M), S \cup Y]) \neq 0$ and thus $S \cup Y \in \mathcal{I}$. We now show that $w(S) \leq w(S_\beta)$ for all $S \in \mathsf{sup}(S_\beta)$.

Claim 11.9 For all $S \in \mathsf{sup}(S_\beta)$, $w(S) \leq w(S_\beta)$.

Proof: For contradiction assume that there exists a set $S_j \in \mathsf{sup}(S_\beta)$ such that $w(S_j) > w(S_\beta)$. Let $\vec{s}_j$ be the vector corresponding to S_j and $\mathcal{W}' = (\mathcal{W} \cup \{\vec{s}_j\}) \setminus \{\vec{s}_\beta\}$. Because $w(S_j) > w(S_\beta)$, we have that $w(\vec{s}_j) > w(\vec{s}_\beta)$ and thus $w'(\mathcal{W}) > w'(\mathcal{W}')$. Now we show that $\mathcal{W}'$ is also a column basis of H_S. This will contradict our assumption that $\mathcal{W}$ is a minimum weight column basis of H_S. Recall that $\vec{s}_\beta = \sum_{i=1}^{\ell} \lambda_i \vec{s}_i$, $\lambda_i \in \mathbb{F}$. Because $S_j \in \mathsf{sup}(S_\beta)$, we have that $\lambda_j \neq 0$. Thus, $\vec{s}_j$ can be written as linear combination of vectors in $\mathcal{W}'$. That is,

$$\vec{s}_j = \lambda_\beta \vec{s}_\beta + \sum_{i=1, i \neq j}^{\ell} \lambda'_i \vec{s}_i. \tag{11.1}$$

Moreover, every vector $\vec{s}_\gamma \notin \mathcal{W}$ can be written as a linear combination of vectors in $\mathcal{W}$:

$$\vec{s}_\gamma = \sum_{i=1}^{\ell} \delta_i \vec{s}_i, \quad \delta_i \in \mathbb{F}. \tag{11.2}$$

By substituting (11.1) into (11.2), we conclude that $\vec{s}_\gamma$ can be written as linear combination of vectors in $\mathcal{W}'$. This shows that $\mathcal{W}'$ is also a column basis of H_S, a contradiction proving the claim. □

Claim 11.9 and the discussions preceding it show that we could take any set $S \in \mathsf{sup}(S_\beta)$ as the desired $\widehat{S}_\beta \in \widehat{S}$. Hence $\widehat{S} \subseteq_{minrep}^q S$ for each Y of size q. This completes the proof for the case $|Y| = q$.

Suppose that $|Y| = q' < q$. Because M is a matroid of rank $k = p+q$, there exists a superset $Y' \in \mathcal{I}$ of Y of size q such that $S_\beta \cap Y' = \emptyset$ and $S_\beta \cup Y' \in \mathcal{I}$. This implies that there exists a set $\widehat{S} \in \widehat{S}$ such that $\det(A_M[\mathbf{R}(A_M), \widehat{S} \cup Y']) \neq 0$ and $w(\widehat{S}) \leq w(S)$. Thus, the columns corresponding to $\widehat{S} \cup Y$ are linearly independent.

The proof is constructive, and the algorithm constructing a representative family of size at most $\binom{p+q}{p}$ can be easily deduced from the proof. The only procedures performed by the algorithm are those computing a determinant and finding a basis. Thus, to argue about the running time of the algorithm, we have to explain how to

(a) Compute determinants, and
(b) Apply fast Gaussian elimination to find a minimum weight column basis.

It is well known that one can compute the determinant of an $n \times n$ matrix in time $\mathcal{O}(n^\omega)$. For a rectangular matrix A of size $d \times n$ (with $d \leq n$), it is possible to compute a minimum weight column basis in time $\mathcal{O}(nd^{\omega-1})$.

See the "Bibliographic notes" section for references. Thus, given a p-family of independent sets $\mathcal{S}$, we can construct the matrix $H_\mathcal{S}$ as follows. For every set S_i, we first compute $\vec{s}_i$. To do this we compute $\det(A_M[I, S_i])$ for every $I \in \binom{[k]}{p}$. This can be done in time $\mathcal{O}(\binom{p+q}{p}p^\omega)$. Thus, we can obtain the matrix $H_\mathcal{S}$ in time $\mathcal{O}(\binom{p+q}{p}tp^\omega)$. Given $H_\mathcal{S}$, we can find a minimum weight basis $\mathcal{W}$ of linearly independent columns of $H_\mathcal{S}$ of total minimum weight in time $\mathcal{O}(t\binom{p+q}{p}^{\omega-1})$. Given $\mathcal{W}$, we can easily recover $\widehat{\mathcal{S}}$. Thus, we can compute $\widehat{\mathcal{S}} \subseteq^q_{minrep} \mathcal{S}$ in $\mathcal{O}\left(\binom{p+q}{p}tp^\omega + t\binom{p+q}{q}^{\omega-1}\right)$ field operations. This concludes the proof for finding $\widehat{\mathcal{S}} \subseteq^q_{minrep} \mathcal{S}$. To find $\widehat{\mathcal{S}} \subseteq^q_{maxrep} \mathcal{S}$, the only change we need to do in the algorithm for finding $\widehat{\mathcal{S}} \subseteq^q_{minrep} \mathcal{S}$ is to find a *maximum weight column basis* $\mathcal{W}$ of $H_\mathcal{S}$. This concludes the proof. □

In Theorem 11.8 we assumed that $\text{rank}(M) = p + q$. However, we remark that one can obtain a similar result even when $\text{rank}(M) > p + q$ using the notion of truncation, see Notes.

11.3 Kernel for VERTEX COVER

In this section, as a warmup to the following sections, we first apply the computation of representative families to obtain a polynomial kernel to our favorite problem: VERTEX COVER.

We have already seen several quadratic kernels for VERTEX COVER earlier in the book. Here, we use matroid theory to obtain a kernel of similar size. A few natural questions that arise in this context are the following:

(a) Which matroid should we associate to VERTEX COVER?
(b) What is the collection $\mathcal{F}$ for which we want to find representatives?
(c) For what value of q should we define q-representatives?

It appears that the answer to (b) is generally easy and that it governs the answers to both (a) and (c). We remark that in combinatorial optimization, $\mathcal{F}$ is the set of constraints that is unbounded and we need to find a representative family for it; a more philosophical viewpoint on this subject is given later. In the context of VERTEX COVER, the constraints correspond to the edges of the input graph G. From now onward, we assume that (G, k) is an input to VERTEX COVER. Let $\mathcal{F} = E(G)$ (each edge is thought of as a set of size 2). Now, let us identify the information we expect from a q-representative of $\mathcal{F}$ to encode. We would like to find a representative family for $\mathcal{F}$, say $\widehat{\mathcal{F}}$, such that G has a vertex cover of size k if and only if there is a k-sized vertex cover hitting all the edges in $\widehat{\mathcal{F}}$. To use the approach of representative sets, it must be the case that the vertex subsets corresponding to edges in $\mathcal{F}$ are independent sets in some matroid.

We associate the following uniform matroid with G. Let $M = (E, \mathcal{I})$ be the matroid where $E = V(G)$ and $\mathcal{I}$ consists of all subsets of $V(G)$ of size at most $k+2$. Now using Theorem 11.8, compute a k-representative $\widehat{\mathcal{F}} \subseteq_{rep}^{k} \mathcal{F}$ in polynomial time. The size of $\widehat{\mathcal{F}}$ is at most $\binom{k+2}{2}$. We show that G has a vertex cover of size k if and only if there is a k-sized vertex cover hitting all the edges in $\widehat{\mathcal{F}}$. The forward direction follows easily as $\widehat{\mathcal{F}}$ is a subset of $E(G)$. For the other direction, let X be a vertex set of size k that hits all the edges corresponding to $\widehat{\mathcal{F}}$. We claim that X is also a vertex cover of G. Toward a contradiction, assume that X does not hit some edge, say uv, of G. Then $X \cap \{u, v\} = \emptyset$, and thus by the definition of representative sets, we have that there exists a set $\{a, b\} \in \widehat{\mathcal{F}}$ such that $X \cap \{a, b\} = \emptyset$. This contradicts the fact that X hits all the edges corresponding to $\widehat{\mathcal{F}}$. This implies that X is indeed a vertex cover of size at most k for G. Let G' be the subgraph of G that has no isolated vertices and $E(G') = \widehat{\mathcal{F}}$. Return G' as the desired kernel. This results in the following.

Theorem 11.10 VERTEX COVER *admits a kernel of size* $\mathcal{O}(k^2)$.

Before we proceed to describe other examples, let us briefly discuss a philosophical viewpoint on representative families. Given a huge dataset, the task of generating an accurate synopsis is of a great significance and it is used in many applications. Objects similar to representative families have been used as a form of synopsis in data-mining. A good representative family in this setting maximizes the amount of information it captures about the original dataset when compared to other subsets of the same size. In combinatorial optimization, the huge dataset corresponds to the huge number of constraints that we need to satisfy. Representative families can be used to prune given sets of constraints to sets of constraints of size polynomial in the parameter while still maintaining the answer. We demonstrate this approach with a few other examples; in particular, refer to the abstraction given in Section 11.5.

11.4 DIGRAPH PAIR CUT

In this section, we give a polynomial kernel for a problem that can be thought of as a generalization of VERTEX COVER and abstracts the difficulty in several cut problems.

11.4 DIGRAPH PAIR CUT

Let D be a directed graph, $s \in V(D)$ and $\{x, y\} \subseteq V(D)$ be a pair of vertices. We say that the pair $\{x, y\}$ is *reachable* from s if there exist paths from s to x and from s to y in D. These paths need not be disjoint. Now, we are ready to state the problem formally. In the DIGRAPH PAIR CUT problem, we are given a directed graph D, a source vertex $s \in V(D)$, a set $\mathcal{P}$ of pairs of vertices, and a non negative integer k. The task is to decide whether there exists a set $X \subseteq V(D) \setminus \{s\}$ such that $|X| \leq k$ and no pair in $\mathcal{P}$ is reachable from s in $D - X$.

Let us remark that a vertex can occur in several pairs of $\mathcal{P}$. We first show that DIGRAPH PAIR CUT is indeed a generalization of VERTEX COVER. Given an instance (G, k) of VERTEX COVER, we obtain an instance of DIGRAPH PAIR CUT as follows. Let D' be an edgeless digraph on $V(G)$. Now, we obtain D from D' by adding a new vertex $s \notin V(D')$ as well as a directed arc from s to every vertex in $V(D')$, that is, D is a star directed away from its center s. Let $\mathcal{P} = E(G)$, that is, the set of the two endpoints of each edge in $E(G)$ belongs to $\mathcal{P}$. Now, it is easy to see that G has a vertex cover of size at most k if and only if there exists a set $X \subseteq V(D) \setminus \{s\}$ such that $|X| \leq k$ and no pair in $\mathcal{P}$ is reachable from s in $D - X$.

It is natural to try the strategy we employed for VERTEX COVER for DIGRAPH PAIR CUT; let us see what happens when we try to do that. As before, we associate a uniform matroid with D. Let $M = (E, \mathcal{I})$ be the matroid, where $E = V(D)$ and $\mathcal{I}$ consists of all subsets of $V(D)$ of size at most $k + 2$. Now using Theorem 11.8, in polynomial time compute a k-representative family $\widehat{\mathcal{P}} \subseteq_{rep}^k \mathcal{P}$. The size of $\widehat{\mathcal{P}}$ is at most $\binom{k+2}{2}$. There are two obvious questions:

(i) Is it true that $(D, s, \mathcal{P}, k)$ is a yes-instance if and only if $(D, s, \widehat{\mathcal{P}}, k)$ is a yes-instance?
(ii) Does this imply that we have a kernel polynomial in k?

We first answer the second question. This method directly does not give us a polynomial kernel—while the number of pairs is polynomial in k, this may not be the case with the size of D. However, it does allow us to upper bound the size of "essential" constraints by a polynomial function of k. We will explain later a simple trick that uses the equivalent instance $(D, s, \widehat{\mathcal{P}}, k)$ to obtain a polynomial size kernel. So for now, we only focus on obtaining an equivalent instance $(D, s, \widehat{\mathcal{P}}, k)$, where $|\widehat{\mathcal{P}}| = k^{\mathcal{O}(1)}$. Let us try to answer the first question. The forward direction is obvious as $\widehat{\mathcal{P}} \subseteq \mathcal{P}$. For the backward direction, let vertex set $X \subseteq V(D) \setminus \{s\}$ be such that $|X| \leq k$ and no pair in $\widehat{\mathcal{P}}$ is reachable from s in $D - X$. The only reason why X may not be a solution for $(D, s, \mathcal{P}, k)$ is that there exists a pair $\{a, b\} \in \mathcal{P} \setminus \widehat{\mathcal{P}}$ such that $\{a, b\}$ is reachable from s in $D - X$. Clearly, then $X \cap \{a, b\} = \emptyset$ and thus by the definition of representative families, there exists a pair $\{a', b'\} \in \widehat{\mathcal{P}}$ such that $X \cap \{a', b'\} = \emptyset$. For VERTEX COVER this immediately implied that X was not the required solution for the reduced instance and hence we arrived at the desired contradiction. However, for DIGRAPH PAIR CUT, the condition $X \cap \{a', b'\} = \emptyset$ does not imply that the pair $\{a', b'\}$ is reachable from s in $D - X$. Indeed, it could be that X hits all the paths from s to either a' or b' somewhere else.

The discussion in the preceding paragraph suggests that our choice of a uniform matroid to define a representative family is not correct. We need a matroid where the fact that $X \cup \{a', b'\}$ is an independent set implies that there are paths from s to a' and b' in $D - X$. It seems very natural to use gammoids in an appropriate manner, and indeed this is what we will do. In this context, note that on the one hand, if $X \cup \{a', b'\}$ is independent, then that would imply that there are $|X| + 2$ vertex disjoint paths from an appropriate source set with its endpoints in $X \cup \{a', b'\}$. On the other hand, if a pair $\{a', b'\}$ is reachable from s, that is, there are paths from s to a' and b', then the witnessing paths are only two and they need not be disjoint. We need to take care of this option appropriately.

All the paths we are considering originate from s, and thus s is a sensible candidate for the source set S of the gammoid we would like to form. However, if some set X needs to be an independent set in a gammoid, then it must be linked to S and thus there must be $|X|$ vertex disjoint paths from S to X. Furthermore, we also need to find a solution that does not include s. To overcome these difficulties, we add $k + 1$ vertices $s_1, \ldots, s_{k+1}$, give them same adjacencies as s, and then delete s. We call this transformed digraph D' and define $S = \{s_1, \ldots, s_{k+1}\}$. It is not difficult to see that $(D, s, \mathcal{P}, k)$ is a yes-instance if and only if there exists a set $X \subseteq V(D') \setminus S$ such that $|X| \leq k$ and no pair in $\mathcal{P}$ is reachable in $D' - X$ from any vertex $s' \in S$. From now onward, we will work with the instance $(D', S, \mathcal{P}, k)$, and for the sake of presentation we denote D' by D. Moreover, from now onward, by slightly abusing notation we will refer to the tuple $(D, S, \mathcal{P}, k)$ as the instance of DIGRAPH PAIR CUT. Having replaced s by S is not sufficient—we still need to perform additional work to define the matroid where all the sets that we want to be independent are indeed independent. This is what we will do next.

Let $M = (E, \mathcal{I})$ be a strict gammoid with $E = V(D)$ and source set S. We would like to compute a k-representative set $\widehat{\mathcal{P}} \subseteq_{rep}^k \mathcal{P}$ with respect to the gammoid we constructed. However, to compute the representative set, it is required that for every pair $\{a, b\} \in \mathcal{P}$, this pair is an independent set in the gammoid. This is a general principle: If we want to compute a representative set for a family $\mathcal{F}$, then every set in $\mathcal{F}$ should be an independent set in the base matroid. Observe that in the current setting, we cannot guarantee that there are

two vertex disjoint paths from S to a pair $\{a,b\}$ in $\mathcal{P}$. We are only guaranteed that there is a path from S to each vertex among a and b (else the pair can be removed from $\mathcal{P}$), but these two paths may not be vertex disjoint. Thus, to make $\{a,b\}$ independent in our gammoid, we apply the following disjointness trick that will be useful in other settings too. We construct a linear matroid M that is a disjoint sum of two gammoids. We make two copies of the digraph D and call them D_1 and D_2. A copy of a vertex $v \in V(D)$ becomes v_1 in D_1 and v_2 in D_2. Furthermore, let S_i, $i \in \{1,2\}$, be the copy of S in D_i. For $i \in \{1,2\}$, let $M_i = (E_i, \mathcal{I}_i)$ be the gammoid with $E_i = V(D_i)$ and the source set S_i. Let $M = M_1 \oplus M_2$. We also modify our family $\mathcal{P}$ as follows.
Let
$$\mathcal{S} = \left\{ \{a_1, b_2\} \mid \{a,b\} \in \mathcal{P} \right\}.$$

Observe that because $|S_i| = k+1$, we have that the largest independent set in $\mathcal{I}_i$ has size $k+1$, and thus the rank of M is $2k+2$. Let $\widehat{\mathcal{S}} \subseteq_{\text{rep}}^{2k} \mathcal{S}$ and $\widehat{\mathcal{P}} = \left\{ \{a,b\} \mid \{a_1, b_2\} \in \widehat{\mathcal{S}} \right\}$. Clearly, $|\widehat{\mathcal{P}}| \leq \binom{2k+2}{2}$.

It remains to prove the following lemma.

Lemma 11.11 $(D, S, \mathcal{P}, k)$ *is a yes-instance of* DIGRAPH PAIR CUT *if and only if* $(D, S, \widehat{\mathcal{P}}, k)$ *is.*

Proof: The forward direction is obvious as $\widehat{\mathcal{P}} \subseteq \mathcal{P}$.

For the reverse direction, let X be a solution to $(D, S, \widehat{\mathcal{P}}, k)$. If X is not a solution for $(D, S, \mathcal{P}, k)$, it means that exists a pair $\{a,b\} \in \mathcal{P} \setminus \widehat{\mathcal{P}}$ such that $\{a,b\}$ is reachable from S in $D - X$. Clearly, then $X \cap \{a,b\} = \emptyset$. The proof would follow easily if we could show that $X_1 \cup \{a_1\}$ ($X_2 \cup \{b_2\}$) is an independent set in $\mathcal{I}_1$ ($\mathcal{I}_2$). Indeed, that would imply that $\{a_1, b_2\} \cup X_1 \cup X_2$ is an independent set in $\mathcal{I}$ and thus there exists a pair $\{a'_1, b'_2\} \in \widehat{\mathcal{S}}$ such that $X_1 \cup \{a'_1\}$ is independent in I_1 and $X_2 \cup \{b'_2\}$ is independent in I_2. This in turn implies that there are $|X|+1$ vertex disjoint paths from S to $X \cup \{a'\}$ in D, hence there is a path from S to a' in $D-X$. Similarly, there is a path from S to b' in $D-X$ and thus $\{a',b'\}$ is reachable from S—a contradiction as X is a solution to $(D, S, \widehat{\mathcal{P}}, k)$. Thus, our goal boils down to finding a solution X for $(D, S, \widehat{\mathcal{P}}, k)$ with the following properties: If there exists a pair $\{a,b\} \in \mathcal{P} \setminus \widehat{\mathcal{P}}$ such that $\{a,b\}$ is reachable from S in $D - X$, then there are $|X|+1$ vertex disjoint paths from S to $X \cup \{a\}$ as well as to $X \cup \{b\}$ in D. Obviously, not every X satisfy these conditions, and *a priori* it is not at all clear that such a solution exists.

To find a solution of the desired kind, we digress at this point. Let S and T be vertex subsets (not necessarily disjoint) of a digraph D, and X be a minimum vertex cut between S and T. That is, X is a minimum sized vertex subset such that in $D - X$ there is no path from a vertex in $S \setminus X$ to a vertex in $T \setminus X$. Moreover, assume that $X \neq S$. Let $R(S, X)$ denote the set of vertices reachable from S in $D - X$. Let u be a vertex in $R(S, X)$. Is it true that there are $|X| + 1$ vertex disjoint paths from S to $X \cup \{u\}$ in $D' = D[R(S, X) \cup X]$? If not then by Menger's theorem there is a set Z in $D[R(S, X) \cup X]$ of size $|X|$ that disconnects S from $X \cup \{u\}$ in D'. Clearly, $Z \neq X$ else we can reach u from S in $D' - Z$. Observe that $R(S, Z) \subsetneq R(S, X)$ and Z is also a minimum vertex cut between S and T. Now, for any vertex $w \in R(S, Z)$, we again ask the following question: Are there $|Z| + 1 = |X| + 1$ vertex disjoint paths from S to $Z \cup \{w\}$ in $D[R(S, Z) \cup Z]$? Observe that this process will stop as D is finite and in each step the size of the reachability set decreases. Thus, we have shown that there exists a minimum vertex cut, say Z, between S and T such that for every vertex $w \in R(S, Z)$, we have that there are $|Z| + 1$ vertex disjoint paths from S to $Z \cup \{w\}$ in $D[R(S, Z) \cup Z]$. In other words, Z is the *unique minimum vertex cut* between S and Z in D. This brings us to the following definition.

Definition 11.12 (Closest set) Let D be a digraph and S and T be vertex subsets (not necessarily disjoint) of $V(D)$.

(i) A set $X \subseteq V(D)$ is *closest* to S if for every vertex $w \in R(S, X)$, there are $|X| + 1$ vertex disjoint paths from S to $X \cup \{w\}$ in $D[R(S, X) \cup X]$. That is, X is the unique minimum vertex cut between S and X. In other words, X is the only vertex cut of size at most $|X|$ for paths from S to X.
(ii) Let Z be a minimum vertex cut between S and T such that for every vertex $w \in R(S, Z)$, there are $|Z| + 1$ vertex disjoint paths from S to $Z \cup \{w\}$ in $D[R(S, Z) \cup Z]$. Such a set Z is called a *T-induced-closest-set*. In other words, Z is the closest to S minimum vertex cut between S and T.

Now we return to the DIGRAPH PAIR CUT problem. Let $(D, S, \mathcal{P}, k)$ be an instance of DIGRAPH PAIR CUT and X be a solution to it. A solution X is called *special* if it is closest to S.

Claim 11.13 *If $(D, S, \mathcal{P}, k)$ is a yes-instance of* DIGRAPH PAIR CUT*, then there exists a special solution to the problem.*

Proof of the claim: Let Y be a solution to $(D, S, \mathcal{P}, k)$ and X be a Y-induced-closest-set. By definition, we have that $|X| \leq |Y|$ and that for every vertex $w \in R(S, X)$, there are $|X| + 1$ vertex disjoint paths from S to $X \cup \{w\}$ in $D[R(S, X) \cup X]$. It only remains to show that X is also a solution to $(D, S, \mathcal{P}, k)$. This follows from the observation that every path from S to a pair $\{a, b\} \in \mathcal{P}$ containing a vertex of Y should also contain a vertex of X. A formal proof is as follows. Suppose that X is not a solution to $(D, S, \mathcal{P}, k)$. This implies that there exists a pair $\{a,b\}$ such that there are paths P_a and P_b from S to a and b, correspondingly, in $D - X$. However, either P_a contains a vertex of Y, or P_b contains a vertex of Y. Without loss of generality assume that P_a contains a vertex of Y. Furthermore, let y be the first occurrence of a vertex from Y on P_a. Let P'_a be the prefix subpath of P_a whose last vertex is y. Thus, in P'_a the only vertex from Y is y. But because X is the Y-induced-closest-set, we have that X is a minimum vertex cut between S and Y. Thus, X contains a vertex of P_a—a contradiction to P_a being a path from S to a in $D - X$. This completes the proof. □

Now, let us conclude the proof the reverse direction of Lemma 11.11. Rather than picking any solution to $(D, S, \widehat{\mathcal{P}}, k)$, we pick a special solution X, whose existence is guaranteed by Claim 11.13. As we have argued earlier, to conclude the proof, it suffices to show that $X_1 \cup \{a_1\}$ ($X_2 \cup \{b_2\}$) is an independent set in $\mathcal{I}_1$ ($\mathcal{I}_2$). However, this follows because X is closest to S, which means that there are $|X|+1$ vertex disjoint paths from S to $X \cup \{a\}$ as well as $|X|+1$ vertex disjoint paths from S to $X \cup \{b\}$. This concludes the proof of the lemma. □

We summarize all that we have said so far in the following lemma.

Lemma 11.14 *Let $(D, S, \mathcal{P}, k)$ be an instance of* DIGRAPH PAIR CUT. *Then, in randomized polynomial time it is possible to obtain a set $\widehat{\mathcal{P}} \subseteq \mathcal{P}$ such that*

- $|\widehat{\mathcal{P}}| = \mathcal{O}(k^2)$, *and*
- $(D, S, \mathcal{P}, k)$ *is a yes-instance if and only if* $(D, S, \widehat{\mathcal{P}}, k)$ *is a yes-instance.*

Proof: The set $\widehat{\mathcal{P}}$ defined in Lemma 11.11 is a representative set of a linear matroid M. The representation A_M is formed from the representation matrices of two gammoids. Each of the gammoids for the graph D has $|S|$ sources. Let U be the set of vertices of the pairs in $\widehat{\mathcal{P}}$. By Theorem 10.8, there is a randomized polynomial-time algorithm with one-sided error bounded by ϵ to compute a representation A of a gammoid of size $|S| \times |U|$ such that every entry of A has bit length $\mathcal{O}(k \log k + \log(\frac{1}{\epsilon}) + \log |V(D)|)$. Thus by Theorem 11.8, the family $\widehat{\mathcal{P}}$ is computable in polynomial time. The rank of M is $2k + 2$, and the family $\widehat{\mathcal{P}}$ is a $2k$-representative family, thus $|\widehat{\mathcal{P}}| = \mathcal{O}(k^2)$. The equivalence of the two instances follows from Lemma 11.11. □

Now we are fully prepared to prove the following theorem. Before that, let us remind that by randomized kernel, we mean that with high probability (say, some constant close to 1), the input and output instances are equivalent.

Theorem 11.15 DIGRAPH PAIR CUT *admits a randomized polynomial kernel.*

Proof: The proof is based on Lemma 11.14. First, we need the following claim.

Claim 11.16 *There exists a randomized algorithm that solves* DIGRAPH PAIR CUT *in time* $2^{\mathcal{O}(k^2)} n^{\mathcal{O}(1)}$.

Proof of the claim: Given an instance $(D, S, \mathcal{P}, k)$ to DIGRAPH PAIR CUT, we first apply Lemma 11.14 and obtain an equivalent instance $(D, S, \widehat{\mathcal{P}}, k)$. Let U be the set of vertices of the pairs in $\widehat{\mathcal{P}}$. A vertex subset $W \subseteq U$ is called *good* if it contains at least one vertex from each pair in $\widehat{\mathcal{P}}$. Now, to check whether the given instance is a yes-instance, we proceed as follows. For every good set W, we check whether it can be separated from S by at most k vertices. If there exists a good W for which we succeed, then we determine that $(D, S, \mathcal{P}, k)$ is a yes-instance, and otherwise we determine that it is a no-instance.

Clearly, if we determine that $(D, S, \mathcal{P}, k)$ is a yes-instance, then it is correct. In the other direction, suppose that $(D, S, \mathcal{P}, k)$ is a yes-instance. Let X be a solution to $(D, S, \mathcal{P}, k)$. We form a set T by picking a vertex from each pair $\{a, b\} \in \mathcal{P}$ such that this vertex is not reachable from S in $D - X$. Clearly, X separates T from S. In fact, every minimum-sized vertex cut that separates S from T is a solution to the instance $(D, S, \mathcal{P}, k)$. As T is a good set, we determine that $(D, S, \mathcal{P}, k)$ is a yes-instance. □

Now, we compress DIGRAPH PAIR CUT into a problem of finding the rank of an independent set in an appropriate matroid. We apply Lemma 11.14 to obtain an equivalent instance $(D, S, \widehat{\mathcal{P}}, k)$. Let U be the set of vertices of the pairs in $\widehat{\mathcal{P}}$. Let $M = (E, \mathcal{I})$ be the gammoid correponding to D with the source set S and the sink set U. Moreover, let A_M be the corresponding representation matrix, so that the size of A_M is $|S| \times |U|$ and every entry has bit length at most $\mathcal{O}(k \log k + \log(\frac{1}{\epsilon}) + \log |V(D)|)$ where ϵ is the probability of failure. (Note that in the matrix A_M, every column corresponds to a vertex.) Thus, for a fixed ϵ, the bit length is bounded by $\mathcal{O}(k \log k + \log |V(D)|)$. Let us remind that a vertex subset $W \subseteq U$ is called *good* if it contains at least one vertex from each pair in $\widehat{\mathcal{P}}$. Thus, $(D, S, \widehat{\mathcal{P}}, k)$ is a yes-instance if and only if there exists a good set $W \subseteq U$ such that there exists a set $X \subseteq V(D)$ of size at most k so that in $D - X$ there is no path from S to W. For any good set $W \subseteq U$, the minimum size of such a set $X \subseteq V(D)$ that separates S from W is equal to the maximum number of vertex disjoint paths from S to W (by Menger's theorem), which is the rank of the set of columns corresponding to W in A_M.

We would like to bound the total number of bits in A_M by a polynomial function of k. Toward this we first check whether $2^{\mathcal{O}(k^2)} \leq |V(D)|$, and if this is the case, then we apply Claim 11.16 and solve the problem in time $2^{\mathcal{O}(k^2)}|V(D)|^{\mathcal{O}(1)} \leq |V(D)|^{\mathcal{O}(1)}$. Thus, in polynomial time we can decide whether the given input is a yes-instance. Otherwise, we have that $|V(D)| \leq 2^{\mathcal{O}(k^2)}$, and therefore $\log |V(D)| \leq \mathcal{O}(k^2)$. This implies that the number of bits in A_M is at most $|S| \cdot |U| \cdot \mathcal{O}(k^2) = \mathcal{O}(k^5)$. Thus, we have obtained an instance of the following LOW-RANK GOOD SET TESTING problem, where the size of the instance is bounded by $\mathcal{O}(k^5)$.

In the LOW-RANK GOOD SET TESTING we are given a matrix A, a family $\mathcal{P}$ of pairs of columns of A and a positive integer k. The task is to decide whether there is a set of columns W that has at least one column from every pair in $\mathcal{P}$, and such that the rank of the submatrix induced by W is at most k.

To derive the existence a kernel for DIGRAPH PAIR CUT, we invoke Theorem 1.6 about polynomial compressions. Observe that LOW-RANK GOOD SET TESTING is in the class NP. Moreover, DIGRAPH PAIR CUT is NP-complete—for example, this can be shown by making use of the reduction from VERTEX COVER, which we gave in the beginning of this section. Thus, by Theorem 1.6, a polynomial compression to LOW-RANK GOOD SET TESTING implies a polynomial kernel for DIGRAPH PAIR CUT. This completes the proof of the theorem. □

11.5 An Abstraction

In this section, we abstract a theme common to the kernels we saw for DIGRAPH PAIR CUT and VERTEX COVER. One way to design a polynomial kernel for a graph problem where the objective is to find a vertex/edge subset of size at most k that satisfies some properties is to try to keep a certificate for every k-sized subset that tells us why it cannot be a solution. For example, for VERTEX COVER for every vertex set X of size at most k that is not a vertex cover, we would like to keep an edge uv such that $X \cap \{u, v\} = \emptyset$. Sometimes we do not keep this certificate for every subset of size at most k that is not a solution, but rather for only those sets that are not a solution and satisfy certain properties. For example, for DIGRAPH PAIR CUT, we know that if there is a solution, then there is a solution that is a closest set to S. This is why for DIGRAPH PAIR CUT it is sufficient that for each closest set X to S of size at most k that is not a solution, we keep a pair $\{u, v\}$ to certify that X is indeed not a solution. In what follows, we abstract and formalize these arguments.

We start by describing a special constraint satisfaction problem (CSP). For a universe U, let $\binom{U}{\leq x}$ denote the family of all subsets of U of size at most x. In the d-SUBSET CSP problem, we are given a universe U, a family $\mathcal{C} \subseteq \binom{U}{\leq d}$, a function $f : \binom{U}{\leq k} \times \mathcal{C} \to \{0, 1\}$ with oracle access, and a non negative integer k. Here, we mean we do not have an explicit representation of f, but given any $(X, c) \in \binom{U}{\leq k}$ we can obtain $f(X, c)$ in polynomial time. The task is to decide whether there exists $X \in \binom{U}{\leq k}$ such that for every $c \in \mathcal{C}, f(X, c) = 1$. We refer to the set X as a *solution* to d-SUBSET CSP.

Example 11.17 To see why VERTEX COVER is a special case of d-SUBSET CSP, for an instance (G, k) of VERTEX COVER, we construct an equivalent instance $(U, \mathcal{C}, f, k)$ of d-SUBSET CSP as follows. We take a universe $U = V(G)$ and a family of constraints $\mathcal{C} = E(G)$. For every $X \in \binom{U}{\leq k}$ and constraint (or edge) $c = uv \in \mathcal{C}$, we put $f(X, c) = 1$ if $X \cap \{u, v\} \neq \emptyset$ and $f(X, c) = 0$ otherwise. Then, X is a vertex cover of size k in G if and only if X is a solution to $(U, \mathcal{C}, f, k)$.

Example 11.18 Similarly, for an instance $(D, s, \mathcal{P}, k)$ of DIGRAPH PAIR CUT, we take $U = V(D)$ and $\mathcal{C} = \mathcal{P}$. For every $X \in \binom{U}{\leq k}$ and $c = \{x, y\} \in \mathcal{C}$, we define $f(X, c) = 1$ if the pair $\{x, y\}$ is not reachable from s in $D - X$ and $f(X, c) = 0$ otherwise. It is easy to see that X is a digraph pair cut of size k in D if and only if X is a solution to $(U, \mathcal{C}, f, k)$.

Our goal is to find a (desirably small) subset of constraints $\mathcal{C}' \subseteq \mathcal{C}$ such that $(U, \mathcal{C}, f, k)$ is a yes-instance if and only if $(U, \mathcal{C}', f, k)$ is a yes-instance. In particular, we would like to bound $|\mathcal{C}'| \leq g(k)$, where g is a polynomial function of k alone.

An approach to find the desired $\mathcal{C}'$ is to find a solution to the following *implicit hitting set* problem. For a set $X \subseteq U$ of size at most k, we define

$$F_X = \Big\{c \in \mathcal{C} \mid f(X, c) = 0\Big\}.$$

Thus, F_X is the set of constraints that X *does not satisfy*. This leads to the following implicit hitting set problem over the universe $\mathcal{C}$. The instance of the problem is of the form

$$\Big(\mathcal{C}, \mathcal{F} = \Big\{F_X \mid X \in \binom{U}{\leq k}\Big\}\Big).$$

We say that $\mathcal{C}' \subseteq \mathcal{C}$ is a *hitting set* for the instance $(\mathcal{C}, \mathcal{F})$, if for every subset X of size at most k, if $F_X \neq \emptyset$, then also $\mathcal{C}' \cap F_X \neq \emptyset$.

The following lemma shows that the family of constraints of a yes-instance to d-SUBSET CSP can be "compressed" to a hitting set of $(\mathcal{C}, \mathcal{F})$.

Lemma 11.19 *Let $\mathcal{C}'$ be a hitting set for the instance $(\mathcal{C}, \mathcal{F})$. Then, $(U, \mathcal{C}, f, k)$ is a yes-instance if and only if $(U, \mathcal{C}', f, k)$ is a yes-instance.*

Proof: The forward direction is straightforward because $\mathcal{C}' \subseteq \mathcal{C}$. For the reverse direction, let X be a solution to $(U, \mathcal{C}', f, k)$. We have to show that X is also a solution to $(U, \mathcal{C}, f, k)$. For a contradiction, assume that this is not the case. Hence there exists a constraint $c \in \mathcal{C}$ such that $f(X, c) = 0$. This implies that F_X is non empty and hence there is a constraint, say c' in $\mathcal{C}' \cap F_X$. Then $f(X, c') = 0$, and hence X is not a solution to $(U, \mathcal{C}', f, k)$. This is a contradiction, completing the proof. □

Thus, the main questions are: for which kind of functions f can we have $|\mathcal{C}'| \leq k^{\mathcal{O}(1)}$, and when can the desired family $\mathcal{C}'$ be found in polynomial time? We call f a *disjointness function*, if for all $X \in \binom{U}{\leq k}$ and $c \in \mathcal{C}$, $f(X, c) = 0$ if and only if $X \cap c = \emptyset$. By definition, the function f from Example 11.17 is a disjointness function, but the function from Example 11.18 is not.

The following theorem is an application of the Sunflower lemma (Theorem 8.2).

Theorem 11.20 *Let $(U, \mathcal{C}, f, k)$ be a yes-instance of d-SUBSET CSP and f be a disjointness function. Then, there exists a hitting set $\mathcal{C}'$ for $(\mathcal{C}, \mathcal{F})$ of size $(kd)^{\mathcal{O}(d)}$ and this set can be found in polynomial time.*

Proof: We give an algorithm computing the required hitting set. At every step of the algorithm, we delete one constraint from the current set of constraints, while maintaining the following condition for every $X \in \binom{U}{\leq k}$: If F_X was non empty before deleting the constraint, then it remains non empty after deleting the constraint. This ensures that a hitting set for the reduced instance is also a hitting set for the original instance. We finally stop when the number of constraints becomes a polynomial function of k and d.

We first check whether $|\mathcal{C}| > d!\,(k+1)^d$. If $|\mathcal{C}| \leq d!\,(k+1)^d$ then we return $\mathcal{C}$ as $\mathcal{C}'$. Otherwise by the Sunflower Lemma (Theorem 8.2), there exists a sunflower with $k+2$ petals and such a sunflower can be computed in time polynomial in $|U|+|\mathcal{C}|+k$. Recall that a sunflower with $k+2$ petals and a core Y is a collection of sets $c_1, c_2, \ldots, c_{k+2} \in \mathcal{C}$ such that $c_i \cap c_j = Y$ for all $i \neq j$; the sets $c_i \setminus Y$ are petals and none of them is empty. Note that a family of pairwise disjoint sets is a sunflower (with an empty core). We would like to show that every hitting set for $(\mathcal{C} \setminus \{c_1\}, \mathcal{F})$ is also a hitting set for $(\mathcal{C}, \mathcal{F})$, and vice versa. Toward this, it is sufficient to prove that for all $X \in \binom{U}{\leq k}$, $F_X \cap \mathcal{C} \neq \emptyset$ if and only if $F_X \cap (\mathcal{C} \setminus \{c_1\}) \neq \emptyset$. Let $X \in \binom{U}{\leq k}$. Clearly, if $F_X \cap (\mathcal{C} \setminus \{c_1\}) \neq \emptyset$ then $F_X \cap \mathcal{C} \neq \emptyset$. For the reverse direction, suppose that $F_X \cap \mathcal{C} \neq \emptyset$ and $c_1 \in F_X$. We aim to show that in this case, F_X also contains one of the constraints in $\{c_2, \ldots, c_{k+2}\}$. Because $c_1 \in F_X$, we have that $f(X, c_1) = 0$, and because f is a disjointness function, this implies that $X \cap c_1 = \emptyset$. Thus, $X \cap Y = \emptyset$. Now because the size of X is at most k and each of the petals is non empty, there exists a constraint $c' \in \{c_2, \ldots, c_{k+2}\}$ such that X does not intersect the petal of c' and thus it does not intersect c' itself. The last assertion implies that $c' \in F_X$ and hence $F_X \cap (\mathcal{C} \setminus \{c_1\}) \neq \emptyset$.

We repeat the algorithm, deleting constraints until it returns a set $\mathcal{C}'$ such that $|\mathcal{C}'| \leq d!\,(k+1)^d \leq (kd)^{\mathcal{O}(d)}$. Because at each step the number of constraints drops by one, we have that the algorithm terminates in at most $|\mathcal{C}|$ steps and thus in polynomial time. This completes the proof. □

We now consider a broad class of functions for which we can find set a $\mathcal{C}'$ of size $k^{\mathcal{O}(1)}$ as in the preceding text in polynomial time. We call a function f *matroidal* if there exists a matroid $M = (E, \mathcal{I})$ such that

- $U \subseteq E$, and
- $f(X, c) = 0$ if and only if $X \cup c \in \mathcal{I}$.

For matroidal functions corresponding to linear matroids, one can show the following theorem, whose proof is simply based on a computation of $\widehat{\mathcal{C}} \subseteq_{rep}^{r-d} \mathcal{C}$ using Theorem 11.8. A formal proof is left as Exercise 11.5.

Theorem 11.21 *Let $(U, \mathcal{C}, f, k)$ be an instance to d-SUBSET CSP and f be a matroidal function. Furthermore, let A_M be a matroid representation for the corresponding matroid M of rank r. Then, in polynomial time we can find a hitting set $\mathcal{C}'$ for $(\mathcal{C}, \mathcal{F})$ of size $\binom{r}{d}$.*

Theorems 11.20 and 11.21 can lead to the derivation of kernels for special cases of d-SUBSET CSP as in polynomial time they shrink $\mathcal{C}$ to be of size polynomial in k, assuming that d is fixed. Let us remind that the objective of this section was to describe a generic way to find a small witness set that preserve all no-instances.

11.6 Combinatorial Approach

In the previous chapter we gave a polynomial kernel for ODD CYCLE TRANSVERSAL. The approach was based on compressing an instance of the problem into a gammoid of polynomial size and then using Cook's theorem to construct a kernel. The drawback of such an approach is that while we know that there exists a polynomial kernel, it is not easy to estimate its size. In this section, we discuss a "combinatorial" approach avoiding this drawback. The approach is based on cut-covering lemma, which we discuss in detail in the following subsection.

11.6.1 Cut-Covering Lemma

In this subsection we use matroids to find a set of vertices that is not too large and "covers all minimum cuts" between a particular source set S and a particular terminal set T. Let us remind that for vertex subsets A and B of a digraph D, a (vertex) (A, B)-cut is a vertex set Z such that every directed path from A to B contains a vertex of Z. The set Z can intersect A and B. We study the following CUT-COVERING problem. For a given digraph D and vertex subsets S and T, the task is to find a set Z (as small as possible) such that for every $A \subseteq S, B \subseteq T$, Z contains a minimum (A, B)-cut.

Of course, we can simply define $V(D)$ as Z. However, we will see how to find Z of size that can be significantly smaller than the size of $V(D)$. The main idea is to identify vertices that are *irrelevant* for our purpose and then discard them appropriately.

We start with the following natural question: *Which conditions force a vertex $w \in V(D)$ to be in the set Z?* If a vertex w appears in *every minimum cut* between some $A \subseteq S$ and $B \subseteq T$, then it must be in Z. These vertices are called *essential vertices*. We will see that just having these essential vertices in Z is almost sufficient. More precisely, we will show that

(a) Either all vertices are essential, or
(b) We can obtain an equivalent instance of the problem with a strictly smaller number of vertices.

We first deal with the second scenario. Toward this, we define the notion of "neighborhood closure" in digraphs.

Definition 11.22 Given a digraph D and a vertex $w \in V(D)$, we say that a digraph D' is obtained by the *neighborhood closure* of w in D if D' is obtained by deleting the vertex w and making a complete bipartite graph between the in-neighbors $N^-(w)$ and out-neighbors $N^+(w)$ of w, with arcs directed from $N^-(w)$ to $N^+(w)$. We denote the result of this operation by $\mathrm{cl}_w(D)$, see Fig. 11.1.

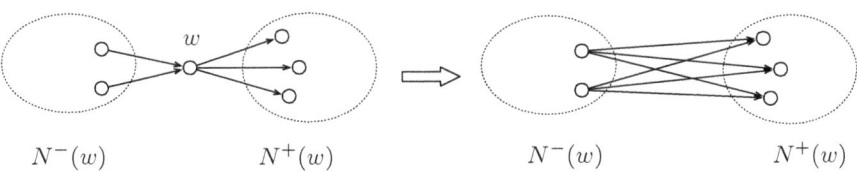

Figure 11.1 Neighborhood closure operation.

In the following two lemmas, we describe the transformation that helps us in eliminating non essential vertices without changing the sizes of minimum vertex cuts between subsets of S and T.

Lemma 11.23 *Let D be a digraph, A and B be vertex subsets and $w \in V(D) \setminus (A \cup B)$. Then,*

$$\text{mincut}_D(A, B) \leq \text{mincut}_{\text{cl}_w(D)}(A, B).$$

Proof: Let Z be a minimum vertex cut between A and B in $\text{cl}_D(w)$. For a contradiction, assume that Z is not a vertex cut between A and B in D. Then, there exist vertices $s \in A$ and $t \in B$ such that there is a path P_{st} between s and t in $D - Z$ that contains w. Let u and v be the in-neighbor and out-neighbor, respectively, of w on $P_{s,t}$. Because of the neighborhood closure operation, we have that $P'_{s,t}$, which is a path without w, is a path in $D' - Z$. This contradicts our assumption about Z. □

Lemma 11.24 *Let D be a digraph, S and T be vertex subsets and $w \in V(D) \setminus (S \cup T)$ be a non essential vertex. Then, for all $A \subseteq S$ and $B \subseteq T$? we have that*

$$\text{mincut}_D(A, B) = \text{mincut}_{\text{cl}_w(D)}(A, B).$$

Proof: Let $D' = \text{cl}_w(D)$. The inequality $\text{mincut}_D(A, B) \leq \text{mincut}_{D'}(A, B)$ follows from Lemma 11.23.

We now show that

$$\text{mincut}_D(A, B) \geq \text{mincut}_{D'}(A, B).$$

Because w is a non essential vertex, there exists a minimum vertex cut between A and B, say Z, that does not contain w. We claim that Z is also a vertex cut between A and B in D'. Suppose that Z is not a vertex cut between A and B, then there exist vertices $s \in A$ and $t \in B$ such that there is a path P_{st} between s and t in $D' - Z$. Clearly, P_{st} must contain at least one arc introduced by neighborhood closure operation. For every arc xy in P_{st} that was introduced by the neighborhood closure operation, we replace xy by a directed path xwy. This gives a directed walk P'_{st} from s to t in $D - Z$. Having P'_{st}, we also derive the existence of a directed path from s to t in $D - Z$, which is a contradiction. Hence, Z is indeed a vertex cut between A and B, and thus $\text{mincut}_D(A, B) \geq \text{mincut}_{D'}(A, B)$. □

The next question we address is how to find essential vertices in polynomial time. Toward this goal, we try to understand the properties of these vertices. Let w be an essential vertex. That is, there exist a subset $A \subseteq S$ and a subset $B \subseteq T$ such that every minimum-sized vertex cut between A and

11.6 Combinatorial Approach

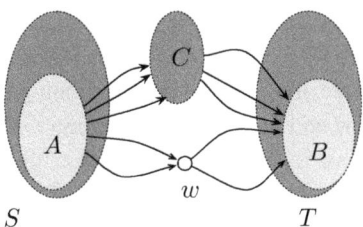

Figure 11.2 Structure of an essential vertex.

B in D includes w. Let $D' = \mathrm{cl}_D(w)$. By Lemma 11.23, we have that $\mathrm{mincut}_D(A, B) \leq \mathrm{mincut}_{D'}(A, B)$. Of course, the previous inequality cannot be replaced by equality, as this would be a contradiction to w being an essential vertex. Thus, we have that

$$\mathrm{mincut}_{D'}(A, B) \geq \mathrm{mincut}_D(A, B) + 1.$$

As we show in the following text, this indicates, for every minimum vertex cut between A and B, the existence of a certain path packing that has two paths between A and B in D that are vertex disjoint apart from having w as a common vertex. See Fig. 11.2 for an illustration.

Formally, we prove Lemma 11.25 ahead. Here, for a digraph D and sets $A, C \subseteq V(D)$, $R(A, C)$ denotes the union of C and the set of vertices in $D - C$ reachable from A and $NR(A, C)$ denotes the union of C and the set of vertices in $D - C$ non reachable from A. Note that in Lemma 11.25, $w \in C$.

Lemma 11.25 *Let D be a digraph, $w \notin A \cup B$ be an essential vertex for sets A and B and C be any minimum vertex cut between A and B. Then,*

(i) *There is a set of $|C| + 1$ paths from A to C in $R(A, C)$ that are pairwise vertex disjoint, except for two of these paths that both end in w, and*
(ii) *There is a set of $|C| + 1$ paths from C to B in $NR(A, C)$ that are pairwise vertex disjoint, except for two of these paths that both start in w.*

Proof: We only prove the first part. The proof of the second part is similar. Because C is a minimum vertex cut between A and B, by Menger's theorem there exist $|C|$ vertex disjoint paths between A and B. Let these paths be $P'_i = a^i_1 \cdots a^i_{i_r}, i \in \{1, \ldots, |C|\}$. Clearly, each of them contains exactly one vertex of C. Let $P_i = a^i_1 \cdots a^i_{i_\ell}, i \in \{1, \ldots, |C|\}$, be the subpaths of $P'_1, \ldots, P'_{|C|}$ where the last vertices on these paths belong to C.

Construct a digraph D' by starting with $D[R(A, C)]$ and then adding a vertex w' and all arcs from the in-neighbors of w to w'. (Note that $C \subseteq R(A, C)$.) That is, w' is copy of w that only has arcs from its in-neighbors. Let β be the size of maximum flow from A to $C \cup \{w'\}$ in D'. If $\beta = |C| + 1$ then we are done, as by Menger's theorem there are $|C| + 1$ vertex disjoint paths from A to $C \cup \{w'\}$ and the paths ending at w and w' in D' both terminate at w in D. Furthermore, all these paths are present in $D[R(A, C)]$. Observe that β cannot be smaller than $|C|$ as the paths P_i, $i \in \{1, \ldots, |C|\}$, belong to D. Thus, let us assume that $\beta = |C|$. This implies that there is a separator Z of size $|C|$ between A and $C \cup \{w'\}$ in D'.

We distinguish four cases based on whether each of w, w' is present in Z or not, and show that none of these cases arise. This will imply that the only case that can occur is that $\beta = |C| + 1$, for which we have already derived the conclusion of the lemma. We start with the observation that because P_i, $i \in \{1, \ldots, |C|\}$, are vertex disjoint paths, (a) each one of them contains exactly one vertex of Z and (b) no two of them contain the same vertex.

(i) $\{w, w'\} \in Z$: This is not possible as it would imply that at least one of the paths P_i, $i \in \{1, \ldots, |C|\}$, does not intersect Z.
(ii) $\{w\} \in Z$ and $\{w'\} \notin Z$: Let P_j be the path that ends in w. Because $w \in Z$, we have that the vertices of P_j^*, defined as the path P_j without the last vertex, does not contain any other vertex of Z. Furthermore, because $w \notin A$, we have that P_j^* is not empty. However, in this case we can get a path from A to w' that avoids Z by first using the path P_j^* and then using an arc to w'. This contradicts the fact that Z separates A and $C \cup \{w'\}$ in D'.
(iii) $\{w'\} \in Z$ and $\{w\} \notin Z$: This case is similar to the previous case.
(iv) $\{w, w'\} \notin Z$: Observe that in this case, we have found a set Z that separates A from C in D and thus separates A from B in D. However, the size of Z is equal to $|C|$. Thus, it is a minimum vertex cut between A and B that avoids the essential vertex w, which is a contradiction.

The preceding case analysis completes the proof. $\square$

Now we will use the properties of essential vertices given in Lemma 11.25 to find non essential vertices.

Lemma 11.26 *Let D be a digraph, S and T be vertex subsets and r denote the size of a minimum vertex cut between S and T. Then in randomized polynomial time, we can find a set $Z \subseteq V(D)$ of size $\binom{|S|+|T|+r}{3}$ that contains all essential vertices in $D \setminus (S \cup T)$.*

Proof: We start with a simple reduction rule. Delete all the vertices in $V(D) \setminus (S \cup T)$ that are either not reachable from S or cannot reach T. Clearly, these

11.6 Combinatorial Approach

vertices are not part of any path from S to T and thus can be discarded. Thus, without loss of generality we can assume that every vertex in $V(D) \setminus (S \cup T)$ is on some path starting from a vertex in S and ending in a vertex of T. To capture essential vertices, we construct a linear matroid M that is a disjoint sum of two gammoids and a uniform matroid.

(i) $M[0]$ is the uniform matroid of rank r. It is defined on the universe $V[0]$, where $V[0]$ is a copy of $V(D)$. For a vertex $v \in V(D)$, we will use $v[0]$ to denote the corresponding vertex in $V[0]$.

(ii) $M[1]$ is a gammoid defined using S. Let $D[1]$ be the digraph constructed as follows. Make a copy of the digraph D, called $D[1]$, with vertex set $V[1]$. Introduce a sink-only vertex $v[1]'$ for every vertex $v[1]$. That is, for every vertex $v[1]$ make a new vertex $v[1]'$ and then make all the in-neighbors of $v[1]$ adjacent to $v[1]'$ as in-neighbors. $M[1]$ is the gammoid $(V[1] \bigcup V[1]', \mathcal{I}[1])$ where $V[1]' = \{v[1]' : v[1] \in V[1]\}$ and $\mathcal{I}[1]$ consists of all the subsets linked to the set $S[1]$.

(iii) $M[2]$ is a gammoid defined using T. Let $D[2]$ be the digraph constructed as follows. Make a copy of the digraph D, called $D[2]$, with vertex set $V[2]$. Reverse every arc of $D[2]$ and get the digraph $D[2]'$. Introduce a sink-only vertex $v[2]'$ for every $v[2]$. That is, for every vertex $v[2]$ make a new vertex $v[2]'$, and then make all the in-neighbors of $v[2]$ in $D[2]'$ adjacent to $v[2]'$ as in-neighbors. $M[2]$ is the gammoid $(V[2] \bigcup V[2]', \mathcal{I}[2])$ where $V[2]' = \{v[2]' : v[2] \in V[2]\}$ and $\mathcal{I}[2]$ consists of all the subsets linked to the set $T[2]$ in $D[2]'$.

Essentially, the idea is that we use $M[1]$ and $M[2]$ to encode properties (i) and (ii), respectively, mentioned in Lemma 11.25 about essential vertices. More precisely, if v is an essential vertex for a pair of sets $A \subseteq S$ and $B \subseteq T$, then observe that for any minimum vertex cut C between A and B, $v \in C$ and we have that $C[1] \cup \{v[1]'\} \in \mathcal{I}[1]$ and $C[2] \cup \{v[2]'\} \in \mathcal{I}[2]$. We will see the application of matroid $M[0]$ later. We form a linear matroid $M = (E, \mathcal{I})$ where $M = M[0] \oplus M[1] \oplus M[2]$. Observe that $\text{rank}(M) = |S| + |T| + r$.

Now we need to define a family of independent sets of rank 3 in M such that each set corresponds to a vertex in D and that will be the family for which we will compute an appropriate representative family. For every vertex $v \in V(D)$, let $f(v) = \{v[0], v[1]', v[2]'\}$. We define

$$\mathcal{F} = \{f(v) \mid v \in V(D) \setminus (S \cup T)\}.$$

Observe that because every vertex in $V(D) \setminus (S \cup T)$ is on some S to T path, we have that each $f(v) \in \mathcal{F}$ is independent. We use Theorem 11.8 to compute

$\widehat{\mathcal{F}} \subseteq_{rep}^{|S|+|T|+r-3} \mathcal{F}$. Clearly, the size of $\widehat{\mathcal{F}}$ is upper bounded by $\binom{|S|+|T|+r}{3}$. We will set $Z := \{v \in V(D) \mid f(v) \in \widehat{\mathcal{F}}\}$.

It only remains to show that Z contains all essential vertices. Toward this it would be sufficient to show the following. For every essential vertex $q \in V(D) \setminus (S \cup T)$, there is an independent set C_q in M such that

- $f(q)$ and C_q are disjoint, and $f(q) \cup C_q$ is an independent set in M, and
- For any other vertex $s \in V(D) \setminus (S \cup T)$,
  - either $f(s) \cup C_q$ is not independent,
  - or $f(s)$ and C_q are not disjoint.

To see why proving the preceding claim is sufficient, observe the following. For every essential vertex q, the preceding claim implies that there exists an independent set C_q such that $f(q)$ is the *unique* independent set in $\mathcal{F}$ for which $C_q \cap f(q) = \emptyset$ and $C_q \cup f(q) \in \mathcal{I}$. Thus, by the definition of representative families, $f(q)$ must be in $\widehat{\mathcal{F}}$. Thus, we obtain all the essential vertices in $\widehat{\mathcal{F}}$ by, in some sense, "isolating" them.

Let $q \in V(D) \setminus (S \cup T)$ be an essential vertex in D with respect to $A \subseteq S$ and $B \subseteq T$, and let C be a minimum vertex cut between A and B. We define

$$C_q = (C[0] \setminus \{q[0]\}) \bigcup ((S[1] \setminus A[1]) \cup C[1]) \bigcup ((T[2] \setminus B[2]) \cup C[2]).$$

Observe that C_q is an independent set of rank at most $|S|+|T|+r-3$. Indeed, $|C[0] \setminus \{q[0]\}| \leq r-1$ because the size of a minimum vertex cut between S and T is r. Moreover, as q is an essential vertex that does not belong to $A \cup B$ and both A and B are vertex cuts between A and B, we have that $|C| \leq \min\{|A|, |B|\} - 1$, and therefore $|(S[1] \setminus A[1]) \cup C[1]| \leq |S| - 1$ and $|(T[2] \setminus B[2]) \cup C[2]| \leq |T| - 1$. In addition, note that $f(q) = \{q[0], q[1]', q[2]'\}$ and C_q are disjoint. We need to show that $f(q) \cup C_q$ is an independent set. Clearly, $q[0] \cup (C[0] \setminus q[0])$ is an independent set in $M[0]$ as its size is upper bounded by r. By Lemma 11.25, there is a set of $|C|+1$ paths from A to C in $R(A,C)$ that are pairwise vertex disjoint, except for two of these paths that intersect in q. Therefore, $(S[1] \setminus A[1]) \cup C[1] \cup \{q[1]'\}$ is independent in $M[1]$. Similarly, one can show that $(T[2] \setminus B[2]) \cup C[2] \cup \{q[2]'\}$ is an independent set in $M[2]$. This proves that $f(q) \cup C_q$ is an independent set in M.

Finally, we want to show that for any other vertex s, $s \neq q$, either $f(s) \cap C_q \neq \emptyset$ or $f(s) \cup C_q \notin \mathcal{I}$. Now for any other vertex s, one of the following three cases happens.

- The vertex $s \in C$. In this case, $f(s)$ and C_q have $s[0]$ as a common element. Thus, $f(s) \cap C_q \neq \emptyset$. This is the only place where we use the uniform matroid in our proof. However, this looks unavoidable.

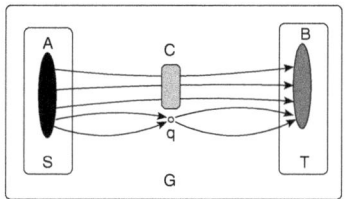
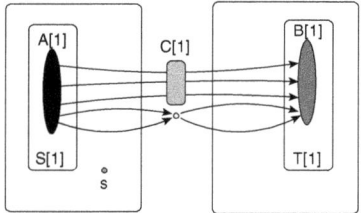

Figure 11.3 An illustration for the proof of Lemma 11.26.

- The vertex s is reachable from A in $D \setminus C$. In other words, the vertex s is not reachable from B in $D \setminus C$. See Fig. 11.3 for an illustration. Observe that $(T[2] \setminus B[2]) \cup C[2] \cup \{s[2]'\}$ is not independent in $D[2]'$. This is because all the paths from $B[2]$ to $s[2]'$ in $D[2]'$ must pass through $C[2]$.
- The vertex s is not reachable from A in $D \setminus C$. Then, $(S[1] \setminus A[1]) \cup C[1] \cup \{s[1]'\}$ is not independent in $M[1]$. This is because all the paths from $A[1]$ to $s[1]'$ pass through $C[1]$.

The preceding case analysis completes the proof. □

Now we combine the results obtained in this section to prove the following main cut-covering result.

Theorem 11.27 (Cut-Covering Theorem) *Let D be a digraph and S and T be vertex subsets. Let r denote the size of a minimum vertex cut between S and T (which may intersect S and T). There exists a set $W \subseteq V(D)$ of size at most $\binom{|S|+|T|+r}{3} + |S| + |T|$ such that for any set $A \subseteq S$ and $B \subseteq T$, it holds that W contains a minimum vertex cut between A and B. Furthermore, one can find such a set in randomized polynomial time with failure probability $\mathcal{O}(2^{-|V(D)|})$.*

Proof: The proof is obtained by iteratively using Lemmata 11.24 and 11.26. Specifically, we apply the following procedure until it is no longer possible.

> Apply Lemma 11.26 on the input and obtain a set Z. If $V(D) \setminus (S \cup T \cup Z)$ is empty, then return the current vertex set of D as W. That is, $W := V(D)$. Otherwise, if there exists a vertex $w \in V(D) \setminus (S \cup T \cup Z)$, let $D' = \mathrm{cl}_D(w)$, and update $D := D'$.

The correctness of the preceding procedure follows from the following facts. Lemma 11.26 implies that when we apply the closure operation with respect to a vertex w, then it is not an essential vertex. Lemma 11.24 implies that because w is a non essential vertex, for all $A \subseteq S$ and $B \subseteq T$ we have that $\mathrm{mincut}_D(A, B) = \mathrm{mincut}_{\mathrm{cl}_D(w)}(A, B)$. Thus, Lemmata 11.24 and 11.26 prove the correctness of the preceding procedure. The size bound follows from the fact that we stop only when all the vertices belong to $S \cup T \cup Z$. This completes the proof. □

Theorem 11.27 has a useful "terminal version," which can be directly applied to derive several kernelization results.

Corollary 11.28 *Let D be a digraph and $X \subseteq V(D)$ be a set of terminals. Then, there exists a set of vertices Z of size $\mathcal{O}(|X|^3)$ such that for any $P, Q, R \subseteq X$, there exists a minimum vertex cut between P and Q in $D - R$ that is contained in Z. Furthermore, one can find such a set in randomized polynomial time with failure probability $\mathcal{O}(2^{-|V(D)|})$.*

Proof: The idea is to construct an auxiliary directed graph where Theorem 11.27 can be applied. For every vertex $x \in X$, we introduce an additional vertex called x^- and make it an in-neighbor to x. That is, x^- is a source whose only neighbor is x. Let the resulting digraph be D', and for a set $A \subseteq X$, we define $A^- = \{y^- \mid y \in A\}$. We let $S = X^-$ and $T = X$, and apply Theorem 11.27 to compute a set W. We return the set $Z := (W \setminus W^-) \cup \{w : w^- \in W^-\} \subseteq V(D)$. Notice that $X \subseteq Z$. Clearly, $|Z| \leq |W| \leq \binom{|S|+|T|+r}{3} + |S| + |T| = \mathcal{O}(|X|^3)$.

It only remains to prove that for any $P, Q, R \subseteq X$, there exists a minimum vertex cut between P and Q in $D - R$ that is contained in Z. For this purpose, consider some subsets $P, Q, R \subseteq X$, and define $A = P^- \cup R^-$ and $B = Q \cup R$. We aim to exhibit a correspondence between a minimum vertex cut between P and Q in $D - R$ and a minimum vertex cut between A and B in D'. First, note that by adding R to any minimum cut between P and Q in $D - R$, we obtain a vertex cut between A and B in D', and thus $\text{mincut}_{D'}(A, B) \leq \text{mincut}_{D-R}(P, Q) + |R|$.

Now, by Theorem 11.27, there exists $C'' \subseteq W$ that is a minimum vertex cut between A and B in D'. Due to the preceding inequality, $|C''| \leq \text{mincut}_{D-R}(P, Q) + |R|$. The minimality of C'' implies that u and u^- cannot both belong to C'', and that $C'' \setminus Q^- = \emptyset$. This in return implies that $C' = (C'' \cup \{u \mid u^- \in C'' \cap P^-\}) \setminus P^-$, which is a subset of $V(D) \cup R^-$, is also a minimum vertex cut between A and B in D'. In particular, $|C'| \leq \text{mincut}_{D-R}(P, Q) + |R|$. Define $C = C' \setminus (R \cup R^-)$, and note that $C \subseteq Z$. We first claim that C is a vertex cut between P and Q in $D - R$. Suppose not, then there exists a path L from a vertex w in P to a vertex in Q in D that avoids $C \cup R$. In this case, observe that $w^- L$ is a path from A to B that avoids the vertices of $C' \cup (R \cup R^-)$, which is a contradiction. Thus, C is indeed a vertex cut between P and Q in $D - R$. Next, observe that by construction and minimality of C', for every vertex $v \in R$, C' must contain exactly one of v and v^-. This implies that $|C| = |C'| - |R| \leq \text{mincut}_{D-R}(P, Q)$. As $|C|$ cannot be smaller than $\text{mincut}_{D-R}(P, Q)$, we have that $|C| = \text{mincut}_{D-R}(P, Q)$. This completes the proof. □

11.6.2 Applications of Cut-Covering Lemma

In this section, we obtain combinatorial polynomial kernels for two problems by applying Theorem 11.27.

DIGRAPH PAIR CUT: Given an instance $(D, S, \mathcal{P}, k)$ of DIGRAPH PAIR CUT, we first apply Lemma 11.14. In randomized polynomial time, this application returns a family $\widehat{\mathcal{P}} \subseteq \mathcal{P}$ such that (a) $|\widehat{\mathcal{P}}| = \mathcal{O}(k^2)$, and (b) $(D, S, \mathcal{P}, k)$ is a yes-instance if and only if $(D, S, \widehat{\mathcal{P}}, k)$ is a yes-instance. Recall that we have done some gadgeteering to transform a single source s into a set S of size $k+1$. Let U be the set of vertices of pairs in $\widehat{\mathcal{P}}$. Now, we apply Theorem 11.27 with $S' := S$ and $T := U$, and obtain a set $W \subseteq V(D)$ of size $\binom{|S'|+|T|+r}{3}+|S'|+|T| = \mathcal{O}(k^6)$ such that for any set $A \subseteq S$ and $B \subseteq U$, it holds that W contains a minimum vertex cut between A and B. Recall that a vertex subset $J \subseteq U$ is called good if it contains at least one vertex from each pair in $\widehat{\mathcal{P}}$. We know that there exists a good set J such that any minimum vertex cut between S and J in D is a solution to the reduced instance $(D, S, \widehat{\mathcal{P}}, k)$. Thus, we know that if there exists a solution, then there is one that is contained in $Z \setminus S$. Now, we obtained an equivalent reduced instance $(D', S, \widehat{\mathcal{P}}, k)$ as follows. Let $v_1, \ldots, v_p \in V(D) \setminus Z$. Let $D_0 := D$. For $i = 1$ to p, let $D_i = \mathrm{cl}_{v_i}(D_{i-1})$. Return $(D_p, S, \widehat{\mathcal{P}}, k)$ as the reduced equivalent instance. The correctness of this step follows from Lemma 11.24. Thus, we have obtained a combinatorial kernel for DIGRAPH PAIR CUT with $\mathcal{O}(k^6)$ vertices. This results in the following theorem.

Theorem 11.29 DIGRAPH PAIR CUT *admits a randomized kernel with $\mathcal{O}(k^6)$ vertices.*

ODD CYCLE TRANSVERSAL: We first recall some of the transformations defined in the previous chapter. Given a graph G, and a set Q such that $G \setminus Q$ is bipartite, we defined another graph G' as follows. Let A and B be a fixed bipartition of $G \setminus Q$. We take two copies of Q, called $Q_a = \{q_a \mid q \in Q\}$ and $Q_b = \{q_b \mid q \in Q\}$. The vertex set of G' is $A \cup B \cup Q_a \cup Q_b$. Edges within $G'[A \cup B]$ are as in G, while for $q \in Q$, the vertex q_a is connected to $N_G(q) \cap A$ and the vertex q_b is connected to $N_G(q) \cap B$.

Let S, T and R be a partition of $Q_a \cup Q_b$. We say that (S, T, R) is a *valid partition* if for every $q \in Q$ either $|\{q_a, q_b\} \cap S| = |\{q_a, q_b\} \cap T| = 1$ or $|\{q_a, q_b\} \cap R| = 2$. By Lemma 10.17, we know that the size of the minimum odd cycle transversal is the minimum over-all valid partitions of $Q_a \cup Q_b = S \cup T \cup R$ of the following value:

$$\frac{|R|}{2} + \mathrm{mincut}_{G'-R}(S, T). \tag{11.3}$$

Observe that we first need a set $Q \subseteq V(G)$ such that $G - Q$ is bipartite. To obtain such a set Q, we make use of the known $\alpha\sqrt{\log n}$ factor approximation algorithm for the optimization version of ODD CYCLE TRANSVERSAL. Specifically, the algorithm mentioned in Theorem 10.18 outputs in polynomial time a set Q of size at most $\alpha\sqrt{\log n} \cdot OPT$, where OPT is the size of a minimum odd cycle transversal for G. If $k \leq \log n$, then run the $\mathcal{O}(3^k mn)$ time algorithm of Theorem 10.16 to find a solution in polynomial time. We return a trivial yes- or no-instance accordingly. Else if $|Q| > k\alpha\sqrt{\log n}$, then output a trivial no-instance. Next, assume that none of the preceding cases occurs, and thus we have $k > \log n$ and $|Q| \leq k\alpha\sqrt{\log n}$. Hence, $|Q| = \mathcal{O}(k^{1.5})$.

Now, we create the graph G' described in the preceding text, and define $X := Q_a \cup Q_b$. Let D be the digraph obtained from G' by replacing every edge $e = uv \in E(G')$ by arcs $\overrightarrow{uv}$ and $\overrightarrow{vu}$. We then apply Corollary 11.28 with $X := Q_a \cup Q_b$ to obtain a set Z of size $\mathcal{O}(|X|^3) = \mathcal{O}(k^{4.5})$ such that for any $P', Q', R' \subseteq X$, a minimum vertex cut between P' and Q' in $D - R'$ is contained in Z. Thus, by Equation 11.3 we know that if there exists an ODD CYCLE TRANSVERSAL of size at most k, then Z covers at least one such ODD CYCLE TRANSVERSAL. Now, we obtain a combinatorial kernel for ODD CYCLE TRANSVERSAL as follows. Let $Z' := (Z \cup Q) \setminus (Q_a \cup Q_b)$. Clearly, $Z' \subseteq V(G)$ and if there exists an ODD CYCLE TRANSVERSAL of size at most k, then there is one contained in Z'. For every pair of vertices $u, v \in Z'$, if there exists a path in G connecting u and v such that none of its internal vertices belongs to Z', then proceed as follows. If there exists such an odd length path, then add an edge between u and v. If there exists such an even length path, then add an edge between u and v and subdivide it. It is possible that for a pair of vertices u and v we have added both an edge and a subdivided edge. Let G' be the resulting graph on Z and the newly added subdivided vertices. Clearly, the number of vertices in $V(G')$ excluding the new subdivided vertices is $\mathcal{O}(k^{4.5})$, thus G' is of size $\mathcal{O}(k^9)$, and G has an odd cycle transversal of size at most k if and only if G' has an odd cycle transversal of size at most k. This results in the following theorem.

Theorem 11.30 ODD CYCLE TRANSVERSAL *admits a randomized kernel of size* $\mathcal{O}(k^9)$.

Exercises

Problem 11.1 (✏) In the d-HITTING SET problem, we are given a family $\mathcal{F}$ of sets of size d over a universe U and a positive integer k. The problem is to decide whether there exists a subset $X \subseteq U$ such that $|X| \leq k$ and for every set

$F \in \mathcal{F}$, $F \cap X \neq \emptyset$. Obtain a $k^{\mathcal{O}(d)}$ kernel for the problem using the method of representative sets.

Problem 11.2 The goal of this exercise is to obtain an alternate proof for bounding the size of representative sets in the case of uniform matroids. Let $A_1, \ldots, A_m$ be p-element sets and $B_1, \ldots, B_m$ be q-element sets such that $A_i \cap B_j = \emptyset$ if and only of $i = j$.

  (i) Show that $m \leq 2^{p+q}$. (Hint: Consider a uniform random partition of $U = \cup_{i=1}^{m}(A_i \cup B_i)$.)
  (ii) Show that $m \leq \binom{p+q}{p}$. (Hint: Consider permutations of U.)
  (iii) Show that the bound of $\binom{p+q}{p}$ on m is tight.
  (iv) Let $\mathcal{S} = \{S_1, \ldots, S_t\}$ be a family of p-element sets. Using the preceding exercises, show that the size of a q-representative family is upper bounded by $\binom{p+q}{p}$.

Problem 11.3 For vertices u, v of a connected graph G, a vertex (u, v)-separator is a set of vertices S such that $u, v \notin S$ and u and v are in different connected components in $G - S$. It is easy to see that an n-vertex graph can contain $\Omega(2^n)$ separators. How many inclusion-wise minimal separators can be in an n-vertex graph? Use representative sets to obtain the upper bound $\mathcal{O}((2-\varepsilon)^n)$ on the number of minimal separators for some $\varepsilon > 0$.

Problem 11.4 Let G be a connected graph on $2n$ vertices and $\mathcal{L}$ be a family of forests of G of size n (i.e., the number of edges is n). Let $\widehat{\mathcal{L}} \subseteq \mathcal{L}$ be a family of forests such that for any forest F of size $n - 1$, if there exists a forest $X \in \mathcal{L}$ such that $F \cup X$ is a spanning tree of G, then there exists a forest $\widehat{X} \in \widehat{\mathcal{L}}$ such that $F \cup \widehat{X}$ is a spanning tree of G. Obtain a non trivial upper bound on the size of $|\widehat{\mathcal{L}}|$ (such as c^n).

Problem 11.5 Prove Theorem 11.21.

Problem 11.6 (☠) Consider the following problem. Given a graph G with a special vertex v and integers s and k, the task is to determine whether we can remove k vertices from $G - v$ such that the connected component of v has at most s vertices. Show that this problem has a randomized polynomial kernel with respect to $s + k$ using representative sets over gammoids. (Hint: Give v "capacity" $k + 1$ to form a gammoid. Next, show that a set X "closest" to v of size at most k is not a solution if and only if there exist $s + 1$ distinct vertices that can each extend X to an independent set in that gammoid.)

Problem 11.7 In the ALMOST 2-SAT problem, we are given a CNF formula φ, where every clause consists of at most two literals, and an integer k. The task is to determine whether it is possible to make φ satisfiable by deleting at most k clauses. Now, in the ALMOST 2-SAT COMPRESSION problem, the input also consists of a set X of clauses whose deletion makes φ satisfiable. Present a parameter-preserving transformation from ALMOST 2-SAT COMPRESSION, parameterized by $k + |X|$, to DIGRAPH PAIR CUT.

Problem 11.8 ALMOST 2-SAT has an $\mathcal{O}(\sqrt{\log n})$-approximation algorithm and an $2.6181^k n^{\mathcal{O}(1)}$-time algorithm, due to Agarwal et al. (2005) and Narayanaswamy et al. (2012), respectively. Having these algorithms and the answer to Exercise 11.7 at hand, show that ALMOST 2-SAT admits a randomized polynomial kernel.

Bibliographic Notes

The $\mathcal{O}(2^n n^2)$ time dynamic programming algorithm for the HAMILTONIAN PATH problem from the introductory section to this chapter is the classical algorithm of Bellman (1962) and Held and Karp (1962). Monien (1985) used representative families for set systems for his LONGEST PATH algorithm. The Two-Families Theorem of Bollobás (1965) for extremal set systems and its generalization to subspaces of a vector space of Lovász (1977) (see also Frankl, 1982) are corner stones in extremal set theory with numerous applications in graph and hypergraph theory, combinatorial geometry and theoretical computer science. We refer to Jukna (2011, Section 9.2.2), surveys of Tuza (1994, 1996), and Gil Kalai's blog[1] for more information on these theorems and their applications.

The current best-known bound ω, that is, $\omega < 2.373$, is due to Williams (2012) and Gall (2014). An algorithm computing the determinant of an $n \times n$ matrix in time $\mathcal{O}(n^\omega)$ can be found, for example, in Bunch and Hopcroft (1974). For a rectangular matrix A of size $d \times n$ (with $d \leq n$), Bodlaender et al. (2015) outlined an algorithm computing a minimum weight column basis in time $\mathcal{O}(nd^{\omega-1})$. The proof of Generalized Laplace expansion (Proposition 11.7) can be found, for example, in Murota (2000, Proposition 2.1.3). The non algorithmic proof of Theorem 11.8, that is, the bound on the size of the minimum representative family, is due to Lovász (1977, Theorem 4.8). The first to provide an algorithmic proof for this lemma was Marx (2009, Lemma 4.2). However, the running time of the algorithm given in Marx

---

[1] http://gilkalai.wordpress.com/2008/12/25/lovaszs-two-families-theorem/.

11.6 Combinatorial Approach 215

(2009) is $f(p,q)(||A||t)^{\mathcal{O}(1)}$ where $f(p,q)$ is a polynomial in $(p+q)^p$ and $\binom{p+q}{p}$; more precisely, $f(p,q) = 2^{\mathcal{O}(p \log k)} \cdot \binom{p+q}{p}^{\mathcal{O}(1)}$. The proof in this book follows the proof of Fomin et al. (2016b). Although it is based on exterior algebra and is essentially the same as the proof given in Lovász (1977), it avoids the terminology from exterior algebra. For other applications of efficient computations of representative sets, see Fomin et al. (2017).

The presentation of randomized polynomial kernel for DIGRAPH PAIR CUT and ODD CYCLE TRANSVERSAL is based on Kratsch and Wahlström (2014). In that paper, the authors present a more careful size bound of $\mathcal{O}(|S| \cdot |T| \cdot r)$ for $|W|$ in the Cut-covering theorem (Theorem 11.27), and of $\mathcal{O}(k^4)$ vertices for DIGRAPH PAIR CUT. Moreover, the authors give a randomized polynomial kernel for ALMOST 2-SAT (on which Exercises 11.7 and 11.8 are based). The ALMOST 2-SAT problem can be used to express several other problems, including ODD CYCLE TRANSVERSAL and VERTEX COVER above a guarantee. In addition, Kratsch and Wahlström (2014) present a randomized polynomial kernel with $\mathcal{O}(k^{s+1})$ vertices for VERTEX MULTIWAY CUT with a fixed number of terminals s (as well as a randomized polynomial kernel for MULTICUT with a fixed number of terminals pairs), a randomized polynomial kernel with $\mathcal{O}(k^3)$ vertices for VERTEX MULTIWAY CUT with deletable terminals and a randomized polynomial kernel for GROUP FEEDBACK VERTEX SET for a group of s elements, where the latter problem is a generalization of ODD CYCLE TRANSVERSAL. We remark that the questions of the existence of polynomial kernels for VERTEX MULTIWAY CUT and GROUP FEEDBACK ARC/VERTEX SET without restrictions as previously mentioned are open. Later, the matroid-based tools of Kratsch and Wahlström (2014) led to the discover of additional randomized polynomial kernels. For example, Hols and Kratsch (2018) obtained a randomized polynomial kernel for the SUBSET FEEDBACK VERTEX SET problem, which is a generalization of FEEDBACK VERTEX SET where we do not need to hit all cycles, but only those passing through at least one "prescribed" vertex. Moreover, Kratsch (2016) obtained a randomized polynomial kernel for a parameterization of VERTEX COVER above a guarantee higher than the one of Kratsch and Wahlström (2014).

We remark that the abstraction based on d-SUBSET CSP is close to the kernelization results for MIN ONES CONSTRAINT SATISFACTION problems by Kratsch and Wahlström (2010). In our case (with matroidal constraints) the constraints must be monotone, but the function f for testing a single constraint may internally depend on the entire variable set U. In the Min Ones setting, the constraints need not be monotone, but may only depend on d values at a time. If the constraints are not monotone, then even when $f(X,c)$ depends on only d values from X for every c, it is not trivial to determine when the problem has a polynomial kernel, and that the answer has a characterization by Kratsch and Wahlström (2010). Exercise 11.6 was given by Wahlström in WorKer Workshop on Kernelization, (2013). Finally, we remark that closest sets occur in the bipedal stage of the algorithm for MULTICUT of Marx and Razgon (2014). There are also similarities between closest sets and the concept of important separators, see Marx (2011).

12
Greedy Packing

In this chapter we consider kernelization algorithms in whose basis lies some greedy packing of constraints. The purpose of the greedy process is to either simply solve the instance or deduce that is has a special structure that can be exploited. This approach is particularly useful in the context of "above guarantee" parameterizations.

For a number of optimization problems, there is some (upper or lower) bound on the size of an optimum solution, and hence the problem becomes trivial for small values of parameter k. This often brings us to results to which we referred (in Section 2.1) as a trivial kernelization. For example, consider the MAXCUT problem, where given a connected graph G and an integer k, we ask whether G contains a cut with at least k edges. Here, if $k \leq |E(G)|/2$, then we have that (G, k) is a yes-instance. Otherwise, (G, k) is already kernel with at most $2k$ edges and $2k + 1$ vertices. In the following text we consider additional simple examples:

- For every boolean CNF formula on m clauses, there is an assignment that satisfies at least $m/2$ clauses.
- In any graph on m edges, there is a cut with at least $m/2$ edges, that is, there is a partition of the vertex set such at least $m/2$ edges lie between the two parts.
- In any planar graph on n vertices, there is an independent set of size at least $n/4$ (as the graph can be properly colored with 4 colors).
- In any graph, the size of any vertex cover is at least as large as the size of a maximum matching. In particular, if a graph on n vertices has a perfect matching, then every vertex cover must have size at least $n/2$. Unlike the previous three examples, this example does not immediately give us a trivial kernel.

To deal with this anomaly, Mahajan and Raman (1999) introduced the notion of parameterization beyond a guarantee. In this scenario, the parameter is not the solution size, but the value of the solution minus the lower bound, which can range from small to moderate values for most instances.

In this chapter we give a kernelization algorithm for a few of these problems. All these kernels have a common theme: They start by computing some greedy packing of constraints. If the packing process can last for sufficiently many steps, we conclude that we have a yes-instance. Otherwise, we obtain a structured input. This structure is exploited to derive a polynomial kernel.

12.1 SET COVER

Our first example is SET COVER, where we consider a parameterization below a trivial bound, rather then above a guarantee as in the next two sections. In a typical covering problem, we are given a universe U of size n, a family S (S could be given implicitly) of size m and an integer k, and the objective is to check whether there exists a subfamily $S' \subseteq S$ of size at most k satisfying some desired properties. If S' is required to contain all the elements of U, then our covering problem is the classical SET COVER problem and S' is called a *solution set family*. The most natural question in this context is whether there exists a solution set family of size at most k. However, it is well known that SET COVER is unlikely to admit a fixed parameter tractable algorithm when parameterized by the solution size.

Observe that n is a trivial upper bound on the size of solution set family. Can we obtain a result more interesting than this trivial bound? This section gives an affirmative answer to this question. Here, we address the $(n-k)$-SET COVER problem, where for a given universe U of size n, a family S of size m and an integer k, the task is to decide whether U can be covered by at most $n - k$ sets from S.

We denote an instance of $(n-k)$-SET COVER by (U, S, k), where U is the universe to be covered, S is the family of sets available, and k is the parameter. The following definition is crucial for our arguments.

Definition 12.1 (*k*-**mini set cover**) For a subfamily $\mathcal{T} \subseteq S$, let $\mathcal{Q}(\mathcal{T})$ be the set of elements covered by $\mathcal{T}$, that is,

$$\mathcal{Q}(\mathcal{T}) = \bigcup_{T \in \mathcal{T}} T.$$

12.1 Set Cover

A collection of sets $\mathcal{T}$ is a *k-mini set cover* of $\mathcal{S}$ if $|\mathcal{T}| \leq k$ and $|\mathcal{Q}(\mathcal{T})| \geq |\mathcal{T}| + k$.

We will implement the following approach.

- If $(U, \mathcal{S}, k)$ contains a k-mini set cover $\mathcal{T}$, then this is a yes-instance of $(n-k)$-Set Cover. Indeed, $\mathcal{T}$ covers at least $|\mathcal{T}|+k$ elements of U. The remaining $n - |\mathcal{T}| - k$ elements can be covered by at most $n - |\mathcal{T}| - k$ sets of $\mathcal{S}$, which overall results in a set cover of size at most $n - k$.
- We start building a k-mini set cover $\mathcal{T}$ in a greedy manner: We add a new set to $\mathcal{T}$ only if it covers at least two elements not already covered by sets from $\mathcal{T}$. If we succeed to build a k-mini set cover, then we are done.
- If we fail to build a k-mini set cover, then we arrive at a very specific situation: No set from $\mathcal{S} \setminus \mathcal{T}$ can cover more than one element not already covered by $\mathcal{T}$. We will use this situation to develop a reduction rule resulting in an equivalent instance with at most $2k^2 - 2$ elements.

In Fig 12.1, we present an algorithm called GreedyMiniSet, which constructs a family $\mathcal{T} \subseteq \mathcal{S}$ with certain properties that we show imply the presence of a k-mini set cover. Starting from an empty set, the family $\mathcal{T}$ is constructed by adding at each step a set T that covers at least two elements not already covered by sets from $\mathcal{T}$. The algorithm stops when either the family $\mathcal{T}$ contains k sets or no set T as in the preceding text can be found.

Lemma 12.2 *If a collection of sets $\mathcal{S}$ satisfies $|\mathcal{Q}(\mathcal{S})| \geq |\mathcal{S}| + k$, then $\mathcal{S}$ contains a k-mini set cover.*

Proof: Let $\mathcal{T}$ be the set returned by GreedyMiniSet($\mathcal{S}, k$). We claim that $\mathcal{T}$ is a k-mini set cover. Suppose that it is not. Then,

$$|\mathcal{Q}(\mathcal{T})| - |\mathcal{T}| < k. \tag{12.1}$$

Algorithm Greedy-mini-set($\mathcal{S}, k$).
Input: Universe U, family of sets $\mathcal{S}$ and integer k.
Output: Family $\mathcal{T}$.

$\mathcal{T} \leftarrow \emptyset$;
while $|\mathcal{T}| < k$ *and* $\exists T \in \mathcal{S} \setminus \mathcal{T}$ *such that* $|\mathcal{Q}(\mathcal{T} \cup \{T\})| \geq |\mathcal{Q}(\mathcal{T})| + 2$ **do**
 $\quad \mathcal{T} \leftarrow \mathcal{T} \cup \{T\}$;

Figure 12.1 Algorithm GreedyMiniSet.

Because at every step of GreedyMiniSet we add to $Q(\mathcal{T})$ at least two new elements, this yields that $|\mathcal{T}| < k$ and that for every set $S \in \mathcal{S} \setminus \mathcal{T}$, $|Q(\{S\}) \setminus Q(\mathcal{T})| \leq 1$. This implies that

$$|Q(\mathcal{S} \setminus \mathcal{T}) \setminus Q(\mathcal{T})| \leq |\mathcal{S} \setminus \mathcal{T}|. \tag{12.2}$$

By (12.1) and (12.2), we deduce that

$$|\mathcal{T}| + |\mathcal{S} \setminus \mathcal{T}| > |Q(\mathcal{T})| - k + |Q(\mathcal{S} \setminus \mathcal{T}) \setminus Q(\mathcal{T})|. \tag{12.3}$$

Because $|\mathcal{S}| = |\mathcal{T}| + |\mathcal{S} \setminus \mathcal{T}|$ and $|Q(\mathcal{S})| = |Q(\mathcal{T})| + |Q(\mathcal{S} \setminus \mathcal{T}) \setminus Q(\mathcal{T})|$, by (12.3), we have that

$$|\mathcal{S}| > |Q(\mathcal{S})| - k,$$

which is a contradiction. This completes the proof of the lemma. □

Lemma 12.3 *An instance $(U, \mathcal{S}, k)$ of $(n - k)$-SET COVER is a yes-instance if and only if $Q(\mathcal{S}) = U$ and there exists a k-mini set cover $\mathcal{T} \subseteq \mathcal{S}$.*

Proof: Suppose that $\mathcal{S}$ contains a k-mini set cover $\mathcal{T}$. By definition, $|Q(\mathcal{T})| \geq |\mathcal{T}| + k$. For every element $u \in U \setminus Q(\mathcal{T})$, we add a set from $\mathcal{S}$ containing u to $\mathcal{T}$. Let $\mathcal{T}'$ denote the family of obtained sets. Clearly, $\mathcal{T}'$ is a set cover. Note that we added at most $n - |Q(\mathcal{T})|$ sets to $\mathcal{T}$ to obtain $\mathcal{T}'$. Therefore, $|\mathcal{T}'| \leq n - |Q(\mathcal{T})| + |\mathcal{T}| \leq n - k$.

If $\mathcal{S}$ contains a set cover $\mathcal{T}$ of size at most $n-k$, then we have that $|\mathcal{T}| \leq n-k$ and $|Q(\mathcal{T})| = n$. Therefore, by Lemma 12.2, $\mathcal{T}$ contains a k-mini set cover. This completes the proof of the lemma. □

Now we are ready to prove the main result of this section.

Theorem 12.4 *There is a polynomial time algorithm that, given an instance $(U, \mathcal{S}, k)$ of $(n-k)$-SET COVER, returns an equivalent instance $(U', \mathcal{S}', k)$ such that $|U'| \leq 2k^2 - 2$.*

Proof: We first verify that $Q(\mathcal{S}) = U$, as otherwise there is no solution and we can return a trivial no-instance. Now, we call GreedyMiniSet($\mathcal{S}, k$) to construct a collection of sets $\mathcal{T}$. If $\mathcal{T}$ is a k-mini set cover, then we are done. Next, suppose that $\mathcal{T}$ is not a k-mini set cover. Then by Lemma 12.3, $|\mathcal{T}| < k$. Hence $|Q(\mathcal{T})| \leq 2k - 2$.

Note that every set in $\mathcal{S} \setminus \mathcal{T}$ covers at most one element from $U \setminus Q(\mathcal{T})$. For $u \in Q(\mathcal{T})$ and $v \in U \setminus Q(\mathcal{T})$, we denote by $\mathcal{S}_{u,v}$ all sets in $\mathcal{S}$ containing both u and v. We carry out a marking procedure that marks in total at most $k(2k - 2)$ elements from $U \setminus Q(\mathcal{T})$. For each element $u \in Q(\mathcal{T})$, we mark k unmarked elements $v \in U \setminus Q(\mathcal{T})$ such that $\mathcal{S}_{u,v} \neq \emptyset$. If there are less than

k such elements, we mark as many as we can. Note that during the marking procedure, no element is marked twice. For an element $u \in \mathcal{Q}(\mathcal{T})$, let M_u denote the elements that were marked for u. We apply the following reduction rule:

> **Reduction nkSC.1** Let $U' = \mathcal{Q}(\mathcal{T}) \cup (\bigcup_{u \in \mathcal{Q}(\mathcal{T})} M_u)$, and $\mathcal{S}' \subseteq \mathcal{S}$ be the family of all sets containing only elements from U'. The new instance is $(U', \mathcal{S}', k)$.

Note that $|U'| = |\mathcal{Q}(\mathcal{T})| + |\bigcup_{u \in \mathcal{Q}(\mathcal{T})} M_u| \leq (2k-2) + k(2k-2) = 2k^2 - 2$, and that the marking procedure can be carried out in polynomial time. Therefore, it only remains for us to show that Rule nkSC.1 is safe. Thus, we proceed to show that the instances $(U', \mathcal{S}', k)$ and $(U, \mathcal{S}, k)$ are equivalent.

In one direction, as every k-mini set cover for $(U', \mathcal{S}', k)$ is also a k-mini set cover for $(U, \mathcal{S}, k)$, Lemma 12.3 implies correctness. To prove the opposite direction, by Lemma 12.3, it is sufficient to show that if there exists a k-mini set cover for $(U, \mathcal{S}, k)$, then there exists a k-mini set cover for $(U', \mathcal{S}', k)$.

Let $\mathcal{T}'$ be a k-mini set cover for $(U, \mathcal{S}, k)$ that has the least number of sets from $\mathcal{S} \setminus \mathcal{S}'$. It is sufficient to show that $\mathcal{T}' \subseteq \mathcal{S}'$, as this will imply that $\mathcal{T}'$ is also a k-mini set cover for $(U', \mathcal{S}', k)$. Targeting a contradiction, suppose that $\mathcal{T}' \not\subseteq \mathcal{S}'$. Pick a set $T \in \mathcal{T}'$ such that $T \notin \mathcal{S}'$. Let $W = T \cap \mathcal{Q}(\mathcal{T})$, and consider the set $T \setminus W$. First, note that $|T \setminus W| \leq 1$, as otherwise we have a contradiction to our greedy construction of $\mathcal{T}$. Moreover, note that there exists an element in $T \setminus W$, which we denote by z, as otherwise $T \subseteq \mathcal{Q}(\mathcal{T}) \subseteq U'$ and therefore T should have been chosen to belong to $\mathcal{S}'$. We also have that $W \neq \emptyset$ because $|T| \geq 2$—if $|T| \leq 1$, then $\mathcal{T}' \setminus \{T\}$ is a k-mini set cover whose number of sets from $\mathcal{S} \setminus \mathcal{S}'$ is smaller than than $|\mathcal{T}' \setminus \mathcal{S}'|$, which is a contradiction.

Consider an element $u \in W$. The fact that $T \notin \mathcal{S}'$ means that $z \notin M_u$. This implies that the marking procedure marked k elements from $U \setminus \mathcal{Q}(\mathcal{T})$ other than z for u. Therefore, $|M_u| = k$. Because $T \setminus \mathcal{Q}(\mathcal{T}) = \{z\}$ and $M_u \subset U \setminus \mathcal{Q}(\mathcal{T})$, we have $T \cap M_u = \emptyset$. Recall that every set in $\mathcal{S}$ contains at most one element from $U \setminus \mathcal{Q}(\mathcal{T})$. This means that every set in $\mathcal{S}$ contains at most one element from M_u. As $|\mathcal{T}' \setminus \{T\}| \leq k-1$, it must be the case that at least one of the elements in M_u is not covered by $\mathcal{T}'$. For every element $u \in W$, we define $r(u)$ to be an element from $M_u \setminus \mathcal{Q}(\mathcal{T}')$. Recall that for distinct $u, v \in W$, the sets M_u and M_v are disjoint by definition. This means that for distinct $u, v \in W$, $r(u) \neq r(v)$. We denote by S_u any set from the collection $\mathcal{S}_{u,r(u)}$ (recall that $\mathcal{S}_{u,r(u)}$ is the collection of sets in $\mathcal{S}$ which contain both u and $r(u)$). Note that $\mathcal{S}_{u,r(u)} \neq \emptyset$ because $r(u) \in M_u$. We now claim that the collection $\mathcal{T}'' = (\mathcal{T}' \setminus \{T\}) \cup \{S_u \mid u \in W\}$ is also a k-mini set cover.

Note that the collection $\mathcal{T}''$ covers every element covered by the collection $\mathcal{T}'$ except z because $W \subseteq \bigcup_{u \in W} S_u \subseteq \mathcal{Q}(\mathcal{T}'')$. However, for each $u \in W$, $\mathcal{T}''$ also covers at least one element that was not covered by $\mathcal{T}'$ (recall that the element $r(u)$ is not covered by $\mathcal{T}'$). Also, because for distinct $u, v \in W$, $r(u) \neq r(v)$, we have $\left|\left(\bigcup_{u \in W} S_u\right) \setminus \mathcal{Q}(\mathcal{T}')\right| \geq |W|$. Thus, $|\mathcal{Q}(\mathcal{T}'')| \geq |\mathcal{Q}(\mathcal{T}')| - 1 + |W|$. Clearly, we have $|\mathcal{T}''| \leq |\mathcal{T}'| + |W| - 1$. Therefore, because $\mathcal{T}'$ was a k-mini set cover, $|\mathcal{Q}(\mathcal{T}'')| \geq |\mathcal{T}'| + k + |W| - 1 \geq |\mathcal{T}''| + k$. Now, by Lemma 12.2, $\mathcal{T}''$ contains a k-mini set cover. Because for every $u \in W$, $S_u \in \mathcal{S}'$, this k-mini set cover uses at least one less set from $\mathcal{S} \setminus \mathcal{S}'$ than $\mathcal{T}'$, which contradicts our choice of $\mathcal{T}'$. Therefore, we conclude that $\mathcal{T}'$ is a k-mini set cover for $(U', \mathcal{S}', k)$. This completes the proof of the theorem. □

Observe that Theorem 12.4 bounds only the size of the universe in the reduced instance. The number of sets in the family of the reduced instance still could be exponential in k. Such kernels are called *partially polynomial kernels*. However, if we further assume that the sets in the family are bounded by some fixed constant r, then a kernel with $\mathcal{O}(k^2)$ size universe has an $\mathcal{O}(k^{2r})$ size set family.

12.2 MAX-LIN-2 above Average

In this section we consider the MAX-LIN-2 problem, defined as follows. The input consists of a system $\mathcal{S}$ and an integer k. The system $\mathcal{S}$ contains m linear equations $e_1, \ldots, e_m$ in n variables $z_1, \ldots, z_n$ over $\mathbb{F}_2$. Each equation e_j, $j = 1, \ldots, m$, is of the form $\sum_{i \in I_j} z_i = b_j$, where $\emptyset \neq I_j \subseteq \{1, \ldots, n\}$, and it has a positive integral weight w_j. The task is to decide whether there is an assignment of values to the variables $z_1, \ldots, z_n$ such that the total weight of the satisfied equations is at least k.

Let us remind that in $\mathbb{F}_2$, which is also known as GF(2) and the Galois field of two elements, we have two elements 0 and 1. Here, the addition operation corresponds to the logical XOR operation, while the multiplication operation corresponds to the logical AND operation. For example, consider the following system:

$$\begin{aligned} z_1 + z_2 + z_4 &= 1 \quad (w_1) \\ z_2 + z_3 &= 0 \quad (w_2) \\ z_2 + z_3 + z_4 &= 1 \quad (w_3) \end{aligned}$$

12.2 MAX-LIN-2 above Average

In this system, the assignment $z_1 = z_2 = z_3 = 1$ and $z_4 = 0$ satisfies the last two equations and thus it is of weight $w_2 + w_3$.

Let $W = w_1 + \cdots + w_m$. The following lemma implies that MAX-LIN-2 admits a trivial polynomial kernel when parameterized by the weight of satisfied equations. An alternative proof is given as Exercise 12.2.

Lemma 12.5 *There exists an assignment such that the total weight of the satisfied equations in S is at least $W/2$.*

Proof: The proof of the lemma is an application of the probabilistic method. Consider a random assignment δ, where each variable z_i is independently at random assigned zero or one with probability $\frac{1}{2}$ each. Equation e_i is satisfied by δ if and only if the sum of the ones modulo 2 in the left side of the equation is equal to the constant b_i in the right side of the equation, which happens with probability exactly $1/2$. By the linearity of expectation, the expected total weight of satisfied equations of S is $\frac{W}{2}$, as

$$\text{E(total weight of satisfied equations)} = \sum_{1 \leq i \leq m} w_i \cdot \Pr(e_i \text{ is satisfied}) = \frac{W}{2}.$$

Because the expected weight in the preceding text of satisfied equations is at least $W/2$, there exists an assignment such that the total weight of satisfied equations in S is at least $W/2$. □

Lemma 12.5 yields that MAX-LIN-2 admits a polynomial kernel when parameterized by the weight of satisfied equations. Indeed, if $2k \leq W$, then by Lemma 12.5, we have a yes-instance. Otherwise, because the weight of each of the equations is at least 1, we have at most $2k$ equations, each of weight at most $2k$, which trivially brings us to a polynomial kernel. Because the "average" weight of all assignments is at least $W/2$, the much more interesting question about MAX-LIN-2 asks whether it admits a kernel when parameterized "above the average" $W/2$.

In this section, we give a kernel for "above average" parameterization for a special variant of MAX-LIN-2, where each equation has at most r variables. We refer to this variant as the MAX-r-LIN-2 problem. In what follows, we give a polynomial kernel for MAX-r-LIN-2 when the parameter is $k' = k - W/2$. In other words, the task is to decide whether there is an assignment of values to the variables $z_1, \ldots, z_n$ such that the total weight of satisfied equations is at least $\frac{W}{2} + k'$.

The ideas behind the kernel for MAX-r-LIN-2 parameterized above average are as follows.

- We start with two reduction rules. The first rule searches for equations on the same set of variables, and if it finds such a pair, it replaces it with another equation. As a result of this rule, we arrive at an equivalent system, where all equations are on different sets of variables. For the second rule, we associate a matrix of coefficients with the system of equations: In this matrix, rows correspond to equations and columns correspond to variables. The second rule reduces the number of variables in the system in such a way that in the new equivalent system the number of variables is equal to the column rank of the coefficient matrix. Both rules also keep the number of variables in each equation upper bounded by r. We apply these rules exhaustively.
- If a resulting irreducible instance has $\mathcal{O}(rk')$ variables, then due to the first reduction rule, all equations should be on different sets of variables. Because each of the equations has at most r variables, we have that the number of equations is $k'^{\mathcal{O}(r)}$. For fixed r, with a simple trick, this would imply that the bit size of the reduced instance is bounded by some polynomial of k' and thus we have a polynomial kernel.
- If we arrive at an irreducible instance with more than $c \cdot rk'$ variables for some constant c, then we prove that we already have a yes-instance. To prove this, we consider a greedy algorithm, which repeatedly selects an equation e and a variable z_i from e. We mark e, eliminate all equations containing z_i by adding e to them, and then apply reduction rules. It is easy to show that such an algorithm can be turned into an assignment satisfying all marked equations.
- It remains to show that it is possible to identify in polynomial time an ordering of the equations such that by feeding the equations to the greedy algorithm in this order, we will mark enough equations to produce an assignment of weight at least $\frac{W}{2} + k'$. To find such an ordering, we crucially rely on the fact that after applying the second reduction rule, we have a system with a full column-rank matrix of coefficients. Based on this, we show that a large irreducible system contains a set of ck' equations K such that none of the system equations can be expressed as a sum of two or more equations from K. By feeding to the greedy algorithm equations from K first, we guarantee that we mark all equations from K, and hence can satisfy equations of sufficient weight.

Let $A(\mathcal{S})$ denote the $m \times n$ matrix of the coefficients of the variables in $\mathcal{S}$. The maximum number of linearly independent columns of $A(\mathcal{S})$ is equal to the rank of the matrix and thus can be obtained by applying Gaussian elimination

12.2 MAX-LIN-2 above Average

algorithm. For an $n \times m$ matrix where $n \leq m$, Gaussian elimination is known to be computable in a number of arithmetic operations bounded by $\mathcal{O}(mn^{w-2})$ where $w < 2.373$ is the matrix multiplication exponent. Because we are working in the field $\mathbb{F}_2$, we obtain the following result.

Lemma 12.6 *For the coefficient matrix $A(\mathcal{S})$, a set of linearly independent columns of maximum size as well as a set of linearly independent rows of maximum size can be found in time $\mathcal{O}(mn^{w-2})$ where $w < 2.373$ is the matrix multiplication exponent.*

We are ready to state our first reduction rule for MAX-LIN-2.

Reduction MLA.1 If there is a subset I of $\{1, 2, \ldots, n\}$ such that $\mathcal{S}$ contains the equation $\sum_{i \in I} z_i = b'$ with weight w' and equation $\sum_{i \in I} z_i = b''$ with weight w'', then proceed as follows. If $b' = b''$, then replace this pair of equations by one with weight $w' + w''$. Otherwise ($b' \neq b''$), keep only the equation with the larger weight, and assign it the new weight $|w' - w''|$. If the resulting weight is 0, delete this equation from the system.

The safeness of Reduction Rule MLA.1 is simple and is left as Exercise 12.3.

Reduction MLA.2 Let t be the rank of $A(\mathcal{S})$, and let $\mathbf{a}^{i_1}, \ldots, \mathbf{a}^{i_t}$ be column vectors of $A(\mathcal{S})$ that are linearly independent. Then, delete all variables not in $\{z_{i_1}, \ldots, z_{i_t}\}$ from the equations of $\mathcal{S}$.

Lemma 12.7 *Reduction Rule MLA.2 is safe.*

Proof: First of all, by Lemma 12.6, the rule is implementable in polynomial time.

Without loss of generality, let us assume that $\{\mathbf{a}^1, \ldots, \mathbf{a}^t\}$ is an independent set of column vectors of $A(\mathcal{S})$ of cardinality equal to the rank of $A(\mathcal{S})$. We will show that there exists an optimal solution (a solution maximizing the weight sum of satisfied equations) such that every variable not in $\{z_1, \ldots, z_t\}$ is assigned zero. We refer to variables in $\{z_1, \ldots, z_t\}$ as to *independent* variables and to all other variables as *dependent* variables. Among all optimal solutions, we choose one with the maximum number of dependent variables that have been assigned zero. Let δ be such an assignment. Targeting a contradiction, let us assume that there exists a dependent variable z_j such that $\delta(z_j) = 1$. Then, for some subset $I \subseteq \{1, \ldots, t\}$, we have $\mathbf{a}^j = \sum_{\ell \in I} \mathbf{a}^\ell$. Let δ' be a new assignment defined as follows:

$$\delta'(z_x) = \begin{cases} \delta(z_x), & \text{if } x \in \{1,\ldots,n\} \setminus (I \cup \{j\}) \\ \delta(z_x) + 1, & \text{otherwise.} \end{cases}$$

Let us remark that in the definition of δ', of course we take $\delta'_x := \delta_x + 1$ modulo 2. Because δ' assigns zero to more dependent variables than δ, it only remains to prove that every equation satisfied by δ is also satisfied by δ'.

Let O and O' be the sets of indices of variables that have been assigned one by δ and δ', respectively. By the definition of O and O', and as we are working over $\mathbb{F}_2$, we have that $O' = (O \setminus (I \cup \{j\})) \cup (I \setminus O)$. Moreover, observe that the assignments δ and δ' are completely characterized by the sets O and O', respectively. From the matrix $A(\mathcal{S})$ we delete all rows corresponding to equations that are not satisfied by δ, and denote the new matrix by $\widetilde{A}$. Furthermore, let $\widetilde{\mathbf{a}}^i$ denote the i-th column of $\widetilde{A}$, and let $\widetilde{\mathbf{b}}$ denote the vector containing right sides of the equations satisfied by δ. Then, we have the following.

$$\begin{aligned} \widetilde{\mathbf{b}} = \sum_{i \in O} \widetilde{\mathbf{a}}^i &= \sum_{i \in O \setminus \{j\}} \widetilde{\mathbf{a}}^i + \widetilde{\mathbf{a}}^j = \sum_{i \in O \setminus \{j\}} \widetilde{\mathbf{a}}^i + \sum_{i \in I} \mathbf{a}^i \\ &= \sum_{i \in O \setminus (I \cup \{j\})} \widetilde{\mathbf{a}}^i + 2 \cdot \sum_{i \in O \cap I} \widetilde{\mathbf{a}}^i + \sum_{i \in I \setminus O} \widetilde{\mathbf{a}}^i \\ &= \sum_{i \in O'} \widetilde{\mathbf{a}}^i \end{aligned}$$

Thus, every equation satisfied by δ is also satisfied by δ', which completes the proof. $\square$

A system $\mathcal{S}$ is called *irreducible* if Reduction Rules MLA.1 and MLA.2 do not apply to $\mathcal{S}$. To proceed analyzing an irreducible system, we need to present a greedy procedure whose usefulness will be argued using the following definition. We remark that in the context of this procedure, we only need to consider Reduction Rule MLA.1. The utility of Reduction Rule MLA.2 will be cleared later.

Definition 12.8 Let $\delta : \mathbf{z} = (z_1, \ldots, z_n) \to \{0, 1\}^n$ be an assignment to the variables of the system $\mathcal{S}$. The *excess* of δ, denoted by $ex_\delta(\mathcal{S})$, is the total weight of equations satisfied by δ minus the total weight of equations falsified by δ. We define the *excess* of a system $\mathcal{S}$ as

$$ex(\mathcal{S}) = \max_\delta ex_\delta(\mathcal{S}),$$

where the maximum is taken over all assignments δ.

12.2 MAX-LIN-2 above Average

Algorithm GreedySystem.
Input: System of equations $A\mathbf{z} = \mathbf{b}$.
Output: Empty system of equations.

while *system $A\mathbf{z} = \mathbf{b}$ is nonempty* **do**

    (i) Choose an arbitrary equation $\sum_{i \in I} z_i = b$, set
$\ell = \min\{i : i \in I\}$, and mark the variable z_ℓ;
    (ii) Mark this equation and delete it from the system;
    (iii) Replace every equation $\sum_{i \in I'} z_i = b'$ containing z_ℓ by the equation $\sum_{i \in I} z_i + \sum_{i \in I'} z_i = b + b'$;
    (iv) Exhaustively apply Reduction Rule MLA.1 to the system.

Figure 12.2 Algorithm GreedySystem.

Recall that $k' = k - W/2$, and let us note that there is an assignment such that the total weight of the satisfied equations is at least $\frac{W}{2} + k'$ if and only if $ex(\mathcal{S}) \geq 2k'$, see Exercise 12.4. In other words, $(\mathcal{S}, k)$ is a yes-instance of MAX-LIN-2 if and only if $ex(\mathcal{S}) \geq 2k'$.

For a system of equations $\mathcal{S}$, consider the algorithm in Fig 12.2. This algorithm, GreedySystem, greedily tries to maximize the total weight of satisfied equations of $A(\mathcal{S})\mathbf{z} = \mathbf{b}$. GreedySystem will be a central component in our kernelization procedure. We denote $A = A(\mathcal{S})$, and assume that initially no equation or variable in $A\mathbf{z} = \mathbf{b}$ is marked.

To understand the intuition underlying this greedy process, first note that at any point of the execution of the algorithm, after already marking some equations, algorithm GreedySystem has replaced $A(\mathcal{S})\mathbf{z} = \mathbf{b}$ with an *equivalent* system under the assumption that the equations marked so far are satisfied; that is, for every assignment of values to the variables $z_1, \ldots, z_n$ that satisfies the equations marked so far, we have the same excess in both original and current systems. Second, note that because $z_\ell + z_\ell = 0$ in $\mathbb{F}_2$, in Step (iii) of the algorithm we are entirely eliminating z_ℓ from the system.

Lemma 12.9 *For any set of equations marked by* GreedySystem, *there exists an assignment of excess at least the size of this set.*

Proof: Let $e_1, e_2, \ldots, e_\ell$ denote the equations marked by some run of GreedySystem, where the indices correspond to the order in which the equations were marked. Accordingly, let $z_1, z_2, \ldots, z_\ell$ denote the marked variables. Moreover, let $\mathcal{S}_i^{\text{pre}}$ denote the system immediately before the algorithm marked e_i, and let $\mathcal{S}_i^{\text{post}}$ denote the system immediately after the application of Step (iii) in the iteration corresponding to e_i. Observe that $\mathcal{S}_1^{\text{pre}}$ is the input system, and that for all $i \geq 2$, is the system immediately after the application of Step (iv) in the iteration corresponding to e_i is exactly $\mathcal{S}_{i+1}^{\text{pre}}$, where we use $\mathcal{S}_{\ell+1}^{\text{pre}}$ to denote the empty system.

We prove by induction on i, where i ranges from $\ell + 1$ to 1, that the excess of the system $\mathcal{S}_i^{\text{pre}}$ is at least $(\ell + 1) - i$. Note that this claim, when $i = 1$, is precisely the claim of the lemma. In the base case, where $i = \ell + 1$, the system is empty and thus the excess is clearly 0. Now, suppose that the claim is true for $i + 1$, and let us prove it for i. By the inductive hypothesis, we have that the excess of $\mathcal{S}_{i+1}^{\text{pre}}$ is at least $(\ell + 1) - (i + 1)$. Due to the safeness of Reduction Rule MLA.1, we have that the excess of $\mathcal{S}_i^{\text{post}}$ is also at least $(\ell + 1) - (i + 1)$. Consider the assignment δ that achieves this excess. We extend this assignment by setting z_i so that the equation e_i is satisfied—this is possible as z_i is not present at all in the system $\mathcal{S}_i^{\text{post}}$. Then, the obtained assignment δ' satisfies all equations satisfied by δ, and in addition it satisfies e_i. This assignment in particular witnesses that the excess of $\mathcal{S}_i^{\text{pre}}$ is at least $(\ell + 1) - i$. This completes the proof. □

The main reason why we require Lemma 12.9 lies in the following observation. By this lemma, we know that if the algorithm executes sufficiently many iterations, that is, at least $2k'$ iterations, then there is an assignment such that the total weight of the satisfied equations is at least $\frac{W}{2} + k'$ (as every assignment has nonzero weight). However, the number of equations marked by GreedySystem depends on the choice of equations to mark in the first step.

In what follows, we will consider the special case of the problem where in the initial system $\mathcal{S}$, each equation has only r variables. Then, it is possible to find a large enough set of equations (in the initial system) that can be marked in successive iterations of GreedySystem. In this case, GreedySystem executes sufficiently many iterations, which allows us to establish a kernel. In other words, an appropriate choice of equations to mark is used in Lemma 12.12 to show that if in an irreducible system the number of variables in each equation is bounded by r and the total number of variables is large enough (lower bounded by a linear function of r), then the excess is at least $2k'$. Lemma 12.11 gives a linear-algebraic basis for the choice used in Lemma 12.12.

Definition 12.10 Let K and M be sets of vectors in $\mathbb{F}_2^n$ such that $K \subseteq M$. We say K is *M-sum-free* if no sum of two or more distinct vectors in K is equal to a vector in M.

Observe that K is M-sum-free if and only if K is linearly independent and no sum of vectors in K is equal to a vector in $M \setminus K$. We will use the properties of M-sum-free sets in the next lemma.

12.2 MAX-LIN-2 above Average

Lemma 12.11 *Let M be a set of vectors in $\mathbb{F}_2^n$ such that M contains a basis of $\mathbb{F}_2^n$. Suppose that each vector of M contains at most r non-zero coordinates. If $k \geq 1$ is an integer and $n \geq r(k-1) + 1$, then in polynomial time we can find a subset K of M of size k such that K is M-sum-free.*

Proof: For $k = 1$, the proof is immediate because every set containing a single vector in M is trivially M-sum-free. Thus, we next assume that $k \geq 2$. Let $\mathbf{1} = (1, \ldots, 1)$ be the vector in $\mathbb{F}_2^n$ in which every coordinate is 1. Because every vector in M has at most r nonzero coordinates, we have that $\mathbf{1} \notin M$. By our assumption, M contains a basis of $\mathbb{F}_2^n$, and by Lemma 12.6, we can find such a basis in polynomial time $\mathcal{O}(n^2|M|)$.

We write $\mathbf{1}$ as a sum of some vectors of this basis B:

$$\mathbf{1} = v_1 + v_2 + \cdots + v_s,$$

where $\{v_1, \ldots, v_s\} \subseteq B$ and $v_1, \ldots, v_s$ are linearly independent. We can find such an expression for $\mathbf{1}$ in polynomial time; indeed, all we have to do is to solve the system of equations $B\mathbf{x} = \mathbf{1}$, which can be done in time $\mathcal{O}(n^2|M|)$.

From now on, our proof strategy is as follows. We want to show that either $\{v_1, \ldots, v_s\} \subseteq B$ is the desired K, or that we can find a strictly smaller expression for $\mathbf{1}$ as a sum of vectors in M. For each $v \in M \setminus \{v_1, \ldots, v_s\}$, consider the set $S_v = \{v, v_1, \ldots, v_s\}$. By Lemma 12.6, in time $\mathcal{O}(n^2|M|)$ we can check whether S_v is linearly independent. We consider two cases:

Case 1: S_v is linearly independent for each $v \in M \setminus \{v_1, \ldots, v_s\}$. Then, $\{v_1, \ldots, v_s\}$ is M-sum-free. Here, we also use the fact that $\{v_1, \ldots, v_s\}$ is linearly independent. Recall that $\mathbf{1} = v_1 + v_2 + \cdots + v_s$, and thus for every coordinate $j \in [n]$, there exists a vector v_i such that the jth coordinate of v_i is one. Because each v_i has at most r positive coordinates, we have that $r(k-1) < n \leq sr$. Hence, $s > k-1$ implying that $s \geq k$. Thus, $\{v_1, \ldots, v_k\}$ is the required set K.

Case 2: S_v is linearly dependent for some $v \in M \setminus \{v_1, \ldots, v_s\}$. Then, we can find (in polynomial time) $I \subseteq [s]$ such that $v = \sum_{i \in I} v_i$. Thus,

$$\mathbf{1} = v_1 + v_2 + \cdots + v_s = \sum_{i \in I} v_i + \sum_{i \in [s] \setminus I} v_i = v + \sum_{i \in [s] \setminus I} v_i.$$

Because $|I| \geq 2$, the preceding is a shorter expression for $\mathbf{1}$. Let $\{v'_1, \ldots, v'_{s'}\} = \{v\} \cup \{v_i : i \notin I\}$. Note that $\{v'_1, \ldots, v'_{s'}\}$ is linearly independent.

Because $s \leq n$ and Case 2 produces a shorter expression for $\mathbf{1}$, after at most n iterations of Case 2 we will arrive at Case 1. □

Our interest in Lemma 12.11 is due to the following result.

Lemma 12.12 *Let S be an irreducible system with m equations and n variables such that each equation contains at most r variables, and $n \geq (2k' - 1)r + 1$. Then, there exists an assignment δ to the variables of S such that $\text{ex}_\delta(S) \geq 2k'$.*

Proof: Recall that $A(S)$ is the matrix of the coefficients of the variables in S. Then, $A(S)$ has m rows and n columns. For each equation e_j, there is a row in $A(S)$ corresponding to it. We think of each row as a vector in $\mathbb{F}_2^n$. Let M be the set of vectors corresponding to the rows.

We claim that M spans $\mathbb{F}_2^n$ or, in other words, M contains a basis of $\mathbb{F}_2^n$. Indeed, because Reduction Rule MLA.2 is not applicable, the column rank of $A(S)$ is n. Because the row rank is equal to the column rank, we have that M contains n linearly independent vectors and thus spans $\mathbb{F}_2^n$.

Thus, M contains a basis for $\mathbb{F}_2^n$. In addition, each vector from M contains at most r nonzero coordinates and $n \geq (2k' - 1)r + 1$. Therefore, using Lemma 12.11 we can find an M-sum-free set $K \subseteq M$ of $2k'$ vectors. Without loss of generality, let us assume that $\{e_1, \ldots, e_{2k'}\}$ are the equations corresponding to the vectors of K. We run algorithm `GreedySystem`, choosing at Step (i) an equation of S from $\{e_1, \ldots, e_{2k'}\}$ each time. Let S' be the resulting system.

We claim that during the execution of `GreedySystem` no equation from $\{e_1, \ldots, e_{2k'}\}$ is deleted before it is marked. Indeed, if this is not the case, then for some $\ell \leq 2k'$, there is an equation e in S such that after $i \leq \ell - 1$ iterations of `GreedySystem`, equations e_ℓ and e contain the same set of variables. Because the system is irreducible, $\ell > 1$. By our choice of pivoting equations in `GreedySystem`, the vector corresponding to equation e_ℓ at the i-th iteration is a sum of at least two vectors from K. Therefore, the vector $\mathbf{v} \in M$ corresponding to e is a sum of at least two vectors from (the original set) K, which contradicts the choice of K as M-sum-free.

Hence, in `GreedySystem` all $2k'$ equations $e_1, \ldots, e_{2k'}$ are marked. Then by Lemma 12.9, there exists an assignment of excess at least $2k'$. □

We are ready to give a polynomial kernel for MAX-r-LIN-2 parameterized "above average."

Theorem 12.13 MAX-r-LIN-2 *admits a kernel of polynomial size for $k' = k - W/2$ with at most $(2k' - 1)r$ variables and $k'^{\mathcal{O}(r)}$ equations.*

Proof: Let (S, k), where S is the system of equations, be an instance of MAX-r-LIN-2. After applying Reduction Rules MLA.1 and MLA.2 exhaustively, we obtain a new irreducible equivalent system $(S^\star, k^\star)$. Because both reduction rules are implementable in polynomial time, the system $(S^\star, k^\star)$ is obtained in polynomial time.

Let n be the number of variables in $\mathcal{S}^\star$, and observe that the number of variables in every equation of $\mathcal{S}^\star$ does not exceed r. If $n \geq (2k'-1)r + 1$, then by Lemma 12.12, $(\mathcal{S}^\star, k^\star)$ is a yes-instance of Max-r-Lin-2. Otherwise, $n \leq (2k'-1)r$, and we have the required number of variables. Furthermore, because $(\mathcal{S}^\star, k^\star)$ is irreducible, we have that no two equations from $\mathcal{S}^\star$ have the same set of variables. Thus, the total number of equations in $\mathcal{S}^\star$ is at most $\sum_{i=1}^{r} \binom{(2k'-1)r}{i}$.

However, although the obtained system $\mathcal{S}^\star$ has $(2k'-1)r$ variables and $k'^{\mathcal{O}(r)}$ equations, it is still not necessary a kernel. The reason is that to encode weights of $\mathcal{S}^\star$, we need $\Omega(\log W)$ bits. Because the weights of the equations in $\mathcal{S}^\star$ can be arbitrarily large, we cannot guarantee that $\log W$ is bounded by some function of $k^\star$. This can be easily resolved as follows. If there exists an equation of weight at least $2k'$, then we can conclude that we have a yes-instance (see Exercise 12.5). Else, every weight can be encoded using $\mathcal{O}(\log k')$ bits. This completes the proof. $\square$

12.3 Max-Er-SAT

Let us remind that in the Max-r-SAT problem we are given a CNF formula φ, where every clause consists of at most r literals, and an integer k. The task is to decide whether there exists an assignment ψ that satisfies at least k clauses of φ. In this section, we consider a more specific variant of the Max-r-SAT problem, called Max-Er-SAT. Here, we assume that the input formula φ is an r-CNF formula for some positive integer r, that is, each clause of φ consists of *exactly* r literals. We also assume that literals in one clause pairwise involve different variables, that is, there are no two identical literals and no literal is the negation of another one. Requiring that each clause consists of exactly r literals makes Max-Er-SAT and Max-r-SAT quite different: For example, we cannot just repeat one of the literals of a clause with less than r literals to increase its size to be exactly r.

For an r-CNF formula one can show the following bound, whose proof is left as Exercise 12.6.

Lemma 12.14 *For an r-CNF formula φ with m clauses, there exists an assignment satisfying at least $\left(1 - \frac{1}{2^r}\right) m$ clauses.*

Lemma 12.14 motivates the following *above average* parameterization of Max-Er-SAT: For a given r-CNF formula φ with m clauses and integer k', the task is to decide whether there is an assignment satisfying at least $\left(1 - \frac{1}{2^r}\right) m + k'$ clauses of φ. In other words, the instance of Max-Er-SAT parameterized above average consists of a pair (φ, k), where the parameter is $k' = k - \left(1 - \frac{1}{2^r}\right) m$.

For a formula φ, we denote its clause set by $\text{Cls}(\varphi)$. We say that a variable x occurs in clause C, denoted by $x \in \text{Vars}(C)$, if C contains x or $\bar{x}$. For a formula φ, we will next define a polynomial P_φ having variables $x_1, \ldots, x_n$. By slightly abusing notation, we do not distinguish here between the variables of P_φ and of φ. Thus, we identify the Boolean values *true* and *false* with the real numbers 1 and -1, respectively. Consequently, an assignment is a function $\psi : \{x_1, x_2, \ldots, x_n\} \to \{-1, 1\}$. Now, the polynomial is defined by the following formula:

$$P_\varphi(x_1, x_2, \ldots, x_n) = \sum_{C \in \text{Cls}(\varphi)} \left(1 - \prod_{x_i \in \text{Vars}(C)} (1 - \varepsilon_i \cdot x_i)\right),$$

where for $x_i \in \text{Vars}(C)$,

$$\varepsilon_i = \begin{cases} -1, & \text{if } \bar{x}_i \in C, \\ 1, & \text{if } x_i \in C. \end{cases}$$

For an assignment ψ, we define $\text{sat}(\varphi, \psi)$ as the number of clauses satisfied by ψ, and we denote $P_\varphi(\psi) = P_\varphi(\psi(x_1), \ldots, \psi(x_n))$.

Lemma 12.15 *For every $k \geq 1$, the following are equivalent*

- *Formula φ has a truth assignment satisfying at least $k + \left(1 - \frac{1}{2^r}\right) m$ clauses.*
- *There is a truth assignment ψ such that $P_\varphi(\psi) \geq 2^r k$.*

Proof: For every truth assignment ψ, $\prod_{x_i \in \text{Vars}(C)}(1 - \varepsilon_i x_i)$ is equal to 2^r if C is not satisfied by ψ and 0 otherwise. Thus,

$$P_\varphi(\psi) = (m - 2^r(m - \text{sat}(\varphi, \psi))) = 2^r \cdot (\text{sat}(\varphi, \psi) - (1 - 2^{-r})m).$$

Hence, $P_\varphi(\psi) \geq 2^r k$ if and only if $\text{sat}(\varphi, \psi) \geq (1 - 2^{-r})m + k$. □

The next lemma shows that there is a polynomial time algorithm that, given an instance (φ, k_1) of MAX-Er-SAT with parameter $k_1' = k_1 - (1 - 2^{-r})m$, constructs in time $m^{\mathcal{O}(r)}$ an equivalent instance $(\mathcal{S}, k_2)$ of MAX-r-LIN-2 with parameter $k_2' = k_2 - W/2$ such that the size of $\mathcal{S}$ is polynomial in k_1'. In other words, we have a compression of MAX-Er-SAT.

Lemma 12.16 *There is an algorithm that for a given r-CNF formula φ with m clauses and an integer k, in time $m^{\mathcal{O}(r)}$ constructs a system of weighted linear equations $\mathcal{S}$ over $\mathbb{F}_2$ such that*

12.3 MAX-Er-SAT

- The system S has $\mathcal{O}(k'r)$ variables, $k'^{\mathcal{O}(r)}$ equations, and the size of S (together with equation weights) is $k'^{\mathcal{O}(r)}$. Here, $k' = k - (1 - 2^{-r})m$.
- There is a truth assignment of φ satisfying at least $(1 - 2^{-r})m + k'$ clauses if and only if there is an assignment of variables of S of weight at least $W/2 + k'$.

Proof: For an r-CNF formula φ, we construct the polynomial P_φ. We rewrite P_φ as the sum of multilinear monomials:

$$P_\varphi = \sum_{I \in \mathcal{F}} c_I \prod_{i \in I} x_i,$$

where $\mathcal{F}$ is a family of nonempty subsets of $\{1, \ldots, n\}$ and $c_I \neq 0$. Let us note that because every clause of φ has r variables, every set $I \in \mathcal{F}$ has at most r elements.

We construct a system of linear equations S with n variables $z_1, \ldots, z_n$ as follows. For every $I \in \mathcal{F}$ and the corresponding multilinear monomial $c_I \prod_{i \in I} x_i$, the equation e_I of S is $\sum_{i \in I} z_i = b_I$, where

$$b_I = \begin{cases} 0, & \text{if } c_I > 0, \\ 1, & \text{if } c_I < 0. \end{cases}$$

The weight w_I of equation e_I is $|c_I|/2^{r-1}$.

Let us note that regrouping P_φ and the construction of S can be easily done in time $mn^{\mathcal{O}(r)}$.

Claim 12.17 *There is an assignment of variables of S of weight at least $W/2 + k'$ if and only if there is a truth assignment of φ satisfying at least $(1 - 2^{-r})m + k'$ clauses.*

Proof: Suppose that there exists an assignment $\delta : \mathbf{z} = (z_1, \ldots, z_n) \to \{0, 1\}^n$ of weight at least

$$\frac{W}{2} + k' = \frac{\sum_{I \in \mathcal{F}} w_I}{2} + k'.$$

We construct a truth assignment ψ such that $P_\varphi(\psi) \geq 2^r \cdot k'$. By Lemma 12.15, this would yield that ψ satisfies at least $(1 - 2^{-r})m + k'$ clauses of φ. In assignment ψ, we set $x_i = (-1)^{\delta(z_i)}$ for all $i \in \{1, \ldots, n\}$. In other words, ψ assigns 1 to x_i if the value of z_i is 0 and -1 if the value of z_i is 1. Then, for every $I \in \mathcal{F}$,

$$\prod_{i \in I} x_i = 1 \text{ if and only if } \sum_{i \in I} z_i = 0,$$

and

$$\prod_{i \in I} x_i = -1 \text{ if and only if } \sum_{i \in I} z_i = 1.$$

By the choice of b_I, we have that if equation e_I is satisfied by δ, then $c_I \prod_{i \in I} x_i = |c_I|$, and if e_I is not satisfied by δ, then $c_I \prod_{i \in I} x_i = -|c_I|$.

Let $\mathcal{I}_{SAT}$ be the family of satisfied sets $I \in \mathcal{F}$, that is, the family of sets such that for every $I \in \mathcal{I}_{SAT}$ equation e_I is satisfied by δ. Moreover, denote $\mathcal{I}_{UNSAT} = \mathcal{F} \setminus \mathcal{I}_{SAT}$. Let us remind that the excess of the assignment δ is at least $2k$, see Exercise 12.4. Thus,

$$ex_\delta(\mathcal{S}) = \sum_{I \in \mathcal{I}_{SAT}} w_I - \sum_{I \in \mathcal{I}_{UNSAT}} w_I \geq 2k'.$$

Therefore,

$$P_\varphi(\psi) = \sum_{I \in \mathcal{F}} c_I \prod_{i \in I} x_i = \sum_{I \in \mathcal{I}_{SAT}} c_I \prod_{i \in I} x_i + \sum_{I \in \mathcal{I}_{UNSAT}} c_I \prod_{i \in I} x_i$$

$$= \sum_{I \in \mathcal{I}_{SAT}} |c_I| - \sum_{I \in \mathcal{I}_{UNSAT}} |c_I|$$

$$= 2^{r-1} \left(\sum_{I \in \mathcal{I}_{SAT}} w_I - \sum_{I \in \mathcal{I}_{UNSAT}} w_I \right) \geq 2^{r-1} \cdot 2k' = 2^r \cdot k'.$$

For the opposite direction, for an assignment ψ of φ, we define $\delta(z_i) = 0$ if $\psi(x_i) = 1$ and $\delta(z_i) = 1$ if $\psi(x_i) = -1$. Then, by exactly the same arguments as mentioned previously, $ex_\delta(\mathcal{S}) \geq 2k$, and the claim follows. ⌟

Finally, by Theorem 12.13, the problem MAX-r-LIN-2 admits a polynomial kernel with at most $\mathcal{O}(k'r)$ variables and $k'^{\mathcal{O}(r)}$ equations for $k' = k - W/2$. Thus, we use Theorem 12.13 to construct such an instance $(\mathcal{S}^\star, k^\star)$. By our construction, (φ, k) is a yes-instance of MAX-Er-SAT if and only if $(\mathcal{S}^\star, k^\star)$ is a yes-instance of MAX-r-LIN-2. □

Lemma 12.16 shows that MAX-Er-SAT admits a "compression" into an instance of another problem. While for fixed r the instance of MAX-r-LIN-2 is bounded by some polynomial of k, this is not a polynomial kernel. Recall that in the definition of a kernelization algorithm, an instance of a problem is mapped into an instance of the same problem, which is not what Lemma 12.16 does.

12.3.1 Kernel for MAX-Er-SAT

We conclude this section with a proof that MAX-Er-SAT above average admits a polynomial kernel.

Theorem 12.18 MAX-Er-SAT *admits a kernel of size* $k'^{\mathcal{O}(1)}$, *where* $k' = k - (1 - 2^{-r})m$.

Proof: By Lemma 12.16, MAX-Er-SAT admits a polynomial compression into MAX-r-LIN-2 transforming every instance $(x, k\tilde{\mathcal{O}})$ of MAX-Er-SAT with $k' = k - (1 - 2^{-r})m$ into an equivalent instance y of MAX-r-LIN-2 of size $k'^{\mathcal{O}(r)}$. Because MAX-Er-SAT is NP-hard and MAX-r-LIN-2 is in NP (the decision versions of both problems are NP-complete), Theorem 1.6 implies that MAX-Er-SAT admits a kernel of size $k'^{\mathcal{O}(1)}$, where $k' = k - (1 - 2^{-r})m$. □

Exercises

Problem 12.1 In MAXCUT, we are given a graph G and integer k, and the task is to determine whether G contains a cut of size k. In other words, we need to decide whether the vertex set of G can be partitioned into two sets such that the number of edges between these sets is at least k. Show that MAXCUT is a special case of MAX-LIN-2.

Problem 12.2 (✐) Prove Lemma 12.5 by induction rather than the probabilistic method. To this end, consider the following approach. Assign values to the variables $z_1, \ldots, z_n$ one by one using the following greedy procedure. Each time a value is assigned to a variable z_i, all equations containing z_i are simplified: If $z_i = 0$ then z_i is simply removed from all such equations, and if $z_i = 1$ then the right hand side b of every such equation is replaced by $1 - b$. As long as there is no equation of the form $z_i = b$, z_i is assigned an arbitrary value. Otherwise, z_i is assigned the value that satisfies those equations of the form $z_i = b$ having total weight at least $W_i/2$, where W_i is the total weight of equations of the form $z_i = b$. Show by induction that the assignment produced by the greedy procedure satisfies equations of total weight at least $W/2$.

Problem 12.3 (✐) Show that Reduction Rule MLA.1 is safe.

Problem 12.4 (✐) Show that $(\mathcal{S}, k)$ is a yes-instance of MAX-LIN-2 AA if and only if $ex(\mathcal{S}) \geq 2k'$.

Problem 12.5 (✐) Complete the proof of Theorem 12.13: Show that if there exists an equation of weight at least $2k'$, then we have a yes-instance.

Problem 12.6 Prove Lemma 12.14: For an r-CNF formula φ with m clauses, there exists an assignment satisfying at least $m(1 - 2^{-r})$ clauses.

Problem 12.7 MAX-LIN-2-ODD is MAX-LIN-2 in which all equations have odd number of variables. Prove that MAX-LIN-2-ODD has a kernel with $\mathcal{O}(k^2)$ variables and equations.

Hint: Write the excess as a symmetric random discrete variable X (X is symmetric if $\mathbb{P}(X = a) = \mathbb{P}(X = -a)$ for every real a). Use the fact that for a symmetric discrete random variable X, we have $\mathbb{P}(X \geq \sqrt{\mathbb{E}(X^2)}) > 0$.

Bibliographic Notes

Parameterizations above and below guarantee were introduced by Mahajan and Raman (1999). In particular, the parameterizations of MAX-LIN-2 and MAX-Er-SAT considered in this chapter were stated in that work. Section 12.1 is largely based on the work of Basavaraju et al. (2016). Crowston et al. (2014) proved that the number of variables of MAX-LIN-2 (without restriction on the number of variables in an equation) can be reduced to $\mathcal{O}(k^2 \log k)$; it is an open problem whether MAX-LIN-2 admits a polynomial kernel. The polynomial kernels for MAX-r-LIN-2 and MAX-r-SAT are largely based on the work of Crowston et al. (2010), but also on results already known due to Gutin et al. (2011b) and further extended by Crowston et al. (2014). An alternative probabilistic approach is due to Alon et al. (2011) and Gutin et al. (2011b). The number of variables in the compressed instance has been further improved by Kim and Williams (2012) and Crowston et al. (2014). We remark that the traditional approach to compute the rank of a matrix A, on which we relied in this chapter, is by Gaussian elimination. For an $m \times n$ matrix with $m \leq n$, it is known that this approach can be implemented in $\mathcal{O}(nm^{w-1})$ field operations (Bunch and Hopcroft, 1974), where w is the matrix multiplication exponent.

Other interesting examples of algorithms and hardness results for above and below guarantee parameterizations include Chen and Zhou (2017), Makarychev et al. (2015), Crowston et al. (2014, 2012b,a, 2013), Gutin et al. (2012, 2011c), Mahajan et al. (2009). In particular, Gutin and Yeo (2012) provide a comprehensive survey of various constraint satisfaction problems parameterized above and below tight bounds. This survey was recently updated (see Gutin and Yeo, 2017). A generalization of Exercise 12.7 was given by Gutin et al. (2011b).

13
Euler's Formula

On planar graphs, there exist many parameterized problems that are known to admit polynomial or even linear kernels, while on general graphs these problems do not admit such kernels. To show such positive results, several kernelization techniques have been developed. In this chapter we give some simple and elegant examples of kernels for problems on planar graphs, while in Chapter 15 we discuss more powerful techniques based on tools from logic. All the kernels in this chapter are based on Euler's formula.

13.1 Preliminaries on Planar Graphs

A graph is *planar* if it can be embedded (drawn) in the plane in such a way that its edges intersect only at their endpoints. Such an embedding is called a *plane graph* or *planar embedding* of the graph. Let G be a plane graph. Note that its edges bound regions. Regions bounded by edges, including the outer region, are called by *faces* of G.

The following is one of the earliest results in Graph Theory.

Theorem 13.1 (Euler's formula) *Let G be a connected plane graph with n vertices, m edges and f faces. Then?*

$$n - m + f = 2.$$

The proof of Euler's formula is left as Exercise 13.1.

We will use the following proposition, whose proof follows from Euler's formula. We leave the proof of it as Exercise 13.2.

Lemma 13.2 *Let G be a triangle-free planar graph with $n > 3$ vertices and m edges. Then, $m \leq 2n - 4$.*

In addition, we will use the following lemma often.

Lemma 13.3 *Let G be a planar graph, $C \subseteq V(G)$, and let N_3 be a set of vertices from $V(G) \setminus C$ such that every vertex from N_3 has at least three neighbors in C. Then, $|N_3| \leq \max\{0, 2|C| - 4\}$.*

Proof: We construct a bipartite graph H with bipartition C and N_3. A vertex of C is adjacent to a vertex from N_3 if and only if these vertices are adjacent in G. On the one hand, H is a triangle-free subgraph of G, and thus by Lemma 13.2,

$$|E(H)| \leq 2|V(H)| - 4 = 2(|C| + |N_3|) - 4.$$

On the other hand, every vertex of N_3 is of degree at least 3 in H, and thus

$$|E(H)| \geq 3 \cdot |N_3|.$$

Hence

$$3 \cdot |N_3| \leq 2|V(H)| - 4 = 2(|C| + |N_3|) - 4$$

and the lemma follows. □

13.2 Simple Planar Kernels

In this section we give two examples of kernels based on the same idea. Our examples are for CONNECTED VERTEX COVER and EDGE DOMINATING SET on planar graphs. Before we proceed, a clarification is required. When we say that some parameterized graph problems admit a kernel on planar graphs, we mean that the input graph is planar as well as that the output graph of the kernelization algorithm must be planar. Thus, in this situation we are allowed to use only reduction rules that do not alter the planarity of the graph.

> Let C be a set of vertices or edges that is a yes-certificate of some parameterized problem. In both of our examples, the vertices outside C will form an independent set. By making use of Lemma 13.3, we estimate that the number of vertices outside solution with at least three neighbors in C does not exceed $2|C|$. Thus, if we manage to design reduction rules leaving at most $f(|C|)$ vertices with at most two neighbors in C, then the number of vertices in the reduced graph does not exceed $|C| + 2|C| + f(|C|)$. In both of our examples, the function f will be linear and reduction will keep the planarity of the graph. Thus, we obtain linear kernels.

13.2.1 Planar CLUSTER VERTEX DELETION

For a graph G, we say that a subset of vertices $S \subseteq V(G)$ is connected if $G[S]$ is connected. Our first example is the following problem. In the CONNECTED VERTEX COVER problem, we are given a graph G and a nonnegative integer k. The task is to decide whether G has a connected vertex cover of size at most k.

We will show in Chapter 19 that a CONNECTED VERTEX COVER does not admit a polynomial kernel. However, on planar graphs not only does this problem admit a polynomial kernel but also it admits a linear-vertex kernel.

Theorem 13.4 CONNECTED VERTEX COVER *on planar graphs admits a* $4k$-*vertex kernel.*

Proof: We apply three reduction rules. The first reduction rule is the same reduction rule we used in Section 2.2 for VERTEX COVER.

Reduction CVC.1 If G contains an isolated vertex v, remove v from G. The new instance is $(G - v, k)$.

If we cannot apply Reduction Rule CVC.1 anymore, we can assume that the input planar graph G is connected because otherwise G has no connected vertex cover.

The second reduction rule is similar to the third reduction rule from Section 2.2.

Reduction CVC.2 If there are two vertices u, v of degree 1 with a common neighbor, then remove one of them, say u. The new instance is $(G - u, k)$.

The proof that Reduction Rule CVC.2 is safe is easy—there is always an optimal vertex cover containing no vertex of degree 1. Let us remark that after exhaustive application of Reduction Rule CVC.2, every vertex of the graph has at most one neighbor of degree 1.

To guarantee that the resulting vertex cover is connected, we use gadgets. The next rule treats vertices of degree 2. Let v be a vertex of degree 2. If v is a cutvertex, that is, after its removal the graph becomes disconnected, then it should be in every connected vertex cover. Otherwise, as we will see in the following text, v can be deleted while both of its neighbors should be in the connected vertex cover.

Reduction CVC.3 Let v be a vertex of degree 2 that is not a cutvertex. Let u and w be the neighbors of v. First, delete v. If u has no neighbor of degree 1, then add a new vertex u' and make it adjacent to u. Similarly, if w has no neighbor of degree 1, then add a new vertex w' and make it adjacent to w.

Claim 13.5 Reduction Rule CVC.3 is safe.

Proof of the claim: Let v be a vertex of degree 2 of G with neighbors u and w and that is not a cutvertex. To prove the claim, it is sufficient to show that there is a connected vertex cover of size k containing v in G if and only if there is a connected vertex cover in $G - v$ of size k containing u and w.

Let C be a connected vertex cover of size k in G. If $v \notin C$, then $u, w \in C$ and we are done. We assume from now that $v \in C$. Because C is connected, at least one neighbor of v should be in C. Let us assume first that exactly one neighbor of v, say u, is in C. Then $w \notin C$. The set $C' = (C \setminus \{v\}) \cup \{w\}$ is obviously a vertex cover of size k. To show that C' is connected we argue as follows. In the graph $G[C]$, vertex v is of degree 1, and thus the set $C \setminus \{v\}$ is also connected. Because v is not a cutvertex, w should have at least one neighbor in G besides v, and because C is a vertex cover, all these neighbors should be in C. Thus, C' is connected.

It only remains to handle the case in which $v, u, w \in C$. Clearly, $C \setminus \{v\}$ is a vertex cover. If $C \setminus \{v\}$ is still a connected set, then we are done. Otherwise, $G[C]$ consists of two connected components. Because v is not a cutvertex, there is an u, w-path in G avoiding v. Because C is a vertex cover, there should be a vertex of the path, say x, adjacent to vertices from each of the two connected components of $C \setminus \{v\}$. However, then $(C \setminus \{v\}) \cup \{x\}$ is connected vertex cover of size k. □

We are ready to conclude the proof of the theorem. Let (G, k) be a reduced yes-instance, hence none of the three rules can be applied to G. Let C be a vertex cover in G of size k. The remaining vertices of $V(G) \setminus C$ can be classified according to the number of neighbors they have in C. We denote by N_1 the set of vertices of $V(G) \setminus C$ with at most one neighbor in C, by N_2 with exactly two neighbors, and N_3 with at least three neighbors.

By Reduction Rules CVC.1 and CVC.2, $|N_1| \leq |C| = k$. Because every cutvertex should be in every connected vertex cover, we have that by Reduction

Rule CVC.3, $|N_2| \leq k$. Finally, by Lemma 13.3, $|N_3| \leq \max\{0, 2|C| - 4\} = 2k - 4$. Therefore,

$$|V(G)| = |C| + |N_1| + |N_2| + |N_3| \leq k + k + 2k - 4 = 4k - 4.$$

□

13.2.2 Planar EDGE DOMINATING SET

In the EDGE DOMINATING SET, we are given a graph G and a nonnegative integer k, and the objective is to determine whether there exists a set X of at most k edges of G such that $G - V(X)$ is edgeless. In other words, we seek a set X of at most k edges such that every edge in G shares an endpoint with at least one edge in X. It is known that EDGE DOMINATING SET admits a kernel with at most $\mathcal{O}(2k^2)$ vertices. When the problem is restricted to planar graph, it is possible to obtain a linear kernel.

Theorem 13.6 EDGE DOMINATING SET *on planar graphs admits a* 14*k-vertex kernel.*

Proof: Let (G, k) be an instance of planar EDGE DOMINATING SET. Our first two rules are exactly the same as for connected vertex cover treating vertices of degree 0 and 1.

> **Reduction EDS.1** If G contains an isolated vertex v, remove v from G. The new instance is $(G - v, k)$.

> **Reduction EDS.2** If there are two vertices u, v of degree 1 with a common neighbor, we remove one of them, say u. The new instance is $(G - u, k)$.

It is easy to show that both rules are safe.

Our next rules treat vertices of degree 2. We say that an edge dominating set D *contains* a vertex v if v is an endpoint of an edge from D. Consider first the following situation, where we have two nonadjacent vertices u, v and at least two vertices of degree 2, say x and y, are adjacent to both u and v; see Fig 13.1.

Claim 13.7 *If G has an edge dominating set of size k, then G has an edge dominating set of size k containing u and v.*

Proof of the claim: Let D be an edge dominating set of G of size k. It should contain at least one of the vertices, u or v. Suppose it does not contain u. Then

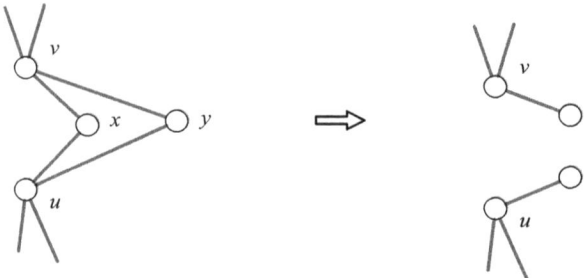

Figure 13.1 Illustration for Reduction Rule EDS.3.

both edges xv and yv must be in D. Because the set D' obtained from D by replacing yv with xu is also an edge dominating set, the claim follows. □

By making use of the claim, we deduce that the following rule is safe.

> **Reduction EDS.3** If there are two nonadjacent vertices u and v, whose common neighborhood $N(u) \cap N(v)$ contains at least two vertices of degree 2, then remove all degree 2 vertices from the common neighborhood of u and v. If u has no neighbor of degree 1, then add a new vertex and make it adjacent to u. Similarly for v, if v has no neighbor of degree 1, then add a new vertex and make it adjacent to v, see Fig 13.1.

Our next observation is as follows.

Claim 13.8 Suppose there is a vertex x of degree 2 adjacent to two adjacent vertices u and v, that is, $xu, xv, uv \in E(G)$. If G has an edge dominating set of size k, then G has an edge dominating set of size k containing u and v.

Proof of the claim: Let D be an edge dominating set of G of size k. Then, D contains at least one of the vertices u and v. Suppose that D does not contain u. Then, to dominate the edge xu, the edge xv must be in D. Because the set D' obtained from D by replacing xv with uv is also edge dominating, the claim follows. □

Based on the preceding claim, we conclude that the following reduction rule is safe.

> **Reduction EDS.4** If there are two adjacent vertices u, v such that their common neighborhood $N(u) \cap N(v)$ contains at least one vertex of degree 2, then remove all degree 2 vertices from the common neighborhood of u and v except one.

Now we are ready to conclude the proof. Let (G, k) be an irreducible yes-instance such that none of the four rules can be applied to G. Let D be an edge dominating set of size k, and let S be the set of vertices contained in D. Then $|S| \leq 2k$. As in Theorem 13.4, we partition the vertices of $V(G) \setminus S$ into the sets N_1, N_2 and N_3 of vertices having at most one, two, and at least three neighbors in S, respectively. Observe that $V(G) \setminus S$ is an independent set, and thus vertices from N_1 are of degree at most 1 and vertices from N_2 are of degree 2. By Reduction Rules EDS.1 and EDS.2, we have that $|N_1| \leq |S|$. By Reduction Rules EDS.3 and EDS.4, for every pair of vertices of S, there is at most one vertex from N_2 adjacent to both. A contraction of an edge incident to a vertex from N_2 results in an edge between two vertices of S. Thus, the size of N_2 is at most the maximum number of edges a planar graph on $|S|$ vertices can have. By Euler's formula, this number is at most $3|S| - 6$. Thus, $|N_2| \leq 3|S|$ and by Lemma 13.3, $|N_3| \leq \max\{0, 2|S| - 4\}$. Putting all together, we arrive at

$$|V(G)| = |S| + |N_1| + |N_2| + |N_3| \leq |S| + |S| + 3|S| - 6 + 2|S| - 4 \leq 14k - 10.$$

□

It is possible to improve the bound on the kernel obtained in Theorem 13.6 to $12k$-vertex kernel, see Exercise 13.4.

13.3 Planar FEEDBACK VERTEX SET

In Section 5.5, we gave a quadratic kernel for FEEDBACK VERTEX SET. Now we show that on planar graphs the problem admits a linear kernel. More importantly, the techniques we use to obtain such a kernel will serve as a prototype of much more powerful techniques (protrusion decompositions and protrusion replacements) discussed in Part II.

The ideas used in the kernelization algorithm for planar FEEDBACK VERTEX SET can be seen as generalization of the arguments we used for planar CONNECTED VERTEX COVER and EDGE DOMINATING SET. These arguments do not work directly for the following reason. Suppose that a graph G has a feedback vertex set of size k and suppose that we succeed to identify a feedback vertex set S of size almost k. (For this purpose, there is a polynomial time 2-approximation algorithm on general graphs and even a polynomial time approximation scheme on planar graphs, see "Bibliographic notes" for details.) By making use of Euler's formula, we bound the number of vertices in $G - S$ having at least three neighbors in S. However, we cannot bound the number of vertices with at most two neighbors in S. Indeed, while as before, we can eliminate vertices of degree 1 and 2, the crucial difference is that $G - S$ is not an independent set and there still can be vertices of high degree in G having only few (say, at most one) neighbors in S. Nevertheless, $G - S$ is a forest, and hence we will implement the following strategy.

- First we show how to enlarge S to a set R_0, still keeping its size linear in k, such that every connected component of $G - R_0$ has at most four neighbors in S.
- Now we can use Euler's formula to argue that the number of different neighborhoods in R_0 of connected components of $G - R_0$ is of order $\mathcal{O}(k)$. We group these components according to their neighborhoods in R_0. In other words, we partition the vertices of G into sets $\{R_0, R_1, \ldots, R_\rho\}$ such that
  - $\max\{\rho, |R_0|\} = \mathcal{O}(k)$,
  - for each $i \in \{1, \ldots, \rho\}$, R_i induces a forest in G, and
  - for each $i \in \{1, \ldots, \rho\}$, $N_G(R_i) \subseteq R_0$ and $|N_G(R_i)| \leq 4$.
- This type of partition is a special case of a protrusion decomposition, that we define in the following chapters. While the number of sets R_i is small, the sizes of these sets are not bounded.
- Our next step will be to reduce the size of each of the sets R_i, $i \geq 1$, to a constant size. This will imply the desired linear kernel. By making use of logic-defined reductions that we develop in the following chapters, one can replace such protrusions to protrusions of constant size. However, for feedback vertex sets we will avoid this step by introducing "handmade" reductions.

We start by constructing the required partition. Let us remark that in the following lemma any bound in $\mathcal{O}(|S|)$ on ρ and R_0 suffices for a linear kernel.

Lemma 13.9 *Let S be a feedback vertex set of a graph G. Then, in polynomial time one can construct a partition of $V(G)$,*

$$\mathcal{R} = \{R_0, R_1, \ldots, R_\rho\},$$

such that

- $\rho \leq 30 \cdot |S|$ *and* $|R_0| \leq 5 \cdot |S|$,
- *For each* $i \in \{1, \ldots, \rho\}$, $G[R_i]$ *is a forest in G, and*
- *For each* $i \in \{1, \ldots, \rho\}$, $N_G(R_i) \subseteq R_0$ *and* $|N_G(R_i)| \leq 4$.

Proof: We start from constructing R_0. For every connected component T of $G - S$ we perform the following procedure. Let us remind that T is a tree. We turn T into a rooted tree by selecting a vertex r of T as a root. For a vertex $t \in V(T)$ we use T_t to denote the subtree of T rooted at t. Consider the case in which T contains a vertex t satisfying the following properties:

- The tree T_t has at least three neighbors in S.
- For every child s of t, T_s has at most two neighbors in S.

In this case, we mark t and remove all vertices of T_t from T. We proceed with marking and removing vertices until T has no subtree with at least 3 neighbors in S. Let Q be the set of all vertices from all components of $G - S$ marked by this procedure.

We claim that $|Q| \leq 2|S|$. To prove it, we consider a bipartite graph B_G with bipartition S and $Q = \{q_1, q_2, \ldots, q_p\}$. For each $i \in \{1, \ldots, p\}$, vertex q_i has exactly the same set of neighbors in S as the subtree of T obtained from the subtree rooted in q_i by removing all subtrees rooted in marked vertices below q_i. In other words, B_G is constructed from G by contracting the corresponding subtree into its marked root and afterward removing edges between the marked vertices. It is clear that B_G is planar. Because every vertex of Q has at least three neighbors in S, by Lemma 13.3, we have that $|Q| \leq 2|S|$.

We enlarge the set Q by replacing it with its least common ancestor closure. In other words, we put $Q := \text{LCA-Closure}(Q)$. Then by Lemma 9.28, the total number of marked vertices Q is at most $4|S|$. We define the set

$$R_0 = S \cup Q.$$

By the preceding arguments, we have that

$$|R_0| \leq 5|S|. \tag{13.1}$$

Another important property of R_0 is that every connected component T of $G - R_0$ has at most four neighbors in R_0. Indeed, T is a connected subgraph of the forest $G - S$, and thus it is a tree. By the selection of the set Q, T has at most two neighbors in S. Moreover, by Lemma 9.27, T has also at most two neighbors in Q. Thus,

$$N_G(T) \subseteq R_0 \text{ and } |N_G(T)| \leq 4. \tag{13.2}$$

We partition the components of $G - R_0$ into classes according to their neighborhoods in R_0. We say that two connected components T and T' of $G - R_0$ are *equivalent* if $N_G(T) = N_G(T')$. Let $R_1, R_2, \ldots, R_\rho$ be the equivalence classes of connected components of $G - R_0$. By (13.2), we have that

$$N_G(R_i) \subseteq R_0 \text{ and } |N_G(R_i)| \leq 4, \text{ for each } 1 \leq i \leq \rho. \tag{13.3}$$

To bound ρ, we use again Lemma 13.3. We construct a bipartite graph R_G with bipartition R_0 and $R = \{r_1, r_2, \ldots, r_\rho\}$. For each $i \in \{1, \ldots, \rho\}$, vertex r_i is adjacent to $N_G(R_i)$. In other words, R_G is constructed from G by replacing each of the classes R_i by a single vertex r_i and making it adjacent to the neighbors (in R_0) of a components—all components from the same class have the same neighborhood—of R_i. It is clear that R_G is planar.

We partition the vertices of R according to their degrees: let N_1 be the set of vertices of degree 1, N_2 of degree 2, and N_3 of degree 3 and 4. Because G is connected there are no isolated vertices in R. The number of vertices in N_1 does not exceed the number of vertices in R_0, thus $|N_1| \leq |R_0|$. Because every vertex from N_2 has a unique neighborhood in R_0, the number of vertices of N_2 does not exceed the maximum number of edges a planar graph on $|R_0|$ vertices can have, which by the Euler formula is at most $3|R_0|$. By Lemma 13.3, the number of vertices from N_3 is at most $2|R_0|$. Hence,

$$\rho \leq 6|R_0| \leq 30|S|. \tag{13.4}$$

By combining (13.1), (13.3), and (13.4), the partition $\{R_0, R_1, \ldots, R_\rho\}$ has the required properties. □

Let (G, k) be a yes-instance of FEEDBACK VERTEX SET. By making use of Lemma 13.9, we proceed with the following strategy.

- We find a feedback vertex set of order $\mathcal{O}(k)$ and use Lemma 13.9 to construct a "protrusion decomposition" $\mathcal{R} = \{R_0, R_1, \ldots, R_\rho\}$ with $|R_0|, \rho \in \mathcal{O}(k)$.
- We use Reduction Rules FVS.1 and FVS.2 to eliminate vertices of degree at most 2. This is not sufficient to obtain the desired kernel, to which end we need one more rule.
- Let us note that while R_0 is a feedback vertex set, we cannot guarantee that it contains even one optimal feedback vertex set. We will show how in polynomial time it is possible to find a superset M of R_0 of size $\mathcal{O}(k)$ such that M contains at least one optimal feedback vertex set.
- Now, having such a set M, we introduce one more reduction rule: Suppose that a vertex $v \in M$ is adjacent to at least two vertices in one connected component of $G - M$. Then, one can argue that the vertex v is relevant, meaning that there is an optimal feedback vertex set containing v, and thus we can take an equivalent instance $(G - v, k - 1)$.
- With the "relevant vertex" reduction rule at hand, we are able to apply Euler's formula to bound the number of vertices in $G - M$ as $\mathcal{O}(k)$.

We proceed with the proof of the main theorem of this section.

13.3 Planar FEEDBACK VERTEX SET

Theorem 13.10 FEEDBACK VERTEX SET *on planar graphs admits a linear kernel.*

Proof: Let (G, k) be an instance of FEEDBACK VERTEX SET, where G is planar. We also assume that G is connected.

Our first reduction rule is Degree-1 Rule (Reduction Rule FVS.1 from Section 5.5): If G contains a vertex of degree 1, then delete this vertex.

Let S be a (not necessarily optimal) feedback vertex set of G. It is well known (see "Bibliographic notes") that there is a 2-approximation algorithm for this problem on general graphs. Moreover, on planar graphs, for each $\varepsilon > 0$ one can find in time $f(1/\varepsilon)n^{\mathcal{O}(1)}$ a feedback vertex set whose size is at most $(1 + \varepsilon)$ the size of an optimal one.

We use Lemma 13.9 to find in polynomial time a partition of the vertex set of G into sets $\{R_0, R_1, \ldots, R_\rho\}$ such that

- Both ρ and $|R_0|$ are in $\mathcal{O}(|S|)$,
- For each $i \in \{1, \ldots, \rho\}$, $G[R_i]$ is a forest in G, and
- For each $i \in \{1, \ldots, \rho\}$, $N_G(R_i) \subseteq R_0$ and $|N_G(R_i)| \leq 4$.

Now, we start construction of the set M. The properties we want are

- $|M| = \mathcal{O}(k)$, and
- If G has a minimum feedback vertex set of size k, then G has a feedback vertex set of size k that is a subset of M.

By (13.3), for each $i \geq 1$, the set $N_G(R_i)$ consists of at most four vertices. Because R_i induces a forest, every minimum feedback vertex set of G contains at most four vertices from $N_G[R_i]$. Our strategy now is to enumerate all possible "configurations" that can occur when the subgraph G_i induced by $N_G[R_i]$ contains at most four vertices from a feedback vertex set. According to this information we identify "relevant" vertices that should be in some optimum solution, and thus can be deleted while decreasing the parameter.

For each $i \in \{1, 2, \ldots, \rho\}$, we do the following. Let $G_i = G[N_G[R_i]]$. For every $X \subseteq N_G(R_i)$ and partition $\{X_1, \ldots, X_\ell\}$, $\ell \leq |X| \leq 4$, of X, we compute a minimum feedback vertex set F of G_i such that

(a) $X = N_G(R_i) \setminus F$. In other words, the vertices of X are exactly the vertices of $N_G(R_i)$ that are not from F;

(b) For every $1 \leq j \leq \ell$, there is a connected component of $G_i - F$ containing X_j. Moreover, for every $j' \neq j$, the connected components containing $X_{j'}$ and X_j are different.

Let us note that it can happen that for some X, either there is no feedback vertex set satisfying condition (b), or the size of a minimum feedback vertex set satisfying (b) is larger than 4. In both these cases, the algorithm does nothing. For all computed feedback vertex sets of all graphs G_i, we mark all vertices contained in these sets. Let M be the set of marked vertices.

How large can M be? For each $i \in \{1, 2, \ldots, \rho\}$, we try all possible subsets X of $N_G(R_i)$. Moreover, for each subset X, we try all possible partitions of X. Thus,

$$|M| \leq \rho \cdot \sum_{p=1}^{4} \sum_{q=0}^{p} \binom{p}{q} B_q,$$

where B_q is the q-th Bell number, the number of partitions of a set with q elements. In particular, $B_0 = 1$, $B_1 = 1$, $B_2 = 2$, $B_3 = 5$, and $B_4 = 15$. We thus arrive at

$$|M| \leq \rho \cdot (5 + 10 + 97) \leq 3360|S|.$$

How long does it take to mark all vertices? Because every feedback vertex set we are searching for is of size at most 4, even by making use of brute force trying all possible subsets of size at most 4, we mark all vertices in polynomial time. By making use of dynamic programming over graphs of bounded treewidth, the technique that will be explained in the next chapters, it is possible to show that such a task can be performed in time linear in n.

Finally, we add to M the set R_0:

$$M := M \cup R_0.$$

Thus,

$$|M| \leq 3365|S|.$$

Next we show that there is always a solution contained in M.

Claim 13.11 A pair (G, k) is a yes-instance if and only if it contains a feedback vertex set F of size at most k such that $F \subseteq M$.

Proof of claim: Targeting toward a contradiction, let us assume that there is a feedback vertex set F of G of size k, but there is no feedback vertex set of size k using only vertices from M. Let us choose F having the maximum number of vertices from M. There is $G_i = G[N_G[R_i]]$ such that F uses some unmarked vertices of G_i. Let $X = N_G(R_i) \setminus F$ and let $\{X_1, \ldots, X_\ell\}$ be the partition of X according to connectivity in $G_i - F$. By this we mean that for every $1 \leq j \leq \ell$, there is a connected component of $G_i - F$ containing X_j, and

13.3 Planar FEEDBACK VERTEX SET

for every $j' \neq j$, the connected components containing $X_{j'}$ and X_j are different. We take a minimum feedback vertex set F_i of G_i such that $X = N_G(R_i) \setminus F_i$ and such that $\{X_1, \ldots, X_\ell\}$ is the partition of X according to connectivity in $G_i - F_i$. By the choice of M, there is F_i consisting of only marked vertices.

We want to show that $F' = (F \setminus N_G[R_i]) \cup F_i$ is a feedback vertex set in G of size at most k. Because F' contains more marked vertices than F, this will contradict the choice of F and prove the claim. If F' was not a feedback vertex set, then $G - F'$ contains a cycle C. This cycle should contain some vertices of G_i and some vertices outside of G_i. But because in $G_i - F$ and in $G_i - F_i$ the "connectivity" partitions $\{X_1, \ldots, X_\ell\}$ are exactly the same, we can reroute the parts of C in G_i avoiding $F \cap N_G[R_i]$, and thus obtain a cycle in $G - F$. The statement that $|F'| \leq k$ follows by noting that $|F_i| \leq |F \cap N_G[R_i]|$. □

Let us note that by Claim 13.11, every connected component of $G - M$ is a tree. We also use Degree-2 Rule (Reduction Rule FVS.2) to eliminate vertices of degree 2. Let us remind that in this rule for neighbors u, w of a degree 2 vertex v, we delete v and add the edge uw if u and w were not adjacent. If they were adjacent, we add a multiple uw edge. Thus, after application of this rule multiple edges can occur. However, by Claim 13.11, between vertices of $G - M$ multiple edges cannot occur, as then every feedback vertex set should contain a vertex outside M. Moreover, we note that the resulting graph remains planar.

Now we are able to state our next reduction rule. Let us remark that we are able to verify the safeness of this rule only because we managed to identify the set of vertices M.

> **Reduction FVS.13 (Relevant Vertex Rule)** Let T be a connected component of $G - M$. If there is $v \in M$ that is either adjacent to a vertex of T using a multiple edge or to at least two vertices of T, then delete v. See Fig 13.2. The new instance is $(G - v, k - 1)$.

Claim 13.12 Reduction Rule FVS.13 is safe.

Indeed, if T contains vertices u, w adjacent to the same vertex $v \in M$, then G contains a cycle with exactly one vertex from M, namely v. Then by Claim 13.11, there is necessarily a solution of size k containing v. Similar arguments apply to the case in which v is adjacent to some vertex of T using a multiple edge. We also remind that no connected component of $G - M$ contains multiple edges.

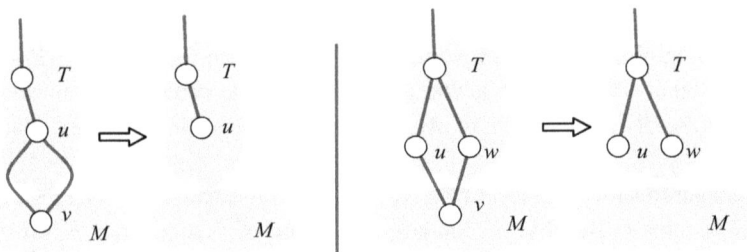

Figure 13.2 Illustration for Reduction Rule FVS.13.

Claim 13.13 Let (G, k) be an irreducible instance of the problem, that is, such that none of the three reduction rules (Degree-1, Degree-2, and Relevant Vertex Rules) can be applied to (G, k). Then, every connected component of $G - M$ has at least three neighbors in M.

Indeed, let T be a connected component of $G-M$. Thus, T is a tree. Because G is connected, T should have at least one neighbor in M. By Degree-1 Rule, every leaf of T is adjacent to a vertex of M. Thus, if T has only one neighbor in M, it consists of one vertex but then it should have been reduced either by Degree-1 Rule or by Relevant Vertex Rule. If T has exactly two neighbors in M, then by Degree-1 Rule, it has at most two leaves. Due to our degree-2 reduction (Reduction Rule FVS.2), we cannot have vertices of degree 2 in T, and thus T consists of exactly two vertices. Let u and v be the vertices of T. By Relevant Vertex Rule, these vertices do not have common neighbors in M, hence these vertices are of degree 2 in G and should have been eliminated by Degree-2 Rule. Thus, T has at least three neighbors in M, and this concludes the proof of Claim 13.13.

We are ready to bound the number of vertices in an irreducible instance (G, k). Let T be a connected component of $G - M$. We cannot apply Degree-1 Rule, thus every leaf of T is adjacent to a vertex in M. By Degree-2 Rule, every vertex of degree 2 in T should be adjacent to M. By Relevant Vertex Rule, vertices of T have no common neighbors in M. This yields that the number of vertices of degree at most 2 in T is at most the number of the vertices from M adjacent to the vertices of T, which is exactly the number of edges from T to M. The number of vertices of degree at least 3 in T does not exceed the number of leaves. Thus, the number of vertices in T is at most twice the number of edges between M and T. Therefore, the number of vertices in $V(G) \setminus M$ does not exceed twice the number of edges between M and $V(G) \setminus M$.

13.3 Planar FEEDBACK VERTEX SET

To bound the number of edges between M and $V(G) \setminus M$, we use Euler's formula. Let $\mathcal{T}$ be the set of connected components of $G - M$. Let us construct a graph G' by contracting every tree $T \in \mathcal{T}$ of $G - M$ into a vertex v_T. Because no pair of vertices of T have the same neighbor in M, in the new graph G' the degree of v_T is exactly the number of edges between T and M. Because G' is planar, by Lemma 13.2, the number of edges in G' between $\{v_T\}_{T \in \mathcal{T}}$ and M does not exceed

$$2(|\mathcal{T}| + |M|).$$

Because degree of each v_T is at least 3, by Lemma 13.3, we have that

$$|\mathcal{T}| \leq 2|M|.$$

Thus, the number of edges in G between M and $V(G) - M$ is at most $6|M|$. Hence the number of vertices in $V(G) - M$ is at most $12|M|$ and the total number of vertices in the reduced graph G is upper bounded by

$$13|M| \leq 13 \cdot 3365|S| = 43745|S|.$$

Because we can select S to be a feedback vertex set of size αk, for some $\alpha \leq 2$, we obtain the linear kernel. $\square$

Let us look once again at the strategy employed in the proof of Theorem 13.10. This viewpoint will be useful later to understand the idea behind protrusion decompositions. First we constructed a partition of G, $\{R_0, R_1, \ldots, R_\rho\}$, and then applied reduction rules. After the exhaustive applications of all reduction rules, for each $i \geq 1$, only a constant number of vertices remained in R_i. Indeed, for each $i \geq 1$, there can be at most

$$\psi = \sum_{p=1}^{4} \sum_{q=0}^{p} \binom{p}{q} B_q = 112$$

marked vertices. Thus, each of the components of $G - M$ has a constant number of neighbors in M. Then, the applications of Degree-1 and Degree-2 rules and the rule excluding marked vertices with at least two neighbors in a tree force that the size of each tree in $G - M$ is a constant. Because every tree should have at least three neighbors in M, the set of trees with the same (constant size) neighborhood in M is also a constant. Thus, each R_i is of constant size. In Chapter 15, these arguments will be generalized to protrusion replacements to obtain meta-theorems for planar kernels.

Exercises

Problem 13.1 Prove Euler's formula: Let G be a connected plane graph with n vertices, m edges, and f faces. Then, $n - m + f = 2$. (Hint: Use induction on the number of edges in a graph.)

Problem 13.2 Prove Lemma 13.2.

Problem 13.3 Show that CONNECTED VERTEX COVER admits a kernel of size exponential in k.

Problem 13.4 Show that the following reduction rules are safe:

- If both adjacent vertices u, v have neighbors of degree 1, then all these neighbors can be deleted after a new vertex of degree 2 adjacent to u and v is added.
- If a vertex of degree 2 is adjacent to the endpoints of an edge uv, then all vertices of degree 1 adjacent to u and v can be removed.

Use these reduction rules to show that EDGE DOMINATING SET on planar graphs admits a kernel with $12k - 10$ vertices.

Problem 13.5 Prove that DOMINATING SET (VC) (DOMINATING SET parameterized by the size k of a minimum vertex cover) on planar graphs admits a linear kernel with $16k$ vertices.

Bibliographic Notes

One of the first results in the area of kernelization on planar graphs was given by Alber et al. (2004a). They gave the first linear sized kernel for the DOMINATING SET problem on planar graphs. The work of Alber et al. (2004a) triggered an explosion of papers on kernelization of problems on planar graphs. Combining the ideas of Alber et al. (2004a) with problem specific data reduction rules, kernels of linear sizes were obtained for a variety of parameterized problems (see Alber et al., 2006, 2004a; Bodlaender and Penninkx, 2008; Bodlaender et al., 2008; Chen et al., 2007; Guo and Niedermeier, 2007b; Guo et al., 2006; Kanj et al., 2011; Lokshtanov et al., 2011a; Moser and Sikdar, 2007). Specifically, linear kernels for FEEDBACK VERTEX SET were given by Bodlaender and Penninkx (2008), Abu-Khzam and Khuzam (2012), Xiao (2014), and Bonamy and Kowalik (2016).

Our presentation of kernelization for connected vertex cover and edge dominating set follows Wang et al. (2013). Kernels of $\mathcal{O}(k^2)$ vertices for

EDGE DOMINATING SET were given by Xiao et al. (2013) and Hagerup (2012). Constant factor approximation algorithms for FEEDBACK VERTEX SET are due to Bar-Yehuda et al. (1998) and Bafna et al. (1999). Moreover, a polynomial time approximation scheme for FEEDBACK VERTEX SET on planar graphs is due to Demaine and Hajiaghayi (2005).

Let us remark that in this chapter, the only property of planarity we use is Euler's formula. This implies, for example, that all the techniques and results of this chapter can be easily generalized to graphs of bounded genus.

PART II

Meta Theorems

14
Introduction to Treewidth

Many NP-hard problems become polynomial time solvable on trees. This has motivated researchers to look for families of graphs that have algorithmic properties similar to those of trees. In particular, the idea of being "treelike" was explored, leading to the notion of *treewidth*. In this chapter, we introduce treewidth and prove some basic properties regarding it. We will use the notion of treewidth to design generic kernelization procedures in the following chapters.

In this chapter we will study a well-known graph parameter, called *treewidth*. The treewidth of a graph G is an integer that measures how close the graph is to being a tree: The lower the treewidth, the more tree-like G is. Treewidth has found numerous applications in algorithms, and has been rediscovered multiple times under different names, so it is no surprise that it is a useful tool also for kernelization. Here we take a minimalistic approach, and tell only the definition of treewidth as well as the properties that are required to prove our kernelization results. There is no disguising that the definition of tree decompositions (and treewidth) is, at a first glance, strange and counterintuitive. The intuition behind the definition of treewidth is as follows. Suppose we wanted to "draw" G inside a tree T. If G is not a tree then the drawing has to self-intersect. Is it possible to draw G inside T without the drawing self-intersecting a great deal? To capture this intuition formally we need to define what it means to draw G inside another graph, and quantify how much such a drawing self-intersects.

The definition of drawing G inside another graph H works as follows. We allow drawing a vertex v of G inside a nonempty *connected* subgraph of H because then we do not need to "lift the pencil" when drawing v. Similarly, if u and v are adjacent in G, we want the drawing of u and the drawing of v in H

to overlap. The point is that we want to be able to draw both u and v inside H without having to lift the pencil. This leads to the following definition.

Definition 14.1 A *model* of a graph G in a graph H is a function $\beta : V(G) \to 2^{V(H)} \setminus \{\emptyset\}$ such that

- For every $v \in V(G)$, $H[\beta(v)]$ is connected, and
- For every $uv \in E(G)$, $\beta(u) \cap \beta(v) \neq \emptyset$.

When measuring how much a model β of G in H self-intersects we simply look at each vertex $b \in V(H)$, and count the number of vertices $v \in V(G)$ such that $b \in \beta(v)$.

Definition 14.2 A model β of G in H has *width*

$$\max_{b \in V(H)} |\{v \in V(G) : b \in \beta(v)\}| - 1.$$

One might wonder about the reason for the "-1" in the definition of the width of a model. The argument is that if G contains even one edge uv, then for any model β of G in H there must be a vertex $b \in H$ where $b \in \beta(u)$ and $b \in \beta(v)$. Thus, without the -1 term the width of any model of a nontrivial graph G in any graph H would be at least 2, which is aesthetically displeasing. We are now ready to define tree decompositions and treewidth.

Definition 14.3 (Tree decomposition) A *tree decomposition* of G is a pair (T, β) where T is a tree and β is a model of G in T. The *width* of a tree decomposition, $\omega(T, \beta)$, is the width of β.

To distinguish the vertices of the graph G and the vertices of the tree T, we usually refer to the vertices of T as to nodes.

Definition 14.4 (Treewidth) The *treewidth* of a graph G is denoted by $\mathrm{tw}(G)$ and is the minimum width $\omega(T, \beta)$ over all tree decompositions (T, β) of G. An *optimal* tree decomposition of G is a tree decomposition of G of width $\mathrm{tw}(G)$.

For a graph G and a model β of G in H, we can define the "inverse" of β as follows. The function χ takes as input a vertex of H and returns the set of vertices in G such that

$$\chi(b) = \{v \in V(G) : b \in \beta(v)\}. \tag{14.1}$$

From (14.1) it follows that

$$\beta(v) = \{b \in V(H) : v \in \chi(b)\}. \tag{14.2}$$

Thus, β uniquely defines χ and χ uniquely defines β.

The equations (14.1) and (14.2) immediately imply that β is a model of G in T if and only if χ satisfies the following properties:

(i) For every $v \in V(G)$, there exists $b \in V(T)$ such that $v \in \chi(b)$,
(ii) For every $v \in V(G)$, $T[\{b : v \in \chi(b)\}]$ is connected, and
(iii) For every $uv \in E(G)$, there exists $b \in V(T)$ such that $\{u, v\} \subseteq \chi(b)$.

In the literature, tree decompositions are often defined using χ rather than β. Specifically, a tree decomposition of G is a pair (T, χ) where T is a tree and χ satisfies the preceding three properties. The width of the decomposition is $\max_{b \in V(T)} |\chi(b)| - 1$. The sets $\chi(b)$ for $b \in V(T)$ are referred to as the *bags* of the decomposition.

We encourage the reader to verify that this definition of tree decompositions is indeed equivalent to Definition 14.3. To truly understand tree decompositions it is crucial that one is able to freely translate between the two definitions.

14.1 Properties of Tree Decompositions

Having defined tree decompositions and treewidth, it is insightful to play around with the notion and prove a few simple properties. We start by showing that by our definition, trees are treelike.

Lemma 14.5 *If G is a tree, then* $\operatorname{tw}(G) \leq 1$.

Proof: Let T be the tree obtained from G by subdividing every edge. For each vertex v of $V(G)$, we set $\beta(v)$ to contain the copy of v in T, as well as all vertices in T that correspond to edges of G that are incident to v. We claim that β is a model of G in T. Indeed, for every v we have that $\beta(v)$ is nonempty and that $T[\beta(v)]$ is connected. Furthermore, for every edge uv, the node $b \in V(T)$ that corresponds to the edge uv satisfies that $b \in \beta(u)$ and $b \in \beta(v)$. Finally, we need to argue that the width of the model β is at most 1.

It is easier to analyze the width using the inverse χ rather than β. For each vertex $b \in V(T)$ that corresponds to a vertex v in G, $\chi(b) = \{v\}$. For each vertex $b \in V(T)$ that corresponds to an edge uv of G, $\chi(b) = \{u, v\}$. Hence the width of the model is at most 1. □

An important property of tree decompositions is that a subtree T' of the decomposition tree T naturally corresponds to a vertex subset $V' \subseteq V(G)$, and that the vertices in V' that have neighbors outside of V' must "live in" vertices of T' with neighbors outside of T'. This is captured by the next lemma.

Definition 14.6 For a graph G and a vertex subset $S \subseteq V(G)$ we define $\partial_G(S) = \{v \in S : N_G(v) \setminus S \neq \emptyset\}$. We refer to $\partial_G(S)$ as the *boundary* of S. When the graph G is clear from context, we omit the subscript.

Definition 14.7 Let (T, χ) be a tree decomposition of G. For any $B \subseteq V(T)$ we define $\chi(B) = \bigcup_{b \in B} \chi(b)$.

Lemma 14.8 Let (T, χ) be a tree decomposition of G and suppose $B \subseteq V(T)$. Then $\partial_G(\chi(B)) \subseteq \chi(\partial_T(B))$.

Proof: Consider a vertex $u \in \partial_G(\chi(B))$. There must exist an edge $uv \in E(G)$ such that $v \notin \chi(B)$. Let b be a vertex in $V(T)$ such that $\{u, v\} \subseteq \chi(b)$, such a bag must exist by the definition of tree decompositions. Because $v \notin \chi(B)$ it follows that $b \notin B$. We have that $u \in \chi(b)$ and furthermore because $u \in \chi(B)$ there is a $b' \in B$ such that $u \in \chi(b')$. Let P be the (unique) path from b' to b in the tree T. By the "connectivity" property of tree decompositions, $u \in \chi(a)$ for each $a \in V(P)$. Let now a be the last vertex on the path P that is in B. Because the path P ends in b, which is not in B, it follows that a has a successor on the path P, and that this successor is not in B. But then $a \in \partial_T(B)$ and $u \in \chi(a)$ yielding $a \in \chi(\partial_T(B))$, completing the proof. □

Another important property is that a set that is connected in the graph must live in a connected subtree of the decomposition.

Definition 14.9 Let (T, β) be a tree decomposition of G. For any $C \subseteq V(G)$ we define $\beta(C) = \bigcup_{v \in C} \beta(v)$.

Lemma 14.10 Let (T, β) be a tree decomposition of G, and let $S \subseteq V(G)$ be such that $G[S]$ is connected. Then $T[\beta(S)]$ is connected.

Proof: The proof is by induction on $|S|$. For $|S| \leq 1$ the statement follows from the connectivity requirement of tree decompositions. Suppose now the statement has been proved for all S with $|S| = p - 1$, we prove it now for any set S of size p. Consider any spanning tree of $G[S]$ and let v be a leaf of this spanning tree. Let u be the neighbor of v in the spanning tree. Then $G[S \setminus \{v\}]$ is connected, and hence by the induction hypothesis $T[\beta(S \setminus \{v\})]$ is connected. We also have that $T[\beta(v)]$ is connected and that $\beta(v) \cap \beta(u) \neq \emptyset$ by the definition of tree decompositions. Thus, $T[\beta(S)]$ is also connected, concluding the proof. □

14.1 Properties of Tree Decompositions

An immediate consequence of Lemma 14.10 is that for any bag $B = \chi(b)$ of a tree decomposition, the images of connected components of $G \setminus \chi(b)$ cannot intersect with more than one component of $T \setminus b$. We formalize this in the following corollary, whose full proof is left as an exercise.

Corollary 14.11 *Let G be a graph and (T, χ) be a tree decomposition of G. For any node $b \in V(T)$ and any connected component C of $G - \chi(b)$ there is a component C_T of $T - b$ such that $\beta(C) \subseteq C_T$.*

Next we inspect how some basic graph operations affect the treewidth of the graph.

Lemma 14.12 *For any vertex $v \in V(G)$ we have $\mathrm{tw}(G) \geq \mathrm{tw}(G - v) \geq \mathrm{tw}(G) - 1$.*

Proof: Consider a tree decomposition (T, β) of G of width $\mathrm{tw}(G)$. The same decomposition (with β restricted to $V(G) \setminus \{v\}$) is a decomposition of $G - v$ of the same (or smaller) width. This proves $\mathrm{tw}(G) \geq \mathrm{tw}(G - v)$. To prove $\mathrm{tw}(G - v) \geq \mathrm{tw}(G) - 1$, we prove $\mathrm{tw}(G - v) + 1 \geq \mathrm{tw}(G)$. Consider now a tree decomposition (T, β) of $G - v$. Setting $\beta(v) = V(T)$ gives a tree decomposition of G of width at most $\mathrm{tw}(G - v) + 1$. □

If one is truly pedantic, the proof of Lemma 14.12 is incomplete. In particular, we need to verify that the constructed tree decompositions satisfy the properties of tree decompositions, and it is a good exercise to verify that they do. Next we inspect the effect of deleting and contracting an edge. Let us remind that for a graph G and its edge uv, we use notation $G - uv$ to denote the graph obtained from G by deleting edge uv and by G/uv the graph obtained from G by contracting uv.

Lemma 14.13 *For any edge $uv \in E(G)$ we have $\mathrm{tw}(G) \geq \mathrm{tw}(G - uv) \geq \mathrm{tw}(G) - 1$.*

Proof: Consider a tree decomposition (T, β) of G of width $\mathrm{tw}(G)$. The same decomposition is a decomposition of $G - uv$ of the same width. This proves $\mathrm{tw}(G) \geq \mathrm{tw}(G - v)$. Furthermore $(G - uv) - v = G - v$ and thus Lemma 14.12 yields $\mathrm{tw}(G - uv) \geq \mathrm{tw}(G - v) \geq \mathrm{tw}(G) - 1$. □

Lemma 14.14 *For any edge $uv \in E(G)$ we have $\mathrm{tw}(G) \geq \mathrm{tw}(G/uv) \geq \mathrm{tw}(G) - 1$.*

Proof: Let x be the new vertex resulting from the contraction of the edge uv, and let (T, β) be a tree decomposition of G of width $\mathrm{tw}(G)$. We make a tree decomposition (T, β') of $\mathrm{tw}(G/uv)$ by setting $\beta'(w) = \beta(w)$ for $w \in V(G) \setminus$

$\{u, v\}$ and setting $\beta'(x) = \beta(u) \cup \beta(v)$. For each $w \in V(G) \setminus \{u, v\}$ we have that $T[\beta'(w)] = T[\beta(w)]$ is a nonempty connected subgraph of T. We also have that $T[\beta'(x)] = T[\beta(u) \cup \beta(v)]$ is a nonempty connected subgraph of T because $T[\beta(u)]$ and $T[\beta(v)]$ are connected, and $\beta(u) \cap \beta(v) \neq \emptyset$ due to $uv \in V(G)$. Hence (T, β') is a tree decomposition of G/uv. Next we consider the width of the decomposition.

For every node $b \in V(T)$ such that $b \notin \beta(u) \cup \beta(v)$ we have that

$$|\{w \in V(G/uv) : b \in \beta'(w)\}| = |\{w \in V(G) : b \in \beta(w)\}|.$$

However, for every node $b \in V(T)$ such that $b \in \beta(u) \cup \beta(v)$ we have that

$$|\{w \in V(G/uv) : b \in \beta'(w)\}| = |(\{w \in V(G) : b \in \beta(w)\} \setminus \{u, v\}) \cup \{x\}|$$
$$\leq |\{w \in V(G) : b \in \beta(w)\}|.$$

This proves the $\mathrm{tw}(G) \geq \mathrm{tw}(G/uv)$ part of the lemma.

For the second inequality, Lemma 14.13 implies $\mathrm{tw}(G/uv) \geq \mathrm{tw}(G - v)$ because one can obtain $G-v$ from $\mathrm{tw}(G/uv)$ by deleting edges. Further, $\mathrm{tw}(G-v) \geq \mathrm{tw}(G) - 1$ by Lemma 14.12, completing the proof. □

Recall that graph H is a *minor* of G if H can be obtained from G by vertex deletions, edge deletions, and edge contractions. Lemmata 14.12, 14.13, and 14.14 directly imply the following theorem.

Theorem 14.15 *If H is a minor of G, then $\mathrm{tw}(H) \leq \mathrm{tw}(G)$.*

14.2 Computing Treewidth

We will now look at a simple algorithm for computing treewidth, namely one that goes over all possible choices for (T, β). It turns out that even getting this algorithm right is nontrivial because it is conceivable that an optimal tree decomposition (T, χ) of some input graph G requires T to be exponentially large in $|V(G)|$. We show now that it is not the case.

Definition 14.16 (Simple tree decomposition) A tree decomposition (T, χ) of G is called *simple* if there is no pair a, b of distinct nodes of T such that $\chi(u) \subseteq \chi(v)$.

We will show that for any graph G there is an optimal simple tree decomposition, and that any simple tree decomposition (T, χ) of G must satisfy $|V(T)| \leq |V(G)|$. To that end, we define a contraction operation on tree decompositions. Let (T, χ) be a tree decomposition of G, $ab \in E(T)$ and let $T' = T/ab$ be the tree obtained from T by contracting ab. Let also x be the node of T' resulting from the contraction of ab. Let $\chi'(c) = \chi(c)$ for all $c \in V(T') \setminus \{x\}$, and let $\chi'(x) = \chi(a) \cup \chi(b)$.

Observation 14.17 (T', χ') is a tree decomposition of G.

Proof: Every vertex of G appears in a bag of (T', χ') because any vertex that was in $\chi(a)$ or $\chi(b)$ is in $\chi'(x)$. For the same reason both endpoints of every edge appear in some bag of (T', χ'). Furthermore, for every vertex $v \in V(G)$ we have that

$$T'[\{b \in V(T') : v \in \chi'(b)\}] = T[\{b \in V(T) : v \in \chi(b)\}]/ab.$$

Thus, for every vertex $v \in V(G)$, the subgraph $T'[\{b \in V(T') : v \in \chi'(b)\}]$ is connected. □

Observation 14.17 naturally leads to the following definition. Let us denote $(T, \chi)/ab = (T/ab, \chi')$ and call $(T, \chi)/ab$ the tree decomposition obtained from (T, χ) by contracting ab.

Lemma 14.18 *There is an algorithm that, given a tree decomposition (T, χ) of G, outputs in time $\mathcal{O}(|V(G)| + |V(T)|\omega(T, \chi))$ a simple tree decomposition (T', χ') of G such that for every $b' \in V(T')$ there is a $b \in V(T)$ such that $\chi(b') = \chi(b)$.*

Proof: The algorithm proceeds as follows; initially the algorithm sets $(T', \chi') = (T, \chi)$. Then, as long as there exists an edge $ab \in E(T')$ such that $\chi'(a) \subseteq \chi'(b)$, the algorithm changes (T', χ') to $(T', \chi')/ab$. If no such edge exists, the algorithm outputs (T', χ').

Because every time an edge ab is contracted we have that $\chi'(a) \subseteq \chi'(b)$, it follows that the algorithm maintains the following property: For every $b' \in V(T')$ there is a $b \in V(T)$ such that $\chi(b') = \chi(b)$. Therefore, all we need to prove is that the tree decomposition (T', χ') is in fact simple. Suppose not, and let a and b be distinct nodes in $V(T)$ such that $\chi'(a) \subseteq \chi'(b)$. Let P be the unique path from a to b in the tree T and let b' be the first node on this path after a. It could be that $b' = b$, but $b' \neq a$ and also we know that $ab' \in E(T)$. In addition, we know that every vertex $v \in V(G)$ such that $v \in \chi'(a)$ also satisfies $v \in \chi'(b)$. By the connectivity property of tree decompositions we have that v must be in the bag of all nodes on P, and specifically $v \in \chi'(b')$. But then $\chi'(a) \subseteq \chi'(b')$ for an edge $ab' \in E(T')$, contradicting that the algorithm terminated. We conclude that (T', χ') must be simple. □

We remark that in the proof of Lemma 14.18 we did not argue that the algorithm runs in time $\mathcal{O}(|V(G)| + |V(T)|\omega(T, \chi))$. Indeed, a naive implementation of the algorithm in Lemma 14.18 would run in time $\mathcal{O}(|V(G)|+|V(T)|^2\omega(T,\chi))$ because we have to go over all edges of T' every time we look for an edge $ab \in E(T')$ such that $\chi'(a) \subseteq \chi'(b)$. However, it is easy to see that it is enough to consider every edge once, and we omit the proof.

Lemma 14.19 *Any simple tree decomposition (T, χ) of G satisfies $|V(T)| \leq |V(G)|$.*

Proof: Pick an arbitrary node $r \in V(T)$ and consider T as a rooted tree with r as the root. By the connectivity property of tree decompositions, for every vertex $v \in V(G)$ the set $\beta(v) = \{b : v \in \chi(b)\}$ induces a connected subtree of T. Thus, there is a unique node $b_v \in V(T)$ that is the node of T closest to r out of all nodes in $\beta(v)$. We say that v *peaks* at b_v. Each vertex $v \in V(G)$ peaks at exactly one node b_v in $V(T)$.

We argue that for every node $b \in V(T)$ there is a vertex $v \in V(G)$ that peaks at b. Suppose not. If b is the root r, this implies that $\chi(b) = \emptyset$, contradicting that (T, χ) is simple. If b is not the root r, then b has a parent b' that is closer to the root r. Because no vertex $v \in V(G)$ peaks at b it follows that $\chi(b) \subseteq \chi(b')$ contradicting that (T, χ) is simple.

We now have that every node b of $V(T)$ has some vertex G that peaks at it, and every vertex v of G peaks in exactly one node of T. Thus, $|V(T)| \leq |V(G)|$. $\square$

Lemmata 14.18 and 14.19 imply the following theorem.

Theorem 14.20 *Every graph G has an optimal simple tree decomposition (T, χ) with $|V(T)| \leq |V(G)|$.*

Theorem 14.20 immediately proves that the problem where we are given as input a graph G and integer k, and have to decide whether $\text{tw}(G) \leq k$, is in NP. A brute force enumeration of all trees on at most n vertices and all functions $\chi : V(T) \to V(G)$ gives an algorithm with running time $2^{\mathcal{O}(n^2)}$. However, it is known that a treewidth can be computed in time $\mathcal{O}(1.7347^n)$. For small values of k one can do much better: There is an algorithm with running $2^{\mathcal{O}(k^3)}n$ to decide whether an input graph G has treewidth at most k. It is also known that if we want a constant-factor approximation, this running time can be speded-up to $2^{\mathcal{O}(k)}n$. The current best polynomial time approximation algorithm for treewidth has ratio $\mathcal{O}(\sqrt{\log \text{tw}(G)})$. On H-minor-free graph classes things are a bit better: For any fixed graph H there is a constant factor approximation for treewidth on graphs excluding H as a minor. Specifically, there is a polynomial time $\frac{3}{2}$-approximation algorithm for treewidth on planar graphs. In fact, it is not even known whether computing treewidth of planar graphs exactly is polynomial time solvable or NP-complete. This remains a challenging open problem in graph algorithms. Summarizing all this, we get the following proposition.

Proposition 14.21 (Seymour and Thomas [1994]; Bodlaender [1996]; Feige et al. [2008]; Fomin et al. [2015a]; Bodlaender et al. [2016a]) *Let G be an n-vertex graph and k be a positive integer. Then, the following algorithms to compute treewidth exist.*

- *There exists an algorithm running in time $\mathcal{O}(1.7347^n)$ to compute* $\mathrm{tw}(G)$.
- *There exists an algorithm with running time $2^{\mathcal{O}(k^3)}n$ to decide whether an input graph G has treewidth at most k.*
- *There exists an algorithm with running time $2^{\mathcal{O}(k)}n$ that either decides that the input graph G does not have treewidth at most k, or concludes that it has treewidth at most 5k.*
- *There exists a polynomial time approximation algorithm with ratio $\mathcal{O}(\sqrt{\log \mathrm{tw}(G)})$ for treewidth.*
- *If G is a planar graph then there is a polynomial time approximation algorithm with ratio $\frac{3}{2}$ for treewidth. Furthermore, if G belongs to a family of graphs that exclude a fixed graph H as a minor, then there is a constant factor approximation for treewidth.*

We remark that all the algorithms in this proposition also compute (in the same running time) a tree decomposition of the appropriate width. For example, the third algorithm either decides that the input graph G does not have treewidth at most k or computes a tree decomposition of width at most $5k$.

14.3 Nice Tree Decompositions

It is often helpful, both in combinatorial arguments and for algorithms on graphs of bounded treewidth, to assume that the tree decomposition has a particular structure. We show that one can modify any simple tree decomposition of G so that it also has this additional structure without increasing the width of the decomposition. We start with the definition of "nice" tree decomposition.

Definition 14.22 (Nice tree decomposition) A tree decomposition (T, χ) of G is *nice* if the following conditions are satisfied.

(i) T is a rooted tree with root r.
(ii) $\chi(r) = \emptyset$, and for every leaf ℓ of T, $\chi(\ell) = \emptyset$.

(iii) Every node b in T has at most two children.
(iv) If b has two children, say b_1 and b_2, then $\chi(b) = \chi(b_1) = \chi(b_2)$.
(v) If b has one child b_1 then $|\chi(b) \setminus \chi(b_1)| + |\chi(b_1) \setminus \chi(b)| \leq 1$.

Lemma 14.23 *There is an algorithm that, given a graph G and a simple tree decomposition (T, χ) of G of width k, outputs a nice tree decomposition (T', χ') of G of width k in time $\mathcal{O}(nk^{O(1)})$. Furthermore, we have $|V(T')| \leq 24(k+2)n$.*

Proof: We start with considering T as an unrooted tree and setting $(T', \chi') = (T, \chi)$. We then proceed to modify (T', χ') for it to have the desired properties. Throughout the process we will maintain that (T', χ') is a tree decomposition of G of width k. First, we attach to every leaf ℓ of T' another leaf ℓ' and set $\chi'(\ell') = \emptyset$. Then, we select an arbitrary leaf of T', call it r, and root the tree T' at r. At this point (T', χ') is a tree decomposition of G satisfying properties (i) and (ii). Further, $|V(T')| \leq 2n$.

As long as T' has a node $a \in V(T')$ with at least three children, we proceed as follows. Let $b_1, b_2, \ldots, b_p$ be the children of a. We make a new node a' and add it to T' in the following manner. The parent of a' is set to a, and for each child b_i of a with $i \geq 2$ we make a' the parent of b_i instead. Finally we set $\chi'(a') = \chi'(a)$. This operation maintains that (T', χ') is a tree decomposition of G. Furthermore it decreases the potential function

$$\sum_{v \in V(T')} \max\{d(v) - 3, 0\}$$

by at least one because the degree of a drops to 3 and the degree of a' is less than the degree of a was before the operation was applied. There is one exception; if a is the root r and r has exactly three children then the operation does not decrease the potential. However, this can happen at most once. Before the process starts the potential is at most

$$\sum_{v \in V(T')} \max\{d(v) - 3, 0\} \leq \sum_{v \in V(T')} d(v) = 2|V(T')| - 2 \leq 4n - 2.$$

Because each step adds one node to the tree and decreases the potential by 1, except for the one step that does nothing to the potential, the number of nodes in $V(T')$ when the process terminates is at most $|V(T')| + 4n \leq 6n$. At this point (T', χ') is a tree decomposition of G satisfying properties (i), (ii), and (iii).

We now run a new process, aimed to make (T', χ') satisfy property (iv) as well. As long as there exists an edge $ab \in E(T')$ with a the parent and b the child, such that a has at least two children and $\chi'(a) \neq \chi'(b)$, we proceed as follows. We add a new node a' to T', make a the parent of a', and change the parent of b to be a'. We set $\chi'(a') = \chi'(a)$. Then (T', χ') is still a tree decomposition of G satisfying properties (i), (ii), and (iii), but the number of edges $ab \in E(T')$ with a the parent and b the child, such that a has at least two children and $\chi'(a) \neq \chi'(b)$ decreases by one. Hence, after at most $6n$ iterations, (T', χ') is a tree decomposition of G satisfying properties (i)–(iv) and $|V(T)| \leq 12n$.

Finally, we run a process aimed at making (T', χ') satisfy property (v). As long as there exists an edge $ab \in E(T')$ such that $|\chi'(a) \setminus \chi'(b)| + |\chi'(b) \setminus \chi'(a)| > 1$, we proceed as follows. Without loss of generality $|\chi'(a) \setminus \chi'(b)| \geq 1$. Let u be a vertex in $\chi'(a) \setminus \chi'(b)$. Make a new node a', remove the edge ab from T' and add the edges aa' and $a'b$ to T'. Set $\chi'(a') = \chi'(a) \setminus \{u\}$. At this point (T', χ') is still a tree decomposition of G satisfying properties (i)–(iv). Additionally, we removed one edge ab, which had positive contribution to the potential function

$$\sum_{pq \in E(T)} \max\left\{|\chi'(p)\chi'(q)| + |\chi'(q)\chi'(p)| - 1, 0\right\},$$

and added two edges aa' and $a'b$. The edge aa' contributes 0 to the potential and $a'b$ contributes one less than ab did. Thus, the potential decreases by one in each step. In the beginning, each edge of T' contributes at most $2(k + 1)$ to the potential, so the process must terminate after at most $12n \cdot 2(k + 1)$ steps. At this point we have that (T', χ') is a tree decomposition of G satisfying properties (i)–(v) and $|V(T)| \leq 24(k + 1)n + 8n \leq 24(k + 2)n$ as required.

The total number of steps in all the processes described in the preceding text is $\mathcal{O}(kn)$ because each step adds a new node to T'. Thus, to make the algorithm run in the desired running time it is sufficient to make each step of each process run in time $k^{\mathcal{O}(1)}$, which is easy to do with appropriate data structures. □

In some situations not all the properties of nice tree decompositions are needed. We will say that a tree decomposition is *seminice* if it satisfies all of the properties of nice decompositions except for the one that the bag of the root should be empty. Clearly every nice decomposition is also seminice.

Definition 14.24 (Seminice tree decomposition) A tree decomposition (T, χ) of G is *seminice* if it satisfies the conditions (i), (iii), (iv), and (v) of Definition 14.24, and for every leaf ℓ of T, $\chi(\ell) = \emptyset$.

14.4 Dynamic Programming

A nice property of trees is that many graph problems that are NP-hard on general graphs are polynomial time solvable when the input graph is a tree. Many algorithms on trees are based on dynamic programming and exploit the fact that trees are fully decomposable by vertex cuts of size one. In some sense, graphs of treewidth k are exactly the graphs that are fully decomposable by vertex cuts of size k. Thus, it is natural to think that some of the dynamic programming algorithms that work for trees could be lifted to also work on graphs of bounded treewidth. This turns out to be the case—with a few notable exceptions most problems that are polynomial time solvable on trees are also polynomial time solvable on graphs of bounded treewidth. We will now show how one can solve many problems on graphs of bounded treewidth in time $f(k)n^{\mathcal{O}(1)}$ if a tree decomposition of width at most k is given as input. We will use the INDEPENDENT SET problem as an example (more examples can be found in the exercises). Recall that an independent set in G is a set S of vertices such that every pair of vertices in S are nonadjacent. In the INDEPENDENT SET problem, we are given as input a graph G and integer t, and the task is to decide whether there exists an independent set of size at least t. In the optimization version of the INDEPENDENT SET problem, the objective is to find a maximum size independent set in G. We will study the optimization version of INDEPENDENT SET in this section.

For a rooted tree T and node $b \in V(T)$, we will refer to the subtree of T rooted at b by T_b. For a nice tree decomposition (T, β) of G and $b \in V(T)$, we define $V_b = \chi(V(T_b))$. In other words, V_b is the set of vertices of G that are contained in the bags of the subtree of T rooted at b.

Consider now the following thought experiment. We fix a node $b \in V(T)$. We want to find an optimal solution $\mathsf{OPT} \subseteq V(G)$ in two stages. First we want to find $\mathsf{OPT} \cap V_b$, and then we want to find $\mathsf{OPT} \setminus V_b$. We have two sets $A \subseteq V_b$ and $B \subseteq V_b$. Are there any situations in which we can automatically conclude that B is a better candidate for $\mathsf{OPT} \cap V_b$ than A is? It turns out that we can. Let us define the following relation $\leq_b$ on subsets of V_b. (We remark that $\leq_b$ is not antisymmetric.)

Definition 14.25 ($\leq_b$ **relation for INDEPENDENT SET**) Let (T, χ) be a nice tree decomposition of graph G, b be a node of T and A, B be subsets of $V(G)$. We say that $A \leq_b B$ if $B \cap \chi(b) = A \cap \chi(b)$ and either

- A is not independent, or
- B is an independent set and $|B| \geq |A|$.

14.4 Dynamic Programming

As shown in the following lemma, $\leq_b$ expresses the preference of some sets over the others.

Lemma 14.26 *If $A \leq_b B$ and there exists an optimal solution $\mathsf{OPT} \subseteq V(G)$ such that $\mathsf{OPT} \cap V_b = A$, then $(\mathsf{OPT} \setminus V_b) \cup B$ is also an optimal solution to G.*

Proof: Consider a maximum size independent set $\mathsf{OPT} \subseteq V(G)$ such that $\mathsf{OPT} \cap V_b = A$. We claim that $\mathsf{OPT}' = (\mathsf{OPT} \setminus V_b) \cup B$ is also a maximum size independent set of G. First we have that

$$|\mathsf{OPT}'| = |(\mathsf{OPT} \setminus V_b) \cup B| = |\mathsf{OPT}| - |A| + |B| \geq |\mathsf{OPT}|,$$

so all we have to prove is that OPT' is an independent set. Toward a contradiction we suppose not, then there are two vertices u and v in OPT' such that $uv \in E(G)$. If both u and v are in $\mathsf{OPT} \setminus V_b$, then $uv \notin E(G)$ because OPT is independent. Furthermore, because OPT is independent it follows that $A = \mathsf{OPT} \cap V_b$ is independent, and therefore $A \leq_b B$ yields that B is independent as well. Thus, if u and v are both in B then $uv \notin E(G)$ as well. Hence one of them must be in $\mathsf{OPT} \setminus V_b$ and the other in B. Without loss of generality $u \in \mathsf{OPT} \setminus V_b$ and $v \in B$.

Because $v \in B$ it follows that $v \in \chi(V(T_b))$, while $u \notin \chi(V(T_b))$. Because $uv \in E(G)$ it follows that $v \in \partial_G(\chi(V(T_b)))$. Lemma 14.8 then yields that $v \in \chi(\partial_T(V(T_b)))$, that is, $v \in \chi(b)$. But then $v \in B \cap \chi(b) = A \cap \chi(b)$ and hence $v \in \mathsf{OPT}$. Now we have two vertices u and v, both in OPT, such that $uv \in E(G)$. This contradicts that OPT is independent. □

Lemma 14.26 brings us to the following definition.

Definition 14.27 (Preference relation for INDEPENDENT SET) A relation $\leq_b$ on subsets of V_b that (a) satisfies the properties of Lemma 14.26 and (b) such that $A \leq_b B$ (for independent sets) yields $A \cap \chi(b) = B \cap \chi(b)$, is a *preference relation*. When $A \leq_b B$, we say that B is *better than* A.

At this point, let us remind that INDEPENDENT SET is an example of dynamic programming over a tree decomposition. The more abstract form of a preference relation described in Definition 14.27 is a template of what a preference relation should express for other problems as well.

Our algorithm for INDEPENDENT SET will compute for each node $b \in V(T)$ a family $\mathcal{F}_b$ of "promising partial solutions," which roughly means that some set in $\mathcal{F}_b$ can be extended to an optimal solution. The next definition captures the notion of $\mathcal{F}_b$ containing "promising partial solutions."

Definition 14.28 A family $\mathcal{F}_b$ of subsets of V_b is called *good* if for any optimal solution $\mathsf{OPT} \subseteq V(G)$ there exists a set $B \in \mathcal{F}_b$ such that $B \cap \chi(b) = \mathsf{OPT} \cap \chi(b)$ and $(\mathsf{OPT} \setminus V_b) \cup B$ is also an optimal solution.

Our algorithm will compute for each node $b \in V(T)$ a good family $\mathcal{F}_b$ of sets. Then the definition of "good" implies that some set $S \in \mathcal{F}_r$ for the root r of T is in fact an optimal solution. Of course, the running time of the algorithm depends on the sizes of the families $\mathcal{F}_b$, so we want to keep $|\mathcal{F}_b|$ as small as possible. To that end, we define the following algorithm.

The algorithm **reduce**() takes as input the family $\mathcal{F}_b$ and outputs a family $\mathcal{F}'_b \subseteq \mathcal{F}_b$. To compute $\mathcal{F}'_b$ it proceeds as follows. Initially $\mathcal{F}'_b = \mathcal{F}_b$, and as long as there is a pair $A, B \in \mathcal{F}'_b$ such that $A \leq_b B$, the algorithm removes A from $\mathcal{F}'_b$. When no such pair remains the algorithm returns $\mathcal{F}'_b$.

Definition 14.29 A family $\mathcal{F}$ of subsets of V_b is an *antichain* of $\leq_b$ if there is no pair $A, B \in \mathcal{F}$ such that $A \leq_b B$.

The family returned by **reduce**($\mathcal{F}_b$) is an antichain of $\leq_b$. We gather additional simple properties of **reduce**() in the next lemma.

Lemma 14.30 *The algorithm* **reduce**() *has the following properties.*

- **reduce**($\mathcal{F}_b$) *runs in time* $\mathcal{O}(|\mathcal{F}_b|^2 n^{\mathcal{O}(1)})$.
- *The family $\mathcal{F}'_b$ returned by* **reduce**($\mathcal{F}_b$) *is an antichain of $\leq_b$.*
- *If $\mathcal{F}_b$ is good, then $\mathcal{F}'_b$ is good.*

Proof: The running time bound on **reduce**($\mathcal{F}_b$) follows from the fact that we only need to check once for every pair $A, B \in \mathcal{F}_b$ whether $A \leq_b B$. The fact that $\mathcal{F}'_b$ is an antichain is an immediate consequence of the definition of the algorithm—otherwise the algorithm would have reduced $\mathcal{F}'_b$ further. All that remains to prove is that if $\mathcal{F}_b$ is good then $\mathcal{F}'_b$ is good. Assume that $\mathcal{F}_b$ is good. Then, initially, when the algorithm sets $\mathcal{F}'_b = \mathcal{F}_b$ we have that $\mathcal{F}'_b$ is good. We proceed to prove that $\mathcal{F}'_b$ is still good after i sets have been removed from it by **reduce**(). The proof is by induction on i. We have already proved the statement for $i = 0$, so what remains is the inductive step.

Assume now that $\mathcal{F}'_b$ is still good after i sets have been removed from it, and let A be the next set to be removed from $\mathcal{F}'_b$. We need to show that $\mathcal{F}'_b$ remains good after A is removed. Suppose not, then there exists an optimal solution OPT of G such that there is no set $B \in \mathcal{F}'_b \setminus \{A\}$ such that $\mathsf{OPT} \cap \chi(b) = B \cap \chi(b)$ and $(\mathsf{OPT} \setminus V_b) \cup B$ is an optimal solution. Because $\mathcal{F}'_b$ is good before A is removed, there exists a set $X \in \mathcal{F}'_b$ such that $\mathsf{OPT} \cap \chi(b) = X \cap \chi(b)$ and $(\mathsf{OPT} \setminus V_b) \cup X$ is an optimal solution. If $X \neq A$, then we have a

14.4 Dynamic Programming

Algorithm `ComputeGoodFamilies`$(G, (T, \chi))$.
Input: A graph G and a seminice tree decomposition (T, χ) of G, with $|V(T)| \leq O(kn)$.
Output: A good family $\mathcal{F}_b$ for each $b \in V(T)$.

Mark all nodes of $V(T)$ as *unprocessed*.
for *every leaf $b \in V(T)$* **do**
$\quad F_b := \{\emptyset\}$
$\quad$ Mark b as *processed*.

while *$V(T)$ has at least one unprocessed node* **do**
$\quad$ Let b be a lowermost unprocessed node in $V(T)$
$\quad$ **if** *b has two children b_1 and b_2* **then**
$\quad\quad \mathcal{F}_b^\star := \{X_1 \cup X_2 \ :\ X_1 \in \mathcal{F}_{b_1}, X_2 \in \mathcal{F}_{b_2}$ and $X_1 \cap \chi(b) = X_2 \cap \chi(b)\}$

$\quad$ **if** *b has exactly one child b_1* **then**
$\quad\quad \mathcal{F}_b^\star := \{X_1 \cup S \ :\ X_1 \in \mathcal{F}_{b_1}$ and $S \subseteq \chi(b) \setminus \chi(b_1)\}$

$\quad \mathcal{F}_b := \textbf{reduce}(\mathcal{F}_b^\star)$
$\quad$ Mark b as *processed*.

Figure 14.1 Algorithm `ComputeGoodFamilies`.

---

contradiction because $X \in \mathcal{F}_b' \setminus \{A\}$. Thus, $X = A$. But A was removed because there is a set $B \in \mathcal{F}_b'$, $B \neq A$, such that $A \leq_b B$. But then, because $\leq_b$ is a preference relation it follows that $\mathsf{OPT} \cap \chi(b) = B \cap \chi(b)$ and $(\mathsf{OPT} \setminus V_b) \cup B$ is an optimal solution. This contradicts the choice of OPT, concluding the proof. $\square$

We are now ready to give the main part of the algorithm for INDEPENDENT SET. The algorithm will compute for each node $b \in V(T)$ a good family $\mathcal{F}_b$. The algorithm processes all the nodes in a bottom-up manner—first it processes all the leaves, and then it repeatedly processes a node b whose children have already been processed. The details of the algorithm can be found in Fig. 14.1.

We now prove that the algorithm performs as expected.

Lemma 14.31 *For each $b \in V(T)$ the family $\mathcal{F}_b$ produced by algorithm* `ComputeGoodFamilies`$(G, (T, \chi))$ *is a good family.*

Proof: We prove that the i-th family computed by the algorithm is good, by induction on i. First, the algorithm computes the family F_b for every leaf b, and sets $F_b := \{\emptyset\}$. Because (T, χ) is a nice tree decomposition of G it follows that $\chi(b) = \emptyset$ and therefore $V_b = \emptyset$. Thus, for any optimal solution OPT of G, there is a set $B \in \mathcal{F}_b$, namely $B = \emptyset$, such that $B \cap \chi(b) = \text{OPT} \cap \chi(b) = \emptyset$ and $(\text{OPT} \setminus V_b) \cup B = \text{OPT}$ is an optimal solution to G.

Assume now that families of the i first nodes processed by the algorithm are all good, and consider the $(i+1)$-st node $b \in V(T)$ to be processed. If b is a leaf, we have already shown that $\mathcal{F}_b$ is good, so assume now that b is not a leaf. All the children of b have been processed. The node b has one or two children in T because (T, β) is a nice tree decomposition. If b has one child b_1 then $\mathcal{F}_{b_1}$ is good by the induction hypothesis. Similarly, if b has two children b_1 and b_2 then $\mathcal{F}_{b_1}$ and $\mathcal{F}_{b_2}$ are both good by the induction hypothesis. It suffices to show that, in either case, the family $\mathcal{F}_b^*$ is good because then the fact that $\mathcal{F}_b$ is good follows directly from Lemma 14.30.

If b has two children b_1 and b_2, then

$$\mathcal{F}_b^* := \{X_1 \cup X_2 \ : \ X_1 \in \mathcal{F}_{b_1}, X_2 \in \mathcal{F}_{b_2} \text{ and } X_1 \cap \chi(b) = X_2 \cap \chi(b)\}.$$

We wish to prove that $\mathcal{F}_b^*$ is good. To that end, consider any optimal solution $\text{OPT} \subseteq V(G)$. Because $\mathcal{F}_{b_1}$ is good, there is a set $X_1 \in \mathcal{F}_{b_1}$ such that $\text{OPT}_1 = (\text{OPT} \setminus V_{b_1}) \cup X_1$ is an optimal solution as well, and $X_1 \cap \chi(b) = \text{OPT} \cap \chi(b)$. Here we used that (T, χ) is a nice tree decomposition, and that therefore $\chi(b_1) = \chi(b_2) = \chi(b)$. Similarly, because $\mathcal{F}_{b_2}$ is good, there is a set $X_2 \in \mathcal{F}_{b_2}$ such that $\text{OPT}_2 = (\text{OPT}_1 \setminus V_{b_1}) \cup X_2$ is an optimal solution, and $X_2 \cap \chi(b) = \text{OPT}_1 \cap \chi(b)$. Consider the set $X = X_1 \cup X_2$. The definition of $\mathcal{F}_b^*$ implies that $X \in \mathcal{F}_b^*$, and $\text{OPT}_2 = (\text{OPT} \setminus V_b) \cup X$ is an optimal solution as well. Finally, $X \cap \chi(b) = \text{OPT} \cap \chi(b)$. We conclude that in this case $\mathcal{F}_b^*$ is good.

If b has one child b_1, then

$$\mathcal{F}_b^* := \{X_1 \cup S \ : \ X_1 \in \mathcal{F}_{b_1} \text{ and } S \subseteq \chi(b) \setminus \chi(b_1)\}.$$

We wish to prove that $\mathcal{F}_b^*$ is good. To that end, consider any optimal solution $\text{OPT} \subseteq V(G)$. Because $\mathcal{F}_{b_1}$ is good there is a set $X_1 \in \mathcal{F}_{b_1}$ such that $\text{OPT}_1 = (\text{OPT} \setminus V_{b_1}) \cup X_1$ is an optimal solution as well, and $X_1 \cap \chi(b_1) = \text{OPT} \cap \chi(b_1)$. Let $S = \text{OPT} \cap (\chi(b) \setminus \chi(b_1))$, and observe that S satisfies $S = \text{OPT}_1 \cap (\chi(b) \setminus \chi(b_1))$ as well. Let $X = X_1 \cup S$, we have that $X \in \mathcal{F}_b^*$, $\text{OPT}_1 = (\text{OPT} \setminus V_b) \cup X$ is an optimal solution, and $\text{OPT} \cap \chi(b) = S \cup (X_1 \cap \chi(b_1) \cap \chi(b)) = X \cap \chi(B)$. Thus, $\mathcal{F}_b^*$ is good in this case as well, concluding the proof. $\square$

Next we give an upper bound on the running time of Algorithm 14.1 in terms of the width of the decomposition (T, χ) and the properties of the relation $\leq_b$.

Definition 14.32 For a graph G, tree decomposition (T, χ) of G and a relation $\leq_b$ on subsets of V_b for each $b \in V(T)$, we define, for each $b \in V(T)$,

14.4 Dynamic Programming

$L(\leq_b)$ to be the size of the largest antichain of $\leq_b$ in 2^{V_b}. Furthermore, set $L = \max_{b \in V(T)} L(\leq_b)$.

Let us upper bound L for the relations $\leq_b$ we defined for INDEPENDENT SET.

Lemma 14.33 *For the relations $\leq_b$ defined for* INDEPENDENT SET, $L \leq 2^{k+2}$.

Proof: Consider an antichain $X_1, \ldots, X_t$ of $\leq_b$ for a node $b \in V(T)$. If $t > 2^{k+2}$ then there exist X_i, X_j, and X_p such that $X_i \cap \chi(b) = X_j \cap \chi(b) = X_p \cap \chi(b)$. Then either at least two of these sets are independent or at least two are not independent. Suppose at least two are independent, without loss of generality it is X_i and X_j. Further, without loss of generality assume that $|X_i| \leq |X_j|$. But then $X_i \leq_b X_j$ contradicting that $X_1, \ldots, X_t$ is an antichain of $\leq_b$. The argument in the case that two of X_i, X_j, and X_p are not independent is identical. □

In the definition of Algorithm 14.1 we required that the nice tree decomposition (T, χ) only had $\mathcal{O}(kn)$ nodes in the decomposition tree. The assumption is not really necessary, as the algorithm works just fine even when the decomposition tree is large. The only reason we have included it is that this allows us to easily state the running time of Algorithm 14.1 in terms of k and n.

Lemma 14.34 *Algorithm 14.1 terminates in $L^4 n^{\mathcal{O}(1)}$ time.*

Proof: Let $M = \max_{b \in V(T)} |\mathcal{F}_b|$. We prove that the running time of the algorithm is upper bounded by $M^4 \cdot n^{\mathcal{O}(1)}$. Because each family $\mathcal{F}_b$ is an antichain of $\leq_b$ by Lemma 14.30, this yields $M \leq L$, thereby proving that the algorithm runs within the claimed running time.

The algorithm processes each of the $\mathcal{O}(kn)$ nodes of the decomposition once. When it processes b and b has two children b_1 and b_2, the algorithm constructs $\mathcal{F}_b^\star$ in time $|\mathcal{F}_{b_1}| \cdot |\mathcal{F}_{b_2}| \cdot n^{\mathcal{O}(1)} = M^2 \cdot n^{\mathcal{O}(1)}$. The construction of $\mathcal{F}_b^\star$ yields $|\mathcal{F}_b^\star| \leq M^2$. Thus, computing $\mathcal{F}_b := \mathbf{reduce}(\mathcal{F}_b^\star)$ takes $M^4 \cdot n^{\mathcal{O}(1)}$ time by Lemma 14.30.

If b has only one child b_1 then the algorithm makes $\mathcal{F}_b^\star$ in time $|\mathcal{F}_{b_1}| \cdot 2^{|\chi(b) \setminus \chi(b_1)|} \cdot n^{\mathcal{O}(1)}$, which is upper bounded by $\mathcal{O}(Mn^{\mathcal{O}(1)})$ because (T, χ) is a nice tree decomposition and therefore $|\chi(b) \setminus \chi(b_1)| \leq 1$. For the same reason $|\mathcal{F}_b^\star| = \mathcal{O}(M)$, and hence, by Lemma 14.30 computing $\mathcal{F}_b := \mathbf{reduce}(\mathcal{F}_b^\star)$ takes $M^2 \cdot n^{\mathcal{O}(1)}$ time. □

Lemmata 14.31, 14.33, and 14.34 immediately yield the following theorem for INDEPENDENT SET.

Theorem 14.35 *There is an algorithm that, given a graph G and a nice tree decomposition (T, χ) of G of width k, finds a maximum independent set of G in time $16^k \cdot n^{\mathcal{O}(1)}$.*

Proof: The algorithm computes a good family $\mathcal{F}_b$ for each node $b \in V(T)$. Then it goes through all the sets in $\mathcal{F}_r$ for the root r of T. By the definition of good families, one of these sets is a maximum size independent set of G. The algorithm outputs an independent set in $\mathcal{F}_r$ of maximum size. Correctness follows from Lemma 14.31, while the running time bound follows from Lemmata 14.34 and 14.34. □

Note that for every n-vertex graph G and subset $U \subseteq V(G)$, it holds that U is a vertex cover if and only if $V(G) \setminus U$ is an independent set. In particular, G has a vertex cover of size at most k if and only if it contains an independent set of size at least $n - k$. Due to this well-known duality of vertex cover and independent set, we have the following corollary.

Corollary 14.36 *There is an algorithm that, given a graph G and a nice tree decomposition (T, χ) of G of width k, finds a minimum vertex cover of G in time $16^k \cdot n^{\mathcal{O}(1)}$.*

Let us note that the running time of the algorithm provided in Theorem 14.35 is not the best possible. It is possible to provide an algorithm for INDEPENDENT SET that runs in time $2^k \cdot k^{\mathcal{O}(1)} \cdot n$ on tree decompositions of width k, see the "Bibliographic Notes" for this chapter for further references.

14.4.1 Reasonable Problems

At this point it is very instructive to go back and notice that there were very few parts of the proof where we used the fact that we were working with the INDEPENDENT SET problem. The only things specific to INDEPENDENT SET that we used were as follows.

- Solutions are vertex subsets. This is used throughout the argument.
- We can check whether a vertex subset is a feasible solution in polynomial time, and we can compare which of two feasible solutions is better in polynomial time. This is only used at the very end, in the proof of Theorem 14.35.
- The definition of the relation $\leq_b$, and the proof of Lemma 14.26 that we have a preference relation.
- The bound of Lemma 14.33 on the size of the longest antichain of $\leq_b$.

14.4 Dynamic Programming

We can now make an abstraction of the properties of INDEPENDENT SET that made the proof go through.

We will say that a graph problem is a *vertex subset problem* if feasible solutions are vertex subsets. Our algorithm for INDEPENDENT SET was based on $\leq_b$ as preference relation. To define preference relation for vertex subset problems, we use directly the properties of Lemma 14.26. Here, maximization problems are handled as well.

Definition 14.37 ($\leq_b$ **relation for vertex subset problem** Π) Let Π be a vertex subset problem and let (T, χ) be a nice tree decomposition of graph G, b be a node of T, and A, B be subsets of $V(G)$. We say that $A \leq_b B$ if the following hold.

- If there exists an optimal solution $\mathsf{OPT} \subseteq V(G)$ of Π such that $\mathsf{OPT} \cap V_b = A$, then $(\mathsf{OPT} \setminus V_b) \cup B$ is also an optimal solution to G.
- If $A \leq_b B$, then $A \cap \chi(b) = B \cap \chi(b)$.

We refer to such a relation $\leq_b$ as to a *preference relation* for Π and say that B is better than A.

A vertex subset problem is *reasonable* if there exists a polynomial time algorithm that verifies whether a given vertex subset is a feasible solution. We will say that a problem *has polynomial time computable preference relations* if there exists a polynomial time algorithm that, given a graph G, nice tree decomposition (T, β) of G, node $b \in V(T)$, and two sets $A, B \subseteq V_b$, computes whether $A \leq_b B$ for some preference relation $\leq_b$. The notion of a *good family* is defined as in Definition 14.28 and the *antichain length* of preference relations is L, as given in Definition 14.32. Then as far as the problem has a polynomial time computable preference relation, the algorithm **reduce**() has the properties provided by Lemma 14.30.

Thus, for polynomial time computable preference relations, the following lemma claims exactly the same as what Lemma 14.30 claimed for INDEPENDENT SET.

Lemma 14.38 *Assume $\leq_b$ is a polynomial time computable preference relation. Then the algorithm* **reduce**() *has the following properties.*

- **reduce**($\mathcal{F}_b$) *runs in time* $\mathcal{O}(|\mathcal{F}_b|^2 n^{\mathcal{O}(1)})$.
- *The family $\mathcal{F}'_b$ returned by* **reduce**($\mathcal{F}_b$) *is an antichain of $\leq_b$.*
- *If $\mathcal{F}_b$ is good, then $\mathcal{F}'_b$ is good.*

Thus, on the way to prove Theorem 14.35 for INDEPENDENT SET, we also proved the following theorem for reasonable vertex subset problems. Here, note that L (defined in Definition 14.32) depends on k.

Theorem 14.39 *For any reasonable vertex subset problem Π that has polynomial time computable preference relations, there is an algorithm that, given an n-vertex graph G and a nice tree decomposition (T, χ) of width k, computes an optimal solution of Π in time $L^4 \cdot n^{\mathcal{O}(1)}$.*

In Section 14.4.2 we show how to apply Theorem 14.39 to give an algorithm for DOMINATING SET on graphs of bounded treewidth, while applications of Theorem 14.39 to other problems are discussed in the exercises.

It is worth mentioning that Algorithm 14.1 runs in a bottom-up fashion, and that therefore one can run the algorithm on a rooted subtree of the input decomposition tree. The algorithm will then compute a good family for every bag of this subtree, and the bags that are not in the subtree do not contribute to the running time of the algorithm.

Lemma 14.40 *For any vertex subset problem that has polynomial time computable preference relations, there is an algorithm that, given a graph G, a seminice tree decomposition (T, χ) of G, and a node $b \in V(T)$, computes a good family $\mathcal{F}_b$ of subsets of V_b, such that $|\mathcal{F}_b| \leq L(\leq_b)$. The running time of the algorithm is upper bounded by $\hat{L}_b^4 \cdot n^{\mathcal{O}(1)}$. Here $\leq_a$ is the polynomial time computable preference relation for every node $a \in V(T)$, and*

$$\hat{L}_b = \max_{a \in V(T_b)} L(\leq_a).$$

Proof: The algorithm simply runs Algorithm 14.40 on all nodes in T_b (the subtree rooted at b) and returns the computed family $\mathcal{F}_b$. The fact that $\mathcal{F}_b$ is good follows from Lemma 14.31. The upper bound on the running time follows immediately from the proof of Lemma 14.34, applied to all nodes in T_b rather than all the nodes of T. □

At a first glance Lemma 14.40 looks useless—why would one want to run an algorithm on half the graph when we could run it on the entire graph? The point is that sometimes we have at hand a tree decomposition of the graph where not all the bags are small, but there are rooted subtrees where all bags are small. Lemma 14.40 allows us to efficiently "analyze" a subtree of the decomposition if all the bags in that subtree are small, regardless of the size of the other bags in the decomposition. Lemma 14.40 will be used in this way in Chapter 15 to give a linear kernel for DOMINATING SET on planar graphs.

14.4 Dynamic Programming 277

Further, the intuition behind Lemma 14.40 is at the core of the techiques discussed in Chapter 16.

14.4.2 Dynamic Programming for DOMINATING SET

Let us remind that *dominating set* in a graph is a vertex set S such that $N[S] = V(G)$. In the DOMINATING SET problem we are given as input a graph G and integer t, and the task is to decide whether there exists a dominating set of size at most t. This can be phrased as a vertex subset problem where the feasible solutions are dominating sets and the objective is to minimize the size of the feasible solution. Thus, in the language of Theorem 14.39, DOMINATING SET is a reasonable vertex subset problem.

If we are given a tree decomposition (T, χ) of the input graph G, we can, for each $b \in V(T)$, define a relation $\leq_b$ on subsets of V_b. Let us remind that we use T_b to denote the subtree of T rooted at b and $V_b = \chi(T_b)$. The relation $\leq_b$ is defined as follows.

Definition 14.41 For two subsets A and B of V_b, $A \leq_b B$ if

- $\chi(T_b) \setminus \chi(b) \subseteq N[B]$ or $\chi(T_b) \setminus \chi(b) \not\subseteq N[A]$,
- $B \cap \chi(b) = A \cap \chi(b)$,
- $N[B] \cap \chi(b) \supseteq N[A] \cap \chi(b)$, and
- $|B| \leq |A|$.

It is easy to see that given A and B we can decide in polynomial time whether $A \leq_b B$. In other words, $\leq_b$ is polynomial time computable. Next we show that $\leq_b$ is a preference relation.

Lemma 14.42 $\leq_b$ *as defined in Definition 14.41 is a preference relation.*

Proof: By definition of $\leq_b$, if $A \leq_B B$ then $A \cap \chi(b) = B \cap \chi(b)$. Thus, we need to prove that if $A \leq_b B$ and there exists an optimal solution $\mathsf{OPT} \subseteq V(G)$ such that $\mathsf{OPT} \cap V_b = A$, then $\mathsf{OPT}' = (\mathsf{OPT} \setminus V_b) \cup B$ is also an optimal solution to G. First we have that

$$|\mathsf{OPT}'| = |(\mathsf{OPT} \setminus V_b) \cup B| = |\mathsf{OPT}| - |A| + |B| \leq |\mathsf{OPT}|,$$

so all we have to prove is that OPT' is a dominating set. The definition of $\leq_b$ implies that $N[A] \cap \chi(T_b) \subseteq N[B] \cap \chi(T_b)$. Further, because the only vertices in $\chi(T_b)$ with neighbors outside $\chi(T_b)$ are in $\chi(b)$ (recall Lemma 14.8) and $B \cap \chi(b) = A \cap \chi(b)$, it follows that $N[A] \subseteq N[B]$. But $\mathsf{OPT}' = (\mathsf{OPT} \setminus A) \cup B$, so

$$N[\mathsf{OPT}] = N[\mathsf{OPT} \setminus A] \cup N[A]$$
$$= N[\mathsf{OPT}' \setminus B] \cup N[A]$$
$$\subseteq N[\mathsf{OPT}' \setminus B] \cup N[B]$$
$$= N[\mathsf{OPT}'].$$

Because OPT is a dominating set, so is OPT'. □

Finally, to invoke Theorem 14.39 we need to bound the antichain length L of the relations $\leq_b$. Recall that for each $b \in V(T)$, $L(\leq_b)$ is defined to be the length of the longest antichain of $\leq_b$.

Lemma 14.43 *For every $b \in V(T)$, $L(\leq_b) < 3^{|\chi(B)|+1}$.*

Proof: Consider an antichain $A_1, A_2, \ldots, A_\ell$ of subsets of V_b and suppose for contradiction that $\ell \geq 3^{|\chi(B)|+1}$. By the pigeonhole principle there are three distinct sets A_p, A_q, and A_r in this antichain such that

$$A_p \cap \chi(b) = A_q \cap \chi(b) = A_r \cap \chi(b)$$

and

$$N[A_p] \cap \chi(b) = N[A_q] \cap \chi(b) = N[A_r] \cap \chi(b).$$

Inspect whether $\chi(T_b) \setminus \chi(b) \subseteq N[A_p]$, $\chi(T_b) \setminus \chi(b) \subseteq N[A_q]$ and whether $\chi(T_b) \setminus \chi(b) \subseteq N[A_r]$. For (at least) two of the three sets the answer to this question is the same. Thus, without loss of generality, we have that either both $\chi(T_b) \setminus \chi(b) \subseteq N[A_p]$ and $\chi(T_b) \setminus \chi(b) \subseteq N[A_q]$ or that $\chi(T_b) \setminus \chi(b) \not\subseteq N[A_p]$ and $\chi(T_b) \setminus \chi(b) \not\subseteq N[A_q]$.

In either of these two cases, A_p and A_q satisfy the three first conditions of both $A_p \leq_b A_q$ and $A_q \leq_b A_p$. Thus, if $|A_p| \leq |A_q|$ then $A_q \leq_b A_p$, whereas if $|A_q| \leq |A_p|$ then $A_p \leq_b A_q$. In either case, this contradicts that $A_1, A_2, \ldots, A_\ell$ is an antichain of $\leq_b$. □

Lemma 14.43 implies that if the width of the tree decomposition (T, χ) is at most k, then the antichain length L of the relations $\leq_b$ is at most 3^{k+2}. Thus, DOMINATING SET is a reasonable vertex subset problem with polynomial time computable preference relations of antichain length at most 3^{k+2}. By Theorem 14.39, there is an algorithm that, given as input a graph G, integer t, and a nice tree decomposition (T, χ) of width at most k, decides whether G has a dominating set of size at most t in $81^k \cdot n^{\mathcal{O}(1)}$ time.

Thus, we have the following theorem.

Theorem 14.44 *There is an algorithm that, given a graph G and a nice tree decomposition (T, χ) of G of width k, finds a minimum dominating set of G in time $81^k \cdot n^{\mathcal{O}(1)}$.*

As in the case with INDEPENDENT SET in Theorem 14.35, the running time of the algorithm provided in Theorem 14.44 is not optimal, and DOMINATING SET can be solved in time $3^k \cdot k^{\mathcal{O}(1)} n$ on graphs of treewidth k, see the "Bibliographic Notes" for references.

14.5 Treewidth and MSO$_2$

The approach we developed in Section 14.4 for solving INDEPENDENT SET and DOMINATING SET on graphs of bounded treewidth can be used for many other problems. In this section, we briefly discuss a general description of properties of a problem that make it amenable to dynamic programming over tree decompositions. This description is in the form of *Monadic second-order logic on graphs*, or **MSO$_2$**. In this section we define **MSO$_2$** and state Courcelle's theorem. Our presentation here is taken from Cygan et al. (2015, Section 7.4). Up to very small changes, Section 14.5.1 is copied from there.

14.5.1 Monadic Second-Order Logic on Graphs

The logic we are about to introduce is called **MSO$_2$**. Instead of providing immediately the formal description of this logic, we first give an example of an **MSO$_2$** formula to work out the main concepts. Consider the following formula **conn**(X), which verifies that a subset X of vertices of a graph $G = (V, E)$ induces a connected subgraph.

$$\mathbf{conn}(X) = \forall_{Y \subseteq V} [(\exists_{u \in X} u \in Y \land \exists_{v \in X} v \notin Y)$$
$$\Rightarrow (\exists_{e \in E} \exists_{u \in X} \exists_{v \in X} \mathbf{inc}(u, e) \land \mathbf{inc}(v, e) \land u \in Y \land v \notin Y)].$$

Translation of this formula into English is
For every subset of vertices Y, if X contains both a vertex from Y and a vertex outside of Y, then there exists an edge e whose endpoints u, v both belong to X, but one of them is in Y and the other is outside of Y.

One can easily see that this condition is equivalent to the connectivity of $G[X]$: The vertex set of G cannot be partitioned into Y and $V(G) \setminus Y$ in such a manner that X is partitioned nontrivially and no edge of $G[X]$ crosses the partition.

As we see in this example, **MSO**$_2$ is a formal language of expressing properties of graphs and objects inside these graphs, such as vertices, edges, or subsets of them. A formula φ of **MSO**$_2$ is nothing else but a string over some mysterious symbols, which we shall decode in the next few paragraphs. One may think that a formula defines a *program* that can be run on an input graph, similarly as, say, a C++ program can be run on some text input. A C++ program is just a sequence of instructions following some syntax, and an **MSO**$_2$ formula is just a sequence of symbols constructed using a specified set of rules. A C++ program can be run on multiple different inputs, and may provide different results of the computation. Similarly, an **MSO**$_2$ formula may be evaluated in different graphs, and it can give different outcomes. More precisely, an **MSO**$_2$ formula can be *true* in a graph or *false*. The result of an application of a formula to a graph will be called the *evaluation* of the formula in the graph.

Similarly to C++ programs, **MSO**$_2$ formulas have *variables* that represent different objects in the graph. Generally, we shall have four *types* of variables: variables for single vertices, single edges, subsets of vertices, and subsets of edges; the last type was not used in formula **conn**(X). At each point of the process of evaluation of the formula, every variable is *evaluated* to some object of appropriate type.

Note that a formula can have "parameters": variables that are given from "outside," whose properties we verify in the graph. In the **conn**(X) example such a parameter is X, the vertex subset whose connectivity is being tested. Such variables will be called *free variables* of the formula. Note that to properly evaluate the formula in a graph, we need to be given the evaluation of these variables. Most often, we will assume that the input graph is *equipped* with evaluation of all the free variables of the considered **MSO**$_2$ formula, which means that these evaluations are provided together with the graph.

If we already have some variables in the formula, we can test their mutual interaction. As we have seen in the **conn**(X) example, we can, for instance, check whether some vertex u belongs to some vertex subset Y ($u \in Y$) or whether an edge e is incident to a vertex u (**inc**(u, e)). These checks can be combined using standard Boolean operators such as $\neg$ (negation, logical NOT), $\wedge$ (conjunction, logical AND), $\vee$ (disjunction, logical OR), and $\Rightarrow$ (implication).

The crucial concept that makes **MSO**$_2$ useful for expressing graph properties are *quantifiers*. They can be seen as counterparts of *loops* in standard programming languages. We have two types of quantifiers, $\forall$ and $\exists$. Each quantifier is applied to some *subformula* ψ, which in the programming language analogy is just a block of code bound by the loop. Moreover, every

14.5 Treewidth and **MSO₂**

quantifier introduces a new variable over which it iterates. This variable can be then used in the subformula.

Quantifier ∀ is called the *universal quantifier*. Suppose we write a formula $\forall_{v \in V} \psi$, where ψ is some subformula that uses variable v. This formula should be then read as "For every vertex v in the graph, ψ holds." In other words, quantifier $\forall_{v \in V}$ iterates through all possible evaluations of variable v to a vertex of the graph, and for each of them it is checked whether ψ is indeed true. If this is the case for *every* evaluation of v, then the whole formula $\forall_{v \in V} \psi$ is true; otherwise it is false.

Quantifier ∃, called the *existential quantifier*, works sort of similarly. Formula $\exists_{v \in V} \psi$ should be read as "There exists a vertex v in the graph, such that ψ holds." This means that $\exists_{v \in V}$ iterates through all possible evaluations of variable v to a vertex of the graph, and verifies whether there is at least one for which ψ is true.

Of course, here we just showed examples of quantification over variables for single vertices, but we can also quantify over variables for single edges (e.g., $\forall_{e \in E}/\exists_{e \in E}$), vertex subsets (e.g., $\forall_{X \subseteq V}/\exists_{X \subseteq V}$), or edge subsets (e.g., $\forall_{C \subseteq E}/\exists_{C \subseteq E}$). Standard Boolean operators can be also used to combine larger formulas; see, for instance, our use of the implication in formula **conn**(X).

Syntax and semantics of MSO₂. Formulas of **MSO₂** can use four types of variables: for single vertices, single edges, subsets of vertices, and subsets of edges. The subscript 2 in **MSO₂** exactly signifies that quantification over edge subsets is also allowed. If we forbid this type of quantification, we arrive at a weaker logic **MSO₁**. The vertex/edge subset variables are called *monadic* variables.

Every formula φ of **MSO₂** can have free variables, which often will be written in parentheses besides the formula. More precisely, whenever we write a formula of **MSO₂**, we should always keep in mind what variables are assumed to be existent in the context in which this formula will be used. The sequence of these variables is called the *signature* over which the formula is written;[1] following our programming language analogy, this is the environment in which the formula is being defined. Then variables from the signature can be used in φ as free variables. The signature will be denoted by Σ. Note that for every variable in the signature we need to know what is its type.

To evaluate a formula φ over signature Σ in a graph G, we need to know how the variables of Σ are evaluated in G. By Σ^G we will denote the sequence

---

[1] For the sake of simplicity, our presentation of notions such as signature is slightly noncompliant with the definitions from model theory.

of evaluations of variables from Σ. Evaluation of a single variable x will be denoted by x^G. Graph G and Σ^G together shall be called the *structure* in which φ is being evaluated. If φ is true in structure $\langle G, \Sigma^G \rangle$, then we shall denote it by

$$\langle G, \Sigma^G \rangle \models \varphi,$$

which should be read as "Structure $\langle G, \Sigma^G \rangle$ is a model for φ."

Formulas of **MSO**$_2$ are constructed inductively from smaller subformulas. We first describe the smallest building blocks, called *atomic formulas*.

- If $u \in \Sigma$ is a vertex (edge) variable and $X \in \Sigma$ is a vertex (edge) set variable, then we can write formula $u \in X$. The semantics is standard: The formula is true if and only if $u^G \in X^G$.
- If $u \in \Sigma$ is a vertex variable and $e \in \Sigma$ is an edge variable, then we can write formula **inc**(u, e). The semantics is that the formula is true if and only if u^G is an endpoint of e^G.
- For any two variables $x, y \in \Sigma$ of the same type, we can write formula $x = y$. This formula is true in the structure if and only if $x^G = y^G$.

Now that we know the basic building blocks, we can start to create larger formulas. As described before, we can use standard Boolean operators ($\neg, \wedge, \vee, \Rightarrow$) working as follows. Suppose that φ_1, φ_2 are two formulas over the same signature Σ. Then we can write the following formulas, also over Σ.

- Formula $\neg \varphi_1$, where $\langle G, \Sigma^G \rangle \models \neg \varphi_1$ if and only if $\langle G, \Sigma^G \rangle \not\models \varphi_1$.
- Formula $\varphi_1 \wedge \varphi_2$, where $\langle G, \Sigma^G \rangle \models \varphi_1 \wedge \varphi_2$ if and only if $\langle G, \Sigma^G \rangle \models \varphi_1$ and $\langle G, \Sigma^G \rangle \models \varphi_2$.
- Formula $\varphi_1 \vee \varphi_2$, where $\langle G, \Sigma^G \rangle \models \varphi_1 \vee \varphi_2$ if and only if $\langle G, \Sigma^G \rangle \models \varphi_1$ or $\langle G, \Sigma^G \rangle \models \varphi_2$.
- Formula $\varphi_1 \Rightarrow \varphi_2$, where $\langle G, \Sigma^G \rangle \models \varphi_1 \Rightarrow \varphi_2$ if and only if $\langle G, \Sigma^G \rangle \models \varphi_1$ implies that $\langle G, \Sigma^G \rangle \models \varphi_2$.

Finally, we can use quantifiers. For concreteness, suppose we have a formula ψ over signature Σ' that contains some vertex variable v. Let $\Sigma = \Sigma' \setminus \{v\}$. Then we can write the following formulas over Σ:

- Formula $\varphi_\forall = \forall_{v \in V} \psi$. Then $\langle G, \Sigma^G \rangle \models \varphi_\forall$ if and only if *for every* vertex $v^G \in V(G)$, it holds that $\langle G, \Sigma^G, v^G \rangle \models \psi$.
- Formula $\varphi_\exists = \exists_{v \in V} \psi$. Then $\langle G, \Sigma^G \rangle \models \varphi_\exists$ if and only if there *exists* a vertex $v^G \in V(G)$ such that $\langle G, \Sigma^G, v^G \rangle \models \psi$.

Similarly, we can perform quantification over variables for single edges ($\forall_{e \in E}/\exists_{e \in E}$), vertex subsets ($\forall_{X \subseteq V}/\exists_{X \subseteq V}$), and edge subsets ($\forall_{C \subseteq E}/\exists_{C \subseteq E}$). The semantics is defined analogously.

14.5 Treewidth and **MSO**$_2$

Observe that in formula **conn**(X) we used a couple of notation "hacks" that simplified the formula, but were formally not compliant to the syntax described previously. We namely allow some shorthands to streamline writing formulas. First, we allow simple shortcuts in the quantifiers. For instance, $\exists_{v \in X} \psi$ is equivalent to $\exists_{v \in V} (v \in X) \wedge \psi$ and $\forall_{v \in X} \psi$ is equivalent to $\forall_{v \in V} (v \in X) \Rightarrow \psi$. We can also merge a number of similar quantifiers into one, for example, $\exists_{X_1, X_2 \subseteq V}$ is the same as $\exists_{X_1 \subseteq V} \exists_{X_2 \subseteq V}$. Another construct that we can use is the subset relation $X \subseteq Y$: It can be expressed as $\forall_{v \in V}(v \in X) \Rightarrow (v \in Y)$, and similarly for edge subsets. We can also express the adjacency relation between two vertex variables: $\mathbf{adj}(u, v) = (u \neq v) \wedge (\exists_{e \in E} \mathbf{inc}(u, e) \wedge \mathbf{inc}(v, e))$. Finally, we use $x \neq y$ for $\neg(x = y)$ and $x \notin X$ for $\neg(x \in X)$. The reader is encouraged to use his or her own shorthands whenever it is beneficial.

Examples. Let us now provide two more complicated examples of graph properties expressible in **MSO**$_2$. We have already seen how to express that a subset of vertices induces a connected graph. Let us now look at 3-colorability. To express this property, we need to quantify the existence of three vertex subsets X_1, X_2, and X_3 that form a partition of V, and where each of them is an independent set.

$$\mathbf{3colorability} \;=\; \exists_{X_1, X_2, X_3 \subseteq V} \mathbf{partition}(X_1, X_2, X_3) \wedge$$
$$\mathbf{indp}(X_1) \wedge \mathbf{indp}(X_2) \wedge \mathbf{indp}(X_3).$$

Here, **partition** and **indp** are two auxiliary subformulas. Formula **partition** has three vertex subset variables X_1, X_2, and X_3 and verifies that (X_1, X_2, X_3) is a partition of the vertex set V. Formula **indp** verifies that a given subset of vertices is independent.

$$\mathbf{partition}(X_1, X_2, X_3) \;=\; \forall_{v \in V} [(v \in X_1 \wedge v \notin X_2 \wedge v \notin X_3)$$
$$\vee (v \notin X_1 \wedge v \in X_2 \wedge v \notin X_3)$$
$$\vee (v \notin X_1 \wedge v \notin X_2 \wedge v \in X_3)];$$

$$\mathbf{indp}(X) \;=\; \forall_{u, v \in X} \neg \mathbf{adj}(u, v).$$

As a second example, let us look at Hamiltonicity: We would like to write a formula that is true in a graph G if and only if G admits a Hamiltonian cycle. For this, let us quantify existentially a subset of edges C that is supposed to comprise the edges of the Hamiltonian cycle we look for. Then we need to verify that (a) C induces a connected graph, and (b) every vertex of V is adjacent to exactly two different edges of C.

$$\mathbf{hamiltonicity} \;=\; \exists_{C \subseteq E} \mathbf{connE}(C) \wedge \forall_{v \in V} \mathbf{deg2}(v, C).$$

Here, **connE**(C) is an auxiliary formula that checks whether the graph (V, C) is connected (using similar ideas as for **conn**(X)), and **deg2**(v, C) verifies that vertex v has exactly two adjacent edges belonging to C:

$$\textbf{connE}(C) = \forall_{Y \subseteq V} \;\; [(\exists_{u \in V} u \in Y \land \exists_{v \in V} v \notin Y)$$
$$\Rightarrow (\exists_{e \in C} \exists_{u \in Y} \exists_{v \notin Y} \textbf{inc}(u, e) \land \textbf{inc}(v, e))];$$

$$\textbf{deg2}(v, C) = \exists_{e_1, e_2 \in C} [(e_1 \neq e_2) \land \textbf{inc}(v, e_1) \land \textbf{inc}(v, e_2) \land$$
$$(\forall_{e_3 \in C} \textbf{inc}(v, e_3) \Rightarrow (e_1 = e_3 \lor e_2 = e_3))].$$

14.5.2 Courcelle's Theorem

In the following, for a formula φ by $||\varphi||$ we denote the length of the encoding of φ as a string.

Theorem 14.45 (Courcelle's theorem, Courcelle [1990]) *Assume that φ is a formula of* **MSO**$_2$ *and G is an n-vertex graph equipped with evaluation of all the free variables of φ. Suppose, moreover, that a tree decomposition of G of width t is provided. Then there exists an algorithm that verifies whether φ is satisfied in G in time $f(||\varphi||, t) \cdot n$, for some computable function f.*

The proof of Courcelle's theorem is beyond the scope of this book, and we refer to other sources for a comprehensive presentation. As we have already seen, the requirement that G be given together with its tree decomposition is not necessary because an optimal tree decomposition of G can be computed within the same complexity bounds.

Recall that in the previous section we constructed formulas **3colorability** and **hamiltonicity** that are satisfied in G if and only if G is 3-colorable or has a Hamiltonian cycle, respectively. If we now apply Courcelle's theorem to these constant-size formulas, we immediately obtain as a corollary that testing these two properties of graphs is fixed-parameter tractable when parameterized by treewidth.

Let us now focus on the VERTEX COVER problem: Given a graph G and integer k, we would like to verify whether G admits a vertex cover of size at most k. The natural way of expressing this property in **MSO**$_2$ is to quantify existentially k vertex variables, representing vertices of the vertex cover, and then verify that every edge of G has one of the quantified vertices as an endpoint. However, observe that the length of such a formula depends linearly on k. This means that a direct application of Courcelle's theorem gives only an $f(k,t) \cdot n$ algorithm, and not an $f(t) \cdot n$ algorithm as was the case for the dynamic-programming routine of Corollary 14.36.

Therefore, we would rather have the following optimization variant of the theorem. Formula φ has some free monadic (vertex or edge) variables $X_1, X_2, \ldots, X_p$, which correspond to the sets we seek in the graph. In the VERTEX COVER example we would have one vertex subset variable X that represents the vertex cover. Formula φ verifies that the variables $X_1, X_2, \ldots, X_p$ satisfy all the requested properties; for instance, that X indeed covers every edge of the graph. Then the problem is to find an evaluation of variables $X_1, X_2, \ldots, X_p$ that minimizes/maximizes the value of some arithmetic expression $\alpha(|X_1|, |X_2|, \ldots, |X_p|)$ depending on the cardinalities of these sets, subject to $\varphi(X_1, X_2, \ldots, X_p)$ being true. We will focus on α being an *affine function*, that is, $\alpha(x_1, x_2, \ldots, x_p) = a_0 + \sum_{i=1}^{p} a_i x_i$ for some $a_0, a_1, \ldots, a_p \in \mathbb{R}$.

The following theorem states that such an optimization version of Courcelle's theorem indeed holds.

Theorem 14.46 (Arnborg et al. [1991]) *Let φ be an $\mathbf{MSO}_2$ formula with p free monadic variables $X_1, X_2, \ldots, X_p$, and let $\alpha(x_1, x_2, \ldots, x_p)$ be an affine function. Assume that we are given an n-vertex graph G together with its tree decomposition of width t, and suppose G is equipped with evaluation of all the free variables of φ apart from $X_1, X_2, \ldots, X_p$. Then there exists an algorithm that in time $f(||\varphi||, t) \cdot n$ finds the minimum (maximum) value of $\alpha(|X_1|, |X_2|, \ldots, |X_p|)$ for sets $X_1, X_2, \ldots, X_p$ for which $\varphi(X_1, X_2, \ldots, X_p)$ is true, where f is some computable function.*

To conclude our VERTEX COVER example, we can now write a simple constant-length formula $\mathbf{vcover}(X)$ that verifies that X is a vertex cover of G: $\mathbf{vcover}(X) = \forall_{e \in E} \exists_{x \in X} \mathbf{inc}(x, e)$. Then we can apply Theorem 14.46 to $\mathbf{vcover}$ and $\alpha(|X|) = |X|$, and infer that finding the minimum cardinality of a vertex cover can be done in $f(t) \cdot n$ time, for some function f.

Note that both in Theorem 14.45 and in Theorem 14.46 we allow the formula to have some additional free variables, whose evaluation is provided together with the graph. This feature can be very useful whenever in the considered problem the graph comes together with some predefined objects, for example, terminals in the STEINER TREE problem or specific vertices that should be contained in a dominating set. For example, we can easily write an $\mathbf{MSO}_2$ formula $\mathbf{BWDominate}(X, B, W)$ for vertex set variables X, B, and W, which is true if and only if X is the subset of B and dominates all vertices from W. Then we can apply Theorem 14.46 to minimize the cardinality of X subject to $\mathbf{BWDominate}(X, B, W)$ being true, where the vertex subsets B, W are given together with the input graph.

Another strengthening of Courcelle's theorem is done by extending the power of $\mathbf{MSO_2}$. In the extended version of $\mathbf{MSO_2}$ we have a new feature that allows to test the cardinality of a set is equal to q modulo r, where q and r are integers such that $0 \leq q < r$ and $r \geq 2$. Such an extension of the $\mathbf{MSO_2}$ is called the *counting monadic second-order logic* ($\mathbf{CMSO_2}$). This $\mathbf{CMSO_2}$ is essentially $\mathbf{MSO_2}$ with the following atomic formula for a set S:

$\mathbf{card}_{q,r}(S) = \mathbf{true}$ if and only if $|S| \equiv q \pmod{r}$.

The name counting for that type of logic is a bit misleading because it cannot really count. For example, we cannot express in this logic that a graph G contains a cycle of length at least $|V(G)|/2$. What $\mathbf{CMSO_2}$ counts modulo some integer. For example, the property that a graph contains a cycle of even length is expressible in $\mathbf{CMSO_2}$. Courcelle's theorem and its extensions (Theorem 14.45 and Theorem 14.46) hold for $\mathbf{CMSO_2}$ as well.

To conclude, let us deliberate briefly on the function f in the bound on the running time of algorithms provided by Theorems 14.45 and 14.46. Unfortunately, it can be proved that this function has to be nonelementary; in simple words, it cannot by bounded by a folded c times exponential function for any constant c. Generally, the main reason why the running time must be so high is the possibility of having alternating sequences of quantifiers in the formula φ. Slightly more precisely, we can define the *quantifier alternation* of a formula φ to be the maximum length of an alternating sequence of nested quantifiers in φ, that is, $\forall \exists \forall \exists \ldots$ (we omit some technicalities in this definition). Then it can be argued that formulas of quantifier alternation at most q give rise to algorithms with at most c-times exponential function f, where c depends linearly on q. However, tracing the exact bound on f even for simple formulas φ is generally very hard and depends on the actual proof of the theorem that is used. This exact bound is also likely to be much higher than optimal. For this reason, Courcelle's theorem and its variants should be regarded primarily as classification tools, whereas designing efficient dynamic-programming routines on tree decompositions requires "getting your hands dirty" and constructing the algorithm explicitly.

14.6 Obstructions to Bounded Treewidth

A tree decomposition of G of small width is often very useful for designing algorithms, as it often reveals the true structure of the graph G. But how do graphs of large treewidth look, and how can we certify that the treewidth of the graph is large without just going through all possibilities for tree decompositions of small width? In this section we investigate obstructions to small treewidth, that is, structures inside G that certify that the treewidth of G is big. We start with the easiest such example.

Lemma 14.47 *The clique K_h on $h > 0$ vertices has treewidth exactly $h - 1$.*

Proving Lemma 14.47 is left as an exercise. Because Theorem 14.15 yields that minors of G have treewidth at most $\mathrm{tw}(G)$, it follows immediately that the treewidth of G is lower bounded by the size of the largest clique minor in G.

Corollary 14.48 *If G contains K_h as a minor, then $\mathrm{tw}(G) \geq h - 1$.*

A natural question is whether the converse of Corollary 14.48 could hold, that is, whether every graph of treewidth at least h must contain a clique on at least h vertices as a minor. This is not true, and one can discover strong evidence for this without having to explicitly construct a graph with treewidth k but no K_k minor. Because the problem of deciding whether an input graph G has treewidth at most k is NP-complete, deciding whether G has treewidth *at least k* is coNP-complete. If the converse of Corollary 14.48 held true, then we could use this to give a witness that the treewidth of G is at least k—every graph of treewidth at least k would have a K_k minor, and this K_k minor would serve as a witness (by Corollary 14.48) that $\mathrm{tw}(G) \geq k$. This would put a coNP-complete problem into NP, proving NP = coNP, which is considered very unlikely. In fact, almost all of the known kernelization lower bounds, and all the bounds covered in Part III are proved under an assumption that is slightly stronger than NP≠coNP. Later in this section we will see an example of graphs that violate the converse of Corollary 14.48 in the strongest possible way; they exclude even the clique K_5 as a minor but can have arbitrarily large treewidth.

Because a graph of bounded treewidth can be "completely decomposed" by separators of small size, one would expect that it is possible to remove few vertices from the graph to leave connected components that are all significantly smaller than the original graph. Our next lemma is a slight strengthening of this statement. For a nonnegative weight function on the vertices of G, say $w : V(G) \to \mathbb{R}_{\geq 0}$, we define the weight of a vertex set to be the sum of the weights of the vertices in the set, namely $w(S) = \sum_{v \in S} w(v)$.

Lemma 14.49 (Balanced Separators) *For any graph G of treewidth k, there is a vertex set B of size at most $k + 1$ such that each connected component C of $G - B$ satisfies $w(C) \leq \frac{w(V(G))}{2}$. Furthermore there is a linear time algorithm that, given a graph G and a tree decomposition (T, χ) of G of width k, outputs a vertex $\hat{b} \in V(T)$ such that $B = \chi(\hat{b})$ has this property.*

Proof: We describe an algorithm that, given G and (T, χ), finds $\hat{b}$. For any edge $ab \in E(T)$, $T - ab$ has two connected components. Let the component containing a be T_a^{ab} and the other be T_b^{ab}. We define $V_a^{ab} = \bigcup_{c \in V(T_a^{ab})} \chi(c) \setminus \chi(b)$ and $V_b^{ab} = \bigcup_{c \in V(T_b^{ab})} \chi(c) \setminus \chi(a)$. The algorithm orients the edge ab toward a if $w(V_a^{ab}) > w(V_b^{ab})$, toward b if $w(V_a^{ab}) < w(V_b^{ab})$, and otherwise arbitrarily. A naive algorithm that computes $w(V_a^{ab})$ and $w(V_b^{ab})$ from scratch for each edge $ab \in E(T)$ would run in polynomial but not linear time. A linear time algorithm is covered in the exercises.

Because T has no cycles, the orientation of T is acyclic. Because every directed acyclic graph has a sink (a vertex with no out-neighbors), T has a node $\hat{b}$ such that all edges incident to $\hat{b}$ are oriented toward $\hat{b}$. We claim now that $B = \chi(\hat{b})$ satisfies the statement of the lemma. Consider any connected component of $G - \chi(\hat{b})$. By Corollary 14.11, we have that any connected component C must satisfy $C \subseteq V_a^{a\hat{b}}$ for some edge $a\hat{b} \in E(T)$. But then $w(C) \leq w(V_a^{a\hat{b}})$ and $w(V_a^{a\hat{b}}) \leq w(V_{\hat{b}}^{a\hat{b}})$ because the edge $a\hat{b}$ is oriented toward $\hat{b}$. Because $V_a^{a\hat{b}}$ and $V_{\hat{b}}^{a\hat{b}}$ are disjoint, it follows that $w(V_a^{a\hat{b}}) + w(V_{\hat{b}}^{a\hat{b}}) \leq w(V(G))$, and hence $w(C) \leq w(V_a^{a\hat{b}}) \leq \frac{w(V(G))}{2}$ as required. After having found the orientation all that is needed to identify $\hat{b}$ is to find a sink in the orientation of T, which clearly can be done in linear time. This concludes the proof. $\square$

A useful consequence of Lemma 14.49 is the following lemma.

Lemma 14.50 *For any graph G of treewidth k and weight function $w : V(G) \to \mathbb{R}_{\geq 0}$ there is a partition of $V(G)$ into L, S and R such that*

$$\max\{w(L), w(R)\} \leq \frac{2w(V(G))}{3},$$

there is no edge from L to R, and $|S| \leq k + 1$. Furthermore there is a linear time algorithm that, given a graph G and a tree decomposition (T, χ) of G of width k, outputs such a partition.

Proof: The algorithm applies Lemma 14.49 and sets S to be the set B returned by Lemma 14.49. In particular, each connected component C of $G - S$ satisfies that $w(C) \leq \frac{w(S)}{2}$. If there are at most two connected components, put one of them into L and the other (if it exists) into R. Because all components have weight at most $\frac{w(S)}{2}$, the statement of the lemma is satisfied.

Suppose now there are at least three components in $G - S$. Let C_1 be of the largest weight, C_2 be of the second largest weight, and C_3 be of the third largest weight component of $G - S$, breaking ties arbitrarily. The algorithm starts by setting $L = C_1$ and $R = C_2$, sets C_3 aside and considers every other component C of $G - S$ one by one. When C is considered it is inserted into the set among L and R that has least weight. After all the components (except C_3) have been processed in this manner, the algorithm inserts C_3 into L or R, whichever is the smallest at the time. Clearly $|S| \leq k + 1$, and there are no edges from L to R; we need only to prove that $\max\{w(L), w(R)\} \leq \frac{2w(V(G))}{3}$.

Let L' and R' be L and R as they were right before C_3 was inserted into either set L or R. We show that $\max\{w(L'), w(R')\} \leq \frac{w(V(G))}{2}$. Suppose that $w(L') \leq w(R')$. Consider the last component C that was added to R, not counting C_3. Let $L^\star$ and $R^\star$ be L and R as they were right before C was inserted into R. Because C was inserted into R, we have that $w(R^\star) \leq w(L^\star)$ at the time. Because $w(C_3) \geq w(C)$ it holds that $w(R^\star \cup C) \leq w(L^\star \cup C_3)$ and $w(R^\star \cup C) + w(L^\star \cup C_3) \leq w(V(G))$ because $R^\star \cup C$ and $L^\star \cup C_3$ are disjoint. But then $w(R') = w(R^\star \cup C) \leq \frac{w(V(G))}{2}$, and because we assumed that $w(L') \leq w(R')$ it follows that $\max\{w(L'), w(R')\} \leq \frac{w(V(G))}{2}$. The case when $w(L') > w(R')$ is identical.

Suppose now that C_3 is inserted into R. Then it holds that $w(R') \leq w(L')$, and because C_3 has not yet been processed it follows that $w(R') \leq \frac{w(V(G)) - w(C_3)}{2}$. But then $w(R) \leq \frac{w(V(G)) + w(C_3)}{2}$. But $w(C_3) \leq \frac{w(V(G))}{3}$ because C_1 and C_2 have at least the same weight as C_3. This yields $w(R) \leq \frac{w(V(G)) + w(C_3)}{2} \leq \frac{2w(V(G))}{3}$. However, $w(L) = w(L') \leq \frac{w(V(G))}{2}$, completing the proof. The case in which C_3 is inserted into L is symmetric. □

We can use Lemma 14.50 to define a witness of G having large treewidth.

Definition 14.51 A vertex set $X \subseteq V(G)$ is called *well-linked* if for every pair X_1, X_2 of disjoint subsets of X there are $\min\{|X_1|, |X_2|\}$ vertex disjoint paths in G with one endpoint in X_1 and the other in X_2.

Even though we will use well-linked sets as "witnesses" for G having high treewidth, they are not witnesses in the usual "NP" sense—it is coNP-complete to decide whether a given set X in G is well-linked. Still one can check this in time $O(2^{|X|} \cdot |X| \cdot n)$ by trying every partition of X into X_1 and X_2 and computing the maximum flow from X_1 to X_2. Indeed, the following observation follows directly from Menger's theorem, by which the maximum number of vertex-disjoint paths between two nonadjacent vertices equals the size of a minimum cut that disconnects them.

Observation 14.52 A set X is well-linked if and only if there do not exist a partition of X into X_1 and X_2 and an X_1-X_2 separator $S \subseteq V(G)$ with $|S| < \min\{|X_1|, |X_2|\}$ (i.e., a set S of size smaller than $\min\{|X_1|, |X_2|\}$) such that no component of $G - S$ contains both a vertex of X_1 and a vertex of X_2).

Lemma 14.50 immediately implies that a graph of treewidth at most k can not contain a large well-linked set.

Lemma 14.53 *If G contains a well-linked set X with $|X| \geq 6(k+2)$, then $\text{tw}(G) > k$.*

Proof: Suppose for contradiction that a graph G of treewidth at most k contains a well-linked set X with $|X| \geq 6(k+2)$. Define a weight function $w : V(G) \to \mathbb{Z}^+$ that assigns 1 to vertices of X and 0 to all other vertices. It follows from Lemma 14.50 that there is a partitioning of $V(G)$ into L, S and R such that $|S| \leq k+1$, there are no edges from L to R, and $\max\{|L \cap X|, |R \cap X|\} \leq \frac{2|X|}{3}$. Without loss of generality $|L \cap X| \leq |R \cap X|$. Then we have that $|L \cap X| \geq \frac{|X|}{3} - (k+1) \geq k+2$ and $|R \cap X| \geq |L \cap X| \geq k+2$. Let $X_1 = L \cap X$ and $X_2 = R \cap X$. Because X is well-linked there are $k+2$ vertex disjoint paths from X_1 to X_2. But each such path must have nonempty intersection with S, contradicting that $|S| \leq k+1$. □

In the beginning of this section we promised a construction of graphs without K_5 as a minor of arbitrarily large treewidth. It turns out that constructing such a graph is quite simple, while proving that the treewidth of this graph is large is more difficult—probably the easiest way to prove this (without the use of characterizations not defined in this book) is to invoke Lemma 14.53. The $k \times k$-grid $⊞_k$ is a graph with vertex set $\{(x, y) : 1 \leq x, y \leq k\}$. Here x and y are always integers, so $⊞_k$ has exactly k^2 vertices. Two vertices (x, y) and (x', y') are adjacent if $|x - x'| + |y - y'| \leq 1$. Thus, the graph $⊞_k$ is planar, and as the name suggests, looks like a k times k grid drawn in the plane. It is easy to see (and it follows from the classic theorem of Kuratowski-Wagner that every planar graph excludes complete graph K_5 and complete bipartite graph $K_{3,3}$ as minors) that $⊞_k$ excludes K_5 as a minor. In the exercise section you will be asked to prove the following facts.

- $⊞_k$ has a tree decomposition of width k.
- $⊞_k$ contains a well-linked set X of size k.

The second point, together with Lemma 14.50 implies that the treewidth of the $k \times k$-grid is at least $\frac{k}{6} - 2$. It is in fact possible (but rather complicated) to show that the treewidth of a grid is exactly k.

Proposition 14.54 (Robertson and Seymour [1986b]) *For every $k > 1$, $\text{tw}(⊞_k) = k$.*

Because $⊞_k$ has treewidth exactly k and excludes K_5 as a minor, this shows that clique minors are not always sufficient as witnesses of the treewidth of G

14.6 Obstructions to Bounded Treewidth

being large. However, if G contains $\boxplus_k$ as a minor, we know that $\mathrm{tw}(G) \geq k$. Is the converse true, that is, does every graph of treewidth at least k contain $\boxplus_k$ as a minor? Of course not, as the clique K_h has treewidth exactly h and does not contain any grids larger than $\boxplus_{\sqrt{h}}$ as a minor. However, in contrast to cliques, every graph of large treewidth does contain a large grid as a minor. This is known as the *Excluded Grid Minor theorem*.

Theorem 14.55 (Excluded Grid Minor) *There exists a constant $c > 0$ such that if $\mathrm{tw}(G) = k$ then G contains $\boxplus_{c \cdot k^{1/20}}$ as a minor and does not contain $\boxplus_{k+1}$ as a minor.*

A weaker variant of Theorem 14.55 that only guarantees the existence of a grid of size $\Omega(\sqrt[5]{\log n})$ was given by Robertson and Seymour. This was later improved to $\Omega(\sqrt[3]{\log n})$ by Kawarabayashi and Kobayashi. It was open for many years whether a polynomial relationship could be established between the treewidth of a graph G and the size of its largest grid minor. In 2013, Chekuri and Chuzhoy established for the first time such a polynomial relationship. Later, Chuzhoy proved Theorem 14.55 (see "Bibliographic Notes").

For a planar graph G it is possible to get a much tighter relationship between the treewidth of G and the size of the largest grid minor that G contains.

Theorem 14.56 (Planar Excluded Grid Minor; Robertson et al. et al. [1994]; Gu and Tamaki [2012]) *For any G excluding H as a minor, such that $\mathrm{tw}(G) \geq \frac{9}{2}t$, G contains $\boxplus_t$ as a minor. Furthermore there exists a polynomial time algorithm that, given G, either outputs a tree decomposition of G of width $\frac{9}{2}t$ or a $\boxplus_t$ minor.*

By saying that an algorithm outputs a $\boxplus_t$ minor, we mean that the algorithm outputs a sequence of edge contractions, and vertex and edges deletions that transform the input graph G to the grid $\boxplus_t$. Alternatively, the output can be defined to be a minor model of $\boxplus_t$ in G, that is, a partition of a subset $U \subseteq V(G)$ into parts that induce connected graphs, with a bijection mapping the vertices of $\boxplus_t$ to these parts such that if two vertices u, v in $\boxplus_t$ are adjacent, then there exist $x \in \varphi(u)$ and $y \in \varphi(v)$ that are adjacent. Observe that in Theorem 14.55 the size of the grid minor is a polynomial in the treewidth while in Theorem 14.55 it is linear. Theorem 14.56 heavily relies on the graph G being planar. It is possible to give such "linear grid minor" theorems for more general classes of graphs, namely any class that excludes a fixed graph H as a minor.

Theorem 14.57 (Kawarabayashi and Kobayashi [2012]; Demaine and Hajiaghayi [2008b]) *For any graph H, there exists a constant h such that*

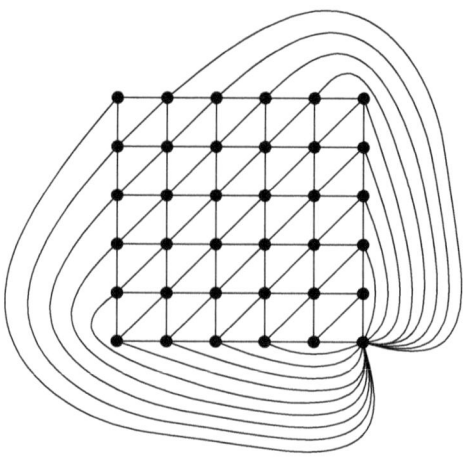

Figure 14.2 The graph Γ_6.

for any G excluding H as a minor, such that $\text{tw}(G) \geq t$, G contains $\boxplus_{ht}$ as a minor. Furthermore there exists a polynomial time algorithm that, given G, either outputs a tree decomposition of G of width t or a $\boxplus_{ht}$ minor.

In the next chapter we will use a variant of Theorem 14.56, which relies on contractions rather than minors. For this we will define a new family of graphs that will play the role of grids. For an integer $k \geq 0$ the graph Γ_k is obtained from the grid $\boxplus_k$ by adding, for every $1 \leq x \leq k-1$, $2 \leq y \leq k$ the edge $(x, y), (x+1, y-1)$, and making the vertex (k, k) adjacent to all vertices with $x \in \{1, k\}$ or $y \in \{1, k\}$. The graph Γ_6 is depicted in Fig. 14.2.

Observe that every face of Γ_k has size 3 (specifically, it is a triangle), therefore adding any edge to Γ_k results in a graph that is nonplanar. Furthermore it is quite easy to start with a grid $\boxplus_{3(k+1)}$ and contract it to a Γ_k. We leave it as an exercise to the reader to prove the following theorem.

Theorem 14.58 *If G is planar and $\text{tw}(G) \geq 13.5(k+1)$ then G contains Γ_k as a contraction. Furthermore there exists a polynomial time algorithm that, given G, either outputs a tree decomposition of G of width $13.5(k+1)$ or a Γ_k contraction.*

Just as it is possible to extend the Planar Excluded Grid Minor theorem to minor free classes, it is possible to extend Theorem 14.58 to classes excluding a fixed graph H as a minor. However, this extension does not work for every choice of graph H. A graph H is *apex* if there exists a vertex $v \in V(H)$ such that $H - v$ is planar. For example, the clique K_5 on 5 vertices is apex. It is possible to lift Theorem 14.58 to classes of graphs excluding an apex graph H as a minor.

Theorem 14.59 (*Fomin et al. [2011b]*) *For any apex graph H there exists a constant h such that for any G excluding H as a minor, such that $\mathrm{tw}(G) \geq t$, G contains Γ_{ht} as a contraction. Furthermore there exists a polynomial time algorithm that, given G, either outputs a tree decomposition of G of width t or a Γ_{ht} contraction.*

Theorem 14.59 is tight in the following sense. Consider the graph $\hat{⊞}_k$ obtained from $⊞_k$ by adding a new vertex u and making u adjacent to all other vertices. The graph $\hat{⊞}_k$ is apex and $\mathrm{tw}(\hat{⊞}_k) = k + 1$. Furthermore any contraction of $\hat{⊞}_k$ will contain a universal vertex, so $\hat{⊞}_k$ does not contain any Γ_h, $h > 3$ as a contraction. Thus, any minor closed class that does exclude any apex graph will contain, for every k, a graph of treewidth at least k and excluding all Γ_h, $h > 3$ as contractions.

Exercises

Problem 14.1 Prove Corollary 14.11.

Problem 14.2 Prove Lemma 14.12.

Problem 14.3 Show that the algorithm described in Lemma 14.18 runs in time $\mathcal{O}(|V(G)| + |V(T)|\omega(T, \chi))$.

Problem 14.4 Prove Lemma 14.47.

Problem 14.5 (♣) Find an example showing that the bound $\mathcal{O}(k|V(G)|)$ on the number of nodes of a nice tree decomposition cannot be strengthened to $\mathcal{O}(|V(G)|)$.

Problem 14.6 (✐) Show that the treewidth of a graph G is equal to the maximum treewidth of its connected components.

Problem 14.7 Prove that every clique of a graph is contained in some bag of its tree decomposition. Infer that $\mathrm{tw}(G) \geq \omega(G) - 1$, where $\omega(G)$ denotes the maximum size of a clique in G.

Problem 14.8 (✐) What is the treewidth of (a) a complete graph; (b) a complete bipartite graph; (c) a forest; and (d) a cycle?

Problem 14.9 (✐) Show that the treewidth of a graph G is equal to the maximum treewidth of its biconnected components.

Problem 14.10 (☠) Prove that a graph has treewidth at most 2 if and only if it does not contain K_4 as a minor.

Problem 14.11 A graph G is outerplanar if it can be drawn in the plane with no edge crossings, such that all vertices are incident to the outer face. Prove that for any outerplanar graph G, $\text{tw}(G) \leq 2$. Are there graphs of treewidth 2 that are not outerplanar?

Problem 14.12 (✐) Prove that the treewidth of a simple graph cannot increase after subdividing any of its edges. Show that in the case of multigraphs the same holds, with the exception that the treewidth can possibly increase from 1 to 2.

Problem 14.13 A graph G is called *d-degenerate* if every subgraph of G contains a vertex of degree at most d. Prove that graphs of treewidth k are k-degenerate.

Problem 14.14 Let G be an n-vertex graph of treewidth at most k. Prove that the number of edges in G is at most kn.

Problem 14.15 (☠) For a graph G given together with its tree decomposition of width t, construct in time $t^{\mathcal{O}(1)}n$ a data structure such that for any two vertices $x, y \in V(G)$, it is possible to check in time $\mathcal{O}(t)$ if x and y are adjacent. You should *not* use any results on hashing, hash tables, and so forth.

Problem 14.16 Show that the following problems can be solved in time $f(k) \cdot n^{\mathcal{O}(1)}$ on an n-vertex graph given together with its tree decomposition of width at most k:

- ODD CYCLE TRANSVERSAL,
- MAXCUT,
- q-COLORING,
- FEEDBACK VERTEX SET,
- HAMILTONIAN PATH and LONGEST PATH,
- HAMILTONIAN CYCLE and LONGEST CYCLE,
- CHROMATIC NUMBER,
- CYCLE PACKING,
- CONNECTED VERTEX COVER,
- CONNECTED DOMINATING SET, and
- CONNECTED FEEDBACK VERTEX SET.

Problem 14.17 LIST COLORING is a generalization of VERTEX COLORING: Given a graph G, a set of colors C, and a list function $L : V(G) \to 2^C$ (i.e., a subset of colors $L(v)$ for each vertex v), the task is to assign a color $c(v) \in L(v)$ to each vertex $v \in V(G)$ such that adjacent vertices receive different colors. Show that on an n-vertex graph G, LIST COLORING can be solved in time $n^{\mathcal{O}(\operatorname{tw}(G))}$.

Problem 14.18 Show that for a fixed graph H, the property "graph G does not contain H as a minor" is expressible in **MSO**$_2$.

Problem 14.19 We define a *k-tree* inductively. A clique on $k+1$ vertices is a k-tree. A new k-tree G can be obtained from a smaller k-tree G' by adding a new vertex and making it adjacent to k vertices of G' that form a clique in G'. Show that every k-tree is a chordal graph of treewidth k. Prove that for every graph G and integer k, G is a subgraph of a k-tree if and only if $\operatorname{tw}(G) \le k$.

Problem 14.20 Show that every maximal treewidth k-graph G, that is, a graph such that adding any missing edge to G increases its treewidth, is a k-tree.

Problem 14.21 Give a linear time algorithm to compute set B described in Lemma 14.49.

Problem 14.22 Prove the following.

- $\boxplus_k$ has a tree-decomposition of width k.
- $\boxplus_k$ contains a well-linked set X of size k.

Problem 14.23 Prove Theorem 14.58 assuming Theorem 14.56.

Problem 14.24 An n-vertex graph G is called an α-*edge-expander* if for every set $X \subseteq V(G)$ of size at most $n/2$ there are at least $\alpha|X|$ edges of G that have exactly one endpoint in X. Show that the treewidth of an n-vertex d-regular α-edge-expander is $\Omega(n\alpha/d)$ (in particular, linear in n if α and d are constants).

Problem 14.25 (☠) Let H be a planar graph. Show that there is a constant c_H such that the treewidth of every H-minor-free graph is at most c_H. Show that planarity requirement in the statement of the exercise is crucial, that is, that K_5-minor-free graphs can be of any treewidth.

Problem 14.26 Prove the following version of the classic result of Lipton and Tarjan on separators in planar graphs. For any planar n-vertex graph G and $W \subseteq V(G)$, there is a set $S \subseteq V(G)$ of size at most $\frac{9}{2}\sqrt{n+1}$ such that every connected component of $G - S$ contains at most $\frac{|W|}{2}$ vertices of W.

Bibliographic Notes

The treewidth of a graph is a fundamental graph parameter. It was introduced by Halin (1976) and rediscovered by Robertson and Seymour (1984, 1986a,b) and, independently, by Arnborg and Proskurowski (1989). Courcelle's theorem is from Courcelle (1992, 1990), and Menger's theorem is from Menger (1927). For a more in-depth coverage, we refer to surveys such as Bodlaender (2006) and Cygan et al. (2015, Ch. 7). Our presentation of the definition of treewidth is inspired by Reed (1997).

Fomin et al. (2015a) gives an algorithm to compute the treewidth of G with running time $\mathcal{O}(1.7347^n)$. For small values of k one can do much better. In particular, Bodlaender (1996) gave a $2^{\mathcal{O}(k^3)}n$ time algorithm to decide whether an input graph G has treewidth at most k. There also exists an algorithm with running time $2^{\mathcal{O}(k)}n$ that either decides that the input graph G does not have treewidth at most k or concludes that it has treewidth at most $5k+4$ (Bodlaender et al., 2016a). The current best polynomial time approximation algorithm for treewidth by Feige et al. (2008) has ratio $\mathcal{O}(\sqrt{\log \mathrm{tw}(G)})$, and it is known that treewidth is hard to approximate within any constant factor in polynomial time under the Small Set Expansion conjecture (Wu et al., 2014). On H-minor-free graph classes things are a bit better; for any fixed graph H there is a constant factor approximation for treewidth on graphs excluding H as a minor. Specifically, on planar graph there is a polynomial time $\frac{3}{2}$ approximation algorithm for treewidth (Seymour and Thomas, 1994), as well as a linear time constant factor approximation algorithm for treewidth (Kammer and Tholey, 2016). In fact, it is not even known whether computing treewidth of planar graphs exactly is polynomial time solvable or NP-complete. This remains a challenging open problem in graph algorithms.

A weaker variant of Theorem 14.55 that only guarantees the existence of a grid of size $\Omega(\sqrt[5]{\log n})$ was given by Robertson and Seymour (1986b). This was later improved to $\Omega(\sqrt[3]{\log n})$ by Kawarabayashi and Kobayashi (2012) and by Leaf and Seymour (2012). It was open for many years whether a polynomial relationship could be established between the treewidth of a graph G and the size of its largest grid minor. Chekuri and Chuzhoy (2016) established for the first time such a polynomial relationship. Later, Chuzhoy proved Theorem 14.55 in Chuzhoy (2015, 2016).

A thorough exposition of dynamic programming algorithms on graph of bounded treewidth, in particular the algorithm of running times $2^k \cdot k^{\mathcal{O}(1)} \cdot n$ for INDEPENDENT SET can be found in the book Cygan et al. (2015). An algorithm of running time $3^k \cdot n^{\mathcal{O}(1)}$ for DOMINATING SET is based on subset convolution. With more ideas, it is possible to implement the subset convolution for DOMINATING SET to run in time $3^k \cdot k^{\mathcal{O}(1)} \cdot n$ van Rooij et al. (2009).

15
Bidimensionality and Protrusions

Bidimensionality provides a general explanation why many problems admit polynomial and linear kernels on planar and other classes of graphs. Roughly speaking, a problem is bidimensional if the solution value for the problem on a $k \times k$-grid is $\Omega(k^2)$ and contraction/removal of edges does not increase the solution value. In this chapter we introduce the theory of bidimensionality, and show how bidimensionality can be used to decompose a graph into a specific type of decomposition called protrusion decomposition. Protrusion decompositions will be used in the following chapter for obtaining meta-kernelization results. In this chapter we show how to use protrusion decomposition to obtain a linear kernel for DOMINATING SET on planar graphs.

Many NP-complete graph problems remain NP-complete even when the input graph is restricted to be planar. Nevertheless, many such problems become significantly easier. For example, consider the DOMINATING SET problem. Here the input is a graph G, and the task is to find a set S as small as possible such that $N[S] = V(G)$. In the decision variant, an integer k is provided and the task is to determine whether such a set of size at most k exists. On general graphs, DOMINATING SET admits no kernel of size $f(k)$ for any f unless FPT = W[1], no $2^{o(n)}$ time algorithm under the Exponential Time Hypothesis, and no $o(\log n)$-approximation algorithm unless P = NP. On planar graphs, DOMINATING SET admits a linear kernel, a $2^{\mathcal{O}(\sqrt{k})} + \mathcal{O}(n)$ time algorithm, and a polynomial time approximation scheme, that is, a $(1 + \epsilon)$ approximation algorithm for every fixed $\epsilon > 0$.

The "bidimensionality" framework introduced by Demaine et al. (2005) allows us to simultaneously explain the existence of linear kernels, subexponential time parameterized algorithms, and polynomial time approximation schemes for a number of problems on planar graphs. The framework also allows us to lift these algorithms to more general classes of graphs, namely, classes of graphs excluding some fixed graph H as a minor. In this chapter and the next, we will describe a "stripped down" version of bidimensionality sufficient to give linear kernels and subexponential time parameterized algorithms for problems on planar graphs. We will not describe how bidimensionality is useful for designing approximation algorithms, and only outline how to lift the kernelization results from planar graphs to more general classes of graphs.

In this chapter, we will prove the graph decomposition theorems that are at the core of bidimensionality, and showcase how these are useful by giving a linear kernel for the DOMINATING SET problem on planar graphs.

15.1 Bidimensional Problems

We will restrict our attention to vertex or edge subset problems. A *vertex subset problem* Π is a parameterized problem where the input is a graph G and an integer k; the parameter is k. Let ϕ be a computable function that takes as input a graph G and a set $S \subseteq V(G)$, and outputs **true** or **false**. The interpretation of ϕ is that it defines the space of *feasible solutions* S for a graph G, by returning a Boolean value denoting whether S is feasible. For example, for the DOMINATING SET problem we have that $\phi(G, S) = $ **true** if and only if $N[S] = V(G)$.

For a function ϕ, we define two parameterized problems, called *vertex-subset problems*: ϕ-MINIMIZATION and ϕ-MAXIMIZATION. In both problems, the input consists of a graph G and a parameter k. ϕ-MINIMIZATION asks whether there exists a set $S \subseteq V(G)$ such that $|S| \leq k$ and $\phi(G, S) = $ **true**. Similarly, ϕ-MAXIMIZATION asks whether there exists a set $S \subseteq V(G)$ such that $|S| \geq k$ and $\phi(G, S) = $ **true**.

Edge subset problems are defined similarly, with the only difference being that S is a subset of $E(G)$ rather than $V(G)$.

Let us remark that the definition of vertex/edge subset problems also captures many problems that, at a first glance, do not look as if they could be captured by this definition. One example is the CYCLE PACKING problem. Here, the input is a graph G and an integer k, and the task is to determine whether there exist k cycles $C_1, \ldots, C_k$ in G that are pairwise vertex-disjoint. This is a vertex subset problem because G has k pairwise vertex-disjoint cycles

15.1 Bidimensional Problems

if and only if there exists a set $S \subseteq V(G)$ of size at least k such that $\phi(G, S)$ is true, where $\phi(G, S)$ is defined as follows.

$\phi(G, S) = \exists V' \subseteq V(G), E' \subseteq E(G)$ such that
- $S \subseteq V(G)$,
- Each connected component of $G' = (V', E')$ is a cycle, and
- Each connected component of G' contains exactly one vertex of S.

This definition may seem a bit silly because checking whether $\phi(G, S)$ is true for a given graph G and set S is NP-complete. In fact, this problem is considered to be more difficult than CYCLE PACKING. Nevertheless, this definition shows that CYCLE PACKING is a vertex subset problem, which will allow us to give a linear kernel for CYCLE PACKING on planar graphs in the next chapter.

For any vertex or edge subset minimization problem Π, we have that $(G, k) \in \Pi$ implies that $(G, k') \in \Pi$ for all $k' \geq k$. Similarly, for a vertex or edge subset maximization problem, we have that $(G, k) \in \Pi$ implies that $(G, k') \in \Pi$ for all $k' \leq k$. Thus, the notion of "optimality" is well defined for vertex and edge subset problems.

Definition 15.1 For a ϕ-MINIMIZATION problem Π, we define

$$OPT_\Pi(G) = \min\{k : (G, k) \in \Pi\}.$$

If there is no k such that $(G, k) \in \Pi$, then we put $OPT_\Pi(G) = +\infty$.
For a ϕ-MAXIMIZATION problem Π, we define

$$OPT_\Pi(G) = \max\{k : (G, k) \in \Pi\}.$$

If there is no k such that $(G, k) \in \Pi$, then we put $OPT_\Pi(G) = -\infty$.

For many problems it holds that contracting an edge cannot increase the size of the optimal solution. We will say that such problems are contraction-closed. Formally, we have the following definition.

Definition 15.2 (Contraction-closed problem) A vertex/edge subset problem Π is *contraction-closed* if for any graph G and edge $uv \in E(G)$, $OPT_\Pi(G/uv) \leq OPT_\Pi(G)$.

We are now ready to give the definition of bidimensional problems. In this definition we use the graph Γ_k, which was defined in Section 14.6.

Definition 15.3 (Bidimensional problem) A vertex-subset problem Π is *bidimensional* if it is contraction-closed, and there exists a constant $c > 0$ such that $OPT_\Pi(\Gamma_t) \geq ct^2$ for every $t > 0$.

There are other kinds of bidimensionality that are not considered in this book. The problems we call bidimensional in this book are usually called contraction-bidimensional in the literature.

It is usually quite easy to determine whether a problem is bidimensional. Take for example INDEPENDENT SET. Contracting an edge can never increase the size of a maximum independent set, so the problem is contraction-closed. Furthermore, in Γ_k, the vertex set

$$\{(x,y) : (x+y) \equiv 0 \mod 2\} \setminus \{(k,k)\}$$

forms an independent set of size at least $\frac{k^2}{2} - 1$. Thus, INDEPENDENT SET is bidimensional.

In Section 14.4, we gave an algorithm for INDEPENDENT SET running in time $2^{\mathcal{O}(t)} n^{\mathcal{O}(1)}$, if a tree-decomposition of the input graph G of width t is given as input. We can use this algorithm, together with the fact that INDEPENDENT SET is bidimensional, to give a subexponential parameterized algorithm for INDEPENDENT SET on connected planar graphs. First, we give a simple but powerful decomposition lemma that works for any bidimensional problem.

Lemma 15.4 (Parameter-treewidth bound) *Let Π be a contraction-bidimensional problem. Then there exists a constant α_Π such that for any planar connected graph G, $\text{tw}(G) \leq \alpha_\Pi \cdot \sqrt{OPT_\Pi(G)}$. Furthermore, there exists a polynomial time algorithm that, given G, produces a tree-decomposition of G of width at most $\alpha_\Pi \cdot \sqrt{OPT_\Pi(G)}$.*

Proof: Consider a bidimensional problem Π and a connected planar graph G. By Theorem 14.58, G contains $\Gamma_{\lfloor \text{tw}(G)/27 \rfloor}$ as a contraction. Because Π is bidimensional, it follows that there exists a constant $c > 0$ such that $OPT_\Pi(\Gamma_k) \geq ck^2$. Because Π is contraction-closed, it then follows that $OPT_\Pi(G) \geq c \lfloor \frac{\text{tw}(G)}{27} \rfloor^2$. Taking the square root on both sides and multiplying both sides by an appropriate constant yields the lemma. □

In the proof of Lemma 15.4 we used the connectivity of G only in the call to Theorem 14.58. In Problem 15.2 we shall see that the condition that G is connected is necessary.

We can use Lemma 15.4 to give a parameterized algorithm for INDEPENDENT SET on connected planar graphs as follows. On input (G,k) construct a tree-decomposition of G of width at most $\alpha_\Pi \cdot \sqrt{OPT_\Pi(G)}$. If the width of this decomposition is at least $\alpha_\Pi \sqrt{k}$, then $OPT_\Pi(G) \geq k$ and the algorithm returns "yes." Otherwise, the algorithm finds a maximum size independent set in G using the algorithm from Section 14.4 in time $2^{\mathcal{O}(\sqrt{k})} n^{\mathcal{O}(1)}$.

In the preceding argument, the only properties of INDEPENDENT SET that we used were that the problem is bidimensional and that it has an efficient algorithm on graphs of bounded treewidth. Thus, the same argument goes through (with different constants) for any bidimensional problem that has an efficient algorithm on bounded treewidth graphs. We have the following result.

Theorem 15.5 (Demaine et al. [2005]) *Let Π be a bidimensional problem such that there exists an algorithm for Π with running time $2^{\mathcal{O}(t)} n^{\mathcal{O}(1)}$ when a tree-decomposition of the input graph G of width t is supplied as input. Then Π is solvable in time $2^{\mathcal{O}(\sqrt{k})} n^{\mathcal{O}(1)}$ on planar connected graphs.*

The proof of Theorem 15.5 is identical to the algorithm we described for INDEPENDENT SET.

15.2 Separability and Treewidth Modulators

We now restrict our attention to problems Π that are somewhat well-behaved in the sense that whenever we have a small separator in the graph that splits the graph in two parts, L and R, the intersection $|X \cap L|$ of L with any optimal solution X to the entire graph is a good estimate of $OPT_\Pi(G[L])$. This restriction allows us to prove decomposition theorems that are very useful for giving kernels. Similar decomposition theorems may also be used to give approximation schemes, but we do not cover this topic here.

Let us recall that for a subset of vertices L of a graph, we use $\partial(L)$ to denote the border of L, that is, the set of vertices of L adjacent to vertices outside L. In other words, the vertices in $\partial(L)$ separate $L \setminus \partial(L)$ from the remaining part of the graph.

Definition 15.6 (Separability) Let $f : \mathbb{N} \cup \{0\} \to \mathbb{Q}^+ \cup \{0\}$ be a function. We say that a vertex subset problem Π is f-*separable* if for any graph G and subset $L \subseteq V(G)$ such that $|\partial(L)| \leq t$, it holds that

$$|OPT_\Pi(G) \cap L| - f(t) \leq OPT_\Pi(G[L]) \leq |OPT_\Pi(G) \cap L| + f(t).$$

Problem Π is called *separable* if there exists a function f such that Π is f-*separable*. Sometimes, when function $f(t)$ is linear, that is, $f(t) = \beta \cdot t$ for some $\beta > 0$, we call the problem *linear-separable*.

Thus for a separable problem Π, for every induced subgraph $G[L]$ of a graph G, the number of vertices in the optimal solution on $G[L]$ is within an additive factor depending only on the size of the border of L from the number of vertices of the global optimal solution contained in L. The abbreviation $(c \cdot t)$-separable stands for f-separable where $f : \mathbb{Z} \to \mathbb{Z}$ is the function that for all $t \in \mathbb{Z}$ assigns $c \cdot t$.

For example, VERTEX COVER is separable. Indeed, if S is a vertex cover of G, then the set $S \cap L$ is also a vertex cover of $G[L]$. Moreover, if S_L is a vertex cover of $G[L]$, then the set $(S \setminus L) \cup \partial(L) \cup S_L$ is a vertex cover of G. Thus,

$$|S \cap L| - t \leq |S_L| \leq |S \cap L|.$$

Similarly, it can be shown INDEPENDENT SET, DOMINATING SET, or CONNECTED DOMINATING SET are separable, and this is left as an exercise (see also Problem 15.3).

A nice feature of separable bidimensional problems is that it is possible to extend Lemma 15.4 to disconnected graphs because the issue of different connected components influencing the value of the optimal solution in a complex way disappears.

Lemma 15.7 (Parameter-treewidth bound for separable problems) *Let Π be bidimensional and separable problem. Then there exists a constant α_Π such that for any planar graph G, $\mathrm{tw}(G) \leq \alpha_\Pi \cdot \sqrt{OPT_\Pi(G)}$. Furthermore, there exists a polynomial time algorithm that, given G, produces a tree-decomposition of G of width at most $\alpha_\Pi \cdot \sqrt{OPT_\Pi(G)}$.*

Proof: The border $\partial(C)$ of every connected component C of the graph G is an empty set. Thus, because Π is separable, there exists a constant c such that for any graph G and connected component C of G, it holds that

$$OPT_\Pi(G[C]) \leq |OPT_\Pi(G) \cap C| + c \leq OPT_\Pi(G) + c.$$

By Lemma 15.4, we can find in polynomial time a tree-decomposition of $G[C]$ of width at most $\alpha_\Pi \cdot \sqrt{OPT_\Pi(G) + c}$. The lemma is proved by increasing the constant α_Π appropriately, and joining the tree-decompositions of the connected components of G to form a tree-decomposition of G. □

It might seem strange that it is possible to give, in one shot, subexponential time algorithms, approximation schemes, and kernels for a wide range of seemingly different problems. One of the reasons why this is possible is the existence of "canonical" bidimensional problems. We say that a set $S \subseteq V(G)$ is a *treewidth-η-modulator* if $\mathrm{tw}(G - S) \leq \eta$. We will consider the following problems, with one problem for every integer $\eta \geq 0$. In the TREEWIDTH-η MODULATOR problem, the input is a graph G and an integer $k \geq 0$, and the question is whether there is a set S such that $|S| \leq k$ and $\mathrm{tw}(G - S) \leq \eta$.

15.2 Separability and Treewidth Modulators

It is a good exercise to prove that for every $\eta \geq 0$, the TREEWIDTH-η MODULATOR problem is bidimensional and separable (see Problem 15.4). We will show that the TREEWIDTH-η MODULATOR problems are canonical bidimensional problems in the following sense.

Lemma 15.8 *For any $\epsilon > 0$, $\beta > 0$, and bidimensional $(\beta \cdot t)$-separable problem Π, there exists an integer $\eta \geq 0$ such that any planar graph G has a treewidth-η-modulator S of size at most $\epsilon \cdot OPT_\Pi(G)$.*

Proof: Let α_Π be the constant from Lemma 15.7. In particular, there exists a polynomial time algorithm that, given a planar graph G, produces a tree-decomposition of G of width at most $\alpha_\Pi \cdot \sqrt{OPT_\Pi(G)}$. Set $\alpha = \max(\alpha_\Pi, 1)$. Further, if $\beta < 1$ then Π is t-separable, and so we may assume without loss of generality that $\beta \geq 1$.

We now define a few constants, and set η based on α, β and ϵ. The reason why these constants are defined the way they are will become clear during the course of the proof.

- Set $\gamma = 4\alpha\beta$,
- Set $\delta = 10\gamma(2\epsilon + 1)$,
- Set $k_0 = (60\gamma)^2 \cdot (1+\frac{1}{\epsilon^2})$, and observe that k_0 satisfies $\frac{2}{3}k_0 + \gamma\sqrt{k_0} \leq k_0 - 1$ and $0 \leq \frac{\epsilon}{3}k_0 - \delta\sqrt{\frac{1}{3}k_0}$, and finally
- Set $\eta = \alpha \cdot \sqrt{k_0}$.

By Lemma 15.7, any graph G such that $OPT_\Pi(G) \leq k_0$ has treewidth at most $\alpha \cdot \sqrt{k_0} = \eta$. Then, G has a treewidth-η-modulator of size 0. To deal with larger values of $OPT_\Pi(G)$, we prove by induction on k that for any $k \geq \frac{1}{3}k_0$, any planar graph G such that $OPT_\Pi(G) \leq k$ has a treewidth-η-modulator of size at most $\epsilon k - \delta\sqrt{k}$. In the base case, we consider any k such that $\frac{1}{3}k_0 \leq k \leq k_0$. Recall that by Lemma 15.7, any graph G such that $OPT_\Pi(G) \leq k_0$ has a treewidth-η-modulator of size 0, and

$$0 \leq \epsilon\frac{1}{3}k_0 - \delta\sqrt{\frac{1}{3}k_0} \leq \epsilon k - \delta\sqrt{k}$$

by the choice of k_0. In the last inequality, we used that the function $\epsilon k - \delta\sqrt{k}$ is monotonically increasing from the first point where it becomes positive.

For the inductive step, let $k > k_0$ and suppose that the statement is true for all values below k. We prove the statement for k. Consider a planar graph G such that $OPT_\Pi(G) \leq k$. By Lemma 15.7, the treewidth of G is at most $tw(G) \leq \alpha \cdot \sqrt{k}$. By Lemma 14.50 applied to the weight function that assigns 1 to vertices of $OPT_\Pi(G)$ and 0 to all other vertices, $V(G)$ has a partition into

L, S, and R such that $|S| \leq \alpha \cdot \sqrt{k} + 1$, $\max |L \cap OPT_\Pi(G)|, |R \cap OPT_\Pi(G)| \leq \frac{2}{3}|OPT_\Pi(G)|$ and there are no edges from L to R. Because L and R are disjoint, there exists a fraction $\frac{1}{3} \leq a \leq \frac{2}{3}$ such that $|L \cap OPT_\Pi(G)| \leq a|OPT_\Pi(G)|$ and $|R \cap OPT_\Pi(G)| \leq (1-a)|OPT_\Pi(G)|$.

Consider now the graph $G[L \cup S]$. Because L has no neighbors in R (in G) and Π is separable, it follows that

$$OPT_\Pi(G[L \cup S]) \leq |OPT_\Pi(G) \cap (L \cup S)| + \beta|S|$$
$$\leq ak + (\alpha\sqrt{k} + 1) + \beta(\alpha\sqrt{k} + 1)$$
$$= ak + (\alpha\sqrt{k} + 1)(\beta + 1) \leq ak + \gamma\sqrt{k}.$$

Here the last inequality follows from the assumption that $k > k_0 \geq 1$ and the choice of γ. Because $k > k_0$, the properties of k_0 imply that $\frac{2}{3}k + \gamma\sqrt{k} \leq k - 1$. Further $ak + \gamma\sqrt{k} \geq \frac{1}{3}k_0$ because $a \geq \frac{1}{3}$. Thus, we may apply the induction hypothesis to $G[L \cup S]$ and obtain a treewidth-η-modulator Z_L of $G[L \cup S]$, such that

$$|Z_L| \leq \epsilon(ak + \gamma\sqrt{k}) - \delta\sqrt{ak + \gamma\sqrt{k}}$$
$$\leq \epsilon(ak + \gamma\sqrt{k}) - \delta\sqrt{k}\sqrt{a}.$$

An identical argument, applied to $G[R \cup S]$, yields a treewidth-η-modulator Z_R of $G[R \cup S]$ such that

$$|Z_R| \leq \epsilon\left((1-a)k + \gamma\sqrt{k}\right) - \delta\sqrt{k}\sqrt{1-a}.$$

We now make a treewidth-η-modulator Z of G as follows. Let $Z = Z_L \cup S \cup Z_R$. The set Z is a treewidth-η-modulator of G because every connected component of $G - Z$ is a subset of L or R, and Z_L and Z_R are treewidth-η-modulators for $G[L \cup S]$ and $G[R \cup S]$, respectively. Finally, we bound the size of Z:

$$|Z| \leq |Z_L| + |Z_R| + |S|$$
$$\leq \epsilon(ak + \gamma\sqrt{k}) - \delta\sqrt{k}\sqrt{a} + \epsilon\left((1-a)k + \gamma\sqrt{k}\right) - \delta\sqrt{k}\sqrt{1-a} + \gamma\sqrt{k}$$
$$\leq \epsilon k - \delta\sqrt{k}\left(\sqrt{1-a} + \sqrt{a}\right) + \sqrt{k}\gamma(2\epsilon + 1)$$
$$\leq \epsilon k - \delta\sqrt{k} + \sqrt{k}\left(\gamma(2\epsilon + 1) - \frac{\delta}{10}\right)$$
$$\leq \epsilon k - \delta\sqrt{k}.$$

In the transition from the third line to the fourth line, we used $\sqrt{1-a} + \sqrt{a} \geq \frac{11}{10}$ for any a between $\frac{1}{3}$ and $\frac{2}{3}$.

15.2 Separability and Treewidth Modulators

Finally, we observe that the statement of the lemma follows from what has just been proved. If $OPT_\Pi(G) \leq k_0$, then G has a treewidth-η-modulator of size $0 \leq \epsilon \cdot OPT_\Pi(G)$. If $OPT_\Pi(G) > k_0$, then G has a treewidth-η-modulator of size at most $\epsilon \cdot OPT_\Pi(G) - \delta\sqrt{OPT_\Pi(G)}$. This completes the proof. □

Lemma 15.8 is quite powerful, but has the significant drawback that it is not constructive, in the sense that it heavily relies on an unknown optimum solution to find the treewidth modulator. Thus, it is not clear how to compute a treewidth-η-modulator of appropriate size when given G as input. This is mostly an issue when designing approximation schemes based on bidimensionality. For the purposes of kernelization, we will be able to circumvent this problem without making Lemma 15.8 constructive. Another issue with Lemma 15.8 is that the constants in the lemma are quite big. Thus, a natural question is whether it is possible to prove constructive variants of Lemma 15.8 for particular choices of problem Π and constant ϵ. We do this now for the DOMINATING SET problem.

Lemma 15.9 *Let Π be the* DOMINATING SET *problem. There is a polynomial time algorithm that, given a connected planar graph G, outputs a set S such that*

- $|S| \leq 6 \cdot OPT_\Pi(G)$,
- $G[S]$ *is connected*,
- $N[S] = V(G)$, *and*
- $tw(G - S) \leq 2$.

For the proof of Lemma 15.9 we will need a claim about the relation between dominating sets and *connected* dominating sets in G. A set S is a *connected dominating set* if S is a dominating set and $G[S]$ is connected. The proof of the following claim is given as an exercise (see Problem 15.5).

Claim 15.10 *There is a polynomial time algorithm that, given as input a connected graph G and a dominating set X of G, computes a connected dominating set S of G such that $X \subseteq S$ and $|S| \leq 3|X|$.*

Proof of Lemma 15.9: The DOMINATING SET problem admits a polynomial time 2-approximation algorithm on planar graphs. (In fact, DOMINATING SET even admits a polynomial time approximation scheme on planar graphs, but for our purposes 2-approximation is sufficient.) We compute a dominating set X of size at most $2 \cdot OPT_\Pi(G)$. We then use Claim 15.10 to compute a connected dominating set S of G of size at most $3|X| \leq 6 \cdot OPT_\Pi(G)$.

We now show that tw$(G - S) \leq 2$. Pick a vertex $v \in S$ and consider a plane embedding of G such that v is on the outer face. This embedding also yields an embedding of $G - S$. Suppose that we wanted to add S back into $G - S$ to form G. Because $G[S]$ is connected, all vertices of S must be inserted in the same face of $G - S$. But v is on the outer face of G, so all vertices of S are to be reinserted into the outer face of $G - S$. Because S is a dominating set, it follows that each vertex in $G - S$ must be incident to the outer face of $G - S$ and hence $G - S$ is outerplanar. We showed in Problem 14.11 that the treewidth of outerplanar graphs is at most 2. This concludes the proof. □

15.3 Protrusion Decompositions

Lemma 15.8, or Lemma 15.9 in the case of DOMINATING SET, allows us to identify a relatively small vertex set, which we call a treewidth modulator, such that the remaining graph has a tree-decomposition of constant width. However, to get a kernel we need a decomposition that controls the interaction between the treewidth modulator and the remaining part of the graph.

We start from the definition of protrusion, the notion playing important role in this and the following chapter. Recall that the *boundary* of a vertex set X in a graph G is the set $\partial(X)$ of vertices in X that have at least one neighbor outside of X.

Definition 15.11 (Protrusion) For integer $t > 0$, a *t-protrusion* in a graph G is a vertex set X such that $\text{tw}(G[X]) \leq t$ and $|\partial(X)| \leq t$.

In other words, while the size of X can be large, the treewidth of $G[X]$ as well as the number of boundary vertices of X is bounded by a constant t. Let us note that in the definition of protrusion we do not require graph $G[X]$ to be connected.

Definition 15.12 (Protrusion decomposition) For integers α, β, and t, an (α, β, t)-*protrusion decomposition* of G is a tree-decomposition (T, χ) of G such that the following conditions are satisfied.

- T is a rooted tree with root r and $|\chi(r)| \leq \alpha$,
- For every node $v \in V(T)$ except r, we have $|\chi(v)| \leq t$, and
- r has degree at most β in T.

Thus, the size of the root bag r of T is at most α, and all other bags are of size at most t. Moreover, $T - r$ has at most β connected components, and for

15.3 Protrusion Decompositions

every connected component B of $T - r$, the set of vertices $\chi(B)$, which is the set of vertices of G contained in bags of B, is a t-protrusion in G.

For kernelization purposes, we will search for an (α, β, t)-protrusion decomposition with α and β being of order k and t a small constant. We will show that in planar graphs, a treewidth-η-modulator S can be used to get a (α, β, t)-protrusion decomposition of G, where t is some function of η. The main idea of the proof is to first construct a protrusion decomposition in which α and t are controlled, while β is not, and then to observe that in planar graphs β is upper bounded by $O(\alpha)$.

Lemma 15.13 *If a planar graph G has a treewidth-η-modulator S, then G has a set $Z \supseteq S$, such that*

- $|Z| \leq 4(\eta + 1)|S| + |S|$, *and*
- *Each connected component of $G - Z$ has at most 2 neighbors in S and at most 2η neighbors in $Z \setminus S$.*

Furthermore, given G, S and a tree-decomposition (T, χ) of $G - S$, Z can be computed in polynonial time.

Proof: Root the tree T at an arbitrary root node r. For a node $v \in V_T$, let T_v be the subtree of T rooted at v. We will iteratively mark some nodes in the decomposition tree T. Initially, the set M_0 of marked nodes is empty. In the i-th iterative step, we let v_i be the lowermost node in T such that some connected component C_i of $G[\chi(T_{v_i} - M_{i-1})]$ has at least three neighbors in S. We mark v_i, or, more formally, we set $M_i = M_{i-1} \cup \{v_i\}$. The process stops when every component C of $G[\chi(T - M_i)]$ has at most 2 neighbors in S. Because $|M_i| = i$, the process must stop after at most $t \leq |V(T)|$ iterations.

We now show that the process has to stop after only $2|S|$ iterations. To that end, consider the sequence of components $C_1, C_2, \ldots, C_t$ encountered during the execution. We will prove that if $j > i$, then $C_j \cap C_i = \emptyset$. Suppose not, and let $x \in C_i \cap C_j$. Observe that $v_j \notin V(T_{v_i})$ because this would contradict the choice of v_i and v_j in the process—in particular, this would mean that v_j is lower than v_i although $i < j$. Furthermore, $C_j \cap \chi(v_j) \neq \emptyset$ because v_j is the *lowermost* node in T such that some connected component C_j of $G[\chi(T_{v_j} - M_{j-1})]$ has at least three neighbors in S. The vertex x cannot be in $\chi(v_i)$ because $v_i \in M_i$ and C_j is disjoint from $\chi(M_i)$. Thus, there exists a node $u \in V(T_{v_i})$, $u \neq v_i$, such that $x \in \chi(u)$. But then $\chi^{-1}(C_j)$ contains a node outside T_{v_i} (namely v_j) and a node inside T_{v_i} (namely u). Thus, $\chi^{-1}(C_j)$ must also contain v_i implying that $C_j \cap \chi(v_i)$ is nonempty. But we have already argued that this set must be empty, a contradiction. Thus, $C_i \cap C_j = \emptyset$.

Next we argue that $t \leq 2|S|$. Consider the graph G' obtained from $G[S \cup C_1 \cup C_2 \ldots \cup C_t]$ by contracting each C_i into a single vertex c_i. Note that G' is a minor of G, and therefore G' is planar. Further, every vertex c_i has at least 3 neighbors in S (because C_i has at least 3 neighbors in S). Thus, by Lemma 13.3, we have that $t \leq 2|S|$.

Let us remind that in Section 9.3.3 we defined the least common ancestor closure operation. We apply this operation here. At this point we set $M =$ LCA-Closure(M_t) and $Z = S \cup \chi(M)$. By Lemma 9.28, we have that $|Z| \leq 4(\eta + 1)|S| + |S|$. Furthermore, each component C of $G - Z$ has at most 2 neighbors in S by the construction of M_t. Finally, $\chi^{-1}(C) \subseteq V(T) \setminus M$. The connected component of $T - M$ that contains $\chi^{-1}(C)$ has at most 2 neighbors in M by Lemma 9.27. Thus, C has at most 2η neighbors in $Z \setminus S$. The preceding existential proof can directly be turned into a polynomial time algorithm for computing Z. □

Next we show how to turn the output of Lemma 15.13 into a protrusion decomposition of G.

Lemma 15.14 *If a planar graph G has a treewidth-η-modulator S, then G has a $((4(\eta+1)+1)|S|, (20(\eta+1)+5)|S|, 3\eta+2)$-protrusion decomposition, such that S is contained in the bag of the root node of the protrusion decomposition. Furthermore, there is a polynomial time algorithm that, given G, S, and a tree-decomposition (T, χ) of $G - S$ of width at most η, computes such a protrusion decomposition of G.*

Proof: By making use of Lemma 15.13, we construct a set Z with $S \subseteq Z$, such that $|Z| \leq 4(\eta + 1)|S| + |S|$, and each connected component of $G - Z$ has at most 2 neighbors in S, and at most 2η neighbors in $Z \setminus S$. Group the components into groups with the same neighborhood in S. More precisely, let $C_1, \ldots, C_t$ be the connected components of $G - Z$. Define sets $X_1, \ldots, X_\ell$ with the following properties. For each $i \leq t$, there is exactly one $j \leq \ell$ such that $C_i \subseteq X_j$, and for all $j' \neq j$ we have $C_i \cap X_{j'} = \emptyset$. Furthermore, for all i, i' and j, it holds that $C_i \subseteq X_j$ and $C_{i'} \subseteq X_j$ if and only if $N(C_i) = N(C_j)$. The definition of the sets $X_1, \ldots, X_\ell$ immediately gives a way to compute them from $C_1, \ldots, C_t$.

For each $i \leq \ell$ we make a tree-decomposition (T_i, χ_i) of $G[X_i \cup N(X_i)]$ by starting with the tree-decomposition (T, χ) of $G - S$, removing all vertices not in X_i from all bags of the decomposition, turning this into a nice tree-decomposition of $G[X_i]$ using Lemma 14.23 and, finally, inserting $N(X_i)$ into all bags of the decomposition. The width of (T_i, χ_i) is at most $\eta + |N(X_i)| \leq 3\eta + 2$.

We now make a tree-decomposition $(\hat{T}, \hat{\chi})$ that is to be our protrusion decomposition. The tree $\hat{T}$ is constructed from $T_1, \ldots, T_\ell$ by adding a new root node r and connecting r to an arbitrary node in each tree T_i. We set $\hat{\chi}(r) = Z$ and, for each node $a \in V(\hat{T})$ that is in the copy of T_i in $\hat{T}$, we set $\hat{\chi}(a) = \chi_i(a)$. It is easy to verify that $(\hat{T}, \hat{\chi})$ is indeed a tree-decomposition of G and that every node $a \in V(T)$ except for r satisfies $|\chi(a)| \leq 3\eta + 2$. Thus, $(\hat{T}, \hat{\chi})$ is a $((4(\eta + 1) + 1)|S|, \ell, 3\eta + 2)$-protrusion decomposition of G. To prove the statement of the lemma it is sufficient to show that $\ell \leq (20(\eta + 1) + 5)|S|$.

Because the neighborhoods of the sets $X_1, \ldots, X_\ell$ are distinct, there are at most $|Z| \leq (4(\eta + 1) + 1)|S|$ sets X_i such that $|N(X_i)| = 1$. By Lemma 13.2, there are at most $2|Z| - 4 \leq (8(\eta + 1) + 2)|S|$ sets X_i such that $|N(X_i)| = 2$. Finally, by Lemma 13.3, there are at most $2|Z| - 4 \leq (8(\eta + 1) + 2)|S|$ sets X_i such that $|N(X_i)| \geq 3$. It follows that $\ell \leq 5|Z| \leq (20(\eta + 1) + 5)|S|$, as claimed. □

Let us remind that by Lemma 15.8, for any bidimensional linear-separable problem Π, there exists an integer $\eta \geq 0$ such that every planar graph G has a treewidth-η-modulator S of size at most $\epsilon \cdot OPT_\Pi(G)$. Combining this with Lemma 15.14, we have the following theorem.

Theorem 15.15 *For any bidimensional linear-separable problem Π, there exists a constant ℓ such that every planar graph G admits an $(\ell \cdot OPT_\Pi(G), \ell \cdot OPT_\Pi(G), \ell)$-protrusion decomposition.*

Let us note that if Π is a minimization problem, then for every yes-instance (G, k) of Π, we have that $k \geq OPT_\Pi(G)$ and hence G admits a $(\ell \cdot k, \ell \cdot k, \ell)$-protrusion decomposition. If Π is a maximization problem, then for every $k \leq OPT_\Pi(G)$, (G, k) is a yes-instance of Π. Then for every parameter $k > 0$ such that G does not admit a $(\ell \cdot k, \ell \cdot k, \ell)$-protrusion decomposition, we have that (G, k) is a yes-instance of Π.

15.4 Kernel for DOMINATING SET on Planar Graphs

We will now show how to use protrusion decompositions to obtain a linear kernel for DOMINATING SET on planar graphs. Recall that a dominating set is a vertex set S such that $N[S] = V(G)$, and the DOMINATING SET problem asks to find a dominating set of size at most k in the input graph. The kernel heavily relies on dynamic programming over graphs of bounded treewidth, so we encourage the reader to refresh the contents of Sections 14.4 and 14.4.2 before proceeding. Before starting to describe the kernel, we need to define *nice* protrusion decompositions. For each node $a \in V(T)$, we define $\hat{T}_a$ to be the subtree of $\hat{T}$ rooted at a, and $\hat{\chi}_a$ to be the restriction of $\hat{\chi}$ to T_a. Then, for each node a of the tree $\hat{T}$ we have that $(\hat{T}_a, \chi_a)$ is a tree-decomposition of $G[\hat{\chi}(T_a)]$.

Let us recall that a tree-decomposition is seminice, see Definition 14.24, if it satisfies all of the properties of nice decompositions except for the one that the bag of the root should be empty.

Definition 15.16 A protrusion decomposition $(\hat{T}, \hat{\chi})$ of G is a *nice* protrusion decomposition if for every non root node a of $\hat{T}$, $(\hat{T}_a, \chi_a)$ is a seminice tree-decomposition of $G[\hat{\chi}(T_a)]$.

Just as it is possible to turn any tree-decomposition into a nice tree-decomposition of the same width, one can make any protrusion decomposition nice.

Lemma 15.17 *There is an algorithm that, given a graph G and an (α, β, γ)-protrusion decomposition $(\hat{T}, \hat{\chi})$ of G, outputs a nice (α, β, γ)-protrusion decomposition $(\hat{T}', \hat{\chi}')$ of G in time $\mathcal{O}((n + |V(T)|)^{\mathcal{O}(1)})$.*

The proof of Lemma 15.17 is almost identical to the proof of Lemma 14.23 and left as an exercise (see Problem 15.6).

Our kernel for planar DOMINATING SET is based on the following ideas.

> Given a planar graph G, suppose that we found a vertex subset Z of size $\mathcal{O}(k)$ such that if G contains a dominating set of size at most k, then there is also some dominating set $S \subseteq Z$ of size at most k. If we have such a set Z, then we can obtain a linear kernel as follows. First, we apply a reduction rule that deletes edges whose both endpoints are not in Z. Because Z contains a dominating set of size k, the reduced instance G' is equivalent to G. In the graph G', the set Z is a vertex cover and we already know that DOMINATING SET (VC) on planar graphs admits a linear kernel (see Problem 13.5).
>
> So to obtain a kernel, it is sufficient to find such a set Z. We achieve this as follows. We construct in polynomial time a nice $(\mathcal{O}(k), \mathcal{O}(k), \mathcal{O}(1))$-protrusion decomposition of G. Then to compute the desired set Z of size $\mathcal{O}(k)$ we will use the dynamic programming algorithm for DOMINATING SET described in Section 14.4.2 but stop the computation before arriving at the root of the decomposition.

We start with the description of how we compute a set Z of size $\mathcal{O}(k)$ such that there exists a minimum dominating set of G that is fully contained in Z.

15.4 Kernel for DOMINATING SET on Planar Graphs

Given an input (G, k) to DOMINATING SET, we apply Lemma 15.9 on G. If the output treewidth-2-modulator S of Lemma 15.9 has size more than $6k$, this implies that G cannot have a dominating set of size at most k, and we may safely return "no." If $|S| \leq 6k$, then we apply Lemma 15.14 on S and obtain a $(78k, 390k, 8)$-protrusion decomposition $(\hat{T}, \hat{\chi})$ of G. Using Lemma 15.17, we can transform $(\hat{T}, \hat{\chi})$ into a nice $(78k, 390k, 8)$-protrusion decomposition of G in polynomial time.

Next, we will use the dynamic programming algorithm for DOMINATING SET described in Section 14.4.2 but stop the computation before arriving at the root of the decomposition. More precisely, we will apply Lemma 14.40 on the tree-decomposition $(\hat{T}, \hat{\chi})$ using the preference relation $\leq_b$ defined in Section 14.4.2. We apply Lemma 14.40 for each child b of the root r of $\hat{T}$. Because all bags of $(\hat{T}, \hat{\chi})$ other than the root have size at most 8, Lemma 14.40 yields that in polynomial time we can compute, for every child b of the root r, a good family $\mathcal{F}_b$ of subsets of $\chi(\hat{T}_b)$, such that $|\mathcal{F}_b| \leq 3^{8+2} = 59049$.

Let Q be the set of children of r in $\hat{T}$. We define a vertex set Z as follows.

$$Z = \hat{\chi}(r) \cup \bigcup_{b \in Q} \bigcup_{A \in \mathcal{F}_b, |A| \leq 9} A.$$

Clearly $|Z| = \mathcal{O}(k)$ because $\chi(r) \leq 78k$, $|Q| \leq 370k$, and for each $b \in Q$ we have $|\mathcal{F}_b| \leq 59049$. Tallying up, we have that $|Z| \leq k(78 + 370 \cdot 59049 \cdot 9) = 196633248k$. Our aim is to show that there exists a minimum size dominating set that is fully contained in Z. Toward this goal we begin with the following observation.

Observation 15.18 For each child b of the root r of $\hat{T}$, $\hat{\chi}(b)$ is a dominating set for $G[\hat{\chi}(T_b)]$.

Proof: Because we constructed the protrusion decomposition $(\hat{T}, \hat{\chi})$ by applying Lemma 15.14 to a connected dominating set S of G, it follows that $\hat{\chi}(r)$ is a dominating set of G. By the properties of tree-decompositions, all the vertices in $\hat{\chi}(r)$ that have neighbors in $\hat{\chi}(T_b)$ lie in $\hat{\chi}(r) \cap \hat{\chi}(b) \subseteq \hat{\chi}(b)$. It follows that every vertex not in $\hat{\chi}(T_v) \setminus \hat{\chi}(b)$ has a neighbor in $\hat{\chi}(b)$, completing the proof. $\square$

The next lemma is an immediate consequence of Observation 15.18.

Lemma 15.19 *For every minimum size dominating set X of G and every child b of the root r in $\hat{T}$, $|X \cap \hat{\chi}(\hat{T}_b)| \leq 9$.*

Proof: Suppose for contradiction that there is some minimum size dominating set X of G and child b of the root r in $\hat{T}$ such that $|X \cap \hat{\chi}(\hat{T}_b)| \geq 10$. Let

$X' = (X \setminus \hat{\chi}(\hat{T}_b)) \cup \hat{\chi}(b)$. We have that $|X'| = |X| - |\hat{\chi}(\hat{T}_b)| + |\hat{\chi}(b)| \leq |X| - 10 + 9 < |X|$. We will show that X' is also a dominating set of G, contradicting the minimality of X.

By Observation 15.18, we have that $\hat{\chi}(\hat{T}_b) \subseteq N[X']$. Because the only vertices in $\hat{\chi}(\hat{T}_b)$ with neighbors outside $\hat{\chi}(\hat{T}_b)$ are in $\chi(b)$, we conclude that $N[X \cap \hat{\chi}(\hat{T}_b)] \subseteq N[X' \cap \hat{\chi}(\hat{T}_b)]$. Furthermore, $X \setminus \hat{\chi}(\hat{T}_b) = X' \setminus \hat{\chi}(\hat{T}_b)$ and therefore $N[X \setminus \hat{\chi}(\hat{T}_b)] = N[X' \cap \hat{\chi}(\hat{T}_b)]$. To conclude,

$$V(G) = N[X] = N[X \cap \hat{\chi}(\hat{T}_b)] \cup N[X \setminus \hat{\chi}(\hat{T}_b)]$$
$$\subseteq N[X' \cap \hat{\chi}(\hat{T}_b)] \cup N[X' \setminus \hat{\chi}(\hat{T}_b)]$$
$$\subseteq N[X'].$$

Thus, X' is a dominating set, yielding the desired contradiction. □

At this point we know that any optimal dominating set should not have a large intersection with $\chi(b)$ for any child b of r, and that for any b we can modify the optimal solution so that its intersection with $\hat{\chi}(\hat{T}_b)$ will be in $\mathcal{F}_b$ and have size at most 9. To prove that we can end up with an optimum dominating set that is a subset of Z, we need to be able to make all of these modifications simultaneously.

Lemma 15.20 *G has a minimum size dominating set X such that $X \subseteq Z$.*

Proof: Out of all minimum size dominating sets of G, let X be a dominating set minimizing $|X \setminus Z|$. Suppose for contradiction that $X \setminus Z \neq \emptyset$. Because $\hat{\chi}(r) \subseteq Z$, there exists a child b of r such that $(X \setminus Z) \cap \hat{\chi}(\hat{T}_b) \neq \emptyset$. Consider the good family $\mathcal{F}_b$. Because the family is good, there exists a set $A \in \mathcal{F}_b$ such that $X' = (X \setminus \hat{\chi}(\hat{T}_b)) \cup A$ is also a minimum dominating set of G. Because $X' \cap \hat{\chi}(\hat{T}_b) = A$ and X' is a minimum size dominating set, Lemma 15.19 implies that $|A| \leq 9$ and that, therefore, $A \subseteq Z$. But then when modifying X into X' we remove at least one vertex not in Z, and only add vertices in Z. Thus, $|X' \setminus Z| < |X \setminus Z|$, contradicting the choice of X. □

Lemma 15.20 leads to a very simple and powerful reduction rule.

Reduction Rule 15.1 Remove all edges with both endpoints in $V(G) \setminus Z$.

To see that Rule 15.1 is safe, note that removing an edge can only turn a yes-instance into a no-instance, never the other way around. However, we know by Lemma 15.20 that if G has a dominating set of size at most k, then it has a dominating set X of size at most k such that $X \subseteq Z$. Removing edges whose both endpoints are not in Z will never remove any edges incident to X. Thus, X stays a dominating set even after Rule 15.1 has been applied. After

15.4 Kernel for DOMINATING SET on Planar Graphs

Rule 15.1 has been applied exhaustively, Z is a vertex cover of G of size at most $196633248k$. We can summarize the discussion so far in the following lemma.

Lemma 15.21 *There is a polynomial time algorithm that, given as input a planar graph G and integer k, outputs a subgraph G' of G and a vertex cover Z of G' of size at most $196633248k$. The graph G' has a dominating set of size at most k if and only if G has.*

Armed with Lemma 15.21, we can now directly apply to G' the kernel from Problem 13.5 for DOMINATING SET (VC) on planar graphs (DOMINATING SET parameterized by vertex cover). This yields the following theorem.

Theorem 15.22 DOMINATING SET (VC) *on planar graphs admits a kernel with* $16 \cdot 196633248k = 3146131968k$ *vertices.*

The main components of the kernel for DOMINATING SET in Theorem 15.22 were a proof of the existence of an $(\mathcal{O}(k), \mathcal{O}(k), \mathcal{O}(1))$-protrusion decomposition, as well as a dynamic programming algorithm for DOMINATING SET on graphs of bounded treewidth. Combining Lemmata 15.8 and 15.14, it is possible to get such protrusion decompositions for all bidimensional, $\mathcal{O}(t)$-separable problems. Further, many problems admit efficient dynamic programming algorithms on graphs of bounded treewidth. Is it possible to make these ideas work for many problems simultaneously? The next chapter is all about achieving this goal.

Exercises

Problem 15.1 Of the following problems, which are contraction-bidimensional?

- DOMINATING SET;
- ODD CYCLE TRANSVERSAL;
- MAXCUT;
- q-COLORING;
- FEEDBACK VERTEX SET;
- INDEPENDENT DOMINATING SET;
- HAMILTONIAN PATH and LONGEST PATH;
- HAMILTONIAN CYCLE and LONGEST CYCLE;
- CHROMATIC NUMBER;
- CYCLE PACKING;

- CONNECTED VERTEX COVER;
- CONNECTED DOMINATING SET; or
- CONNECTED FEEDBACK VERTEX SET.

Problem 15.2 (i) Make a vertex-subset maximization Π such that

$$\mathsf{OPT}^\star_\Pi(G) = \max{(0, is(G) - 2 \cdot isolated(G))}$$

where $is(G)$ returns the size of the maximum independent set of G and $isolated(G)$ returns the number of vertices in G of degree 0.
(ii) Prove that the problem Π is contraction-bidimensional.
(iii) For every $k \geq 0$, construct a graph G such that $\mathsf{OPT}^\star_\Pi(G) = 0$ and $\mathrm{tw}(G) \geq k$.

Problem 15.3 Which of the problems from Problem 15.1 are separable?

Problem 15.4 Prove that for every $\eta \geq 0$, the TREEWIDTH-η MODULATOR problem is contraction-bidimensional and separable.

Problem 15.5 Prove Claim 15.10.

Problem 15.6 Prove Lemma 15.17.

Bibliographic Notes

Many problems that admit no polynomial kernel on general graphs, admit linear kernels on sparse classes of graphs, including planar graphs. More than a decade ago, Alber et al. (2004b) proposed a linear kernel for DOMINATING SET on planar graphs. This breakthrough led to a flurry of research of linear kernels for problems on planar graphs, such as FEEDBACK VERTEX SET by Bodlaender and Penninkx (2008), CYCLE PACKING (Bodlaender et al., 2008), INDUCED MATCHING (Kanj et al., 2011; Moser and Sikdar, 2007), FULL-DEGREE SPANNING TREE (Guo et al., 2006) and CONNECTED DOMINATING SET (Lokshtanov et al., 2011a). To generalize these results, it was shown by Guo and Niedermeier (2007b) that problems satisfying a certain "distance property" admit a linear kernel on planar graphs. Bodlaender et al. (2009a) subsumed this result by obtaining a meta-theorem for problems admitting linear kernels on planar graphs or, more generally, on bounded-genus graphs. Later, this was further extended in Fomin et al. (2010) for bidimensional problems on H-minor-free graphs and apex-minor-free graphs. Such meta-theorems, based on protrusion decompositions, are the subject of the next chapter.

For DOMINATING SET specifically, it is known that, on general graphs, these problems have no kernel of size $f(k)$ for any f unless FPT $=$ W[1] (see Downey and Fellows, 1999). Under the Exponential Time Hypothesis, DOMINATING SET admits $2^{o(n)}$ time algorithm (see e.g., Lokshtanov et al., 2011b), and it admits no polynomial time $o(\log n)$-approximation unless P $=$NP (Feige, 1998). On the positive side, on planar graphs, in addition to the linear kernel mentioned previously, DOMINATING SET admits a $2^{\mathcal{O}(\sqrt{k})} + \mathcal{O}(n)$ time algorithm, see Alber et al. (2002), as well as a polynomial time approximation scheme (see e.g., Baker, 1994).

Bidimensionality was first introduced by Demaine et al. (2005); see also surveys (Demaine and Hajiaghayi, 2008a; Dorn et al., 2008). Besides kernelization, the framework could be used to obtain parameterized subexponential as well as efficient polynomial-time approximation schemes (EPTASes). For kernelization algorithms based on bidimensional arguments we refer to Fomin et al. (2012b, 2010, 2012a). Applications for designing EPTASes are discussed in Demaine and Hajiaghayi (2005) and Fomin et al. (2011a, 2018).

The notion of separability, in slightly different form, was introduced by Demaine and Hajiaghayi (2005). Lemma 15.8 about TREEWIDTH-η MODULATOR of bidimensional problems is from Fomin et al. (2010, 2018). Protrusions and protrusion decompositions were introduced by Bodlaender et al. (2009a), see also Bodlaender et al. (2016b). The definition of protrusion decomposition is from Bodlaender et al. (2016b) and it slightly differs the one we give in this book. There for integers α, β, and t, an (α, β, t)-protrusion decomposition of G was defined as a partition of $V(G)$ into sets $R_0, R_1, \ldots, R_\beta$, such that the size of R_0 is at most α, and each of the sets $N_G[R_i]$, $1 \leq i \leq \beta$, is a t-protrusion and $N(R_i) \subseteq R_0$. Up to constants, these definitions are equivalent, in a sense that an (α, β, t)-protrusion decomposition from this book is also an (α, β, t)-protrusion decomposition from Bodlaender et al. (2016b), while an (α, β, t)-protrusion decomposition from Bodlaender et al. (2016b) is also an $(\alpha, \beta, 2t)$-protrusion decomposition from this book.

16
Surgery on Graphs

In this chapter, we discuss a general kernelization technique of graph surgery. We find a large protrusion, cut it from the graph, and attach a smaller protrusion. First, we set up the conditions whose satisfaction enables us to apply the technique; in particular, we discuss the notion of a finite integer index. Then, we present a general reduction rule that finds a large protrusion and replaces it by a smaller one. This rule leads to the establishment of meta-theorems concerning kernelization. In most parts of the book we neglected the analysis of running times of kernelization algorithms, being satisfied that the running times are polynomial in the input size. In this chapter we make an exception and spend a significant amount of efforts to obtain linear running times. The techniques discussed here are fundamental and can be used as subroutines for many kernelization algorithms, thus finding the best possible polynomial dependence for them is an important task.

In this chapter we formalize the approach described in the following text, and apply it to give linear kernels for a wide range of problems on planar graphs.

For many problems, whenever there is a constant size separator in a graph, the left side of the separator may only "affect" the right side of it in a constant number of ways. For each of the (constant number of) possible ways that the left side could affect the right side, we could store a single representative "left side" graph that would affect the right side in exactly that way. If an input instance can be separated to a left side and a right side by a constant size separator, we could proceed as follows. First, we "analyze" the left part of the instance and determine in which way (out of the constant number of possibilities) it affects the rest of the graph. We then retrieve the representative "left-hand side" graph which would affect the rest of the instance in the same way. Then we "replace" the left part of the instance with the representative graph. Because the part of the graph we deleted affects the graph in exactly the same way as the representative graph we inserted, this is a safe reduction rule. If the left-hand side of the instance before the reduction rule had more vertices than the representative we replace it with, the reduction rule makes the input instance smaller. We think of such reduction rules as performing surgery on the input graph—parts of the graph are cut away and replaced with smaller gadgets that effectively have the same function as the part that was cut away.

To deploy the strategy outlined in the preceding text, first we need to formalize what exactly we mean by two different "left-hand side" graphs affecting the rest in the same way. It turns out that the right definition is that of *finite integer index*, first defined by Bodlaender and van Antwerpen-de Fluiter (2001) in the late 1990s. Indeed it turns out that every separable (see Definition 15.6) CMSO-optimization problem (see Definition 16.1) has finite integer index. Thus, the outlined strategy applies to all such problems.

The definition of finite integer index leads in a natural way to the *existence* of a constant size set of "representative" left-hand side graphs, such that any left-hand side graph affects the rest of the graph in exactly the same way as one of the representatives. However, we need our kernelization algorithms to *know* a set of representatives. We will get around this problem in the following way: Because the set of representative left-hand side graphs is a constant size set of constant size graphs, we will only show *existence* of kernelization algorithms, and assume that the set of representatives is hard-coded in the source code of the kernelization algorithm. Thus, the kernelization theorems in this chapter are non constructive in the following way: They state that a kernelization algorithm *exists* for a number of problems, but there is no way to deduce the (source code of the) algorithm from the theorem. Similarly, we know that the sizes of the obtained kernels are linear, but the functions hidden in the $\mathcal{O}$-notation are determined non constructively and we cannot derive bounds on the kernel sizes from the proof.

The next step is to "analyze" the left side of the instance, namely to determine in which way it affects the rest of the graph and retrieve the representative left-hand side graph that affects the rest of the instance in the same way. Notice that so far all we have required of the input graph to apply our strategy is the existence of a small separator in the graph. However, any constant degree vertex v gives rise to such a small separator: The neighbors of v form a separator that splits G into a right side, namely v, and a left side containing everything else. If we were able to "analyze" in polynomial time the left-hand side of the instance and replace it with a constant size representative, then the reduced instance would have constant size and we could solve the problem in polynomial time by brute forcing the reduced instance. Thus, for NP-hard problems (that remain NP-hard even on instances that contain at least one vertex of constant degree) we do not hope to analyze *all* possible "left-hand side graphs" in polynomial time. Instead we focus on left-hand side graphs that for some reason are easy to analyze. Here we will only consider *protrusions*— left-hand side graphs that have constant treewidth protrusion.

Recall that the *boundary* of a vertex set X in a graph G is the set $\partial(X)$ of vertices in X that have at least one neighbor outside of X. An *r-protrusion* in a graph G is a vertex set X such that $\text{tw}(G[X]) \leq r$ and $|\partial(X)| \leq r$. Thus, for any (α, β, η)-protrusion decomposition $(\hat{T}, \hat{\chi})$ of G, and child b of the root r of $\hat{T}$, $\chi(\hat{T}_b)$ is an $(\eta + 1)$-protrusion in G. For problems that have finite integer index, protrusions are the perfect candidates for "left-hand side" graphs. Indeed, we will (essentially) show that for any problem that has finite integer index, one can in linear time "analyze" a protrusion and produce the representative left-hand side graph that is equivalent to it. Doing this exhaustively results in an instance where, for some constant η, there are no η-protrusions of super-constant size. In Chapter 15 we showed that for bidimensional and $\mathcal{O}(t)$-separable problems on planar graphs, every non trivial instance can be decomposed such that all but $\mathcal{O}(\text{OPT})$ vertices are in one of $\mathcal{O}(\text{OPT})$ protrusions. It follows that a reduced instance must have size upper bounded by $\mathcal{O}(\text{OPT})$.

Definition 16.1 (CMSO-optimization problem) A vertex/edge subset problem with feasibility function ϕ is a CMSO-optimization problem if there exists a CMSO sentence ψ such that $\phi(G, S) = $ **true** if and only if $(G, S) \models \psi$.

Now we can state the main result of this chapter.

Theorem 16.2 *Every bidimensional, $\mathcal{O}(t)$-separable CMSO-optimization problem admits a linear kernel on planar graphs.*

For example, the problems in the next corollary are bidimensional, $\mathcal{O}(t)$-separable CMSO-optimization problems, see Problems 15.1 and 16.1. Thus, we have that

Corollary 16.3 *The following problems*

- VERTEX COVER, FEEDBACK VERTEX SET, *and more generally,* TREEWIDTH-η MODULATOR,
- DOMINATING SET,
- CONNECTED DOMINATING SET,
- CONNECTED VERTEX COVER, *and*
- CONNECTED FEEDBACK VERTEX SET

admit linear kernels on planar graphs.

This chapter is devoted to proving Theorem 16.2 using the strategy described previously. The protrusion replacing technique is very general and can be applied to many problems. Due to this, we also spend a significant amount of space to describe efficient algorithms computing protrusions. Combined with additional ideas, this will bring us to kernelization algorithms that run in linear time.

16.1 Boundaried Graphs and Finite Integer Index

Our strategy calls for replacing the "left-hand side" of a separator in a graph by a different "left-hand side" that is equivalent to it. The part that is being replaced lives inside our input instance G. However, prior to being inserted into G, the part that we insert into G exists independently of any graph. We now set up the formalism to talk about "left-hand side" graphs that live in the wild without any "right-hand side" to accompany them. We call such objects *boundaried graphs*.

Definition 16.4 (Boundaried graphs) A *boundaried graph* is a graph G with a set $B \subseteq V(G)$ of distinguished vertices and an injective labeling λ from B to the set $\mathbb{Z}^+$. The set B is called the *boundary* of G and the vertices in B are called *boundary vertices* or *terminals*. Given a boundaried graph G, we denote its boundary by $\delta(G)$, we denote its labeling by λ_G, and we define its *label set* by $\Lambda(G) = \{\lambda_G(v) \mid v \in \delta(G)\}$. Given a finite set $I \subseteq \mathbb{Z}^+$, we define $\mathcal{F}_I$ to denote the class of all boundaried graphs whose label set is I. Similarly, we define $\mathcal{F}_{\subseteq I} = \bigcup_{I' \subseteq I} \mathcal{F}_{I'}$. We also denote by $\mathcal{F}$ the class of all boundaried graphs. Finally, we say that a boundaried graph is a *t-boundaried graph* if $\Lambda(G) \subseteq \{1, \ldots, t\}$.

Attaching two boundaried graphs together along the boundary yields a normal (non boundaried) graph, as defined in the following text (see Fig. 16.1).

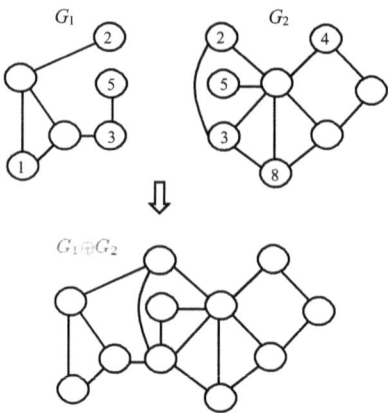

Figure 16.1 Gluing two boundaried graphs.

Definition 16.5 (Gluing by ⊕) Let G_1 and G_2 be two boundaried graphs. We denote by $G_1 \oplus G_2$ the graph (not boundaried) obtained by taking the disjoint union of G_1 and G_2 and identifying equally labeled vertices of the boundaries of G_1 and G_2. In $G_1 \oplus G_2$ there is an edge between two labeled vertices if there is an edge between them in G_1 or in G_2.

Definition 16.6 Let $G = G_1 \oplus G_2$ where G_1 and G_2 are boundaried graphs. We define the *glued* set of G_i as the set $B_i = \lambda_{G_i}^{-1}(\Lambda(G_1) \cap \Lambda(G_2)), i = 1, 2$.

Let $\mathcal{G}$ be a class of (not boundaried) graphs. By slightly abusing notation, we say that a boundaried graph *belongs to a graph class* $\mathcal{G}$ if the underlying graph belongs to $\mathcal{G}$.

Finite integer index We are using boundaried graphs as our notion of "left-hand side graph." Next we need to define what it means for two left-hand side graphs to "affect the rest of the graph in the same way." The definition of "affecting the rest in the same way" depends on the problem that we are working with. For example, two boundaried graphs that are equivalent when working with VERTEX COVER may not be equivalent for DOMINATING SET and vice versa. For technical reasons, this definition needs an extended notion of parameterized problems that allows the parameter value to be negative, but where either all instances with negative parameter value are "yes" instances, or all such instances are "no" instances. The reason for this technicality will become clear in Lemma 16.11.

Definition 16.7 (Extended parameterized problem) An extended parameterized problem Π is a subset of $\Sigma^* \times \mathbb{Z}$, such that either (i) for all I, k with

$k < 0$ we have $(I, k) \in \Pi$, or (ii) for all I, k with $k < 0$ we have $(I, k) \notin \Pi$. In case (i) Π is called a *positive* extended parameterized problem; in case (ii) Π is called a *negative* extended parameterized problem. An extended parameterized problem Π' *agrees* with a parameterized problem Π if $\Pi' \cap (\Sigma^* \times \mathbb{N}) = \Pi$. For a parameterized problem Π there are exactly one positive extended parameterized problem Π^+ and exactly one negative extended parameterized problem Π^- that agrees with Π. These are called the positive and negative extensions of Π, respectively.

The reason that instances $(G, k) \in \Pi$ are called "yes" instances of Π is that parameterized problems Π are often defined as the set of pairs (G, k) for which the answer to some question is "yes." For example, does G contain an independent set of size at least k? Does G have a vertex cover of size at most k? For such questions, involving "at least k" or "at most k," the answer is monotone—if G has an independent set of size at least k, it also has an independent set of size at least $k - 1$ (but not necessarily one of size $k + 1$). If G has a vertex cover of size at most k, it also has one of size at most $k + 1$, but not necessarily one of size $k - 1$. For this reason, for some problems (typically maximization problems) it is more natural to interpret all instances with negative parameter value as "yes" instances, while for others (typically minimization problems) it is more natural to interpret all instances with negative parameter value as "no" instances. Indeed, every graph has an independent set of size at least -1, but no graph has a vertex cover of size at most -1. The positive and negative extensions of a parameterized problem are meant to capture this difference. Thus, for (the decision version of) maximization problems we will typically consider their positive extension, while for minimization problems we will consider their negative extension.

We are now ready to define what it means for two left-hand side graphs to affect the rest of the graph in the same way.

Definition 16.8 (Canonical equivalence on boundaried graphs) Let Π be an extended parameterized graph problem whose instances are pairs of the form (G, k). Given two boundaried graphs $G_1, G_2 \in \mathcal{F}$, we say that $G_1 \equiv_\Pi G_2$ if $\Lambda(G_1) = \Lambda(G_2)$ and there exists a *transposition constant* $c \in \mathbb{Z}$ such that

$$\forall (F, k) \in \mathcal{F} \times \mathbb{Z}, \ (G_1 \oplus F, k) \in \Pi \Leftrightarrow (G_2 \oplus F, k + c) \in \Pi.$$

Note that the relation $\equiv_\Pi$ is an equivalence relation (you are asked to prove this in Exercise 16.2). Observe that c could be negative in the preceding definition. This is the reason we extended the definition of parameterized problems to include negative parameters also.

Notice that two boundaried graphs with different label sets belong to different equivalence classes of $\equiv_\Pi$. Hence, for every equivalence class $\mathcal{C}$ of $\equiv_\Pi$ there exists some finite set $I \subseteq \mathbb{Z}^+$ such that $\mathcal{C} \subseteq \mathcal{F}_I$. We are now in position to define what it means that for a problem Π, for every fixed boundary size, there are only finitely many essentially different (with respect to $\equiv_\Pi$) left-hand side graphs with that boundary size.

Definition 16.9 (Finite Integer Index) An *extended* parameterized graph problem Π whose instances are pairs of the form (G, k) has *Finite Integer Index* (or simply has *FII*), if and only if for every finite $I \subseteq \mathbb{Z}^+$, the number of equivalence classes of $\equiv_\Pi$ that are subsets of $\mathcal{F}_I$ is finite. A parameterized graph problem Π whose instances are pairs of the form (G, k) has FII if either its positive extension or its negative extension has FII.

In Exercise 16.3, it is asked to show that the number of equivalence classes above depends only on $|I|$.

For problems Π that have FII, it is natural to use the following reduction rule. Suppose that the input graph G can be decomposed as $G = G_1 \oplus F$, where G_1 is "simple" and F is "difficult." If the "simple" part G_1 is really large, one could hope to replace G_1 by something that affects the rest in the same way. Specifically, if we have at hand G_2 such that $G_1 \equiv_\Pi G_2$ and $|V(G_2)| < |V(G_1)|$, then by Equation 16.1 there exists a $c \in \mathbb{Z}$ such that $(G_1 \oplus F, k) \in \Pi \Leftrightarrow (G_2 \oplus F, k + c)$. Then we can replace the instance (G, k) with the equivalent instance $(G_2 \oplus F, k + c)$.

There are several issues to be overcome with the preceding approach. Where do we take the graph G_2 from? How do we *compute* the constant c? What if the constant c is positive—then our reduction rule *increases* the parameter value k, which, if left unchecked could ruin a kernelization algorithm. We will handle all these issues, starting with the last one. Next we show that we can always find a set of potential replacement graphs G_2 that have negative value of c with *every* other graph in the same equivalence class of $\equiv_\Pi$.

Definition 16.10 (Progressive representatives) Let Π be an extended parameterized graph problem whose instances are pairs of the form (G, k) and let $\mathcal{C}$ be some equivalence class of $\equiv_\Pi$. We say that $J \in \mathcal{C}$ is a *progressive representative* of $\mathcal{C}$ if for every $H \in \mathcal{C}$ there exists $c \in \mathbb{Z}^-$, such that

$$\forall (F, k) \in \mathcal{F} \times \mathbb{Z} \quad (H \oplus F, k) \in \Pi \Leftrightarrow (J \oplus F, k + c) \in \Pi. \quad (16.1)$$

The following lemma guaranties the existence of a progressive representative for each equivalence class of $\equiv_\Pi$.

Lemma 16.11 *Let Π be an extended parameterized graph problem whose instances are pairs of the form (G, k). Then each equivalence class of $\equiv_\Pi$ has a progressive representative.*

Proof: We only consider the case when Π is a negative extended parameterized problem. In other words, every instance of Π with a negative valued parameter is a no-instance. The case when Π is a positive extended parameterized problem is left to the reader as Exercise 16.4.

Let $\mathcal{C}$ be an equivalence class of $\equiv_\Pi$. We distinguish two cases:

Case 1. Suppose first that for every $H \in \mathcal{C}$, every $F \in \mathcal{F}$, and every integer $k \in \mathbb{Z}$ it holds that $(H \oplus F, k) \notin \Pi$. Then we set J to be an arbitrary chosen graph in $\mathcal{C}$ and $c = 0$. In this case, it is obvious that (16.1) holds for every $(F, k) \in \mathcal{F} \times \mathbb{Z}$.

Case 2. Suppose now that for some $H_0 \in \mathcal{C}$, $F_0 \in \mathcal{F}$, and $k_0 \in \mathbb{Z}$ it holds that that $(H_0 \oplus F_0, k_0) \in \Pi$. Among all such triples, choose the one where the value of k_0 is minimized. Because every instance of Π with a negative valued parameter is a no-instance, it follows that k_0 is well defined and is non negative. We claim that H_0 is a progressive representative.

Let $H \in \mathcal{C}$. As $H_0 \equiv_\Pi H$, there is a constant c such that

$$\forall (F, k) \in \mathcal{F} \times \mathbb{Z}, \quad (H \oplus F, k) \in \Pi \Leftrightarrow (H_0 \oplus F, k + c) \in \Pi.$$

It suffices to prove that $c \leq 0$. Assume for a contradiction that $c > 0$. Then, by taking $k = k_0 - c$ and $F = F_0$, we have that

$$(H \oplus F_0, k_0 - c) \in \Pi \Leftrightarrow (H_0 \oplus F_0, k_0 - c + c) \in \Pi.$$

Because $(H_0 \oplus F_0, k_0) \in \Pi$ it follows that $(H \oplus F_0, k_0 - c) \in \Pi$ contradicting the choice of H_0, F_0, k_0. $\square$

Lemma 16.11 implies that for every extended parameterized problem Π "the set of progressive representatives" is well defined.

Definition 16.12 (The progressive representatives of Π) Let Π be an extended parameterized problem. For each $I \subseteq \mathbb{Z}^+$, we define $\mathcal{S}_I$ to be a set containing exactly one progressive representative of each equivalence class of $\equiv_\Pi$ that is a subset of $\mathcal{F}_I$. We also define $\mathcal{S}_{\subseteq I} = \bigcup_{I' \subseteq I} \mathcal{S}_{I'}$.

16.2 Which Problems Have Finite Integer Index?

It takes some practice to get used to Definition 16.9. In this section we give an example of how to show that a concrete problem has finite integer index, an easy to use sufficient condition for a problem to have finite integer index, and an example of how to show that a concrete problem does not have finite integer index.

Independent Set has finite integer index. Consider the INDEPENDENT SET problem—here (G, k) is a yes instance if G contains an independent set of size at least k. To prove that INDEPENDENT SET has finite integer index, we consider the positive extension of it, for which we need to prove that for every finite $I \subseteq \mathbb{Z}^+$, the number of equivalence classes of $\equiv_\Pi$ that are subsets of $\mathcal{F}_I$ is finite. In other words, for every fixed boundary (size) the number of equivalence classes of $\equiv_\Pi$ is finite. We will show that the number of equivalence classes is bounded by $(|I| + 1)^{2^{|I|}}$.

The proof idea is to define a *signature* function $\zeta_G : 2^I \to \mathbb{Z}$ for each boundaried graph $G \in \mathcal{F}_I$, and then to show that the signature function satisfies the following two properties.

(i) For every boundaried graph $G \in \mathcal{F}_I$ it holds that
$\max_{S \subseteq I} \zeta_G(S) - \min_{S \subseteq I} \zeta_G(S) \leq |I|$.
(ii) For every pair $G_1, G_2 \in \mathcal{F}_I$, if there exists an integer c^* (that depends on G_1 and G_2) such that for every $S \subseteq I$, $\zeta_{G_1}(S) = \zeta_{G_2}(S) + c^*$, then $G_1 \equiv_\Pi G_2$.

It is an easy exercise to show that the two facts together imply that the number of equivalence classes is bounded by $(|I| + 1)^{2^{|I|}}$ (see Exercise 16.5). We now proceed to execute this plan.

Given a boundaried graph $G \in \mathcal{F}_I$, we define the signature function $\zeta_G : 2^I \to \mathbb{Z}$ as follows. Each subset $S \subseteq I$ can be thought of as a set of labels of vertices in $\delta(G)$. Hence $\lambda_G^{-1}(S)$ maps S to the set of boundary vertices of G whose label set is S.

Consider now the largest independent set J in G such that the intersection $J \cap \delta(G)$ of the independent set with the boundary is contained in $\lambda_G^{-1}(S)$. The signature function ζ_G maps S to $|J|$. We define ζ_G as follows:

$$\zeta_G(S) = \max_J |J|,$$

where the maximum is taken over all independent sets J in G such that $J \cap \delta(G) \subseteq \lambda_G^{-1}(S)$. We now prove the first point of our plan.

Lemma 16.13 *For every boundaried graph $G \in \mathcal{F}_I$, it holds that*

$$\max_{S \subseteq I} \zeta_G(S) - \min_{S \subseteq I} \zeta_G(S) \leq |I|.$$

16.2 Which Problems Have Finite Integer Index? 325

Proof: Let ℓ be the size of the largest independent set X of $G \setminus \delta(G)$. Because $X \cap \delta(G) = \emptyset$ we have that $X \cap \delta(G) \subseteq \lambda_G^{-1}(S)$ for *every* choice of $S \subseteq I$. Therefore, $\min_{S \subseteq I} \zeta_G(S) \geq \ell$. Further, let Y be a largest independent set of G, irrespective of $Y \cap \delta(G)$. We have that $|Y| \leq \ell + |I|$ because otherwise $Y \setminus \delta(G)$ would be larger than X, contradicting the choice of X. Because Y is a largest independent set of G it holds that $\max_{S \subseteq I} \zeta_G(S) \leq |Y| \leq \ell + |I|$. The claim follows. □

Next we prove the second point of our plan.

Lemma 16.14 *For every pair $G_1, G_2 \in \mathcal{F}_I$, if there exists an integer c^* (that depends on G_1 and G_2) such that for every $S \subseteq I$, $\zeta_{G_1}(S) = \zeta_{G_2}(S) + c^*$, then $G_1 \equiv_\Pi G_2$.*

Proof: We recall the definition of $\equiv_\Pi$. We have that $G_1 \equiv_\Pi G_2$ if $\Lambda(G_1) = \Lambda(G_2)$ and there exists a $c \in \mathbb{Z}$ such that

$$\forall (F, k) \in \mathcal{F} \times \mathbb{Z}, \ (G_1 \oplus F, k) \in \Pi \Leftrightarrow (G_2 \oplus F, k + c) \in \Pi.$$

The first condition holds because $\Lambda(G_1) = \Lambda(G_2) = I$. For the second condition we will prove that it holds with $c = c^*$. We now prove the forward direction of the implication.

Let $(F, k) \in \mathcal{F} \times \mathbb{Z}$ be such that $(G_1 \oplus F, k) \in \Pi$. We need to prove that $(G_2 \oplus F, k + c) \in \Pi$. Note that k might be negative, but this will not affect our arguments because we look at the positive extension of the problem. When Π is the INDEPENDENT SET problem, this means that $G_1 \oplus F$ has an independent set J_1 of size at least k, and we need to prove that $G_2 \oplus F$ has an independent set J_2 of size at least $k + c$. Let $S = \lambda_{G_1}(J_1 \cap \delta(G_1))$. Because $J_1 \cap V(G_1)$ is an independent set with $\lambda_{G_1}(J_1 \cap \delta(G_1)) \subseteq S$ it follows that $\zeta_{G_1}(S) \geq |J_1 \cap V(G_1)|$. By assumption we have that

$$\zeta_{G_2}(S) = \zeta_{G_1}(S) + c \geq |J_1 \cap V(G_1)| + c.$$

Let J_2^* be an independent set in G_2 that witnesses the value of $\zeta_{G_2}(S)$. Specifically, let J_2^* be an independent set in G_2 such that $|J_2^*| = \zeta_{G_2}(S)$ and $\lambda_{G_2}(J_2^* \cap \delta(G_2)) \subseteq S$.

We set $J_2 = J_2^* \cup (J_1 \setminus V(G_1))$. It is easy to see that J_2 is an independent set in $G_2 \oplus F$: Indeed J_2^* and $(J_1 \setminus V(G_1))$ are both independent sets. Thus, an edge uv between two vertices of J_2 must have one endpoint u in $(J_1 \setminus V(G_1))$ and the other endpoint v in J_2^*. If $v \in \delta(G_2)$ then $\lambda(v) \in S$ by the choice of J_2^*. However, in F there are no edges with one endpoint in $(J_1 \cap V(F)) \setminus \delta(F) = J_1 \setminus V(G_1)$ and the other endpoint in $\delta(F)$ being some vertex with a label in S, contradicting the existence of the edge uv. If $v \notin \delta(G_2)$ then $v \in V(G_1) \setminus \delta(G_1)$, again contradicting the existence of the edge uv because $G_1 \oplus F$ does not have any edges with one endpoint in $V(G_1) \setminus \delta(G_1)$ and the other in $V(F) \setminus \delta(F)$. This proves that J_2 is indeed an independent set. Finally,

$$|J_2| = |J_2^*| + |J_1 \setminus V(G_1)| \geq |J_1 \cap V(G_1)| + c + |J_1 \setminus V(G_1)| = |J_1| + c.$$

This completes the forward direction of the implication. The proof of the backward direction is identical with the roles of G_1 and G_2 reversed, and every $+c$ changed to $-c$. □

Theorem 16.15 INDEPENDENT SET *has finite integer index.*

Proof: For every boundaried graph $G \in \mathcal{F}_I$ define its *truncated signature* $\hat{\zeta}_G : 2^I \to \mathbb{Z}$ such that for every $S \subseteq I$, $\hat{\zeta}_G(S) = \zeta_G(S) - \min_{S \subseteq I} \zeta_G(S)$. By Lemma 16.13 we have that $\hat{\zeta}_G(S) \in \{0, 1, \ldots, |I|\}$, and that therefore there can be at most $(|I| + 1)^{2^{|I|}}$ different truncated signatures. By Lemma 16.14 two boundaried graphs with the same truncated signature are equivalent (with respect to $\equiv_\Pi$ for the positive extension of the problem). Hence the number of equivalence classes of $\equiv_\Pi$ is at most $(|I| + 1)^{2^{|I|}}$, completing the proof. □

Separable CMSO-optimization problems. An astute reader can notice the similarity between the proof of Theorem 16.15 and a proof that INDEPENDENT SET parameterized by treewidth is FPT. Specifically, the signature function ζ_G together with Lemma 16.14 can be used to give a dynamic programming algorithm for INDEPENDENT SET on graphs of treewidth. To prove that INDEPENDENT SET has finite integer index it is sufficient to complement Lemma 16.14 by a proof that the minimum and maximum value of the signature differ only by $|I|$.

It turns out that the proof of Theorem 16.15 can be carried over to a host of CMSO-optimization problems, see Definition 16.1.

In particular, we have the following sufficient condition.

Theorem 16.16 (Fomin et al. [2016a]) *Every separable CMSO-optimization problem has FII.*

Independent Dominating Set does not have Finite Integer Index. Let us consider the negative extension of INDEPENDENT DOMINATING SET (the positive case is left as an exercise). To show that it does not have FII, we exhibit a set of boundaried graphs $\mathcal{G}$ with the same label set $\{1, 2\}$ such that

- No two graphs in $\mathcal{G}$ belong to the same equivalence class of $\equiv_\Pi$, and
- For every $\ell \in \mathbb{N}$, the set $\mathcal{G}$ will include a unique graph G_ℓ.

The second condition shows that $\mathcal{G}$ is infinite, and hence the first condition implies that the number of equivalence classes of $\equiv_\Pi$ is infinite.

We construct the graph G_ℓ as follows. We define the boundary of G_ℓ to contain exactly two vertices, u and v, where the label of u is 1 and the label of v is 2, and we insert an edge between u and v. In addition, we add ℓ new vertices that are leaves adjacent to v. This completes the description of G_ℓ.

Let us pick some integers $\ell, \ell' \in \mathbb{N}$ with $\ell < \ell'$, and show that G_ℓ and $G_{\ell'}$ are not equivalent. To this end, suppose by way of contradiction that these two graphs are equivalent, and let c be the corresponding transposition constant. We denote $F_2 = G_{2\ell'}$, and we define F_1 to be the boundaried graph F_2 where the labels of the two boundary vertices are swapped.

On the one hand, in the graph $G_\ell \oplus F_1$, the minimum size of an independent dominating set is $\ell + 1$, and in the graph $G_{\ell'} \oplus F_1$ it is $\ell' + 1$. Because G_ℓ and $G_{\ell'}$ are equivalent, for any $(F, k) \in \mathcal{F} \times \mathbb{Z}$, it holds that $(G_\ell \oplus F, k) \in \Pi \Leftrightarrow (G_{\ell'} \oplus F, k+c) \in \Pi$. In particular, it holds that $(G_\ell \oplus F_1, \ell+1) \in \Pi \Leftrightarrow (G_{\ell'} \oplus F_1, \ell+1+c) \in \Pi$. Because $(G_\ell \oplus F_1, \ell+1) \in \Pi$ and $(G_{\ell'} \oplus F_1, r) \notin \Pi$ for any integer $r < \ell' + 1$ (because we consider the negative extension), we have that $c \geq \ell' - \ell \geq 1$.

On the other hand, in the graph $G_\ell \oplus F_2$, the minimum size of an independent dominating set is 1, and in the graph $G_{\ell'} \oplus F_2$ it is also 1. Moreover, it holds that $(G_\ell \oplus F_2, 0) \in \Pi \Leftrightarrow (G_{\ell'} \oplus F, c) \in \Pi$. Because $(G_\ell \oplus F_2, 0) \notin \Pi$, we have that $(G_{\ell'} \oplus F, c) \notin \Pi$. However, $(G_{\ell'} \oplus F, r) \in \Pi$ for any integer $r \geq 1$, and because $c \geq 1$, we have reached a contradiction. We thus conclude that no two graphs in $\mathcal{G}$ belong to the same equivalence class of $\equiv_\Pi$.

16.3 A General Reduction Rule

In this section we provide a reduction rule for graph problems that have FII. Informally, this reduction rule does the following.

- Find a large protrusion.
- Replace it by a smaller one.

Of course, there are a great deal of questions hidden under the carpet with this generic reduction rule. First, why does this rule imply a kernel? How to find a protrusion efficiently? How to replace one protrusion by a smaller one efficiently, and why will such a replacement work? In this section we uncover the hidden parts of the puzzle, and when finally all the parts are assembled together, we obtain linear linear kernels for many parameterized problems on planar graphs.

Replacing a protrusion. We start from the procedure of replacing a large protrusion by a smaller one. Let c be some constant and suppose that we have a t-protrusion X of size c that we want to replace by a smaller protrusion. We do not know how to implement such a replacement efficiently when the size of X can be arbitrarily large. The following lemma says that we can always extract from X a protrusion of constant size that is still larger than c.

Lemma 16.17 *If a graph G contains a t-protrusion X where $|X| > c > 0$, then it also contains a $(2t + 1)$-protrusion $Y \subseteq X$ where $c < |Y| \leq 2c$. Moreover, given a tree-decomposition of $G[X]$ of width at most t, a tree-decomposition of Y of width at most $2t$ can be found in $\mathcal{O}(|X|)$ steps.*

Proof: If $|X| \leq 2c$, we are done. Assume that $|X| > 2c$ and let (T, χ) be a nice tree-decomposition of $G[X]$, rooted at some arbitrarily chosen, node r of T. Given a node x of the rooted tree T, we denote by T_x the subtree of T rooted at x. We also define $V_x = \chi(V(T_x))$, which is the set of vertices of X contained in the bags of the nodes corresponding to x and its descendants.

Let $B \subseteq V(T)$ be the set of nodes of T such that for every $x \in B$, $|V_x| > c$. In other words, for every $x \in B$ the total number of vertices of G contained in the bags of the nodes corresponding to x and its descendants is more than c. As $|X| > 2c$, B is a non empty set. We choose b to be a member of B whose descendants in T do not belong to B. The choice of b and the fact that T is a binary tree ensure that $c < |V_b| \leq 2c$. Note that we obtain the upper bound $2c$ rather than $2c + t$ because (T, χ) is nice. We define $Y = \partial_G(X) \cup V_b$ and observe that (T_b, χ'), where χ' is the restriction of χ on nodes of T_b, is a tree-decomposition of $G[Y]$. As $|\partial_G(X)| \leq t$, the width of this tree-decomposition is at most $2t$. Moreover, it holds that $\partial_G(Y) \subseteq \partial_G(X) \cup \chi(b)$, therefore Y is a $(2t + 1)$-protrusion of G. □

We are ready to prove the main reduction lemma about replacing protrusions.

Lemma 16.18 (Protrusion Replacement Lemma) *Let Π be a problem that has FII. Then for every $t \in \mathbb{Z}^+$, there exists a $c \in \mathbb{Z}^+$ (depending on Π and t), and an algorithm that, given an instance (G, k) of Π and a t-protrusion X in G with $|X| > c$, outputs in $\mathcal{O}(|G|)$ steps an equivalent instance (G^*, k^*) of Π where $|V(G^*)| < |V(G)|$ and $k^* \leq k$.*

16.3 A General Reduction Rule

Proof: Recall that by $\mathcal{F}_{\subseteq[2t+1]}$ we denote the set of boundaried graphs with label sets from $\{1, \ldots, 2t+1\}$ and by $\mathcal{S}_{\subseteq[2t+1]}$ a set of (progressive) representatives for $\equiv_\Pi$ for graphs from $\mathcal{F}_{\subseteq[2t+1]}$. Let

$$c = \max \left\{ |V(Y)| \;:\; Y \in \mathcal{S}_{\subseteq[2t+1]} \right\}.$$

Our algorithm has a hard-wired table in its source code that stores for each boundaried graph G_Y in $\mathcal{F}_{\subseteq[2t+1]}$ on at most $2c$ vertices a boundaried graph $G'_Y \in \mathcal{S}_{\subseteq[2t+1]}$ and a constant $\mu \leq 0$ such that $G_Y \equiv_\Pi G'_Y$. Specifically, for every pair $(F, k) \in \mathcal{F} \times \mathbb{Z}$, we have

$$(G_Y \oplus F, k) \in \Pi \iff (G'_Y \oplus F, k + \mu) \in \Pi. \tag{16.2}$$

The existence of such a constant $\mu \leq 0$ is guaranteed by the fact that $\mathcal{S}_{\subseteq[2t+1]}$ is a set of progressive representatives (see Lemma 16.11). Thus, the size of the table is bounded by some constant $f(c)$, which is roughly proportional to the number of non isomorphic labeled graphs on $2c$ vertices.

We now apply Lemma 16.17 and find in $G[X]$ a $(2t+1)$-protrusion Y of G such that $c < |Y| \leq 2c$. We split G into two boundaried graphs $G_Y = G[Y]$ and $G_R = G - (Y \setminus \partial(Y))$ as follows. Both G_R and G_Y have boundary $\partial(Y)$. Because $|\partial(Y)| \leq 2t+1$, we may label the boundaries of G_Y and G_R with labels from $\{1, \ldots, 2t+1\}$ such that $G = G_Y \oplus G_R$. As $c < |V(G_Y)| \leq 2c$, the algorithm can look up in its table and find a $G'_Y \in \mathcal{S}_{\subseteq[2t+1]}$ and a constant μ such that $G_Y \equiv_\Pi G'_Y$ and G_Y, G'_Y and μ satisfy (16.2). The algorithm outputs

$$(G^*, k^*) = (G'_Y \oplus G_R, k + \mu).$$

Because $|V(G'_Y)| \leq c < |V(G_Y)|$ and $k^* \leq k + \mu \leq k$, it remains to argue that the instances (G, k) and (G^*, k^*) are equivalent. However, this is directly implied by (16.2).

Now, we consider the running time. By Lemma 16.17, the new protrusion Y can be found in $\mathcal{O}(X)$ steps. Splitting G into two graphs can be done in $\mathcal{O}(|G|)$ steps. The time required to look up in the table a representative equivalent to Y is proportional to the size of the table and thus requires a constant number of steps. Here we crucially use the fact that the size of Y does not exceed a constant. Finally, the gluing operation $G'_Y \oplus G_R$ can be done in a number of steps proportional to the number of edges of G. $\square$

Finding a protrusion. Given a graph G and integers t and c, how to find a t-protrusion X whose size is between c and $2c$, if there is any?

First, how to identify that a given set X is a t-protrusion? Following the definition, we have to verify that the size of its boundary and its treewidth do not exceed t. We can do it in time $\mathcal{O}(|G|)$ as follows. We construct the graph $G[X]$ in time $\mathcal{O}(|G|)$ and run the algorithm of Bodlaender (1996), see Proposition 14.21, to decide whether the treewidth of $G[X]$ is at most t in time $\mathcal{O}(|X|)$. Finally, we check in time $\mathcal{O}(|G|)$ whether $\partial(X)$ is of size at most t by going through the vertices of X and counting how many of them have a neighbor outside X.

Because at the end we are looking for a t-protrusion whose size is between $c+1$ and $2c$ for some constant c, we can try all possible vertex subsets of such sizes and check in time $\mathcal{O}(n)$ whether each of the guessed set is a t-protrusion. Running this brute-force approach on an n-vertex graph will bring us to an algorithm of running time $n^{\mathcal{O}(c)}$, which is polynomial. By making use of Lemma 16.17, we can invoke a better strategy: Go through all possible boundary sets S of a t-protrusion. More precisely, we have the following lemma.

Lemma 16.19 *Given an n-vertex graph G and integers $t, c > 0$, there is an algorithm that in time $n^{\mathcal{O}(t)}$ either finds a $(4t + 1)$-protrusion of size between $c + 1$ and $2c$ or concludes correctly that G has no t-protrusion of size more than c.*

Proof: For a vertex set S of size at most t we denote by $\mathcal{C}_S$ the family of vertex sets of the connected components of $G - S$ such that for every $C \in \mathcal{C}_S$ the treewidth of $G[C \cup S]$ is at most t. Let X_S be the set of vertices that are either in S or in some of the vertex sets of $\mathcal{C}_S$. Note that $\partial(X_S) \subseteq S$ and that the treewidth of $G[X_S]$ is at most $2t$. Hence, the set X_S is a $2t$-protrusion. Moreover, every t-protrusion X in G is contained in X_S for $S = \partial(X)$.

Our algorithm goes through every vertex subset S of size at most t and constructs the set X_S (this construction can be done in $\mathcal{O}(n)$ time by checking whether the treewidth of each subgraph $G[C \cup X]$ is at most t). If for each set S the size of the constructed protrusion does not exceed c, we conclude that G has no t-protrusion of size more than c. Otherwise, if for some S we found a $2t$-protrusion X_S of size more than c, we use Lemma 16.17 to construct a $(4t + 1)$-protrusion of size between $c + 1$ and $2c$.

The running time of this algorithm is dominated by the number of times we have to guess sets S, which is $n^{\mathcal{O}(t)}$. ☐

Let us note that the running time $n^{\mathcal{O}(t)}$ in the lemma is not optimal. We explain later how to improve it significantly.

Meta-kernel: Putting things together. Let us recall the definition of the protrusion decomposition of a graph. For integers α, β, and t, an (α, β, t)-protrusion decomposition of G is a rooted tree-decomposition (T, χ) of G such

16.3 A General Reduction Rule

that the degree of the root is at most β, the root bag is of size α, and all other bags are of size at most t. Hence, the vertex set of G can be partitioned into sets $R_0, R_1, \ldots, R_\beta$, such that the size of R_0 is at most α, and each of the sets $N_G[R_i]$, $1 \leq i \leq \beta$, is a t-protrusion and $N(R_i) \subseteq R_0$.

We need the following simple lemma that says that if a graph has a protrusion decomposition and is of a large size, then it should contain a sufficiently large protrusion.

Lemma 16.20 *For every $c, t, k > 0$, a graph G with $(t \cdot k, t \cdot k, t)$-protrusion decomposition and more than $(t \cdot k)(c + 1)$ vertices contains a t-protrusion of size at least $c + 1$.*

Proof: Let (T, χ) be a $(t \cdot k, t \cdot k, t)$-protrusion decomposition of G. For the root r of T we have $|\chi(r)| \leq t \cdot k$. The remaining vertices of the graph are contained in at most $t \cdot k$ t-protrusions. Thus, at least one of these t-protrusions should contain at least

$$\left\lceil \frac{(t \cdot k)(c + 1) + 1 - t \cdot k}{t \cdot k} \right\rceil = c + 1$$

vertices. □

Now all is set to prove the kernelization meta-theorem.

Theorem 16.21 *Every bidimensional linearly separable problem Π that has FII admits a kernel of linear size. The running time of the kernelization algorithm is polynomial, where the exponent of the polynomial depends on the problem Π only.*

Proof: On an instance (G, k) of a bidimensional linearly separable problem Π that has FII and for constants c, t and ℓ we run the following algorithm.

For the input (G, k) apply the protrusion-finder algorithm from Lemma 16.19 on G.

- If the algorithm finds a $(4t + 1)$-protrusion X of size between $c + 1$ and $2c$, apply the protrusion-replacing algorithm from Lemma 16.18 and obtain an equivalent instance (G^*, k^*) of Π. Restart the algorithm with new the input $(G := G^*, k := k^*)$.
- If the algorithm reports that G has no t-protrusion, then
  - If G has more than $\ell \cdot k$ vertices, and Π is a minimization problem, then report that (G, k) is a no-instance.

- If G has more than $\ell \cdot k$ vertices, and Π is a maximization problem, then report that (G, k) is a yes-instance.
- If G has at most $\ell \cdot k$ vertices, then output (G, k).

The algorithm runs in polynomial time: By Lemma 16.18, at every recursive call we decrease the number of vertices in the input graph. Thus, on an n-vertex graph we make at most n recursive calls. For each call the algorithm computes a $(4t + 1)$-protrusion, which by Lemma 16.19 can be done in time $n^{\mathcal{O}(t)}$, and then replaces protrusion, which by Lemma 16.18, takes $\mathcal{O}(n)$ steps.

What remains is to argue that it is possible to select constants c, t, and ℓ such that the algorithm works correctly. We select these constants as follows.

By Theorem 15.15, there is a constant x, depending on Π only, such that G has a $(x \cdot OPT_\Pi(G), x \cdot OPT_\Pi(G), x)$-protrusion decomposition. We select $t = x$.

Lemma 16.18 guarantees that there is a constant y, depending on Π and t only, such that for every graph G with a $(4t + 1)$-protrusion of size between y and $2y$ and an integer k, the instance (G, k) can be reduced to an equivalent instance (G^*, k^*) of Π, where the graph G^* has less vertices than G and $k^* \leq k$. We select $c = y$. Finally, we define $\ell = t(c + 1)$.

The algorithm halts when it cannot select a $(4t+1)$-protrusion of size more than c. By Lemma 16.19, this happens only when G has no t-protrusion of size at least $c + 1$. Suppose that the number of vertices in G is at least $\ell \cdot k + 1$. We claim that $k < OPT_\Pi(G)$. Indeed, if $k \geq OPT_\Pi(G)$, then graph G has a $(t \cdot k, t \cdot k, t)$-protrusion decomposition and, by Lemma 16.20, should contain a t-protrusion of size at least $c + 1$, which is a contradiction.

But when $k < OPT_\Pi(G)$ and Π is a minimization problem, then (G, k) is a no-instance. Similarly, if Π is a maximization problem, then (G, k) is a yes-instance.

Finally, if the size of G is at most $\ell \cdot k$, the algorithm outputs (G, k). Hence the described algorithm is a kernel of linear size. □

Combined with Theorem 16.16, Theorem 16.21 implies the following corollary, which is exactly Theorem 16.2.

Corollary 16.22 *Every bidimensional linearly separable CMSO-optimization problem Π admits a kernel of linear size.*

16.4 Kernelization in Quadratic Running Time

The running time of the meta-kernelization algorithm from Theorem 16.21 is polynomial, however the exponent of the polynomial depends on problem Π. The most time-consuming part of the algorithm is the brute-force search for a t-protrusion of certain size. In this section we explain a much more efficient way of performing this part of the algorithm, which will bring us to an algorithm with quadratic running time.

Let us remind that a vertex set X of a graph G is connected if $G[X]$ is connected. The faster protrusion-finding algorithm is based on the following lemma about the number of connected sets in a graph.

Lemma 16.23 *Let G be a graph. For every $v \in V(G)$, and $p, q \geq 0$, the number of connected vertex subsets $P \subseteq V(G)$ such that*

(i) $v \in P$,
(ii) $|P| = p + 1$, *and*
(iii) $|N_G(P)| = q$,

is at most $\binom{p+q}{p}$. Moreover, there is an algorithm that, given as input a graph G, a vertex $v \in V(G)$ and integers p and q, outputs in time $\mathcal{O}(|E(G)| + |V(G)| \cdot \binom{p+q}{p} \cdot (p+q)^{\mathcal{O}(1)})$ all pairs (P, Q) such that P is a connected vertex set of size $p + 1$ containing v, $Q = N_G(P)$ and $|Q| = q$.

Proof: We assume that the input graph G is provided with the following additional data structure. For every vertex $u \in V(G)$, we can output in time polynomial in p and q the degree of u in G. Moreover, if the degree of u is at most $p + q + 1$, then this structure should allow us to output the list of neighbors of u. Such a data structure can be easily constructed in time $\mathcal{O}(|E(G)| + |V(G)|)$. From now on we assume that we run this preprocessing step and constructed required structure.

For a vertex $v \in V(G)$ and integers $p, q \geq 0$, we denote by $\mathcal{P}_{p,q}(v)$ the family of all sets satisfying the conditions of the lemma. Thus, $\mathcal{P}_{p,q}(v)$ is a family of pairs (P, Q) such that P is a connected set containing v, and such that $|P| = p + 1$, and $Q = N(P)$ is of size q. To prove the lemma, we give an algorithm that enumerates all elements of $\mathcal{P}_{p,q}(v)$ in time $\binom{p+q}{p} \cdot (p+q)^{\mathcal{O}(1)}$. Let us underline that the running time of the algorithm does not depend on the size of graph G. Of course, for that we will strongly use our assumption that the input has already been preprocessed.

To enumerate all sets from $\mathcal{P}_{p,q}(v)$, we use a recursive (or branching) algorithm constructing triples of sets (I, B, U) with the following properties.

- The sets I, B, and U are pairwise disjoint.
- The set I of *inner* vertices is connected; it contains v and $|I| \leq p + 1$.
- The set B of *boundary* vertices satisfies $B \subseteq N(I)$ and $|B| \leq q$.
- The set U of *undecided* vertices satisfies $U \cup B = N(I)$.
- Finally, $|I \cup B \cup U| \leq p + q + 1$.

We refer to such a triple as a *legitimate* triple. The intuition behind the definition of a legitimate triple (I, B, U) is that if $I \cup B \cup U \subseteq P \cup Q$ for some $(P, Q) \in \mathcal{P}_{p,q}(v)$, then the inner vertices of I are in P, the boundary vertices of B belong to Q, and the undecided vertices of U can go either in P or in Q.

More formally, for a legitimate triple $X = (I, B, U)$ we define $\mathcal{P}(X)$ as the family of all sets $(P, Q) \in \mathcal{P}_{p,q}(v)$ such that

- $I \subseteq P$, $B \subseteq Q$, and $U \subseteq P \cup Q$.

When a triple X is not legitimate, we put $\mathcal{P}(X) = \emptyset$.

The recursive algorithm is based on the following observations.

Observation 16.24 $\mathcal{P}(v, \emptyset, N(v)) = \mathcal{P}_{p,q}(v)$.

Proof: For every $(P, Q) \in \mathcal{P}_{p,q}(v)$, the set P should contain v and every vertex of $N(v)$ should be either in P or in Q. □

The next observation follows directly from the definition of the family $\mathcal{P}$.

Observation 16.25 For every pair $(P, Q) \in \mathcal{P}_{p,q}(v)$, $\mathcal{P}(P, Q, \emptyset) = (P, Q)$. Also for every legitimate triple $X = (I, B, U)$ with $|I| = p + 1$, $|B| = q$ and $U = \emptyset$, $\mathcal{P}(X) = (I, B)$.

Observation 16.26 For every legitimate triple $X = (I, B, U)$, and every $u \in U$, $\mathcal{P}(X) = \mathcal{P}(Y) \cup \mathcal{P}(Z)$, where

- $Y = (I \cup \{u\}, B, (U \cup N(u)) \setminus (I \cup \{u\} \cup B))$, and
- $Z = (I, B \cup \{u\}, U \setminus \{u\})$.

Proof: The fact that $\mathcal{P}(X) \supseteq \mathcal{P}(Y) \cup \mathcal{P}(Z)$ follows from the definition of triples Y and Z.

To show that $\mathcal{P}(X) \subseteq \mathcal{P}(Y) \cup \mathcal{P}(Z)$, observe the following. For every $(P, Q) \in \mathcal{P}(X)$, we have $U \subseteq P \cup Q$. Therefore, every vertex $u \in U$ is either in P or in Q.

If $u \in P$, we claim that $(P, Q) \in \mathcal{P}(Y)$. Let us check first that Y is legitimate. Because I is connected and u is adjacent to one of the vertices of I, the set $I \cup \{u\}$ is connected. We have $I \cup \{u\} \subseteq P$, hence $|I \cup \{u\}| \leq p + 1$. The set B satisfies $B \subseteq N(I)$ and because $u \notin B$, $B \subseteq N(I \cup \{u\})$. Also the set B and the set of undecided vertices $(U \cup N(u)) \setminus (I \cup \{u\} \cup B)$ of Y form a partition of the set $N(I \cup \{u\})$. Because $I \cup \{u\} \subseteq P$ and $B \subseteq N(P) = Q$, we have that $(P, Q) \in \mathcal{P}(Y)$.

The proof that for $u \in Q$ we have $(P, Q) \in \mathcal{P}(Z)$ is very similar. In this case, $B \cup \{u\}$ is a subset of $N(P)$. Thus, Z is legitimate and $(P, Q) \in \mathcal{P}(Z)$. □

To enumerate all sets from $\mathcal{P}_{p,q}(v)$ in time independent of the size of the graph G, we need one more observation.

Observation 16.27 If a legitimate triple $X = (I, B, U)$ contains a vertex $u \in U$ with degree at least $p + q + 1$, then $\mathcal{P}(X) = \mathcal{P}(Z)$, where $Z = (I, B \cup \{u\}, U \setminus \{u\})$.

Proof: Let $u \in U$ be a vertex of degree at least $p+q+1$. By Observation 16.26, $\mathcal{P}(X) = \mathcal{P}(Y) \cup \mathcal{P}(Z)$, where $Y = (I \cup \{u\}, B, (U \cup N(u)) \setminus (I \cup \{u\} \cup B))$. But the triple Y is not legitimate because it has in total more than $p+q+1$ vertices in its sets, thus $\mathcal{P}(Y) = \emptyset$ and $\mathcal{P}(X) = \mathcal{P}(Z)$. □

By Observations 16.24, to enumerate all sets from $\mathcal{P}_{p,q}(v)$, it is sufficient to compute $\mathcal{P}(\{v\}, \emptyset, N(v))$.

The recursive algorithm computing $\mathcal{P}(v, \emptyset, N(v))$ starts with the triple $(\{v\}, \emptyset, N(v))$. To compute $\mathcal{P}(X)$ for a legitimate triple $X = (I, B, U)$, the algorithm does the following.

- (Non branching step) If U contains a vertex u of degree at least $p + q + 1$, put $\mathcal{P}(X) = \mathcal{P}(Z)$, where $Z = (I, B \cup \{u\}, U \setminus \{u\})$.
- (Branching step) Select (arbitrarily) a vertex $u \in U$ and put $\mathcal{P}(X) = \mathcal{P}(Y) \cup \mathcal{P}(Z)$, where $Y = (I \cup \{u\}, B, (U \cup N(u)) \setminus (I \cup \{u\} \cup B))$, and $Z = (I, B \cup \{u\}, U \setminus \{u\})$.

By Observations 16.24, 16.25, 16.26, and 16.27, the algorithm outputs all sets $P \in \mathcal{P}_{p,q}(v)$.

Now, let us consider the running time of the algorithm. Due to the preprocessing procedure computing the vertex degrees of the graph, the non branching step of the algorithm is performed in time polynomial in the sizes of the sets B and U, which is $(p+q)^{\mathcal{O}(1)}$. Due to the non branching step, every vertex of U is of degree at most $p + q$. Then we are able to construct the new triples Y and Z in time $(p+q)^{\mathcal{O}(1)}$. Let us note that this is exactly the place where we need the non branching step because otherwise the construction of $U \cup N(u)$ would take time proportional to the number of edges of G.

Hence, up to a factor polynomial in $p+q$, the running time of the algorithm is proportional to the number of its recursive calls, which in turn is at most

$\mathcal{P}(\{v\}, \emptyset, N(v))$. To bound the size of $\mathcal{P}(\{v\}, \emptyset, N(v))$, we prove inductively that for every legitimate triple (I, B, U) appearing in the algorithm, $|\mathcal{P}(I, B, U)| \leq \binom{i+b}{b}$ where $i = p + 1 - |I|$ and $b = q - |B|$. The base of the induction with $i = 0$ and $b = 0$ corresponds to the case in which $|I| = p+1$, $|B| = q$ and $U = \emptyset$. In this case by Observation 16.25, $\mathcal{P}(I, B, U) = I$.

For the inductive step, for the triple $X = (I, B, U)$, we branch into two subproblems Y and Z. In the first subproblem Y, the size of the inner set is decreased by at least one, and in the subproblem Z, the size of the boundary set is decreased by at least one. Thus,

$$|\mathcal{P}(X)| \leq |\mathcal{P}(Y)| + |\mathcal{P}(Z)| \leq \binom{i+b-1}{b} + \binom{i+b-1}{b-1} = \binom{i+b}{b}.$$

Hence, the running time of the algorithm enumerating all pairs from $\mathcal{P}_{p,q}(v)$ is, up to a factor polynomial in p and q, bounded by

$$|\mathcal{P}(\{v\}, \emptyset, N(v))| \leq \binom{p+q}{q}.$$

Finally, running the algorithm for each vertex v, we obtain the statement of the lemma. □

By making use of Lemma 16.23, we can efficiently enumerate in time $2^{\mathcal{O}(p+q)}(n+m)$ all connected sets of a graph G of size at most p and with neighborhood size at most q. Every set is defined by the vertices contained in that set. Actually, the algorithm does a bit more. The algorithm can also output in time $2^{\mathcal{O}(p+q)}(n+m)$ not only the sets P but also the subgraphs $G[P]$ induced by these sets P. However, in the claimed running time the algorithm cannot output the graphs $G[P \cup Q]$. This is due to the way we handle the vertices of high degrees in the non branching step of the algorithm. In this step, if we find a vertex of high degree in the set U, we move it to the set Q. However, we are not able to control the adjacencies of the vertices in Q in time depending on p and q only. So far this is not important, but we will have to come back to this issue in the next section, where we give a linear time implementation of the meta-kernelization algorithm.

For algorithmic purposes, we need a procedure that efficiently partitions sets according to their neighborhoods.

Definition 16.28 (Neighborhood partition) Let $\mathcal{S} = \{S_1, \ldots, S_p\}$ be a family of vertex subsets of a graph G. A partition $\{\mathcal{P}_1, \ldots, \mathcal{P}_t\}$ of $\mathcal{S}$ is the *neighborhood partition of $\mathcal{S}$* if for every $1 \leq i, j \leq p$, the sets S_i and S_j belong to the same class $\mathcal{P}_k$ of the partition if and only if $N_G(S_i) = N_G(S_j)$.

16.4 Kernelization in Quadratic Running Time

In other words, the neighborhood partition of S is the partition of S into its neighborhood-equivalent classes.

Lemma 16.29 *There exists an algorithm with the following specifications. It takes as input a graph G on n vertices and m edges, a family $S = \{S_1, S_2, \ldots, S_\ell\}$ of vertex sets together with the family $\mathcal{N} = \{N_1, \ldots, N_\ell\}$, where $N_i = N_G(S_i)$, and $|N_i| \leq q$ for $i \in \{1, \ldots, \ell\}$. The algorithm runs in time $\mathcal{O}((|S| + n) \cdot q \log q)$ and outputs the neighborhood partition of S.*

Proof: We assume that the vertices of G are labeled by integers from $\{1, \ldots, n\}$. The algorithm starts by sorting each of the sets N_i in increasing order. This takes time $\mathcal{O}(|S| \cdot q \log q)$. Then the algorithm goes over every $j \in \{1, \ldots, q\}$ in increasing order. For each choice of j the algorithm sorts the sets $\{S_1, S_2, \ldots, S_\ell\}$ by the label of the jth vertex of the corresponding set in $\mathcal{N}$ using a stable bucket sort.

Each such bucket sort takes time $\mathcal{O}(|S| + n)$, hence the total running time is $\mathcal{O}((|S| + n) \cdot q \log q)$. When the sorting algorithm is finished, the sets in S are now lexicographically sorted according to their neighborhoods. Because sets with equal neighborhoods appear consecutively in this ordering, going through the ordering in one pass provides the neighborhood partition of S. □

The "bottleneck" in the running time of the kernelization algorithm in Theorem 16.21 is the costly $n^{\mathcal{O}(t)}$-tme procedure of finding an $\mathcal{O}(t)$-protrusion of reasonable size. By making use of Lemmata 16.23 and 16.29, and slightly decreasing the size of the protrusion, we can make this running time linear.

Lemma 16.30 *Given a graph G with n vertices and m edges, and integers $c > 3t > 0$, there is a constant α and an algorithm that in time $f(t,c) \cdot (n+m)$, for some function f of c and t only, either finds an $\alpha \cdot t$-protrusion of size between c/α^t and $2c$, or concludes correctly that G has no t-protrusion of size more than c.*

Proof: Suppose that G has a t-protrusion of size at least c. Then by Lemma 16.17, G has a $(2t + 1)$-protrusion X of size at least $c + 1$ and at most $2c$. Let $S = \partial(X)$ and let $\mathcal{C}_S$ be the family of connected components of $G[X] - S$. Every set $C \in \mathcal{C}_S$ is a connected set of size at most $2c$ and because $N(C) \subseteq S$, the size of its neighborhood is at most $2t + 1$. Also $\text{tw}(G[C]) \leq 2t + 1$.

Because for each $C \in \mathcal{C}_S$ we have $N(C) \subseteq S$, there are at most $2^{|S|} \leq 2^{2t+1}$ different neighborhoods of sets $C \in \mathcal{C}_S$. Let us consider a neighborhood partition $\{\mathcal{P}_1, \ldots, \mathcal{P}_p\}$ of the sets of $\mathcal{C}_S$. Then $p \leq 2^{2t+1}$. Because the total number of vertices in all components $C \in \mathcal{C}_S$ is at least $c - |S| \geq c - 2t - 1$, we have that at least in one of these classes the number of vertices contained in the sets of this class is at least $(c - 2t - 1)/2^{2t+1}$.

Summarizing, if G has a t-protrusion of size at least c, then there is a family of (disjoint) connected sets $C_1, \ldots, C_\ell$, such that

(i) Each of these sets C_i is of size at most $2c$ and the treewidth of the graph induced by $N[C_i]$ is at most $2t + 1$,
(ii) All sets belong to the same neighborhood class, that is $N(C_1) = \cdots = N(C_\ell)$, and the size of this neighborhood is at most $2t + 1$, and
(iii) The total number of vertices of G belonging to these components is at least $(c - 2t - 1)/2^{2t+1}$.

However, the union N of the sets $N[C_1], \ldots, N[C_\ell]$, where sets $C_1, \ldots, C_\ell$ satisfy conditions (i) – (iii), is a $(4t + 1)$-protrusion of size at least $(c - 2t - 1)/2^{2t+1}$. Indeed, the boundary vertices of N are contained in $N(C_1)$. A tree-decomposition of $G[N]$ of width at most $4t + 1$ can be constructed from the forest of tree-decompositions of graphs induced by $N[C_i]$ by adding to each of their bags the vertices of $N(C_1)$ and then adding edges to turn the forest into a tree. We know that by Lemma 16.17, such a protrusion N contains a $(8t + 3)$-protrusion of size at least $(c - 2t - 1)/2^{2t+1}$ and at most $2c$.

To find a family of sets satisfying conditions (i) – (iii), for every $0 \leq p \leq 2c$ and $0 \leq q \leq 2t + 1$, we use Lemma 16.23 to enumerate all pairs (P, Q), where P is a connected set of size $p + 1$ and Q is the neighborhood of P of size q. Then we eliminate all sets P such that $\text{tw}(G[P \cup Q])$ is more than $2t + 1$. Let S be the resulting family.

We use Lemma 16.29 to compute the neighborhood partition of S. If there is an equivalence class in this partition whose sets contain at least $(c - 2t - 1)/2^{2t+1}$ vertices, then the union of these sets and their neighborhoods is a $(4t + 1)$-protrusion X of size at least $(c - 2t - 1)/2^{2t+1}$. We use Lemma 16.17 to obtain from X a $(8t+3)$-protrusion Y whose size is between $(c-2t-1)/2^{2t+1}$ and $2c$. By picking α such that $\alpha \cdot t \geq 8t + 1$ and $(c - 2t - 1)/2^{2t+1} \geq c/\alpha^t$, for example $\alpha = 9$, we obtain the required $\alpha \cdot t$-protrusion. Otherwise, we can correctly report that G has no t-protrusion of size larger than c.

Now, let us consider the running time. By Lemma 16.23, we enumerate all connected sets P of size $p + 1$ and with neighborhood Q of size q in time $2^{\mathcal{O}(c+t)}(n + m)$. For every set P we also output the subgraph $G[P]$. Computing the treewidth of $G[P]$ can be done in time $\mathcal{O}(2^{t^3} \cdot c)$ by making use the algorithm of Bodlaender (1996); see Proposition 14.21. The size of S is $2^{\mathcal{O}(c+t)}n$. Thus, the running time required to compute S is $\mathcal{O}(2^{\mathcal{O}(c+t)} \cdot 2^{t^3} \cdot (n + m))$.

16.4 Kernelization in Quadratic Running Time

By Lemma 16.29, the neighborhood partition of S can be computed in $2^{\mathcal{O}(c+t)}(n+m)$. This gives us the set X. Constructing graph $G[X]$ and then computing its tree-decomposition of width $\mathcal{O}(t)$ will require time $\mathcal{O}((n+m) + 2^{t^3}|X|)$. Then by Lemma 16.17, computing Y is done in time $\mathcal{O}(|X|)$. Thus, the total running time of the algorithm is $\mathcal{O}(2^{t^3} \cdot 2^{\mathcal{O}(t+c)}(n+m)) = f(t,c)(n+m)$.

Let us note that if, instead of using Bodlaender's algorithm, we use a single-exponential linear-time treewidth approximation algorithm (see Proposition 14.21), then the running time of the algorithm would be $\mathcal{O}(2^{\mathcal{O}(t+c)}(n+m))$ but the constant α is larger. □

With the faster protrusion-finder provided by Lemma 16.30, we can modify the proof of Theorem 16.21 such that the running time of the algorithm becomes $\mathcal{O}(n^2)$.

Theorem 16.31 *Every bidimensional linearly separable problem Π that has FII admits a kernel of linear size. For an n-vertex input graph, the running time of the kernelization algorithm is $\mathcal{O}(n^2)$.*

Proof: We run exactly the same algorithm with constants c, t, and ℓ as in Theorem 16.21, except that for finding a $4t$-protrusion we use a linear time algorithm for finding an $\alpha \cdot t$-protrusion from Lemma 16.30: If the algorithm finds an $\alpha \cdot t$-protrusion X of size between $c+1$ and $2c$, apply the protrusion-replacing algorithm from Lemma 16.18 and obtain an equivalent instance (G^*, k^*) of Π. Here α is the constant from Lemma 16.30.

As in Theorem 16.21, the algorithm concludes that

- If G has more than $\ell \cdot k$ vertices, and Π is a minimization problem, then (G, k) is a no-instance;
- If G has more than $\ell \cdot k$ vertices, and Π is a maximization problem, then (G, k) is a yes-instance; and
- If G has at most $\ell \cdot k$ vertices, then the algorithm outputs (G, k).

By Lemma 16.30, it takes time $\mathcal{O}(n+m)$ to find a required $\alpha \cdot t$-protrusion. Because at every step of the algorithm we decrease the number of vertices in the input graph, the total running time is $\mathcal{O}(n^2)$.

The correctness of the algorithm for a specific choice of constants c, t, and ℓ is almost identical to the proof of Theorem 16.21. We observe these small differences and skip the full proof.

The choice of constant t is the same as in Theorem 16.21. That is, t is a constant such that G has a $(t \cdot OPT_\Pi(G), t \cdot OPT_\Pi(G), t)$-protrusion decomposition. By Lemma 16.18, there is a constant y, depending on Π and t only, such that for every graph G with an $\alpha \cdot t$-protrusion of size between y and

$2y$ and integer k, the instance (G,k) can be reduced to an equivalent instance (G^*, k^*) of Π, where graph G^* has less vertices than G and $k^* \leq k$. We select $c = y \cdot \alpha^t$ and put $\ell = t(c+1)$. □

16.5 Linear Time Algorithm

The kernelization algorithm from the previous section uses quadratic time for the following reasons. It repeats n times the following two operations: finding a protrusion and replacing it. Each of these operations requires linear time, and this is why in total we have quadratic running time.

Suppose that we can perform protrusion replacement in time linear in the size of the replaced protrusion and independent of the size of the graph. While Protrusion Replacement Lemma (Lemma 16.18) does not do it, a close investigation of its proof reveals that the only cases requiring scanning the adjacency lists of the whole graph are when we cut and glue protrusions. In particular, for performing ⊕ operation, we need to know the adjacencies between the vertices in the boundary of a protrusion. As we will see, by constructing in linear time a specific data structure, we will be able to perform such an adjacency check efficiently and thus implement protrusion replacements in time $\mathcal{O}(|X|)$, linear in the size of the protrusion and independent of the size of the input graph. However, we need one more idea to get the linear running time.

The second idea is the following. For kernelization we used the argument that if the input graph G is sufficiently large, say larger than $\alpha \cdot OPT_\Pi(G)$ for some contant α, then it should contain a t-protrusion of size at least c, for some constants t and c. With some work these arguments can be extended: For some ε, if the size n of G is at least $\alpha \cdot OPT_\Pi(G)$, then G contains at least εn protrusions of size at least c. By applying fast protrusion replacement to each of these protrusions, we replace each of these protrusions by a smaller one. Thus, in time linear (in n) we obtain an equivalent instance on at most $(1-\delta)n$ vertices.

We apply the same procedure until we are able to find a new set of protrusions. If we are able to compute such a set of protrusions in time linear in the size of the graph, the total running time would be proportional to

$$\mathcal{O}(n + (1-\delta)n + (1-\delta)^2 n + \cdots) = \mathcal{O}\left(\frac{n}{\delta}\right) = \mathcal{O}(n).$$

We say that sets $X, Y \subseteq V(G)$ *touch* if $N_G[X] \cap Y \neq \emptyset$. In other words, sets touch if they have a vertex in common or G has an edge between them. The following notion of protrusion cover will be used through all this section.

16.5 Linear Time Algorithm

Definition 16.32 (Protrusion cover) For integers $c, t > 0$ and graph G, a (c, t)-*protrusion cover* of G is a family $\mathcal{Z} = \{Z_1, \ldots, Z_q\}$ of sets such that

- For every i, $N[Z_i]$ is a t-protrusion in G and $|Z_i| \geq c$, and
- For every $i \neq j$, sets Z_i and Z_j do not touch.

The number q of elements in $\mathcal{Z}$ is the order of $\mathcal{Z}$ and is denoted by $|\mathcal{Z}|$.

Let us remark that according to this definition, families of sets in the protrusion cover do not necessarily cover all the vertices of the graph. However, in the main application of protrusion covers, we construct families of order $\varepsilon \cdot |V(G)|$, for some $\varepsilon > 0$, thus covering a significant part of the graph. Hence, the origin of the name protrusion cover.

Then on the input graph G, the new algorithm will execute the following plan.

- Find a (c, t)-protrusion cover of order $\varepsilon \cdot |V(G)|$,
- Replace each of the protrusions from the cover by a smaller one, and
- Proceed with the reduced graph.

In what follows, we explain why the algorithm is correct, why we obtain a kernel of linear size, and how to implement the algorithm to run in linear time.

We proceed in several steps. Let Π be a bidimensional separable problem.

- The first step is purely combinatorial and is required to prove the correctness of the algorithm. We show that for any choice of parameters c, t, there exists a function $f(c, t)$ and $\varepsilon > 0$ such that every planar graph with more than $f(c, t) \cdot OPT_\Pi(G)$ vertices contains a (c, t)-protrusion cover of order at least $\varepsilon \cdot |V(G)|$.
- We need a fast variant of Lemma 16.18 that allows us to replace a protrusion with a smaller one in time linear in the size of the protrusion.
- We also need a linear time algorithm that, given parameters c, t, and a graph G, either constructs for some $\alpha > 0$ a $(c/\alpha^t, \alpha t)$-protrusion cover of order $\Omega(n)$ or concludes that G has no (c, t)-protrusion cover of order $\Omega(n)$. Note that in the latter case we use the first step to conclude that we have a trivial no-instance (when Π is a minimization problem) or yes-instance (when Π is a maximization problem).

The combination of these steps will bring us a linear time linear kernel.

From protrusion decompositions to protrusion covers. We start from a combinatorial result relating protrusion covers to protrusion decompositions. This result is proved using a sequence of lemmata.

The first lemma shows that if a graph is of small treewidth and of large size, then it has a protrusion cover of large order.

Lemma 16.33 *For integers $c > t \geq 2$ there exists a constant $\varepsilon \geq \frac{1}{122c}$ such that every graph G of treewidth t and with $n \geq 1/\varepsilon$ vertices, contains a $(c, 2t+1)$-protrusion cover of order at least $\varepsilon \cdot n$.*

Proof: Let (T, χ) be a nice tree-decomposition of an n-vertex graph G of width t, where T is a rooted tree with root r. For a subset of nodes $Q \subseteq V(T)$, we define the *size* of Q as the size of

$$\chi(Q) = \bigcup_{q \in Q} \chi(q).$$

In other words, $\chi(Q)$ is the set of vertices of G that are contained in the bags of Q.

For a node $v \in T$, a connected component C of $T - v$ is said to be *below* v if all vertices of C are descendants of v in T. We start by constructing a set $S \subseteq V(T)$ and a family $\mathcal{C} = \{C_1, \ldots, C_{|S|}\}$ of connected components of $T - S$ using the following greedy procedure.

Initially, we put $S = \emptyset$, $\mathcal{C} = \emptyset$, and $T_0 = T$. We maintain the invariant that T_i is the connected component of $T - S$ containing r. At the ith step of the greedy procedure we pick a lowermost node v_i in $V(T_{i-1})$ such that there is a connected component C_i of $T_{i-1} - v_i$ below v_i of size $|\chi(C_i)| \geq 3c + 7(t+1)$. We add v_i to S, C_i to $\mathcal{C}$, and update T_i accordingly. That is, we select T_i to be the connected component of $T_{i-1} - v_i$ containing r.

The procedure terminates when no node v in T_i has this property. Hence, when the procedure terminates, for each node $v \in T_i$ and each of the components C of $T_i - v$ below v, it follows that $|\chi(C)| < 3c + 7(t+1)$. For every node v_i, the sum of the sizes of the components of $T_i - v_i$ below v_i does not exceed $2 \cdot (3c + 7(t+1))$. This is because T is a binary tree and because at every step of the procedure we select the lowermost node v_i such that the size of every connected component of $T_i - v_i$ below v_i is at most $3c + 7(t+1)$, Hence, for every component C of $T - S$,

$$|\chi(C)| < 6c + 14(t+1) \leq 20c. \qquad (16.3)$$

We use (16.3) to bound $|S|$, the cardinality of $\mathcal{C}$. We have that the set of nodes S, together with the nodes of connected components of $T - S$, covers all nodes of T. The tree T is binary, thus $T - S$ has at most $2|S| + 1 \leq 3|S|$ connected components. Every bag $\chi(v)$ is of size at most $(t+1) \leq c$ and by (16.3), for every component C of $T-S$, $|\chi(C)| \leq 20c$. Therefore, $|S| \cdot (t+1) + 3|S| \cdot 20c \geq n$. Because $c \geq t+1$, this implies that $|S| \geq \frac{n}{61c}$.

Having constructed S and $C_1, \ldots, C_{|S|}$, we let $S' = \text{LCA-Closure}(S)$. By Lemma 9.28, $|S'| \leq 2|S|$. Let $S^* = S' \setminus S$. Because $|S^*| \leq |S|$, at most $\frac{|S|}{2}$ of the connected components $C_1, \ldots, C_{|S|}$ contain at least two nodes of S^*. This implies that at least $\frac{|S|}{2}$ of the components $C_1, \ldots, C_{|S|}$ contains at most one node of S^*. Without loss of generality, we assume that each of the components $C_1, \ldots, C_{\lfloor \frac{|S|}{2} \rfloor}$ contains at most one node of S^*. For every $i \leq |S|/2$, if C_i does not contain a node of S^*, then $C'_i = C_i$ is a component of $C \setminus S'$ with $|\chi(C'_i)| \geq 3c + 7(t+1) \geq c + 2(t+1)$. If C_i contains one node v of S^*, because v has degree at most 3 and $|\chi(C_i)| \geq 3c + 7(t+1)$, we have that $T[C_i \setminus \{v\}]$ has at least one component C'_i with $|\chi(C'_i)| \geq c + 2(t+1)$. Thus, we have constructed a set S' and a collection of disjoint connected components $C'_1, \ldots, C'_{\lfloor \frac{|S|}{2} \rfloor}$ of $T - S'$, each with $|\chi(C'_i)| \geq c + 2(t+1)$. By Lemma 9.27, every C'_i has at most two neighbors in T.

We construct protrusion cover $\mathcal{Z}$ as follows. For every $i \leq |S|/2$ let $Z_i = \chi(C'_i) \setminus \chi(S')$. Because C'_i has at most two neighbors in T, it follows that $|N(Z_i)| \leq 2(t+1)$; thus $N[Z_i]$ is a $2(t+1)$-protrusion. Also $|Z_i| \geq c + 2(t+1) - 2(t+1) = c$. Moreover, for any $i \neq j$, sets Z_i do not touch Z_j. Hence, $\mathcal{Z}$ is a $(c, 2(t+1))$-protrusion cover of G of order $\frac{|S|}{2} \geq \frac{n}{122c}$. □

Lemma 16.33 implies the following lemma.

Lemma 16.34 *For any integers $c > t \geq 2$, there exist constants $\delta > 0$ and $d > 0$ such that for every $k > 0$, if a graph G with $n \geq d \cdot k \cdot t$ vertices admits a $(t \cdot k, t \cdot k, t)$-protrusion decomposition, then G has a $(c, 2 \cdot t + 1)$-protrusion cover of order at least $\delta \cdot n$.*

Proof: Let $\varepsilon = \frac{1}{122c}$ be the constant from Lemma 16.33. We define $\delta = \varepsilon/2$ and $d = 2(1 + \frac{1}{\varepsilon^2})$. The reason why these constants are defined the way they are will become clear during the course of the proof.

Because G admits a $(t \cdot k, t \cdot k, t)$-protrusion decomposition, it implies that its vertex set can be partitioned into sets $R_0, R_1, \ldots, R_{tk}$ such that $|R_0| \leq t \cdot k$, and for each $1 \leq i \leq t \cdot k$ we have that $N(R_i) \subseteq R_0$, and $N_G[R_i]$ is a t-protrusion. Then,

$$\sum_{i=1}^{k \cdot t} |R_i| \geq n - t \cdot k. \tag{16.4}$$

Because for every $i \geq 1$, $N(R_i)$ is in R_0, we have that for any $i \neq j \in \{1, \ldots, k \cdot t\}$, sets R_i and R_j do not touch. Thus, the union of protrusion covers of the graphs $G[R_1], \ldots, G[R_{tk}]$ is also a protrusion cover of the graph G. Because for each $i \geq 1$, the treewidth of $G[R_i]$ is at most t, by Lemma 16.33 every $G[R_i]$ with $|R_i| \geq 1/\varepsilon$ contains a $(c, 2t + 1)$-protrusion cover of order at least $\varepsilon \cdot |R_i|$. The total number of vertices contained in all sets R_i of size less that $1/\varepsilon$ is at most $(1/\varepsilon) \cdot k \cdot t$. Therefore, G has a $(c, 2t + 1)$-protrusion cover of order at least

$$\sum_{i=1}^{k \cdot t} \varepsilon |R_i| - (1/\varepsilon) \cdot k \cdot t.$$

By (16.4), we have that

$$\sum_{i=1}^{k \cdot t} \varepsilon |R_i| - (1/\varepsilon) \cdot k \cdot t \geq \varepsilon \cdot \left(n - k \cdot t \cdot \left(1 + \frac{1}{\varepsilon^2} \right) \right).$$

By the choice of constants $\delta = \varepsilon/2$ and $d = 2(1 + \frac{1}{\varepsilon^2})$, and the condition $n \geq d \cdot k \cdot t$, we conclude that

$$\varepsilon \cdot \left(n - k \cdot t \cdot \left(1 + \frac{1}{\varepsilon^2} \right) \right) \geq \varepsilon \frac{n}{2} = \delta n.$$

Hence, G has a $(c, 2t + 1)$-protrusion cover of order δn. □

We summarize the connection between bidimensional problems and protrusion covers in the following theorem.

Theorem 16.35 *Let Π be a bidimensional separable problem and $c > 0$. Then there exist an integer $t > 0$ (depending on Π only), and constants $\varepsilon > 0$ and $d > 0$, such that every planar graph G with more than $d \cdot t \cdot OPT_\Pi(G)$ vertices contains a $(c, 2t)$-protrusion cover of order at least $\varepsilon \cdot |V(G)|$.*

Proof: Because Π is a bidimensional separable problem, by Theorem 15.15, there is a constant t', depending on Π only, such that every planar graph G has a $(t' \cdot OPT_\Pi(G), t' \cdot OPT_\Pi(G), t')$-protrusion decomposition. Let $\delta > 0$ and $d > 0$ be the constants from Lemma 16.34. We put $\varepsilon = \delta$ and $t = 2t' + 1$. Because G has more than $d \cdot t \cdot OPT_\Pi(G) > d \cdot t' \cdot OPT_\Pi(G)$ vertices, by Lemma 16.34 it admits a (c, t)-protrusion cover of order at least $\varepsilon \cdot |V(G)|$. □

Algorithmic part. We assume that graph is represented by adjacency list. Following Cormen et al. (2009), we use an implementation in which the vertices of a graph are represented by index numbers. In this implementation we use an array indexed by vertex numbers. For each vertex the corresponding cell of the array points to a singly linked list of the neighboring vertices of

16.5 Linear Time Algorithm

that vertex. For each vertex u, we call this list the *adjacency list of u*. In this model, to check whether a vertex u is adjacent to a vertex v, one either goes through the adjacency list of u or through the adjacency list of v, which can take time proportional to the number of vertices in the graph. Every protrusion is a set of vertices and is represented as an array of vertices. In this model, to check whether two vertices of a protrusion are adjacent, we might spend time $\Omega(n)$.

For the linear time algorithm, we need a representation that for any two vertices u and v of any protrusion of constant size can check their adjacency in constant time. The representation should also allow us to update the information when we replace one protrusion with another. Roughly, such a representation should keep for every protrusion X the subgraph $G[X]$ induced by X and allow us to update this information when the graph is changing. While the number of protrusions of constant size we are dealing with will be $\mathcal{O}(n)$, a naive approach of going through every pair of vertices of each protrusion and checking their adjacencies could take time $\mathcal{O}(n^2)$ simply because some pairs can be in $\Omega(n)$ protrusions. Thus, we have to be a bit more careful.

Definition 16.36 (Explicit induced subgraph representation) For a graph G and vertex set $X \subseteq V(G)$, an *explicit representation* of $G[X]$ is a list containing the identification numbers of the vertices in X and a list that for every ordered pair (u, v) such that $uv \in E(G[X])$ contains a pointer to the position of u in the adjacency list of v. We refer to the list of edge-pointers as the *edge list*.

If a protrusion X is given together with its explicit representation, then the protrusion replacement from Lemma 16.18 can be performed in time $\mathcal{O}(|X|)$. Indeed, the only operations concerning Lemma 16.18 that required time $\mathcal{O}(n + m)$ were the operations of cutting the graph along the boundary of X and gluing a new protrusion along this boundary. But with an explicit representation of X, these operations clearly can be done in time proportional to the number of edges in $G[X]$, which is $\mathcal{O}(|X|)$. Thus, we obtain the following lemma.

Lemma 16.37 (Fast Protrusion Replacement Lemma) *Let Π be a problem that has FII. Then for every $t \in \mathbb{Z}^+$, there exists a $c \in \mathbb{Z}^+$ (depending on Π and t) and an algorithm that, given an instance (G, k) of Π, a t-protrusion X in G with $|X| > c$, and an explicit representation of X, outputs in $\mathcal{O}(|X|)$ steps an equivalent instance (G^*, k^*) of Π where $|V(G^*)| < |V(G)|$ and $k^* \leq k$.*

The next lemma shows how to compute explicit representations for a family of sets.

Lemma 16.38 *Given a graph G together with a family of vertex sets* $\mathcal{X} = \{X_1, \ldots, X_p\}$, *each of the sets of size at most c, an explicit representation of all $X_i \in \mathcal{X}$ can be computed in time* $\mathcal{O}(c^{\mathcal{O}(1)}(|V(G)| + |E(G)| + |\mathcal{X}|))$.

Proof: Without loss of generality we can assume that all adjacency lists of all vertices of G are sorted in increasing order by their identification numbers. This assumption is justified by listing all edges of G and then sorting them in linear time using two stable bucket sorts, first sorting on the second endpoint and then on the first endpoint.

For each set X_i we produce a list of all the $\mathcal{O}(c^2)$ *potential edges* of X_i. Here by potential edge we mean an ordered triple (u, v, i), where $u, v \in X_i$. We merge the list of potential edges into one list L. Notice that $|L| = \mathcal{O}(c^2) \cdot |\mathcal{X}|$ and that L can be computed in time $\mathcal{O}(|L|)$. Next we sort L in lexicographical order using three stable bucket sorts, first on the third, then the second, and finally on the first coordinate of triples. This also takes time $\mathcal{O}(|L| + |V(G)|)$.

We will now construct the edge lists of the sets $X_1, \ldots, X_p$. Initially all the lists are empty and we make an array of size p, where the ith entry of the array points to the edge list of X_i. We scan through all vertices $u \in V(G)$ in increasing order by their identification numbers. For each $u \in V(G)$, we scan through the adjacency list of u. Notice that this list is also sorted in increasing order. We also maintain a pointer p_L to a position in the list L. Initially this pointer points to the first entry of the list.

When we consider the entry of the adjacency list of u corresponding to an edge uv, we proceed as follows. While p_L points to a potential edge (u', v', i) such that (u', v') is lexicographically smaller than (u, v), we move p_L to the next entry of L. Then while p_L points to a potential edge (u, v, i), we add a pointer to the position of v in the adjacency list of u to the edge list of X_i, and then move p_L to the next entry of L.

Because each entry of L is considered once, and each edge $uv \in E(G)$ is considered twice, the total running time is as claimed.

To see the correctness of the construction, observe that for every vertex u and $v \in N(u)$, when the algorithm considers the pair (u, v), the pointer p_L will scan through all potential edges of the form (u, v, i). This is because all entries of L and all adjacency lists are lexicographically sorted. □

As far as we have learned how to compute in linear time explicit representation of a family of sets, we are to able give a linear time algorithm computing a protrusion cover.

Lemma 16.39 *For every $c > t \geq 2$ there exist $\gamma > 0$ and an algorithm $\mathcal{A}$ with the following specification.*

16.5 Linear Time Algorithm

- The input to $\mathcal{A}$ is a graph G with n vertices and m edges.
- The output of $\mathcal{A}$ is a $(c/\gamma^t, \gamma \cdot t)$-protrusion cover $\mathcal{V} = \{V_1, \ldots, V_z\}$ of G such that the size of each set V_i is at most $6c$.
- The running time of the algorithm is $\mathcal{O}(n+m)$.

Moreover, for every $\varepsilon > 0$, there exists $\delta > 0$ such that if input graph G admits a (c,t)-protrusion cover of order εn, then the order z of the protrusion cover $\mathcal{V}$ is at least δn.

Proof: The correctness of our algorithm is based on the combinatorial result that guarantees the existence of a protrusion cover with specific properties. Informally, we want to show that if G contains a (c, t)-protrusion cover of order εn, then it also contains a protrusion cover of order εn with certain properties. The properties we want of protrusion cover $\{Z_1, \ldots, Z_q\}$ are as follows.

- Every set Z_i is of size $\Theta(c)$.
- For each set Z_i, its connected components in $G[Z_i]$ have equal neighborhoods.

Let $\mathcal{X} = \{X_1, \ldots, X_q\}$ be a (c, t)-protrusion cover of order εn in G.

Claim 16.40 *The graph G contains a $(c, 2t+1)$-protrusion cover $\mathcal{Y} = \{Y_1, \ldots, Y_q\}$ of order εn such that every set Y_i is of size at most $5c$.*

Proof Each set $N[X_i]$ is a t-protrusion of size at least $c + t + 1$. By Lemma 16.17, for every $i \in \{1, \ldots, q\}$, there is a $(2t+1)$-protrusion $X_i \subseteq Y_i$, such that $c \leq |X_i| \leq 2(c+t+1) \leq 5c$. Then $\mathcal{Y} = \{Y_1, \ldots, Y_q\}$ is the required protrusion cover.

Claim 16.41 *The graph G contains a $(\frac{c}{2^{2t+1}}, 2t+1)$-protrusion cover $\mathcal{Z} = \{Z_1, \ldots, Z_q\}$ of order εn such that every set Z_i is of size at most $5c$ and for every set Z_i, all connected components of the graph $G[Z_i]$ have exactly the same neighborhood in G. In other words, for any connected component C of $G[Z_i]$, $N_G(C) = N_G(Z_i)$.*

Proof By Claim 16.40, G contains a $(c, 2t+1)$-protrusion cover $\mathcal{Y} = \{Y_1, \ldots, Y_q\}$ of order εn such that every set Y_i is of size at most $5c$. By the definition of a protrusion cover, each of the sets Y_i has a neighborhood $N(Y_i)$ of size at most $2t+1$. Because the neighborhood of each of the connected components of $G[Y_i]$ belongs to $N(Y_i)$, the neighborhood partition of the connected components of $G[Y_i]$ contains at most 2^{2t+1} equivalent classes. Because the size of Y_i is at least c, the components of at least one of the neighborhood equivalence classes contain in total at least $\frac{c}{2^{2t+1}}$ vertices. This means that there is a set $Z_i \subseteq Y_i$ such that for every connected component C of $G[Z_i]$, $N(C) = N(Z_i) \subseteq N(Y_i)$. Then $\mathcal{Z} = \{Z_1, \ldots, Z_q\}$ is the required protrusion cover.

We put $\gamma = 5$, then $2^{2t+1} \leq \gamma^t$ and $\gamma \cdot t \geq 2t + 1$.

We consider the following Algorithm $\mathcal{A}$ operating in several steps. It takes as input a graph G and integers c, t, and outputs a family $\mathcal{V} = \{V_1, \ldots, V_z\}$ of vertex subsets of G.

Step 1. Use Lemma 16.23 to produce all pairs (P_i, Q_i), $1 \leq i \leq \ell$, such that P_i is a connected vertex set of size at most $5c$ and $Q = N_G(P)$ is of size at most $\gamma \cdot t$.

Step 2. Use Lemma 16.38 to construct explicit representations of all sets $P_i \cup Q_i$, $1 \leq i \leq \ell$.

Step 3. Eliminate all pairs (P, Q) such that the treewidth of $G[P \cup Q]$ is more than γt. Let (P_i, Q_i), $1 \leq i \leq \ell$ be the remaining pairs.

Step 4. Define $\mathcal{P} = \{P_1, P_2, \ldots, P_\ell\}$ and use Lemma 16.29 to compute the neighborhood partition of $\mathcal{P}$. Let $\{\mathcal{P}_1, \ldots, \mathcal{P}_r\}$ be the neighborhood partition of $\mathcal{P}$.

Step 5. Eliminate all equivalent classes whose sets contain in total less than c/γ^t vertices. For each remaining equivalence class $\mathcal{P}_i = \{P_1^i, \ldots, P_s^i\}$, we club the sets P_s^i into groups such that the total number of vertices in each of the groups is at least c/γ^t and at most $6c$. In other words, we obtain a partition of the vertex vertex set $P_1^i \cup \cdots \cup P_s^i$ into sets $W_1^i, \ldots, W_x^i$ such that for each $j \in \{1, \ldots, x\}$, $c/\gamma^t \leq |W_j^i| \leq 6c$. Let us note that because all sets P_j^i are of size at most $5c$, such a partition is always possible. Also because each of the sets W_j^i is the union of some sets from the same class $\mathcal{P}_i$ of the neighborhood partition, we have that $N_G(W_j^i) = N_G(P_1^i)$ for every $j \in \{1, \ldots, x\}$. Finally, let $\mathcal{W} = \{W_1, \ldots, W_y\}$ be the family of all sets W_j^i, $i \in \{1, \ldots, s\}$ and $j \in \{1, \ldots, x\}$.

Step 6. Construct an auxiliary graph $G_\mathcal{W}$. The vertices of $G_\mathcal{W}$ are sets of $\mathcal{W}$, and two vertices are adjacent if and only if the corresponding sets touch. Let Δ be the maximum vertex degree of $G_\mathcal{W}$. Find an independent set of size at least $|V(G_\mathcal{W})|/(\Delta + 1)$ in $G_\mathcal{W}$. Let $\mathcal{V} = \{V_1, \ldots, V_z\}$, $z \geq |V(G_\mathcal{W})|/(\Delta + 1)$ be the family of the corresponding (pairwise non touching) sets from $\mathcal{W}$.

Step 7. Output $\mathcal{V} = \{V_1, \ldots, V_z\}$.

First of all, $\mathcal{V} = \{V_1, \ldots, V_z\}$ is a $(c/\gamma^t, \gamma \cdot t)$-protrusion cover and the size of each set V_i is at most $6c$. Indeed, by the construction of $\mathcal{W} = \{W_1, \ldots, W_y\}$,

16.5 Linear Time Algorithm

for each $1 \leq i \leq y$, the set $N[W_i]$ is a $\gamma \cdot t$ protrusion, and the size of set W_i is at least c/γ^t and at most $6c$. The only reason why $\mathcal{W}$ may not be a $(\frac{c}{\gamma^t}, \gamma \cdot t)$-protrusion cover is that the sets of $\mathcal{W}$ can touch each other. Thus, when we select a subset $\mathcal{V} = \{V_1, \ldots, V_z\}$ of sets from $\mathcal{W}$ that are pairwise non touching, we obtain a $(c/\gamma^t, \gamma \cdot t)$-protrusion cover.

Now we argue now that if G has a (c, t)-protrusion cover of order εn, then:

- The set $\mathcal{V} = \{V_1, \ldots, V_z\}$ produced by the algorithm is the required protrusion cover, and
- The algorithm can be implemented to run in linear time.

We prove each of the arguments as a separate claim.

Claim 16.42 *If G admits a (c, t)-protrusion cover of order εn, then $\mathcal{V} = \{V_1, \ldots, V_z\}$ is a $(c/\gamma^t, \gamma \cdot t)$-protrusion cover of order δn, where*

$$\delta \geq \frac{\varepsilon}{6\gamma^t} \cdot \frac{1}{\binom{5c+\gamma t}{\gamma t} \cdot (6c + \gamma t)^2 + 1}.$$

Proof By Claim 16.41, G contains a $(\frac{c}{\gamma^t}, \gamma \cdot t)$-protrusion cover $\mathcal{Z} = \{Z_1, \ldots, Z_q\}$ of order $q = \varepsilon n$ such that every set Z_i is of size at most $5c$ and for every set Z_i, all connected components of the graph $G[Z_i]$ have exactly the same neighborhood in G.

Each of the vertex sets Z_i is of size at most $5c$, the size of its neighborhood is at most γt and the treewidth of $G[Z_i \cup N(Z_i)]$ is at most γt. In Step 1 we enumerate all sets P_i of size at most $5c$ with neighborhood Q_i of size at most γt. In Step 3 we eliminated all pairs whose induced subgraph is of treewidth more than γt. Thus, after Step 3, for every connected component C of $G[Z_i]$, there is a set $P \in \mathcal{P} = \{P_1, P_2, \ldots, P_\ell\}$ such that $C = P$. Therefore, all vertices contained in sets of $\mathcal{Z}$ with the same neighborhood are also contained in the sets of the same class of neighborhood partition of $\mathcal{P}$. In other words, let $\{\mathcal{Z}_1, \ldots, \mathcal{Z}_a\}$ be the neighborhood partition of $\mathcal{Z} = \{Z_1, \ldots, Z_q\}$. Then we can denote a neighborhood partition of $\mathcal{P}$ by $\{\mathcal{P}_1, \ldots, \mathcal{P}_r\}$ with $r \geq a$ such that for every $i \leq a$, $\mathcal{Z}_i \subseteq \mathcal{P}_i$. (By writing $\mathcal{Z}_i \subseteq \mathcal{P}_i$ for families of sets $\mathcal{Z}_i$ and $\mathcal{P}_i$, we mean that for every set $Z \in \mathcal{Z}_i$ there is a set $P \in \mathcal{P}_i$ such that $Z = P$.) In particular, every vertex v of G that is contained in some set from the equivalence class $\mathcal{Z}_i$ also belongs to some set from $\mathcal{P}_i$.

Because each of the sets from $\mathcal{Z}_i$ contains at least c/γ^t vertices, we have that the number of vertices of G covered by sets from $\mathcal{Z}_i$ is at least

$$\frac{c \cdot |\mathcal{Z}_i|}{\gamma^t}. \tag{16.5}$$

Here we use $|\mathcal{Z}_i|$ to denote the number of sets in the family $\mathcal{Z}_i$. With this notation, the number q of sets in the protrusion cover $\mathcal{Z} = \{Z_1, \ldots, Z_q\}$ is

$$q = \sum_{i=1}^{a} |\mathcal{Z}_i|.$$

Every set W^i_j, which was formed by grouping sets of $\mathcal{P}_i = \{P^i_1, \ldots, P^i_s\}$ in Step 5, is of size at most $6c$. Thus, the number of sets $W^i_1, \ldots, W^i_x$ we create at this step is at least the number of vertices covered by all sets from $\mathcal{P}_i$ divided by $6c$. Because $\mathcal{Z}_i \subseteq \mathcal{P}_i$, by (16.5), we have that for each i we created at least

$$\frac{|\mathcal{Z}_i|}{6c \cdot \gamma^t}$$

sets. Because the sets of the protrusion cover $\mathcal{Z}$ do not touch, and thus disjoint, we have that the family $\mathcal{W} = \{W_1, \ldots, W_y\}$, produced in Step 5, is of order

$$y \geq \sum_{i=1}^{a} \frac{|\mathcal{Z}_i|}{6c \cdot \gamma^t} = \frac{q}{6c \cdot \gamma^t} = \frac{\varepsilon n}{6c \cdot \gamma^t}.$$

Moreover, the size of each of the sets W_i is at least c/γ^t and $N[W_i]$ is a γt-protrusion. However, sets from $\mathcal{W}$ can touch each other.

In Step 6 we produce a maximal subfamily $\mathcal{V} = \{V_1, \ldots, V_z\}$ of pairwise non touching sets of $\mathcal{W}$. Thus, the family $\mathcal{V}$ is a $(\frac{c}{\gamma^t}, \gamma \cdot t)$-protrusion cover, so it only remains to bound its order z. By Lemma 16.23, every vertex $v \in W_i$ is contained in at most $\binom{5c+\gamma t}{\gamma t} \cdot (5c + \gamma t)$ sets W_j. Hence, the number of sets intersecting W_i is at most

$$\binom{5c + \gamma t}{\gamma t} \cdot (5c + \gamma t) \cdot |W_i|.$$

Similarly, the number of sets intersecting the neighborhood of W_i is at most

$$\binom{5c + \gamma t}{\gamma t} \cdot (5c + \gamma t) \cdot |N(W_i)|.$$

Thus, each set W_i touches at most

$$\binom{5c + \gamma t}{\gamma t} \cdot (5c + \gamma t) \cdot (|N(W_i)| + |W_i|) \leq \binom{5c + \gamma t}{\gamma t}(6c + \gamma t)^2 \quad (16.6)$$

sets. By Brook's theorem, the chromatic number of an n-vertex graph of maximum vertex degree Δ is at most $\Delta + 1$. Thus, such a graph contains an

16.5 Linear Time Algorithm

independent set of size at least $n/(\Delta + 1)$. The graph $G_{\mathcal{W}}$ has $y \geq \frac{q}{6\gamma^t} = \frac{\varepsilon n}{6\gamma^t}$ vertices and its maximum vertex degree is at most

$$\binom{5c + \gamma t}{\gamma t}(6c + \gamma t)^2.$$

Hence, the order z of the $(\frac{c}{\gamma^t}, \gamma \cdot t)$-protrusion cover $\mathcal{V}$ is at least

$$\frac{\varepsilon n}{6\gamma^t} \cdot \frac{1}{\binom{5c+\gamma t}{\gamma t} \cdot (6c + \gamma t)^2 + 1} = \delta n.$$

Claim 16.43 *Algorithm $\mathcal{A}$ can be implemented to run in time $\mathcal{O}(n + m)$.*

Proof We analyze the running time of the algorithm step by step.

By Lemma 16.23, in Step 1 the number of pairs (P_i, Q_i) produced by the algorithm is at most $n \cdot \binom{5c+\gamma t}{\gamma t} \cdot (5c+\gamma t)^{\mathcal{O}(1)}$ and all these pairs are enumerated in time $\mathcal{O}(m + n \cdot \binom{5c+\gamma t}{\gamma t} \cdot (5c + \gamma t)^{\mathcal{O}(1)}) = \mathcal{O}(n + m)$.

In Step 2 we compute explicit representations of all sets $P_i \cup Q_i$. By Lemma 16.38, this takes time $\mathcal{O}((n + m + \binom{5c+\gamma t}{\gamma t}) \cdot (5c + \gamma t)^{\mathcal{O}(1)})$. As far as we have explicit representations of all the sets $P_i \cup Q_i$, deciding whether the treewidth of the graph $G[P_i \cup Q_i]$ is at most γt takes time $\mathcal{O}((5c+\gamma t) \cdot 2^{\mathcal{O}(t^2)})$, see Proposition 14.21. Thus, Step 3 takes time

$$\mathcal{O}(2^{\mathcal{O}(t^2)}) \cdot n \cdot \binom{5c + \gamma t}{\gamma t} \cdot (5c + \gamma t)^{\mathcal{O}(1)}) = \mathcal{O}(n + m).$$

By Lemma 16.29, the time required to find the neighborhood partition $\{\mathcal{P}_1, \ldots, \mathcal{P}_r\}$ of $\mathcal{P}$ in Step 4 is

$$\mathcal{O}((m + n) \cdot \binom{5c + \gamma t}{\gamma t} \cdot (5c + \gamma t)^{\mathcal{O}(1)}) = \mathcal{O}(n + m).$$

In Step 5 we can use a greedy algorithm that for each neighborhood-partition class $\mathcal{P}_i = \{P_1^i, \ldots, P_s^i\}$ groups its sets in time $\mathcal{O}(|P_1^i \cup \cdots \cup P_s^i|)$. Thus, $\mathcal{W} = \{W_1, \ldots, W_y\}$ is constructed in time linear in n and m.

Finally, for Step 6 we again use a greedy algorithm. An independent set of size $k/(\Delta + 1)$ in a k-vertex graph of degree Δ can be obtained by repeating the following procedure. We pick a vertex, add it to the independent set, and delete its neighbors from the graph. Thus, in the algorithm, we select a set W_i to be added to $\mathcal{V}$ and delete all sets touching W_i. By (16.6), the number of sets touching W_i is a constant depending on c, t, and γ only. Therefore, the construction of the family $\mathcal{V}$ also takes time $\mathcal{O}(|\mathcal{W}|) = \mathcal{O}(n + m)$.

The proof of the lemma follows from Claims 16.42 and 16.43. □

We are ready to prove the main result of this section.

Theorem 16.44 *Every bidimensional linearly separable problem Π that has FII admits a kernel of linear size. For an n-vertex input planar graph, the running time of the kernelization algorithm is $\mathcal{O}(n)$.*

Proof: The outline of the algorithm is very similar to the algorithm from Theorem 16.21. The main difference is that instead of finding a protrusion, we compute a protrusion cover and replace all protrusions in parallel.

On an instance (G, k) of a bidimensional linearly separable problem Π that has FII and for constants c, t, ε and ℓ, we run the following algorithm.

> Let γ be the constant defined in Lemma 16.39. For an input (G, k), we apply the algorithm that computes a protrusion cover from Lemma 16.39 on G.
>
> - If the algorithm finds a $(c/\gamma^t, \gamma t)$-protrusion cover $\mathcal{V} = \{V_1, \ldots, V_z\}$ of order $z = \delta \cdot |V(G)|$, where δ is the constant from Lemma 16.39 that depends only on ε, γ, c, and t (this dependence is given in Claim 16.42), then for each protrusion $N_G[V_i]$, we apply the Fast Protrusion Replacement Lemma (Lemma 16.37). Thus, we obtain an equivalent instance (G^*, k^*) of Π. Then, we restart the algorithm with $(G := G^*, k := k^*)$ as input.
> - If the algorithm fails to find a $(c/\gamma^t, \gamma t)$-protrusion cover of order $z = \delta \cdot |V(G)|$, then
>   - If G has more than $\ell \cdot k$ vertices, and Π is a minimization problem, then report that (G, k) is a no-instance.
>   - If G has more than $\ell \cdot k$ vertices, and Π is a maximization problem, then report that (G, k) is a yes-instance.
>   - If G has at most $\ell \cdot k$ vertices, then output (G, k).

We need to show that the algorithm can be implemented to run in linear time and that for a certain choice of constants it works correctly. We start with the running time.

By Lemma 16.39, the protrusion cover $\mathcal{V} = \{V_1, \ldots, V_z\}$ is computed in time $\mathcal{O}(|V(G)| + |E(G)|)$. Because G is planar, $\mathcal{O}(|V(G)| + |E(G)|) = \mathcal{O}(|V(G)|)$. Moreover, in the process of implementation of the algorithm of Lemma 16.39, we compute explicit representations of all γt-protrusions $N[V_i]$, $i \in \{1, \ldots, z\}$. Each of the sets V_i is of size at most $6c$, thus the size of the protrusion is $|N[V_i]| \leq 6c + \gamma t$. By the Fast Protrusion Replacement Lemma, the replacement step for each protrusion takes time $\mathcal{O}(6c + \gamma t) = \mathcal{O}(1)$. Hence, computing the new instance (G^*, k^*) takes time $\mathcal{O}(|\mathcal{V}|) = \mathcal{O}(|V(G)|)$.

16.5 Linear Time Algorithm

Because at each iteration of the algorithm we reduce at least $\delta |V(G)|$ disjoint sets of the protrusion cover, the size of the reduced graph G^* is at most $(1 - \delta)|V(G)|$. Hence, the total running time of the algorithm is $\mathcal{O}(n + (1 - \delta)n + (1 - \delta)^2 n + \cdots) = \mathcal{O}(\frac{n}{\delta}) = \mathcal{O}(n)$.

It only remains to argue that it is possible to select constants c, t, ε, and ℓ such that the algorithm works correctly. We select these constants as follows.

By Theorem 16.35, there exists an integer $t > 0$ (depending on Π only) and constants $\varepsilon > 0$ and $d > 0$ such that every planar graph G with more than $d \cdot t \cdot OPT_\Pi(G)$ vertices contains a (c, t)-protrusion cover of order at least $\varepsilon \cdot |V(G)|$. We take c, t, ε from this theorem and $\ell = dt$.

By Lemma 16.39, if the algorithm does not find a $(c/\gamma^t, \gamma \cdot t)$-protrusion cover of order δn, then G has no (c, t)-protrusion cover of order $\varepsilon \cdot |V(G)|$. Then by Theorem 16.35, if the number of vertices in G is at least $\ell \cdot k + 1$, then $k < OPT_\Pi(G)$. Hence, when $k < OPT_\Pi(G)$ and Π is a minimization problem, we can correctly conclude that (G, k) is a no-instance. Similarly, if Π is a maximization problem, then (G, k) is a yes-instance.

Finally, if the size of G is at most $\ell \cdot k$, the algorithm outputs (G, k) and thus the described algorithm is a kernel of linear size. □

Combined with Theorem 16.16, Theorem 16.44 implies the following corollary.

Corollary 16.45 *Every bidimensional linearly separable CMSO-optimization problem Π admits a kernel of linear size. For an n-vertex input planar graph, the running time of the kernelization algorithm is $\mathcal{O}(n)$.*

Exercises

Problem 16.1 Prove that

- VERTEX COVER,
- FEEDBACK VERTEX SET,
- TREEWIDTH-η MODULATOR,
- DOMINATING SET,
- CONNECTED DOMINATING SET,
- CONNECTED VERTEX COVER, and
- CONNECTED FEEDBACK VERTEX SET

are CMSO-optimization problems.

Problem 16.2 Prove that the relation $\equiv_\Pi$ is an equivalence relation.

Problem 16.3 Let Π be a parameterized graph problem that has FII. For a finite $I \subseteq \mathbb{Z}^+$, show that the number of equivalence classes of $\equiv_\Pi$ that are subsets of $\mathcal{F}_I$ depends only on $|I|$.

Problem 16.4 Prove Lemma 16.11 when Π is a positive extended parameterized problem.

Problem 16.5 Let Π be a parameterized graph problem with a signature function that satisfies the two properties in Section 16.2, then Π has FII.

Problem 16.6 Prove that LONGEST PATH does not have FII.

Problem 16.7 Prove that the negative extension of INDEPENDENT SET does not have FII.

Bibliographic Notes

The idea of graph replacement for algorithms dates back to Fellows and Langston (1989). Arnborg et al. (1993) proved that every set of graphs of bounded treewidth that is definable by a Monadic Second Order Logic (MSO) formula is also definable by reduction. By making use of algebraic reductions, Arnborg et al. (1993) obtained a linear time algorithm for MSO-expressible problems on graphs of bounded treewidth. Bodlaender and de Fluiter (1996), Bodlaender and van Antwerpen-de Fluiter (2001), and de Fluiter (1997) generalized these ideas in several ways—in particular, they applied it to a number of optimization problems. We also mention the work of Bodlaender and Hagerup (1998), who used the concept of graph reduction to obtain parallel algorithms for MSO-expressible problems on graphs of bounded treewidth.

The notion of Finite Integer Index was introduced in the thesis of de Fluiter (1997); see also Bodlaender and de Fluiter (1996).

The general framework of meta-kernelization and protrusion replacing technique was developed in Bodlaender et al. (2009a, 2016b). Kernelization of bidimensional problems was obtained in Fomin et al. (2010, 2016a). The proof of Theorem 16.16 is given in Fomin et al. (2016a).

The results discussed in this chapter could be extended to more general classes of graphs. The planar excluded grid theorem (Theorem 14.56) can be generalized to graphs excluding some fixed graph H as a minor, that is, H-minor-free graphs. Demaine and Hajiaghayi (2008b) proved that for every fixed graph H and integer $t > 0$, every H-minor-free graph G of treewidth more than $\alpha_H t$ contains $\boxplus_t$ as a minor, where α_H is a constant depending on H only. Using this, it is possible to show that the treewidth-parameter bound $\mathrm{tw}(G) \leq \alpha_Q \cdot \sqrt{OPT_Q(G)}$ holds for much more general classes of apex-minor-free graphs. An apex graph is a graph obtained from a planar graph G by adding one vertex and making it adjacent to an arbitrary subset of vertices of G. Then a class of graphs is apex-minor-free if every graph in this class does not contain some fixed apex graph as a minor. Thus, for example, the arguments we use in this chapter can be easily adapted to imply a linear kernel for DOMINATING SET on apex-minor-free graphs, but do not imply such an algorithm for general H-minor-free graphs. While DOMINATING SET admits a linear kernel on H-minor-free graphs, the algorithm requires additional ideas, see Fomin et al. (2012a) and Drange et al. (2016a).

When we relax the notion of (contraction) bidimensionality to minor bidimensionality, that is, we require that the problem Q is minor-closed and $OPT_Q(\boxplus_t) = \Omega(t^2)$, then for minor-bidimensional problems the kernelization algorithm from this section hold even for H-minor-free graphs. Therefore, for example, FEEDBACK VERTEX SET admits linear kernel on graphs excluding a fixed minor.

Lemma 16.23 is due to Fomin and Villanger (2012). It can be seen as a variation of the Two-Families theorem of Bollobás (1965). The observation on the size of an independent set in graphs of bounded degree in Lemma 16.39 is based on Brooks theorem from Brooks (1941).

The notion of protrusion cover (in a slightly different form) is taken from Fomin et al. (2012b). Linear time kernelization algorithm follows ideas from Fomin et al. (2012b) and Fomin et al. (2015b).

The kernelization algorithm discussed in this chapter are non constructive in the following sense. The theorems show the existence of kernelization algorithms, but they do not provide a way to construct such algorithms. Non constructiveness is due to the protrusion replacing procedure. Here we prove that if the size of a protrusion is larger than some constant c, which depends on the sizes of graphs in progressive representatives of the corresponding boundary graph, then we can replace this protrusion. However, the algorithm does not provide a way to compute this constant c. This issue is addressed in the work of Garnero et al. (2015).

Other kernelization meta-theorems based on the techniques explained in this chapter, can be found in Fomin et al. (2016c), Gajarský et al. (2017), Kim et al. (2016), and Ganian et al. (2016).

PART III

Lower Bounds

17
Framework

In this chapter we define the framework that will be used to establish lower bounds on some problem kernels. We define polynomially bounded distillation algorithms and prove a fundamental theorem about such algorithms. We use this theorem to show that LONGEST PATH does not admit polynomial kernels subject to a popular assumption from complexity theory. Then we define OR-cross-compositions of languages, and use this to show that STEINER TREE and CLIQUE (VC) do not admit polynomial kernels either.

The starting point of this book was Lemma 1.4. This lemma implies that a problem has a kernel if and only if it is fixed-parameter tractable. The tools offered by Parameterized Complexity allow us to distinguish between fixed-parameter tractable and intractable problems. However, we are interested in kernels that are as small as possible, and a kernel obtained using Lemma 1.4 has size that equals the dependence on k in the running time of the best-known FPT algorithm for the problem. The natural question is—can we do better? In particular, can we get polynomial-sized kernels for problems that admit FPT algorithms? As we saw in the previous chapters, many such problems admit polynomial kernels. However, for some problems like EDGE CLIQUE COVER (Theorem 2.12), we were able to provide only a kernel of exponential (in k) size. The goal of this part of the book is to provide the intractability theory of kernelization that allows us to identify problems that are unlikely to have polynomial kernels.

To begin with, we consider the following problem. In LONGEST PATH, we are given an undirected graph G and a nonnegative integer k. The task is to decide whether G contains a (simple) path of length at least k.

It is well known that the LONGEST PATH problem is fixed-parameter tractable. There are many parameterized algorithms developed for this problem, see Cygan et al. (2015) for an overview of different algorithms for LONGEST PATH. In particular, the problem can be solved in time $2^{\mathcal{O}(k)} n^{\mathcal{O}(1)}$, where n is the number of vertices in the input graph G. Thus by Lemma 1.4, we deduce that LONGEST PATH admits a kernel of size $2^{\mathcal{O}(k)}$. But what about a kernel of polynomial size?

We argue that intuitively this should not be possible. Assume that LONGEST PATH admits a polynomial kernel of size k^c, where c is some fixed constant. We take many instances,

$$(G_1, k), (G_2, k), \ldots, (G_t, k),$$

of the LONGEST PATH problem, where in each instance $|V(G_i)| = n$, $1 \leq i \leq t$, and $k \leq n$. If we make a new graph G by just taking the disjoint union of the graphs $G_1, \ldots, G_t$, we see that G contains a path of length k if and only if G_i contains a path of length k for some $i \leq t$. Now run the kernelization algorithm on G. Then kernelization algorithm would in polynomial time return a new instance (G', k') such that $|V(G')| \leq k^c \leq n^c$, a number potentially much smaller than t, for example set $t = n^{1000c}$. This means that in some sense, the kernelization algorithm considers the instances $(G_1, k), (G_2, k), \ldots, (G_t, k)$ and in *polynomial time* figures out which of the instances are the most likely to contain a path of length k. More precisely, if we have to preserve the value of the OR of our instances while being forced to forget at least one of the inputs entirely, then we have to make sure that the input being forgotten was not the only one whose answer is yes (otherwise we turn a yes-instance into a no-instance). However, at least intuitively, this seems almost as difficult as solving the instances themselves, and because the LONGEST PATH problem is NP-complete, this seems unlikely. In what follows, we formalize this intuition.

17.1 OR-Distillation

We start with the crucial definition.

Definition 17.1 (Distillation algorithm) Let $L, R \subseteq \{0, 1\}^*$ be a pair of languages and let $t \colon \mathbb{N} \to \mathbb{N} \setminus \{0\}$ be a function. Then a *t-bounded* OR-*distillation* algorithm from L into R is an algorithm that for every n, given as input $t(n)$ strings $x_1, \ldots, x_{t(n)}$ with $|x_i| = n$ for all i,

- Runs in polynomial time, and
- Outputs a string y of length at most $t(n) \cdot \log n$ such that $y \in R$ if and only if $x_i \in L$ for some $i \in \{1, \ldots, t(n)\}$.

The strategy of using distillation to rule out the existence of polynomial kernels is to combine the following facts.

- As we will see in Theorem 17.3, the existence of a polynomially bounded distillation for any NP-hard language implies a complexity-theoretic collapse, and is therefore considered very unlikely.
- For some parameterized problems L, one can show that the existence of a polynomial kernel would imply the existence of a polynomially bounded distillation for an NP-hard problem related to L. Hence, it is unlikely that such a polynomial kernel exists.

Distillation algorithms are also often called OR-distillation because the answer to the output instance of R is equivalent to the logical OR of the answers to the input instances of L.

The main property of distillation algorithms is provided in Theorem 17.3. To state this theorem, let us recall the definition of complexity class NP/poly. For more details on computational complexity we refer to Arora and Barak (2009).

Definition 17.2 (**Class** NP/poly) We say that a language L belongs to the complexity class NP/poly if there is a Turing machine M and a sequence of strings $(\alpha_n)_{n=0,1,2,\ldots}$, called *advice*, such that:

- Machine M, when given an input x of length n, has access to the string α_n and has to decide whether $x \in L$. Machine M works in *nondeterministic polynomial time*.
- $|\alpha_n| \leq p(n)$ for some polynomial $p(\cdot)$.

In the first condition, nondeterministic polynomial time means that the run of the algorithm is nondeterministic, and by deciding a problem nondeterministically, we mean that if the answer is yes, then at least one computation path answers yes, and if the answer is no, then all computation paths answer no. Note that in this definition α_n depends only on n. Thus, for each n we need to design a "global" advice α_n that will work for all the inputs of length n.

As the basis of additional lower bounds on kernelization, it is assumed that the containment coNP $\subseteq$ NP/poly is not true (see the "Bibliographic Notes" in this chapter). Briefly, the containment coNP $\subseteq$ NP/poly may be viewed as a variant of the hypothesis coNP = NP, and it is considered to be highly implausible.

For language $L \subseteq \{0, 1\}^*$, we let $\bar{L} = \{0, 1\}^* \setminus L$ denote the complement of L. We remark that in what follows, we use the term *NP-hard* with respect to Karp reductions.

Theorem 17.3 *If there is a t-bounded OR-distillation algorithm from a language $L \subseteq \{0, 1\}^*$ into a language $R \subseteq \{0, 1\}^*$ for some polynomially bounded function t, then $\bar{L} \in \text{NP}/\text{poly}$.*

In particular, if L is NP-hard then $\text{coNP} \subseteq \text{NP}/\text{poly}$.

Proof: The idea of the proof is to show that there is a nondeterministic Turing machine that, with the help of a polynomial amount of advice, decides $\bar{L}$ in polynomial time. Specifically, by using a distillation and advice, one can obtain a polynomial-time verifiable witness of nonmembership of an instance x_1 in a language as follows: If y is known to be a no-instance hard-coded in the advice, and there is some series of inputs $x_2, \ldots, x_t$ that together with x_1 is mapped to y by the distillation (verifiable in polynomial time), then the answer of x_1 must be false because the OR is false.

We start with a simple lemma, which will allow us to implement the approach previously mentioned. To understand the relevance of this lemma, think of β in the context of the functionality of distillation, and remember that we want to find y that "implies" the classification of as many inputs x as possible.

Lemma 17.4 *Let X, Y be finite sets, p be a natural number, and*

$$\beta: \underbrace{X \times \cdots \times X}_{p} \to Y$$

be a mapping. We say that $y \in Y$ covers $x \in X$ if there exist $x_1, \ldots, x_p \in X$ such that $x_i = x$ for some i, $1 \leq i \leq p$, and $\beta((x_1, \ldots, x_p)) = y$. Then at least one element from Y covers at least $|X|/\sqrt[p]{|Y|}$ elements of X.

Proof: Let $X^p = \underbrace{X \times \cdots \times X}_{p}$. By the pigeonhole principle, there is $y \in Y$ such that β maps at least $|X|^p/|Y|$ elements of X^p to y. Let $\mathcal{X}_y$ be the set of tuples in X^p mapped to y. Let Z be the set of elements occurring in at least one tuple in $\mathcal{X}_y$; then all elements in Z are covered by y. Because $\mathcal{X}_y$ consists of at least $|X|^p/|Y|$ tuples, each of which consists of p elements of Z, it follows that $|Z|^p \geq |X|^p/|Y|$. □

For $n \in \mathbb{N}$, let $\bar{L}_n = \{x \in \bar{L} \mid |x| = n\}$. Thus, $\bar{L}_n$ consists of all strings of length n that are not in L.

17.1 OR-Distillation

We set $\alpha(n) = t(n) \log t(n)$. Let $\mathcal{A}$ be a t-bounded OR-distillation algorithm from L into R. Then for each input $x_1, \ldots, x_{t(n)}$ such that for all $i \in [t(n)]$, $x_i \in \bar{L}_n$, $\mathcal{A}$ outputs a string y of length at most $\alpha(n)$ such that $y \in \bar{R}$. We define $\bar{R}_{\alpha(n)} = \{y \in \bar{R} \mid |y| \leq \alpha(n)\}$. Thus, to each $t(n)$-tuple $x_1, \ldots, x_{t(n)}$ with $x_i \in \bar{L}_n$ for all $1 \leq i \leq t(n)$, the distillation algorithm $\mathcal{A}$ maps a string from $\bar{R}_{\alpha(n)}$. Because our alphabet is binary, the cardinality of the set $\bar{R}_{\alpha(n)}$ is at most $2^{\alpha(n)} = 2^{t(n)\log t(n)} = t(n)^{t(n)}$.

By Lemma 17.4, there is $y_1 \in \bar{R}_{\alpha(n)}$ such that the number of elements of $\bar{L}_n$ that it covers is at least

$$\frac{|\bar{L}_n|}{|\bar{R}_{\alpha(n)}|^{1/t(n)}} \geq \frac{|\bar{L}_n|}{t(n)}.$$

Denote $Z_1 = \{x \in \bar{L}_n : y_1 \text{ covers } x\}$. By applying Lemma 17.4 again, there is a string $y_2 \in \bar{L}_{\alpha(n)} \setminus \{y_1\}$ covering at least $\frac{|\bar{L}_n \setminus Z_1|}{(|\bar{R}_{\alpha(n)}|-1)^{1/t(n)}} \geq \frac{|\bar{L}_n \setminus Z_1|}{|\bar{R}_{\alpha(n)}|^{1/t(n)}} = \frac{|\bar{L}_n \setminus Z_1|}{t(n)}$ elements of $\bar{L}_n \setminus Z_1$. Denote $Z_2 = \{x \in \bar{L}_n \setminus Z_1 : y_2 \text{ covers } x\}$. Generally, we denote by $y_i \in \bar{L}_{\alpha(n)} \setminus \{y_1, \ldots, y_{i-1}\}$ a string that covers at least

$$\frac{|\bar{L}_n \setminus (Z_1 \cup \ldots \cup Z_{i-1})|}{t(n)}$$

elements of $\bar{L}_n \setminus (Z_1 \cup \ldots \cup Z_{i-1})$, where Z_i is the set of new elements covered by y_i.

We claim that for all $i \leq t(n)$, the number of elements of $\bar{L}_n$ that $y_1, y_2, \ldots, y_i$ cover together is either all elements of $\bar{L}_i$ or at least $C_i|\bar{L}_n|$ for $C_i = \frac{t(n)-1}{t(n)} C_{i-1} + \frac{1}{t(n)}$ where $C_1 = \frac{1}{t(n)}$. We have already shown that the base case holds. Now, suppose that the claim holds for $i-1$, and let us prove it for i. Then, by the inductive hypothesis, the number of elements of $\bar{L}_n$ that $y_1, y_2, \ldots, y_i$ cover together, if it is not already all elements of $\bar{L}_n$, is at least

$$|Z_1| + \ldots + |Z_i| \geq |Z_1| + \ldots + |Z_{i-1}| + \frac{|\bar{L}_n \setminus (Z_1 \cup \ldots \cup Z_{i-1})|}{t(n)}$$
$$\geq C_{i-1}|\bar{L}_n| + \frac{|\bar{L}_n| - C_{i-1}|\bar{L}_n|}{t(n)} = \left(\frac{t(n)-1}{t(n)} C_{i-1} + \frac{1}{t(n)}\right) \cdot |\bar{L}_n|.$$

This proves our claim. Now, note that the recurrence in the preceding text evaluates to

$$C_i = \frac{1}{t(n)} \cdot \sum_{j=0}^{i-1} \left(\frac{t(n)-1}{t(n)}\right)^j = 1 - \left(1 - \frac{1}{t(n)}\right)^i.$$

Thus, by setting $i = 2t(n) \cdot n$, we have $C_i|\bar{L}_n| = (1 - (1 - \frac{1}{t(n)})^{2t(n) \cdot n})|\bar{L}_n| \geq (1 - \frac{1}{e^n})|\bar{L}_n|$. Because $|\bar{L}_n| \leq 2^n$, this means that all elements of $\bar{L}_n$ are then covered.

We thus conclude that there is a set $S_n \subseteq \bar{R}_{\alpha(n)}$ of size $(t(n))^{\mathcal{O}(1)}$ such that S_n covers every element of $\bar{L}_n$. Because $t(n)$ is bounded by some polynomial of n, we have that $|S_n| = n^{\mathcal{O}(1)}$. By construction, S_n has the following properties. For every string x of length n:

(S1) If $x \in \bar{L}_n$, then there is a set of strings $x_1, \ldots, x_{t(n)}$ of length n with $x_i = x$ for some i, $1 \leq i \leq t(n)$, such that on input $x_1, \ldots, x_{t(n)}$, algorithm $\mathcal{A}$ outputs a string from S_n.

(S2) If $x \notin \bar{L}_n$, then as x is of length n, we have that $x \in L$. Then for every input set of strings $x_1, \ldots, x_{t(n)}$ of length n with $x_i = x$ for some i, $1 \leq i \leq t(n)$, the distillation algorithm $\mathcal{A}$ outputs a string from R, and thus not a string from $S_n \subseteq \bar{R}$.

The NP/poly machine M that decides the language $\bar{L}$ is described as follows. For $x \in \{0, 1\}^n$ given as input, M takes as advice the set S_n. The nondeterministic machine M guesses a set of $t(n)$ strings $x_1, \ldots, x_{t(n)} \in \{0, 1\}^n$, each of the strings of length n, and such that at least one of these strings is x. Then it runs in polynomial time the distillation algorithm $\mathcal{A}$ on the guessed input $x_1, \ldots, x_{t(n)}$. If $\mathcal{A}$ outputs a string from the advice set S_n, then M accepts. Otherwise it rejects. This completes the description of M.

It is clear that M runs in polynomial time. By (S1) and (S2), $x \in \bar{L}$ if and only if M accepts x, that is, M has a computation path that accepts x. Thus, $\bar{L} \in \text{NP/poly}$.

Furthermore, if L is NP-hard then $\bar{L}$ is coNP-hard. Then every problem in coNP is polynomial-time reducible to $\bar{L}$. Thus, coNP $\subseteq$ NP/poly. This completes the proof. $\square$

We apply Theorem 17.3 immediately and prove that LONGEST PATH is unlikely to admit a polynomial kernel.

Theorem 17.5 LONGEST PATH *parameterized by k, the length of the path, does not admit a polynomial kernel unless* coNP $\subseteq$ NP/poly.

Proof: Suppose that LONGEST PATH admits a polynomial kernel of size k^c and let $\mathcal{K}$ be the corresponding kernelization algorithm.

Let us remind that in HAMILTONIAN PATH, we are given an undirected graph G and the task is to decide whether it contains a path spanning all its vertices. This is exactly the LONGEST PATH problem with k being the number of vertices of G. We also say that a graph is *Hamiltonian* if it contains a Hamiltonian path, that is, a path containing all its vertices. Deciding whether a graph is Hamiltonian is a well-known NP-hard problem.

17.1 OR-Distillation

We fix some reasonable encoding of undirected graphs by binary strings. The property of the encoding we require is that the length of the string is polynomial in the size of the graph it encodes and that two strings of equal length encode graphs with the same number of vertices. For example, we can encode every graph by the sequence of rows of its adjacency matrix. We define the language

$$L = \{x \in \{0, 1\}^* : x \text{ encodes a Hamiltonian graph}\}.$$

Observe that deciding whether $x \in L$ is NP-hard.

We want to prove that kernelization algorithm $\mathcal{K}$ for LONGEST PATH gives rise to a polynomially bounded distillation algorithm from L to a language R, which is

$$R = \{y \in \{0, 1\}^* : y \text{ encodes a yes-instance of LONGEST PATH}\}.$$

Thus, every string y of R encodes a pair (G, k) such that the undirected graph G contains a path of length k. Then for every string $y = (z, k)$, the kernelization algorithm $\mathcal{K}$ outputs in polynomial time a string $y' = (z', k')$ such that $|z'|+k' \leq k^c$ and $y \in R$ if and only if $y' \in R$.

Let $t(n) = n^c$. The algorithm $\mathcal{A}$ does the following.

- For every n, $\mathcal{A}$ receives as input $t(n)$ strings $x_1, \ldots, x_{t(n)}$, each of the strings of length exactly n. We assume that each of the strings x_i encodes a p-vertex graph G_i, where $p \leq n$. More precisely, if some of the strings do not encode a p-vertex graph, we omit these strings and consider only those strings that do encode a p-vertex graph.
- For the graph $G = G_1 \cup \cdots \cup G_{t(n)}$ and the integer p, algorithm $\mathcal{A}$ calls kernelization algorithm $\mathcal{K}$ with (G, p) as input, and outputs a string y corresponding to the encoding of the reduced instance (G', k').

Algorithm $\mathcal{A}$ has the following properties. First, by construction, the pair (G, p) is a yes-instance of LONGEST PATH if and only if the graph G contains a path of length at least p, which in turn, is if and only if at least one of the graphs G_i is Hamiltonian. Thus, the kernelization algorithm $\mathcal{K}$ outputs a yes-instance (G', k'), and hence $\mathcal{A}$ outputs a string $y \in R$, if and only if at least one of the strings x_i is in L. Second, the kernelization algorithm runs in polynomial time and outputs an instance (G', k') of LONGEST PATH such that the length of the corresponding string y is at most $n^c = t(n)$.

Thus, $\mathcal{A}$ is a polynomially bounded OR-distillation algorithm from L into R. By Theorem 17.3, the existence of such an algorithm for an NP-hard problem would imply that coNP $\subseteq$ NP/poly. Hence, unless coNP $\subseteq$ NP/poly, LONGEST PATH does not admit a polynomial kernel. □

17.2 Cross-Composition

In this section we build on the ideas used in the proof of Theorem 17.5. In particular, these ideas will bring us to *cross-composition*, a technique that is handy to rule out polynomial kernels. By making use of cross-composition, it is sufficient to compose the OR of any classical NP-hard problem into an instance of the parameterized problem Q for which we want to prove a lower bound. The term *cross* in the name comes from the fact that the source and target problems might not be the same. Also, instead of the parameter being bounded by a polynomial in the parameter of the original problem, it is required that the parameter of the output is bounded by a polynomial in largest input size. In addition, cross-composition allows the output parameter to depend on the logarithm of the number of input instances, which often simplifies the constructions and proofs.

We start with the definition of polynomial equivalence relation.

Definition 17.6 (Polynomial equivalence relation) An equivalence relation $\mathcal{R}$ on the set Σ^* is called a *polynomial equivalence relation* if the following conditions are satisfied:

(i) There exists an algorithm that, given strings $x, y \in \Sigma^*$, resolves whether x is equivalent to y in time polynomial in $|x| + |y|$.
(ii) For any finite set $S \subseteq \Sigma^*$ the equivalence relation $\mathcal{R}$ partitions the elements of S into at most $(\max_{x \in S} |x|)^{\mathcal{O}(1)}$ classes.

As an example of a polynomial equivalence relation, let us take some problem defined on undirected graphs. We fix some encoding of graphs. Now, we put into one equivalence class all the strings from Σ^* that do not encode any graph. We refer to such instances as *malformed*. All other strings encoding graphs are *well-formed*. We can assume that we can choose the encoding in such a way that graphs with encoding of length at most n have at most n vertices and at most n edges. Then $\mathcal{R}$ can be a relation such that two well-formed instances are equivalent if the corresponding graphs have the same numbers of vertices and edges. In this scenario, if all strings in a set $S \subseteq \Sigma^*$ are of length at most n, then S is divided by $\mathcal{R}$ into at most $n^2 + 1$ classes ($+1$ comes from the malformed class) and condition (b) is satisfied. Of course, provided that we chose a reasonable encoding, condition (a) holds as well. For parameterized problems, when the input to the problem consists of a graph and an integer k, encoded in unary, then we could in addition refine $\mathcal{R}$ by requiring that the instances x and y have the same value of $k \leq n$. Indeed, this would just increase the bound on the number of equivalence classes in S from $n^2 + 1$ to $n^3 + 1$.

We now proceed to the main definition.

17.2 Cross-Composition

Definition 17.7 (OR-**cross-composition**) Let $L \subseteq \Sigma^*$ be a language and $Q \subseteq \Sigma^* \times \mathbb{N}$ be a parameterized language. We say that L *cross-composes* into Q if there exists a polynomial equivalence relation $\mathcal{R}$ and an algorithm $\mathcal{A}$, called a *cross-composition*, satisfying the following conditions. The algorithm $\mathcal{A}$ takes as input a sequence of strings $x_1, x_2, \ldots, x_t \in \Sigma^*$ that are equivalent with respect to $\mathcal{R}$, runs in time polynomial in $\sum_{i=1}^{t} |x_i|$, and outputs one instance $(y, k) \in \Sigma^* \times \mathbb{N}$ such that:

(i) $k \leq p(\max_{i=1}^{t} |x_i| + \log t)$ for some polynomial $p(\cdot)$, and
(ii) $(y, k) \in Q$ if and only if there exists at least one index i such that $x_i \in L$.

Cross-composition is very convenient. As we will see soon in the proof of Theorem 17.8, having a cross-composition of a language L into a parameterized language Q that admits a polynomial kernel (and even more generally, a polynomial compression) implies that L admits a polynomially bounded distillation. By the results of the previous section, this is highly unlikely when L is NP-hard.

Thus, to prove that a problem Q is unlikely to admit a polynomial kernel, all we need is to cross-compose some NP-hard problem L into it!

It is important to understand the role of $\mathcal{R}$ in the definition of cross-composition. Observe that in the proof of Theorem 17.5, we defined the HAMILTONIAN PATH problem as a set of strings that denote adjacency matrices of graphs with hamiltonian cycles. The main reason to define the problem in this way was that when the size of strings were equal, then they denoted graphs on the same number of vertices. This kind of situations can easily be handled by a polynomial time equivalence relation $\mathcal{R}$. For example, for the HAMILTONIAN PATH problem, we can say that two strings $x, y \in \{0, 1\}^*$ are equivalent if $|x| = |y|$ and the graphs described by x and y have the same number of vertices.

Note that in this definition, contrary to OR-distillation, it is only the output parameter that is small, while the whole output string y may be even as huge as the concatenation of the input instances. Moreover, the output parameter can also depend poly-logarithmically on the number of input instances.

In Definition 1.5, we introduced the notion of compression, which is a more general form of kernelization. Often, when we talk about compression, we do not specify the target language R from Definition 1.5. Then we just mean the existence of a polynomial compression of a language L into *any* language R.

The machinery developed in the next theorem allows to rule out polynomial compressions as well.

Our plan now is to show that pipelining the cross-composition from an NP-hard problem with a polynomial kernel will yield an OR-distillation of the NP-hard problem. Then we would be able to employ Theorem 17.3 for refuting the existence of a larger class of preprocessing routines.

Theorem 17.8 *Let $L \subseteq \Sigma^*$ be an NP-hard language. If L cross-composes into a parameterized problem Q and Q has a polynomial compression, then* coNP $\subseteq$ NP/ poly.

Proof: Suppose that Q has a polynomial compression into some language R. Using the premises of the theorem, we give a t-bounded OR-distillation algorithm for L, where t is a polynomially bounded function, into the language OR(R) consisting of strings of the form $z_1\#z_2\#\ldots\#z_q$ such that for at least one index i it holds that $z_i \in R$. Together with Theorem 17.3, this will prove the theorem.

We start with observations that can be derived from the given assumptions.

(c_1) Language L cross-composes into Q, and let $\mathcal{R}$ denote the corresponding polynomial equivalence relation. Thus, given a set of $\mathcal{R}$-equivalent strings $x_1, \ldots, x_p$ one can obtain in polynomial time an instance (y, k) such that $k \leq (\max_{i=1}^{p} |x_i| + \log p)^{c_1}$ for some constant c_1, and $(y, k) \in Q$ if and only there exists at least one index, $1 \leq i \leq p$, such that $x_i \in L$.

(c_2) Language Q has a polynomial compression into R. Thus, given an instance (y, k) of Q, in polynomial time, one can obtain an instance z of R such that $|z| \leq k^{c_2}$ for some constant c_2.

(c_3) Because $\mathcal{R}$ is the polynomial equivalence relation, there is a constant c_3 such that for every integer n, any set S of strings of length n can be partitioned in polynomial time into at most n^{c_3} $\mathcal{R}$-equivalent classes.

Let $t(n) = n^{2(c_1 \cdot c_2 + c_3)}$ be a polynomially bounded function.

Because $\mathcal{R}$ is the polynomial equivalence relation, for every integer n we have the following. For a given set S of $t(n)$ instances of L of length n, namely $x_1, \ldots, x_{t(n)}$, it is possible in polynomial time to partition S into $\mathcal{R}$-equivalent classes $X_1, \ldots, X_r$, where $r \leq n^{c_3}$.

We apply the cross-composition algorithm on each of the classes X_i, $i \in \{1, \ldots, r\}$. We can do it because all the instances in X_i are $\mathcal{R}$-equivalent. Let the output of the cross-composition algorithm be (y_i, k_i) for X_i, where (y_i, k_i) is an instance of Q. By the definition of cross-composition and by (c1), for all $1 \leq i \leq r$, k_i is at most $(n + \log t(n))^{c_1}$.

In the next step of the algorithm, we compress each of the r instances of Q to build instances of R whose sizes are polynomial in the parameter. Let the instances after compression be z_i for $1 \le i \le r$, where $|z_i| \le k_i^{c_2}$. Observe that $z = z_1 \# z_2 \# \ldots \# z_r$ is an instance of $\mathrm{OR}(R)$.

Thus, we constructed a polynomial-time algorithm that for a given set of strings $x_1, \ldots, x_{t(n)}$ of length n, constructs a string z such that $z \in \mathrm{OR}(R)$ if and only if for at least one index $i \in \{1, \ldots, t(n)\}$, $x_i \in L$. The length of $z = z_1 \# z_2 \# \ldots \# z_r$ is at most

$$\begin{aligned}
|z| &\le r + r \cdot \max_{1 \le i \le r} |z_i| \\
&= r + r \cdot \max_{1 \le i \le r} k_i^{c_2} \le r + r \cdot (n + \log t(n))^{c_1 c_2} \\
&\le n^{c_3} + n^{c_3} \cdot (n + \log t(n))^{c_1 c_2} \\
&\le n^{2 c_3} \cdot (n \log t(n))^{c_1 c_2} \le n^{2(c_3 + c_1 c_2)} = t(n).
\end{aligned}$$

Thus, we have the desired t-bounded distillation algorithm from language L to language $\mathrm{OR}(R)$, where t is a polynomially bounded function. This together with Theorem 17.3 completes the proof. □

17.3 Examples of Compositions

Let us see how the developed framework can be used to derive the impossibility (under assumption that $\mathrm{coNP} \subseteq \mathrm{NP}/\mathrm{poly}$ does not hold) of kernelization for some concrete optimization problems.

17.3.1 Lower Bound for STEINER TREE

In the STEINER TREE problem we are given a graph G, a subset $T \subseteq V(G)$ of terminals, and an integer k. The task is to decide whether there exists a tree H in G on at most k vertices such that $T \subseteq V(H)$. Such a tree is called a *Steiner tree*. We will assume that $k \le |V(G)|$, else the instance is trivial to solve. STEINER TREE can be solved in time $2^{\mathcal{O}(|T|)} |V(G)|^{\mathcal{O}(1)}$ and thus is FPT parameterized by the number of terminals. In this section we show that STEINER TREE does not admit a polynomial compression being parameterized by the size of the solution k. Because k is always at least $|T|$ (if the answer is yes), this would also imply that STEINER TREE does not admit polynomial kernel and compression when parameterized by $|T|$.

Theorem 17.9 STEINER TREE *parameterized by the size of the solution k does not admit a polynomial compression unless* $\mathrm{coNP} \subseteq \mathrm{NP}/\mathrm{poly}$.

Proof: We give a cross-composition from STEINER TREE to itself. For the cross-composition, we first need a polynomial equivalence relation $\mathcal{R}$. We define $\mathcal{R}$ such that the triples (G_i, T_i, k_i), (G_j, T_j, k_j) go to the same equivalence class if and only if $|V(G_i)| = |V(G_j)|$, $|T_i| = |T_j|$, and $k_i = k_j$. All the remaining malformed instances, which do not form an instance of STEINER TREE, form another equivalence class. Clearly, this relation satisfies both the properties of a polynomial equivalence relation: Given pairs (G_i, T_i, k_i), (G_j, T_j, k_j) of well-formed instances of STEINER TREE, we can check in polynomial time if they have the same number of vertices, same-sized terminal sets, and that $k_i = k_j$. For any finite set $S \subseteq \Sigma^*$, the equivalence relation $\mathcal{R}$ partitions the elements of S into at most $(\max_{x \in S} |x|)^{\mathcal{O}(1)}$ classes as in a well-formed instance, $|T_i| \leq |V(G_i)|$ and $k_i \leq |V(G_i)|$.

Now, we have to give a cross-composition algorithm for instances belonging to the same equivalence class. For the equivalence class containing malformed instances, we output a trivial no-instance. Thus, from now on, we assume that we have an equivalence class $(G_1, T_1, k), \ldots, (G_t, T_t, k)$ and the number of the vertices, the number of terminals, and the size of a solution that is asked for, are the same for all triples in this class. Let $|V(G_i)| = n$ and $|T_i| = \ell$ for all $1 \leq i \leq t$. Suppose that $\ell \geq 1$, else the solution is trivial.

We construct an instance (G', T', k') of STEINER TREE, where $|T'| = \ell$ and $k' = k + \ell n$. We start the construction by taking a disjoint union of graphs G_i. Let the vertices of T_i be denoted by $t_1^i, \ldots, t_\ell^i$. We add new vertices, $w_1, \ldots, w_\ell$, which will form the set of terminal vertices T' of G'. Now, we add a path on $n + 1$ vertices from w_j to t_j^i, for all $j \in \{1, \ldots, \ell\}$ and $i \in \{1, \ldots, t\}$. Let the resulting graph be G', see Fig. 17.1 for an illustration.

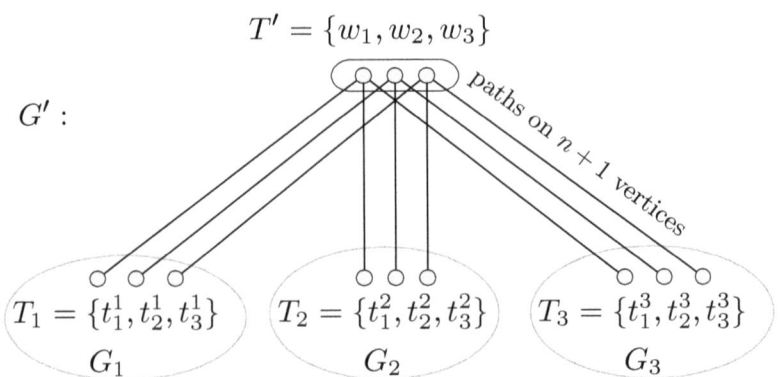

Figure 17.1 Constructing a new instance (G', T', k') in STEINER TREE cross-composition.

Now we prove the required equivalence. If G_i is a yes-instance of STEINER TREE, then we start with the Steiner tree H in G_i. Because $T_i \subseteq V(H)$, we can add the vertices of T' by the corresponding paths to the vertices in T_i. Because H is connected, we have that even after adding these paths the subgraph remains connected. The total number of vertices is at most the number of vertices in $V(H)$ and the corresponding paths, hence it is at most $k+\ell n$. For the reverse direction, observe that if we have a Steiner tree in G' that contains the vertices of T' and is of size at most $k' = k + \ell n$, then it cannot contain vertices from two distinct instances G_x and G_y. Indeed, any connected subgraph of G' that contains the vertices of T' should contain a path from w_j to some vertex t_j^i, for all $j \in \{1, \ldots, \ell\}$, and the number of vertices on all these paths together is at least $\ell(n+1)$. However, if this connected subgraph contains vertices from two distinct instances G_x and G_y, then it must contain some vertex w_j with paths to both vertices t_j^x and t_j^y. So, if a connected subgraph of G' that contains the vertices of T' also contains vertices from two distinct instances G_x and G_y, then its size must be at least $\ell(n+1) + n > k + \ell n$. This implies that a Steiner tree H in G' containing the vertices of T' of size at most $k' = k + \ell n$ contains vertices from at most one instance, say G_x. Let H' be the subtree of H containing only the vertices from G_x. By construction, we have that $T_x \subseteq V(H')$ and the connectivity of H forces H' to be connected. The size of $V(H')$ is at most k and thus we know that G_x is a yes-instance of STEINER TREE.

Now by applying Theorem 17.8, we derive the desired result. This completes the proof. □

17.3.2 CLIQUE Parameterized by Vertex Cover

Let us remind that in the CLIQUE problem, we are given a graph G and an integer ℓ. The task is to decide whether there exists a set of ℓ vertices of G that is a clique in G. When being parameterized by the size of the clique ℓ, CLIQUE is W[1]-hard and thus does not admit even an exponential kernel. However, when parameterized by the size of a given vertex cover, the problem becomes FPT. More precisely, in the CLIQUE parameterized by the vertex cover number (CLIQUE (VC) for short) we are given a graph G, integers k, ℓ, and a vertex cover $S \subseteq V$ such that $|S| = k$. The parameter is k and the task is to decide whether G has a clique on ℓ vertices.

The reason why CLIQUE (VC) is FPT is the following. Let S be a vertex cover and K be a clique of G. Then $V(G) \setminus S$ is an independent set, and thus it contains at most one vertex of K. Whether a clique of size ℓ is entirely in S, or all but one are in S, can be checked by bruteforce in time $2^k \cdot n^{\mathcal{O}(1)}$. In what follows, we prove that CLIQUE (VC) does not admit a polynomial kernel unless coNP $\subseteq$ NP/poly.

Theorem 17.10 CLIQUE *parameterized by vertex cover number does not admit a polynomial compression unless* coNP $\subseteq$ NP/poly.

Proof: We prove the theorem by showing that the NP-complete problem CLIQUE cross-composes into CLIQUE (VC).

For the cross-composition, we first need a polynomial equivalence relation $\mathcal{R}$. We define $\mathcal{R}$ such that all the pairs $(G_i, \ell_i), (G_j, \ell_j)$ are in the same equivalence class if and only if $|V(G_i)| = |V(G_j)|$ and $\ell_i = \ell_j$. We put all the instances that are malformed, as well as instances where the size of the clique that is asked for exceeds the number of vertices in the graph, in another equivalence class. Then this relation satisfies both the properties of a polynomial equivalence relation: Given pairs $(G_i, \ell_i), (G_j, \ell_j)$ of well-formed instances of CLIQUE, we can check in polynomial time if they have the same number of vertices and that $\ell_i = \ell_j$. For any finite set $S \subseteq \Sigma^*$, the equivalence relation $\mathcal{R}$ partitions the elements of S into at most $(\max_{x \in S} |x|)^{\mathcal{O}(1)}$ classes, as in a well-formed instance we have $\ell_i \leq |V(G_i)|$.

Now we give a cross-composition algorithm for instances belonging to the same equivalence class. For the equivalence class containing the malformed instances, we output a trivial no-instance. So, all that is left is to give a composition algorithm for an equivalence class where the number of vertices and the size of clique that is asked for are the same. Let $(G_1, \ell), \ldots, (G_t, \ell)$ be instances of the same equivalence class, such that $|V(G_i)| = n$ for all $i \in \{1, \ldots, t\}$. For all $i \in \{1, \ldots, t\}$, we think of the vertices in $V(G_i)$ as being bijectively labeled by integers in $\{1, \ldots, n\}$. Using these instances, we make an instance (G', Z', k', ℓ') of CLIQUE (VC), which consists of a graph G' with vertex cover $Z' \subseteq V(G)$ of size k' and an integer ℓ'.

We number the vertices in each of the G_is from 1 to n arbitrarily. We construct G' as follows.

(i) We make ℓn new vertices $v_{i,j}$ with $i \in \{1, \ldots, \ell\}$ and $j \in \{1, \ldots, n\}$, and connect two vertices $v_{i,j}$ and $v_{i',j'}$ if $i \neq i'$ and $j \neq j'$. Let C denote the set of these vertices. It is easy to see that any clique in G' can contain only one vertex $v_{i,m}$ for all $m \in \{1, \ldots, n\}$ for each choice of $i \in \{1, \ldots, \ell\}$. Similarly, a clique in G' can contain only one vertex $v_{m,j}$ for all $m \in \{1, \ldots, \ell\}$ for each choice of $j \in \{1, \ldots, n\}$. Thus, any clique contains at most ℓ vertices from C. One can think of these vertices as being placed on an $\ell \times n$ grid and the vertices in each row and each

17.3 Examples of Compositions

column form an independent set. Furthermore, any two vertices that are neither in the same column nor in the same row are adjacent.

(ii) For each pair $\{p,q\}$, $1 \le p < q \le n$, create three new vertices: $w_{p,q}$, $w_{p,\hat{q}}$, and $w_{\hat{p},q}$. Let D denote the set of these $3 \cdot \binom{n}{2}$ vertices. We make vertices of D adjacent to vertices of C as follows.

   (a) $w_{p,q}$ is adjacent to all vertices from C.
   (b) $w_{p,\hat{q}}$ is adjacent to all vertices from C except for $v_{i,q}$ for all $i \in \{1, \ldots, \ell\}$. That is, if we view the vertices of C placed on the $\ell \times n$-grid, then the only vertices $w_{p,\hat{q}}$ is not adjacent to belong to the q-th column.
   (c) $w_{\hat{p},q}$ is adjacent to all vertices from C except for $v_{i,p}$ for all $i \in \{1, \ldots, \ell\}$. That is, the only vertices $w_{\hat{p},q}$ is not adjacent to belong to the p-th column.

For each $p < q$, we refer to $w_{p,q}$, $w_{p,\hat{q}}$ as the (p,q)-*cloud*. Each cloud is an independent set. We add all edges between different clouds. That is, we add all edges between vertices in D that correspond to distinct pairs from $\{1, \ldots, n\}$. Any clique can contain at most one out of the three vertices from each cloud.

(iii) For each graph G_i, we introduce a new vertex u_i and connect it to all vertices in C. Let B be the set of these t vertices. The adjacency between each u_i and D is as follows:

   (a) Make u_i adjacent to $w_{p,q}$ if pq is an edge in G_i.
   (b) Otherwise make u_i adjacent to $w_{p,\hat{q}}$ and $w_{\hat{p},q}$.

We put $\ell' := \ell + 1 + \binom{n}{2}$ and $Z' = C \cup D$. Clearly, Z' is a vertex cover for G' because the remaining vertices are in B, which is an independent set. Also, $|Z'| = n\ell + 3\binom{n}{2}$. So, the parameter, $k' = |Z'| = n\ell + 3\binom{n}{2}$ is bounded by a polynomial in n as well as the largest input size. Also, it is easy to see that the construction can be done in polynomial time in the size of input. So, all we need to show is that (G', Z', k', ℓ') is a yes-instance of CLIQUE (VC), if and only if (G_i, ℓ) is a yes-instance of CLIQUE for some $i \in \{1, \ldots, t\}$.

($\Rightarrow$) Let (G', Z', k', ℓ') be a yes-instance of CLIQUE (VC). Let S' be a clique of size $\ell + 1 + \binom{n}{2}$ in G'. As argued in the preceding text, any clique in G' can take at most ℓ vertices from C, at most $\binom{n}{2}$ vertices from D and at most one vertex from B. Let

$$S = \{j \in \{1, \ldots, n\} : v_{i,j} \in S' \text{ for some } i \in \{1, \ldots, \ell\}\}.$$

The size of the set S is ℓ because for each $i \in \{1, \ldots, \ell\}$, S' can contain at most one $v_{i,\cdot}$ and no two vertices $v_{i,j}$ and $v_{i',j'}$ from S' can have indices $j = j'$. Let the vertex in S' from B be u_{i^*}. We argue that (G_{i^*}, ℓ) is a yes-instance of CLIQUE, and the vertices of S form a clique in G_{i^*}.

Let p, q be any two vertices in S. We look at the vertices in D corresponding to (p, q), namely $w_{p,q}$, $w_{p,\hat{q}}$ and $w_{\hat{p},q}$. Because these three vertices form an independent set, at most one of them is in S'. Also, because we want $\binom{n}{2}$ vertices from D, each such triple contributes exactly one vertex to the clique. By the construction of S, the clique S' must contain two vertices $v_{i,p}$ and $v_{i',q}$ for some i and i'. Now, the clique cannot contain any of the vertices $w_{p,\hat{q}}$ and $w_{\hat{p},q}$ from D because they are not adjacent to $v_{i',q}$ and $v_{i,p}$, respectively, which are vertices in the clique. So, $w_{p,q}$ is contained in the clique along with u_{i^*}, which means that pq is an edge in G_{i^*}. Therefore, S is a clique of size ℓ in G_{i^*}, and thus (G_{i^*}, ℓ) is a yes-instance of CLIQUE.

($\Leftarrow$) Let (G_{i^*}, ℓ) be a yes-instance of CLIQUE for some i^*. Let $S = \{p_1, \ldots, p_\ell\} \subseteq \{1, \ldots, n\}$ be the clique of size ℓ in G_{i^*}. We show that (G', Z', k', ℓ') is a yes-instance by constructing a clique S' of size $\ell + 1 + \binom{n}{2}$ in G'.

First, we insert the vertex u_{i^*} into S'. Also, for each p_i in S, we add v_{i,p_i} to S'. All these vertices are adjacent to u_{i^*} by construction. They are also pairwise adjacent because for no two vertices $v_{i,j}$ and $v_{i',j'}$ added to S', $i = i'$ or $j = j'$. This contributes $\ell + 1$ vertices to the clique. To construct a clique of size $\ell + 1 + \binom{n}{2}$, we have to add exactly one vertex from each cloud, that is from $w_{p,q}$, $w_{p,\hat{q}}$ and $w_{\hat{p},q}$ for $1 \leq p < q \leq n$.

For each pair $\{p, q\}$, we look at the following two cases:

- If p is adjacent to q in G_{i^*}, then the vertex u_{i^*} is adjacent to $w_{p,q}$ in G' and $w_{p,q}$ is adjacent to all vertices of C. In this case, we add $w_{p,q}$ to S'.
- Otherwise, u_{i^*} is adjacent to both $w_{p,\hat{q}}$ and $w_{\hat{p},q}$. Because p and q are not adjacent in G_{i^*}, S cannot contain both p and q. If S contains p (and does not contain q), then we add the vertex $w_{p,\hat{q}}$ to S'. The vertex $w_{p,\hat{q}}$ is adjacent to all the vertices in S' that are added already because the only vertices in C it is not adjacent to are of the form $v_{\cdot,q}$, which are not added to S' by construction. Symmetrically, if S contains q (and does not contain p), then we add the vertex $w_{\hat{p},q}$ to S'.

Hence, we get a clique S' of size $\ell' = \ell + 1 + \binom{n}{2}$ in G' and (G', Z', k', ℓ') is a yes-instance of CLIQUE (VC). This concludes the proof of the construction. Now by applying Theorem 17.8, we derive the desired result. This completes the proof. □

Exercises

Problem 17.1 Show that coNP $\subseteq$ NP/poly if and only if NP $\subseteq$ coNP/poly.

Problem 17.2 Show that CLIQUE parameterized by maximum vertex degree does not admit a polynomial kernel unless coNP $\subseteq$ NP/poly.

Problem 17.3 Recall the TEST COVER problem from Exercise 2.8. Show that this problem does not admit a polynomial kernel unless coNP $\subseteq$ NP/poly.

Bibliographic Notes

The definition of a distillation algorithm adapted in this book is slightly different from the definition used in Cygan et al. (2015, Definition 15.1). The main difference in the definitions is that, in our definition, the length of the string y outputted by a distillation algorithm is bounded by $t(n) \cdot \log n$. For deriving lower bounds on kernels in the next two chapters, where we rule out polynomial kernels, this constraint is not required. However, this difference will become useful in Chapter 20, where we obtain concrete polynomial lower bounds on the sizes of the kernels. Let us also remark that for the proofs of the lower bounds that we provide in this book, a slightly lighter condition $t(n)$ on the length of string x in the definition of the distillation algorithm will suffice. However, because the proof of Theorem 17.3 works also for the bound $t(n) \cdot \log n$, we decided to have this bound in the definition.

For an introduction to complexity theory, and in particular to the concepts used in this chapter such as the assumption coNP $\subseteq$ NP/poly, we refer to the book of Arora and Barak (2009).

Theorem 17.3 is the quantitative version of the main result proved in Fortnow and Santhanam (2011). This theorem will allow us to derive polynomial lower bounds in the upcoming chapters. The framework for proving kernelization lower bounds was initially proposed by Bodlaender et al. (2009b). They called the technique OR-*composition*. OR-composition is a slightly weaker form of the cross-composition framework that was presented in this chapter. More precisely, the formalism presented in Bodlaender et al. (2009b) does not use polynomial equivalence relations, assumes that the source and target languages of a composition are the same, and does not allow the output parameter to depend poly-logarithmically on the number of input instances. The cross-composition framework was proposed by Bodlaender et al. (2014).

The term *cross-composition* was used to underline that this composition allows "cross-fertilization" between different languages.

The bound for CLIQUE parameterized by vertex cover (Theorem 17.10) is due to Bodlaender et al. (2014). The paper (Bodlaender et al., 2014), as well as the thesis of Jansen (2013), contain more examples of cross-composition. The lower bounds for LONGEST PATH (Theorem 17.5) and STEINER TREE (Theorem 17.9), using different approaches, were obtained in Bodlaender et al. (2009b) and Dom et al. (2014), respectively. Exercise 17.3 is taken from Gutin et al. (2013b).

18
Instance Selectors

In this chapter we introduce Instance Selector, an approach for deriving OR-cross-compositions. We use it to obtain lower bounds on the sizes of kernels for DISJOINT FACTORS, CNF-SAT parameterized by the number of variables, and COLORED RED-BLUE DOMINATING SET.

In the previous chapter, we defined what is a cross-composition from a language L to a parameterized language Q, that is, an algorithm that, given t strings $x_1, x_2, \ldots, x_t$ belonging to the same equivalence class of $\mathcal{R}$, computes an instance $(x^*, k^*) \in \Sigma^* \times \mathbb{N}$ in time polynomial in $\sum_{i=1}^{t} |x_i|$ such that (i) $(x^*, k^*) \in Q \Leftrightarrow x_i \in L$ for some $1 \leq i \leq t$, and (ii) k^* is bounded by a polynomial in $\max_{i=1}^{t} |x_i| + \log t$. Observe that the magnitude of the parameter of the output is allowed to be $(\log t)^{\mathcal{O}(1)}$.

In this chapter we describe cross-composition algorithms for various problems. In all these examples we will compose a problem into itself. All these algorithms have the following theme in common. Instead of building a composition for t instances simultaneously, in many cases it can be much easier to construct the composition by explaining how to compose from only two instances.

The description of these algorithms generally revolves around a single function, which we will call $\rho : \{0, 1\}^* \times \{0, 1\}^* \to \{0, 1\}^*$, that accepts two instances and returns one. We want the function ρ to have the following properties:

- For two instances x_1 and x_2 belonging to the same equivalence class, $\rho((x_1, k), (x_2, k))$ outputs (x^*, k^*) such that $(x^*, k^*) \in Q$ if and only if at least one among (x_1, k) and (x_2, k) is in Q. Thus, for two instances,

ρ selects an instance equivalent to their logical OR. This is where the name *instance selector* comes from.
- The output of $\rho((x_1,k),(x_2,k))$ is computed in time polynomial in $|x_1|+|x_2|+k$.
- The parameter k^* in the new instance should be "small." In most typical situations, we demand $k^* \leq k + c$ for some constant c.

Let us note that constructing such a function ρ is sufficient for constructing a cross-composition. Indeed, given strings $(x_1,k),(x_2,k),\ldots,(x_t,k)$, we group them into $t/2$ pairs and apply ρ to each pair. Then we group the obtained instances into pairs again, and use ρ on the new instances. After repeating these steps $\log_2 t$ times, we obtain a string (x^*,k^*) such that $(x^*,k^*) \in Q$ if and only if at least one of the instances (x_i,k) is in Q. The parameter k^* is at most $k + c \cdot \log_2 t$ and thus we obtain a cross-composition.

We can visualize the repeating steps of instance selector in the form of a complete binary tree $\mathbb{T}$ with $2t-1$ nodes. For convenience, we generally assume that $t = 2^\ell$. (Such an assumption can usually be easily justified.) This makes the tree ℓ levels deep. The input instances are plugged in at the leaves of $\mathbb{T}$. We inductively compute the contents of a given node as being $\rho(a,b)$, where a and b are the instances obtained at the children of this node. The output of the composed algorithm is what is obtained at the root of this tree (as shown in the Fig. 18.1).

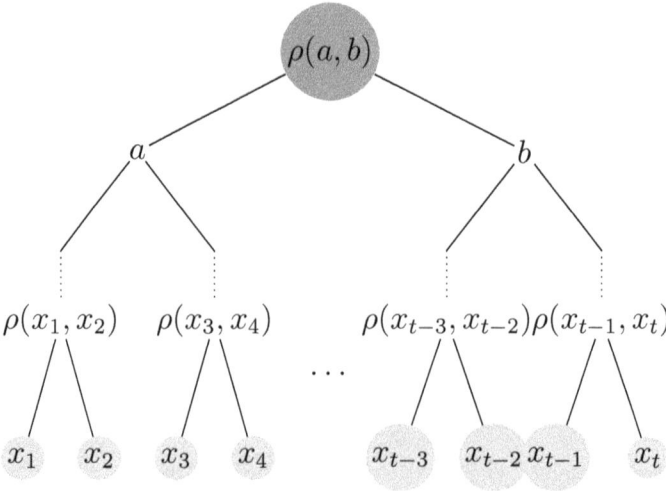

Figure 18.1 General framework for composition: A composition tree.

18.1 Disjoint Factors

Our first example of an instance selector concerns DISJOINT FACTORS.

Let $L_k = \{w_1, \ldots, w_k\}$ be an alphabet consisting of k letters. We denote by L_k^* the set of strings on L_k. A *factor* of a string $s \in L_k^*$ is a substring $w_i \cdots w_i \in L_k^*$ of s. Thus, a factor starts and ends with the same letter and has length at least two. A string s has the *disjoint factor property* if one can find disjoint factors $F_1, \ldots, F_k$ in s such that the factor F_i starts and ends by the letter w_i.

For example, the word 123235443513 has all the r-factors, $r \in \{1, \ldots, k\}$, but not as many disjoint factors. It has disjoint 2, 3, and 4 factors, but, for instance, the only 5-factor overlaps with the 4-factor, and the only 1-factor overlaps with all other factors. Of course, other combinations of disjoint factors are attainable from this word, but it clearly does not have the disjoint factor property. The problem we would be interested in is the following.

In the DISJOINT FACTORS problem, we are given a word $w \in L_k^*$ and the task is to decide whether w admits the disjoint factors property. Observe that the difficulty lies in the fact that the factors F_i do not necessarily appear in increasing order, otherwise detecting them would be computable in $\mathcal{O}(n)$, where n is the length of w. The problem is known to be NP-complete. We record this without a proof.

Lemma 18.1 DISJOINT FACTORS *is* NP-*complete*.

It is immediate that DISJOINT FACTORS is FPT. Because the problem can be solved in time that is linear in the length of the word given the ordering of the factors, we simply iterate over all possible orderings of factors—this gives us an algorithm with runtime $\mathcal{O}(k! \cdot n)$. However, less obvious is a $2^k \cdot n^{\mathcal{O}(1)}$ algorithm for the problem; see Exercise 18.1.

Next we give a cross-composition algorithm for DISJOINT FACTORS following the framework described in Section 17.2.

Theorem 18.2 DISJOINT FACTORS *parameterized by the size of the alphabet k does not admit a polynomial compression unless* coNP $\subseteq$ NP/ poly.

Proof: We prove the theorem by showing that DISJOINT FACTORS cross-composes into itself. We define a polynomial equivalence relation $\mathcal{R}$ such that all bit-strings that do not encode a valid instance of DISJOINT FACTORS are equivalent. Of the remaining instances, any two well-formed instances (s_1, k) and (s_2, k) are equivalent if and only if they satisfy $|s_1| = |s_2|$.

We define the instance selector ρ as follows. Let (s_1, k) and (s_2, k), where s_1 and s_2 are strings from L_k^*, be two equivalent under $\mathcal{R}$ instances of DISJOINT

FACTORS. Let b be a new letter not from the alphabet L_k and let $s = bs_1bs_2b$. Thus, $s \in L_{k+1}^*$ is obtained by appending b to s_1 from both ends, then appending s_2 and again appending b. We put

$$\rho((s_1, k), (s_2, k)) = (s, k + 1).$$

We claim that $(s, k + 1)$ is a yes-instance of DISJOINT FACTORS if and only if at least one among (s_1, k) and (s_2, k) is.

Indeed, let $F_1, \ldots, F_{k+1}$ be disjoint factors of s. Then factor F_{k+1}, the factor that starts and ends with b, should contain the middle b. (If it contains the first and the last bs, then it overlaps with all other factors of s.) But then all other k disjoint factors should be from either s_1 or s_2. Hence, at least one among (s_1, k) and (s_2, k) is a yes-instance of DISJOINT FACTORS.

In the opposite direction, if s_1 has disjoint factors $F_1, \ldots, F_k$ (the case of s_2 is symmetric), then the $k + 1$ disjoint factors of s are the k factors of s_1 and the factor formed by the middle and the last b. Thus, $(s, k + 1)$ is a yes-instance of DISJOINT FACTORS.

The instance selector ρ is clearly computable in polynomial time. The parameter in the selector increases by 1. We are basically done with the proof. As we have already discussed in the introductory part of this chapter, such an instance selector implies the existence of a cross-composition algorithm, which in turn, combined with Lemma 18.1 and Theorem 17.8, implies the desired result.

In what follows, we explain once again in detail, why the construction of an instance selector ρ for DISJOINT FACTORS gives a cross-composition algorithm. In all the remaining examples of this chapter, we will be skipping such reasonings.

Let $s_1, s_2, \ldots, s_t$ be strings from L_k^* that are equivalent under $\mathcal{R}$. We may assume that the number of instances $t = 2^\ell$ for some ℓ, else we can duplicate the instances to get the desired number of instances. To obtain a cross-composition algorithm $\mathcal{A}$, which composes the input set of words into a word s^*, we do the following. We partition $s_1, s_2, \ldots, s_t$ into pairs and use ρ to construct new $s_1^1, s_2^1, \ldots, s_{t/2}^1$ instances over alphabet L_{k+1}^*. As we have already proved, every new string s_i^1 is a yes-instance of DISJOINT FACTORS if and only if at least one of the two old instances used to select it is a yes-instance of DISJOINT FACTORS. We continue this procedure until we obtain one string $s^\ell \in L_{k+\ell-1}^*$; see Fig. 18.2. Algorithm $\mathcal{A}$ outputs s^ℓ. By inductive arguments, one can argue that $(s^\ell, k + \ell)$ is a yes-instance if and only if at least one of the instances (s_i, k), $i \in \{1, \ldots, t\}$ is. The construction can be done in time polynomial in $|s_1| + \cdots + |s_t|$, and thus $\mathcal{A}$ is a cross-composition. $\square$

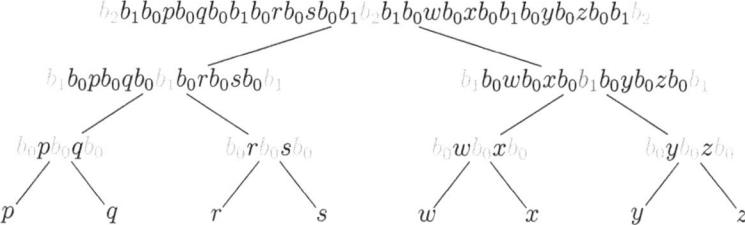

Figure 18.2 Disjoint Factors Composition: An example with $\{p, q, r, s, w, x, y, z\}$ as input strings. The output string is composed from the input strings by adding three additional letters. Notice how a solution in the root can be traced to some unique solution in the leaves and conversely.

18.2 SAT Parameterized by the Number of Variables

In this section we study the parameterized version of CNF-SAT where parameter is the number of variables. Let us remind that in CNF-SAT, we are given a propositional formula φ on n Boolean variables $\mathtt{Vars} = \{x_1, x_2, \ldots, x_n\}$ in conjunctive normal form,

$$\varphi = C_1 \wedge C_2 \wedge \ldots \wedge C_m.$$

Here, each C_i is a *clause* of the form

$$C_i = \ell_1^i \vee \ell_2^i \vee \ldots \vee \ell_{r_i}^i,$$

where ℓ_j^i are literals of some variables of $\mathtt{Vars}$. The task is to decide whether φ is satisfiable. Here we prove the lower bound on the compression of CNF-SAT when parameterized by the number of variables n.

The problem is evidently in FPT, as an algorithm merely has to iterate over all possible assignments to the variables, there being 2^n of them. The runtime of this algorithm is $\mathcal{O}(2^n \cdot m)$, where m is the input length.

Theorem 18.3 CNF-SAT *parameterized by the number of variables n does not admit a polynomial compression unless* coNP $\subseteq$ NP/poly.

Proof: We prove the theorem by showing that CNF-SAT parameterized by the number of variables cross-composes into itself. We define a polynomial equivalence relation $\mathcal{R}$ such that all bit-strings that do not encode a valid instance of CNF-SAT are equivalent. Of the remaining instances, any two well-formed instances (φ_1, n) and (φ_2, n) are equivalent if and only if they satisfy $|\varphi_1| = |\varphi_2|$. Let $\varphi_1, \varphi_2, \ldots, \varphi_t$ be equivalent CNF formulas. All these formulas are on n variables and we assume that each formula has the same set of variables $\mathtt{Vars} = \{x_1, x_2, \ldots, x_n\}$. Further, let $m := \max_{i \in \{1, \ldots, t\}} |\varphi_i|$.

Instead of building a cross-composition, we only describe an instance selector ρ. To define the instance selector, we need the following operation on CNF formulas. For a formula $\varphi = C_1 \wedge C_2 \wedge \ldots \wedge C_m$ and a boolean variable x, we define $\varphi \vee x$ as the formula obtained from φ by adding x to every clause C_i of φ. Then for two equivalent instances (φ_1, n) and (φ_2, n) on variables $\{x_1, x_2, \ldots, x_n\}$, we define

$$\rho((\varphi_1, n), (\varphi_2, n)) = (\varphi, n+1),$$

where

$$\varphi = (\varphi_1 \vee x_{n+1}) \wedge (\varphi_2 \vee \neg x_{n+1}).$$

For example, for $\varphi_1 = (x_1 \vee x_2) \wedge (x_1 \vee \neg x_2) \wedge (x_2 \vee \neg x_3)$ and variable x_4, the result of $\varphi_1 \vee x_4$ is the formula $(x_1 \vee x_2 \vee x_4) \wedge (x_1 \vee \neg x_2 \vee x_4) \wedge (x_2 \vee \neg x_3 \vee x_4)$. For φ_1 and $\varphi_2 = (x_1 \vee x_3) \wedge (x_1 \vee \neg x_2) \wedge (x_2 \vee x_3)$, the instance selector outputs $\rho((\varphi_1, n), (\varphi_2, n)) = (\varphi, n+1)$, where

$$\varphi = (\varphi_1 \vee x_4) \wedge (\varphi_2 \vee \neg x_4)$$
$$= (x_1 \vee x_2 \vee x_4) \wedge (x_1 \vee \neg x_2 \vee x_4) \wedge (x_2 \vee \neg x_3 \vee x_4)$$
$$\wedge (x_1 \vee x_3 \vee \neg x_4) \wedge (x_1 \vee \neg x_2 \vee \neg x_4) \wedge (x_2 \vee x_3 \vee \neg x_4).$$

We claim that there is a truth assignment satisfying φ if and only if there is a truth assignment satisfying at least one among φ_1 and φ_2.

Let ψ be a truth assignment satisfying φ. If $\psi(x_{n+1}) = \top$, then every clause of φ_2 should be satisfied by ψ. Otherwise, if $\psi(x_{n+1}) = \bot$, then ψ satisfies φ_1.

Suppose now that ψ is a truth assignment satisfying at least one of the formulas φ_1 and φ_2. Then the truth assignment ψ' on φ that coincides with ψ for the first n variables and

$$\psi'(x_{n+1}) = \begin{cases} \bot, & \text{if } \psi \text{ satisfies } \varphi_1, \\ \top, & \text{otherwise (in which case } \psi \text{ satisfies } \varphi_2), \end{cases}$$

satisfies φ.

The instance selector ρ for CNF-SAT brings us immediately to an algorithm $\mathcal{A}$ that in time polynomial in m and t constructs a CNF formula φ such that

- φ is satisfiable if and only if for at least one $i \in \{1, \ldots, t\}$ formula φ_i is satisfiable, and
- The number of variables in φ is $n + \log_2 t$.

Hence $\mathcal{A}$ is a cross-composition.

Because CNF-SAT is NP-hard, the proof of the theorem now follows from Theorem 17.8. □

18.3 Colored Red-Blue Dominating Set

Our last example of the instance selector technique concerns a variant of DOMINATING SET. An instance of RED-BLUE DOMINATING SET (RBDS) comprises of a bipartite graph G with bipartition T and N, and an integer k. We ask whether there exists a vertex set $X \subseteq N$ of size at most k such that every vertex in T has at least one neighbor in X.

In the literature, the sets T and N are usually called *blue* and *red* vertices, respectively, and this is why the problem is called RED-BLUE DOMINATING SET. Here, we call the vertices "terminals" and "nonterminals" to avoid confusion with the colored version of the problem that we are going to introduce. RBDS is equivalent to SET COVER and HITTING SET.

Let us remind that an input to HITTING SET consists of a universe U, a family $\mathcal{F}$ of subsets of U, and an integer k. The goal is to choose a set X of at most k elements from U such that every set from the family $\mathcal{F}$ contains at least one element from X. To see that HITTING SET and RBDS are equivalent, note that, given a HITTING SET instance $(U, \mathcal{F}, k)$, one may set $T = \mathcal{F}, N = U$ and make each set $A \in \mathcal{F}$ adjacent to all its elements; the condition that every set from $\mathcal{F}$ contains an element from X translates to the condition that every vertex from T is adjacent to a vertex from X in the constructed graph. SET COVER is the dual of HITTING SET, where the task is to find at most k sets from the family $\mathcal{F}$ covering all elements of U.

HITTING SET, and therefore RBDS, is NP-complete. Due to equivalence with HITTING SET, RBDS is also W[2]-hard being parameterized by k. However, it is trivially FPT parameterized by the size of N. It is also FPT parameterized by the size of T; see Exercise 18.3. However, RBDS does not admit a polynomial kernel being parameterized by neither $|T|$ nor $|N|$ unless coNP $\subseteq$ NP/poly. Here we prove the lower bound for RBDS when parameterized by $|T|$. The lower bound for parameterization by $|N|$ is left as an exercise (Exercise 19.3).

Observe that RBDS becomes polynomial for $k \geq |T|$ (each vertex $v \in T$ may simply greedily pick one "private" neighbor in N), so the parameterization by $|T| + k$ is equivalent to the parameterization by $|T|$.

We do not know how to construct a cross-composition for RBDS directly. This is why the proof is performed in two steps. In this section we describe an auxiliary variant of RBDS and show that it is compositional. In the next chapter, we will reduce to RBDS from the auxiliary variant and thus rule out the existence of a polynomial kernel for RBDS parameterized by $|T|$.

The auxiliary problem is called COLORED RED-BLUE DOMINATING SET (COL-RBDS for short). In this problem we are given a bipartite graph G with bipartition N and T, and an integer k. The set of nonterminal vertices N is partitioned into k sets, $N = N^1 \cup N^2 \cup \ldots \cup N^k$, and the solution set X is required to contain exactly one vertex from each set N^i. We will think of sets $N^1, N^2, \ldots, N^k$ as of *colors*, provided by a function col : $N \to \{1, \ldots, k\}$. Thus, a solution $X \subseteq N$ is not only required to be of size at most k, but it should also contain exactly one vertex of each color. We refer to such a solution X as a *k-colored dominating set*. We parameterize COL-RBDS by $|T| + \ell$, that is, we add the number of colors to the parameter. Let us note that while for RBDS the parameterization by $|T| + k$ is equivalent to the parameterization by $|T|$, this is not the case for COL-RBDS.

Theorem 18.4 COL-RBDS *does not admit a polynomial compression unless* coNP $\subseteq$ NP/ poly.

Proof: We describe a cross-composition for a sequence
$$(G_1 = (T_1 \cup N_1, E_1), k, \text{col}_1), \ldots, (G_t = (T_t \cup N_t, E_t), k, \text{col}_t)$$
of COL-RBDS instances with $|T_1| = |T_2| = \cdots = |T_t| = p$. Again, instead of providing a description of a cross-composition, we define an instance selector for COL-RBDS.

For a bipartite graph G with bipartition T and N and k-coloring of N, we let $\lambda(G)$ denote the graph obtained from G after adding a set $\mathcal{S}$ of $2(k-1)$ new vertices $u(r)$ and $v(r)$, $r \in \{1, \ldots, k-1\}$, to the terminal vertex set T of G, and the following edges to the edge set:

$$E_1 = \{xu(r) : x \in N_r \text{ and } r \in \{1, \ldots, k-1\}\}, \text{ and}$$
$$E_2 = \{xv(r) : x \in N_k \text{ and } r \in \{1, \ldots, k-1\}\}.$$

Thus, all vertices that have color $r \in \{1, \ldots, k-1\}$ are made adjacent to $u(r)$, and all vertices with color k are adjacent to $v(r)$ for all $r \in \{1, \ldots, k-1\}$. The terminal set of $\lambda(G)$ is $T \cup \mathcal{S}$; see Fig. 18.3.

We similarly define $\bar{\lambda}(G)$. Here, the vertex set of G is expanded by vertices $\mathcal{S} = \{u(r), v(r), : r \in \{1, \ldots, k-1\}\}$, and new edges as follows:

$$E_1 = \{xv(r) : x \in N_r \text{ and } r \in \{1, \ldots, k-1\}\}, \text{ and}$$
$$E_2 = \{xu(r) : x \in N_k \text{ and } r \in \{1, \ldots, k-1\}\}.$$

The terminal set of $\bar{\lambda}(G)$ is $T \cup \mathcal{S}$. Here, all vertices that have color $1 \le r < k$ are adjacent to $v(r)$ and all vertices with color k are adjacent to $u(r)$, for all r. Let us note that if a set $X \subseteq N$ is a k-colored dominating set in a graph G, then in $\lambda(G)$ (and in $\bar{\lambda}(G)$) it also dominates all the vertices of $\mathcal{S}$ as well as "old" terminal vertices of G, and thus is a k-colored dominating set in $\lambda(G)$ (and in

18.3 Colored Red-Blue Dominating Set

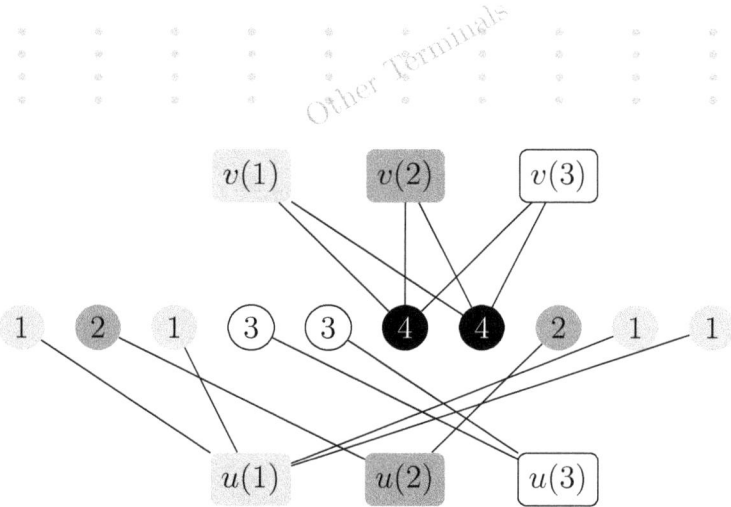

Figure 18.3 Composition of COL-RBDS. An illustration of the application of λ to a graph. The subscripts on the u and v vertices are omitted for clarity, as are the edges between terminals and nonterminals. Note that such a illutstration for $\bar{\lambda}$ would be identical with the u and v labels flipped.

$\bar{\lambda}(G)$). The converse is also true: If X is a k-colored dominating set in $\lambda(G)$ or in $\bar{\lambda}(G)$, then it is also a k-colored dominating set in G.

To describe ρ, we need to define the operation of *identifying* two vertices. For two nonadjacent vertices u and v of a graph G, the graph H obtained by identifying u and v is the graph obtained from G by deleting u and v, adding a new vertex w, and making it adjacent to all neighbors of u and all neighbors of v in G. This operation intuitively amounts to merging u and v into a common vertex and using the union of their neighborhoods as the neighborhood of the common vertex.

Let G_1 and G_2 be two equivalent (subject to $\mathcal{R}$) bipartite graphs with bipartitions T_i, $|T_i| = p$, and N_i, and k-colorings col_i of N_i, $i = 1, 2$. We define

$$\rho((G_1, k, \text{col}_1), (G_2, k, \text{col}_2)) = (G, k, \text{col}),$$

where G and col are defined as follows.

The graph G is obtained by merging of graphs $\lambda(G_1)$ and $\bar{\lambda}(G_2)$, where we identify the pairs of their terminal vertices. More precisely, the terminal set of $\lambda(G_1)$ consists of the terminal set of graph G_1, namely $T_1 = \{x_1, \ldots, x_p\}$, plus $2(k-1)$ new vertices of $\mathcal{S}_1 = \{u^1(r), v^1(r) : r \in \{1, \ldots, k-1\}\}$, added by λ. The terminal set of $\bar{\lambda}(G_2)$ is the union of the terminal set of G_2,

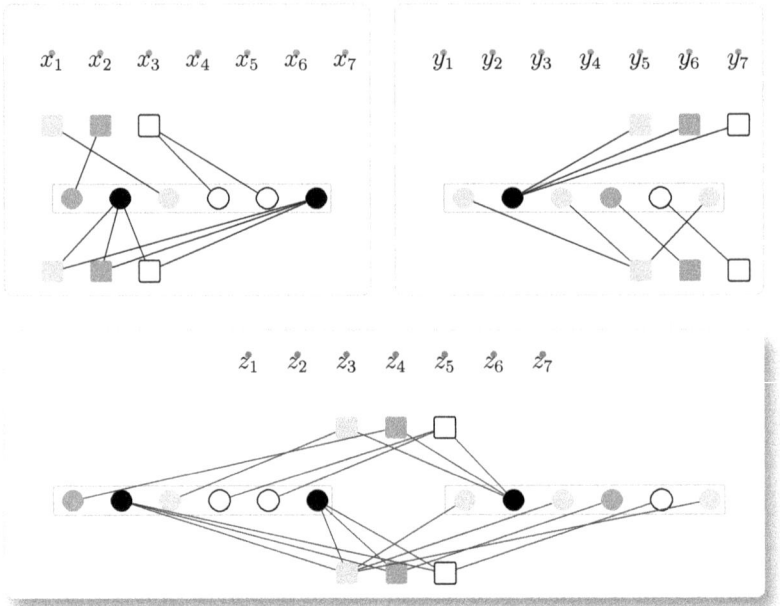

Figure 18.4 Composing col-RBDS. An example of a selector ρ from $\lambda(G_1)$ and $\overline{\lambda}(G_2)$. Here terminals x_is get identified with the y_is. The merge of x_i and y_i is labeled z_i in the resulting graph, and we do not show in the figure how these terminals are connected to nonterminal vertices. The terminal vertices from $\mathcal{S}_i$ are shown by squares, and they are also pairwise-identified. For the nonterminals, we take a simple union.

namely $T_2 = \{y_1, \ldots, y_p\}$, plus the new vertices of $\mathcal{S}_2 = \{u^2(r), v^2(r) : r \in \{1, \ldots, k-1\}\}$, added by $\overline{\lambda}$. Then G is obtained from the union of $\lambda(G_1) \cup \overline{\lambda}(G_2)$ by identifying all pairs of terminal vertices of the form $\{x_i, y_i\}$ for all $i \in \{1, \ldots, p\}$, and $\{u^1(r), u^2(r)\}$ and $\{v^1(r), v^2(r)\}$ for all $r \in \{1, \ldots, k-1\}$. We call the set of vertices of G obtained by identifying pairs from $\mathcal{S}_1$ and $\mathcal{S}_2$ by $\mathcal{S} = \{u(r), v(r), r \in \{1, \ldots, k-1\}\}$.

The terminal set T of G consists of p "old" terminal vertices and the $2(k-1)$ "new" vertices of $\mathcal{S}$. The nonterminal set N of G is the disjoint union $N = N_1 \cup N_2$. The coloring col of N is formed from colorings col_1 and col_2 of N_1 and N_2, respectively. This means that every vertex v of N inherits its color either from N_1 or from N_2. See Fig. 18.4.

Claim 18.5 *G has a k-colored dominating set if and only if at least one of the instances G_i, $i = 1, 2$, has a k-colored dominating set.*

Proof Let G_i, $i = 1, 2$, be a yes-instance of COL-RBDS and let X be a k-colored dominating set in G_i. Then in G, X dominates all "old" terminal vertices and all terminals from $\mathcal{S}$. Indeed, by construction, X should dominate old terminals. Every vertex $u(r)$ or $v(r)$ of $\mathcal{S}$ is adjacent either to all nonterminal vertices colored r or to all nonterminal vertices colored k, and thus it is also dominated by X.

For the converse, suppose that G has a k-colored dominating set $X = \{x_1, x_2, \ldots, x_k\}$, where x_i is the vertex for which $\text{col}(x_i) = i$. We argue that all vertices of X are from exactly one of the G_is, $i = 1, 2$, and then it is immediate that they must dominate all the terminals of G_i.

Targeting toward a contradiction, suppose that the vertices of X do not belong only to one graph among G_1 and G_2. Let us further first assume that $x_k \in G_1$, and we pick any $r \neq k$ such that $x_r \in G_2$. Due to the applicability of transformations λ and $\bar{\lambda}$, vertex $u(r)$ of $\mathcal{S}$ in G can be dominated either by x_k or by x_r. However, it cannot be adjacent to x_r because $x_r \in V(G_2)$ and in $\bar{\lambda}(G_2)$, $u(r)$ is adjacent only to vertices colored k. It also cannot be adjacent to $x_k \in V(G_1)$ because in $\lambda(G_1)$ u_r is adjacent to vertices colored $r \neq k$. Thus, $u(r)$ is not dominated by X in G, which is a contradiction. In the case $x_k \in G_2$ and $x_r \in G_2$ for some $r \neq k$, symmetric arguments show that $v(r)$ is not dominated by X in G.

The described instance selector for COL-RBDS immediately implies the existence of a cross-composition. The only detail that is different for COL-RBDS, when compared to other examples considered in this section, is that in the new instance the parameter grows by more than a constant. Let us remind that we parameterized by k, the size of a colored dominating set, plus the cardinality of the terminal set T. While we still seek a k-colored dominating set in the new graph G, the size of the terminal set of G increases by $2(k-1)$ because we have added to it the vertices of $\mathcal{S}$. By applying the selection ℓ times for $t = 2^\ell$ instances with terminal sets of size p, we cross-compose t into an instance with terminal set T of size

$$|T| = p + 2\ell \cdot (k-1).$$

Because the size of the parameter $|T| + k$ is bounded by a polynomial in $\max_{i=1}^{t} |G_i| + \log t$, we obtain a cross-composition for COL-RBDS. □

Exercises

Problem 18.1 Give an algorithm solving DISJOINT FACTORS in time $2^k \cdot n^{\mathcal{O}(1)}$.

Problem 18.2 Show that DISJOINT FACTORS is NP-complete.

Problem 18.3 Give an algorithm solving RED-BLUE DOMINATING SET in time $2^{|T|} \cdot n^{\mathcal{O}(1)}$.

Bibliographic Notes

The idea of an instance selector originated in the work of Dom et al. (2014). The formalism used in this chapter is inspired by the Master thesis by Misra (2010) and the survey by Misra et al. (2011).

The lower bound for DISJOINT FACTORS was shown by Bodlaender et al. (2011), and the bound for CNF-SAT (Theorem 18.3) was obtained in Fortnow and Santhanam (2011). Bounds for COLORED RED-BLUE DOMINATING SET were obtained in Dom et al. (2014).

Other applications of the instance selector technique can be found in Cygan et al. (2014b, 2012, 2014a).

19
Polynomial Parameter Transformation

In this chapter we introduce a type of reduction suitable for deriving kernelization lower bounds, namely, polynomial parameter transformation (PPT). We give several examples of how PPTs can be used.

Notions of reduction are generally popular as they lie at the heart of most known hardness results. To establish NP-hardness for some problem P, we rarely use the definition of NP-hardness but instead reduce an already known NP-hard problem to P. A very similar situation occurs with kernelization. Instead of constructing a distillation or a cross-composition every time we want to establish a lower bound for some problem, often it is easier to deduce the hardness of one problem by reducing to it another hard problem. To this end, we need an appropriate notion of reduction.

We start with the definition of the required transformation.

Definition 19.1 Let $P, Q \subseteq \Sigma^* \times \mathbb{N}$ be two parameterized problems. An algorithm $\mathcal{A}$ is called PPT from P to Q if, given an instance (x, k) of problem P, $\mathcal{A}$ works in polynomial time and outputs an equivalent instance $(\hat{x}, \hat{k})$ of problem Q, that is, $(x, k) \in P$ if and only if $(\hat{x}, \hat{k}) \in Q$, such that $\hat{k} \leq p(k)$ for some polynomial $p(\cdot)$.

Thus, in PPT we do not put any constraints on the size of $\hat{x}$, and only the polynomial bound on the parameter $\hat{k}$ is essential.

The motivation for defining PPT will become clear from the following theorem.

Theorem 19.2 *Let P and Q be parameterized problems such that there is a PPT from P to Q. If Q has a polynomial compression, then P also has a polynomial compression.*

Proof: Suppose that Q admits a polynomial compression to some language L. We show that there is a polynomial time compression of P to L.

Consider the following algorithm, which for an input pair (x, k), first calls a PPT $\mathcal{A}$ on (x, k). Let (y, k') be the output given by $\mathcal{A}$. Then $(x, k) \in P$ if and only if $(y, k') \in Q$ and k' is bounded by some polynomial of k. Now, we apply the polynomial compression algorithm (say $\mathcal{K}$) from Q to L on (y, k'). Let z be the output of $\mathcal{K}$. Thus, $(y, k') \in Q$ if and only if $z \in L$, and the size of z is bounded by a polynomial of k'. Pipelining algorithms $\mathcal{A}$ and $\mathcal{K}$, we obtain a polynomial compression of P to L. □

In this chapter we give examples of PPTs from a problem P to a problem Q such that the problem P does not admit a polynomial compression unless coNP $\subseteq$ NP/poly. Such a transformation together with Theorem 19.2 would imply that Q does not admit a polynomial compression unless coNP $\subseteq$ NP/poly. For some of the examples we deal with, we are not aware of any obvious cross-composition algorithms. In these situations, PPT is a very reasonable alternative to the strategy of showing a cross-composition algorithm for ruling out polynomial kernels.

19.1 Packing Paths and Cycles

We start with simple illustrative examples. Consider the following extension of the LONGEST PATH problem. In the PATH PACKING problem, we are given a graph G and a positive integer k. The task is to decide whether there exists a collection of k mutually vertex-disjoint paths of length k in G.

This problem is known to be fixed parameter tractable by Alon et al. (1995). Because PATH PACKING reminds LONGEST PATH, it is natural to guess that PATH PACKING also does not admit a polynomial kernel. However, the "disjoint union" trick that we used for LONGEST PATH, does not directly apply here.

Theorem 19.3 PATH PACKING *parameterized by k does not admit a polynomial kernel unless* coNP $\subseteq$ NP/poly.

Proof: We give a PPT from the LONGEST PATH problem. Given an instance (G, k) of LONGEST PATH, we construct a graph G' from G by adding $k - 1$ vertex disjoint paths of length k. Then, G contains a path of length k if and only if G' contains k mutually vertex-disjoint paths of length k. Because LONGEST PATH does not admit a polynomial compression unless coNP $\subseteq$ NP/poly (Theorem 17.5), by Theorem 19.2 so does PATH PACKING. □

19.1 Packing Paths and Cycles

Closely related to PATH PACKING is the CYCLE PACKING problem. Here we are given a graph G and a nonnegative integer k, and the task is to decide whether G contains at least k vertex-disjoint cycles. The problem of CYCLE PACKING is strongly related to the FEEDBACK VERTEX SET problem. Clearly, if a graph has more than k vertex-disjoint cycles, then it cannot have a feedback vertex set of size k or less, as any feedback vertex set has to pick at least one vertex from every cycle. If there are at most k vertex disjoint cycles, the implications are less immediate, but an upper bound of $\mathcal{O}(k \log k)$ on the size of an optimal feedback vertex set is known, due to a classic result by Erdős and Pósa. For FEEDBACK VERTEX SET, we have already seen polynomial kernels in earlier chapters. Note also that the variant of the problem called EDGE DISJOINT CYCLE PACKING, where instead of vertex-disjoint cycles, we have to find edge-disjoint cycles, admits a polynomial kernel; see Exercise 19.1. In contrast, we show that the CYCLE PACKING problem does not admit a polynomial kernel, and we establish this by showing a PPT from DISJOINT FACTORS. Because DISJOINT FACTORS parameterized by the size of the alphabet k does not admit a polynomial compression unless coNP $\subseteq$ NP/ poly (Theorem 18.2), this would imply that CYCLE PACKING also does not admit a polynomial compression.

Theorem 19.4 CYCLE PACKING *parameterized by k does not admit a polynomial compression unless* coNP $\subseteq$ NP/ poly.

Proof: Let L_k be an alphabet consisting of k letters, for simplicity we assume that $L_k = \{1, \ldots, k\}$, and let $s = w_1 \cdots w_n \in L_k^*$ be an input to DISJOINT FACTORS. We build a graph G_s as follows. First, we take n vertices $v_1, \ldots, v_n$, and edges $\{v_i, v_{i+1}\}$ for $1 \leq i < n$, that is, these vertices form a path of length n. Let P denote this path. Then, for each $i \in \{1, \ldots, k\}$ we add to G_s a vertex x_i, and make x_i adjacent to all vertices v_j of P such that in the string s, the letter s_j is i. See Fig. 19.1 for an illustration.

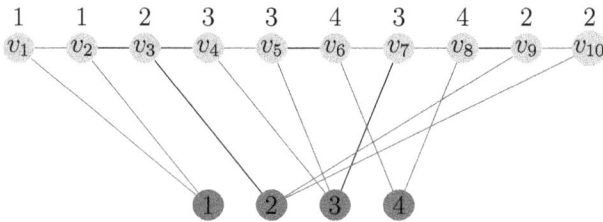

Figure 19.1 PPT from DISJOINT FACTORS to CYCLE PACKING, where $s = 1123343422$.

We claim that the graph G_s has k disjoint cycles if and only if s has the requested k disjoint factors. Suppose that G_s has k disjoint cycles $C_1, \ldots, C_k$. As P is a path, each of these cycles must contain at least one vertex not on P, that is of the form x_j. Also it is easy to see that none of these cycles can contain more than one of the x_j vertices, else we could not have k cycles. Hence, for every $1 \leq j \leq k$, the cycle C_j thus consists of x_j and a subpath of P. This subpath must start and end with a vertex adjacent to x_j. These two endpoints represent letters in s equal to j. Let F_j be the factor of s corresponding to the vertices on P in C_j. Now, $F_1, \ldots, F_k$ are disjoint factors, each of length at least two (as the cycles have length at least three), and F_j starts and ends with j, for all $1 \leq j \leq k$.

Conversely, if we have disjoint factors $F_1, \ldots, F_k$, we build k vertex-disjoint cycles as follows: For each j, $1 \leq j \leq k$, take the cycle consisting of x_j and the vertices corresponding to factor F_j. Thus, we have shown the desired result. This concludes the proof. □

19.2 RED-BLUE DOMINATING SET

In the previous chapter (Theorem 18.4), we gave a cross-composition for COL-ORED RED-BLUE DOMINATING SET (COL-RBDS). Our real interest, however, is in showing the hardness of obtaining polynomial kernels for the following fundamental problems: HITTING SET and SET COVER. Recall that a convenient equivalent graph-theoretic formulation of these problems is in the form of RED-BLUE DOMINATING SET (RBDS). We start by reducing RBDS from COL-RBDS.

Recall that in RBDS we are given a bipartite graph $G = (T \cup N, E)$ and an integer k, and we are asked whether there exists a vertex set $X \subseteq N$ of size at most k such that every vertex in T has at least one neighbor in X. We also refer to the vertices T as *terminals* and to the vertices of N as *nonterminals*.

In the colored version COL-RBDS, which we showed to be compositional, the vertices of N are colored with colors chosen from $\{1, \ldots, k\}$, that is, we are additionally given a function col : $N \to \{1, \ldots, k\}$, and X is required to contain exactly one vertex of each color.

Theorem 19.5 RBDS *parameterized by* $|T|$ *does not admit a polynomial compression unless* coNP $\subseteq$ NP/ poly.

Proof: By Theorem 18.4, COL-RBDS parameterized by $|T|+k$ does not admit a polynomial compression unless coNP $\subseteq$ NP/ poly. To prove the theorem, we give a PPT from COL-RBDS parameterized by $|T|+k$ to RBDS parameterized by $|T|$.

Given an instance $(G = (T \cup N, E), k, \mathrm{col})$ of COL-RBDS, we construct an instance $(G' = (T' \cup N, E'), k)$ of RBDS.

In G', the set T' consists of all vertices from T plus k additional vertices $v_1, \ldots, v_k$. The edge set E' consists of all edges from E plus the edges

$$\{uv_i \;:\; i \in \{1, \ldots, k\} \;\wedge\; u \in N \;\wedge\; \mathrm{col}(u) = i\}.$$

See Fig. 19.2 for an illustration.

First, observe that G is a yes-instance of COL-RBDS if and only if G' is a yes-instance of COL-RBDS. Clearly, every k-colored dominating set in G is also a k-dominating set in G'. In the opposite direction, every vertex v_i can be dominated only by a vertex from N colored i. Because we seek a dominating set of size k, every k-dominating of G' should contain exactly one vertex of each color, and thus should be a k-colored dominating set.

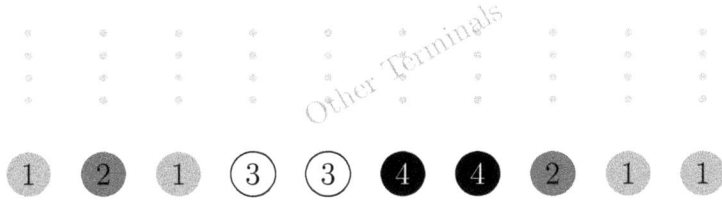

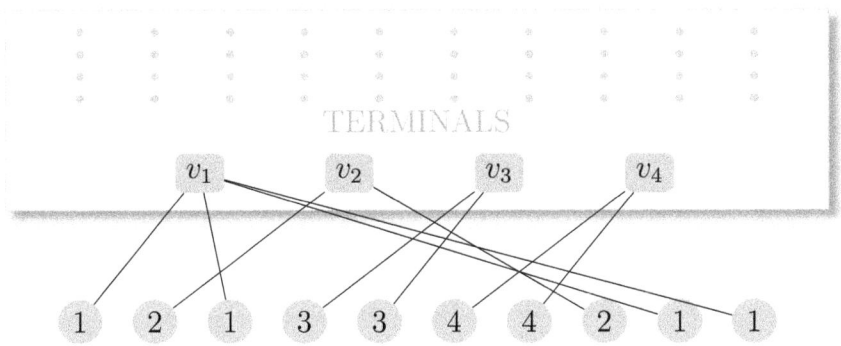

Figure 19.2 The PPT from the colored version of RBDS to RBDS.

Finally, we parameterize COL-RBDS by $|T| + k$. Because the size of the terminal set of G is $|T'| = |T| + k$, the described construction provides us with a PPT. □

As we have already mentioned in the previous chapter, RBDS becomes polynomial-time solvable when $k \geq |T|$. To see this, greedily pick for each vertex $v \in T$ one "private" neighbor in N. Thus, the parameterization by $|T|+k$ is equivalent to the parameterization by $|T|$. Hence, by Theorem 19.5, we have the following corollary.

Corollary 19.6 RBDS *parameterized by* $|T|+k$ *(and thus by k) does not admit a polynomial compression unless* $\text{coNP} \subseteq \text{NP/poly}$.

As we have also already discussed in the previous chapter, RBDS is equivalent to HITTING SET. Recall that an input to HITTING SET consists of a universe U, a family $\mathcal{F}$ of subsets of U, and an integer k. The goal is to choose a set X of at most k elements from U such that every set from the family $\mathcal{F}$ contains at least one element from X. To see that RBDS and HITTING SET are equivalent, note that, given a HITTING SET instance $(U, \mathcal{F}, k)$, one may set $N = U$, $T = \mathcal{F}$, and make each set $A \in \mathcal{F}$ adjacent to all its elements; for a set $X \subseteq U$, the condition that every set from $\mathcal{F}$ contains an element from X is equivalent to saying that X is a dominating set in the constructed graph.

HITTING SET is dual to SET COVER. Let us remind that an input to SET COVER consists of a universe U, a family $\mathcal{F}$ of subsets of U, and an integer k. The goal is to choose at most k sets from the family $\mathcal{F}$ that cover the entire universe U. That is, we are looking for a subfamily $\mathcal{X} \subseteq \mathcal{F}$ such that $|\mathcal{X}| \leq k$ and $\bigcup \mathcal{X} = U$. To see that RBDS and SET COVER are equivalent, note that, given a SET COVER instance $(U, \mathcal{F}, k)$, one may set $N = \mathcal{F}$, $T = U$ and make each set $A \in \mathcal{F}$ adjacent to all its elements; the condition that a family of sets $X \subseteq \mathcal{F}$ covers U translates to X dominates T in the constructed graph.

Hence by Theorem 19.5, we have the following

Theorem 19.7 SET COVER *parameterized by the size of the universe U and* HITTING SET *parameterized by the size of the family $\mathcal{F}$ do not admit a polynomial compression unless* $\text{coNP} \subseteq \text{NP/poly}$.

RBDS is handy for making PPTs to different problems. As a warm-up exercise, let us consider STEINER TREE. Recall that in Theorem 17.9, which was proved by constructing a cross-composition, we stated that STEINER TREE parameterized by the size of the solution k does not admit a polynomial compression unless $\text{coNP} \subseteq \text{NP/poly}$. An alternative and simpler proof of Theorem 17.9 is by the following PPT from RBDS to STEINER TREE.

19.2 RED-BLUE DOMINATING SET

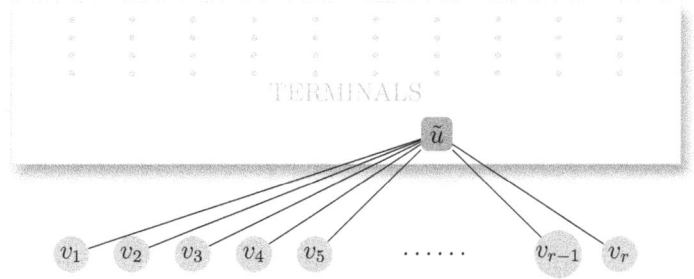

Figure 19.3 PPT from STEINER TREE to RBDS.

Let $(G = (T \cup N, E), k)$ be an instance of RBDS. To transform it into an instance (G', T', k') of STEINER TREE define $T' = T \cup \{\tilde{u}\}$, where $\tilde{u}$ is a new vertex and let

$$E(G') = E \cup \{\tilde{u}v \,:\, v \in N\},$$

and

$$k' = k + |T| + 1.$$

See Fig. 19.3 for an illustration. It is easy to see that there is a one-to-one correspondence between solutions for STEINER TREE on (G', T', k') and solutions for RBDS on (G, k). Indeed, every dominating set $X \subseteq N$ of size k can be turned into a Steiner tree in G' by adding to X the terminal vertices T and $\tilde{u}$. Moreover, for every Steiner tree in G', with vertex set $T \cup \{\tilde{u}\} \cup X$, every vertex of T should be adjacent to some vertex of X. Thus, X is a dominating set in G.

Our next example is CONNECTED VERTEX COVER. Here we are given a graph G and an integer k, and asked for a vertex cover of size at most k that induces a connected subgraph in G. It is known, see Exercise 19.2, that CONNECTED VERTEX COVER is FPT.

The PPT from CONNECTED VERTEX COVER to RBDS is almost the same as the reduction from STEINER TREE. The only trick is based on the following observation. If we have a vertex v adjacent to a vertex u of degree 1, then there is always a minimal (connected) vertex cover containing v. Thus, by attaching vertices of degree one we "anchor" their neighbors to be in the solution.

More formally, let $(G = (T \cup N, E), k)$ be an instance of RBDS. We transform it first into a graph G' by adding a vertex $\tilde{u}$ and making it adjacent to all the vertices of N. The graph G'' is then obtained from G' by attaching a leaf to every vertex in T'. Now, G'' has a connected vertex cover of size

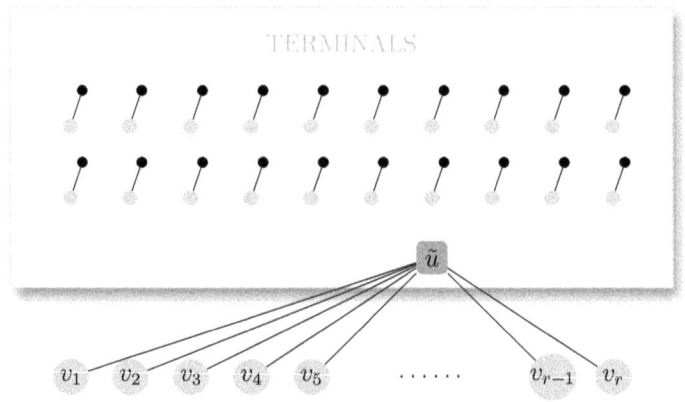

Figure 19.4 PPT from RBDS to CONNECTED VERTEX COVER.

$k'' = |T| + 1 + k$ if and only if G' has a Steiner tree of size k'', which happens if and only if in G all vertices from T can be dominated by k vertices from N. See Fig. 19.4 for an illustration.

Thus, we have the following theorem.

Theorem 19.8 CONNECTED VERTEX COVER *parameterized by the size of the solution k does not admit a polynomial compression unless* coNP $\subseteq$ NP/ poly.

Interestingly, Theorem 19.8 is a sharp contrast to the fact that VERTEX COVER admits a kernel of size $\mathcal{O}(k^2)$.

Another variant of VERTEX COVER is CAPACITATED VERTEX COVER, where we are asked to find a vertex cover in a graph where the vertices have capacities associated with them, and every vertex can cover at most as many edges as its capacity. The CAPACITATED VERTEX COVER problem takes as input a graph G, a capacity function cap : $V(G) \to \mathbb{N}^+$ and an integer k, and the task is to find a vertex cover $C \subset V(G)$ of size at most k for which there is a a mapping from $E(G)$ to C such that *(i)* for every edge $e \in E(G)$ mapped to a vertex $v \in C$, v is incident to e, and *(ii)* at most cap(v) edges are mapped to every vertex $v \in C$.

A PPT from RBDS to CAPACITATED VERTEX COVER is as follows. Let $(G = (T \cup N, E), k)$ be an instance of RBDS. We transform G into graph G' as follows. The vertex set of G' consists of sets T' and N. Each vertex $u \in T$ of G is replaced in G' by a clique with four vertices u^0, u^1, u^2, u^3. Thus, $|T'| = 4|T|$. For every edge $uv \in E(G)$ with $u \in T$ and $v \in N$, we add the edge $u^0 v$ to G'. The capacities of the vertices are defined as follows:

For each vertex $u \in T$, the vertices $u^1, u^2, u^3 \in T'$ have capacity 1 and the vertex u^0 has capacity $\deg_{G'}(u^0) - 1$. Each vertex $v \in N$ has capacity $\deg_{G'}(v)$. Clearly, to cover the edges of the size-4 cliques inserted for the vertices of T, every capacitated vertex cover for G', for every $u \in T$, must contain all the vertices u^0, u^1, u^2, u^3. Moreover, because the capacity of each vertex u^0 is too small to cover all the edges incident to it, at least one neighbor v of u^0 must be selected into every capacitated vertex cover for G'. Therefore, G' has a capacitated vertex cover of size $k' = 4 \cdot |T| + k$ if and only if all vertices from T can be dominated in G by k vertices from N.

This brings us to the following theorem.

Theorem 19.9 CAPACITATED VERTEX COVER *parameterized by the size of the solution k does not admit a polynomial compression unless* coNP $\subseteq$ NP/ poly.

Exercises

Problem 19.1 (☠) In the EDGE DISJOINT CYCLE PACKING problem, we are given an undirected graph G and a positive integer k, and the objective is to test whether G has k pairwise edge disjoint cycles. Obtain a polynomial kernel for EDGE DISJOINT CYCLE PACKING (parameterized by k).

Problem 19.2 (✐) Show that CAPACITATED VERTEX COVER and CONNECTED VERTEX COVER parameterized by the solution size are FPT.

Problem 19.3 Prove that RED-BLUE DOMINATING SET parameterized by $|N|$ does not admit a polynomial kernel unless coNP $\subseteq$ NP/ poly.

Bibliographic Notes

The first usage of a PPT to establish lower bounds on kernel sizes is due to Bodlaender et al. (2011), see also Binkele-Raible et al. (2012). The example of PATH PACKING is from Lokshtanov (2009). The bounds for RED-BLUE DOMINATING SET, HITTING SET, and SET COVER were originally established by Dom et al. (2014).

Other examples of applications of PPTs can be found in Cygan et al. (2012), Jansen (2013), and Kratsch and Wahlström (2013).

20
Polynomial Lower Bounds

In this chapter we introduce the notion of a weak cross-composition, used to obtain lower bounds for problems that admit polynomial kernels. In particular, we use a weak cross-composition to establish a lower bound for d-HITTING SET. Specifically, for any $\varepsilon > 0$, the d-HITTING SET problem parameterized by the solution size does not admit a polynomial compression with bitsize $\mathcal{O}(k^{d-\varepsilon})$, unless coNP $\subseteq$ NP/poly.

In previous chapters, we saw how one can rule out polynomial kernels (and even compressions) for specific problems. So far, these techniques were applied to rule out the existence of polynomial kernels. Interestingly, with a small modification, the same approach can also be used to obtain concrete lower bounds on the kernel sizes of problems admitting polynomial kernels. For example, we have already seen that VERTEX COVER and FEEDBACK VERTEX SET admit kernels of bit-size $\mathcal{O}(k^2)$ and that d-HITTING SET admits a kernel of bit-size roughly k^d. The technique we develop in this chapter is used to show that most likely these bounds on the kernel sizes are tight.

20.1 Weak Cross-Composition

So far, in our strategy of using cross-composition to rule out the existence of polynomial-size compressions of NP-hard problems, we used the following chain of arguments. First, we know that a polynomially bounded OR-distillation of an NP-hard language L is not possible unless coNP $\subseteq$ NP/poly (Theorem 17.3). Second, the possibility of cross-composing a language L into a polynomially compressible language Q implies that L admits a polynomially bounded OR-distillation (Theorem 17.8). Thus, if L can be cross-composed into Q, then Q cannot be compressed.

Quite surprisingly, almost the same approach can be used for deriving lower bounds on kernel sizes for problems admitting polynomial kernels! The rough idea is the following. Let us recall Definition 17.7 of cross-composition on page 366. A cross-composition algorithm outputs a pair (y, k) with a string y from a set of t strings, $x_1, \ldots, x_t$, such that k is bounded by $p(\max_{i=1}^{t} |x_i| + \log t)$ for some polynomial $p(\cdot)$. The dependence $p(\log t)$ in the bound for k was used in Theorem 17.8 to show that cross-composition with compression can be used to design an OR-distillation, that is, an algorithm producing a string of length at most t.

But the proof of Theorem 17.8 will work also if we slightly change the settings. For example, suppose that VERTEX COVER, which has a polynomial kernel, admits a "weaker" cross-composition into Q, such that for $(y, k) \in Q$ the bound on the parameter k is weaker, say $k \leq p(\max_{i=1}^{t} |x_i|) \cdot t^{\frac{1}{2}+\delta}$ for every $\delta > 0$. Then the assumption that Q has a bitsize $k^{2-\varepsilon}$ compression for some $\varepsilon > 0$ pipelined with such a composition, would allow us to design an OR-distillation. Thus, if we succeed to construct such a weaker cross-composition, this would imply that VERTEX COVER does not admit a bitsize $k^{2-\varepsilon}$ compression unless coNP $\subseteq$ NP/poly.

To formalize this idea, we need to define a weak cross-composition.

Definition 20.1 (Weak cross-composition) Let $L \subseteq \Sigma^*$ be a language and $Q \subseteq \Sigma^* \times \mathbb{N}$ be a parameterized language. We say that L *weakly-cross-composes* into Q if there exists a real constant $d \geq 1$, called the *dimension*, a polynomial equivalence relation $\mathcal{R}$, and an algorithm $\mathcal{A}$, called the *weak cross-composition*, satisfying the following conditions. The algorithm $\mathcal{A}$ takes as input a sequence of strings $x_1, x_2, \ldots, x_t \in \Sigma^*$ that are equivalent with respect to $\mathcal{R}$, runs in time polynomial in $\sum_{i=1}^{t} |x_i|$, and outputs one instance $(y, k) \in \Sigma^* \times \mathbb{N}$ such that:

(i) For every $\delta > 0$, there exists a polynomial $p(\cdot)$ such that for every choice of t and input strings $x_1, x_2, \ldots, x_t$, it holds that $k \leq p(\max_{i=1}^{t} |x_i|) \cdot t^{\frac{1}{d}+\delta}$, and

(ii) $(y, k) \in Q$ if and only if there exists at least one index i such that $x_i \in L$.

A theorem for cross-composition of bounded cost analogous to the one for cross-composition is as follows. Its proof goes along the lines of Theorem 17.8 except for having slightly different calculations.

Theorem 20.2 *Assume that an NP-hard language L admits a weak cross-composition of dimension d into a parameterized language Q. Assume further that Q admits a polynomial compression with bitsize $\mathcal{O}(k^{d-\varepsilon})$, for some $\varepsilon > 0$. Then $\mathrm{coNP} \subseteq \mathrm{NP}/\,\mathrm{poly}$.*

Proof: Because the proof of this theorem and Theorem 17.8 are very similar, here we give details only for the parts of the proof that differ in these theorems.

Suppose that Q admits a polynomial compression with bitsize $\mathcal{O}(k^{d-\varepsilon})$, for some $\varepsilon > 0$, into a language R. As in Theorem 17.8, we show that this implies the existence of a t-bounded OR-distillation algorithm for L, where t is a polynomially bounded function, into the language $\mathrm{OR}(R)$ consisting of strings of the form $z_1\#z_2\#\ldots\#z_q$.

We define the following constants.

(c_1) Language L weakly cross-composes into Q. Therefore, there is $c_1 > 0$ such that, given a set of $\mathcal{R}$-equivalent strings $x_1,\ldots,x_t$, the composition algorithm outputs a string (y,k) equivalent to the OR of the strings x_i and such that $k \leq (\max_{i=1}^{t} |x_i|)^{c_1} \cdot t^{\frac{1}{d}+\delta}$ for every $\delta > 0$.

(c_2) Because $\mathcal{R}$ is the polynomial equivalence relation, there is a constant c_2 such that for every integer n, any set S of strings of length n can be partitioned in polynomial time into at most n^{c_2} $\mathcal{R}$-equivalent classes.

Let

$$t(n) = (2n^{c_2 + c_1(d-\varepsilon)})^{\frac{1}{\varepsilon d}}$$

be a polynomially bounded function. The reason why we define $t(n)$ in this way will become clear from the arguments in the following text. As in the proof of Theorem 17.8, we pipeline a weak cross-composition with a compression. Thus, from an input of $t = t(n)$ strings, we first obtain a set of instances of Q, denoted by (y_i, k_i), $i \in \{1,\ldots,r\}$. After compressing each (y_i, k_i), we construct an instance of $\mathrm{OR}(R)$, which is a string $z = z_1\#z_2\#\ldots\#z_r$. Thus, each substring z_i is obtained from compressing a string obtained by weakly cross-composing an equivalent class of input strings. Here, $r \leq n^{c_2}$ and

$$|z| \leq r + r \cdot \max_{1 \leq i \leq r} |z_i| \leq n^{c_2} + n^{c_2} \cdot \max_{1 \leq i \leq r} |z_i| \leq 2n^{c_2} \cdot \max_{1 \leq i \leq r} |z_i|.$$

(For the last inequality we assume that $\max_{1 \leq i \leq r} |z_i| \geq 1$.) Because of the compression, we have that for every $i \in \{1, \ldots, r\}$,

$$|z_i| \leq k_i^{d-\varepsilon}.$$

By the definition of a weak cross-composition, we have that

$$|k_i| \leq n^{c_1} \cdot t^{\frac{1}{d}+\delta}.$$

Putting all these together and by defining $\delta = \varepsilon/d^2$, we have that

$$|z| \leq 2n^{c_2} n^{c_1(d-\varepsilon)} \cdot t^{1+d\delta - \varepsilon/d - \varepsilon d}$$
$$\leq 2n^{c_2} n^{c_1(d-\varepsilon)} \cdot t^{1-\varepsilon d} = t^{\varepsilon d} \cdot t^{1-\varepsilon d} = t.$$

This provides the desired t-bounded distillation algorithm from the language L to the language $\mathrm{OR}(R)$, and completes the proof. □

20.2 Lower Bound for VERTEX COVER

To use Theorem 20.2 for some specific problem, we need to construct a weak cross-composition. There is no universal recipe for constructing such compositions.

We have earlier seen that VERTEX COVER admits a kernel with at most $2k$ vertices and $\mathcal{O}(k^2)$ edges; thus it admits a kernel of bitsize $\mathcal{O}(k^2)$. In what follows, we prove that VERTEX COVER does not admit any kernel or compression of size $\mathcal{O}(k^{2-\epsilon})$ for any $\epsilon > 0$ unless $\mathrm{coNP} \subseteq \mathrm{NP/poly}$.

By Theorem 20.2, to refute the existence of a polynomial compression for VERTEX COVER with subquadratic bitsize, it is sufficient to design a weak cross-composition of dimension 2 from some NP-hard problem to VERTEX COVER. While it is possible, the success of the whole construction depends on the correct choice of the starting problem. We will compose from MULTICOLORED BICLIQUE. In the MULTICOLORED BICLIQUE problem we are given a bipartite graph G with a bipartition U and W such that U is partitioned into k color classes $U_1, U_2, \ldots, U_k$, each of size n, and W is partitioned into k color classes $W_1, W_2, \ldots, W_k$, each of size n as well. The task is to decide whether G contains a *multicolored biclique* with $2k$ vertices. In other words, the task is to decide whether one can pick one vertex from each class U_i and one vertex from each class W_i such that the graph induced by the chosen vertices is isomorphic to the complete bipartite graph $K_{k,k}$.

The MULTICOLORED BICLIQUE problem is known to be NP-hard, and we record this without a proof.

Lemma 20.3 MULTICOLORED BICLIQUE *is* NP-*hard*.

We are ready to show that MULTICOLORED BICLIQUE weakly cross-composes into VERTEX COVER, which will bring us to the following theorem.

Theorem 20.4 *For any $\varepsilon > 0$, the* VERTEX COVER *problem parameterized by the solution size does not admit a polynomial compression with bitsize $\mathcal{O}(k^{2-\varepsilon})$, unless* coNP $\subseteq$ NP/ poly.

Proof: For our proof we give a weak cross-composition of dimension 2. We define a polynomial equivalence relation $\mathcal{R}$ such that all bit-strings that do not encode a valid instance of MULTICOLORED BICLIQUE are equivalent. Of the remaining instances, any two well-formed instances I_1 and I_2 are equivalent if and only if they have the same number (say k) of color classes and every color class in both instances is of the same size.

Let $B_1, B_2, \ldots, B_t$ be the instances of MULTICOLORED BICLIQUE belonging to the same equivalence class of $\mathcal{R}$. Thus, we can assume that every instance B_i has the same number k of groups in each side of its bipartition, and every group in every instance B_i has the same size n. Furthermore, we can assume that $\sqrt{t}$ is an integer. (If not, we copy a few instances, not increasing the number of instances by more than a factor of 2.) It is very useful to view the instances $B_1, B_2, \ldots, B_t$ as the entries of a $\sqrt{t} \times \sqrt{t}$ matrix B. From this point of view, we can refer to the instances of MULTICOLORED BICLIQUE as $B_{i,j}$, where $1 \leq i,j \leq \sqrt{t}$. We also use the notation $U_{i,j}$ and $W_{i,j}$ to refer to the bipartition of $B_{i,j}$.

First, we modify each of the $B_{i,j}$ such that all graphs $B_{i,j}[U_{i,j}]$ and $B_{i,j}[W_{i,j}]$ become complete k-partite graphs. We do so by adding edges between any two vertices of $U_{i,j}$ if they are in different color classes. We do the same with the vertices in $W_{i,j}$. We call the new graphs $B'_{i,j}$. Clearly, every original graph $B_{i,j}$ has a multicolored biclique $K_{k,k}$ if and only if $B'_{i,j}$ has a clique on $2k$ vertices.

Now, we construct a graph G by introducing $2\sqrt{t}$ sets $U^1, \ldots, U^{\sqrt{t}}$ and $W^1, \ldots, W^{\sqrt{t}}$ of kn vertices each. Thus, $|V(G)| = 2\sqrt{t}kn$. Each of the sets U_i and W_i is colored in k colors, each color class is of size n. The edge set of G is constructed in such a way that for each pair of indices $1 \leq i,j \leq \sqrt{t}$, the subgraph of G induced by $U^i \cup W^j$ is a copy of $B'_{i,j}$. In other words, for each $i \in \{1, \ldots, \sqrt{t}\}$, we make the vertices of U^i with different colors pairwise adjacent. We do the same with W^i. Thus, each of the graphs $G[U^i]$ and $G[W^i]$ becomes a complete k-partite graph. Then for each pair of indices $1 \leq i,j \leq \sqrt{t}$, we add edges between U_i and W_j in such a manner that the subgraph $G[U^i \cup W^j]$ is isomorphic to $B'_{i,j}$.

20.2 Lower Bound for VERTEX COVER

Claim 20.5 *The graph G has a $2k$-clique if and only if at least one of the graphs $B'_{i,j}$ has a $2k$-clique.*

Proof If one of the $B'_{i,j}$s has a $2k$-clique, then G has a $2k$-clique because there is a graph isomorphic to every $B'_{i,j}$ that is a subgraph of G. Now, for the forward direction, suppose that G has a $2k$-sized clique. We observe that there are no edges between U^i and $U^{i'}$ in G for $i \neq i'$. Similarly, there are no edges between W^j and $W^{j'}$ in G for $j \neq j'$. Thus, the $2k$ clique of G is contained in $G[U^i \cup W^j]$ for some $1 \leq i, j \leq \sqrt{t}$. But each $G[U^i \cup W^j]$ is isomorphic to $B'_{i,j}$. Therefore, $B'_{i,j}$ has a $2k$-sized clique.

As argued earlier, the original graph $B_{i,j}$ had a multicolored biclique if and only if $B'_{i,j}$ has a clique on $2k$ vertices. Now by Claim 20.5, the original graph $B_{i,j}$ has a multicolored biclique if and only if G has a $2k$-clique. To complete our reduction, we map the t instances of MULTICOLORED BICLIQUE to the following instance of VERTEX COVER, $(\overline{G}, |V(\overline{G})| - 2k)$. Here, $\overline{G}$ is the complement graph of G. We know that G has a $2k$-sized clique if and only if $\overline{G}$ has a $|V(\overline{G})| - 2k$-sized vertex cover. Hence, we output $(\overline{G}, |V(\overline{G})| - 2k)$ as an instance of VERTEX COVER, which is a yes-instance if and only if at least one of the t instances of MULTICOLORED BICLIQUE is a yes-instance. The only thing that remains to show is to bound the size of $|V(\overline{G})| - 2k$. However,

$$|V(\overline{G})| - 2k \leq |V(\overline{G})| \leq 2t^{\frac{1}{2}}kn.$$

Hence, our construction is a weak cross-composition. Thus, by making use of Lemma 20.3 and Theorem 20.2, we obtain the desired result. □

Theorem 20.4 implies the bounds on the kernel size for FEEDBACK VERTEX SET. There is a simple polynomial parameter transformation that takes as input an instance (G, k) of VERTEX COVER and outputs an equivalent instance (H, k) of FEEDBACK VERTEX SET. The graph H is obtained from G as follows. For every edge $uv \in E(G)$, we add a new vertex w_{uv} and make it adjacent to u and to v, thus creating a triangle that must be hit by every feedback vertex set. Therefore,

Corollary 20.6 *For any $\varepsilon > 0$, the FEEDBACK VERTEX SET problem parameterized by the solution size does not admit a polynomial compression with bitsize $\mathcal{O}(k^{2-\varepsilon})$, unless* coNP $\subseteq$ NP/ poly.

It is interesting to compare the lower bounds for VERTEX COVER and FEEDBACK VERTEX SET with the known upper bounds. By Theorem 20.4 and Corollary 20.6, obtaining kernels for these problems with a strictly subquadratic number of edges is implausible (because $\mathcal{O}(k^{2-\varepsilon})$ edges can be encoded in $\mathcal{O}(k^{2-\varepsilon} \log k)$ bits). VERTEX COVER admits a kernel that has a linear number of vertices (kernel with $2k$ vertices is given in Theorem 6.2). For FEEDBACK VERTEX SET the best-known kernel, see Theorem 5.14, has $\mathcal{O}(k^2)$ vertices. By making use of weak cross-composition we can only bound the size of the kernel, but cannot obtain more specific information on its structure.

20.3 Lower Bound for d-HITTING SET

In this section we obtain a concrete lower bound for a generalization of VERTEX COVER, namely d-HITTING SET. Let us remind that in this problem, we are given a family $\mathcal{A}$ of sets over a universe U, where each set in the family has cardinality at most d, and a positive integer k. The objective is to decide whether there is a subset $H \subseteq U$ of size at most k such that H contains at least one element from each set in $\mathcal{A}$. Thus, VERTEX COVER is d-HITTING SET for $d = 2$.

It is convenient for our purposes to restate d-HITTING SET in the language of hypergraphs: In a d-uniform hypergraph H (i.e., every hyperedge in $E(H)$ is a d-sized subset of $V(H)$), we are looking for a set of vertices of size k hitting every hyperedge of H. For our arguments, we need to define what is a hyperclique in a hypergraph. To this end, let H be a d-uniform hypergraph. A *hyperclique* of H is a subset $W \subseteq V(G)$ such that every d-element set $X \subseteq W$ is a hyperedge of H. Let $\overline{H}$ be the complement of the hypergraph H. That is, $\overline{H}$ is a d-uniform hypergraph on the same vertex set as H, where a d-sized vertex set X is a hyperedge of $\overline{H}$ if and only if it is not a hyperedge of H.

Let us reflect a bit on how we established the lower bound for VERTEX COVER in Theorem 20.4. For the NP-hard problem MULTICOLORED BICLIQUE, we provided an embedding of t instances of MULTICOLORED BICLIQUE of length n into a carefully constructed graph G on $\sqrt{t}\,\mathrm{poly}(n)$ vertices. The property of the embedding was that G contained a clique of the specific size ℓ if and only if at least one of the t instances of MULTICOLORED BICLIQUE was a yes-instance. Because the vertex cover of $\overline{G}$ did not exceed $|V(G)| - \ell$, this provided us with the required weak cross-composition.

For $d > 2$, our approach is similar. This time it is more convenient to show that 3-SAT weakly cross-composes into d-HITTING SET. We construct an embedding of t instances of 3-SAT into a carefully selected d-uniform hypergraph H with $t^{1/d}\,\mathrm{poly}(n)$ vertices such that H contains a hyperclique of specific size ℓ if and only if at least one of the t instances of 3-SAT is satisfiable.

20.3 Lower Bound for d-HITTING SET

We will use the following simple result. In graphs, this result states that for every independent set I in a graph G (or for every clique in the complement of G), the vertices $V(G) \setminus I$ form a vertex cover of G.

Lemma 20.7 *Let $d \geq 2$ and let C be a vertex subset of a d-uniform hypergraph H. Then, C is a hyperclique if and only if the set $W = V(H) \setminus C$ intersects all hyperedges of $\overline{H}$.*

Proof: Let C be a hyperclique in H. Then for each hyperedge e of $\overline{H}$ its vertex set cannot be entirely in C and thus is intersected by W.

In the opposite direction, suppose that $W = V(H) \setminus C$ intersects all hyperedges of $\overline{H}$. Then every vertex set $X \subseteq C$ of size d, because it does not intersect W, should induce a hyperedge of H. Thus, C is a hyperclique. □

In Theorem 8.3, we proved that d-HITTING SET admits a kernel with at most $d! \, k^d$ sets and at most $d! \, k^d \cdot d^2$ elements. The following theorem provides a lower bound for kernelization of d-HITTING SET.

Theorem 20.8 *For every integer $d \geq 2$ and any $\varepsilon > 0$, the d-HITTING SET problem parameterized by the solution size does not admit a polynomial compression with bitsize $\mathcal{O}(k^{d-\varepsilon})$, unless coNP $\subseteq$ NP/poly.*

Proof: We give a weak cross-composition of dimension d from 3-SAT to d-HITTING SET. The 3-SAT problem is a variant of CNF-SAT, where every clause contains exactly three literals. It is well known to be NP-complete.

We define a polynomial equivalent relation $\mathcal{R}$ such that all bit-strings that do not encode a valid instance of 3-SAT are equivalent. Of the remaining instances, any two well-formed instances φ_1 and φ_2 are equivalent if and only if they have the same number of variables and the same number of clauses.

Let $\varphi_1, \ldots, \varphi_t$ be t instances of 3-SAT with the same number of variables and the same number of clauses. Because the number of variables in all instances is the same, we can assume that they are over the same set of variables $\{x_1, \ldots, x_n\}$. (Observe that if they were not the same we could rename the variables.) We identify these variables by integers from $\{1, \ldots, n\}$. We also assume that $t^{1/d}$ is an integer, else we can duplicate the instances so that we have this property.

For a triple of integers $S = \{i, j, k\}$, $i \neq j \neq k$ and $i, j, k \in \{1, \ldots, n\}$, we call a mapping $f \colon S \to \{\bot, \top\}$ a *partial assignment*. Thus, for each triple S we have eight different partial assignments. Let $\mathcal{F}$ be a family of all partial assignments of all triples. Then the size of $\mathcal{F}$ is $|\mathcal{F}| = 8 \cdot \binom{n}{3}$. We construct a consistency graph P, whose vertices are assignments from $\mathcal{F}$, and two partial assignments f and f' are adjacent if and only if they are consistent on the intersection of their domains. That is, if $f \colon S \to \{0, 1\}$ and $f' \colon S' \to \{\bot, \top\}$, then for all

$u \in S \cap S'$ we have $f(u) = f'(u)$. Observe that the graph P contains a clique of size $\binom{n}{3}$: Take partial assignments corresponding to any fixed assignment from $\{1, \ldots, n\}$ to $\{\bot, \top\}$. However, P does not have a clique of size more than $\binom{n}{3}$. Toward this, observe that for every triple S, the vertices of P corresponding to all the eight partial assignments of S form an independent set.

We use the graph P to construct an instance of d-HITTING SET as follows. First, we construct a d-uniform hypergraph H where we will be seeking a clique of an appropriate size and then take the complement of this hypergraph as an instance for d-HITTING SET.

It is convenient to view the input instances $\varphi_1, \ldots, \varphi_t$ as elements of a d-dimensional array. In other words, we fix a bijection, say,

$$g: \{1, \ldots, t\} \to \{1, \ldots, t^{1/d}\}^d.$$

Thus, every integer $i \in \{1, \ldots, t\}$ is mapped by g to a d-dimensional vector $(i_1, \ldots, i_d)$ with $i_j \in \{1, \ldots, t^{1/d}\}$ for all $j \in \{1, \ldots, d\}$. Then every instance φ_i can be written as $\varphi_{i_1, \ldots, i_d}$, where $g(i) = (i_1, \ldots, i_d)$.

The vertex set of hypergraph H consists of $dt^{1/d}$ groups of vertices. We denote these groups by $V_{a,b}$ for $a \in \{1, \ldots, d\}$ and $b \in \{1, \ldots, t^{1/d}\}$. These groups have the following properties.

- For each $b \in \{1, \ldots, t^{1/d}\}$, $|V_{1,b}| = |V(P)|$. Thus, in total we have $t^{1/d}$ copies of the vertex set of the consistency graph P. Let us remind that every vertex of P is a partial assignment to a triple of variables. Thus, every subset $X \subseteq V_{1,b}$ corresponds to a set of partial assignments of triples.
- For each $a \in \{2, \ldots, d\}$ and $b \in \{1, \ldots, t^{1/d}\}$, $V_{a,b} = \{v_{ab}\}$. That is, it is a singleton set.

Thus, $V(H) = \bigcup_{a,b} V_{a,b}$. Now we define the set of hyperedges of H. A subset e of d elements of $V(H)$ is a hyperedge of H if and only if it satisfies the following properties.

(i) For each $a \in \{1, \ldots, d\}$, there is at most one $b \in \{1, \ldots, t^{1/d}\}$ such that $e \cap V_{a,b} \neq \emptyset$. We denote such b by $b(a)$.
(ii) The intersection $e \cap V_{1,b(1)}$ is a clique in the graph P.
(iii) If $e \cap V_{a,b(a)} \neq \emptyset$ for all $a \in \{1, \ldots, d\}$, then the (unique) partial assignment $\sigma \in e \cap V_{1,b(1)}$ does not set any clause of $\varphi_{b(1), \ldots, b(d)}$ to false.

This completes the construction of a d-uniform hypergraph H. Hyperedges with $|e \cap V_{1,b(1)}| > 1$ play the role of checking consistency of assignments, and hyperedges with $|e \cap V_{a,b(a)}| = 1$ for all $a \in \{1, \ldots, d\}$ select an instance $\varphi_{b(1), \ldots, b(d)}$ and check whether that instance is satisfied.

20.3 Lower Bound for d-HITTING SET

We set $\ell = \binom{n}{3} + d - 1$. Now we show that at least one of the formulas $\varphi_1, \ldots, \varphi_t$ is satisfiable if and only if H has a hyperclique of size ℓ.

For the forward direction, let us assume that φ_i is satisfiable and $\psi: \{1, \ldots, n\} \to \{\bot, \top\}$ is a satisfying assignment. Furthermore, assume that $g(i) = (b_1, \ldots, b_d) \in \{1, \ldots, t^{1/d}\}^d$. Let W be the set of vertices in P that correspond to 3-variable partial assignments formed by ψ and let W_1 be its copy in V_{1,b_1}. Thus, $|W_1| = \binom{n}{3}$. We take

$$C = \left\{ v_{jb_j} : j \in \{2, \ldots, d\} \right\} \bigcup W_1$$

and claim that C is a hyperclique in H of size ℓ. The size bound follows from the construction. Clearly, every $e \subseteq C$ of size d satisfies the first property of being an hyperedge of H. The set $e \cap V_{1,b_1}$ forms a clique in P as these vertices correspond to a fixed assignment ψ. The final assertion in the definition of hyperedges follows from the fact that ψ is a satisfying assignment for φ_i. This completes the proof in the forward direction.

For the reverse direction, assume that C is a hyperclique of size ℓ in H. Because C is a hyperclique, the first property of the hyperedges of H implies that for every $j \in \{1, \ldots, d\}$, there is at most one b_j such that $C \cap V_{j,b_j} \neq \emptyset$. Because the graph P has a clique of size exactly $\binom{n}{3}$, we have that $C \cap V_{1,b_1}$ contains at most $\binom{n}{3}$ vertices and the other vertices that C could contain are $d - 1$ vertices of $\cup_{j \geq 2} V_{j,b_j}$. However, the cardinality constraint on C implies that $|C \cap V_{1,b_1}| = \binom{n}{3}$ and $|C \cap V_{j,b_j}| = 1$ for all $j \in \{2, \ldots, d\}$. Let $i = g^{-1}(b_1, \ldots, b_d)$. We claim that $\varphi_i = \varphi_{b_1, \ldots, b_d}$ is satisfiable. The second property of hyperedges and the properties of P imply that $C \cap V_{1,b_1}$ corresponds to an assignment $\zeta: \{1, \ldots, n\} \to \{\bot, \top\}$. By the third property of hyperedges, the corresponding partial assignment does not set any clause of $\varphi_{b_1, \ldots, b_d}$ to false. But because ζ sets a value for each variable, this means that ζ satisfies $\varphi_{b_1, \ldots, b_d}$.

Finally, we take $(\overline{H}, |V(H)| - \ell)$ as the instance of d-HITTING SET. By Lemma 20.7 and the preceding construction, we know that at least one of $\varphi_1, \ldots, \varphi_t$ is satisfiable if and only if there is a set of size $|V(H)| - \ell$ intersecting all the sets of $\overline{H}$. Thus, the parameter size is upper bounded by

$$|V(H)| - \ell \leq |V(H)| \leq t^{1/d} \binom{n}{3} + (d-1)t^{1/d} = \mathcal{O}(n^3 t^{1/d}).$$

This shows that our construction is a weak cross-composition. Now by applying Theorem 20.2, we obtain the desired result. This concludes the proof. □

20.4 Ramsey

The classical Ramsey's theorem on graphs says that for every integer $k > 0$, there is a computable function $R(k)$ such that every graph with $R(k)$ vertices contains an independent set of size k or a clique of size k.

A natural decision version of this problem is defined as follows. In the Ramsey problem, we are given a graph G and an integer k. The task is to decide whether G contains a clique of size k or an independent set of size k.

It is well known that Ramsey is an NP-complete problem. The problem of finding an independent set of size k in a graph and the problem of finding a clique of size k in a graph are not expected to have an algorithm with running time of the form $f(k) \cdot n^{\mathcal{O}(1)}$. However, Ramsey is fixed parameter tractable for the following reason. We know that every graph with $R(k)$ vertices has either a clique of size k or an independent set of size k. Thus, given an instance (G, k), if $R(k) \leq |V(G)|$ then we know that it is a yes-instance. Else, we have that $|V(G)| \leq R(k)$ and, thus, in time $f(R(k))$ we can check whether there exists a set X in G of size k that is either a clique or an independent set. Thus, a valid question to ask is whether Ramsey has a polynomial kernel. Using the framework described previously, we will show that Ramsey does not admit a compression of size $k^{2-\epsilon}$ unless coNP $\subseteq$ NP/poly. This result is not optimal—by making use of the techniques discussed in the next chapter, it is possible to show that Ramsey does not admit any polynomial compression unless coNP $\subseteq$ NP/poly. However, the proof of this fact is quite technical. However, the proof of $k^{2-\epsilon}$ is relatively simple and it serves as a good example of a weak cross-composition.

We will give a weak cross-composition of dimension 2 from the following promise version of Ramsey. In this version, we are guaranteed that the input graph G has both a clique of size $k - 1$ and an independent set of size $k - 1$, and we ask whether G has a clique of size k or independent set of size k.

We start by showing that Refinement Ramsey is NP-hard.

Lemma 20.9 Refinement Ramsey *is NP-hard.*

Proof We give a reduction from Ramsey. Given an instance (G, k) of Ramsey, we construct an instance (G', k') of Refinement Ramsey such that (G, k) is a yes-instance if and only if (G', k') is a yes-instance.

Let us remind that the disjoint union of vertex-disjoint graphs G and H is the graph $G \dot\cup H$ with the vertex set $V(G) \cup V(H)$ and the edge set $E(G) \cup E(H)$. The join $\otimes$ of vertex-disjoint graphs G and H is the graph with the vertex set $V(G) \cup V(G)$ and the edge set $E(G) \cup E(H) \cup \{uv \colon u \in V(G), \in V(H)\}$.

We construct G' by first taking a disjoint union of G and a clique C on $k-1$ vertices and then joining this graph (disjoint union of C and G) with an independent set I of size k. That is, $G' = (G \dot\cup C) \otimes I$. We also set $k' = k+1$.

We first show that G' has both a clique and independent set each of size k. The clique C combined with any vertex of I is a clique of size k, and I is an independent set of size k.

Now we show the desired equivalences. If (G, k) is a yes-instance of RAMSEY, then

- **Case 1:** G has a clique of size k. In this case, we get a clique of size $k+1$ in G' by combining the clique in G with any vertex in I.
- **Case 2:** G has an independent set of size k. In this case, we combine it with one of the vertices in C to get an independent set in G' of size $k+1$.

Conversely, if (G', k') is a yes-instance of REFINEMENT RAMSEY, then

- **Case 1:** G' has a clique of size $k+1$. We observe that the clique cannot come from $I \cup C$ alone because the largest clique in $I \cup C$ is of size k. So, it has at least one vertex from G, which forces at most one vertex from I and no vertices from C, because there are no edges between G and C. Hence, all but one vertex of the $k+1$ sized clique have to come from G, and thus G has a k-sized clique.
- **Case 2:** G' has an independent set of size $k+1$. We again observe that the independent set cannot come from $I \cup C$ alone because the largest independent set in $I \cup C$ is of size k. So, it has at least one vertex from G, which forces at most one vertex from C and no vertices from I, because all the vertices of G are adjacent to all the vertices of I. Hence, all but one vertex of the $k+1$-sized independent set have to come from G, and thus G has a k sized independent set.

This completes the proof. □

Now we are ready to give the main proof of this section.

Theorem 20.10 RAMSEY *has no compression of size* $\mathcal{O}(k^{2-\epsilon})$ *for any* $\epsilon > 0$ *unless* coNP $\subseteq$ NP/ poly.

Proof: For our proof we give a weak cross-composition of dimension 2 from REFINEMENT RAMSEY to RAMSEY. We define a polynomial equivalence relation $\mathcal{R}$ such that all bit-strings that do not encode a valid instance of REFINEMENT RAMSEY are equivalent. Of the remaining instances, any two well-formed instances (G_1, k_1) and (G_2, k_2) are equivalent if and only if $|V(G_1)| = |V(G_2)|$ and $k_1 = k_2$.

Let $(G_1, k), \ldots, (G_t, k)$ be t instances of REFINEMENT RAMSEY, where all the instances belong to the same equivalence class. We also assume that $\sqrt{t}$ is an integer. We can guarantee this condition by copying some instances and thus increasing their number by (at most) a factor 2.

Now, we divide the t instances arbitrarily into $\sqrt{t}$ groups of size $\sqrt{t}$ each. Then we perform a *join operation* for every two instances that are in the same group, to get graphs $Y_1, \ldots, Y_{\sqrt{t}}$. That is, if $G_1, \ldots, G_p$ are in the same group then we add an edge between any two vertices of different graphs. We refer to the disjoint union of these $\sqrt{t}$ graphs as G'. That is,

$$G' = \dot{\cup}_{i=1}^{\sqrt{t}} Y_i.$$

We output (G', k') as an instance of RAMSEY where $k' = (k-1)\sqrt{t} + 1$.

Now we show that (G', k') is a yes-instance of RAMSEY if and only if (G_i, k) is a yes instance of REFINEMENT RAMSEY for some $i \in \{1, \ldots, t\}$.

We first assume that (G_i, k) is a yes-instance of REFINEMENT RAMSEY.

- **Case 1**: G_i has a clique of size k. In this case, we get a clique of size $k' = (k-1)\sqrt{t} + 1$ in G' by combining this k-sized clique with all the cliques of different graphs in Y_j in which G_i belongs. This is possible because all the graphs have a clique of size $k-1$ (they are instances of REFINEMENT RAMSEY) and all possible edges between any two graphs are present.
- **Case 2**: G_i has an independent set of size k. In this case, we take $\sqrt{t} - 1$ independent sets of size $k-1$ from all Y_js except the one in which G_i belongs. Then we combine it with the independent set of size k in G_i to get an independent set of size $k' = (k-1)\sqrt{t} + 1$ in G'. This is because all the independent sets come from different Y_js and there is no edge between them.

For the reverse direction we assume that (G', k') is a yes-instance of RAMSEY. We have the following two cases.

- **Case 1**: G' has a clique of size $(k-1)(\sqrt{t}-1) + k = (k-1)\sqrt{t} + 1$. This clique has to come from one Y_i because there is no edge between vertices of two different Y_is. Because there are $\sqrt{t}$ graphs in Y_i, there exists one graph, say G_j, that contributes k vertices to the clique. Because the adjacencies inside any of the original instances is not changed, (G_j, k) is a yes-instance of REFINEMENT RAMSEY.
- **Case 2**: G' has an independent set of size $(k-1)\sqrt{t} + 1$. In this case, by the pigeonhole principle, at least k vertices come from some Y_i. Now, inside Y_i, no two vertices of different G_js can be part of the independent set because the join operation adds all edges between two vertices belonging to different

graphs. Hence, all these k vertices come from a graph G_j, and thus (G_j, k) is a yes-instance of REFINEMENT RAMSEY.

It is easy to see that the composition runs in time polynomial in the input size. Also, we see that $k' = \sqrt{t} \cdot n^{O(1)}$. Thus, by combining Lemma 20.9 and Theorem 20.2, we get the desired result. □

Bibliographic Notes

The idea of using OR-distillation for obtaining polynomial lower bounds for kernels is attributed to Dell and van Melkebeek (2014), who also obtained the bounds for VERTEX COVER, FEEDBACK VERTEX SET, and d-HITTING SET.

The definition of weak composition originates in the work of Hermelin and Wu (2012); see also Dell and Marx (2012). Our presentation of the formalism of using weak cross-composition is based on Bodlaender et al. (2014). The presented lower bounds for kernelization of VERTEX COVER and d-HITTING SET are taken from Dell and Marx (2012).

Ramsey's theorem is due to Ramsey (1930). The fact that RAMSEY is FPT was observed by Khot and Raman (2002) as the special case of a more general framework. The polynomial lower bound for RAMSEY follows the description from Kratsch (2014).

For more examples on polynomial kernel lower bounds see Cygan et al. (2012) and Dell and Marx (2012).

21
Extending Distillation

In this chapter we conclude the overview of techniques for obtaining lower bounds on kernelization. All bounds we discussed in this part of the book are built on Theorem 17.3 about bounded OR-distillations of languages. It was realized that this theorem can be extended in several ways. First, a result similar to Theorem 17.3 can be obtained for "oracle communication protocols." We use communication protocols to obtain a "structural" lower bound on the kernelization of POINT LINE COVER. Then we briefly look at the settings where we can exploit co-nondeterminism and discuss kernelization for RAMSEY. Finally, we discuss AND-composition and AND-distillation and how these concepts can be used to obtain lower kernelization bounds for problems like TREEWIDTH.

21.1 Oracle Communication Protocol

In this section, we define a two-player communication protocol.

Suppose we have two players, ALICE and BOB. Let $L \subseteq \{0, 1\}^*$ be a language. ALICE has a string $x \in \{0, 1\}^*$, and she wants to know whether $x \in L$. For example, let L be CNF-SAT. Then, ALICE wants to know whether the formula she has is satisfiable or not. However, she is not very powerful (i.e., she is just a polynomial time machine), while BOB is very powerful. Of course, one way for ALICE to find out the answer is to send the whole of x to BOB and ask him. However, sending messages to BOB are very expensive, and thus ALICE first wants to "compress" x to something equivalent but much smaller than x, and only then send it to BOB. Because ALICE wants to compress her instance, the idea of

21.1 Oracle Communication Protocol

polynomial kernelization or polynomial compression immediately comes into picture. What makes the two-player communication protocol more powerful is that ALICE does not need to send the whole input in one go. She can send a part of it and based on the answer of BOB, she can send some other part or something else, and use all these pieces of information to decide whether $x \in L$. This adaptivity of ALICE in a two-player communication protocol is what makes it more powerful.

In what follows, we formalize this idea and see where it can bring us.

Definition 21.1 (**Oracle communication protocol**) An oracle communication protocol $\mathscr{P}$ for a language L is a communication protocol between two players. The first player is given the input x and has to run in time polynomial in the length of the input; the second player is computationally unbounded but is not given any part of x. At the end of the protocol, the first player should be able to decide whether $x \in L$. The cost of the protocol is the number of bits of communication from the first player to the second player.

We refer to the second player as an oracle. Observe that the bits communicated from the second player to the first player do not count in the cost.

The first player is modeled by a polynomial time Turing machine M, and the second player by a function f. The machine M has a special oracle query tape, oracle query symbol, and oracle answer tape. Whenever M writes the special oracle query symbol on the oracle query tape, in a single computation step the contents of the answer tape is replaced by $f(q)$, where q represents the contents of the oracle query tape at that time. In the oracle communication protocol, the second player has no access to the input. To model this, the function f is independent of the input given to M. Moreover, we assume that the oracle query tape is write-only and one way, so that the previous queries are available to the function. This is used to model that the strategy used by the second player can be adaptive. We can also assume that $f(q)$ takes no more than a polynomial number of bits in the input size for any q. This assumption is valid because if $f(q)$ does not satisfy this property, then we can truncate the later bits as the machine M cannot read all of them given that it is a polynomial time Turing machine. Next, we define the notion of communication transcript.

Definition 21.2 (**Communication Transcript**) Let $\mathscr{P}$ be an oracle communication protocol for a language L. A communication transcript on a given input x consists of the sequence of all queries the protocol $\mathscr{P}$ makes on input x as well as the answers $f(q)$ to each of the oracle queries q. That is, $\mathscr{P}$ stores the content of M's oracle query tape at the end of the protocol as well as every answer given along its execution.

We say that an oracle communication protocol decides a parameterized problem $Q \subseteq \Sigma^* \times \mathbb{N}$ if M with oracle f accepts an input (x, k) if and only if $(x, k) \in Q$. The cost **cost**(k) of the protocol is the maximum number of bits written on the oracle query tape over all inputs x with parameter k.

21.2 Hardness of Communication

In this section we prove a theorem that is analogous to Theorem 17.3, on which all compression lower bounds seen so far were based. Let us remind that Theorem 17.3 says that if there is a polynomially bounded OR-distillation algorithm from a language $L \subseteq \{0, 1\}^*$ into a language $R \subseteq \{0, 1\}^*$, then $\bar{L} \in$ NP/ poly, or equivalently, $L \in$ coNP/ poly. In other words, if there is a polynomial-time algorithm that, for input strings $x_1, x_2, \ldots, x_{t(n)}$ of length n where $t(n)$ is some polynomial, outputs a string y of length at most $t(n) \log t(n)$ such that $y \in R$ if and only if at least one of the strings x_i is in L, then $\bar{L} \in$ NP/ poly.

The proof for the next theorem is similar to Theorem 17.3. One can skip this proof in the first reading.

Theorem 21.3 *Let L be a language and $t : \mathbb{N} \to \mathbb{N} \setminus \{0\}$ be a polynomially bounded function such that the problem of deciding whether at least one out of $t(n)$ inputs of length at most n belongs to L has an oracle communication protocol of cost $\mathcal{O}(t(n) \log t(n))$. Then $\bar{L} \in$ NP/ poly.*

Proof: Suppose that deciding whether at least one, out of $t(n)$ inputs of length at most n belongs to L, has an oracle communication protocol $\mathscr{P}$ of cost $\mathcal{O}(t(n) \log t(n))$. In other words, this means that we have an oracle communication protocol $\mathscr{P}$ of cost $\mathcal{O}(t(n) \log t(n))$ for the language OR(L) consisting of strings of the form $x_1 \# x_2 \# \ldots \# x_{t(n)}$ such that for at least one index i it holds that $x_i \in L$. Here, recall that a deterministic oracle communication protocol $\mathscr{P}$ is modeled by a deterministic polynomial-time Turing machine M and a function f. To prove the theorem, we design a nondeterministic polynomial time Turing machine with polynomial advice that, given an input string x, outputs YES on at least one path if $x \in \bar{L}$ and No on all paths if $x \notin \bar{L}$.

We start with the following observation, which is the key insight behind the arguments that follow. An instance x of bitsize n belongs to $\bar{L}$ (i.e., does not belong to L) if and only if there exists a sequence $x_2, \ldots, x_{t(n)}$ of instances of bitsize n such that $\mathscr{P}(x, x_2, \ldots, x_{t(n)})$ rejects. For the forward direction, given $x \notin L$, we take $x_i = x$ for $i \in \{1, 2, \ldots, t(n)\}$. Clearly, because $x \notin L$, it holds that $\mathscr{P}(x, x_2, \ldots, x_{t(n)})$ rejects. For the reverse direction, note that if $\mathscr{P}(x, x_2, \ldots, x_{t(n)})$ rejects, then we know that $x, x_2, \ldots x_{t(n)} \notin L$. Then, in particular, $x \notin L$.

We device the proof system for $\bar{L}$ as follows. It includes as advice both a large set $\mathcal{A}$ of communication transcripts and the value of $t(n)$. The definition of $\mathcal{A}$ will be determined later. Here, it is crucial to understand that every transcript in $\mathcal{A}$ (by the definition of being a transcript) is not an arbitrary string, but it describes a sequence of questions asked by the first player and the "correct" answer given to each one of these questions by the second player. We have no means to compute these answers because the second player is "all powerful," but we do not need to do that as the answers are simply "given" to us.

Given an input instance x of bitsize n, we proceed as follows:

(i) Guess a sequence $x_2, \ldots, x_{t(n)}$, where each x_i has bitsize n.
(ii) For every communication transcript τ in $\mathcal{A}$, perform the following computation:

- Run the first player on input $(x, x_2, \ldots, x_{t(n)})$. Whenever the first player sends a bit to the second player (by writing on the oracle query tape), verify that it agrees with the corresponding bit in τ. If a disagreement is detected, proceed to the next transcript (if one exists). Whenever the first player expects a bit from the second player (by reading from the oracle answer tape), use the corresponding bit in τ. If no such bit exists, proceed to the next transcript (if one exists).
- If the first player rejects, then accept.

(iii) If no run in the previous step terminated with the decision to accept, then reject.

Let us see what does the computation in the preceding text achieve.

- $x \notin \bar{L}$: In this case, $x \in L$. Then, for any choice of $x_2, \ldots, x_{t(n)}$, it holds that $\mathscr{P}(x, x_2, \ldots, x_{t(n)})$ accepts. Consider some such choice $x_2, \ldots, x_{t(n)}$. Then, for any communication transcript τ in $\mathcal{A}$, one of the following occurs.

  - If an inconsistency is detected, then we do not accept (we proceed to the next transcript).
  - Otherwise, no inconsistency is detected. This means that the first player obtains answers to all the questions that it asks and all these answers are exactly the answers that the second player would have supplied.

This implies that we have an accurate simulation of $\mathcal{P}(x, x_2, \ldots, x_{t(n)})$ and therefore the first player accepts. Thus, the proof system does not accept.

This means that the choice of $x_2, \ldots, x_{t(n)}$ leads to rejection. Because this choice was arbitrary, the proof system says No on all computational paths.

- $x \in \overline{L}$: In this case, $x \notin L$. Suppose that for every $x' \notin L$, there is a choice of $x_2, \ldots, x_{t(n)}$ such that the transcript τ resulting from running the protocol $\mathcal{P}$ on $(x', x_2, \ldots, x_{t(n)})$ belongs to $\mathcal{A}$, and $\mathcal{P}$ rejects on τ. Then, we have a computation path where the proof system says YES.

In what follows, we show that indeed there exists a set $\mathcal{A}$ of the "desired kind" (that makes the proof of the case in which $x \in \overline{L}$ goes through) of size polynomial in n. By desired kind, we mean that for every $x \in \overline{L}$, there is a choice of $x_2, \ldots, x_{t(n)}$ such that the transcript τ resulting from running the protocol $\mathcal{P}$ on $(x, x_2, \ldots, x_{t(n)})$ is in $\mathcal{A}$, and $\mathcal{P}$ rejects on τ. Clearly, if we take $\mathcal{A}$ to be the set of all transcripts, then it is a set of the "desired kind"—to see this, consider the proof of the forward direction of the key observation mentioned earlier. However, the problem is that the set of all transcripts can be huge, and our advice must be of polynomial size. Thus, we need $\mathcal{A}$ to be both of the "desired kind" and of size polynomial in n. This will also show that the running time of the constructed machine is polynomial in n.

Consider instances $x_1, \ldots, x_{t(n)}$ of L of bitsize n, and let $\mathcal{T}(x_1, \ldots, x_{t(n)})$ denote the communication transcript of $\mathcal{P}$ on input $(x_1, \ldots, x_{t(n)})$. We think of $\mathcal{T}$ as a function mapping the input to its transcript. Because the second player is not given the input $(x_1, \ldots, x_{t(n)})$, the transcript $\mathcal{T}(x_1, \ldots, x_{t(n)})$ is determined solely by the bits sent from the first player to the second player. Therefore, the number of such distinct transcripts is at most $2^{\mathbf{cost}(n)+1}$, where $\mathbf{cost}(n)$ denotes the cost of the protocol on inputs consisting of $t(n)$ instances of bitsize n each. We say that a rejecting transcript τ *covers* an instance $x \in \overline{L}$ of bitsize n if there exists a sequence $x_2, \ldots, x_{t(n)}$ of instances of bitsize n each such that $\mathcal{T}(x, x_2, \ldots, x_{t(n)}) = \tau$. From the preceding discussion, it suffices to show that a small $\mathcal{A}$ exists that covers every $x \in \overline{L}$. We construct $\mathcal{A}$ in the following iterative way.

We start with $\mathcal{A}_s = \emptyset$ and successively pick a rejecting communication transcript τ that covers the largest number of instances $x \in \overline{L}$ of length n that were not covered so far, and add τ to $\mathcal{A}$. This should remind us the proof strategy we employed in Theorem 17.3. We keep doing so until there are no more instances $x \in \overline{L}$ of bitsize n left to cover.

Consider a step in the construction of $\mathcal{A}$ and let $\mathcal{U}$ denote the set of uncovered instances $x \in \overline{L}$ of bitsize n at the beginning of the step. Because

21.2 Hardness of Communication

every tuple in $\mathcal{U}^{t(n)}$ is mapped by $\mathcal{T}$ to one of the rejecting transcripts in the preceding text and there are less than $2^{\text{cost}(n)+1}$ distinct such transcripts, there exists a rejecting transcript τ^* such that at least a fraction $\frac{1}{2^{\text{cost}(n)+1}}$ of the tuples in $\mathcal{U}^{t(n)}$ are mapped by $\mathcal{T}$ to this particular τ^*. That is,

$$|\mathcal{T}^{-1}(\tau^*) \cap \mathcal{U}^{t(n)}| \geq \frac{|\mathcal{U}|^{t(n)}}{2^{\text{cost}(n)+1}}.$$

By Lemma 17.4, τ^* covers at least $\frac{|\mathcal{U}|}{2^{(\text{cost}(n)+1)/t(n)}}$ instances $x \in \mathcal{U}$. Let $\varphi(n) = \frac{1}{2^{(\text{cost}(n)+1)/t(n)}}$.

Let e be the base of the natural logarithm. In every step, we are covering a φ fraction of the remaining instances in $\bar{L}$. Initially, there are at most 2^n instances to start with, so after ℓ steps, we are left with at most

$$(1 - \varphi(n))^\ell \cdot 2^n \leq e^{-\varphi(n)\ell} \cdot 2^n$$

instances. Thus, there will be no instances left to cover after $\mathcal{O}(n/\varphi(n))$ steps. Clearly, $n/\varphi(n)$ is polynomially bounded in n if $1/\varphi(n)$ is polynomially bounded in n. However, $1/\varphi(n) = 2^{(\text{cost}(n)+1)/t(n)}$ is polynomially bounded in $t(n)$ and hence in n (for polynomially bounded $t(n)$) as long as $\text{cost}(n) = \mathcal{O}(t(n) \log t(n))$. Thus, $\mathcal{A}$ covers all instances in $\bar{L}$ and the number of transcripts, as well as the length of each transcript, is polynomially bounded. So, the advise length is polynomially bounded in n. Also, the running time of the proof system is also polynomially bounded in n and hence the resulting algorithm for $\bar{L}$ is suitable for NP/poly. This finishes the proof. □

Note that we have described the model where ALICE is a deterministic Turing machine M. One can get other variants of oracle communication protocols by

- Allowing M to be randomized, or
- Allowing M to be a polynomial time co-nondeterministic Turing machine.

In particular, when M is a polynomial time co-nondeterministic Turing machine, whenever there are multiple possible valid executions (as in the case of co-nondeterministic protocols), one can define the cost as the maximum cost over all of them, that is, we consider the worst case. Then Theorem 21.3 can be proved even for the model where the first player can be co-nondeterministic. The only difference in the proof is that for co-nontederministic protocols, we define $\mathcal{T}(x_1, \ldots, x_{t(n)})$ to be an arbitrary transcript of an execution on which $\mathcal{P}$ produces the correct output. The first step of the proof system remains the same. In the second step, instead of deterministically simulating the first player, now we simulate nondeterministically. The advise remains the same. Clearly, if $x \notin \overline{L}$, then being a co-nondeterministic protocol, none of the transcripts of $\mathscr{P}$ will reject and hence the proof system will say No. If $x \in \overline{L}$ then we argue as before that that is a polynomial-sized advise that covers all the instances in $\overline{L}$. Clearly, if $(x, x_2, \ldots, x_{t(n)}) \notin \text{OR}(L)$ then there will be a valid path in $\mathscr{P}$ that will lead to a rejection. Here, the proof system will guess that path, validate it, and then finally accept the string. The counting arguments carry over the same way as in the deterministic case.

As an example of an immediate application of Theorem 21.3, let us see how it can be applied to d-HITTING SET. In Theorem 20.8, we provide a lower bound on the kernel size for this problem. Now, Theorem 21.3 gives an even stronger lower bound for d-HITTING SET.

Theorem 21.4 *Let $d \geq 2$ and ϵ be a positive real number. There is no protocol of cost $\mathcal{O}(k^{d-\epsilon})$ for d-HITTING SET unless* coNP $\subseteq$ NP/ poly.

Proof: Let us assume that we have a protocol $\mathscr{P}$ of cost $\mathcal{O}(k^{d-\epsilon})$ for d-HITTING SET. Let L denote 3-SAT and let $\phi_1, \ldots, \phi_{t(n)}$ be instances of 3-SAT of length at most n. In Theorem 20.8, we gave a weak cross-composition of dimension d from L to d-HITTING SET. In particular, the size of the parameter in the constructed instance of d-HITTING SET was $\mathcal{O}(n^3 t^{1/d})$. By applying this polynomial time reduction and running the protocol $\mathscr{P}$ for d-HITTING SET on the instance obtained after reduction, we obtain a protocol for OR(L), whose cost is

$$\mathcal{O}((n^3 \cdot t(n)^{\frac{1}{d}})^{d-\epsilon}).$$

Because $(d - \epsilon) < d$, the last expression is bounded by $\mathcal{O}(t(n))$ for a polynomial $t(n)$ with a sufficiently large exponent. Theorem 21.3 then shows that $\overline{L}$ is in coNP, which is equivalent to coNP $\subseteq$ NP/ poly. $\square$

Let us note that by the preceding discussion on co-nondeterministic protocols, Theorem 21.4 holds even when the first player is co-nondeterministic.

21.3 Lower Bounds for POINT LINE COVER

We have earlier seen that VERTEX COVER admits a kernel with at most $2k$ vertices and $\mathcal{O}(k^2)$ edges and thus it admits a kernel of size $\mathcal{O}(k^2)$. We also showed that VERTEX COVER does not admit any kernel or compression of bitsize $\mathcal{O}(k^{2-\epsilon})$ for any $\epsilon > 0$ unless coNP $\subseteq$ NP/ poly (Theorem 20.4). Observe that graphs with m edges (and no isolated vertices) can be represented with $\mathcal{O}(m \log m)$ bits. Thus, if we have a kernel with $\mathcal{O}(k^{2-\epsilon})$ edges then it

21.3 Lower Bounds for POINT LINE COVER

would imply that we have kernel of size $\mathcal{O}(k^{2-\epsilon'})$ and thus VERTEX COVER does not admit a kernel with $\mathcal{O}(k^{2-\epsilon})$ edges. One can similarly show that there is no kernel for VERTEX COVER with at most $\mathcal{O}(k^{1-\epsilon})$ vertices.

However, besides VERTEX COVER, there are not so many known lower bounds on "specific parts of kernels" matching the known upper bounds. For example, we know that d-HITTING SET admits a kernel with universe size $\mathcal{O}(k^{d-1})$ and total bitsize $\mathcal{O}(k^d)$. However, the lower bound $k^{d-\varepsilon}$ on the size of the kernel rules out only a possibility of a kernel with the universe size $\mathcal{O}(k^{1-\epsilon})$. So there is still a large gap between he known upper and lower bounds on the size of the universe in a kernel for d-HITTING SET. A similar situation occurs for many other problems, including FEEDBACK VERTEX SET and ODD CYCLE TRANSVERSAL.

However, we will now see how a simple strategy can be used to derive a non trivial lower bound on part of the input for a specific problem. Our example is the POINT LINE COVER problem. Recall that in this problem, we are given a set of n points $\mathcal{P}$ in the plane, and a positive integer k. The task is to decide whether there is a set of at most k lines in the plane that cover all the points in $\mathcal{P}$.

In the beginning of this book, we gave a very simple kernel for this problem with at most k^2 points. Now we show a lower bound matching this upper bound. That is, we address the question of whether there exists a kernel with $k^{2-\epsilon}$ points for some $\epsilon > 0$. It is not hard to show, by the PPT reduction from VERTEX COVER, that POINT LINE COVER is unlikely to have a kernel of bitsize $k^{2-\epsilon}$ for $\epsilon > 0$. However, ruling out a kernel with $k^{2-\epsilon}$ points requires new ideas.

In what follows, we give an outline of an argument that shows that unless coNP $\subseteq$ NP/poly, there is no kernel for POINT LINE COVER with less than $k^{2-\epsilon}$ points for some $\epsilon > 0$. We will use the following strategy.

(A) Obtain a lower bound on the size/cost of kernel/compression/protocol. For POINT LINE COVER, we show that it admits no oracle communication protocol of cost $\mathcal{O}(k^{2-\epsilon})$ unless coNP $\subseteq$ NP/poly.

(B) Obtain a kernel/compression/protocol in the parameter for which we want to prove the lower bound. For POINT LINE COVER, we give a an oracle communication protocol of cost $\mathcal{O}(n \log n)$ which can decide instances with n points.

Finally, compare the bounds in (A) and (B) to get the desired lower bound on the parameter in question. In particular, the existence of a kernel with $\mathcal{O}(k^{2-\epsilon})$ points for POINT LINE COVER combined with (B) would contradict (A).

We start with a size bound, for which the following lemma will be useful. The proof of Lemma 21.5 is based on a polynomial parameter transformation from VERTEX COVER to POINT LINE COVER that maps k to $2k$. We do not provide this proof here.

Lemma 21.5 (Kratsch et al. [2016]) *There is a polynomial-time reduction from* VERTEX COVER *to* POINT LINE COVER *that maps instances (G, k) of* VERTEX COVER *to equivalent instances $(\mathcal{P}, 2k)$ of* POINT LINE COVER.

Let us remind that by Theorem 20.4, VERTEX COVER parameterized by k does not admit a polynomial compression with bitsize $\mathcal{O}(k^{2-\varepsilon})$, unless coNP $\subseteq$ NP/poly for any $\varepsilon > 0$. Hence by Lemma 21.5, POINT LINE COVER does not admit a polynomial compression with bitsize $\mathcal{O}(k^{2-\varepsilon})$ as well. But this lower bound does not rule out the existence of a kernel for POINT LINE COVER with $\mathcal{O}(k^{2-\varepsilon})$ points. Indeed, the best-known polynomial-time encoding of an arbitrary POINT LINE COVER instance with n points requires roughly n^2 bits. Thus, the lower bound $\mathcal{O}(k^{2-\varepsilon})$ on the bitsize provides us only with an $\mathcal{O}(k^{1-\varepsilon})$ lower bound on the number of points.

Theorem 21.6 *Let $\epsilon > 0$. The* POINT LINE COVER *problem admits no oracle communication protocol of cost $\mathcal{O}(k^{2-\epsilon})$ for deciding instances $(\mathcal{P}, k)$, unless* coNP $\subseteq$ NP/poly.

Proof: For a contradiction, assume that POINT LINE COVER admits an oracle communication protocol $\mathscr{P}$ of cost $\mathcal{O}(k^{2-\epsilon})$ that decides any instance $(\mathcal{P}, k)$. We will use the communication protocol $\mathscr{P}$ to design a protocol for VERTEX COVER of the same cost. Given an instance (G, k) of VERTEX COVER, we first apply Lemma 21.5 and obtain an instance $(\mathcal{P}, 2k)$ of POINT LINE COVER such that G has a vertex cover of size k if and only if $2k$ lines cover all the points in $\mathcal{P}$. Now we apply $\mathscr{P}$ on $(\mathcal{P}, 2k)$ and obtain a protocol of cost $\mathcal{O}(k^{2-\epsilon})$ for VERTEX COVER. However, by Theorem 21.4, we know that VERTEX COVER does not admit a protocol of cost $\mathcal{O}(k^{2-\epsilon})$ unless coNP $\subseteq$ NP/poly. This completes the proof. $\square$

Theorem 21.6 proves the requirement of **(A)**. If we could somehow show that POINT LINE COVER admits an oracle communication protocol of cost $\mathcal{O}(n(\log n)^{\mathcal{O}(1)})$ on n-points instances, then that would immediately imply that unless coNP $\subseteq$ NP/poly there is no kernel for POINT LINE COVER with less than $k^{2-\epsilon}$ points for some $\epsilon > 0$. Next, we outline such an oracle communication protocol for POINT LINE COVER.

Informally, the idea of the communication protocol we will describe later is based on the following generic idea. Let $L \subseteq \{0, 1\}^*$ denote a language.

21.3 Lower Bounds for POINT LINE COVER

Suppose that we are able to group all strings of length n into some $f(n)$ classes such that any two strings in the same class either both belong to L or both do not belong to L. Let Z denote a set of size $f(n)$ containing a representative from each equivalence class and furthermore let us assume that the set Z is computable. Now one can use the set Z to obtain an oracle communication protocol for L of cost $\mathcal{O}(\log f(n))$. In this protocol, the second player (BOB) wants to know the input the first player (ALICE) is holding. Toward this, ALICE and BOB do as follows. Given an input x, ALICE computes the representative y contained in the set Z such that x and y belong to the same class. BOB computes the set Z and arranges them in the lexicographical order. Now, BOB find the string y ALICE is holding by doing a binary search on Z. That is, when BOB sends an input z, ALICE, compares it with her string and returns whether her string is equal to z, larger than z or smaller than z. This can be conveyed in a constant number of bits, and thus in $\mathcal{O}(\log f(n))$ bits BOB can know the string ALICE is holding. Once BOB knows the string, it just solves it and returns YES or No accordingly. This communication protocol has cost $\mathcal{O}(\log f(n))$.

We will show that, essentially, there are at most $n^{\mathcal{O}(n)}$ distinct inputs on n points for POINT LINE COVER. We assume the presence of an arbitrary but fixed Cartesian coordinate system. All geometric objects are referenced in the context of this coordinate system. We use p_x and p_y to denote the x and y coordinates, respectively, of a point p. A set of points in the plane is said to be *in general position* if no three of them are collinear; a set of points that is not in general position is said to be *degenerate*. For two points $p \neq q$ in the plane, we use $\overline{pq}$ to denote the unique line in the plane that passes through p and q; we say that the line $\overline{pq}$ is *defined by* the pair p, q.

Let a, b, c be three points in the plane. We say that the *orientation* of the ordered triple $\langle a, b, c \rangle$ is $+1$ if the points lie in counter-clockwise position, -1 if they lie in clockwise position, and 0 if they are collinear. Formally, let

$$M(\langle a, b, c \rangle) = \begin{pmatrix} 1 & a_x & a_y \\ 1 & b_x & b_y \\ 1 & c_x & c_y \end{pmatrix}.$$

Then, $orientation(\langle a, b, c \rangle) = sgn(\det M(\langle a, b, c \rangle))$ where sgn is the sign function and det is the determinant function. Note that the determinant above is zero if and only if the rows are linearly dependent, in which case, without loss of generality, $\langle 1, a_x, a_y \rangle = \lambda \langle 1, b_x, b_y \rangle + \mu \langle 1, c_x, c_y \rangle$. Comparing the first coordinates on both sides of the inequality, we see that $\mu = 1 - \lambda$, which is equivalent to saying that one of the points is a convex combination of the other two. Hence, $orientation(\langle a, b, c \rangle)$ is zero exactly when a, b, and c are collinear.

Let $\mathcal{P} = \langle p_1, \cdots, p_n \rangle$ be an ordered set of points, where $p_i = (x_i, y_i) = \mathcal{P}[i]$. Denote by $\binom{[n]}{3}$ the set of ordered triples $\langle i, j, k \rangle$ where $i < j < k$ and $i, j, k \in [n]$. Define $\sigma : \binom{[n]}{3} \mapsto \{+1, 0, -1\}$ to be the function $\sigma(\langle i, j, k \rangle) = orientation(p_i, p_j, p_k)$. The function σ is called the *order type* of $\mathcal{P}$. Observe that the order type of a point set depends on the order of points and not just on the set of points. Two point sets $\mathcal{P}, \mathcal{Q}$ of the same size n are said to be *combinatorially equivalent* if there exist orderings $\mathcal{P}'$ of $\mathcal{P}$ and $\mathcal{Q}'$ of $\mathcal{Q}$ such that the order types of $\mathcal{P}'$ and $\mathcal{Q}'$—which are both functions of type $\binom{[n]}{3} \mapsto \{+1, 0, -1\}$—are identical. Otherwise we say that $\mathcal{P}$ and $\mathcal{Q}$ are *combinatorially distinct*. If two order types come from combinatorially equivalent (distinct) point sets, we call the order types combinatorially equivalent (distinct).

It is not difficult to see that combinatorial distinction is a correct criterion for telling nonequivalent instances of POINT LINE COVER apart. Formally, we prove the following.

Lemma 21.7 *Let* $(\mathcal{P}, k), (\mathcal{Q}, k)$ *be two instances of* POINT LINE COVER. *If the point sets* $\mathcal{P}, \mathcal{Q}$ *are combinatorially equivalent, then* $(\mathcal{P}, k)$ *and* $(\mathcal{Q}, k)$ *are equivalent instances of* POINT LINE COVER.

Proof: Let $\mathcal{P}, \mathcal{Q}$ be combinatorially equivalent, let $|\mathcal{P}| = |\mathcal{Q}| = n$, and let $\mathcal{P}', \mathcal{Q}'$ be orderings of $\mathcal{P}$ and $\mathcal{Q}$, respectively, with identical order types. Observe first that the combinatorial equivalence provides us with a natural bijection $\pi : \mathcal{P} \mapsto \mathcal{Q}$, defined as follows. Let $p \in \mathcal{P}$, and let $i \in [n]$ be such that $\mathcal{P}'[i] = p$. Then $\pi(p) = \mathcal{Q}'[i]$.

For any subset $T \subseteq \mathcal{P}$, let $\pi(T)$ denote the set $\{\pi(t) : t \in T\}$. Let $S \subseteq \mathcal{P}$ be collinear. For any triple $a, b, c \in \pi(S)$, we have that

$$orientation(\langle a, b, c \rangle) = orientation(\langle \pi(a), \pi(b), \pi(c) \rangle) = 0,$$

where the first equality follows from the combinatorial equivalence of $\mathcal{P}$ and $\mathcal{Q}$ and the second equality follows from the collinearity of every triple of points in S. This implies that every triple of points in $\pi(S)$ are collinear, which is equivalent to saying that $\pi(S)$ is a collinear subset of $\mathcal{Q}$. Similarly, because π is a bijection, if $\pi(S)$ is collinear for some $S \subseteq \mathcal{P}$, then S is also collinear. Thus, S is a collinear subset of $\mathcal{P}$ if and only if $\pi(S)$ is a collinear subset of $\mathcal{Q}$.

Let $(\mathcal{P}, k)$ be a yes-instance, and let Ł be a set of at most k lines that cover all points in $\mathcal{P}$. Without loss of generality, each of the lines in Ł passes through at least two points in $\mathcal{P}$ because we can always replace a line through a single point by a line through two or more points. For each $\ell \in$ Ł, denote by S_ℓ the subset of points of $\mathcal{P}$ that ℓ covers. Because S_ℓ is collinear, so is $\pi(S_\ell)$ and

21.3 Lower Bounds for POINT LINE COVER   423

thus we can define ℓ' to be the line through $\pi(S_\ell)$. Then, $Ł' = \{\ell' : \ell \in Ł\}$ covers $\mathcal{Q}$ because for every $q \in \mathcal{Q}$ there is line $\ell \in Ł$ that covers $\pi^{-1}(q)$. This implies that $(\mathcal{Q}, k)$ is a yes-instance. Again, because π is a bijection, we have that if $(\mathcal{Q}, k)$ is a yes-instance, then $(\mathcal{P}, k)$ is a yes-instance. Thus, $(\mathcal{P}, k)$ is a yes-instance if and only if $(\mathcal{Q}, k)$ is a yes-instance. □

We are interested in order types is because of the following lemma, which we state without the proof.

Lemma 21.8 (Alon [1986]) *There are at most $n^{\mathcal{O}(n)}$ combinatorially distinct order types defined by n points in $\mathbb{R}^2$. Furthermore, there exists an algorithm that enumerates, for each $n \in \mathbb{N}$, all order types defined by n points in the plane.*

Now using Lemmata 21.7 and 21.8, we are ready to describe the desired oracle communication protocol for POINT LINE COVER.

Lemma 21.9 *There is an oracle communication protocol of cost $\mathcal{O}(n \log n)$ for deciding instances of POINT LINE COVER with n points.*

Proof: We describe the claimed oracle communication protocol for deciding POINT LINE COVER instances. ALICE and BOB both use the following scheme to represent order types as strings over the alphabet $\{+1, 0, -1\}$. Recall that the order type of an ordered set of n points $\mathcal{P} = \langle 1, \ldots, n \rangle$ is a certain function $\sigma : \binom{[n]}{3} \mapsto \{+1, 0, -1\}$. To form the string representing σ, we first arrange the set $\binom{[n]}{3}$ in increasing lexicographic order to get a list Ł. Then we replace each $x \in Ł$ by $\sigma(x)$. This gives us the desired string; we denote it the Order Type Representation (OTR) of the ordered set. Observe that each OTR can be encoded using $\mathcal{O}(n^3)$ bits.

From Lemma 21.8 we know that the number of combinatorially distinct order types of n-point sets is $n^{\mathcal{O}(n)}$. We use this in the following protocol to decide POINT LINE COVER.

(i) ALICE sends the value n of the number of points in the input set to BOB in binary encoding.
(ii) ALICE fixes an arbitrary ordering of the input point set. She then computes the OTR of this ordered set.
(iii) BOB generates a list of all $n^{\mathcal{O}(n)}$ possible order types; by Lemma 21.8 this is a computable task. He then computes the OTRs of these order types and sorts them in lexicographically increasing order.
(iv) ALICE and BOB now engage in a conversation where Bob uses binary search on the sorted list to locate the OTR that ALICE holds. BOB sends

the median OTR M in his list to ALICE. ALICE replies, in two bits, whether the OTR she holds is smaller, equal to, or larger than M in lexicographic order. If the answer is not "equal," BOB prunes his list accordingly, throwing out all OTRs that cannot be the one held by ALICE. By repeating this procedure $\mathcal{O}(\log(n^{\mathcal{O}(n)})) = \mathcal{O}(n \log n)$ times, BOB is left with a single OTR n that is identical to the one held by Alice.

(v) BOB now computes the size of a smallest point-line cover of any point set that has the order type n and sends this number to ALICE. ALICE compares this number with the input k and answers YES or NO accordingly.

It is not difficult to see that ALICE can do her part of this procedure in polynomial time and that all tasks that Bob has to do are computable. The total cost of the protocol is $\log n + \mathcal{O}(n \log n) = \mathcal{O}(n \log n)$, as claimed. $\square$

Theorem 21.10 *Let $\epsilon > 0$. Unless* coNP $\subseteq$ NP/ poly, *there is no polynomial-time algorithm that reduces every instance $(\mathcal{P}, k)$ of* POINT LINE COVER *to an equivalent instance with $\mathcal{O}(k^{2-\epsilon})$ points.*

Proof: By Lemma 21.9, such a kernelization would directly give an oracle communication protocol for POINT LINE COVER of cost $\mathcal{O}(k^{2-\epsilon'})$: Given an instance $(\mathcal{P}, k)$, Alice applies the (polynomial-time) kernelization that generates an equivalent instance with $\mathcal{O}(k^{2-\epsilon})$ points. Then she proceeds by using the protocol from the proof of Lemma 21.9.

As we have already showed in Theorem 21.6, there is no $\mathcal{O}(k^{2-\epsilon'})$ protocol for POINT LINE COVER for any $\epsilon' > 0$, unless coNP $\subseteq$ NP/ poly. This completes the proof. $\square$

21.4 Lower Bounds Using Co-Nondeterminism

Let us also mention the usage of co-nondeterminism to derive lower bounds. Here, we only state (without details) the relevant definition, theorem to serve as a tool for proofs, and an example of an application.

Definition 21.11 (Co-nondeterministic OR-cross-composition) Let $L \subseteq \Sigma^*$ be a language, let $\mathcal{R}$ be a polynomial equivalence relation and let $Q \subseteq \Sigma^* \times \mathbb{N}$ be a parameterized problem. We say that L co-nondeterministically cross-composes into Q (with respect to $\mathcal{R}$) if there is a co-nondeterministic algorithm $\mathcal{A}$ that, given t strings $x_1, x_2, \ldots, x_t$ belonging to the same equivalence class of $\mathcal{R}$, takes time polynomial in $\sum_{i=1}^{t} |x_i|$ and outputs on each computation path an instance $(x^*, k^*) \in \Sigma^* \times \mathbb{N}$ such that the following conditions hold:

(i) k^* is bounded by $t^{o(1)}(\max_{i=1}^{t} |x_i|)^{\mathcal{O}(1)}$.
(ii) If at least one instance x_i is a yes-instance, then all computation paths lead to the output of a yes-instance (x^*, k^*).
(iii) Otherwise, if all instances x_i are no-instances, then at least one computation path leads to the output of a no-instance.

The proof is along the similar lines as Theorem 17.8 and it invokes Theorem 21.3 inside the proof.

Theorem 21.12 (Kratsch [2014]) *Let $L \subseteq \Sigma^*$ be an NP-hard language. If L co-nondeterministically cross-composes into a parameterized problem Q, then Q does not admit a polynomial compression, unless* coNP $\subseteq$ NP/ poly.

Using Theorem 21.12, one can show the following theorem.

Theorem 21.13 (Kratsch [2014]) RAMSEY *does not admit a polynomial compression unless* coNP $\subseteq$ NP/ poly.

21.5 AND-Distillations and AND-Compositions

A very natural question is whether the results on distillations and compositions obtained in the previous chapters are valid if one would like to substitute OR with AND. While the answer to this question is yes, the proofs for AND are much more complicated.

Let us define a *t-bounded* AND-*distillation algorithm* by replacing the second condition of a distillation algorithm (Definition 17.1) with the requirement that the output string y belongs to R if and only if *all* the input strings x_i belong to L. The following theorem is the analogue of Theorem 17.3 for OR-distillation. However, the proof of this theorem is much more complicated.

Theorem 21.14 (Drucker [2015]) *Let $L, R \subseteq \Sigma^*$ be two languages. If there exists a polynomially bounded* AND-*distillation of L into R, then $L \in$* coNP/ poly.

Having Theorem 21.14 at hand, one can use it similarly to Theorem 17.3. In particular, AND-cross-composition is defined by replacing condition (ii) of cross-composition by requiring that the resulting instance (y, k) belongs to Q if and only if *all* the input strings x_i belong to L. The proof of Theorem 17.8 is oblivious to whether we use the OR function or the AND function; the outcome of the constructed distillation will be just an instance of AND(R) instead of OR(R). Therefore, by replacing the usage of Theorem 17.3 with that of Theorem 21.14, we obtain the following result.

Theorem 21.15 *Assume that an* NP*-hard language L* AND*-cross-composes into a parameterized language Q. Then Q does not admit a polynomial compression unless* NP $\subseteq$ coNP/ poly.

As an example of a problem admitting a trivial AND-cross-composition take the TREEWIDTH problem: Given a graph G and a parameter k, verify whether tw(G) $\leq k$. Because treewidth of a disjoint union of a family of graphs is equal to the maximum over the treewidths of these graphs, the disjoint union yields an AND-cross-composition from the unparameterized version of TREEWIDTH into the parameterized one. Computing the treewidth of a graph is NP-hard, so by Theorem 21.15 we infer that TREEWIDTH does not admit a polynomial kernel unless NP $\subseteq$ coNP/ poly. The same reasoning can be performed for other graph parameters that behave similarly under the disjoint union, for instance for pathwidth, cutwidth, and rankwidth.

Exercises

Problem 21.1 Show that if $L \subseteq \{0, 1\}^* \times \mathbb{N}$ has a kernel of size $f(k)$, then L has an oracle communication protocol of cost $f(k)$.

Problem 21.2 Use Theorem 21.15 to show that EDGE CLIQUE COVER does not admit a polynomial kernel.

Bibliographic Notes

Our exposition of oracle communication protocol follows the work of Dell and van Melkebeek (2014). The bound for POINT LINE COVER follows the paper of Kratsch et al. (2016). Lemma 21.8 is due to Alon (1986). The proof that RAMSEY does not admit a polynomial kernel can be found in Kratsch (2014). Theorem 21.14 is due to Drucker (2015). A shorter proof of this theorem is announced by Dell (2014).

PART IV

Beyond Kernelization

22
Turing Kernelization

In this chapter we discuss Turing kernelization. We define what a Turing kernel is and give examples of such kernels for CLIQUE (VC), MAX LEAF SUBTREE, and PLANAR LONGEST CYCLE.

In Part III we discussed the framework for ruling out the existence of polynomial kernels for many parameterized problems. However, such lower bounds are definitely not the end of the story. Even if we do not have a polynomial kernel, an algorithm producing a polynomial (in the input length) number of outputs of size polynomial in the parameter and such that the original instance can be solved once all the output instances are solved would be still a desirable option from a practitioner's point of view. In other words, even if it turns out to be impossible to reduce an input to a single small equivalent input, the following type of preprocessing would still be desirable: a preprocessing algorithm that "splits" the input (x, k) into $\text{poly}(|x|)$ instances of size $\text{poly}(k)$, such that once their answers are known, the answer to (x, k) can efficiently be found.

In Section 17.3.2, we discussed the problem of finding a clique in a graph G where the parameter is the vertex cover number of G. More precisely, in the CLIQUE (VC) problem we are given a graph G, integers k, ℓ and a vertex cover $S \subseteq V(G)$ of G such that $|S| = k$. The parameter is k and the task is to decide whether G has a clique on ℓ vertices. As we have already seen in Section 17.3.2, CLIQUE (VC) does not admit a polynomial compression unless coNP $\subseteq$ NP/poly.

However, the set $I = V(G) \setminus S$ is an independent set, and hence no clique of G can have more than one vertex from I. Thus, if C is a clique of size ℓ in an n-vertex graph G, then at least $\ell - 1$ vertices of C should be in S. Without loss of generality, the set I can be assumed to be nonempty. Therefore, C should be contained in at least one of the $|I|$ sets $\{v\} \cup S$, where $v \in I$. Moreover, for every $v \in V(G)$, the set S is also a vertex cover of the induced subgraph $G[S \cup \{v\}]$. This yields that (G, S, k, ℓ) is a yes-instance of CLIQUE (VC) if and only if at least one of the $|I|$ instances $(G[S \cup \{v\}], S, k, \ell)$, $v \in I$, is a yes-instance of CLIQUE (VC).

To summarize, CLIQUE (VC) exhibits an interesting behavior. While the problem is unlikely to admit a polynomial kernel, there is a polynomial time algorithm producing at most n instances with at most $k + 1$ vertices each, such that the original instance is a yes-instance if and only if at least one of the output instances is a yes-instance.

The type of "kernelization" we have seen for CLIQUE (VC) can be formalized as follows. Suppose that we have an oracle that can answer "short" questions: For a parameterized problem Q and a function f, the oracle can answer if a given instance of size at most $f(k)$ belongs to Q or not. Then, a Turing kernelization is an algorithm solving the problem in polynomial time and by making use of a polynomial number of queries to the oracle. More precisely,

Definition 22.1 (Turing kernelization) Let Q be a parameterized problem and let $f : \mathbb{N} \to \mathbb{N}$ be a computable function. A *Turing kernelization*, or a *Turing kernel*, for Q of size f is an algorithm that decides whether a given instance $(x, k) \in \Sigma^* \times \mathbb{N}$ belongs to Q in time polynomial in $|x| + k$, when given access to an oracle that decides membership in Q for any instance (x', k') with $|x'|, k' \leq f(k)$ in a single step.

As in the case of normal kernels, we say that a Turing kernel is *polynomial* if f is a polynomial function. A few remarks are in order. First, normal polynomial kernels are polynomial Turing kernels too. This is just because in polynomial time they produce an instance that can be decided in one oracle call. Second, a Turing kernelization is an adaptive algorithm: Its action and queries can depend on the answers to previous queries.

With this definition at hand, our discussion about CLIQUE (VC) can be summarized in the following theorem.

Theorem 22.2 CLIQUE (VC) *admits a Turing kernel of size* $\mathcal{O}(k^2)$.

Proof: For a given instance (G, S, k, ℓ) of CLIQUE (VC), for every $v \in V(G)$ we construct an instance $(G[S \cup \{v\}], S, k, \ell)$ of CLIQUE (VC). Thus, we end up with at most $|V(G)|$ instances and (G, S, k, ℓ) is a yes-instance if and only if at least one of the produced instances is a yes-instance. Because the size of each of the new instances is $\mathcal{O}(k^2)$, the oracle can make decisions on instances of such size. Then, Turing kernelization routine makes at most $|V(G)|$ calls to the oracle. If the answer to at least one call is yes, we return yes. Otherwise we return no. □

22.1 MAX LEAF SUBTREE

Our next example is MAX LEAF SUBTREE. Let us remind that this is the problem of deciding whether a given graph G contains a tree with at least k leaves. This problem does not admit a polynomial compression, see Problem 22.5. However, by Theorem 3.8, when the input graph G is connected, the complexity of the problem changes and MAX LEAF SUBTREE admits a polynomial kernel. This allows us to construct a Turing kernel for this problem.

Theorem 22.3 *The* MAX LEAF SUBTREE *problem admits a Turing kernel of size* $\mathcal{O}(k^2)$.

Proof: Let (G, k) be an instance of MAX LEAF SUBTREE, where G is an n-vertex graph and $C_1, \ldots, C_r$ are the connected components of G. For each of the connected components C_i, we invoke Theorem 3.8. As the result, we obtain at most $r \leq n$ instances (C'_i, k'), where $|V(C'_i)| = \mathcal{O}(k)$ and $k' \leq k$. Moreover, (G, k) is a yes-instance if and only if at least one (C'_i, k') is a yes-instance. Because the size of each of the new instances is $\mathcal{O}(k^2)$, it can be processed by the corresponding oracle. Then Turing kernelization routine makes at most r calls to an oracle for each instance (C'_i, k'). If any of these answers is positive then we can return yes, and otherwise it is safe to return no. □

22.2 PLANAR LONGEST CYCLE

In this section we construct a Turing kernelization for PLANAR LONGEST CYCLE. The problem does not admit a polynomial compression unless coNP $\subseteq$ NP/poly; see Problem 22.6. This kernel differs from the Turing kernels we considered before. The kernelization algorithms for MAX LEAF SUBTREE and CLIQUE (VC) did not exploit the full power of the definition of a Turing kernel—we did not fully take advantage of the presence of an oracle (which is able to answer queries about instances of size polynomial in the parameter) in the following sense. Our queries were independent, while a Turing kernel can work adaptively, formulating its next question based on the answers it has received so far. Our last example of a Turing kernelization takes the full advantage of the oracle.

We say that a connected graph G is 3-connected if for every set $S \subseteq V(G)$ of size at most 2, $G - S$ is connected. Let us remark that we do not exclude the option that G can have at most three vertices. The crucial property of 3-connected planar graphs is that they have sufficiently large cycles. More precisely,

Theorem 22.4 (Chen and Yu [2002]) *Every n-vertex 3-connected planar graph contains a cycle of length at least $n^{\log_3 2}$.*

From the perspective of kernelization, Theorem 22.4 shows that PLANAR LONGEST CYCLE admits a trivial polynomial kernel on 3-connected graphs: If the input graph has at least $k^{\log_2 3}$ vertices, then it contains a cycle of length at least k. The idea behind the Turing kernelization is as follows.

For a planar graph G, we construct in polynomial time a tree decomposition (T, χ) of G such that

- The intersection of every two different bags of the decomposition is of size at most 2.
- For every bag $\chi(a)$ of the decomposition, if we contract all edges of G except the edges with two endpoints in $\chi(a)$, then the resulting minor of G is 3-connected.

By Theorem 22.4, if there is a bag of (T, χ) with more than $k^{\log_2 3}$ vertices, then G is a yes-instance of PLANAR LONGEST CYCLE. (If a minor of G contains a cycle of length at least k, so does G.) When every bag of (T, χ) is of size at most $k^{\log_2 3}$, we run an algorithm very similar to the dynamic programming algorithms on graphs of bounded treewidth we discussed in Section 14.4. The most crucial difference is that instead of going through all possible subsets of each of the bags, we send a query to the oracle.

Let us formalize first what is the tree decomposition we want to construct.

For two adjacent nodes a, b of T, the set of vertices $\chi(a) \cap \chi(b)$ is called the *adhesion* of edge ab.

Definition 22.5 (Torso of a tree decomposition) For a node $a \in V(T)$ of a tree decomposition (T, χ), the *torso* of a is the graph H_a obtained from $G[\chi(a)]$ by adding all the edges uv such that $u, v \in \chi(a) \cap \chi(b)$, where $b \neq a$.

In other words, let $a_1, \ldots, a_p$ be the nodes of T adjacent to a. Then we construct H_a from $G[\chi(a)]$ by turning each of the sets $\chi(a) \cap \chi(a_i)$ into a clique. Let us note that a torso is not necessary a subgraph or a minor of the graph G.

22.2 PLANAR LONGEST CYCLE

Definition 22.6 (Separators and minimal separators) For a pair of vertices u, v from the same connected component of a graph G, a vertex set S is a (u, v)-*separator* if $u, v \notin S$ and u and v are in different connected components of $G - S$. A (u, v)-separator is *minimal* if it does not contain any other (u, v)-separator as a proper subset. Finally, a set S is a *minimal separator* if S is a minimal (u, v)-separator for some $u, v \in V(G)$.

Let us remark that a minimal separator S can properly contain another minimal separator S'. Indeed, this can happen if S' separates other pair of vertices than S.

The following theorem is a reformulation of the classical result of Tutte (1966).

Theorem 22.7 (Tutte [1966]) *Every graph G has a tree decomposition (T, χ) such that*

- *Each torso of (T, χ) is 3-connected and is a minor of G, and*
- *For every pair of nodes $a, b \in V(T)$, $a \neq b$, $|\chi(a) \cap \chi(b)| \leq 2$.*

By the result of Hopcroft and Tarjan (1973), this decomposition can be computed in linear time.

We refer a tree decomposition satisfying conditions of Theorem 22.7 as a *Tutte decomposition*.

Definition 22.8 By PLANAR LONGEST CYCLE oracle, we mean an oracle that, for a given planar graph G with at most $k + (3k + 1)k^{\log_2 3}$ vertices, decides if G contains a cycle of length at least k.

We remark that in the definition of PLANAR LONGEST CYCLE oracle, one can change requirement on the size of the graph to any polynomial of sufficiently high degree. We selected the polynomial to be $k+(3k+1)k^{\log_2 3}$ in the definition just because this is the minimum requirement for the proof of Theorem 22.10 to go through. Similarly, we use $(3k + 1)k^{\log_2 3}$ in the auxiliary Lemma 22.9 to be able to plug it in later in the proof of Theorem 22.10.

Lemma 22.9 *Let G be a planar graph with at most $(3k+1)k^{\log_2 3}$ vertices and containing no cycle of length at least k. Let u, v be a pair of adjacent vertices in G. Then the maximum length of a uv-path in G can be identified in at most k calls to the PLANAR LONGEST CYCLE oracle.*

Proof: We prove the lemma by the following self-reduction arguments. Because u and v are adjacent and there is no k-cycle in G, we conclude that there is no uv-path in G of length $k - 1$ or more.

We construct graph G_1 by adding to G a new vertex w and making it adjacent to u and v. Notice that G is still planar and has at most $(3k+1)k^{\log_2 3} + 1$ vertices. We query the PLANAR LONGEST CYCLE oracle about G_1. If the answer is affirmative—there is a cycle of length at least k in G_1—then this cycle should pass through w and is of length exactly k. Then the graph G, in this situation, has a uv-path of length $k - 2$ and does not have a uv-path of length at least $k - 1$.

Now it should be clear how to proceed. We continue with this construction for each $i \in \{1, \ldots, k - 1\}$. Specifically, the graph G_i is constructed from G by adding i new vertices $w_1, w_2, \ldots, w_i$ and connecting u and v by a path $uw_1w_2 \cdots w_iv$ of length $i + 1$. Again, G_i is planar and has at most $(3k + 1)k^{\log_2 3} + i \leq (3k + 1)k^{\log_2 3} + k$ vertices. Moreover, if G_i has no k-cycle, then there is no uv-path in G of length at least $k - i - 1$.

For $i = 1$ to $k - 1$, we ask the oracle whether G_i contains a k-cycle. Then for the minimum i such that the oracle confirms the existence of a k-cycle in G_i, we conclude that the maximum length of a uv-path in graph G is $k - i - 1$. □

We are ready to give the Turing kernelization for PLANAR LONGEST CYCLE.

Theorem 22.10 PLANAR LONGEST CYCLE *admits a polynomial Turing kernel.*

Proof We prove the theorem by providing a polynomial time algorithm that is using $\mathcal{O}(kn)$ queries to the PLANAR LONGEST CYCLE oracle.

Let us observe that every cycle in a graph is contained entirely in a 2-connected component of that graph. We can use the linear time algorithm of Hopcroft and Tarjan to compute the 2-connected components of the input planar graph G and solve the problem on each of them separately.

From now on, we assume that G is 2-connected. We use Theorem 22.7 to construct a Tutte decomposition (T, χ) of G. By Theorem 22.7, every torso H_a of (T, χ), $a \in V(T)$ is a minor of G (and hence planar) and 3-connected. Therefore, if there is a torso H_a with at least $k^{\log_2 3}$ vertices, then by Theorem 22.4 H_a contains a cycle with at least k vertices. Because every torso is a minor of G, this implies that G also contains a cycle with at least k vertices.

Let us note that because G is 2-connected, for every pair of adjacent nodes a and b of T, the size of $\chi(a) \cap \chi(b)$ is exactly 2. Let $\{u, v\} = \chi(a) \cap \chi(b)$. In each torso H_a of size more than 2 and containing $\{u, v\}$, these vertices are adjacent. Indeed, let x be a vertex of H_a different from u and v, and let y be a vertex of G such that x and y are in different connected components C_x and C_y of $G - \{u, v\}$. Because the graph G is 2-connected, there are paths P_u and P_v from x to y such

22.2 PLANAR LONGEST CYCLE

that P_u avoids u and P_v avoids v. The union of these paths contains a cycle C passing through u and v. Moreover, $V(C) \cap C_y$ is a uv-path with all internal vertices outside C_x, and thus u and v should be adjacent in the torso H_a.

We root the tree at some node r and proceed bottom-up from leaves to r. For a node $a \in V(T)$ we will refer to the subtree of T rooted at a by T_a. We define

$$V_a = \bigcup_{a \in V_a} \chi(a).$$

For each leaf $a \in V(T)$ we use the oracle to compute the following. We query the oracle if the torso H_a contains a cycle of length at least k. If the answer is yes, we conclude that G contains a cycle of length at least k and stop. Otherwise, let b be the parent of a and let $\{u, v\}$ be the adhesion $\chi(a) \cap \chi(b)$. Then u and v are adjacent in H_a and by making use of Lemma 22.9, in at most k calls to the oracle, we compute in polynomial time the maximum length of a uv-path in H_a.

For a nonleaf node $a \in V(T)$, $a \neq r$, let $C = \{c_1, \ldots, c_\ell\}$ be its set of children and p be its parent node. Let us note that due to the 2-connectivity condition, we have that the size of $\chi(a) \cap \chi(c_i)$ is exactly 2 for each $1 \leq i \leq \ell$. Suppose inductively that for node a and for each of its children $c_i \in C$, we computed the maximum length k_i of a path in $G[V_{c_i}]$ with the endpoints in the adhesion $\chi(c_i) \cap \chi(a)$. We also can assume that $k_i \leq k - 2$ because otherwise we are able to conclude that G contains a cycle of length at least k. Because the torso H_a is planar, by Euler's formula (Theorem 13.1) there are at most $3 \cdot |V(H_a)| \leq 3k^{\log_2 3}$ edges in H_a. Because every pair of vertices from the same adhesion is adjacent, we have that $\ell \leq 3k^{\log_2 3}$.

We construct an auxiliary graph F_a from $G[\chi(a)]$ by adding for every child $c_i \in C$ a path of length k_i connecting the pair of vertices from $\chi(a) \cap \chi(c_i)$. The properties of the auxiliary graph F_a are summarized in the following claims.

Claim 22.11 *Graph F_a is a subgraph of $G[V_a]$, and thus it is planar.*

Indeed, graph F_a can be obtained from $G[V_a]$ by deleting for every child c_i of a all edges except edges of a path of length k_i with endpoints in $\chi(a) \cap \chi(c_i)$.

Claim 22.12 *Graph F_a has at most $3 \cdot k^{\log_2 3} k$ vertices.*

This claim follows because F_a is formed from the $k^{\log_2 3}$-vertex graph H_a by adding $\ell \leq 3k^{\log_2 3}$ paths, each of length at most $k - 2$. Thus, it has at most $k^{\log_2 3} + 3 \cdot k^{\log_2 3}(k - 2) \leq 3 \cdot k^{\log_2 3} k$ vertices.

Claim 22.13 *There is a cycle of length at least k in $G[V_a]$ if and only if there a cycle of length at least k in F_a.*

This is true because the intersection of the longest cycle in $G[V_a]$ with each of the graphs $G[V_{c_i}]$ is either empty or of length k_i. Thus, if $G[V_a]$ contains a cycle of length t, so does F_a. The opposite assertion holds because F_a is a subgraph of $G[V_a]$

Claim 22.14 Let b be the parent of a in T and $\{u, v\} = \chi(a) \cap \chi(b)$. If $G[V_a]$ has no cycle of length at least k, then the maximum length of a uv-path in $G[V_a]$ is equal to the maximum length of a uv-path in F_a.

The arguments proving this claim are as for Claim 22.13.

Let a be a nonroot node, b be its parent, and $\{u, v\} = \chi(a) \cap \chi(b)$. Now assuming that the maximum lengths k_i of paths in $G[V_{c_i}]$ are computed, we can in polynomial time, and by making use of at most k calls to the oracle, correctly decide whether $G[V_a]$ contains a cycle of length at least k, and if the answer is negative then compute the maximum length of a uv-path in $G[V_a]$ as follows:

- Construct the auxiliary graph F_a. Because the values k_i are known, this construction takes polynomial time.
- By Claim 22.12, F_a has at most $3 \cdot k^{\log_2 3} k$ vertices and by Claim 22.11, it is planar. Thus, we can use Lemma 22.9, which in at most k calls to the oracle, decides in polynomial time whether F_a contains a cycle of length at least k, and if the answer is negative then compute the maximum length of a uv-path in F_a. By Claims 22.13 and 22.14, for both possible outputs, we can make exactly the same conclusion about $G[V_a]$.

Thus, by proceeding inductively from leaves to root, we are able to construct the graph F_r for the root vertex r. In polynomial time and by making use of $\mathcal{O}(nk)$ calls to the oracle. By querying the oracle about F_r, we decide whether $G = G[V_r]$ contains a cycle of length at least k. □

22.2.1 Hardness of Turing Kernelization

As of now, there is no known framework for refuting the existence of Turing kernelizations under standard complexity assumptions. As a mean to cope with the lack of progress on this subject, a hierarchy for kernelization called the WK-hierarchy was defined by Hermelin et al. (2015), and some problems were conjectured to be hard for Turing kernelization. In particular, the class of WK[1]-complete problems includes problems such as HITTING SET parameterized by the number of sets, CONNECTED VERTEX COVER parameterized by the solution size, and MIN-ONES-r-SAT. All WK[1]-complete problems are equivalent through PPTs, and it is conjectured that none of these problems admits a polynomial Turing kernel.

Let us now elaborate more on this hierarchy. Toward the definition of the WK-hierarchy, we need to consider the following definition.

Definition 22.15 For integers $t \geq 0$ and $d \geq 1$, the classes of formulas $\Gamma_{t,d}$ and $\Delta_{t,d}$ are defined inductively as follows.

$$\begin{aligned}
\Gamma_{0,d} &= \{\lambda_1 \wedge \cdots \wedge \lambda_c \mid c \in \{1,\ldots,d\}, \lambda_1, \ldots, \lambda_c \text{ are literals}\}. \\
\Delta_{0,d} &= \{\lambda_1 \vee \cdots \vee \lambda_c \mid c \in \{1,\ldots,d\}, \lambda_1, \ldots, \lambda_c \text{ are literals}\}. \\
\Gamma_{t+1,d} &= \{\wedge_{i \in I} \delta_i \mid I \neq \emptyset \text{ is a finite set}, \delta_i \in \Delta_{t,d} \text{ for all } i \in I\}. \\
\Delta_{t+1,d} &= \{\vee_{i \in I} \delta_i \mid I \neq \emptyset \text{ is a finite set}, \delta_i \in \Gamma_{t,d} \text{ for all } i \in I\}.
\end{aligned}$$

In addition, $\Gamma_{t,d}$-WSAT($k \log n$) is the problem where, given a formula $\phi \in \Gamma_{t,d}$ with n variables and an integer k, the objective is to decide whether ϕ has a satisfying assignment that assigns true to exactly k variables. Here, the parameter is $k \log n$.

Then, the WK-hierarchy is defined as follows.

Definition 22.16 Let $t \geq 1$ be an integer. Then,

$$\text{WK}[t] = \bigcup_{d \in \mathbb{N}} [\Gamma_{t,d}\text{-WSAT}(k \log n)]_{\leq ppt},$$

where $[L]_{\leq ppt}$ denotes the closure of L under PPTs.

The basic problems complete for this hierarchy are given in the following theorem. Here, $\Gamma_{t,d}^-$ ($\Gamma_{t,d}^+$) is the restriction of $\Gamma_{t,d}^-$ to formulas that contain only negative (respectively, positive) literals.

Theorem 22.17 (Hermelin et al. [2015]) Let $t \geq 1$ be an integer. Then,

- $\Gamma_{1,2}^-$-WSAT($k \log n$) is WK[1]-complete.
- $\Gamma_{t,1}^-$-WSAT($k \log n$) is WK[1]-complete for odd $t > 1$.
- $\Gamma_{t,1}^+$-WSAT($k \log n$) is WK[1]-complete for even $t > 1$.

Problems that are WK[1]-hard are conjectured not to have polynomial Turing kernels. Among the problems shown to be W[1]-complete, we have CLIQUE parameterized by $k \log n$ (note that parameterization by k alone would have not made sense for our purpose because then the problem is W[1]-hard, and our objective is to refute the existence of polynomial Turing kernels for problems that are in FPT), MIN-ONES-r-SAT with $r \geq 3$ parameterized by k, the upper bound on the number of variables assigned true, HITTING SET parameterized by the number of sets, SET COVER parameterized by the number of elements, CONNECTED VERTEX COVER parameterized by the solution size, CYCLE PACKING parameterized by the sought number of cycles, and STEINER TREE parameterized by the solution size (including the number of terminals). In particular, to prove that a problem is WK[1]-hard, it suffices to given a PPT from a problem already known to be WK[1]-hard.

Exercises

Problem 22.1 Show that CLIQUE parameterized by the maximum vertex degree admits a polynomial Turing kernel.

Problem 22.2 A graph G is a *grid graph* if it is an induced subgraph of $\boxplus_t$ for some $t \in \mathbb{N}$. Show that LONGEST PATH parameterized by the solution size admits a quadratic Turing kernel on subgraphs of grid graphs.

Problem 22.3 Show that LONGEST CYCLE parameterized by the solution size admits a quadratic Turing kernel on subgraphs of grid graphs.

Problem 22.4 A *disk graph* G is the intersection graph of a set of disks D in the (Euclidean) plane. That is, there is a bijective function $f : V(G) \to D$ such that any two vertices are adjacent in G if and only if their disks $f(u)$ and $f(v)$ intersect. It is known that for any clique C in G, there exist $\mathcal{O}(1)$ points in the plane such that for every vertex $v \in V(C)$, it holds that $f(v)$ contains at least one of these points (Har-Peled et al., 2018).

Show that CLIQUE parameterized by the solution size admits a linear Turing kernel on disk graphs (where the geometric representation is given as input).

Problem 22.5 Show that the MAX LEAF SUBTREE problem, studied in the chapter, does not admit a polynomial compression with parameter k unless coNP $\subseteq$ NP/poly.

Problem 22.6 Show that the PLANAR LONGEST CYCLE, studied in the chapter, does not admit a polynomial compression with parameter k unless coNP $\subseteq$ NP/poly.

Bibliographic Notes

The formal foundation for Turing kernelization is the concept of *oracle Turing machines* (see Flum and Grohe [2006]), where we constrain the power of the oracle to being able to answer only queries that are short in terms of the parameter. The definition of Turing kernelization is from Binkele-Raible et al. (2012).

The first example of Turing kernels of polynomial size were obtained for the DIRECTED MAX LEAF problem by Binkele-Raible et al. (2012); see also Daligault and Thomassé (2009) for further improvements. Currently, the smallest known kernel for MAX LEAF SUBTREE on connected graphs has at most $3.75k$ vertices (Estivill-Castro et al., 2005).

The Turing kernel for LONGEST PATH is due to Jansen (2017), who was first to exploit the adaptiveness in the definition of Turing kernelization. In this paper, it was also shown that LONGEST PATH admits a polynomial Turing kernel on bounded-degree and $K_{3,t}$-minor-free graphs. These results were significantly extended to classes of graphs excluding a fixed graph as a topological minor by Jansen et al. (2017). Our exposition of the theorem of Tutte (1966) follows Jansen (2017).

The WK-hierarchy is defined in Hermelin et al. (2015), and we refer interested readers to that work for further details on it. In this regard, we remark that it is not known whether LONGEST PATH WK[1]-hard. Finally, we point out a discussion on Turing kernelization by Weller (2013), and refer to the work by Jansen and Marx (2015) for Turing kernels for several subgraph isomorphism and packing problems. Exercises 22.2, 22.3, and 22.4 are due to Bart M.P. Jansen (private communication).

23
Lossy Kernelization

All the kernels we have seen in this book are lossless. That is, an input instance is a yes-instance if and only if the reduced instance is a yes-instance. What about kernels that are "lossy" in nature? In these kind of kernels, as before, given an instance we would like the kernelization algorithm to output a reduced instance of size polynomial in the parameter; however we relax the notion of equivalence in the following way. Given a solution to the reduced instance (some approximate solution, say a c-approximate solution) we return a solution to the original instance that is an αc-approximate solution to the original instance. The factor α is the loss we incurred while going from reduced instance to the original instance. Observe that the kernel lower bounds we have shown for various problems no more hold in this setting. In this chapter we first setup the formal framework to study lossy kernels, and then give lossy kernels for CONNECTED VERTEX COVER, PARTIAL VERTEX COVER, CYCLE PACKING, and STEINER TREE.

Despite the success of kernelization, the basic definition has an important drawback: "Theoretically it does not combine well with approximation algorithms or with heuristics." This is a serious problem because after all the ultimate goal of parameterized algorithms, or for that matter of any algorithmic paradigm, is to eventually solve the given input instance. Thus, the application of a preprocessing algorithm is always followed by an algorithm that finds a solution to the reduced instance. In practice, even after applying a preprocessing procedure, the reduced instance may not be small enough to be solved to optimality within a reasonable time bound. In these cases, one gives up on optimality and resorts to approximation algorithms or heuristics instead. Thus, it is *crucial* that the solution obtained by an approximation algorithm or heuristic when run on the reduced instance provides a good solution to the original instance, or at least *some* meaningful information about the original instance. The current definition of kernels allows for kernelization algorithms with the unsavory property that running an approximation algorithm or heuristic on the reduced instance provides *no insight whatsoever* about the original instance. In particular, the *only* thing guaranteed by the definition of a kernel is that the reduced instance (I', k') is a yes instance if and only if the original instance (I, k) is. If we have an α-approximate solution to (I', k'), there is no guarantee that we will be able to get an α-approximate solution to (I, k), or even able to get any feasible solution to (I, k).

The main reason that the existing notion of kernelization does not combine well with approximation algorithms is that the definition of a kernel is deeply rooted in decision problems. The starting point of our new framework is an extension of kernelization to optimization problems. This allows us to define α-approximate kernels. Loosely speaking, an (α)-approximate kernel of size $g(k)$ is a polynomial time algorithm that, given an instance (I, k), outputs an instance (I', k') such that $|I'| + k' \leq g(k)$ and any c-approximate solution s' to the instance (I', k') can be turned in polynomial time into a $(c \cdot \alpha)$-approximate solution s to the original instance (I, k) In this chapter, we first set up the formal framework to study lossy kernels and then give lossy kernels for CONNECTED VERTEX COVER, PARTIAL VERTEX COVER, CYCLE PACKING, and STEINER TREE.

23.1 Framework

We will be dealing with approximation algorithms and solutions that are not necessarily optimal but also at the same time relatively "close" to being optimal. To properly discuss these concepts they have to be formally defined. Our starting point is a parameterized analogue of the notion of an *optimization problem* from the theory of approximation algorithms.

Definition 23.1 (Parameterized optimization problem) A parameterized optimization (minimization or maximization) problem Π is a computable function

$$\Pi \colon \Sigma^* \times \mathbb{N} \times \Sigma^* \to \mathbb{R} \cup \{\pm\infty\}.$$

The *instances* of a parameterized optimization problem Π are pairs $(I, k) \in \Sigma^* \times \mathbb{N}$, and a *solution* to (I, k) is simply a string $s \in \Sigma^*$, such that $|s| \leq |I| + k$. The *value* of the solution s is $\Pi(I, k, s)$. Just as for "classical" optimization problems, the instances of Π are given as input, and the algorithmic task is to find a solution with the best possible value, where *best* means minimum for minimization problems and maximum for maximization problems.

Definition 23.2 (Optimum value) For a parameterized minimization problem Π, the *optimum value* of an instance $(I, k) \in \Sigma^* \times \mathbb{N}$ is

$$\text{OPT}_\Pi(I, k) = \min_{\substack{s \in \Sigma^* \\ |s| \leq |I|+k}} \Pi(I, k, s).$$

For a parameterized maximization problem Π, the optimum value of (I, k) is

$$\text{OPT}_\Pi(I, k) = \max_{\substack{s \in \Sigma^* \\ |s| \leq |I|+k}} \Pi(I, k, s).$$

For an instance (I, k) of a parameterized optimization problem Π, an *optimal solution* is a solution s such that $\Pi(I, k, s) = \text{OPT}_\Pi(I, k)$.

When the problem Π is clear from context, we will often drop the subscript and refer to $\text{OPT}_\Pi(I, k)$ as $\text{OPT}(I, k)$. Observe that in the definition of $\text{OPT}_\Pi(I, k)$, the set of solutions over which we are minimizing/maximizing Π is finite, therefore the minimum or maximum is well defined. We remark that the function Π in Definition 23.1 depends *both* on I and on k. Thus, it is possible to define parameterized problems such that an optimal solution s for (I, k) is not necessarily optimal for (I, k').

Let us remind that for an instance (I, k), the *size* of the instance is $|I| + k$ while the integer k is referred to as the *parameter* of the instance. For decision problems "solving" an instance means to determine whether the input instance is a yes- or no-instance to the problem. Next, we define what it means to "solve" an instance of a parameterized optimization problem and define fixed parameter tractability for parameterized optimization problems.

Definition 23.3 Let Π be a parameterized optimization problem. An *algorithm for* Π is an algorithm that, given as input an instance (I, k), outputs a solution s and halts. The algorithm *solves* Π if, for every instance (I, k), the solution s output by the algorithm is optimal for (I, k). We say that a parameterized optimization problem Π is *decidable* if there exists an algorithm that solves Π.

Definition 23.4 (FPT optimization problem) A parameterized optimization problem Π is *fixed parameter tractable* (FPT) if there is an algorithm that solves Π, such that the running time of the algorithm on instances of size n with parameter k is upper bounded by $f(k)n^{\mathcal{O}(1)}$ for a computable function f.

We remark that Definition 23.3 differs from the usual formalization of what it means to "solve" a decision problem. Solving a decision problem amounts to always returning "yes" on "yes"-instances and "no" on "no"-instances. For parameterized optimization problems, the algorithm has to produce an optimal solution. This is analogous to the definition of optimization problems most commonly used in approximation algorithms.

Parameterizations by the value of the solution. At this point, it is useful to consider a few concrete examples and to discuss the relationship between parameterized optimization problems and decision variants of the same problem. For a concrete example, consider the VERTEX COVER problem. Here the input is a graph G, and the task is to find a smallest possible *vertex cover* of G: a subset $S \subseteq V(G)$ is a *vertex cover* if every edge of G has at least one endpoint in S. This is quite clearly an optimization problem. Indeed, the feasible solutions are the vertex covers of G and the objective function is the size of S.

In the most common formalization of the VERTEX COVER problem as a *decision problem* parameterized by the solution size, the input instance G comes with a parameter k and the instance (G, k) is a yes-instance if G has a vertex cover of size at most k. Thus, the parameterized decision problem "does not care" whether G has a vertex cover of size even smaller than k; the only thing that matters is whether a solution of size at most k is present.

To formalize VERTEX COVER as a parameterized optimization problem, we need to determine for every instance (G, k) which value to assign to potential solutions $S \subseteq V(G)$. We can encode the set of feasible solutions by giving finite values for vertex covers of G and ∞ for all other sets. We want to distinguish between graphs that do have vertex covers of size at most k and the ones that do not. At the same time, we want the computational problem of solving the instance (G, k) to become easier as k decreases. A way to achieve this is to assign $|S|$ to all vertex covers S of G of size at most k, and $k + 1$ for all other vertex covers. Thus, one can formalize the VERTEX COVER problem as a parameterized optimization problem as follows.

$$VC(G, k, S) = \begin{cases} \infty & \text{if } S \text{ is not a vertex cover of } G, \\ \min(|S|, k + 1) & \text{otherwise.} \end{cases}$$

Note that this formulation of VERTEX COVER "cares" about solutions of size less than k. One can think of k as a threshold: For solutions of size at most k we care about what their size is, while all solutions of size larger than k are equally bad in our eyes, and are assigned value $k + 1$.

Clearly any FPT algorithm that solves the parameterized optimization version of VERTEX COVER also solves the (parameterized) decision variant. Using standard self-reducibility techniques, one can make an FPT algorithm for the decision variant solve the optimization variant as well.

We have seen how a minimization problem can be formalized as a parameterized optimization problem parameterized by the value of the optimum. Next, we give an example for how to do this for maximization problems. In the CYCLE PACKING problem we are given as input a graph G, and the task is to find a largest possible collection $\mathcal{C}$ of pairwise vertex disjoint cycles. Here a *collection of vertex disjoint cycles* is a collection $\mathcal{C}$ of vertex subsets of G such that for every $C \in \mathcal{C}$, $G[C]$ contains a cycle and for every $C, C' \in \mathcal{C}$ we have $V(C) \cap V(C') = \emptyset$. We will often refer to a collection of vertex disjoint cycles as a *cycle packing*.

We can formalize the CYCLE PACKING problem as a parameterized optimization problem parameterized by the value of the optimum in a manner similar to what we did for VERTEX COVER. In particular, if $\mathcal{C}$ is a cycle packing, then we assign it value $|\mathcal{C}|$ if $|\mathcal{C}| \leq k$ and value $k+1$ otherwise. If $|\mathcal{C}|$ is not a cycle packing, we give it value $-\infty$.

$$CP(G, k, \mathcal{C}) = \begin{cases} -\infty & \text{if } \mathcal{C} \text{ is not a cycle packing,} \\ \min(|\mathcal{C}|, k+1) & \text{otherwise.} \end{cases}$$

Thus, the only (formal) difference between the formalization of parameterized minimization and maximization problems parameterized by the value of the optimum is how infeasible solutions are treated. For minimization problems infeasible solutions get value ∞, while for maximization problems they get value $-\infty$. However, there is also a "philosophical" difference between the formalization of minimization and maximization problems. For minimization problems we do not distinguish between feasible solutions that are "too bad"; solutions of size more than k are all given the same value. However, for maximization problems all solutions that are "good enough," that is, of size at least $k+1$, are considered equal.

Observe that the "capping" of the objective function at $k+1$ *does not make sense for approximation algorithms* if one insists on k being the (unparameterized) optimum of the instance I. The parameterization discussed in the preceding text is *by the value of the solution that we want our algorithms to output*, not by the unknown optimum. We will discuss this topic in more detail in the paragraph "**Capping the objective function at $k+1$**," after the notion of approximate kernelization has been formally defined.

Structural parameterizations. We now give an example that demonstrates that the notion of parameterized optimization problems is robust enough to capture not only parameterizations by the value of the optimum but also parameterizations by structural properties of the instance that may or may not be connected to the value of the best solution. In the OPTIMAL LINEAR

ARRANGEMENT problem, we are given as input a graph G, and the task is to find a bijection $\sigma : V(G) \to \{1, \ldots, n\}$ such that

$$val(\sigma, G) = \sum_{uv \in E(G)} |\sigma(u) - \sigma(v)|$$

is minimized. A bijection $\sigma : V(G) \to \{1, \ldots, n\}$ is called a *linear layout*, and $val(\sigma, G)$ is called the *value* of the layout σ.

We will consider the OPTIMAL LINEAR ARRANGEMENT problem for graphs that have a relatively small vertex cover. This can be formalized as a parameterized optimization problem as follows:

$$OLA((G, S), k, \sigma) = \begin{cases} -\infty & \text{if } S \text{ is not vertex cover of } G \\ & \text{of size at most } k, \\ \infty & \text{if } \sigma \text{ is not a linear layout,} \\ val(\sigma, G) & \text{otherwise.} \end{cases}$$

In the preceding definition the first case takes precedence over the second: If S is not vertex cover of G of size at most k and σ is not a linear layout, $OLA((G, S), k, \sigma)$ returns $-\infty$. This ensures that malformed input instances do not need to be handled.

Note that the input instances to the parameterized optimization problem previously described are pairs $((G, S), k)$ where G is a graph, S is a vertex cover of G of size at most k and k is the parameter. This definition allows algorithms for OPTIMAL LINEAR ARRANGEMENT parameterized by vertex cover to assume that the vertex cover S is given as input.

Kernelization of parameterized optimization problems. The notion of a kernel (or kernelization algorithm) is a mathematical model for polynomial time preprocessing for decision problems. We will now define the corresponding notion for parameterized optimization problems. To that end, we first need to define a polynomial time preprocessing algorithm.

Definition 23.5 (Polynomial time preprocessing algorithm) Polynomial time preprocessing algorithm $\mathcal{A}$ for a parameterized optimization problem Π is a pair of polynomial time algorithms. The first one is called the **reduction algorithm** and computes a map $\mathcal{R}_\mathcal{A} : \Sigma^* \times \mathbb{N} \to \Sigma^* \times \mathbb{N}$. Given as input an instance (I, k) of Π, the reduction algorithm outputs another instance $(I', k') = \mathcal{R}_\mathcal{A}(I, k)$.

The second algorithm is called the **solution-lifting algorithm**. This algorithm takes as input an instance $(I, k) \in \Sigma^* \times \mathbb{N}$ of Π, the output instance (I', k') of the reduction algorithm, and a solution s' to the instance (I', k'). The solution-lifting algorithm works in time polynomial in $|I|,k,|I'|,k'$ and s' and outputs a solution s to (I,k). Finally, if s' is an optimal solution to (I',k') then s is an optimal solution to (I,k).

Observe that the solution-lifting algorithm could contain the reduction algorithm as a subroutine. Thus, on input (I,k,I',k',s') the solution-lifting algorithm could start by running the reduction algorithm (I,k) and produce a transcript of *how* the reduction algorithm obtains (I',k') from (I,k). Hence, when designing the solution-lifting algorithm we may assume without loss of generality that such a transcript is given as input. For the same reason, it is not really necessary to include (I',k') as input to the solution-lifting algorithm. However, to avoid starting every description of a solution-lifting algorithm with "we compute the instance (I',k') from (I,k)," we include (I',k') as input.

The notion of polynomial time preprocessing algorithms could be extended to *randomized* polynomial time preprocessing algorithms, by allowing both the reduction algorithm and the solution-lifting algorithm to draw random bits, and *fail* with a small probability. With such an extension, it matters whether the solution-lifting algorithm has access to the random bits drawn by the reduction algorithm because these bits might be required to reconstruct the transcript of how the reduction algorithm obtained (I',k') from (I,k). If the random bits of the reduction algorithm are provided to the solution-lifting algorithm, the preceding discussion applies.

A kernelization algorithm is a polynomial time preprocessing algorithm for which we can prove an upper bound on the size of the output instances in terms of the parameter of the instance to be preprocessed. Thus, the *size* of a polynomial time preprocessing algorithm $\mathcal{A}$ is a function $\text{size}_\mathcal{A} : \mathbb{N} \to \mathbb{N}$ defined as follows.

$$\text{size}_\mathcal{A}(k) = \sup\{|I'| + k' : (I',k') = \mathcal{R}_\mathcal{A}(I,k), I \in \Sigma^*\}.$$

In other words, we look at all possible instances of Π with a fixed parameter k and measure the supremum of the sizes of the output of $\mathcal{R}_\mathcal{A}$ on these instances. At this point, recall that the *size* of an instance (I,k) is defined as $|I|+k$. Note that this supremum may be infinite; This happens when we do not have any bound on the size of $\mathcal{R}_\mathcal{A}(I,k)$ in terms of the input parameter k only. Kernelization algorithms are exactly these polynomial time preprocessing algorithms whose output size is finite and bounded by a computable function of the parameter.

23.1 Framework

Definition 23.6 (Kernel for optimization problem) A *kernelization* (or *kernel*) for a parameterized optimization problem Π is a polynomial time preprocessing algorithm $\mathcal{A}$ such that size$_\mathcal{A}$ is upper bounded by a computable function $g : \mathbb{N} \to \mathbb{N}$.

If the function g in Definition 23.6 is a polynomial, we say that Π admits a *polynomial kernel*. Similarly, if g is a linear, quadratic or cubic function of k we say that Π admits a linear, quadratic, or cubic kernel, respectively.

One of the basic theorems in Parameterized Complexity is that a decidable parameterized decision problem admits a kernel if and only if it is fixed parameter tractable (Theorem 1.4). We now show that this result also holds for parameterized optimization problems. We say that a parameterized optimization problem Π is *decidable* if there exists an algorithm that solves Π, where the definition of "solves" is given in Definition 23.3.

Proposition 23.7 *A decidable parameterized optimization problem Π is FPT if and only if it admits a kernel.*

Proof: The backward direction is trivial; on any instance (I, k) one may first run the reduction algorithm to obtain a new instance (I', k') of size bounded by a function $g(k)$. Because the instance (I', k') has bounded size and Π is decidable, one can find an optimal solution s' to (I', k') in time upper bounded by a function $g'(k)$. Finally, one can use the solution-lifting algorithm to obtain an optimal solution s to (I, k).

For the forward direction we need to show that if a parameterized optimization problem Π is FPT then it admits a kernel. Suppose there is an algorithm that solves instances Π of size n with parameter k in time $f(k)n^c$. On input (I, k) the reduction algorithm runs the FPT algorithm for n^{c+1} steps. If the FPT algorithm terminates after at most n^{c+1} steps, the reduction algorithm outputs an instance (I', k') of constant size. The instance (I', k') is hard-coded in the reduction algorithm and does not depend on the input instance (I, k). Thus, $|I'|+k'$ is upper bounded by a constant. If the FPT algorithm does not terminate after n^{c+1} steps the reduction algorithm halts and outputs the instance (I, k). Note that in this case $f(k)n^c > n^{c+1}$, which implies that $f(k) > |I|$. Hence, the size of the output instance is upper bounded by a function of k.

We now describe the solution-lifting algorithm. If the reduction algorithm outputs (I, k) then the solution-lifting algorithm just returns the same solution that it gets as input. If the reduction algorithm outputs (I', k') this means that the FPT algorithm terminated in polynomial time, which means that the solution-lifting algorithm can use the FPT algorithm to output an optimal solution to (I, k) in polynomial time, regardless of the solution to (I', k') it gets as input. This concludes the proof. □

Parameterized approximation and approximate kernelization. For some parameterized optimization problems we are unable to obtain FPT algorithms, and we are also unable to find satisfactory polynomial time approximation algorithms. In this case, one might aim for FPT-approximation algorithms, algorithms that run in time $f(k)n^c$ and provide good approximate solutions to the instance.

Definition 23.8 (Parameterized approximation algorithm) Let $\alpha \geq 1$ be constant. A *fixed parameter tractable α-approximation algorithm for a parameterized optimization problem* Π is an algorithm that takes as input an instance (I, k), runs in time $f(k)|I|^{\mathcal{O}(1)}$, and outputs a solution s such that $\Pi(I, k, s) \leq \alpha \cdot \mathsf{OPT}(I, k)$ if Π is a minimization problem, and $\alpha \cdot \Pi(I, k, s) \geq \mathsf{OPT}(I, k)$ if Π is a maximization problem.

Note that Definition 23.8 only defines constant factor FPT-approximation algorithms. The definition can in a natural way be extended to approximation algorithms whose approximation ratio depends on the parameter k, on the instance I, or on both.

We are now ready to define one of the key new concepts of the chapter—the concept of an α-approximate kernel. We defined kernels by first defining polynomial time preprocessing algorithms (Definition 23.5) and then adding size constraints on the output (Definition 23.6). In a similar manner we will first define α-approximate polynomial time preprocessing algorithms, and then define α-approximate kernels by adding size constraints on the output of the preprocessing algorithm.

Definition 23.9 Let $\alpha \geq 1$ be a real number and Π be a parameterized optimization problem. An *α-approximate polynomial time preprocessing algorithm* $\mathcal{A}$ for Π is a pair of polynomial time algorithms. The first one is called the *reduction algorithm* and computes a map $\mathcal{R}_\mathcal{A} : \Sigma^* \times \mathbb{N} \to \Sigma^* \times \mathbb{N}$. Given as input an instance (I, k) of Π, the reduction algorithm outputs another instance $(I', k') = \mathcal{R}_\mathcal{A}(I, k)$.

The second algorithm is called the *solution-lifting algorithm*. This algorithm takes as input an instance $(I, k) \in \Sigma^* \times \mathbb{N}$ of Π, the output instance (I', k') of the reduction algorithm, and a solution s' to the instance (I', k'). The solution-lifting algorithm works in time polynomial in $|I|, k, |I'|, k'$ and s', and outputs a solution s to (I, k). If Π is a minimization problem, then

$$\frac{\Pi(I, k, s)}{\mathsf{OPT}(I, k)} \leq \alpha \cdot \frac{\Pi(I', k', s')}{\mathsf{OPT}(I', k')}.$$

If Π is a maximization problem, then

$$\frac{\Pi(I,k,s)}{\mathsf{OPT}(I,k)} \cdot \alpha \geq \frac{\Pi(I',k',s')}{\mathsf{OPT}(I',k')}.$$

Definition 23.9 only defines constant factor approximate polynomial time preprocessing algorithms. The definition can in a natural way be extended to approximation ratios that depend on the parameter k, on the instance I, or on both. Additionally, the discussion following Definition 23.5 also applies here. In particular, we may assume that the solution-lifting algorithm also gets as input a transcript of how the reduction algorithm obtains (I',k') from (I,k). The size of an α-approximate polynomial time preprocessing algorithm is defined in exactly the same way as the size of a polynomial time preprocessing algorithm (from Definition 23.5).

Definition 23.10 (α-approximate kernelization) An α-approximate kernelization (or α-approximate kernel) for a parameterized optimization problem Π, and real $\alpha \geq 1$, is an α-approximate polynomial time preprocessing algorithm $\mathcal{A}$ such that size$_\mathcal{A}$ is upper bounded by a computable function $g : \mathbb{N} \to \mathbb{N}$.

Just as for regular kernels, if the function g in Definition 23.10 is a polynomial, we say that Π admits an α-approximate polynomial kernel. If g is a linear, quadratic, or cubic function, then Π admits a linear, quadratic, or cubic α-approximate kernel, respectively.

Proposition 23.7 establishes that a parameterized optimization problem Π admits a kernel if and only if it is FPT. Next, we establish a similar equivalence between FPT-approximation algorithms and approximate kernelization.

Proposition 23.11 *For every $\alpha \geq 1$ and decidable parameterized optimization problem Π, Π admits a fixed parameter tractable α-approximation algorithm if and only if Π has an α-approximate kernel.*

The proof of Proposition 23.11 is identical to the proof of Proposition 23.7, but with the FPT algorithm replaced by the fixed parameter tractable α-approximation algorithm, and the kernel replaced with the α-approximate kernel. On an intuitive level, it should be easier to compress an instance than it is to solve it. For α-approximate kernelization this intuition can be formalized.

Theorem 23.12 *For every $\alpha \geq 1$ and decidable parameterized optimization problem Π, Π admits a polynomial time α-approximation algorithm if and only if Π has an α-approximate kernel of constant size.*

The proof of Theorem 23.12 is simple. On the one hand, if there is an α-approximate kernel of constant size one can brute force the reduced instance and lift the optimal solution of the reduced instance to an α-approximate solution to the original. On the other hand, if there is a factor α approximation algorithm, the reduction algorithm can just output any instance of constant size. Then, the solution-lifting algorithm can just directly compute an α-approximate solution to the original instance using the approximation algorithm.

We remark that Proposition 23.11 and Theorem 23.12 also apply to approximation algorithms and approximate kernels with a super-constant approximation ratio. We also remark that with our definition of α-approximate kernelization, by setting $\alpha = 1$ we essentially get back the notion of kernel for the same problem. The difference arises naturally from the different goals of decision and optimization problems. In decision problems we aim to correctly classify the instance as a yes- or a no- instance. In an optimization problem we just want as good a solution as possible for the instance at hand. In traditional kernelization, a yes/no answer to the reduced instance translates without change to the original instance. With our definition of approximate kernels, a sufficiently good solution (i.e., a witness of a yes answer) will always yield a witness of a yes answer to the original instance. However, the *failure* to produce a sufficiently good solution to the reduced instance does not stop us from *succeeding* at producing a sufficiently good solution for the original one. From the perspective of optimization problems, such an outcome is a win.

Capping the objective function at $k + 1$. We now return to the topic of parameterizing optimization problems by the value of the solution and discuss the relationship between (approximate) kernels for such parameterized optimization problems and (traditional) kernels for the parameterized decision version of the optimization problem.

Consider a traditional optimization problem, say VERTEX COVER. Here, the input is a graph G, and the goal is to find a vertex cover S of G of minimum possible size. When *parameterizing* VERTEX COVER by the objective function value we need to provide a parameter k such that solving the problem on the same graph G becomes progressively easier as k decreases. In parameterized complexity this is achieved by considering the corresponding *parameterized decision* problem where we are given G and k and asked whether there exists a vertex cover of size at most k. Here k is the parameter. If we also required an algorithm for VERTEX COVER to produce a solution, then the preceding parameterization can be interpreted as follows. Given G and k, output a vertex cover of size at most k or fail (i.e., return that the algorithm could not find a vertex cover of size at most k). If there exists a vertex cover of size at most k, then the algorithm is not allowed to fail.

A c-approximation algorithm for the VERTEX COVER problem is an algorithm that, given G, outputs a solution S of size no more than c times the size of the smallest vertex cover of G. So, how do approximation and parameterization mix? For $c \geq 1$, there are *two* natural ways to define a parameterized c-approximation algorithm for VERTEX COVER.

(a) Given G and k, output a vertex cover of size at most k or fail (i.e., return that the algorithm could not find a vertex cover of size at most k). If there exists a vertex cover of size at most k/c, then the algorithm is not allowed to fail.
(b) Given G and k, output a vertex cover of size at most ck or fail (i.e., return that the algorithm could not find a vertex cover of size at most ck.) If there exists a vertex cover of size at most k, then the algorithm is not allowed to fail.

Note that if we required the approximation algorithm to run in *polynomial time*, then both preceding definitions would yield exactly the definition of polynomial time c-approximation algorithms by a linear search or binary search for the appropriate value of k. In the parameterized setting, the running time depends on k, and the two formalizations are different, but nevertheless equivalent up to a factor c in the value of k. That is, $f(k) \cdot n^{\mathcal{O}(1)}$ time algorithms and $g(k)$ size kernels for parameterization (b) translate to $f(ck) \cdot n^{\mathcal{O}(1)}$ time algorithms and $g(ck)$ kernels for parameterization (a) and vice versa.

By defining the parameterized optimization problem for VERTEX COVER in such a way that the objective function depends on the parameter k, one can achieve either one of the two discussed formulations. By defining

$$VC(G, k, S) = \min\{|S|, k + 1\}$$

for vertex covers S we obtain formulation (a). By defining

$$VC(G, k, S) = \min\{|S|, \lceil ck \rceil + 1\}$$

for vertex covers S we obtain formulation (b). It is more meaningful to define the computational problem *independently of the (approximation factor of) algorithms for the problem*. For this reason we stick to formulation (a) in this chapter.

Reduction Rules and Strict α-Approximate Kernels. Kernelization algorithms are commonly described as a set of *reduction rules*. Here we discuss reduction rules in the context of parameterized optimization problems.

A reduction rule is simply a polynomial time preprocessing algorithm, see Definition 23.5. The reduction rule *applies* if the output instance of the reduction algorithm is not the same as the input instance. Most kernelization algorithms consist of a set of reduction rules. In every step, the algorithm checks whether any of the reduction rules apply. If a reduction rule applies, the kernelization algorithm runs the reduction algorithm on the instance and proceeds by working with the new instance. This process is repeated until the instance is *reduced*, that is, none of the reduction rules apply. To prove that this is indeed a kernel (as defined in Definition 23.6) one proves an upper bound on the size of any reduced instance.

To be able to make kernelization algorithms as described previously, it is important that reduction rules can be *chained*. That is, suppose that we have an instance (I, k) and run a preprocessing algorithm on it to produce another instance (I', k'). Then we run another preprocessing algorithm on (I', k') to get a third instance $(I^\star, k^\star)$. Given an optimal solution $s^\star$ to the last instance, we can use the solution-lifting algorithm of the second preprocessing algorithm to get an optimal solution s' to the instance (I', k'). Then we can use the solution-lifting algorithm of the first preprocessing algorithm to get an optimal solution s to the original instance (I, k).

Unfortunately, one can not chain α-approximate polynomial time preprocessing algorithms, as defined in Definition 23.9, in this way. In particular, each successive application of an α-approximate preprocessing algorithm increases the gap between the approximation ratio of the solution to the reduced instance and the approximation ratio of the solution to the original instance output by the solution-lifting algorithm. For this reason we need to define *strict* approximate polynomial time preprocessing algorithms.

Definition 23.13 Let $\alpha \geq 1$ be a real number and Π be a parameterized optimization problem. An α-approximate polynomial time preprocessing algorithm is said to be *strict* if, for every instance (I, k), reduced instance $(I', k') = \mathcal{R}_A(I, k)$ and solution s' to (I', k'), the solution s to (I, k) output by the solution-lifting algorithm when given s' as input satisfies the following.

- If Π is a minimization problem, then
$$\frac{\Pi(I, k, s)}{\text{OPT}(I, k)} \leq \max\left\{\frac{\Pi(I', k', s')}{\text{OPT}(I', k')}, \alpha\right\}.$$

- If Π is a maximization problem, then
$$\frac{\Pi(I, k, s)}{\text{OPT}(I, k)} \geq \min\left\{\frac{\Pi(I', k', s')}{\text{OPT}(I', k')}, \frac{1}{\alpha}\right\}.$$

The intuition behind Definition 23.13 is that an α-strict approximate preprocessing algorithm may incur error on near-optimal solutions, but that they have to preserve factor α-approximation. If s' is an α-approximate solution to (I', k'), then s must be a α-approximate solution to (I, k) as well. Furthermore, if the ratio of $\Pi(I', k', s')$ to $\mathsf{OPT}(I', k')$ is *worse* than α, then the ratio of $\Pi(I, k, s)$ to $\mathsf{OPT}(I, k)$ should not be worse than the ratio of $\Pi(I', k', s')$ to $\mathsf{OPT}(I', k')$.

We remark that a reduction algorithm $\mathcal{R}_\mathcal{A}$ and a solution-lifting algorithm that together satisfy the conditions of Definition 23.13 also automatically satisfy the conditions of Definition 23.9. Therefore, to prove that $\mathcal{R}_\mathcal{A}$ and a solution-lifting algorithm constitute a strict α-approximate polynomial time preprocessing algorithm, it is not necessary to prove that they constitute a α-approximate polynomial time preprocessing algorithm first. The advantage of Definition 23.13 is that strict α-approximate polynomial time preprocessing algorithms do chain—the composition of two strict α-approximate polynomial time preprocessing algorithms is again a strict α-approximate polynomial time preprocessing algorithm.

We can now formally define what a reduction rule is. A reduction rule for a parameterized optimization problem Π is simply a polynomial time algorithm computing a map $\mathcal{R}_\mathcal{A} : \Sigma^* \times \mathbb{N} \to \Sigma^* \times \mathbb{N}$. In other words, a reduction rule is "half" of a polynomial time preprocessing algorithm. A reduction rule is only useful if the other half is there to complete the preprocessing algorithm.

Definition 23.14 A reduction rule is said to be α-*safe for* Π if there exists a solution-lifting algorithm, such that the rule together with the solution-lifting algorithm constitute a strict α-approximate polynomial time preprocessing algorithm for Π. A reduction rule is *safe* if it is 1-safe.

In some cases, even the final kernelization algorithm is a strict α-approximate polynomial time preprocessing algorithm. This happens if, for example, the kernel is obtained only by applying α-safe reduction rules. Strictness yields a tighter connection between the quality of solutions to the reduced instance and the quality of the solutions to the original instance output by the solution-lifting algorithms. Thus, we would like to point out which kernels have this additional property. For this reason we define strict α-approximate kernels.

Definition 23.15 An α-approximate kernel $\mathcal{A}$ is called *strict* if $\mathcal{A}$ is a strict α-approximate polynomial time preprocessing algorithm.

Polynomial Size Approximate Kernelization Schemes. In approximation algorithms, the best one can hope for is usually an *approximation scheme*, that is, an approximation algorithm that can produce a $(1+\epsilon)$-approximate solution for every $\epsilon > 0$. The algorithm runs in polynomial time for every fixed value of ϵ. However, as ϵ tends to 0 the algorithm becomes progressively slower in such a way that the algorithm cannot be used to obtain optimal solutions in polynomial time.

In the setting of approximate kernelization, we could end up in a situation in which it is possible to produce a polynomial $(1 + \epsilon)$-approximate kernel for every fixed value of ϵ, but that the size of the kernel grows so fast when ϵ tends to 0 that this algorithm cannot be used to give a polynomial size kernel (without any loss in solution quality). This can be formalized as a polynomial size approximate kernelization scheme (PSAKS).

Definition 23.16 (Polynomial size approximate kernelization scheme) A PSAKS for a parameterized optimization problem Π is a family of α-approximate polynomial kernelization algorithms, with one such algorithm for every $\alpha > 1$.

Definition 23.16 states that a PSAKS is a *family* of algorithms, one for every $\alpha > 1$. However, many PSAKSes are *uniform*, in the sense that there exists an algorithm that, given α, outputs the source code of an α-approximate polynomial kernelization algorithm for Π. In other words, one could think of a uniform PSAKS as a single α-approximate polynomial kernelization algorithm where α is part of the input, and the size of the output depends on α. From the definition of a PSAKS, it follows that the size of the output instances of a PSAKS when run on an instance (I, k) with approximation parameter α can be upper bounded by $f(\alpha) \cdot k^{g(\alpha)}$ for some functions f and g independent of $|I|$ and k.

Definition 23.17 (fEfficient PSAKS) A *size efficient* PSAKS, or simply an *efficient* PSAKS (EPSAKS) is a PSAKS such that the size of the instances output when the reduction algorithm is run on an instance (I, k) with approximation parameter α can be upper bounded by $f(\alpha) \cdot k^c$ for a function f of α and constant c independent of I, k, and α.

Notice here the analogy to efficient polynomial time approximation schemes, which are nothing but α-approximation algorithms with running time $f(\alpha) \cdot n^c$. A PSAKS is required to run in polynomial time for every fixed value of α, but the running time is allowed to become worse as α tends to 1. We can define *time-efficient* PSAKSs analagously to how we defined EPSAKSs.

Definition 23.18 (Time-efficient PSAKS) A PSAKS is said to be *time efficient* if (a) the running time of the reduction algorithm when run on an instance (I, k) with approximation parameter α can be upper bounded by $f(\alpha) \cdot |I|^c$ for a function f of α and constant c independent of I, k, α, and (b) the running time of the solution-lifting algorithm when run on an instance (I, k), reduced instance (I', k'), and solution s' with approximation parameter α can be upper bounded by $f'(\alpha) \cdot |I|^c$ for a function f' of α and constant c independent of I, k, and α.

Just as we distinguished between normal and strict α-approximate kernels, we say that a PSAKS is *strict* if it is a strict α-approximate kernel for every $\alpha > 1$.

The following facts are useful in later sections to show the desired approximate kernels.

Fact 23.1 For any positive reals x, y, p, and q, $\min\left(\frac{x}{p}, \frac{y}{q}\right) \leq \frac{x+y}{p+q} \leq \max\left(\frac{x}{p}, \frac{y}{q}\right)$.

Fact 23.2 For any $y \leq \frac{1}{2}$, $(1-y)^y \geq \left(\frac{1}{4}\right)^y$.

23.2 Cycle Packing

In this section, we design a strict polynomial size 6-approximate kernel for the CYCLE PACKING problem. The CYCLE PACKING problem is formally defined as follows.

$$CP(G, k, P) = \begin{cases} -\infty & \text{if } P \text{ is not a set of vertex disjoint cycles in } G \\ \min\{|P|, k+1\} & \text{otherwise.} \end{cases}$$

In this subsection we give a polynomial size 6-approximate kernel. We start by defining feedback vertex sets of a graph. Given a graph G and a vertex subset $F \subseteq V(G)$, F is called a *feedback veretx set* of G if $G - F$ is a forest. We will make use of the following well-known lemma of Erdős and Pósa (1965) relating feedback vertex set and the number of vertex disjoint cycles in a graph.

Lemma 23.19 (Erdős and Pósa [1965]) *There exists a constant c' such that every (multi-) graph either contains k vertex disjoint cycles or it has a feedback vertex set of size at most $c'k \log k$. Moreover, there is a polynomial time algorithm that takes a graph G and an integer k as input, and outputs either k vertex disjoint cycles or a feedback vertex set of size at most $c'k \log k$.*

In our 6-approximate kernelization algorithm we apply the following reduction rules in the given order exhaustively.

Reduction LCP.1 Compute a shortest cycle C in G. If $|C| \leq 6$ then output $G' = G - C$ and $k' = k - 1$.

Lemma 23.20 *Reduction Rule LCP.1 is 6-safe.*

Proof: The solution-lifting algorithm takes a cycle packing P' of G' and adds the cycle C to it. The resulting cycle packing P is a cycle packing in G with one more cycle. Thus, $CP(G, k, P) \geq CP(G', k', P') + 1$. Next we show that $\mathsf{OPT}(G', k') \geq \mathsf{OPT}(G, k) - 6$. To see this, consider an optimal cycle packing P^* in G. Remove all cycles in P that contain a vertex in C to get a cycle packing $\tilde{P}$ in G'. Because $|C| \leq 6$ it follows that $|\tilde{P}| \geq |P^*| - 6$, and hence $\mathsf{OPT}(G', k') \geq \mathsf{OPT}(G, k) - 6$. Hence, we have that

$$\frac{CP(G, k, P)}{\mathsf{OPT}(G, k)} \geq \frac{CP(G', k', P') + 1}{\mathsf{OPT}(G', k') + 6} \geq \min\left(\frac{CP(G', k', P')}{\mathsf{OPT}(G', k')}, \frac{1}{6}\right).$$

The last transition follows from Fact 23.1. This concludes the proof. □

Reduction LCP.2 If G has a vertex of degree at most 1, then remove it.

Reduction LCP.3 If G has a degree 2 vertex u with neighbors x, y, then delete u and add an edge (x, y).

It is easy to see that the Reduction Rules LCP.2 and LCP.3 are 1-safe. Because Reduction Rule LCP.1 is not applicable while applying Reduction rule LCP.3, the reduced instance after applying Reduction Rule LCP.3 will still be a simple graph. We are now almost in a position to prove the size bound for the kernel. First, we need to state another graph theoretic lemma regarding feedback vertex sets in graphs with no short cycles.

Lemma 23.21 (Raman et al. [2006]) *Let G be a graph on n vertices with minimum degree 3 and no cycles of length at most 6. Then every feedback vertex set of G has size at least $\sqrt{n/2}$.*

Theorem 23.22 CYCLE PACKING *admits a strict 6-approximate kernel with $\mathcal{O}((k \log k)^2)$ vertices.*

Proof: The kernelization algorithm applies rules LCP.1, LCP.2, and LCP.3 exhaustively. Let (G, k) be the reduced instance. If $|V(G)| < 2(c'k \log k)^2$, where c' is the constant from Lemma 23.19, then we are done, so assume that $|V(G)| \geq 2(c'k \log k)^2$. By Lemma 23.21, every feedback vertex set of

G has size at least $c'(k \log k)$. Thus, executing the algorithm of Lemma 23.19 will give us a cycle packing of size k, which the kernelization algorithm may output. Because the kernel was obtained by an exhaustive application of 6-safe rules, it follows that the kernel is strict. □

23.3 Partial Vertex Cover

In the PARTIAL VERTEX COVER problem the input is a graph G on n vertices and an integer k. The task is to find a vertex set $S \subseteq V(G)$ of size k, maximizing the number of edges with at least one endpoint in S. We will consider the problem parameterized by the solution *size* k. Note that the solution size is *not* the objective function value. We define PARTIAL VERTEX COVER as a parameterized optimization problem as follows.

$$PVC(G, k, S) = \begin{cases} -\infty & |S| > k \\ \text{number of edges incident on } S & \text{otherwise.} \end{cases}$$

PARTIAL VERTEX COVER is W[1]-hard by Guo et al. (2007), thus we do not expect an FPT algorithm or a kernel of *any* size to exist for this problem.

Theorem 23.23 PARTIAL VERTEX COVER *admits EPSAKS.*

Proof: We give an α-approximate kernelization algorithm for the problem for every $\alpha > 1$. Let $\epsilon = 1 - \frac{1}{\alpha}$ and $\beta = \frac{1}{\epsilon}$. Let (G, k) be the input instance. Let $v_1, v_2, \ldots, v_n$ be the vertices of G in the nonincreasing order of degree, that is, $d_G(v_i) \geq d_G(v_j)$ for all $1 \geq i > j \geq n$. The kernelization algorithm has two cases based on degree of v_1.

Case 1: $d_G(v_1) \geq \beta\binom{k}{2}$. In this case $S = \{v_1, \ldots, v_k\}$ is an α-approximate solution. The number of edges incident to S is at least $(\sum_{i=1}^{k} d_G(v_i)) - \binom{k}{2}$ because, at most, $\binom{k}{2}$ edges have both endpoints in S and they are counted twice in the sum $(\sum_{i=1}^{k} d_G(v_i))$. The value of the optimum solution is at most $\sum_{i=1}^{k} d_G(v_i)$. Now consider the value, $\frac{PVC(G,k,S)}{\mathsf{OPT}(G,k)}$.

$$\frac{PVC(G, k, S)}{\mathsf{OPT}(G, k)} \geq \frac{(\sum_{i=1}^{k} d_G(v_i)) - \binom{k}{2}}{\sum_{i=1}^{k} d_G(v_i)} \geq 1 - \frac{\binom{k}{2}}{d_G(v_1)} \geq 1 - \frac{1}{\beta} = \frac{1}{\alpha}.$$

The preceding inequality implies that S is an α-approximate solution. So the kernelization algorithm outputs a trivial instance $(\emptyset, 0)$ in this case.

Case 2: $d_G(v_1) < \beta\binom{k}{2}$. Let $V' = \{v_1, v_2, \ldots, v_{k\lceil \beta\binom{k}{2}\rceil+1}\}$. In this case the algorithm outputs (G', k), where $G' = G[N_G[V']]$. We first claim that

$\mathsf{OPT}(G',k) = \mathsf{OPT}(G,k)$. Because G' is a subgraph of G, $\mathsf{OPT}(G',k) \leq \mathsf{OPT}(G,k)$. Now it is enough to show that $\mathsf{OPT}(G',k) \geq \mathsf{OPT}(G,k)$. Toward that, we prove that there is an optimum solution that contains only vertices from the set V'. Suppose not, then consider the solution S that is lexicographically smallest in the ordered list $v_1, \ldots v_n$. The set S contains at most $k-1$ vertices from V' and at least one from $V \setminus V'$. Because the degree of each vertex in G is at most $\lceil \beta \binom{k}{2} \rceil - 1$ and $|S| \leq k$, we have that $|N_G[S]| \leq k\lceil \beta \binom{k}{2} \rceil$. This implies that there exists a vertex $v \in V'$ such that $v \notin N_G[S]$. Hence, by including the vertex v and removing a vertex from $S \setminus V'$, we can cover at least as many edges as S can cover. This contradicts our assumption that S is lexicographically smallest. Because G' is a subgraph of G, any solution of G' is also a solution of G. Thus, we have shown that $\mathsf{OPT}(G',k) = \mathsf{OPT}(G,k)$. So the algorithm returns the instance (G',k) as the reduced instance. Because G' is a subgraph of G, in this case, the solution-lifting algorithm takes a solution S' of (G',k) as input and outputs S' as a solution of (G,k). Because $\mathsf{OPT}(G',k) = \mathsf{OPT}(G,k)$, it follows that

$$\frac{PVC(G,k,S')}{\mathsf{OPT}(G,k)} = \frac{PVC(G',k,S')}{\mathsf{OPT}(G',k)}.$$

The number of vertices in the reduced instance is $\mathcal{O}(k \cdot \lceil \frac{1}{\epsilon} \binom{k}{2} \rceil^2) = \mathcal{O}(k^5)$. The running time of the algorithm is polynomial in the size of G. Because the algorithm either finds an α-approximate solution (Case 1) or reduces the instance by a 1-safe reduction rule (Case 2), this kernelization scheme is strict. $\square$

23.4 Connected Vertex Cover

In this section we design a PSAKS for CONNECTED VERTEX COVER. The parameterized optimization problem CONNECTED VERTEX COVER is defined as follows.

$$CVC(G,k,S) = \begin{cases} \infty & \text{if } S \text{ is not a connected vertex cover} \\ & \text{of the graph } G \\ \min\{|S|, k+1\} & \text{otherwise.} \end{cases}$$

We show that CONNECTED VERTEX COVER has a polynomial size strict α-approximate kernel for every $\alpha > 1$. Let (G,k) be the input instance. Without loss of generality assume that the input graph G is connected. Let d be the least positive integer such that $\frac{d}{d-1} \leq \alpha$. In particular, $d = \lceil \frac{\alpha}{\alpha-1} \rceil$. For a graph G

and an integer k, define H to be the set of vertices of degree at least $k + 1$. We define I to be the set of vertices that are not in H and whose neighborhood is a subset of H. That is, $I = \{v \in V(G) \setminus H \mid N_G(v) \subseteq H\}$. The kernelization algorithm works by applying two reduction rules exhaustively. The first of the two rules is the following.

> **Reduction LCVC.1** Let $v \in I$ be a vertex of degree $D \geq d$. Delete $N_G[v]$ from G and add a vertex w such that the neighborhood of w is $N_G(N_G(v)) \setminus \{v\}$. Then add k degree 1 vertices $v_1, \ldots, v_k$ whose neighbor is w. Output this graph G', together with the new parameter $k' = k - (D - 1)$.

Lemma 23.24 *Reduction Rule LCVC.1 is α-safe.*

Proof: To show that Rule LCVC.1 is α-safe we need to give a solution-lifting algorithm to go with the reduction. Given a solution S' to the instance (G', k'), if S' is a connected vertex cover of G' of size at most k' the algorithm returns the set $S = (S' \setminus \{w, v_1, \ldots, v_k\}) \cup N_G[v]$. Otherwise the solution-lifting algorithm returns $V(G)$. We now need to show that the reduction rule together with the preceding solution-lifting algorithm constitutes a strict α-approximate polynomial time preprocessing algorithm.

First, we show that $\mathsf{OPT}(G', k') \leq \mathsf{OPT}(G, k) - (D - 1)$. Consider an optimal solution S^* to (G, k). We have two cases based on the size of S^*. If $|S^*| > k$ then $CVC(G, k, S) = k + 1$; in fact, $\mathsf{OPT}(G, k) = k + 1$. Furthermore, any connected vertex cover of G' has value at most $k' + 1 = k - (D - 1) + 1 \leq \mathsf{OPT}(G, k) - (D - 1)$. Now we consider the case when $|S^*| \leq k$. If $|S^*| \leq k$ then $N_G(v) \subseteq S^*$, because the degree of all the vertices in $N_G(v)$ is at least $k + 1$ and S^* is a vertex cover of size at most k. Then $(S^* \setminus N_G[v]) \cup \{w\}$ is a connected vertex cover of G' of size at most $|S^*| - (D - 1) = \mathsf{OPT}(G, k) - (D - 1)$.

Now we show that $CVC(G, k, S) \leq CVC(G', k', S') + D$. If S' is a connected vertex cover of G' of size strictly more than k' then

$$CVC(G, k, S) \leq k + 1 = k' + D < k' + 1 + D = CVC(G', k', S') + D.$$

Suppose now that S' is a connected vertex cover of G' of size at most k'. Then $w \in S'$ because w has degree at least k in G'. Thus, $|S| \leq |S'| - 1 + D + 1 \leq |S'| + D$. Finally, $G[S]$ is connected because $G[N_G[v]]$ is connected and $N_G(N_G[v]) = N_{G'}(w) \setminus \{v_1, \ldots, v_k\}$. Hence, S is a connected vertex cover of G. Thus, $CVC(G, k, S) \leq CVC(G', k', S') + D$. Therefore, we have that

$$\frac{CVC(G, k, S)}{\mathsf{OPT}(G, k)} \leq \frac{CVC(G', k', S') + D}{\mathsf{OPT}(G', k') + (D - 1)} \leq \max\left(\frac{CVC(G', k', S')}{\mathsf{OPT}(G', k')}, \alpha\right).$$

The last transition follows from Fact 23.1. This concludes the proof. □

The second rule is easier than the first: If any vertex v has at least $k + 1$ false twins, then remove v. A *false twin* of a vertex v is a vertex u such that $uv \notin E(G)$ and $N(u) = N(v)$.

> **Reduction LCVC.2** If a vertex v has at least $k+1$ false twins, then remove v, that is, output $G' = G - v$ and $k' = k$.

Lemma 23.25 *Reduction Rule LCVC.2 is 1-safe.*

Proof: The solution-lifting algorithm takes as input a set S' to the reduced instance and returns the same set $S' = S$ as a solution to the original instance. To see that $\mathsf{OPT}(G', k) \leq \mathsf{OPT}(G, k)$, consider a smallest connected vertex cover S^* of G. Again, we will distinguish between two cases: either $|S^*| > k$ or $|S^*| \leq k$. If $|S^*| > k$ then $\mathsf{OPT}(G', k) \leq k + 1 = \mathsf{OPT}(G, k)$. Thus, assume $|S^*| \leq k$. Then, there is a false twin u of v that is not in S^*, and therefore $(S^* \setminus \{v\}) \cup \{u\}$ is a connected vertex cover of $G - v$ of size at most k.

Next we show that $CVC(G, k, S) \leq CVC(G', k', S')$. If $|S'| > k' = k$, then clearly $CVC(G, k, S) \leq k + 1 = k' + 1 = CVC(G', k', S')$. So let us assume that $|S'| \leq k$. Observe that, as v has $k + 1$ false twins, all vertices in $N(v)$ have degree at least $k + 1$ in $G - v$. Thus, $N(v) \subseteq S' = S$ and S is a connected vertex cover of G, and hence $CVC(G, k, S) \leq CVC(G', k', S')$. As a result,

$$\frac{CVC(G, k, S)}{\mathsf{OPT}(G, k)} \leq \frac{CVC(G', k', S')}{\mathsf{OPT}(G', k')}.$$

This concludes the proof. □

Lemma 23.26 *Let (G, k) be an instance irreducible by rules LCVC.1 and LCVC.2, such that $\mathsf{OPT}(G, k) \leq k$. Then $|V(G)| \leq \mathcal{O}(k^d + k^2)$.*

Proof: Because $\mathsf{OPT}(G, k) \leq k$, G has a connected vertex cover S of size at most k. We analyze separately the size of the three sets H, I, and $V(G) \setminus (H \cup I)$. First, $H \subseteq S$ so $|H| \leq k$. Furthermore, every vertex in I has degree at most $d-1$, otherwise Rule LCVC.1 applies. Thus, there are at most $\binom{k}{d-1}$ different subsets X of $V(G)$ such that there is a vertex v in I such that $N(v) = I$. Because each vertex v has at most k false twins it follows that $|I| \leq \binom{k}{d-1} \cdot (k + 1) = \mathcal{O}(k^d)$.

Finally, every edge that has no endpoint in H, has at least one endpoint in $S \setminus H$. Because each vertex in $S \setminus H$ has degree at most k, it follows that there are at most $k|S| \leq k^2$ such edges. Each vertex that is neither in H nor in I must be incident to at least one edge with no endpoint in H. Thus, there are at most $2k^2$ vertices in $V(G) \setminus (I \cup H)$ concluding the proof. □

Theorem 23.27 CONNECTED VERTEX COVER *admits a strict time efficient PSAKS with* $\mathcal{O}(k^{\lceil \frac{\alpha}{\alpha-1} \rceil} + k^2)$ *vertices.*

Proof: The kernelization algorithm applies the rules LCVC.1 and LCVC.2 exhaustively. If the reduced graph G has more than $\mathcal{O}(k^d + k^2)$ vertices then, by Lemma 23.26, $\mathsf{OPT}(G,k) = k+1$ and the algorithm may return any conneccted vertex cover of G as an optimal solution. Thus, the reduced graph has at most $\mathcal{O}(k^d + k^2)$ vertices because $d = \lceil \frac{\alpha}{\alpha-1} \rceil$ the size bound follows. The entire reduction procedure runs in polynomial time (independent of α), hence the PSAKS is time efficient. □

23.5 Steiner Tree

Let us remind that in the STEINER TREE problem we are given as input a graph G, a subset R of $V(G)$ whose vertices are called *terminals* and a weight function $w : E(G) \to \mathbb{N}$. A *Steiner tree* is a subtree T of G such that $R \subseteq V(T)$, and the *cost* of a tree T is defined as $w(T) = \sum_{e \in E(T)} w(e)$. The task is to find a Steiner tree of minimum cost. We may assume without loss of generality that the input graph G is complete and that w satisfies the triangle inequality: for all $u, v, w \in V(G)$ we have $w(uw) \leq w(uv) + w(vw)$. This assumption can be justified by adding for every pair of vertices u,v the edge uv to G and making the weight of uv equal the shortest path distance between u and v. If multiple edges are created between the same pair of vertices, only the lightest edge is kept.

Most approximation algorithms for the STEINER TREE problem rely on the notion of a k-restricted Steiner tree, defined as follows. A *component* is a tree whose leaves coincide with a subset of terminals, and a k-component is a component with at most k leaves. A k-restricted Steiner tree $\mathcal{S}$ is a collection of k-components, such that the union of these components is a Steiner tree T. The cost of $\mathcal{S}$ is the sum of the costs of all the k-components in $\mathcal{S}$. Thus, an edge that appears in several different k-components of $\mathcal{S}$ will contribute several times to the cost of $\mathcal{S}$ but only once to the cost of T. The following result by Borchers and Du (1997) shows that for every $\epsilon > 0$ there exists a k such that the cost of the best k-restricted Steiner tree $\mathcal{S}$ is not more than $(1+\epsilon)$ times the cost of the best Steiner tree. Thus, approximation algorithms for STEINER TREE only need to focus on the best possible way to "piece together" k-components to connect all the terminals.

Proposition 23.28 (Borchers and Du [1997]) *For every $k \geq 1$, graph G, terminal set R, weight function $w : E(G) \to \mathbb{N}$, and Steiner tree T, there is a k-restricted Steiner tree S in G of cost at most $(1 + \frac{1}{\lceil \log_2 k \rceil}) \cdot w(T)$.*

Proposition 23.28 can easily be turned into a PSAKS for STEINER TREE parameterized by the number of terminals, defined as follows.

$$ST((G,R), k', T) = \begin{cases} -\infty & \text{if } |R| > k' \\ \infty & \text{if } T \text{ is not a Steiner tree for } R \\ w(T) & \text{otherwise.} \end{cases}$$

To get a $(1+\epsilon)$-approximate kernel it is sufficient to pick k based on ϵ, compute for each k-sized subset $R' \subseteq R$ of terminals an optimal Steiner tree for R', and only keep vertices in G that appear in these Steiner trees. This reduces the number of vertices of G to $\mathcal{O}(k|R|^k)$, but the edge weights can still be large making the bitsize of the kernel super-polynomial in $|R|$. However, it is quite easy to show that keeping only $\mathcal{O}(\log |R|)$ bits for each weight is more than sufficient for the desired precision.

Theorem 23.29 STEINER TREE *parameterized by the number of terminals admits a PSAKS.*

Proof: Start by computing a 2-approximate Steiner tree T_2 using the classic factor 2 approximation algorithm, see for example, Vazirani (2001). For every vertex $v \notin R$ such that $\min_{x \in R} w(vx) \geq w(T_2)$ delete v from G as v may never participate in any optimal solution. By the triangle inequality we may now assume without loss of generality that for every edge $uv \in E(G)$ we have $w(uv) \leq 3w(T_2) \leq 6\mathsf{OPT}(G, R, w)$.

Working toward a $(1+\epsilon)$-approximate kernel of polynomial size, set k to be the smallest integer such that $\frac{1}{\lceil \log_2 k \rceil} \leq \epsilon/2$. For each subset R' of R of size at most k, compute an optimal Steiner tree $T_{R'}$ for the instance (G, R', w) in time $\mathcal{O}(3^k |E(G)||V(G)|)$ using the algorithm of Dreyfus and Wagner (1971). Mark all the vertices in $V(T_{R'})$. After this process is done, some $\mathcal{O}(k|R|^k)$ vertices in G are marked. Obtain G' from G by deleting all the unmarked vertices in $V(G) \setminus R$. Clearly every Steiner tree in G' is also a Steiner tree in G. We argue that $\mathsf{OPT}(G', R, w) \leq (1 + \frac{\epsilon}{2})\mathsf{OPT}(G, R, w)$.

Consider an optimal Steiner tree T for the instance (G, R, w). By Proposition 23.28 there is a k-restricted Steiner tree S in G of cost at most $(1 + \frac{1}{\lceil \log_2 k \rceil}) \cdot w(T) \leq (1 + \frac{\epsilon}{2})\mathsf{OPT}(G, R, w)$. Consider a k-component $C \in S$, and let R' be the set of leaves of C—note that these are exactly the terminals appearing in C. C is a Steiner tree for R', and so $T_{R'}$ is a Steiner tree for R' with $w(T_{R'}) \leq w(C)$. Then $S' = (S \setminus \{C\}) \cup \{T_{R'}\}$ is a k-restricted Steiner

23.5 Steiner Tree

tree of cost no more than $(1 + \frac{\epsilon}{2})\mathsf{OPT}(G, R, w)$. Repeating this argument for all k-components of $\mathcal{S}$ we conclude that there exists a k-restricted Steiner tree $\mathcal{S}$ in G of cost at most $(1 + \frac{\epsilon}{2})\mathsf{OPT}(G, R, w)$, such that all k-components in $\mathcal{S}$ only use marked vertices. The union of all the k-components in $\mathcal{S}$ is then a Steiner tree in G' of cost at most $(1 + \frac{\epsilon}{2})\mathsf{OPT}(G, R, w)$.

We now define a new weight function $\hat{w} : E(G') \to \mathbb{N}$, by setting

$$\hat{w}(e) = \left\lfloor w(e) \cdot \frac{8|R|}{\epsilon \cdot w(T_2)} \right\rfloor.$$

Note that because $w(e) \leq 3 \cdot w(T_2)$ it follows that $\hat{w}(e) \leq \frac{24|R|}{\epsilon}$. Thus, it takes only $\mathcal{O}(\log |R| + \log \frac{1}{\epsilon})$ bits to store each edge weight. It follows that the bitsize of the instance $(G', R, \hat{w})$ is $|R|^{2^{\mathcal{O}(1/\epsilon)}}$. We now argue that, for every $c \geq 1$, a c-approximate Steiner tree T' for the instance $(G', R, \hat{w})$ is also a $c(1 + \epsilon)$-approximate Steiner tree for the instance (G, R, w).

First, observe that the definition of $\hat{w}$ implies that for every edge e we have the inequality

$$\begin{aligned} w(e) &\leq \hat{w}(e) \cdot \frac{\epsilon \cdot w(T_2)}{8|R|} + \frac{\epsilon \cdot w(T_2)}{8|R|} \\ &\leq \hat{w}(e) \cdot \frac{\epsilon \cdot \mathsf{OPT}(G, R, w)}{4|R|} + \frac{\epsilon \cdot \mathsf{OPT}(G, R, w)}{4|R|}. \end{aligned}$$

In a complete graph that satisfies the triangle inequality, a Steiner tree on $|R|$ terminals has at most $|R| - 1$ nonterminal vertices. Thus, it follows that T' has at most $2|R|$ edges. Therefore,

$$w(T') \leq \hat{w}(T') \cdot \frac{\epsilon \cdot \mathsf{OPT}(G, R, w)}{4|R|} + \frac{\epsilon}{2}\mathsf{OPT}(G, R, w).$$

Consider now an optimal Steiner tree Q for the instance (G', R, w). We have that

$$w(Q) \cdot \frac{4|R|}{\epsilon \cdot \mathsf{OPT}(G, R, w)} \geq \hat{w}(Q),$$

which in turn implies that

$$\mathsf{OPT}(G', R, w) \geq \mathsf{OPT}(G', R, \hat{w}) \cdot \frac{\epsilon \cdot \mathsf{OPT}(G, R, w)}{4|R|}.$$

We can now wrap up the analysis by comparing $w(T')$ with $\mathsf{OPT}(G, R, w)$.

$$\begin{aligned} w(T') &\leq \hat{w}(T') \cdot \frac{\epsilon \cdot \mathsf{OPT}(G, R, w)}{4|R|} + \frac{\epsilon}{2}\mathsf{OPT}(G, R, w) \\ &\leq c \cdot \mathsf{OPT}(G', R, \hat{w}) \cdot \frac{\epsilon \cdot \mathsf{OPT}(G, R, w)}{4|R|} + \frac{\epsilon}{2}\mathsf{OPT}(G, R, w) \\ &\leq c \cdot \mathsf{OPT}(G', R, w) + \frac{\epsilon}{2}\mathsf{OPT}(G, R, w) \\ &\leq c \cdot (1 + \epsilon/2) \cdot \mathsf{OPT}(G, R, w) + \frac{\epsilon}{2}\mathsf{OPT}(G, R, w) \\ &\leq c \cdot (1 + \epsilon) \cdot \mathsf{OPT}(G, R, w) \end{aligned}$$

This implies that T' is a $c(1 + \epsilon)$-approximate Steiner tree for the instance (G, R, w), concluding the proof. □

Exercises

Problem 23.1 Prove Proposition 23.11.

Problem 23.2 Show that CLIQUE (VC) admits EPSAKS.

Problem 23.3 Show that VERTEX COVER/TREEWIDTH-η MODULATOR admits EPSAKS.

Problem 23.4 Show that FEEDBACK VERTEX COVER/TREEWIDTH-η MODULATOR admits EPSAKS.

Problem 23.5 (♞) Show that PATH CONTRACTION admits PSAKS.

Problem 23.6 (♞) Show that TREE CONTRACTION admits PSAKS.

Problem 23.7 Show that if a parameterized optimization problem Π admits PTAS (or EPTAS) then Π admits a constant size PSAKS (or EPSAKS) under any parameterization.

Problem 23.8 Show that CHROMATIC NUMBER/VC admits a $\frac{3}{2}$-approximate kernel.

Bibliographic Notes

The notion of lossy kernelization was defined by Lokshtanov et al. (2017), and the kernels described in this chapter are from that work. The PSAKS for PARTIAL VERTEX COVER (Theorem 23.23) is based on the work of Marx

(2008), and the PSAKS for STEINER TREE (Theorem 23.29) on Byrka et al. (2013). In Lokshtanov et al. (2017), it was also shown how to interpret the work of Fellows et al. (2016) as an approximate kernel for OPTIMAL LINEAR ARRANGEMENT parameterized by vertex cover number. The existence of EPSAKSs for the problems considered in this chapter is an open problem. We refer to Lokshtanov et al. (2017) and Appendix A of this book for additional open problems. We also remark that definitions of parameterized optimization problems existing prior to this work, particularly those given for parameterized approximation algorithms by Marx (2008), could have also served as a basis to define parameterized approximate kernels. The difference between the definitions of parameterized optimization problems present here and those currently used in parameterized approximation algorithms are mostly notational.

The CONNECTED VERTEX COVER problem is known to admit a factor 2 approximation (Arkin et al., 1993; Savage, 1982), and is known not to admit a factor $(2-\epsilon)$-approximation algorithm assuming the Unique Games conjecture (Khot and Regev, 2008). Further, an approximation algorithm with ratio below 1.36 would imply that P = NP (Dinur and Safra, 2005). From the perspective of kernelization, it is easy to show that CONNECTED VERTEX COVER admits a kernel with at most 2^k vertices (Cygan et al., 2015), where k is the solution size. However, Dom et al. (2014) showed that CONNECTED VERTEX COVER does not admit a kernel of polynomial size, unless NP $\subseteq$ coNP/Poly.

The 6-approximate kernel described for CYCLE PACKING is not the best known. Lokshtanov et al. (2017) already developed a PSAKS for this problem. CYCLE PACKING admits a factor $\mathcal{O}(\log n)$ approximation algorithm (Salavatipour and Verstraëte, 2005), and is known not to admit an approximation algorithm (Friggstad and Salavatipour, 2011) with factor $\mathcal{O}((\log n)^{\frac{1}{2}\epsilon})$ for any $\epsilon > 0$, unless all problems in NP can be solved in randomized quasipolynomial time. With respect to kernelization, CYCLE PACKING is known not to admit a polynomial kernel (Bodlaender et al., 2011), unless NP $\subseteq$ coNP/Poly.

The observation that a lossy preprocessing can simultaneously achieve a better size bound than normal kernelization algorithms as well as a better approximation factor than the ratio of the best approximation algorithms is not new. In particular, motivated by this observation Fellows et al. (2018) initiated the study of lossy kernelization. Fellows et al. (2018) proposed a definition of lossy kernelization called α-fidelity kernels. Essentially, an α-fidelity kernel is a polynomial time preprocessing procedure such that an optimal solution to the reduced instance translates to an α-approximate solution to the original. Unfortunately, this definition suffers from the same serious drawback as the original definition of kernels—it does not combine well with approximation algorithms or with heuristics. Indeed, in the context of lossy preprocessing this drawback is even more damning, as there is no reason why one should allow a loss of precision in the preprocessing step, but should demand that the reduced instance has to be solved to optimality. Furthermore, the definition of α-fidelity kernels is usable only for problems parameterized by the value of the optimum and falls short for structural parameterizations. Even though the definition of α-approximate kernels crucially differs from the definition of α-fidelity kernels (Fellows et al., 2018), it seems that most of the preprocessing algorithms that establish the existence of α-approximate kernels can be used to establish the existence of α-fidelity kernels and vice versa.

The work by Lokshtanov et al. (2017) also contains a framework to obtain hardness results concerning approximate kernels. This framework was devised by amalgamating the notion of cross-compositions, used to show kernelization lower bounds, with gap-creating reductions, used to show hardness of approximation bounds, thus defining gap creating cross-compositions. Having set up the framework, it is shown that for any $\alpha \geq 1$, LONGEST PATH does not admit an α-approximate kernel of polynomial size unless $NP \subseteq coNP/Poly$. Other stronger lower bounds, which require additional work on top of the basic framework, are then given for SET COVER and HITTING SET.

We refer to Eiben et al. (2018), Siebertz (2017), Krithika et al. (2016), Agrawal et al. (2017), Dvořák et al. (2017) for further work on lossy kernels. Exercises 23.5 and 23.6 are taken from Krithika et al. (2016).

Appendix A
Open Problems

In this appendix we provide a list of some of the most interesting (in our opinion) open problems concerning kernelization. A comprehensive list of open problems in parameterized complexity can be found at http://fptschool.mimuw.edu.pl/opl.pdf. We also do not mention here open questions concerning lossy kernelization: The concluding part of Lokshtanov et al. (2017) contains a great deal of open questions about this subject.

A.1 Polynomial Kernels

DIRECTED FEEDBACK VERTEX SET
Input: A directed graph G and an integer k.
Question: Is there a set X of k vertices such that each directed cycle of G contains a member of X?

The problem was shown to be in FPT by Chen et al. (2008). The running time of the algorithm is $4^k k! \, n^{\mathcal{O}(1)}$. It remains open whether DIRECTED FEEDBACK VERTEX SET admits a polynomial kernel parameterized by k. The special case in which the input is a planar directed graph is also open. The undirected variant of the problem, FEEDBACK VERTEX SET, admits a polynomial a kernel with $\mathcal{O}(k^2)$ vertices Thomassé (2010) (see Chapter 5).

PLANAR VERTEX DELETION
Input: A graph G and an integer k.
Question: Does there exist a set X of at most k vertices of G such that $G - X$ is planar?

PLANAR VERTEX DELETION is solvable in time $k^{\mathcal{O}(k)}n$; see Jansen et al. (2014). Whether it admits a polynomial (in k) kernel is open. This problem can be seen as a special case of $\mathcal{F}$-DELETION, which is defined as follows. Let $\mathcal{F}$ be a finite set of graph. Then for a given graph G and an integer k, we seek for a set of vertices X of size k such that $G - X$ contains no graph from $\mathcal{F}$ as a minor. Thus, PLANAR VERTEX DELETION is exactly $\mathcal{F}$ for $\mathcal{F} = \{K_5, K_{3,3}\}$. When the set $\mathcal{F}$ contains at least planar graph, $\mathcal{F}$-DELETION admits a kernel of size $k^{f(\mathcal{F})}$ for some function f; see Fomin et al. (2012b).

INTERVAL COMPLETION
Input: A graph G and an integer k.
Question: Can G be transformed into an interval graph by adding at most k edges?

Let us remind that a graph G is interval graph if it is an intersection graph of open intervals of the real line. Bliznets et al. (2016) gave an algorithm solving INTERVAL COMPLETION in time $k^{\mathcal{O}(\sqrt{k})}n^{\mathcal{O}(1)}$. No polynomial (in k) kernel is known for this problem. Related completion problems, namely, CHORDAL COMPLETION and PROPER INTERVAL COMPLETION, admit polynomial kernels; see Kaplan et al. (1999) and Bessy and Perez (2013).

PARTITION INTO MONOTONE SUBSEQUENCES
Input: A permutation π of $\{1, \ldots, n\}$ and an integer k.
Question: Is it possible to parition π in at most k monotone subsequences?

For example, the permutation $\pi = (1, 5, 4, 2, 3, 6)$ can be partitioned into two monotone subsequences, one increasing and one decreasing, namely $(1, 3, 6)$ and $(5, 4, 2)$. This problem is equivalent to deciding whether a permutation graph admits a cocoloring with at most k colors. The problem was shown to be in FPT by Heggernes et al. (2013). The running time of their algorithm is $2^{\mathcal{O}(k^2 \log k)} n^{\mathcal{O}(1)}$. It remains open whether PARTITION INTO MONOTONE SUBSEQUENCES admits a polynomial kernel parameterized by k.

VERTEX MULTIWAY CUT
Input: A graph G with a set of terminals T, and an integer k.
Question: Is there a set of vertices $X \subseteq V(G) \setminus T$ of size at most k such that in the graph $G - X$ no pair of terminals from T is in the same connected component? In other words, for every pair of distinct vertices $p, r \in T$ every s, t-path in G contains a vertex of X.

VERTEX MULTIWAY CUT is solvable in time $2^k \cdot n^{\mathcal{O}(1)}$. It is not known whether it admits a polynomial kernel when parameterized by k. The variant of the problem where X is allowed to contain terminals admits a polynomial kernel; see Kratsch and Wahlström (2012). Kratsch and Wahlström (2012) gave a randomized kernel with k^{t+1} vertices, which is polynomial when the number of terminals t is a constant. Pilipczuk et al. (2014) proved that the problem admits a polynomial kernel on planar graphs.

T-CYCLE

Input: A graph G with a set of terminals T.
Question: Is there a cycle in G containing all vertices of T? Here the parameter is the cardinality of T.

For the special case $T = V(G)$, T-CYCLE is equivalent to deciding whether G is Hamiltonian. The problem was shown to be solvable in time $2^{|T|} \cdot n^{\mathcal{O}(1)}$ by Björklund et al. (2012). Wahlström (2013) proved that T-CYCLE admits a polynomial compression of size $\mathcal{O}(|T|^3)$. However, this is a compression that maps a graph G with terminal set T to a matrix M whose entries are polynomials. Then the determinant polynomial of M contains a certain type of term if and only if (G, T) is a yes-instance of T-CYCLE. Finding the required terms in the determinant polynomial is not known to be in NP, and thus the standard trick of transforming a polynomial compression into a polynomial kernel does not work here. Whether T-CYCLE admits a polynomial kernel is open. More generally, we are not aware of any strong evidence that there exist problems that do not admit a polynomial kernel but admit a polynomial compression. Finding an example demonstrating that polynomial compression is a strictly more general concept than polynomial kernelization is an extremely interesting open problem.

A.2 Structural Kernelization Bounds

VERTEX COVER

Input: A graph G and an integer k.
Question: Does there exist a set X of at most k vertices of G such that $G - X$ is edgeless?

By Chen et al. (2001), VERTEX COVER admits a kernel with $2k$ vertices; see Chapter 6. By the lower bounds of Dell and van Melkebeek (2014) (see Chapter 20), it is unlikely that VERTEX COVER admits a kernel of bitsize $k^{2-\varepsilon}$ for any $\varepsilon > 0$. However, this does not rule out that VERTEX COVER admits a kernel with $(2 - \varepsilon)$ vertices for some $\varepsilon > 0$. There is a common misconception that lower bounds on non approximability of a problem automatically yield the corresponding lower bounds for kernels. In particular, the result of Dinur and Safra (2005) that the optimization version of VERTEX COVER is NP-hard to approximate to within a factor of 1.3606 does not imply directly that a kernel with $1.3606k$ vertices for VERTEX COVER would imply that P = NP. Similarly, the existence of a $(2 − \varepsilon)$ vertex kernel does not directly refute the Unique Game Conjecture. We are not aware of $(1 + \varepsilon)k$ lower bound on the number of vertices in kernel for the problem for any $0 < \varepsilon < 1$. Thus, the problem of obtaining lower bounds on the number of vertices in a kernel for VERTEX COVER is widely open. The problem is interesting even for a very special case, when the input graph is planar.

Similar questions are valid for FEEDBACK VERTEX SET and d-HITTING SET, as we explain in the following text.

FEEDBACK VERTEX SET

Input: A graph G and an integer k.
Question: Does there exist a set X of at most k vertices of G such that $G − X$ is a forest?

By Thomassé (2010) (see also, Chapter 5), FEEDBACK VERTEX SET admits a kernel with $\mathcal{O}(k^2)$ vertices. As it was shown by Dell and van Melkebeek (2014), the problem does not admit a polynomial compression with bitsize $\mathcal{O}(k^{2-\varepsilon})$, unless coNP $\subseteq$ NP/ poly. However, whether FEEDBACK VERTEX SET admits a kernel with $\mathcal{O}(k^{2-\varepsilon})$ vertices is open.

d-HITTING SET

Input: A universe U, a family $\mathcal{A}$ of sets over U, where each set in $\mathcal{A}$ is of size at most d, and an integer k.
Question: Does there exist a set $X \subseteq U$ of size at most k that has a nonempty intersection with every set of $\mathcal{A}$?

By Dell and van Melkebeek (2014), d-HITTING SET does not admit a polynomial compression with bitsize $\mathcal{O}(k^{d-\varepsilon})$, unless coNP $\subseteq$ NP/ poly. Abu-Khzam (2010b) showed that d-HITTING SET admits a kernel with at most $(2d − 1)k^{d−1} + k$ elements. Could it be that d-HITTING SET admits a kernel with a polynomial in k number of elements where the degree of the polynomial does not depend on d? This does not look like a plausible conjecture, but we do not know how to refute it either.

CLUSTER VERTEX DELETION

Input: A graph G and an integer k.
Question: Does there exist a set X of at most k vertices of G such that $G − X$ is a cluster graph? Here, a cluster graph is a graph where every connected component is a clique.

Le et al. (2018) showed that the problem admits a kernel with $\mathcal{O}(k^{5/3})$ vertices. The existence of a linear-vertex kernel for CLUSTER VERTEX DELETION is open.

FEEDBACK VERTEX SET IN TOURNAMENTS
Input: A tournament G and an integer k.
Question: Is there a set X of k vertices such that each directed cycle of G contains a member of X?

Similar to CLUSTER VERTEX DELETION, Le et al. (2018) gave a subquadratic $\mathcal{O}(k^{5/3})$ (in the number of vertices) kernel. No linear-vertex kernel for FEEDBACK VERTEX SET IN TOURNAMENTS is known.

EDGE DOMINATING SET
Input: A graph G and an integer k.
Question: Does there exist a set X of at most k edges of G such that $G - V(X)$ is edgeless?

Xiao et al. (2013) gave a kernel for this problem with $\mathcal{O}(k^2)$ vertices and of size $\mathcal{O}(k^3)$. Whether these upper bounds are optimal is open.

A.3 Deterministic Kernels

In Chapters 10 and 11, we saw how matroid-based techniques can be used to obtain polynomial kernels. Specifically, we made use of a computation of representative families for linear representations of gammoids. Because all known efficient constructions of linear representations of gammoids are randomized, the kernels based on them are randomized. However, there is no evidence that the only way of constructing polynomial kernels for the problem in Chapters 10 and 11 is by making use of gammoids. This brings us to the following set of questions.

ODD CYCLE TRANSVERSAL
Input: A graph G and an integer k.
Question: Does there exist a set $X \subseteq V(G)$ of at most k vertices of G such that $G - X$ is bipartite?

Recall that a randomized polynomial kernel for ODD CYCLE TRANSVERSAL parameterized by k was given by Kratsch and Wahlström (2014) (see Chapter 10). The existence of a deterministic polynomial kernel for ODD CYCLE TRANSVERSAL is open even when the input graph is planar.

ALMOST 2-SAT

Input: A CNF formula φ, where every clause consists of at most two literals, and an integer k.
Question: Is it possible to make φ satisfiable by deleting at most k clauses?

VERTEX COVER ABOVE LP

Input: A graph G and an integer k.
Question: Does there exist a set X of at most k vertices of G such that $G - X$ is edgeless?

Note that this is the same problem as VERTEX COVER, but the name VERTEX COVER ABOVE LP indicates of an above guarantee parameterization with the optimum solution $lp(G)$ to the linear programming relaxation of the problem as a lower bound. That is, the parameter is $k - lp(G)$.

SUBSET FEEDBACK VERTEX SET

Input: A graph G with a set of terminal vertices T and an integer k.
Question: Does there exist a set X of at most k vertices of G such that graph $G - X$ has no cycle passing through any vertex of T?

Let us note that FEEDBACK VERTEX SET is the special case of SUBSET FEEDBACK VERTEX SET when $T = V(G)$. A randomized polynomial in k kernel for SUBSET FEEDBACK VERTEX SET was obtained by Hols and Kratsch (2018). This algorithm also uses a linear representation of a gammoid.

So far, even the existence of deterministic quasi polynomial time kernels for these problems is open.

A.4 Turing Kernels

LONGEST PATH

Input: A graph G and an integer k.
Question: Does there exist a path in G of length at least k?

LONGEST PATH is solvable in time $2^{\mathcal{O}(k)} n^{\mathcal{O}(1)}$, however it does not admit a polynomial kernel when parameterized by k; see Chapter 17. However, as it was shown by Jansen (2017), it admits a polynomial Turing kernel when the input graph is planar; see also Chapter 22. The existence of Turing kernel for LONGEST PATH was lifted to graphs excluding a fixed graph as a topological minor by Jansen et al. (2017). The existence of a polynomial Turing kernel for LONGEST PATH on general graphs is open. Similar questions are open for

LONGEST CYCLE (finding a cycle of length at least k or finding a cycle of length exactly k).

In general, the reason why we have no evidence that LONGEST PATH does not admit a polynomial Turing kernel on general graphs is the lack of tools for obtaining such type of results. Developing instruments that can be used to rule out polynomial Turing kernels is a big research challenge. Hermelin et al. (2015) constructed a large group of problems that equivalently (un)likely have Turing kernels.

Appendix B
Graphs and SAT Notation

A *graph* is a pair $G = (V, E)$ of sets such that E is a set of 2-elements subsets of V. The elements of V are the *vertices* and the elements of E are the edges of G. Sometimes the vertex set of a graph G is referred to as $V(G)$ and its edge set as $E(G)$. In this book, graphs are always finite, that is, the sets V and E are finite, and simple, which means that not two elements of E are equal. Unless specified otherwise, we use parameters $n = |V|$ and $m = |E|$. An edge of an undirected graph with endpoints u and v is denoted by $\{u, v\}$; the endpoints u and v are said to be *adjacent*, and one is said to be a *neighbor* of the other. In a directed graph an arc going from vertex u to vertex v is denoted by (u, v). In arc $a = (u, v)$, u is the *tail* and v is the *head* of a. Often we write edge $\{u, v\}$ or (u, v) as uv. Graph G/e is obtained from G by *contracting* edge $e = uv$, which is removal of edge e and identifying its endpoints u and v.

The *complement* of undirected graph $G = (V, E)$ is denoted by $\overline{G}$; its vertex set is V and its edge set is $\overline{E} = \{\{u, v\} : \{u, v\} \notin E, u \neq v\}$. For any non empty subset $W \subseteq V$, the subgraph of G induced by W is denoted by $G[W]$; its vertex set is W and its edge set consists of all those edges of E with both endpoints in W. For $S \subseteq V$, we often use $G - S$ to denote the graph $G[V \setminus S]$. We also write $G - v$ instead of $G - \{v\}$. The *neighborhood* of a vertex v in G is $N_G(v) = \{u \in V : \{u, v\} \in E\}$ and the *closed neighborhood* of v is $N_G[v] = N_G(v) \cup \{v\}$. For a vertex set $S \subseteq V$ we denote by $N_G(S)$ the set $\bigcup_{v \in S} N_G(v) \setminus S$. We denote by $d_G(v)$ the *degree* of a vertex v in graph G. We may omit indices if the graph under consideration is clear from the context. The minimum degree of a graph G is denoted by $\delta(G)$. The maximum degree of a graph G is denoted by $\Delta(G)$. A graph G is called *r-regular* if all vertices of G have degree r. A 3-regular graph is also called a *cubic* graph.

A *walk* of length k is a nonempty graph $W = (V, E)$ of the form

$$V = \{v_0, v_1, \ldots, v_k\} \quad E = \{v_0 v_1, v_1 v_2, \ldots, v_{k-1} v_k\}.$$

A walk is a *path*, if the v_i are all distinct. If $P = v_0 v_1 \ldots v_k$ is a path, then the graph obtained fro P by adding edge $x_k x_0$ is called a *cycle* of length k. The *girth* of a graph G is the shortest length of a cycle in G. A *Hamiltonian path (cycle)* in a graph G is a path (cycle) passing through all vertices of G. We denote by $d(v, w)$ the *distance* between v and w in the graph G, which is the shortest length of a path between v and w. For any integer $k \geq 1$ and any vertex v of G, we denote by $N^k(v)$ the set of all vertices w satisfying $d(v, w) = k$.

A *matching* M in graph G is a set of pairwise non adjacent edges, a vertex of G is *saturated* if it is incident to an edge in the matching. Otherwise the vertex is *unsaturated*. For a given a matching M, an *alternating path* is a path in which the edges belong alternatively to the matching and not to the matching. An *augmenting* path is an alternating path that starts from and ends on unsaturated vertices. A *perfect matching* is a matching M covering all vertices of the graph, that is, every vertex of the graph is an endpoint of an edge in M.

A nonempty graph G is *connected* if, for every pair u, v of its vertices, there is a path between u and v. A *connected component* of the graph is its maximal connected subgraph. A vertex v is a *cutvertex* of a graph, if the number of connected components in G is less that in $G - v$. In other words, cut vertex separates some connected component of G. A *tree* T is a connected graph without cycles. A *forest* F is a graph without cycle; thus, all the connected components of F are trees. A *spanning tree* T of a graph G is a tree such that $V(T) = V(G)$ and $E(T) \subseteq E(G)$.

An *independent set* I of a graph $G = (V, E)$ is a subset of the vertex set V such that the vertices of I are pairwise non adjacent. The maximum size of an independent set of a graph G is denoted by $\alpha(G)$. A *clique* C of a graph $G = (V, E)$ is a subset of the vertex set V such that the vertices of C are pairwise adjacent. By $\omega(G)$ we denote the maximum clique-size of a graph G. Let us remark that $\alpha(G) = \omega(\overline{G})$. A *dominating set* D of a graph $G = (V, E)$ is a subset of the vertex set V such that every vertex of $V \setminus D$ has a neighbor in D. By $\gamma(G)$ we denote the minimum size of a dominating set of a graph G.

A *coloring* of a graph G assigns a *color* to each vertex of G such that adjacent vertices receive distinct colors. The *chromatic number* of G denoted by $\chi(G)$ is the minimum k such that there is coloring of G using k colors.

A *vertex cover* C of a graph $G = (V, E)$ is a subset of the vertex set V such that C covers the edge set E, that is, every edge of G has at least one endpoint in C. An *edge cover* C of a graph $G = (V, E)$ is a subset of the edge set E such that C covers the vertex set V, that is, every vertex of G is endpoint of at least one of the edges in C.

Two graphs $G = (V, E)$ and $H = (W, F)$ are *isomorphic*, denoted by $G \cong H$, if there is a bijection $I : V \to W$ such that for all $u, v \in V$ holds $\{u, v\} \in$

$E \Leftrightarrow \{f(u), f(v)\} \in F$. Such a bijection I is called an *isomorphism*. If $G = H$, it is called an *automorphism*. A mapping $h : V \to W$ is a *homomorphism* from graph $G = (V, E)$ to graph $H = (W, F)$ if for all $u, v \in V$: $\{u, v\} \in E$ implies $\{f(u), f(v)\} \in F$.

For more information on Graph Theory we refer to the textbooks by Bondy and Murty (2008), Diestel (2005), and Berge (1973).

SAT Notation

Let Vars $= \{x_1, x_2, \ldots, x_n\}$ be a set of *Boolean variables*. A variable x or a negated variable $\neg x$ is called a *literal*. A propositional formula φ is in *conjunctive normal form*, or is a *CNF formula*, if it is of the form:

$$\varphi = C_1 \wedge C_2 \wedge \ldots \wedge C_m.$$

Here, each C_i is a *clause* of the form

$$C_i = \ell_1^i \vee \ell_2^i \vee \ldots \vee \ell_{r_i}^i,$$

where ℓ_j^i are literals of some variables of Vars. The number of literals r_i in a clause C_i is called the *length* of the clause and is denoted by $|C_i|$. The *size* of formula φ is defined as $|\varphi| = \sum_{i=1}^{m} |C_i|$. The set of clauses of a CNF formula is usually denoted by Cls.

For $q \geq 2$, a CNF formula φ is in *q-CNF* if every clause from φ has at most q literals. If φ is a formula and X a set of variables, then we denote by $\varphi - X$ the formula obtained from φ after removing all the clauses that contain a literal of a variable from X.

For a CNF formula φ on variables Vars, a *truth assignment* is a mapping $\psi : \text{Vars} \to \{\bot, \top\}$. Here, we denote the false value as $\bot$, and the truth value as $\top$. This assignment can be naturally extended to literals by taking $\psi(\neg x) = \neg \psi(x)$ for each $x \in \text{Vars}$. A truth assignment ψ *satisfies* a clause C of φ if and only if C contains some literal ℓ with $\psi(\ell) = \top$; ψ satisfies formula φ if it satisfies all the clauses of φ. A formula is *satisfiable* if it is satisfied by some truth assignment; otherwise it is *unsatisfiable*.

The notion of a truth assignment can be naturally generalized to partial assignments that valuate only some subset $X \subseteq \text{Vars}$; that is, ψ is a mapping from X to $\{\bot, \top\}$. Here, a clause C is satisfied by ψ if and only if C contains some literal ℓ whose variable belongs to X, and that, moreover, satisfies $\psi(\ell) = \top$.

Appendix C
Problem Definitions

2-SAT
Input:
A CNF formula φ, where every clause consists of at most two literals.
Question:
Does there exist a satisfying assignment for φ?

3-Coloring
Input:
A graph G.
Question:
Does there exist a coloring $c : V(G) \to \{1, 2, 3\}$ such that $c(u) \neq c(v)$ for every $uv \in E(G)$?

d-Hitting Set
Input:
A universe U, a family $\mathcal{A}$ of sets over U, where each set in $\mathcal{A}$ is of size at most d, and an integer k.
Question:
Does there exist a set $X \subseteq U$ of size at most k that has a nonempty intersection with every set of $\mathcal{A}$?

d-Set Packing
Input:
A universe U, a family $\mathcal{A}$ of sets over U, where each set in $\mathcal{A}$ is of size at most d, and an integer k.
Question:
Does there exist a family $\mathcal{A}' \subseteq \mathcal{A}$ of k pairwise-disjoint sets?

d-Subset CSP
Input:
A universe U, a family $\mathcal{C}$ of subsets of size at most d of U, oracle access to a function $f : \binom{U}{\leq k} \times \mathcal{C} \to \{0, 1\}$, and an integer k.
Question:
Does there exist a set $X \subseteq U$ of size at most k such that for every $c \in \mathcal{C}, f(X, c) = 1$?

$(k, n-k)$-MaxCut
Input:
A graph G, and integers k and p.
Question:
Does there exist a partition $A \uplus B$ of $V(G)$ such that $|A| = k$ and at least p edges of G have one endpoint in A and the other endpoint in B?

$K_{1,d}$-Packing
Input:
A graph G and an integer k.
Question:
Does G contain at least k vertex-disjoint copies of the star $K_{1,d}$?

$(n-k)$-Set Cover
Input:
A universe U of size n, a family $\mathcal{F}$ over U, and an integer k.
Question:
Does there exist a subfamily $\mathcal{F}' \subseteq \mathcal{F}$ of size at most $n - k$ such that $\bigcup \mathcal{F}' = U$?

ALMOST 2-SAT
Input:
A CNF formula φ, where every clause consists of at most two literals, and an integer k.
Question:
Is it possible to make φ satisfiable by deleting at most k clauses?

ALMOST INDUCED MATCHING
Input:
A graph G and an integer k.
Question:
Does there exist a set X of at most k vertices of G such that $G - X$ is an induced matching?

CAPACITATED VERTEX COVER
Input:
A graph G, a capacity function cap : $V(G) \to \mathbb{N}^+$ and an integer k.
Question:
Does there exist a set X of k vertices of G that is a vertex cover in G for which there is a mapping from $E(G)$ to X such that *(i)* for every edge $e \in E(G)$ mapped to a vertex $v \in X$, v is incident to e, and *(ii)* at most cap(v) edges are mapped to every vertex $v \in X$?

CLIQUE
Input:
A graph G and an integer k.
Question:
Does there exist a set of k vertices of G that is a clique in G?

CNF-SAT
Input:
A CNF formula φ.
Question:
Does there exist a satisfying assignment for φ?

COMPONENT ORDER CONNECTIVITY
Input:
A graph G, and integers k and ℓ.
Question:
Does there exist a set X of at most k vertices such that every connected component of $G - X$ consists of at most ℓ vertices?

CLUSTER EDITING
Input:
A graph G and an integer k.
Question:
Does there exist a set $A \subseteq \binom{V(G)}{2}$ of size at most k such that the graph $(V(G), (E(G) \setminus A) \cup (A \setminus E(G)))$ is a cluster graph? Here, a cluster graph is a graph where every connected component is a clique.

CLUSTER VERTEX DELETION
Input:
A graph G and an integer k.
Question:
Does there exist a set X of at most k vertices of G such that $G - X$ is a cluster graph? Here, a cluster graph is a graph where every connected component is a clique.

COGRAPH COMPLETION
Input:
A graph G and an integer k.
Question:
Does there exist a set $F \subseteq V(G) \times V(G)$ such that $G' = (V(G), E(G) \cup F)$ is a cograph, that is, G' does not contain P_4 as an induced subgraph?

COLORED RED-BLUE DOMINATING SET
Input:
A bipartite graph G with bipartition classes $R \uplus B = V(G)$, an integer ℓ and a partition of R into ℓ sets $R^1, R^2, \ldots, R^\ell$.
Question:
Does there exist a set $X \subseteq R$ that contains exactly one element of every set R^i, $1 \leq i \leq \ell$ and such that $N_G(X) = B$?

CONNECTED DOMINATING SET
Input:
A graph G and an integer k.
Question:
Does there exist a set X of at most k vertices of G such that $G[X]$ is connected and $N_G[X] = V(G)$?

CONNECTED VERTEX COVER
Input:
A graph G and an integer k.
Question:
Does there exist a set X of at most k vertices of G such that $G[X]$ is connected and $G - X$ is edgeless?

CYCLE PACKING
Input:
A graph G and an integer k.
Question:
Does there exist in G a family of k pairwise vertex-disjoint cycles?

Problem Definitions

DIGRAPH PAIR CUT
Input:
A directed graph G, a designated vertex $s \in V(G)$, a family of pairs of vertices $\mathcal{F} \subseteq \binom{V(G)}{2}$, and an integer k.
Question:
Does there exist a set X of at most k vertices of G, such that for each pair $\{u, v\} \in \mathcal{F}$, at least one vertex among u and v is not reachable from s in the graph $G - X$?

DISJOINT FACTORS
Input:
A word w over an alphabet $\Gamma = \{\gamma_1, \gamma_2, \ldots, \gamma_s\}$.
Question:
Does there exist pairwise disjoint subwords $u_1, u_2, \ldots, u_s$ of w such that each u_i is of length at least two and begins and ends with γ_i?

DOMINATING SET
Input:
A graph G and an integer k.
Question:
Does there exist a set X of at most k vertices of G such that $N_G[X] = V(G)$?

DUAL COLORING
Input:
A graph G and an integer k.
Question:
Does there exist a coloring $c : V(G) \to [n-k]$ such that $c(u) \neq c(v)$ for every edge uv?

EDGE CLIQUE COVER
Input:
A graph G and an integer k.
Question:
Does there exist k subgraphs $H_1, H_2, \ldots, H_k$ of G such that each H_i is a clique and $E(G) = \bigcup_{i=1}^{k} E(H_i)$?

EDGE DISJOINT CYCLE PACKING
Input:
A graph G and an integer k.
Question:
Does there exist in G a family of k pairwise edge-disjoint cycles?

EDGE DOMINATING SET
Input:
A graph G and an integer k.
Question:
Does there exist a set X of at most k edges of G such that $G - V(X)$ is edgeless?

FEEDBACK ARC SET IN TOURNAMENTS
Input:
A tournament G and an integer k.
Question:
Does there exist a set X of at most k edges of G such that $G - X$ is acyclic?

FEEDBACK VERTEX SET
Input:
A graph G and an integer k.
Question:
Does there exist a set X of at most k vertices of G such that $G - X$ is a forest?

HAMILTONIAN PATH
Input:
A graph G.
Question:
Does there exist a simple path P in G such that $V(P) = V(G)$?

HITTING SET
Input:
A universe U, a family $\mathcal{A}$ of sets over U, and an integer k.
Question:
Does there exist a set $X \subseteq U$ of size at most k that has a nonempty intersection with every element of $\mathcal{A}$?

INDEPENDENT DOMINATING SET
Input:
A graph G and an integer k.
Question:
Does there exist a set X of at most k vertices of G such that $G[X]$ is edgeless and $N_G[X] = V(G)$?

INDEPENDENT SET
Input:
A graph G and an integer k.
Question:
Does there exist a set X of at most k vertices of G such that $G[X]$ is edgeless?

LONGEST CYCLE
Input:
A graph G and an integer k.
Question:
Does there exist a cycle of G of length at least k?

LONGEST PATH
Input:
A graph G and an integer k.
Question:
Does there exist a path in G of length at least k?

MAX LEAF SPANNING TREE
Input:
A graph G and an integer k.
Question:
Does there exist a spanning tree of G with at least k leaves?

MAX LEAF SUBTREE
Input:
A graph G and an integer k.
Question:
Does there exist a subgraph of G that is a tree with at least k leaves?

MAX-r-LIN-2
Input:
A system S of m linear equations, $e_1, \ldots, e_m$, in n variables $z_1, \ldots, z_n$ over $\mathbb{F}_2$, and integer k. Each equation e_j is of the form $\sum_{i \in I_j} z_i = b_j$, where $\emptyset \neq I_j \subseteq \{1, \ldots, n\}$ is of size at most r, and has a positive integral weight w_j.
Question:
Does there exist an assignment to $z_1, \ldots, z_n$ such that the total weight of the satisfied equations is at least k?

MAX-LIN-2
Input:
A system S of m linear equations, $e_1, \ldots, e_m$, in n variables $z_1, \ldots, z_n$ over $\mathbb{F}_2$, and integer k. Each equation e_j is of the form $\sum_{i \in I_j} z_i = b_j$, where $\emptyset \neq I_j \subseteq \{1, \ldots, n\}$, and has a positive integral weight w_j.
Question:
Does there exist an assignment to $z_1, \ldots, z_n$ such that the total weight of the satisfied equations is at least k?

MAX-r-SAT
Input:
A CNF formula φ where every clause consists of at most r literals, and an integer k.
Question:
Does there exist an assignment ψ that satisfies at least k clauses of φ?

MAX-Er-SAT
Input:
A CNF formula φ where every clause consists of exactly r literals and these literals correspond to different variables, and an integer k.
Question:
Does there exist an assignment ψ that satisfies at least k clauses of φ?

MAX-INTERNAL SPANNING TREE
Input:
A graph G and an integer k.
Question:
Does there exist a spanning tree of G with at least k internal vertices?

MAXCUT
Input:
A graph G and an integer k.
Question:
Does there exist a partition $A \uplus B$ of $V(G)$ such that at least k edges of G have one endpoint in A and the second endpoint in B?

MAXIMUM SATISFIABILITY
Input:
A CNF formula φ and an integer k.
Question:
Does there exist an assignment ψ that satisfies at least k clauses of φ?

MIN-ONES-2-SAT
Input:
A CNF formula φ, where every clause consists of at most two literals, and an integer k.
Question:
Does there exist an assignment ψ that satisfies φ and sets at most k variables to true?

MIN-WEIGHT-2-IP
Input:
An instance I of integer programming with two variables per inequality (IP2), and an integer k.
Question:
Does I have a feasible solution of weight at most k?

Multicolored Biclique

Input:
A bipartite graph G with bipartition classes $A \uplus B = V(G)$, an integer k, a partition of A into k sets $A_1, A_2, \ldots, A_k$, and a partition of B into k sets $B_1, B_2, \ldots, B_k$.

Question:
Does there exist a set $X \subseteq A \cup B$ that contains exactly one element of every set A_i and B_i, $1 \leq i \leq \ell$ and that induces a complete bipartite graph $K_{k,k}$ in G?

Non-Blocker

Input:
A graph G and an integer k.

Question:
Does there exist a set $X \subseteq V(G)$ of at least k vertices such that every vertex in X has a neighbor outside X?

Odd Cycle Transversal

Input:
A graph G and an integer k.

Question:
Does there exist a set $X \subseteq V(G)$ of at most k vertices of G such that $G - X$ is bipartite?

Odd Subgraph

Input:
A graph G and an integer k.

Question:
Does there exist a subgraph of G on k edges where all vertices are of odd degrees?

Optimal Linear Arrangement

Input:
A graph G and an integer k.

Question:
Does there exist a bijection $\sigma : V(G) \to \{1, \ldots, n\}$ such that $\sum_{uv \in E(G)} |\sigma(u) - \sigma(v)| \leq k$?

Partial Vertex Cover

Input:
A graph G and integers k and r.

Question:
Does there exist a set X of at most k vertices of G such that at least r edges of G are incident to at least one vertex of X?

Planar Vertex Deletion

Input:
A graph G and an integer k.

Question:
Does there exist a set X of at most k vertices of G such that $G - X$ is planar?

Planar Longest Cycle

Input:
A planar graph G and an integer k.

Question:
Does there exist a cycle in G of length at least k?

Path Packing

Input:
A graph G and an integer k.

Question:
Does there exist in G a family of k pairwise vertex disjoint paths of length k?

Point Line Cover

Input:
A set P of points on the plane and an integer k.

Question:
Does there exist a family L of at most k lines on the plane such that every point in P lies on some line from L?

Ramsey

Input:
A graph G and an integer k.

Question:
Does there exist a set X of exactly k vertices of G such that $G[X]$ is a clique or $G[X]$ is edgeless?

Red-Blue Dominating Set

Input:
A bipartite graph G with bipartition classes $R \uplus B = V(G)$ and an integer k.

Question:
Does there exist a set $X \subseteq R$ of size at most k such that $N_G(X) = B$?

Set Cover

Input:
A universe U, a family $\mathcal{F}$ over U, and an integer k.

Question:
Does there exist a subfamily $\mathcal{F}' \subseteq \mathcal{F}$ of size at most k such that $\bigcup \mathcal{F}' = U$?

Set Splitting

Input:
A universe U and a family $\mathcal{F}$ of sets over U.

Question:
Does there exist a set $X \subseteq U$ such that $A \cap X \neq \emptyset$ and $A \setminus X \neq \emptyset$ for every $A \in \mathcal{F}$?

Steiner Tree
Input:
A graph G, a set $K \subseteq V(G)$, and an integer k.
Question:
Does there exist a connected subgraph of G that contains at most k edges and contains all vertices of K?

Treewidth
Input:
A graph G and an integer k.
Question:
Is the treewidth of G at most k?

Treewidth-η Modulator
Input:
A graph G and an integer k.
Question:
Does there exist a set X of at most k vertices of G such that $G - X$ has treewidth at most η?

Vertex Cover Above LP
Input:
A graph G and an integer k.
Question:
Does there exist a set X of at most k vertices of G such that $G - X$ is edgeless? Note that this is the same problem as Vertex Cover, but the name Vertex Cover Above LP is usually used in the context of above guarantee parameterization with an optimum solution to a linear programming relaxation as a lower bound.

Vertex Cover
Input:
A graph G and an integer k.
Question:
Does there exist a set X of at most k vertices of G such that $G - X$ is edgeless?

References

Abu-Khzam, Faisal N. 2010a. An improved kernelization algorithm for r-Set Packing. *Information Processing Letters*, **110**(16), 621–624.

Abu-Khzam, Faisal N. 2010b. A kernelization algorithm for d-Hitting Set. *Journal of Computer and System Sciences*, **76**(7), 524–531.

Abu-Khzam, Faisal N., and Khuzam, Mazen Bou. 2012. An improved kernel for the Undirected Planar Feedback Vertex Set Problem. Pages 264–273 of: *Proceedings of the 7th International Symposium on Parameterized and Exact Computation (IPEC)*. Lecture Notes in Computer Science, vol. 7535. Springer.

Abu-Khzam, Faisal N., Collins, Rebecca L., Fellows, Michael R., Langston, Michael A., Suters, W. Henry, and Symons, Christopher T. 2004. Kernelization algorithms for the Vertex Cover Problem: Theory and experiments. Pages 62–69 of: *Proceedings of the 6th Workshop on Algorithm Engineering and Experiments and the 1st Workshop on Analytic Algorithmics and Combinatorics (ALENEX/ANALC)*. SIAM.

Abu-Khzam, Faisal N., Fellows, Michael R., Langston, Michael A., and Suters, W. Henry. 2007. Crown structures for vertex cover kernelization. *Theory of Computing Systems*, **41**(3), 411–430.

Agarwal, Amit, Charikar, Moses, Makarychev, Konstantin, and Makarychev, Yury. 2005. $O(\sqrt{\log n})$ approximation algorithms for Min UnCut, Min 2CNF deletion, and directed cut problems. Pages 573–581 of: *Proceedings of the 37th Annual ACM Symposium on Theory of Computing (STOC)*. ACM.

Agrawal, Akanksha, Kolay, Sudeshna, Lokshtanov, Daniel, and Saurabh, Saket. 2016a. A faster FPT algorithm and a smaller kernel for Block Graph Vertex Deletion. Pages 1–13 of: *Proceedings of the 12th Latin American Theoretical Informatics Symposium (LATIN)*. Lecture Notes in Computer Science, vol. 9644. Springer.

Agrawal, Akanksha, Lokshtanov, Daniel, Mouawad, Amer E., and Saurabh, Saket. 2016b. Simultaneous Feedback Vertex Set: A parameterized perspective. Pages 7:1–7:15 of: *Proceedings of the 33rd International Symposium on Theoretical Aspects of Computer Science (STACS)*. Leibniz International Proceedings in Informatics (LIPIcs), vol. 47. Schloss Dagstuhl - Leibniz-Zentrum fuer Informatik.

Agrawal, Akanksha, Saurabh, Saket, and Tale, Prafullkumar. 2017. On the parameterized complexity of contraction to generalization of trees. Pages 1:1–1:12 of:

Proceedings of the 12th International Symposium on Parameterized and Exact Computation (IPEC). Leibniz International Proceedings in Informatics (LIPIcs), vol. 89. Schloss Dagstuhl - Leibniz-Zentrum fuer Informatik.

Alber, Jochen, Bodlaender, Hans L., Fernau, Henning, Kloks, Ton, and Niedermeier, Rolf. 2002. Fixed parameter algorithms for dominating set and related problems on planar graphs. *Algorithmica*, **33**(4), 461–493.

Alber, Jochen, Fernau, Henning, and Niedermeier, Rolf. 2004a. Parameterized complexity: Exponential speed-up for planar graph problems. *Journal of Algorithms*, **52**(1), 26–56.

Alber, Jochen, Fellows, Michael R., and Niedermeier, Rolf. 2004b. Polynomial-time data reduction for dominating set. *Journal of ACM*, **51**(3), 363–384.

Alber, Jochen, Betzler, Nadja, and Niedermeier, Rolf. 2006. Experiments on data reduction for optimal domination in networks. *Annals OR*, **146**(1), 105–117.

Alon, Noga. 1986. The number of polytopes, configurations and real matroids. *Mathematika*, **33**(1), 62–71.

Alon, Noga, Yuster, Raphael, and Zwick, Uri. 1995. Color-coding. *Journal of ACM*, **42**(4), 844–856.

Alon, Noga, Gutin, Gregory, Kim, Eun Jung, Szeider, Stefan, and Yeo, Anders. 2011. Solving MAX-r-SAT above a tight lower bound. *Algorithmica*, **61**(3), 638–655.

Arkin, Esther M., Halldórsson, Magnús M., and Hassin, Refael. 1993. Approximating the tree and tour covers of a graph. *Information Processing Letters*, **47**(6), 275–282.

Arnborg, Stefan, and Proskurowski, Andrzej. 1989. Linear time algorithms for NP-hard problems restricted to partial k-trees. *Discrete Applied Mathematics*, **23**(1), 11–24.

Arnborg, Stefan, Lagergren, Jens, and Seese, Detlef. 1991. Easy problems for tree-decomposable graphs. *Journal of Algorithms*, **12**(2), 308–340.

Arnborg, Stefan, Courcelle, Bruno, Proskurowski, Andrzej, and Seese, Detlef. 1993. An algebraic theory of graph reduction. *Journal of ACM*, **40**(5), 1134–1164.

Arora, Sanjeev, and Barak, Boaz. 2009. *Computational Complexity—A Modern Approach*. Cambridge University Press.

Bafna, Vineet, Berman, Piotr, and Fujito, Toshihiro. 1999. A 2-approximation algorithm for the undirected feedback vertex set problem. *SIAM Journal on Discrete Mathematics*, **12**(3), 289–297.

Baker, Brenda S. 1994. Approximation algorithms for NP-complete problems on planar graphs. *Journal of ACM*, **41**(1), 153–180.

Balasubramanian, R., Fellows, Michael R., and Raman, Venkatesh. 1998. An improved fixed-parameter algorithm for vertex cover. *Information Processing Letters*, **65**(3), 163–168.

Bansal, Nikhil, Blum, Avrim, and Chawla, Shuchi. 2004. Correlation clustering. *Machine Learning*, **56**(1–3), 89–113.

Bar-Yehuda, Reuven, Geiger, Dan, Naor, Joseph, and Roth, Ron M. 1998. Approximation algorithms for the feedback vertex set problem with applications to constraint satisfaction and Bayesian inference. *SIAM Journal of Computing*, **27**(4), 942–959.

Bartlett, Andrew, Chartier, Timothy P., Langville, Amy N., and Rankin, Timothy D. 2008. Integer programming model for the Sudoku problem. *The Journal of Online Mathematics and Its Applications*, **8**.

Basavaraju, Manu, Francis, Mathew C., Ramanujan, M. S., and Saurabh, Saket. 2016. Partially polynomial kernels for set cover and test cover. *SIAM Journal of Discrete Mathematics*, **30**(3), 1401–1423.

Bellman, Richard. 1962. Dynamic programming treatment of the travelling salesman problem. *Journal of ACM*, **9**(1), 61–63.

Berge, Claude. 1973. *Graphs and Hypergraphs*. North-Holland Mathematical Library, vol. 6. Amsterdam, The Netherlands: North-Holland Publishing Co.

Bessy, Stéphane, and Perez, Anthony. 2013. Polynomial kernels for proper interval completion and related problems. *Information and Computation*, **231**, 89–108.

Bessy, Stéphane, Fomin, Fedor V., Gaspers, Serge, Paul, Christophe, Perez, Anthony, Saurabh, Saket, and Thomassé, Stéphan. 2011. Kernels for feedback arc set in tournaments. *Journal of Computer and System Sciences*, **77**(6), 1071–1078.

Binkele-Raible, Daniel, Fernau, Henning, Fomin, Fedor V., Lokshtanov, Daniel, Saurabh, Saket, and Villanger, Yngve. 2012. Kernel(s) for problems with no kernel: On out-trees with many leaves. *ACM Transactions on Algorithms*, **8**(4), 38.

Björklund, Andreas, Husfeldt, Thore, and Taslaman, Nina. 2012. Shortest cycle through specified elements. Pages 1747–1753 of: *Proceedings of the 23rd Annual ACM-SIAM Symposium on Discrete Algorithms (SODA)*. SIAM.

Bliznets, Ivan, Fomin, Fedor V., Pilipczuk, Marcin, and Pilipczuk, Michał. 2016. Subexponential parameterized algorithm for interval completion. Pages 1116–1131 of: *Proceedings of the 27th Annual ACM-SIAM Symposium on Discrete Algorithms (SODA)*. SIAM.

Bodlaender, Hans L. 1996. A linear-time algorithm for finding tree-decompositions of small treewidth. *SIAM Journal of Computing*, **25**(6), 1305–1317.

Bodlaender, Hans L. 2006. Treewidth: Characterizations, applications, and computations. Pages 1–14 of: *Proceedings of the 32nd International Workshop on Graph-Theoretic Concepts in Computer Science (WG)*. Lecture Notes in Computer Science, vol. 4271. Springer.

Bodlaender, Hans L. 2009. Kernelization: New upper and lower bound techniques. Pages 17–37 of: *Proceedings of the 4th International Workshop on Parameterized and Exact Computation (IWPEC)*. Lecture Notes in Computer Science, vol. 5917. Springer.

Bodlaender, Hans L., and de Fluiter, Babette. 1996. Reduction algorithms for constructing solutions in graphs with small treewidth. Pages 199–208 of: *Proceedings of the Second Annual International Conference on Computing and Combinatorics (COCOON)*. Lecture Notes Computer Science, vol. 1090. Springer.

Bodlaender, Hans L., and Hagerup, Torben. 1998. Parallel algorithms with optimal speedup for bounded treewidth. *SIAM Journal on Computing*, **27**(6), 1725–1746.

Bodlaender, Hans L., and Penninkx, Eelko. 2008. A linear kernel for planar feedback vertex set. Pages 160–171 of: *Proceedings of the 3rd International Workshop on Parameterized and Exact Computation (IWPEC)*. Lecture Notes in Computer Science, vol. 5018. Springer.

Bodlaender, Hans L., and van Antwerpen-de Fluiter, Babette. 2001. Reduction algorithms for graphs of small treewidth. *Information and Computation*, **167**(2), 86–119.

Bodlaender, Hans L., and van Dijk, Thomas C. 2010. A cubic kernel for feedback vertex set and loop cutset. *Theory of Computing Systems*, **46**(3), 566–597.

Bodlaender, Hans L., Penninkx, Eelko, and Tan, Richard B. 2008. A linear kernel for the *k*-disjoint cycle problem on planar graphs. Pages 306–317 of: *Proceedings of the 19th International Symposium on Algorithms and Computation (ISAAC)*. Lecture Notes in Computer Science, vol. 5369. Springer.

Bodlaender, Hans L., Fomin, Fedor V., Lokshtanov, Daniel, Penninkx, Eelko, Saurabh, Saket, and Thilikos, Dimitrios M. 2009a. (Meta) kernelization. Pages 629–638 of: *Proceedings of the 50th Annual Symposium on Foundations of Computer Science (FOCS)*. IEEE.

Bodlaender, Hans L., Downey, Rodney G., Fellows, Michael R., and Hermelin, Danny. 2009b. On problems without polynomial kernels. *Journal of Computer and System Sciences*, **75**(8), 423–434.

Bodlaender, Hans L., Thomassé, Stéphan, and Yeo, Anders. 2011. Kernel bounds for disjoint cycles and disjoint paths. *Theoretical Computer Science*, **412**(35), 4570–4578.

Bodlaender, Hans L., Jansen, Bart M. P., and Kratsch, Stefan. 2013. Kernel bounds for path and cycle problems. *Theoretical Computer Science*, **511**, 117–136.

Bodlaender, Hans L., Jansen, Bart M. P., and Kratsch, Stefan. 2014. Kernelization lower bounds by cross-composition. *SIAM Journal on Discrete Mathematics*, **28**(1), 277–305.

Bodlaender, Hans L., Cygan, Marek, Kratsch, Stefan, and Nederlof, Jesper. 2015. Deterministic single exponential time algorithms for connectivity problems parameterized by treewidth. *Information and Computation*, **243**, 86–111.

Bodlaender, Hans L., Drange, Pål Grønås, Dregi, Markus S., Fomin, Fedor V., Lokshtanov, Daniel, and Pilipczuk, Michał. 2016a. A $c^k n$ 5-approximation algorithm for treewidth. *SIAM Journal on Computing*, **45**(2), 317–378.

Bodlaender, Hans L., Fomin, Fedor V., Lokshtanov, Daniel, Penninkx, Eelko, Saurabh, Saket, and Thilikos, Dimitrios M. 2016b. (Meta) kernelization. *Journal of ACM*, **63**(5), 44:1–44:69.

Bollobás, Béla. 1965. On generalized graphs. *Acta Mathematica Academiae Scientiarum Hungaricae*, **16**(3–4), 447–452.

Bonamy, Marthe, and Kowalik, Lukasz. 2016. A 13k-kernel for planar feedback vertex set via region decomposition. *Theoretical Computer Science*, **645**, 25–40.

Bondy, Adrian, and Murty, Ram M. 2008. *Graph Theory*. Graduate Texts in Mathematics, vol. 244. Springer.

Bonsma, Paul S., Brüggemann, Tobias, and Woeginger, Gerhard J. 2003. A faster FPT algorithm for finding spanning trees with many leaves. Pages 259–268 of: *Proceedings of the 28th Symposium on Mathematical Foundations of Computer Science (MFCS)*. Lecture Notes in Computer Science, vol. 2747. Springer.

Borchers, Al, and Du, Ding-Zhu. 1997. The k-Steiner ratio in graphs. *SIAM Journal on Computing*, **26**(3), 857–869.

Brooks, Leonard R. 1941. On colouring the nodes of a network. *Mathematical Proceedings of the Cambridge Philosophical Society*, **37**(2), 194–197.

Bunch, James R., and Hopcroft, John E. 1974. Triangular factorization and inversion by fast matrix multiplication. *Mathematics of Computation*, **28**(125), 231–236.

Burrage, Kevin, Estivill-Castro, Vladimir, Fellows, Michael R., Langston, Michael A., Mac, Shev, and Rosamond, Frances A. 2006. The undirected feedback vertex set problem has a poly(k) kernel. Pages 192–202 of: *Proceedings of the 2nd International Workshop on Parameterized and Exact Computation (IWPEC)*. Lecture Notes in Computer Science, vol. 4169. Springer.

Buss, Jonathan F., and Goldsmith, Judy. 1993. Nondeterminism within P. *SIAM Journal of Computing*, **22**(3), 560–572.

Byrka, Jaroslaw, Grandoni, Fabrizio, Rothvoß, Thomas, and Sanità, Laura. 2013. Steiner tree approximation via iterative randomized rounding. *Journal of ACM*, **60**(1), 6:1–6:33.

Cai, Leizhen, and Cai, Yufei. 2015. Incompressibility of H-free edge modification problems. *Algorithmica*, **71**(3), 731–757.

Cai, Liming, Chen, Jianer, Downey, Rodney G., and Fellows, Michael R. 1997. Advice classes of parameterized tractability. *Annals of Pure and Applied Logic*, **84**(1), 119–138.

Cao, Yixin, and Chen, Jianer. 2012. Cluster editing: Kernelization based on edge cuts. *Algorithmica*, **64**(1), 152–169.

Chekuri, Chandra, and Chuzhoy, Julia. 2016. Polynomial bounds for the Grid-Minor Theorem. *Journal of ACM*, **63**(5), 40:1–40:65.

Chen, Guantao, and Yu, Xingxing. 2002. Long cycles in 3-connected graphs. *Journal of Combinatorial Theory Series B*, **86**(1), 80–99.

Chen, Jianer, and Lu, Songjian. 2009. Improved parameterized set splitting algorithms: A probabilistic approach. *Algorithmica*, **54**(4), 472–489.

Chen, Jianer, and Meng, Jie. 2012. A $2k$ kernel for the cluster editing problem. *Journal of Computer and System Sciences*, **78**(1), 211–220.

Chen, Jianer, Kanj, Iyad A., and Jia, Weijia. 2001. Vertex cover: Further observations and further improvements. *Journal of Algorithms*, **41**(2), 280–301.

Chen, Jianer, Fernau, Henning, Kanj, Iyad A., and Xia, Ge. 2007. Parametric duality and kernelization: Lower bounds and upper bounds on kernel size. *SIAM Journal of Computing*, **37**(4), 1077–1106.

Chen, Jianer, Liu, Yang, Lu, Songjian, O'Sullivan, Barry, and Razgon, Igor. 2008. A fixed-parameter algorithm for the directed feedback vertex set problem. *Journal of ACM*, **55**(5), 21:1–21:19.

Chen, Xue, and Zhou, Yuan. 2017. Parameterized algorithms for Constraint Satisfaction problems above average with global cardinality constraints. Pages 358–377 of: *Proceedings of the 27th Annual ACM-SIAM Symposium on Discrete Algorithms (SODA)*. SIAM.

Chen, Zhi-Zhong, Jiang, Tao, and Lin, Guohui. 2003. Computing phylogenetic roots with bounded degrees and errors. *SIAM Journal of Computing*, **32**(4), 864–879.

Chlebík, Miroslav, and Chlebíková, Janka. 2008. Crown reductions for the Minimum Weighted Vertex Cover problem. *Discrete Applied Mathematics*, **156**(3), 292–312.

Chor, Benny, Fellows, Michael R., and Juedes, David W. 2004. Linear kernels in linear time, or how to save k colors in $O(n^2)$ steps. Pages 257–269 of: *Proceedings of the 30th Workshop on Graph-Theoretic Concepts in Computer Science (WG)*. Lecture Notes in Computer Science, vol. 3353. Springer.

Chuzhoy, Julia. 2015. Improved bounds for the Flat Wall Theorem. Pages 256–275 of: *Proceedings of the 26th Annual ACM-SIAM Symposium on Discrete Algorithms (SODA)*. SIAM.

Chuzhoy, Julia. 2016. Improved bounds for the Excluded Grid Theorem. *CoRR*, **abs/1602.02629**.

Condon, Anne, Edelsbrunner, Herbert, Emerson, E. Allen, Fortnow, Lance, Haber, Stuart, Karp, Richard M., Leivant, Daniel, Lipton, Richard J., Lynch, Nancy, Parberry, Ian, Papadimitriou, Christos H., Rabin, Michael, Rosenberg, Arnold, Royer, James S., Savage, John, Selman, Alan L., Smith, Carl, Tardos, Eva, and Vitter, Jeffrey Scott. 1999. *Challenges for Theory of Computing: Report for an NSF-Sponsored Workshop on Research in Theoretical Computer Science*. Available at https://www.cse.buffalo.edu/~selman/report/Report.html.

Cormen, Thomas H., Leiserson, Charles E., Rivest, Ronald L., and Stein, Clifford. 2009. *Introduction to Algorithms (3 ed.)*. MIT Press.

Corneil, Derek G., Perl, Yehoshua, and Stewart, Lorna K. 1985. A linear recognition algorithm for cographs. *SIAM Journal of Computing*, **14**(4), 926–934.

Courcelle, Bruno. 1990. The monadic second-order logic of graphs I: Recognizable sets of finite graphs. *Information and Computation*, **85**(1), 12–75.

Courcelle, Bruno. 1992. The monadic second-order logic of graphs III: Treewidth, forbidden minors and complexity issues. *Informatique Théorique*, **26**(3), 257–286.

Crowston, Robert, Gutin, Gregory, and Jones, Mark. 2010. Note on Max Lin-2 above average. *Information Processing Letters*, **110**(11), 451–454.

Crowston, Robert, Jones, Mark, and Mnich, Matthias. 2012a. Max-Cut Parameterized above the Edwards-Erdős Bound. Pages 242–253 of: *Proceedings of the 39th International Colloquium of Automata, Languages and Programming (ICALP)*. Lecture Notes in Computer Science, vol. 7391. Springer.

Crowston, Robert, Gutin, Gregory, Jones, Mark, and Yeo, Anders. 2012b. A new lower bound on the maximum number of satisfied clauses in Max-SAT and its algorithmic applications. *Algorithmica*, **64**(1), 56–68.

Crowston, Robert, Jones, Mark, Muciaccia, Gabriele, Philip, Geevarghese, Rai, Ashutosh, and Saurabh, Saket. 2013. Polynomial kernels for lambda-extendible properties parameterized above the poljak-turzik bound. Pages 43–54 of: *IARCS Annual Conference on Foundations of Software Technology and Theoretical Computer Science (FSTTCS)*. Leibniz International Proceedings in Informatics (LIPIcs), vol. 24. Schloss Dagstuhl–Leibniz-Zentrum fuer Informatik.

Crowston, Robert, Fellows, Michael R., Gutin, Gregory, Jones, Mark, Kim, Eun Jung, Rosamond, Frances A., Ruzsa, Imre Z., Thomassé, Stéphan, and Yeo, Anders. 2014. Satisfying more than half of a system of linear equations over GF(2): A multivariate approach. *Journal of Computer and System Sciences*, **80**(4), 687–696.

Cygan, Marek, Kratsch, Stefan, Pilipczuk, Marcin, Pilipczuk, Michał, and Wahlström, Magnus. 2011. Clique cover and graph separation: New incompressibility results. *CoRR*, **abs/1111.0570**.

Cygan, Marek, Pilipczuk, Marcin, Pilipczuk, Michał, and Wojtaszczyk, Jakub Onufry. 2012. Kernelization hardness of connectivity problems in d-degenerate graphs. *Discrete Applied Mathematics*, **160**(15), 2131–2141.

Cygan, Marek, Kratsch, Stefan, Pilipczuk, Marcin, Pilipczuk, Michał, and Wahlström, Magnus. 2014a. Clique cover and graph separation: New incompressibility results. *ACM Transactions on Computation Theory*, **6**(2), 6:1–6:19.

Cygan, Marek, Pilipczuk, Marcin, Pilipczuk, Michał, and Wojtaszczyk, Jakub Onufry. 2014b. Solving the 2-Disjoint connected subgraphs problem faster than 2^n. *Algorithmica*, **70**(2), 195–207.

Cygan, Marek, Fomin, Fedor V., Kowalik, Lukasz, Lokshtanov, Daniel, Marx, Dániel, Pilipczuk, Marcin, Pilipczuk, Michał, and Saurabh, Saket. 2015. *Parameterized Algorithms*. Springer.

Cygan, Marek, Grandoni, Fabrizio, and Hermelin, Danny. 2017. Tight kernel bounds for problems on graphs with small degeneracy. *ACM Transactions on Algorithms*, **13**(3), 43:1–43:22.

Daligault, Jean, and Thomassé, Stéphan. 2009. On finding directed trees with many leaves. Pages 86–97 of: *Proceedings of the 4th International Workshop on Parameterized and Exact Computation (IWPEC)*. Lecture Notes in Computer Science, vol. 5917. Springer.

Daligault, Jean, Gutin, Gregory, Kim, Eun Jung, and Yeo, Anders. 2010. FPT algorithms and kernels for the Directed k-Leaf problem. *Journal of Computer and System Sciences*, **76**(2), 144–152.

de Fluiter, Babette. 1997. *Algorithms for Graphs of Small Treewidth*. Ph thesis, Utrecht University.

Dehne, Frank K. H. A., Fellows, Michael R., and Rosamond, Frances A. 2003. An FPT algorithm for set splitting. Pages 180–191 of: *Proceedings of the 29th International Workshop on Graph-Theoretic Concepts in Computer Science (WG)*. Lecture Notes in Computer Science, vol. 2880. Springer.

Dehne, Frank K. H. A., Fellows, Michael R., Rosamond, Frances A., and Shaw, Peter. 2004. Greedy localization, iterative compression, modeled crown reductions: New FPT techniques, an improved algorithm for set splitting, and a novel 2k kernelization for vertex cover. Pages 271–280 of: *Proceedings of the 1st International Workshop on Parameterized and Exact Computation (IWPEC)*. Lecture Notes in Computer Science, vol. 3162. Springer.

Dehne, Frank K. H. A., Fellows, Michael R., Fernau, Henning, Prieto-Rodriguez, Elena, and Rosamond, Frances A. 2006. Nonblocker: Parameterized algorithmics for minimum dominating set. Pages 237–245 of: *SOFSEM 2006: Theory and Practice of Computer Science, 32nd Conference on Current Trends in Theory and Practice of Computer Science, Merín, Czech Republic, January 21–27, 2006, Proceedings*.

Dell, Holger. 2014. AND-compression of NP-complete problems: Streamlined proof and minor observations. Pages 184–195 of: *Proceedings of the 9th International Symposium on Parameterized and Exact Computation (IPEC)*. Lecture Notes in Computer Science, vol. 8894. Springer.

Dell, Holger, and Marx, Dániel. 2012. Kernelization of packing problems. Pages 68–81 of: *Proceedings of the 23rd Annual ACM-SIAM Symposium on Discrete Algorithms (SODA)*. SIAM.

Dell, Holger, and van Melkebeek, Dieter. 2014. Satisfiability allows no nontrivial sparsification unless the polynomial-time hierarchy collapses. *Journal of ACM*, **61**(4), 23.

Demaine, Erik D., and Hajiaghayi, MohammadTaghi. 2005. Bidimensionality: New connections between FPT algorithms and PTASs. Pages 590–601 of: *Proceedings of the 16th Annual ACM-SIAM Symposium on Discrete Algorithms (SODA)*. SIAM.

Demaine, Erik D., and Hajiaghayi, MohammadTaghi. 2008a. The Bidimensionality Theory and its algorithmic applications. *The Computer Journal*, **51**(3), 292–302.

Demaine, Erik D., and Hajiaghayi, MohammadTaghi. 2008b. Linearity of grid minors in treewidth with applications through bidimensionality. *Combinatorica*, **28**(1), 19–36.

Demaine, Erik D., Fomin, Fedor V., Hajiaghayi, MohammadTaghi, and Thilikos, Dimitrios M. 2005. Subexponential parameterized algorithms on graphs of bounded genus and H-minor-free graphs. *Journal of ACM*, **52**(6), 866–893.

DeMillo, Richard A., and Lipton, Richard J. 1978. A probabilistic remark on algebraic program testing. *Information Processing Letters*, **7**(4), 193–195.

Diestel, Reinhard. 2005. *Graph theory*. 3rd ed. Graduate Texts in Mathematics, vol. 173. Springer-Verlag.

Dinur, Irit, and Safra, Samuel. 2005. On the hardness of approximating minimum vertex cover. *Annals of Mathematics (2)*, **162**(1), 439–485.

Dom, Michael, Guo, Jiong, Hüffner, Falk, Niedermeier, Rolf, and Truß, Anke. 2010. Fixed-parameter tractability results for feedback set problems in tournaments. *Journal of Discrete Algorithms*, **8**(1), 76–86.

Dom, Michael, Lokshtanov, Daniel, and Saurabh, Saket. 2014. Kernelization lower bounds through colors and IDs. *ACM Transactions on Algorithms*, **11**(2), 13.

Dorn, Frederic, Fomin, Fedor V., and Thilikos, Dimitrios M. 2008. Subexponential parameterized algorithms. *Computer Science Review*, **2**(1), 29–39.

Downey, Rodney G., and Fellows, Michael R. 1999. *Parameterized complexity*. Springer-Verlag.

Downey, Rodney G., and Fellows, Michael R. 2013. *Fundamentals of Parameterized Complexity*. Texts in Computer Science. Springer.

Drange, Pål Grønås, Dregi, Markus Sortland, Fomin, Fedor V., Kreutzer, Stephan, Lokshtanov, Daniel, Pilipczuk, Marcin, Pilipczuk, Michał, Reidl, Felix, Villaamil, Fernando Sánchez, Saurabh, Saket, Siebertz, Sebastian, and Sikdar, Somnath. 2016a. Kernelization and sparseness: The case of dominating set. Pages 31:1–31:14 of: *Proceedings of the 33rd International Symposium on Theoretical Aspects of Computer Science (STACS)*. LIPIcs, vol. 47. Schloss Dagstuhl - Leibniz-Zentrum fuer Informatik.

Drange, Pål Grønås, Dregi, Markus S., and van't Hof, Pim. 2016b. On the computational complexity of vertex integrity and component order connectivity. *Algorithmica*, **76**(4), 1181–1202.

Dreyfus, Stuart E., and Wagner, Robert A. 1971. The Steiner problem in graphs. *Networks*, **1**(3), 195–207.

Drucker, Andrew. 2015. New limits to classical and quantum instance compression. *SIAM Journal on Computing*, **44**(5), 1443–1479.

Dvořák, Pavel, Feldmann, Andreas Emil, Knop, Dušan, Masařík, Tomáš, Toufar, Tomáš, and Veselý, Pavel. 2017. Parameterized approximation schemes for steiner trees with small number of steiner vertices. *CoRR*, **abs/1710.00668**.

Dvorák, Zdenek, and Lidický, Bernard. 2017. Independent sets near the lower bound in bounded degree graphs. Pages 28:1–28:13 of: *Proceedings of the 34th International Symposium on Theoretical Aspects of Computer Science (STACS)*. Leibniz International Proceedings in Informatics (LIPIcs), vol. 66. Schloss Dagstuhl - Leibniz-Zentrum fuer Informatik.

Dvorak, Zdenek, and Mnich, Matthias. 2014. Large independent sets in triangle-free planar graphs. Pages 346–357 of: *Proceedings of the 22nd Annual European Symposium on Algorithms (ESA)*. Lecture Notes in Computer Science, vol. 8737. Springer.

Edmonds, Jack, and Fulkerson, Delbert R. 1965. *Transversals and Matroid Partition*. Defense Technical Information Center.

Eiben, Eduard, Kumar, Mithilesh, Mouawad, Amer E., Panolan, Fahad, and Siebertz, Sebastian. 2018. Lossy kernels for connected dominating set on sparse graphs. Pages 29:1–29:15 of: *Proceedings of the 35th International Symposium on Theoretical Aspects of Computer Science (STACS)*. Leibniz International Proceedings in Informatics (LIPIcs), vol. 96. Schloss Dagstuhl - Leibniz-Zentrum fuer Informatik.

Erdős, Paul, and Pósa, Louis. 1965. On independent circuits contained in a graph. *Canadian Journal of Mathematics*, **17**, 347–352.

Erdős, Paul, and Rado, Richard. 1960. Intersection theorems for systems of sets. *Journal of the London Mathematical Society*, **35**, 85–90.

Estivill-Castro, Vladimir, Fellows, Michael R., Langston, Michael A., and Rosamond, Frances A. 2005. FPT is P-Time Extremal Structure I. Pages 1–41 of: *Proceedings of the First Workshop Algorithms and Complexity in Durham (ACID)*, vol. 4. Texts in Algorithmics 4, King's College, London.

Eves, H. 1969. Mathematical Circles. Prindle, Weber, and Schmidt.

Feige, Uriel. 1998. A threshold of ln n for approximating set cover. *Journal of ACM*, **45**(4), 634–652.

Feige, Uriel, Hajiaghayi, MohammadTaghi, and Lee, James R. 2008. Improved approximation algorithms for minimum weight vertex separators. *SIAM Journal of Computing*, **38**(2), 629–657.

Fellows, Michael R. 2003. Blow-ups, win/win's, and crown rules: Some new directions in FPT. In: *Proceedings of the 29th Workshop on Graph-Theoretic Concepts in Computer Science (WG)*. Lecture Notes in Computer Science, vol. 2880. Springer.

Fellows, Michael R. 2006. The lost continent of polynomial time: Preprocessing and kernelization. Pages 276–277 of: *Proceedings of the 2nd International Workshop on Parameterized and Exact Computation (IWPEC)*. Lecture Notes in Computer Science, vol. 4169. Springer.

Fellows, Michael R., and Langston, Michael A. 1989. On search, decision and the efficiency of polynomial time algorithms (extended abstract). Pages 501–512 of: *Proceedings of the 21st Annual ACM Symposium on Theory of Computing (STOC)*. ACM.

Fellows, Michael R., and Rosamond, Frances A. 2007. The complexity ecology of parameters: An illustration using bounded max leaf number. Pages 268–277 of: *Proceedings of the 3rd Conference on Computability in Europe (CiE)*. Lecture Notes in Computer Science, vol. 4497. Springer.

Fellows, Michael R., Heggernes, Pinar, Rosamond, Frances A., Sloper, Christian, and Telle, Jan Arne. 2004. Finding k disjoint triangles in an arbitrary graph. Pages 235–244 of: *Proceedings of the 30th International Workshop on Graph-Theoretic Concepts in Computer Science (WG)*. Lecture Notes in Computer Science, vol. 3353. Springer.

Fellows, Michael R., Lokshtanov, Daniel, Misra, Neeldhara, Mnich, Matthias, Rosamond, Frances A., and Saurabh, Saket. 2009. The complexity ecology of parameters: An illustration using bounded max leaf number. *Theory of Computing Systems*, **45**(4), 822–848.

Fellows, Michael R., Guo, Jiong, Moser, Hannes, and Niedermeier, Rolf. 2011. A generalization of Nemhauser and Trotters local optimization theorem. *Journal of Computer and System Sciences*, **77**(6), 1141–1158.

Fellows, Michael R., Hermelin, Danny, Rosamond, Frances A., and Shachnai, Hadas. 2016. Tractable parameterizations for the minimum linear arrangement problem. *ACM Transactions on Computation Theory*, **8**(2), 6:1–6:12.

Fellows, Michael R., Kulik, Ariel, Rosamond, Frances A., and Shachnai, Hadas. 2018. Parameterized approximation via fidelity preserving transformations. *Journal of Computer and System Sciences*, **93**, 30–40.

Flum, Jörg, and Grohe, Martin. 2006. *Parameterized Complexity Theory*. Texts in Theoretical Computer Science: An EATCS Series. Springer-Verlag.

Fomin, Fedor V., and Saurabh, Saket. 2014. Kernelization methods for fixed-parameter tractability. Pages 260–282 of: *Tractability*. Cambridge University Press.

Fomin, Fedor V., and Strømme, Torstein. 2016. Vertex cover structural parameterization revisited. Pages 171–182 of: *Proceedings of the 42nd International Workshop on Graph-Theoretic Concepts in Computer Science (WG)*. Lecture Notes in Computer Science, vol. 9941. Springer.

Fomin, Fedor V., and Villanger, Yngve. 2012. Treewidth computation and extremal combinatorics. *Combinatorica*, **32**(3), 289–308.

Fomin, Fedor V., Lokshtanov, Daniel, Saurabh, Saket, and Thilikos, Dimitrios M. 2010. Bidimensionality and kernels. Pages 503–510 of: *Proceedings of the 21st Annual ACM-SIAM Symposium on Discrete Algorithms (SODA)*. SIAM.

Fomin, Fedor V., Lokshtanov, Daniel, Raman, Venkatesh, and Saurabh, Saket. 2011a. Bidimensionality and EPTAS. Pages 748–759 of: *Proceedings of the 22nd Annual ACM-SIAM Symposium on Discrete Algorithms (SODA)*. SIAM.

Fomin, Fedor V., Golovach, Petr A., and Thilikos, Dimitrios M. 2011b. Contraction obstructions for treewidth. *Journal of Combinatorial Theory Series B*, **101**(5), 302–314.

Fomin, Fedor V., Lokshtanov, Daniel, Misra, Neeldhara, Philip, Geevarghese, and Saurabh, Saket. 2011c. Hitting forbidden minors: Approximation and Kernelization. Pages 189–200 of: *Proceedings of the 28th International Symposium on Theoretical Aspects of Computer Science (STACS)*. Leibniz International Proceedings in Informatics (LIPIcs), vol. 9. Schloss Dagstuhl - Leibniz-Zentrum fuer Informatik.

Fomin, Fedor V., Lokshtanov, Daniel, Saurabh, Saket, and Thilikos, Dimitrios M. 2012a. Linear kernels for (connected) dominating set on H-minor-free graphs. Pages 82–93 of: *Proceedings of the 23rd Annual ACM-SIAM Symposium on Discrete Algorithms (SODA)*. SIAM.

Fomin, Fedor V., Lokshtanov, Daniel, Misra, Neeldhara, and Saurabh, Saket. 2012b. Planar F-Deletion: Approximation, kernelization and optimal FPT algorithms. Pages 470–479 of: *Proceedings of the 53rd Annual Symposium on Foundations of Computer Science (FOCS)*. IEEE.

Fomin, Fedor V., Gaspers, Serge, Saurabh, Saket, and Thomassé, Stéphan. 2013. A linear vertex kernel for maximum internal spanning tree. *Journal of Computer and System Sciences*, **79**(1), 1–6.

Fomin, Fedor V., Jansen, Bart M. P., and Pilipczuk, Michał. 2014. Preprocessing subgraph and minor problems: When does a small vertex cover help? *Journal of Computer and System Sciences*, **80**(2), 468–495.

Fomin, Fedor V., Todinca, Ioan, and Villanger, Yngve. 2015a. Large induced subgraphs via triangulations and CMSO. *SIAM Journal on Computing*, **44**(1), 54–87.

Fomin, Fedor V., Lokshtanov, Daniel, Misra, Neeldhara, Ramanujan, M. S., and Saurabh, Saket. 2015b. Solving d-SAT via backdoors to small treewidth. Pages 630–641 of: *Proceedings of the 26th Annual ACM-SIAM Symposium on Discrete Algorithms (SODA)*. SIAM.

Fomin, Fedor V., Lokshtanov, Daniel, Saurabh, Saket, and Thilikos, Dimitrios M. 2016a. Bidimensionality and Kernels. *CoRR*, **abs/1606.05689**.

Fomin, Fedor V., Lokshtanov, Daniel, Panolan, Fahad, and Saurabh, Saket. 2016b. Efficient computation of representative families with applications in parameterized and exact algorithms. *Journal of ACM*, **63**(4), 29:1–29:60.

Fomin, Fedor V., Lokshtanov, Daniel, Misra, Neeldhara, Philip, Geevarghese, and Saurabh, Saket. 2016c. Hitting forbidden minors: Approximation and kernelization. *SIAM Journal on Discrete Mathematics*, **30**(1), 383–410.

Fomin, Fedor V., Lokshtanov, Daniel, Panolan, Fahad, and Saurabh, Saket. 2017. Representative families of product families. *ACM Transactions on Algorithms*, **13**(3), 36:1–36:29.

Fomin, Fedor V., Lokshtanov, Daniel, and Saurabh, Saket. 2018. Excluded grid minors and efficient polynomial-time approximation schemes. *Journal of ACM*, **65**(2), 10:1–10:44.

Ford Jr., Lester R., and Fulkerson, Delbert R. 1956. Maximal flow through a network. *Canadian Journal of Mathematics*, **8**, 399–404.

Fortnow, Lance, and Santhanam, Rahul. 2011. Infeasibility of instance compression and succinct PCPs for NP. *Journal of Computer and System Sciences*, **77**(1), 91–106.

Frank, András, Király, Tamás, and Kriesell, Matthias. 2003. On decomposing a hypergraph into k connected sub-hypergraphs. *Discrete Applied Mathematics*, **131**(2), 373–383.

Frankl, Peter. 1982. An extremal problem for two families of sets. *European Journal of Combinatorics*, **3**(2), 125–127.

Friggstad, Zachary, and Salavatipour, Mohammad R. 2011. Approximability of packing disjoint cycles. *Algorithmica*, **60**(2), 395–400.

Gajarský, Jakub, Hlinený, Petr, Obdrzálek, Jan, Ordyniak, Sebastian, Reidl, Felix, Rossmanith, Peter, Villaamil, Fernando Sánchez, and Sikdar, Somnath. 2017. Kernelization using structural parameters on sparse graph classes. *Journal of Computer and System Sciences*, **84**, 219–242.

Gall, François Le. 2014. Powers of tensors and fast matrix multiplication. Pages 296–303 of: *Proceedings of the International Symposium on Symbolic and Algebraic Computation (ISSAC)*. ACM.

Gallai, Tibor. 1961. Maximum-minimum Sätze und verallgemeinerte Faktoren von Graphen. *Acta Mathematica Academiae Scientiarum Hungaricae*, **12**(1–2), 131–173.

Gallai, Tibor. 1967. Transitiv orientierbare Graphen. *Acta Mathematica Academiae Scientiarum Hungaricae*, **18**(1–2), 25–66.

Ganian, Robert, Slivovsky, Friedrich, and Szeider, Stefan. 2016. Meta-kernelization with structural parameters. *Journal of Computer and System Sciences*, **82**(2), 333–346.

Garnero, Valentin, Paul, Christophe, Sau, Ignasi, and Thilikos, Dimitrios M. 2015. Explicit linear kernels via dynamic programming. *SIAM Journal on Discrete Mathematics*, **29**(4), 1864–1894.

Gramm, Jens, Guo, Jiong, Hüffner, Falk, and Niedermeier, Rolf. 2005. Graph-modeled data clustering: Exact algorithms for clique generation. *Theory of Computing Systems*, **38**(4), 373–392.

Gramm, Jens, Guo, Jiong, Hüffner, Falk, and Niedermeier, Rolf. 2008. Data reduction and exact algorithms for clique cover. *ACM Journal of Experimental Algorithmics*, **13**, article 2.

Gu, Qian-Ping, and Tamaki, Hisao. 2012. Improved bounds on the planar branchwidth with respect to the largest grid minor size. *Algorithmica*, **64**(3), 416–453.

Guillemot, Sylvain, Havet, Frédéric, Paul, Christophe, and Perez, Anthony. 2013. On the (non-) existence of polynomial kernels for P_l-free edge modification problems. *Algorithmica*, **65**(4), 900–926.

Guo, Jiong. 2007. Problem kernels for NP-complete edge deletion problems: Split and related graphs. Pages 915–926 of: *Proceedings of the 18th International Symposium on Algorithms and Computation (ISAAC)*. Lecture Notes in Computer Science, vol. 4835. Springer.

Guo, Jiong. 2009. A more effective linear kernelization for cluster editing. *Theoretical Computer Science*, **410**(8–10), 718–726.

Guo, Jiong, and Niedermeier, Rolf. 2007a. Invitation to data reduction and problem kernelization. *SIGACT News*, **38**(1), 31–45.

Guo, Jiong, and Niedermeier, Rolf. 2007b. Linear problem kernels for NP-hard problems on planar graphs. Pages 375–386 of: *Proceedings of the 34th International Colloquium of Automata, Languages and Programming (ICALP)*. Lecture Notes in Computer Science, vol. 4596. Springer.

Guo, Jiong, Niedermeier, Rolf, and Wernicke, Sebastian. 2006. Fixed-parameter tractability results for full-degree spanning tree and its dual. Pages 203–214 of: *Proceedings of the 2nd International Workshop on Parameterized and Exact Computation (IWPEC)*. Lecture Notes in Computer Science, vol. 4169. Springer.

Guo, Jiong, Niedermeier, Rolf, and Wernicke, Sebastian. 2007. Parameterized complexity of vertex cover variants. *Theory of Computing Systems*, **41**(3), 501–520.

Gutin, Gregory, and Yeo, Anders. 2012. Constraint satisfaction problems parameterized above or below tight bounds: A survey. Pages 257–286 of: *The Multivariate Algorithmic Revolution and Beyond*. Springer.

Gutin, Gregory, and Yeo, Anders. 2017. Parameterized constraint satisfaction problems: A survey. Pages 179–203 of: Krokhin, Andrei A., and Zivny, Stanislav (eds.), *The Constraint Satisfaction Problem: Complexity and Approximability*. Dagstuhl Follow-Ups, vol. 7. Schloss Dagstuhl - Leibniz-Zentrum fuer Informatik.

Gutin, Gregory, Jones, Mark, and Yeo, Anders. 2011a. Kernels for below-upper-bound parameterizations of the hitting set and directed dominating set problems. *Theoretical Computer Science*, **412**(41), 5744–5751.

Gutin, Gregory, Kim, Eun Jung, Szeider, Stefan, and Yeo, Anders. 2011b. A probabilistic approach to problems parameterized above or below tight bounds. *Journal of Computer and System Sciences*, **77**(2), 422–429.

Gutin, Gregory, Kim, Eun Jung, Lampis, Michael, and Mitsou, Valia. 2011c. Vertex cover problem parameterized above and below tight bounds. *Theory of Computing Systems*, **48**(2), 402–410.

Gutin, Gregory, van Iersel, Leo, Mnich, Matthias, and Yeo, Anders. 2012. Every ternary permutation constraint satisfaction problem parameterized above average has a kernel with a quadratic number of variables. *Journal of Computer and System Sciences*, **78**(1), 151–163.

Gutin, Gregory, Rafiey, Arash, Szeider, Stefan, and Yeo, Anders. 2013a. Corrigendum: The linear arrangement problem parameterized above guaranteed value. *Theory of Computing Systems*, **53**(4), 690–691.

Gutin, Gregory, Muciaccia, Gabriele, and Yeo, Anders. 2013b. (Non-)existence of polynomial kernels for the Test Cover problem. *Information Processing Letters*, **113**(4), 123–126.

Gyárfás, András. 1990. A simple lower bound on edge coverings by cliques. *Discrete Mathematics*, **85**(1), 103–104.

Habib, Michel, and Paul, Christophe. 2010. A survey of the algorithmic aspects of modular decomposition. *Computer Science Review*, **4**(1), 41–59.

Hagerup, Torben. 2012. Kernels for edge dominating set: Simpler or smaller. Pages 491–502 of: *Proceedings of the 37th International Symposium on Mathematical Foundations of Computer Science (MFCS)*. Lecture Notes in Computer Science, vol. 7464. Springer.

Halin, Rudolf. 1976. S-functions for graphs. *Journal of Geometry*, **8**(1–2), 171–186.

Hall, Philip. 1935. On representatives of subsets. *Journal of the London Mathematical Society*, **10**(1), 26–30.

Har-Peled, Sariel, Kaplan, Haim, Mulzer, Wolfgang, Roditty, Liam, Seiferth, Paul, Sharir, Micha, and Willert, Max. 2018. Stabbing pairwise intersecting disks by five points. *CoRR*, **abs/1801.03158**.

Heggernes, Pinar, Kratsch, Dieter, Lokshtanov, Daniel, Raman, Venkatesh, and Saurabh, Saket. 2013. Fixed-parameter algorithms for cochromatic number and disjoint rectangle stabbing via iterative localization. *Information and Computation*, **231**, 109–116.

Held, Michael, and Karp, Richard M. 1962. A dynamic programming approach to sequencing problems. *Journal of SIAM*, **10**(1), 196–210.

Hermelin, Danny, and Wu, Xi. 2012. Weak compositions and their applications to polynomial lower bounds for kernelization. Pages 104–113 of: *Proceedings of the 23rd Annual ACM-SIAM Symposium on Discrete Algorithms (SODA)*. SIAM.

Hermelin, Danny, Kratsch, Stefan, Soltys, Karolina, Wahlström, Magnus, and Wu, Xi. 2015. A completeness theory for polynomial (turing) kernelization. *Algorithmica*, **71**(3), 702–730.

Hochbaum, Dorit S. (ed). 1997. *Approximation Algorithms for NP-Hard Problems*. PWS Publishing Co.

Hols, Eva-Maria C., and Kratsch, Stefan. 2018. A randomized polynomial kernel for subset feedback vertex set. *Theory of Computing Systems*, **62**(1), 63–92.

Hopcroft, John E., and Karp, Richard M. 1973. An $n^{5/2}$ algorithm for maximum matchings in bipartite graphs. *SIAM Journal of Computing*, **2**(3), 225–231.

Hopcroft, John E., and Tarjan, Robert E. 1973. Dividing a graph into triconnected components. *SIAM Journal of Computing*, **2**(3), 135–158.

Hüffner, Falk, Niedermeier, Rolf, and Wernicke, Sebastian. 2008. Techniques for practical fixed-parameter algorithms. *The Computer Journal*, **51**(1), 7–25.

Iwata, Yoichi. 2017. Linear-time kernelization for feedback vertex set. Pages 68:1–68:14 of: *Proceedings of the 44th International Colloquium of Automata, Languages and Programming (ICALP)*. Leibniz International Proceedings in Informatics (LIPIcs), vol. 80. Schloss Dagstuhl - Leibniz-Zentrum fuer Informatik.

Jansen, Bart M. P. 2012. Kernelization for maximum leaf spanning tree with positive vertex weights. *Journal of Graph Algorithms and Applications*, **16**(4), 811–846.

Jansen, Bart M. P. 2013. The power of data reduction: Kernels for fundamental graph problems. Ph thesis, Utrecht University.

Jansen, Bart M. P. 2017. Turing kernelization for finding long paths and cycles in restricted graph classes. *Journal of Computer and System Sciences*, **85**, 18–37.

Jansen, Bart M. P., and Bodlaender, Hans L. 2013. Vertex cover kernelization revisited: Upper and lower bounds for a refined parameter. *Theory of Computing Systems*, **53**(2), 263–299.

Jansen, Bart M. P., and Marx, Dániel. 2015. Characterizing the easy-to-find subgraphs from the viewpoint of polynomial-time algorithms, kernels, and Turing kernels. Pages 616–629 of: *Proceedings of the 26th Annual ACM-SIAM Symposium on Discrete Algorithms (SODA)*. SIAM.

Jansen, Bart M. P., Lokshtanov, Daniel, and Saurabh, Saket. 2014. A Near-optimal planarization algorithm. Pages 1802–1811 of: *Proceedings of the 25th Annual ACM-SIAM Symposium on Discrete Algorithms (SODA)*. SIAM.

Jansen, Bart M. P., Pilipczuk, Marcin, and Wrochna, Marcin. 2017. Turing kernelization for finding long paths in graph classes excluding a topological minor. *CoRR*, **abs/1707.01797**.

Jukna, Stasys. 2011. *Extremal Combinatorics*. 2nd ed. Texts in Theoretical Computer Science. An EATCS Series. Springer. Extremal Combinatorics: With Applications in Computer Science.

Kaibel, Volker, and Koch, Thorsten. 2006. Mathematik für den Volkssport. *DMV Mitteilungen*, **14**(2), 93.

Kammer, Frank, and Tholey, Torsten. 2016. Approximate tree decompositions of planar graphs in linear time. *Theoretical Computer Science*, **645**, 60–90.

Kanj, Iyad A., Pelsmajer, Michael J., Schaefer, Marcus, and Xia, Ge. 2011. On the induced matching problem. *Journal of Computer and System Sciences*, **77**(6), 1058–1070.

Kaplan, Haim, Shamir, Ron, and Tarjan, Robert E. 1999. Tractability of parameterized completion problems on chordal, strongly chordal, and proper interval graphs. *SIAM Journal of Computing*, **28**(5), 1906–1922.

Karzanov, Alexander V. 1974. The problem of finding the maximal flow in a network by the method of preflows. *Dokl. Akad. Nauk SSSR*, **215**(1), 49–52.

Kawarabayashi, Ken-ichi, and Kobayashi, Yusuke. 2012. Linear min-max relation between the treewidth of H-minor-free graphs and its largest grid. Pages 278–289 of: *Proceedings of the 29th International Symposium on Theoretical Aspects of Computer Science (STACS)*. Leibniz International Proceedings in Informatics (LIPIcs), vol. 14. Schloss Dagstuhl–Leibniz-Zentrum fuer Informatik.

Khot, Subhash, and Raman, Venkatesh. 2002. Parameterized complexity of finding subgraphs with hereditary properties. *Theoretical Computer Science*, **289**(2), 997–1008.

Khot, Subhash, and Regev, Oded. 2008. Vertex cover might be hard to approximate to within 2-epsilon. *Journal of Computer System Sciences*, **74**(3), 335–349.

Khuller, Samir. 2002. Algorithms column: The vertex cover problem. *SIGACT News*, **33**(2), 31–33.

Kim, Eun Jung, and Kwon, O-joung. 2017. A polynomial kernel for block graph deletion. *Algorithmica*, **79**(1), 251–270.

Kim, Eun Jung, and Williams, Ryan. 2012. Improved parameterized algorithms for above average constraint satisfaction. Pages 118–131 of: *Proceedings of the 6th International Symposium on Parameterized and Exact Computation (IPEC)*. Lecture Notes in Computer Science, vol. 7112. Springer.

Kim, Eun Jung, Langer, Alexander, Paul, Christophe, Reidl, Felix, Rossmanith, Peter, Sau, Ignasi, and Sikdar, Somnath. 2016. Linear kernels and single-exponential algorithms via protrusion decompositions. *ACM Transactions on Algorithms*, **12**(2), 21:1–21:41.

Kleitman, Daniel J., and West, Douglas. B. 1991. Spanning trees with many leaves. *SIAM Journal of Discrete Mathematics*, **4**(1), 99–106.

Kőnig, Dénes. 1916. Über Graphen und ihre Anwendung auf Determinantentheorie und Mengenlehre. *Mathematische Annalen*, **77**(4), 453–465.

Kratsch, Stefan. 2014. Co-nondeterminism in compositions: A kernelization lower bound for a ramsey-type problem. *ACM Transactions on Algorithms*, **10**(4), 19:1–19:16.

Kratsch, Stefan. 2016. A randomized polynomial kernelization for Vertex Cover with a smaller parameter. Pages 59:1–59:17 of: *Proceedings of the 24th Annual European Symposium on Algorithms (ESA)*. Leibniz International Proceedings in Informatics (LIPIcs), vol. 57. Schloss Dagstuhl - Leibniz-Zentrum fuer Informatik.

Kratsch, Stefan, and Wahlström, Magnus. 2009. Two edge modification problems without polynomial kernels. Pages 264–275 of: *Parameterized and Exact Computation*,

4th International Workshop (IWPEC). Lecture Notes in Computer Science, vol. 5917. Springer.

Kratsch, Stefan, and Wahlström, Magnus. 2010. Preprocessing of min ones problems: A dichotomy. Pages 653–665 of: *Proceedings of the 37th International Colloquium of Automata, Languages and Programming (ICALP)*. Lecture Notes in Computer Science, vol. 6198. Springer.

Kratsch, Stefan, and Wahlström, Magnus. 2012. Representative sets and irrelevant vertices: New tools for kernelization. Pages 450–459 of: *Proceedings of the 53rd Annual Symposium on Foundations of Computer Science (FOCS)*. IEEE.

Kratsch, Stefan, and Wahlström, Magnus. 2013. Two edge modification problems without polynomial kernels. *Discrete Optimization*, **10**(3), 193–199.

Kratsch, Stefan, and Wahlström, Magnus. 2014. Compression via matroids: A randomized polynomial kernel for odd cycle transversal. *ACM Transactions on Algorithms*, **10**(4), 20.

Kratsch, Stefan, Philip, Geevarghese, and Ray, Saurabh. 2016. Point line cover: The easy kernel is essentially tight. *ACM Transactions on Algorithms*, **12**(3), 40:1–40:16.

Krithika, R., Misra, Pranabendu, Rai, Ashutosh, and Tale, Prafullkumar. 2016. Lossy kernels for graph contraction problems. Pages 23:1–23:14 of: *Proceedings of the 36th IARCS Annual Conference on Foundations of Software Technology and Theoretical Computer Science (FSTTCS)*. Leibniz International Proceedings in Informatics (LIPIcs), vol. 65. Schloss Dagstuhl - Leibniz-Zentrum fuer Informatik.

Kumar, Mithilesh, and Lokshtanov, Daniel. 2016. A $2lk$ kernel for l-component order connectivity. Pages 20:1–20:14 of: *Proceedings of the 11th International Symposium on Parameterized and Exact Computation (IPEC)*. Leibniz International Proceedings in Informatics (LIPIcs), vol. 63. Schloss Dagstuhl - Leibniz-Zentrum fuer Informatik.

Lampis, Michael. 2011. A kernel of order $2k - c \log k$ for vertex cover. *Information Processing Letters*, **111**(23–24), 1089–1091.

Lawler, Eugene L. 2001. *Combinatorial Optimization: Networks and Matroids*. Dover Books on Mathematics Series. Dover Publications.

Le, Tien-Nam, Lokshtanov, Daniel, Saurabh, Saket, Thomassé, Stéphan, and Zehavi, Meirav. 2018. Subquadratic kernels for Implicit 3-Hitting Set and 3-Set Packing problems. Pages 331–342 of: *Proceedings of the 28th Annual ACM-SIAM Symposium on Discrete Algorithms (SODA)*. SIAM.

Leaf, Alexander, and Seymour, Paul D. 2012 (manuscript). Treewidth and planar minors. https://web.math.princeton.edu/pds/papers/treewidth/paper.pdf.

Li, Wenjun, Cao, Yixin, Chen, Jianer, and Wang, Jianxin. 2017. Deeper local search for parameterized and approximation algorithms for maximum internal spanning tree. *Information and Computation*, **252**, 187–200.

Linial, Nathan, and Sturtevant, Dean G. 1987. Unpublished result.

Lokshtanov, Daniel. 2009. New methods in parameterized algorithms and complexity. Ph thesis, University of Bergen.

Lokshtanov, Daniel, and Saurabh, Saket. 2009. Even faster algorithm for set splitting! Pages 288–299 of: *Proceedings of the 4th International Workshop on*

Parameterized and Exact Computation (IWPEC). Lecture Notes in Computer Science, vol. 5917. Springer.

Lokshtanov, Daniel, and Sloper, Christian. 2005. Fixed parameter set splitting, linear kernel and improved running time. Pages 105–113 of: *Proceedings of the First Algorithms and Complexity in Durham Workshop (ACiD)*. Texts in Algorithmics, vol. 4. King's College, London.

Lokshtanov, Daniel, Mnich, Matthias, and Saurabh, Saket. 2011a. A linear kernel for a planar connected dominating set. *Theoretical Computer Science*, **412**(23), 2536–2543.

Lokshtanov, Daniel, Marx, Dániel, and Saurabh, Saket. 2011b. Lower bounds based on the Exponential Time Hypothesis. *Bulletin of the EATCS*, **105**, 41–72.

Lokshtanov, Daniel, Narayanaswamy, N. S., Raman, Venkatesh, Ramanujan, M. S., and Saurabh, Saket. 2014. Faster parameterized algorithms using linear programming. *ACM Transactions on Algorithms*, **11**(2), 15.

Lokshtanov, Daniel, Panolan, Fahad, Ramanujan, M. S., and Saurabh, Saket. 2017. Lossy kernelization. Pages 224–237 of: *Proceedings of the 49th Annual ACM Symposium on Theory of Computing (STOC)*. ACM.

Lokshtanov, Daniel, Misra, Pranabendu, Panolan, Fahad, Saurabh, Saket, and Zehavi, Meirav. 2018. Quasipolynomial representation of transversal matroids with applications in parameterized complexity. Pages 32:1–32:13 of: *9th Innovations in Theoretical Computer Science Conference, ITCS 2018, January 11–14, 2018, Cambridge, MA*.

Loréa, Michel. 1975. Hypergraphes et matroides. *Cahiers du Centre d'tudes de Recherche Operationnelle*, **17**, 289–291.

Lovász, László. 1970. A generalization of Kőnig's theorem. *Acta Mathematica Academiae Scientiarum Hungaricae*, **21**(3–4), 443–446.

Lovász, László. 1977. Flats in matroids and geometric graphs. Pages 45–86 of: *Combinatorial Surveys (Proceedings of the Sixth British Combinatorial Conference, Royal Holloway Coll., Egham)*. Academic Press.

Lovász, László, and Plummer, Michael D. 2009. *Matching Theory*. AMS Chelsea Publishing.

Mahajan, Meena, and Raman, Venkatesh. 1999. Parameterizing above guaranteed values: MaxSat and MaxCut. *Journal of Algorithms*, **31**(2), 335–354.

Mahajan, Meena, Raman, Venkatesh, and Sikdar, Somnath. 2009. Parameterizing above or below guaranteed values. *Journal of Computer and System Sciences*, **75**(2), 137–153.

Majumdar, Diptapriyo, Raman, Venkatesh, and Saurabh, Saket. 2015. Kernels for structural parameterizations of Vertex Cover-case of small degree modulators. Pages 331–342 of: *Proceedings of the 10th International Symposium on Parameterized and Exact Computation (IPEC)*. Leibniz International Proceedings in Informatics (LIPIcs), vol. 43. Schloss Dagstuhl–Leibniz-Zentrum fuer Informatik.

Makarychev, Konstantin, Makarychev, Yury, and Zhou, Yuan. 2015. Satisfiability of ordering CSPs above average is fixed-parameter tractable. Pages 975–993 of: *Proceedings of the 56th Annual Symposium on Foundations of Computer Science (FOCS)*. IEEE.

Marx, Dániel. 2008. Parameterized complexity and approximation algorithms. *The Computer Journal*, **51**(1), 60–78.
Marx, Dániel. 2009. A parameterized view on matroid optimization problems. *Theoretical Computer Science*, **410**(44), 4471–4479.
Marx, Dániel. 2011. Important Separators and Parameterized Algorithms. Pages 5–10 of: *Graph-Theoretic Concepts in Computer Science—37th International Workshop, WG 2011, Teplá Monastery, Czech Republic, June 21–24, 2011. Revised Papers.*
Marx, Dániel, and Razgon, Igor. 2014. Fixed-parameter tractability of multicut parameterized by the size of the cutset. *SIAM Journal on Computing*, **43**(2), 355–388.
McConnell, Ross M., and de Montgolfier, Fabien. 2005. Linear-time modular decomposition of directed graphs. *Discrete Applied Mathematics*, **145**(2), 198–209.
McConnell, Ross M., and Spinrad, Jeremy P. 1999. Modular decomposition and transitive orientation. *Discrete Mathematics*, **201**(1–3), 189–241.
McCuaig, William, and Shepherd, F. Bruce. 1989. Domination in graphs with minimum degree two. *Journal of Graph Theory*, **13**(6), 749–762.
Menger, Karl. 1927. Zur allgemeinen Kurventheorie. *Fund. Math.*, **10**(1), 96–115.
Misra, Neeldhara. 2010. Infeasibility of polynomial kernelization. MPhil thesis, Institute of Mathematical Sciences.
Misra, Neeldhara, Narayanaswamy, N. S., Raman, Venkatesh, and Shankar, Bal Sri. 2010. Solving Min Ones-2-SAT as Fast as Vertex Cover. Pages 549–555 of: *Proceedings of the 35th International Symposium on Mathematical Foundations of Computer Science (MFCS).* Lecture Notes in Computer Science, vol. 6281. Springer.
Misra, Neeldhara, Raman, Venkatesh, and Saurabh, Saket. 2011. Lower bounds on kernelization. *Discrete Optimization*, **8**(1), 110–128.
Misra, Neeldhara, Philip, Geevarghese, Raman, Venkatesh, and Saurabh, Saket. 2012a. On parameterized independent feedback vertex set. *Theoretical Computer Science*, **461**, 65–75.
Misra, Pranabendu, Raman, Venkatesh, Ramanujan, M. S., and Saurabh, Saket. 2012b. Parameterized algorithms for even cycle transversal. Pages 172–183 of: *Proceedings of the 38th International Workshop on Graph-Theoretic Concepts in Computer Science (WG).* Lecture Notes in Computer Science, vol. 7551. Springer.
Misra, Pranabendu, Raman, Venkatesh, Ramanujan, M. S., and Saurabh, Saket. 2013. A polynomial kernel for feedback arc set on bipartite tournaments. *Theory of Computing Systems*, **53**(4), 609–620.
Möhring, R. H., and Radermacher, F. J. 1984. Substitution decomposition for discrete structures and connections with combinatorial optimization. Pages 257–355 of: *Algebraic and Combinatorial Methods in Operations Research.* North-Holland Math. Stud., vol. 95. North-Holland.
Monien, Burkhard. 1985. How to find long paths efficiently. Pages 239–254 of: *Analysis and Design of Algorithms for Combinatorial Problems (Udine, 1982).* North-Holland Math. Stud., vol. 109. North-Holland.
Moser, Hannes. 2009. A problem kernelization for graph packing. Pages 401–412 of: *Proceedings of the 35th Conference on Current Trends in Theory and Practice*

of Computer Science (SOFSEM). Lecture Notes in Computer Science, vol. 5404. Springer.

Moser, Hannes, and Sikdar, Somnath. 2007. The parameterized complexity of the induced matching problem in planar graphs. Pages 325–336 of: *Proceedings First Annual International Workshop: Frontiers in Algorithmics (FAW)*. Lecture Notes in Computer Science, vol. 4613. Springer.

Murota, Kazuo. 2000. *Matrices and Matroids for Systems Analysis*. Algorithms and Combinatorics, vol. 20. Springer-Verlag.

Narayanaswamy, N. S., Raman, Venkatesh, Ramanujan, M. S., and Saurabh, Saket. 2012. LP can be a cure for parameterized problems. Pages 338–349 of: *Proceedings of the 29th International Symposium on Theoretical Aspects of Computer Science (STACS)*. Leibniz International Proceedings in Informatics (LIPIcs), vol. 14. Schloss Dagstuhl–Leibniz-Zentrum fuer Informatik.

Nemhauser, George L., and Trotter Jr., Leslie E. 1974. Properties of vertex packing and independence system polyhedra. *Mathematical Programming*, **6**(1), 48–61.

Niedermeier, Rolf. 2006. *Invitation to Fixed-Parameter Algorithms*. Oxford Lecture Series in Mathematics and its Applications, vol. 31. Oxford University Press.

Niedermeier, Rolf. 2010. Reflections on multivariate algorithmics and problem parameterization. Pages 17–32 of: *Proceedings of the 27th International Symposium on Theoretical Aspects of Computer Science (STACS)*. Leibniz International Proceedings in Informatics (LIPIcs), vol. 5. Schloss Dagstuhl - Leibniz-Zentrum fuer Informatik.

Oxley, James G. 2010. *Matroid Theory*. 2nd ed. Oxford Graduate Texts in Mathematics, vol. 21. Oxford University Press.

Perfect, Hazel. 1968. Applications of Menger's graph theorem. *Journal of Mathematical Analysis and Applications*, **22**(1), 96 – 111.

Philip, Geevarghese, Raman, Venkatesh, and Sikdar, Somnath. 2012. Polynomial kernels for dominating set in graphs of bounded degeneracy and beyond. *ACM Transactions on Algorithms*, **9**(1), 11.

Pilipczuk, Marcin, Pilipczuk, Michał, Sankowski, Piotr, and van Leeuwen, Erik Jan. 2014. Network sparsification for steiner problems on planar and bounded-genus graphs. Pages 276–285 of: *Proceedings of the 55th Annual Symposium on Foundations of Computer Science (FOCS)*. IEEE Computer Society.

Prieto, Elena. 2005. Systematic kernelization in FPT algorithm design. Ph thesis, The University of Newcastle.

Prieto, Elena, and Sloper, Christian. 2003. Either/or: Using vertex cover structure in designing FPT-algorithms: The case of k-internal spanning tree. Pages 474–483 of: *Proceedings of the 8th International Workshop on Algorithms and Data Structures (WADS 2003)*. Lecture Notes in Computer Science, vol. 2748. Springer.

Prieto, Elena, and Sloper, Christian. 2005. Reducing to independent set structure: The case of k-internal spanning tree. *Nordic Journal of Computing*, **12**(June), 308–318.

Prieto, Elena, and Sloper, Christian. 2006. Looking at the stars. *Theoretical Computer Science*, **351**(3), 437–445.

Raman, Venkatesh, and Saurabh, Saket. 2008. Short cycles make W-hard problems hard: FPT algorithms for W-hard problems in graphs with no short cycles. *Algorithmica*, **52**(2), 203–225.

Raman, Venkatesh, Saurabh, Saket, and Subramanian, C. R. 2006. Faster fixed parameter tractable algorithms for finding feedback vertex sets. *ACM Transactions on Algorithms*, **2**(3), 403–415.

Ramsey, Frank P. 1930. On a problem of formal logic. *Proceedings of the London Mathematical Society*, **S2-30**, 264–286.

Reed, Bruce A. 1997. Tree width and tangles: A new connectivity measure and some applications. Pages 87–162 of: *Surveys in Combinatorics*. London Mathematical Society Lecture Note Series, vol. 241. Cambridge University Press.

Reed, Bruce A., Smith, Kaleigh, and Vetta, Adrian. 2004. Finding odd cycle transversals. *Operations Research Letters*, **32**(4), 299–301.

Robertson, Neil, and Seymour, Paul D. 1984. Graph minors. III. Planar tree-width. *Journal of Combinatorial Theory Series B*, **36**(1), 49–64.

Robertson, Neil, and Seymour, Paul D. 1986a. Graph minors. II. Algorithmic aspects of tree-width. *Journal of Algorithms*, **7**(3), 309–322.

Robertson, Neil, and Seymour, Paul D. 1986b. Graph minors. V. Excluding a planar graph. *Journal of Combinatorial Theory Series B*, **41**(1), 92–114.

Robertson, Neil, Seymour, Paul D., and Thomas, Robin. 1994. Quickly excluding a planar graph. *Journal of Combinatorial Theory Series B*, **62**(2), 323–348.

Salavatipour, Mohammad R., and Verstraëte, Jacques. 2005. Disjoint cycles: Integrality gap, hardness, and approximation. Pages 51–65 of: *Proceedings of the 11th International Conference on Integer Programming and Combinatorial Optimization (IPCO)*, vol. 3509. Springer.

Saurabh, Saket, and Zehavi, Meirav. 2016. $(k, n - k)$-Max-Cut: An $O^*(2^p)$-time algorithm and a polynomial kernel. Pages 686–699 of: *Proceedings of the 12th Latin American Theoretical Informatics Symposium (LATIN)*. Lecture Notes in Computer Science, vol. 9644. Springer.

Savage, Carla. 1982. Depth-first search and the vertex cover problem. *Information Processing Letters*, **14**(5), 233–235.

Schrijver, Alexander. 2003. *Combinatorial Optimization: Polyhedra and Efficiency*. Vol. A. Springer-Verlag.

Schwartz, Jacob T. 1980. Fast probabilistic algorithms for verification of polynomial identities. *Journal of ACM*, **27**(4), 701–717.

Seymour, Paul D., and Thomas, Robin. 1994. Call routing and the ratcatcher. *Combinatorica*, **14**(2), 217–241.

Shamir, Ron, Sharan, Roded, and Tsur, Dekel. 2004. Cluster graph modification problems. *Discrete Applied Mathematics*, **144**(1–2), 173–182.

Siebertz, Sebastian. 2017. Lossy kernels for connected distance-r domination on nowhere dense graph classes. *CoRR*, **abs/1707.09819**.

Soleimanfallah, Arezou, and Yeo, Anders. 2011. A kernel of order $2k - c$ for Vertex Cover. *Discrete Mathematics*, **311**(10–11), 892–895.

Telle, Jan Arne, and Villanger, Yngve. 2012. FPT algorithms for domination in biclique-free graphs. Pages 802–812 of: *Proceedings of the 20th Annual European Symposium on Algorithms (ESA)*. Lecture Notes Computer Science, vol. 7501. Springer.

Thomassé, Stéphan. 2010. A quadratic kernel for feedback vertex set. *ACM Transactions on Algorithms*, **6**(2), 32.1–32.8.

Tutte, William T. 1966. *Connectivity in Graphs.* Mathematical Expositions, No. 15. University of Toronto Press and Oxford University Press.

Tuza, Zsolt. 1994. Applications of the set-pair method in extremal hypergraph theory. Pages 479–514 of: *Extremal Problems for Finite Sets (Visegrád, 1991).* Bolyai Society Mathematical Studies, vol. 3. János Bolyai Mathematical Society.

Tuza, Zsolt. 1996. Applications of the set-pair method in extremal problems. II. Pages 459–490 of: *Combinatorics, Paul Erdős is Eighty, Vol. 2 (Keszthely, 1993).* Bolyai Society Mathematical Studies, vol. 2. János Bolyai Mathematical Society.

van Rooij, Johan M. M., Bodlaender, Hans L., and Rossmanith, Peter. 2009. Dynamic programming on tree decompositions using generalised fast subset convolution. Pages 566–577 of: *Proceedings of the 17th Annual European Symposium on Algorithms (ESA).* Lecture Notes in Computer Science, vol. 5757. Springer.

Vazirani, Vijay V. 2001. *Approximation Algorithms.* Springer-Verlag.

Wahlström, Magnus. 2013. Abusing the Tutte M=matrix: An algebraic instance compression for the K-set-cycle problem. Pages 341–352 of: *Proceedings of the 30th International Symposium on Theoretical Aspects of Computer Science (STACS).* Leibniz International Proceedings in Informatics (LIPIcs), vol. 20. Schloss Dagstuhl - Leibniz-Zentrum fuer Informatik.

Wang, Jianxin, Ning, Dan, Feng, Qilong, and Chen, Jianer. 2010. An improved kernelization for P_2-packing. *Information Processing Letters,* **110**(5), 188–192.

Wang, Jianxin, Yang, Yongjie, Guo, Jiong, and Chen, Jianer. 2013. Planar graph vertex partition for linear problem kernels. *Journal of Computer System Sciences,* **79**(5), 609–621.

Weller, Mathias. 2013. Aspects of preprocessing applied to combinatorial graph problems. Ph thesis, Universitatsverlag der TU Berlin.

Welsh, Dominic J. A. 2010. *Matroid Theory.* Courier Dover Publications.

Williams, Virginia Vassilevska. 2012. Multiplying matrices faster than Coppersmith-Winograd. Pages 887–898 of: *Proceedings of the 44th Symposium on Theory of Computing Conference (STOC 2012).* ACM.

Wu, Yu, Austrin, Per, Pitassi, Toniann, and Liu, David. 2014. Inapproximability of treewidth and related problems. *Journal of Artificial Intelligence Research,* **49**, 569–600.

Xiao, Mingyu. 2014. A new linear kernel for undirected Planar Feedback Vertex Set: Smaller and simpler. Pages 288–298 of: *Proceedings of the 10th International Conference on Algorithmic Aspects in Information and Managemen (AAIM).* Lecture Notes in Computer Science, vol. 8546. Springer.

Xiao, Mingyu. 2017a. Linear kernels for separating a graph into components of bounded size. *Journal of Computer System Sciences,* **88**, 260–270.

Xiao, Mingyu. 2017b. On a generalization of Nemhauser and Trotter's local optimization theorem. *Journal of Computer System Sciences,* **84**, 97–106.

Xiao, Mingyu, and Guo, Jiong. 2015. A quadratic vertex kernel for feedback arc set in bipartite tournaments. *Algorithmica,* **71**(1), 87–97.

Xiao, Mingyu, and Kou, Shaowei. 2016. Almost induced matching: Linear kernels and parameterized algorithms. Pages 220–232 of: *Proceedings of the 42nd International Workshop on Graph-Theoretic Concepts in Computer Science (WG).* Lecture Notes in Computer Science, vol. 9941. Springer.

Xiao, Mingyu, Kloks, Ton, and Poon, Sheung-Hung. 2013. New parameterized algorithms for the edge dominating set problem. *Theoretical Computer Science*, **511**, 147–158.

Zippel, Richard. 1979. Probabilistic algorithms for sparse polynomials. Pages 216–226 of: *Proceedings of the International Symposium on Symbolic and Algebraic Computation (EUROSAM)*. Lecture Notes in Computer Science, vol. 72. Springer.

Author Index

Abu-Khzam, Faisal N., 59, 60, 132, 252, 470
Agarwal, Amit, 182, 214
Agrawal, Akanksha, 83, 466
Alber, Jochen, 252, 314, 315
Alon, Noga, 236, 390, 423, 426
Arkin, Esther M., 465
Arnborg, Stefan, 285, 296, 354
Arora, Sanjeev, 361, 375
Austrin, Per, 296

Bafna, Vineet, 47, 49, 253
Baker, Brenda S., 315
Balasubramanian, R., 31
Bansal, Nikhil, 162
Barak, Boaz, 361, 375
Bartlett, Andrew, 11
Bar-Yehuda, Reuven, 49, 253
Basavaraju, Manu, 236
Bellman, Richard, 214
Berge, Claude, 476
Berman, Piotr, 47, 49, 253
Bessy, Stephane, 468
Betzler, Nadja, 252
Binkele-Raible, Daniel, 49, 397, 438, 439
Björklund, Andreas, 469
Bliznets, Ivan, 468
Blum, Avrim, 162
Bodlaender, Hans L., xii, 11, 31, 49, 59, 83, 214, 252, 265, 296, 314–315, 317, 330, 338, 354, 375–376, 388, 397, 411, 465
Bollobás, Béla, 214, 355
Bonamy, Marthe, 252
Bondy, Adrian, 476
Bonsma, Paul S., 48
Borchers, Al, 461, 462
Brooks, Leonard R., 355
Brüggemann, Tobias, 48
Bunch, James R., 214, 236
Burrage, Kevin, 49, 83

Buss, Jonathan F., 31
Byrka, Jaroslaw, 465

Cai, Leizhen, 163
Cai, Liming, 11
Cai, Yufei, 163
Cao, Yixin, 120, 162
Charikar, Moses, 182, 214
Chartier, Timothy P., 11
Chawla, Shuchi, 162
Chekuri, Chandra, 296
Chen, Guantao, 432
Chen, Jianer, 11, 60, 104, 120, 162, 252, 467, 469
Chen, Xue, 236
Chen, Zhi-Zhong, 162
Chlebík, Miroslav, 60, 104
Chlebíková, Janka, 60, 104
Chor, Benny, 59
Chuzhoy, Julia, 296
Collins, Rebecca L., 59
Condon, Anne, xi
Cook, Stephen A., 11
Cormen, Thomas H., 344
Corneil, Derek G., 162
Courcelle, Bruno, 279, 284, 296, 354
Crowston, Robert, 236
Cygan, Marek, xiii, 7, 11, 30–31, 51, 132, 182, 214, 279, 296, 360, 375, 388, 397, 411, 465

Daligault, Jean, 49, 439
de Fluiter, Babette, 354
Dehne, Frank K. H. A., 49, 120
Dell, Holger, 411, 426, 469, 470
Demaine, Erik D., 253, 291, 297, 301, 315, 354
DeMillo, Richard A., 168
de Montgolfier, Fabien, 162

Diestel, Reinhard, 476
Dinur, Irit, 465, 470
Dom, Michael, 31, 163, 376, 388, 397, 465
Dorn, Frederic, 315
Downey, Rodney G., xii, 8, 11, 30, 315, 375–376
Drange, Pål Grønås, 83, 265, 296, 355
Dregi, Markus S., 83, 265, 296
Dregi, Markus Sortland, 355
Dreyfus, Stuart E., 462
Drucker, Andrew, 425, 426
Du, Ding-Zhu, 461–462
Dvořák, Pavel, 466
Dvorak, Zdenek, 30

Edelsbrunner, Herbert, xi
Edmonds, Jack, 182
Eiben, Eduard, 466
Emerson, E. Allen, xi
Erdős, Paul, 132, 455
Estivill-Castro, Vladimir, 48, 49–83, 439

Feige, Uriel, 265, 296, 315
Feldmann, Andreas Emil, 466
Fellows, Michael R., xii, 8, 11, 30–31, 48–49, 59, 60, 83, 104, 120, 236, 314, 315, 354, 375–376, 439, 465–466
Feng, Qilong, 60
Fernau, Henning, 49, 252, 315, 397, 438–439
Flum, Jörg, 11, 30, 132, 438
Fomin, Fedor V., xiii, 7, 11, 30–31, 49, 51, 83, 120, 163, 182, 215, 265, 279, 293, 296, 297, 301, 314–315, 326, 354, 355, 360, 375, 397, 438, 439, 465, 468
Ford Jr., Lester R., 182
Fortnow, Lance, xi, 375, 388
Francis, Mathew C., 236
Frank, András, 107, 120
Frankl, Peter, 214
Friggstad, Zachary, 465
Fujito, Toshihiro, 47, 49, 253
Fulkerson, Delbert R., 182

Gajarský, Jakub, 355
Gall, François Le, 182, 214
Gallai, Tibor, 83, 162
Ganian, Robert, 355
Garnero, Valentin, 355
Gaspers, Serge, 31, 120, 163
Geiger, Dan, 49, 253
Goldsmith, Judy, 31
Golovach, Petr A., 293
Gramm, Jens, 31, 162
Grandoni, Fabrizio, 132, 465
Grohe, Martin, 11, 30, 132, 438
Gu, Qian-Ping, 291
Guillemot, Sylvain, 163

Guo, Jiong, 11, 31, 104, 162–163, 252, 314, 457
Gutin, Gregory, 31, 49, 236, 376
Gyárfás, András, 31

Haber, Stuart, xi
Habib, Michel, 162
Hagerup, Torben, 253, 354
Hajiaghayi, MohammadTaghi, 253, 265, 291, 296, 297, 301, 315, 354
Halin, Rudolf, 296
Hall, Philip, 50, 59
Halldórsson, Magnús M., 465
Har-Peled, Sariel, 438
Hassin, Refael, 465
Havet, Frédéric, 163
Heggernes, Pinar, 60, 468
Held, Michael, 214
Hermelin, Danny, xii, 132, 375–376, 411, 436–437, 439, 465, 473
Hlinený, Petr, 355
Hols, Eva-Maria C., 215, 472
Hopcroft, John E., 51, 59, 214, 236, 433, 434
Hüffner, Falk, 11, 31, 162–163
Husfeldt, Thore, 469

Iwata, Yoichi, 11

Jansen, Bart M. P., 31, 48–49, 59, 375, 376, 397, 411, 439, 468, 472
Jia, Weijia, 104, 469
Jiang, Tao, 162
Jones, Mark, 49, 236
Juedes, David W., 59
Jukna, Stasys, 132, 214

Kaibel, Volker, 11
Kalai, Gil, 214
Kammer, Frank, 296
Kanj, Iyad A., 104, 252, 314, 469
Kaplan, Haim, 438, 468
Karp, Richard M., xi, 51, 59, 214
Karzanov, Alexander V., 59
Kawarabayashi, Ken-ichi, 291, 296
Khot, Subhash, 411, 465
Khuller, Samir, 104
Khuzam, Mazen Bou, 252
Kim, Eun Jung, 49, 83, 236, 355
Király, Tamás, 107, 120
Kleitman, Daniel J., 34–35
Kloks, Ton, 253, 315, 471
Knop, Dušan, 466
Kobayashi, Yusuke, 291, 296
Koch, Thorsten, 11
Kolay, Sudeshna, 83
König, Dénes, 50, 59
Kou, Shaowei, 83

Kowalik, Lukasz, xiii, 7, 11, 30, 51, 182, 252, 279, 296, 360, 375, 465
Kratsch, Dieter, 468
Kratsch, Stefan, 31, 59, 163, 169, 182, 214–216, 375–376, 388, 397, 411, 420, 425, 426, 436–437, 439, 469, 471–473
Kreutzer, Stephan, 355
Kriesell, Matthias, 107, 120
Krithika, R., 466
Kulik, Ariel, 465, 466
Kumar, Mithilesh, 83, 104, 466
Kwon, O-joung, 83

Lagergren, Jens, 285
Lampis, Michael, 104, 236
Langer, Alexander, 355
Langston, Michael A., 48–49, 59, 83, 104, 354, 439
Langville, Amy N., 11
Lawler, Eugene L., 182
Le, Tien-Nam, 83, 163, 471
Leaf, Alexander, 296
Lee, James R., 265, 296
Leiserson, Charles E., 344
Leivant, Daniel, xi
Li, Wenjun, 120
Lidický, Bernard, 30
Lin, Guohui, 162
Linial, Nathan, 34–35
Lipton, Richard J., xi, 168
Liu, David, 296
Liu, Yang, 467
Lokshtanov, Daniel, xiii, 7, 11, 30, 48–49, 51, 59, 83, 104, 120, 163, 182, 215, 252, 265, 279, 296, 314, 315, 326, 354–355, 360, 375–376, 388, 397, 438–439, 464–468, 471
Loréa, Michel, 107
Lovász, László, 59, 120, 214–215
Lu, Songjian, 120, 467
Lynch, Nancy, xi

Mac, Shev, 49, 83
Mahajan, Meena, 218, 236
Majumdar, Diptapriyo, 31
Makarychev, Konstantin, 182, 214, 236
Makarychev, Yury, 182, 214, 236
Marx, Dániel, xiii, 7, 11, 30, 51, 182, 214–215, 279, 296, 360, 375, 411, 465
Masařík, Tomáš, 466
McConnell, Ross M., 162
McCuaig, William, 47
Meng, Jie, 162
Menger, Karl, 182, 296
Misra, Neeldhara, 11, 48–49, 83, 104, 315, 355, 388, 468
Misra, Pranabendu, 83, 163, 182, 466

Mitsou, Valia, 236
Mnich, Matthias, 30, 48, 236, 252, 314
Möhring, R. H., 162
Monien, Burkhard, 214
Moser, Hannes, 60, 104, 252, 314
Mouawad, Amer E., 83, 466
Muciaccia, Gabriele, 31, 236, 376
Mulzer, Wolfgang, 438
Murota, Kazuo, 214
Murty, Ram M., 476

Naor, Joseph, 49, 253
Narayanaswamy, N. S., 104, 182, 214
Nederlof, Jesper, 214
Nemhauser, George L., 104
Niedermeier, Rolf, 11, 30, 31, 104, 162–163, 252, 314–315, 457
Ning, Dan, 60

Obdržálek, Jan, 355
Ordyniak, Sebastian, 355
O'Sullivan, Barry, 467
Oxley, James G., 182

Panolan, Fahad, 182, 215, 464–467
Papadimitriou, Christos H., xi
Parberry, Ian, xi
Paul, Christophe, 31, 162–163, 355
Pelsmajer, Michael J., 252, 314
Penninkx, Eelko, 252, 314–315, 354
Perez, Anthony, 31, 163, 468
Perfect, Hazel, 182
Perl, Yehoshua, 162
Philip, Geevarghese, 31, 83, 132, 236, 355, 420, 426
Pilipczuk, Marcin, xiii, 7, 11, 30–31, 51, 182, 279, 296, 355, 360, 375, 388, 397, 411, 439, 465, 468–469, 472
Pilipczuk, Michał, 265, 296, 355, 468, 469
Pitassi, Toniann, 296
Plummer, Michael D., 59
Poon, Sheung-Hung, 253, 471
Pósa, Louis, 455
Prieto, Elena, 49, 59–60, 83, 120
Prieto-Rodriguez, Elena, 49
Proskurowski, Andrzej, 296, 354

Rabin, Michael, xi
Radermacher, F. J., 162
Rado, Richard, 121, 132
Rafiey, Arash, 31
Rai, Ashutosh, 236, 466
Raman, Venkatesh, 11, 31, 83, 104, 132, 163, 182, 214, 218, 236, 315, 388, 411, 456, 468
Ramanujan, M. S., 83, 163, 182, 214, 236, 355, 464–467

Ramsey, Frank P., 411
Rankin, Timothy D., 11
Ray, Saurabh, 420, 426
Razgon, Igor, 216, 467
Reed, Bruce A., 182, 296
Regev, Oded, 465
Reidl, Felix, 355
Rivest, Ronald L., 344
Robertson, Neil, 290–291, 296
Roditty, Liam, 438
Rosamond, Frances A., 48–49, 60, 83, 120, 236, 439, 465–466
Rosenberg, Arnold, xi
Rossmanith, Peter, 296, 355
Roth, Ron M., 49, 253
Rothvoß, Thomas, 465
Royer, James S., xi
Ruzsa, Imre Z., 236

Safra, Samuel, 465, 470
Salavatipour, Mohammad R., 465
Sanità, Laura, 465
Sankowski, Piotr, 469
Santhanam, Rahul, 375, 388
Sau, Ignasi, 355
Saurabh, Saket, xiii, 7, 11, 30, 31, 48–49, 51, 83, 120, 163, 182, 214–215, 236, 252, 279, 296, 314–315, 326, 354–355, 360, 375–376, 388, 397, 438–439, 456, 464–468, 471
Savage, Carla, 465
Savage, John, xi
Schaefer, Marcus, 252, 314
Schrijver, Alexander, 59
Schwartz, Jacob T., 168
Seese, Detlef, 285, 354
Seiferth, Paul, 438
Selman, Alan L., xi
Seymour, Paul D., 265, 290–291, 296
Shachnai, Hadas, 465, 466
Shamir, Ron, 162, 468
Shankar, Bal Sri, 104
Sharan, Roded, 162
Sharir, Micha, 438
Shaw, Peter, 120
Shepherd, F. Bruce, 47
Siebertz, Sebastian, 355, 466
Sikdar, Somnath, 31, 132, 236, 252, 314–355
Slivovsky, Friedrich, 355
Sloper, Christian, 49, 59–60, 120
Smith, Carl, xi
Smith, Kaleigh, 182
Soleimanfallah, Arezou, 104
Soltys, Karolina, 436, 437, 439, 473
Spinrad, Jeremy P., 162
Stein, Clifford, 344
Stewart, Lorna K., 162

Strømme, Torstein, 31
Sturtevant, Dean G., 34–35
Subramanian, C. R., 456
Suters, W. Henry, 59, 104
Symons, Christopher T., 59
Szeider, Stefan, 31, 236, 355

Tale, Prafullkumar, 466
Tamaki, Hisao, 291
Tan, Richard B., 252, 314
Tardos, Eva, xi
Tarjan, Robert E., 433, 434, 468
Taslaman, Nina, 469
Telle, Jan Arne, 60, 132
Thilikos, Dimitrios M., 293, 297, 301, 314–315, 326, 354–355
Tholey, Torsten, 296
Thomas, Robin, 265, 291, 296
Thomassé, Stéphan, 11, 31, 120, 163, 236, 388, 397, 465
Todinca, Ioan, 265, 296
Toufar, Tomáš, 466
Trotter, Leslie E., Jr., 104
Truß, Anke, 31, 163
Tsur, Dekel, 162
Tutte, William T., 433, 439
Tuza, Zsolt, 214

van Antwerpen-de Fluiter, Babette, 317, 354
van Dijk, Thomas C., 49, 83
van Iersel, Leo, 236
van Leeuwen, Erik Jan, 469
van Melkebeek, Dieter, 411, 426, 469, 470
van Rooij, Johan M. M., 296
van 't Hof, Pim, 83
Vazirani, Vijay V., 462
Verstraëte, Jacques, 465
Veselý, Pavel, 466
Vetta, Adrian, 182
Villaamil, Fernando Sánchez, 355
Villanger, Yngve, 49, 132, 265, 296, 355, 397, 438, 439
Vitter, Jeffrey Scott, xi

Wagner, Robert A., 462
Wahlström, Magnus, 31, 163, 469
Wang, Jianxin, 60, 120, 252
Weller, Mathias, 439
Welsh, Dominic J. A., 182
Wernicke, Sebastian, 11, 252, 314, 457
West, Douglas B., 34–35
Willert, Max, 438
Williams, Ryan, 236
Williams, Virginia Vassilevska, 214

Author Index

Woeginger, Gerhard J., 48
Wojtaszczyk, Jakub Onufry, 388, 397, 411
Wrochna, Marcin, 439, 472
Wu, Xi, 411, 436, 437, 439, 473
Wu, Yu, 296

Xia, Ge, 252, 314
Xiao, Mingyu, 49, 83, 104, 163, 252, 253, 471

Yang, Yongjie, 252
Yeo, Anders, 11, 31, 49, 104, 236, 376, 388, 397, 465
Yu, Xingxing, 432
Yuster, Raphael, 390

Zehavi, Meirav, 31, 83, 163, 182, 471
Zhou, Yuan, 236
Zippel, Richard, 168
Zwick, Uri, 390

Index

$+$, 185
M-sum-free, 228
$[n]$, 185
NP/poly, 361
$\alpha(G)$, 475
$\boxplus_k$
    see $k \times k$-grid, 290
•, 185
○, 185
coNP $\subseteq$ NP/poly, 361
$\gamma(G)$, 475
$\mathbb{F}_2$, 222, 480
$\omega(G)$, 475
$\oplus$, 165
$k \times k$-grid, 290
k-CNF formula, 89
k-colored dominating set, 384
k-mini set cover, 219
q-CNF, **476**
q-star, 61
x-flower, 76
$\binom{[n]}{i}$, 185
$\mathcal{G}$-module, 138
(2SAT), 93
(IP2), 92
INTEGER LINEAR PROGRAMMING (IP), 84
LINEAR PROGRAMMING (LP), 84
rwb-dominating set, 22

adhesion, 432
algorithm
    ApproximatingCOC, 71
    ComputeGoodFamilies, 271
    ComputeMaximalModule, 136
    GreedyMiniSet$(\mathcal{S}, k)$, 219
    GreedySystem, 227

antichain length, 275
apex graph, 355
apex-minor-free graph, 355
assignment
    weight, 89
atomic formula, 282
automorphism, 476

bag, 259
Bell number, 248
bidimensional problem, **300**
bidimensionality, **300**, 298–313
bitsize, **10**
Boolean variable, 89, 381
boundary, 260
bridge, 35
Brook's theorem, 350, 355

Cauchy-Schwarz inequality, 161
chess, 1
chromatic number, 54, 350
clause, 89, **381**, **476**
clique, 475
closest set, 196
CMSO-optimization problem, **318**, 318, 353
CNF, 89
CNF formula, 89, **476**
    closure, 91
cochromatic number, 468
cocoloring, 468
communication transcript, 413
complement, 54
complement of a hypergraph, 404
composition
    AND-, 425
    AND-cross-, 425–426

510

cross-, **366**, 367, 368, 376, 426
OR-, 375
weak, 411
weak cross-, **399**, 400
compression, 177, 367, 469
conjunctive normal form, 89, **476**
connected component, 475
connected dominating set, 305
connected set, 239, 333
contraction-bidimensional, 300
Cook-Levin theorem, 11
Cook's theorem, 202
cotree, 148
Counting Monadic Second Order logic
    $CMSO_2$, 286
Courcelle's theorem, 284–286
critical clique, 139
Crown Decomposition, 50, 51
CSP
    constraint satisfaction problem, 199
cut
    vertex, 203
cut-covering lemma, 202
cut-width, 426
cutvertex, 475
cycle, 475

degree modulator, 25
dimension, 399
directed non-blocker set, 48
disjoint factor property, 379
disjoint union $\dot{\cup}$, 147
distance, 475
distillation, 360
    AND-, 425
    bounded-, **360**
    OR-, **360**, 368
dominating set, 22, 47, 277
double clique, 42

edge
    subdivided, 36
edge cover, 475
efficient polynomial size approximate
    kernelization scheme, **454**
EPSAKS
    see, efficient polynomial size approximate
        kernelization scheme, 454
Erdős-Rado lemma, 121
Euler's formula, 237, 243, 435
excess, 226, 234

Excluded Grid Minor theorem, 291
expander, 295
expansion
    q-expansion, 62
    weighted q-expansion, 66, 67, 98
explicit induced subgraph representation, 345
exponential time hypothesis, 8

factor, 379
feedback arc set, 21
feedback vertex set, 40
finite integer index, 322, 339, 354
fixed-parameter tractability, 7
fixed-parameter tractable, **7**
forest, 475
Four Color Theorem, 17
function
    disjointness, 201
    matroidal, 202

Galois field, 222
gammoid, 194, 182
Gaussian elimination, 170
Generalized Laplace expansion, 187
GF(2), 222
girth, 475
good family, 270, 275
graph, 474
    3-connected, 432
    K_4-minor-free, 294
    P_4, 147
    d-degenerate, 124
    k-tree, 295
    boundaried, 319
    cluster, 139
    cograph, 147
    connected, 475
    expander, 295
    Gaifmann, 105
    implication digraph of CNF formula, 90
    incidence, 105
    outerplanar, 294
    planar, 17, 237
    primal, 105
    prime, 134
    quotient, 137
    variable-clause incidence, 56

half-integral solution, 86
Hall's Theorem, 50
    strong Hall's condition, 106

512 Index

Hamiltonian cycle, 475
Hamiltonian graph, 364
Hamiltonian path, 364, 475
Hopcroft-Karp algorithm, 51
hyperclique, 404
hyperforest, 105
hypergraph, 105
   2-coloring, 108
   partition-connected, 107
hypertree, 105

independent set, 17, 475
inductive priorities, 32
instance
   malformed, **366**, 366
   well-formed, **366**, 366
instance selector, 378
interval graph, 468
isomorphic graphs, 475
isomorphism, 476
iterative compression, 173

join $\otimes$, 147

Kőnig's Minimax Theorem, 50, 88
kernel
   for optimization problem, 447
   polynomial, 8
   size, 8
kernelization, 8
   approximate, 449
   trivial, 16

least common ancestor, 153
least common ancestor closure, 153, 245, 308
linear separability, 301
linear-separable problem, 301
linked, 168
literal, 89, **476**
lossy kernelization, 441–464

matching, 50, 88, 475
matroid, 164
   basis, 165
   direct sum $\oplus$, 165
   dual, 167
   gammoid, 168
   graphic, 167
   linear, 165
   partition, 166
   rank, 165
   representable, 165
   transversal, 167
   uniform, 166
matroid axioms, 164
matroid property
   hereditary, **165**
maximum matching, 89
Menger's theorem, 169, 196, 198, 206
minimal separator, 433
minor, 295, 432
model, 258
modular partition, 134
   factor, 138
   maximal, 134
   nontrivial, 134
   trivial, 134
module, 133
   $\mathcal{G}$-, 138
   maximal, 134
   strong, 134
   trivial, 134
   undirected, 133
Monadic Second Order logic
   MSO_1, 281
   MSO_2, 279, 281
multicolored biclique, 401

neighborhood closure, 203
neighborhood partition, 336, 347
node, 258
nonblocker set, 47

odd cycle transversal, 173
operation
   $+$, 185
   $\bullet$, 185
   $\circ$, 185
   $\dot{\cup}$, 147, 408
   $\otimes$, 147, 408
   $\oplus$, 165
oracle, 430
oracle communication protocol, 413
oracle Turing machines, 438
Order Type Representation, 423

parameterized problem, **6**
partially polynomial kernel, 222
partition connectedness, 106
path, 475
   alternating, 475
   augmentig, 475

Index

pathwidth, 426
permutation graph, 468
polynomial compression, **9**, 9–11, 367–403
polynomial equivalence relation, **366**, 375
polynomial parameter transformation, **389**, 403
polynomial size approximate kernelization scheme, **454**, 454
PPT, 389, 437
preference relation, 269, 275, 277, 311
problem
    bidimensional, 318, 331–332, 353
    $(k, n-k)$-MAXCUT, 30–31, 477
    $(n-k)$-SET COVER, 218–220, 477
    2-SAT, 93, 95, 477
    3-COLORING, 477
    3-SAT, 404–405, 418
    $K_{1,d}$-PACKING, 48, 477
    T-CYCLE, 469
    $\mathcal{F}$-COMPLETION, 163
    $\mathcal{F}$-DELETION, 163
    $\mathcal{F}$-EDITING, 163
    $\mathcal{F}$-deletion, 49, 468
    ϕ-MAXIMIZATION, 298–299
    ϕ-MINIMIZATION, 298–299
    d-HITTING SET, 59–60, 122–123, 132, 212, 398, 404–407, 411, 418–419, 470, 477
    d-SET PACKING, 59, 123–124, 132, 477
    d-SUBSET CSP, 200–202, 215, 477
    q-COLORING, 294, 313
    ALMOST 2-SAT, 213–215, 472, 478
    ALMOST INDUCED MATCHING, 82, 83, 478
    BLOCK DELETION SET, 82, 83
    CAPACITATED VERTEX COVER, 396, 397, 478
    CHORDAL COMPLETION, 468
    CHROMATIC NUMBER/VC, 464
    CHROMATIC NUMBER, 294, 313
    CLIQUE (VC), 359, 371–374, 429–431, 464
    CLIQUE, 7, 371–376, 437–438, 478
    CLUSTER EDITING, 29, 133, 139, 145, 162, 478
    CLUSTER VERTEX DELETION, 65, 83, 470, 471, 478
    CMSO-optimization, **318**, 332, 353
    CNF-SAT, 6, 7, 11, 16, 377, 381, 382, 388, 405, 412, 478
    COGRAPH COMPLETION, 133, 147, 150–151, 153, 155, 163, 478
    COLORED RED-BLUE DOMINATING SET, 377, 383–388, 392–394, 478
    COMPONENT ORDER CONNECTIVITY, 61, 70–71, 82–84, 96, 98–99, 101–104, 478
    CONNECTED DOMINATING SET, 48, 294, 302, 314, 319, 353, 478
    CONNECTED FEEDBACK VERTEX SET, 294, 314, 319, 353
    CONNECTED VERTEX COVER, 238–239, 243, 252, 294, 314, 319, 353, 395–397, 436, 438, 440–441, 458, 461, 465, 478
    contraction-bidimensional, 313
    contraction-closed, 299
    CUT-COVERING, 203
    CYCLE PACKING, 294, 298–299, 313–314, 391, 438, 440–441, 444, 455–456, 465, 478
    DIGRAPH PAIR CUT, 193–200, 211, 214–215, 479
    DIRECTED FEEDBACK VERTEX SET, 467
    DIRECTED MAX LEAF, 49, 439
    DISJOINT FACTORS, 377, 379–380, 387–388, 391, 479
    DOMINATING SET (VC), 252, 310, 313
    DOMINATING SET, 8, 15, 22, 24, 31, 124–126, 129, 132, 252, 276–279, 296–298, 302, 305, 306, 309–311, 313–315, 319, 353, 355, 383, 479
    DUAL COLORING, 50, 52, 54–55, 479
    EDGE CLIQUE COVER, 15–16, 28, 31, 359, 426, 479
    EDGE DISJOINT CYCLE PACKING, 391, 397, 479
    EDGE DOMINATING SET, 238, 241, 243, 252, 253, 471, 479
    EVEN CYCLE TRANSVERSAL, 82, 83
    FAST, 21, 31, 133, 158–160, 163
    FEEDBACK ARC SET IN TOURNAMENTS, 15–16, 21, 479
    FEEDBACK VERTEX COVER/TREEWIDTH-η MODULATOR, 464
    FEEDBACK VERTEX SET, 11, 32, 40–41, 47, 49, 61, 73–81, 83, 215, 243, 246–247, 252–253, 294, 313–314, 319, 353, 355, 391, 398, 403–404, 411, 419, 467, 470, 472, 479
    FEEDBACK VERTEX SET IN TOURNAMENTS, 163, 471
    HAMILTONIAN CYCLE, 294, 313
    HAMILTONIAN PATH, 114, 183–184, 214, 294, 313, 364, 367, 479

problem (cont.)
   HITTING SET, 132, 383, 392, 394, 397, 436–437, 466, 479
   INDEPENDENT DOMINATING SET, 313, 326, 479
   INDEPENDENT FEEDBACK VERTEX SET, 82–83
   INDEPENDENT SET, 17, 30, 268–269, 271, 273–276, 279, 296, 300–302, 324–326, 354, 479
   INTERVAL COMPLETION, 468
   linear-separable, 301
   LIST COLORING, 294–295
   LONGEST CYCLE (VC), 29, 57–58
   LONGEST CYCLE, 50, 57, 294, 313, 438, 473, 479
   LONGEST PATH, 183–184, 214, 294, 313, 354, 359–360, 364–365, 376, 390, 438, 439, 466, 472–473, 480
   LOW-RANK GOOD SET TESTING, 199
   MAX LEAF SPANNING TREE, 33, 48, 480
   MAX LEAF SUBTREE, 32–34, 36, 38–40, 47, 48, 429, 431, 438, 439, 480
   MAX-3-SAT, 15–17
   MAX-r-LIN-2, 223, 230–232, 234–236, 480
   MAX-r-SAT, 231, 236, 480
   MAX-Er-SAT, 231–232, 234–236, 480
   MAX-INTERNAL SPANNING TREE/VC, 58
   MAX-INTERNAL SPANNING TREE, 58–59, 105, 114, 120, 480
   MAX-LIN-2, 222–223, 225, 227, 235–236, 480
   MAX-LIN-2 AA, 235
   MAXCUT, 109, 217, 235, 294, 313, 480
   MAXIMUM SATISFIABILITY, 16, 50, 55–57, 480
   MIN-ONES-2-SAT, 84, 90, 92–93, 95, 480
   MIN-ONES-r-SAT, 436–437
   MIN-WEIGHT-2-IP, 84, 95, 480
   MULTICOLORED BICLIQUE, 401–404, 481
   MULTICUT, 216
   NONBLOCKER, 47, 481
   ODD CYCLE TRANSVERSAL, 164, 173, 174, 177, 179, 180, 182, 183, 202, 211–212, 215, 294, 313, 419, 471, 481
   ODD SUBGRAPH, 29, 481
   OPTIMAL LINEAR ARRANGEMENT, 31, 445, 465, 481
   parameterized optimization, 441
   PARTIAL VERTEX COVER, 440, 441, 457, 464, 481
   PARTITION CUT-FLOW, 169, 173
   PARTITION INTO MONOTONE SUBSEQUENCES, 468
   PATH CONTRACTION, 464
   PATH PACKING, 390–391, 397
   PLANAR INDEPENDENT SET, 15–17
   PLANAR LONGEST CYCLE, 429, 431–434, 438, 481
   PLANAR VERTEX DELETION, 467–468, 481
   POINT LINE COVER, 4, 6, 29, 412, 419–424, 426, 481
   PROPER INTERVAL COMPLETION, 468
   RAMSEY, 408–412, 426, 481
   RED-BLUE DOMINATING SET, 125–126, 128–129, 383–384, 388, 392–397, 481
   REFINEMENT RAMSEY, 408–411
   separable, 301, 314, 318, 331–332, 339, 353
   SET COVER, 218, 383, 392, 394, 397, 437, 466, 481
   SET SPLITTING, 105, 108–111, 113, 114, 119, 120, 481
   SIMULTANEOUS FEEDBACK VERTEX SET, 82–83
   STEINER TREE, 285, 359, 369–371, 376, 394, 395, 438, 440–441, 461–462, 465, 482
   SUBSET FEEDBACK VERTEX SET, 472
   TREE CONTRACTION, 464
   TREEWIDTH-η MODULATOR, 302, 303, 314–315, 319, 353, 482
   TREEWIDTH, 412, 426, 482
   VERTEX COLORING, 294
   VERTEX COVER, 4, 8, 15–16, 18–20, 25, 30–31, 35, 50, 52–54, 59, 61, 70, 76, 84, 86–87, 90, 92–93, 95, 104, 191–194, 199–200, 215, 239, 284–285, 302, 319, 353, 396, 398–399, 401–404, 411, 418–420, 443–444, 450–451, 469–470, 472, 482
   VERTEX COVER (DEGREE-1-MODULATOR), 25, 31
   VERTEX COVER (DEGREE-2-MODULATOR), 30–31, 82, 83
   VERTEX COVER (FVS), 30–31
   VERTEX COVER ABOVE LP, 472, 482
   VERTEX COVER/TREEWIDTH-η MODULATOR, 464
   VERTEX MULTIWAY CUT, 215, 468
   WEIGHTED FEEDBACK VERTEX SET, 82
protrusion, **306**, 306–310, 318, 327–353
protrusion cover, **341**, 340–353

Index

protrusion decomposition, 244, **306**, 306–310, 315, 327–353
   nice, 310
protrusion replacement, 328
PSAKS, 454
   see, polynomial size approximate kernelization scheme, 454

quantifier
   alternation, 286
   existential, 281, **282**
   universal, 281, **282**

Ramsey's theorem, 408
rankwidth, 426
reasonable problem, 275
reduction rule, 15
   safeness, 15
   soundness, 15
representative family, 186

SAT, 381
saturated vertex, 475
separability, 301
separable problem, 301, 314
separator, 433
   minimal, 213
set
   closest, 196
signature, **281**, 324
Steiner tree, 369, 396
structure, 282
sudoku, 2
sunflower, **121**, 121–123, 124
   core, 121
   lemma, 121, 201
   petal, 121
Sunflower Lemma, 201

torso, **432**
touch, 340
tournament, 21, 159, 471
   acyclic, 21
   transitive, 21
transitive ordering, 21
transversal matroid, 182
tree, 475
tree decomposition, **258**, 258, 432
   nice, 265
   optimal, 258
   seminice, 267, 310
   simple, 262
treewidth, **258**, 257–293
treewidth-η-modulator, **302**
truth assignment, 89, **476**
Turing kernel, *see* Turing kernelization, **430**
Turing kernelization, 48, 430–439, 473
Tutte decomposition, **433**
Two-Families Theorem, 214
Two-Families theorem, 355

Vandermonde matrix, 166
variable, 280
   Boolean, **476**
   free, 280–281, 285
   monadic, 281
vertex
   branch, 36
   internal, 114
   subdivider, 36
vertex cover, 475
vertex subset problem, 275

walk, 474
well-linked set, 289
width
   model, 258

For EU product safety concerns, contact us at Calle de José Abascal, 56–1°,
28003 Madrid, Spain or eugpsr@cambridge.org.

www.ingramcontent.com/pod-product-compliance
Ingram Content Group UK Ltd.
Pitfield, Milton Keynes, MK11 3LW, UK
UKHW022257240426
470365UK00007B/106